ANNUAL 1997-98

Published by Invincible Press, an imprint of HarperCollins*Publishers*, 77-85 Fulham Palace Road, Hammersmith, London W6 8JB

First published 1887

The copyrights of the League Fixture Lists are owned by The Football Association, Football League and Scottish League, and these fixtures have been reproduced with their permission.

Editorial compilation by Hayters, Humatt House, 146-148 Clerkenwell Road, London EC1R 5DP

Typesetting by Letterpart Limited, Reigate, Surrey

Printed and bound in Great Britain

Distributed by The Magazine Marketing Company, Octagon House, White Hart Meadows, Ripley, Woking, Surrey GU23 6HR. Telephone (01483) 211222

ISBN 0 00 218784 1

FRONT COVER

RUUD GULLIT becomes the first foreign coach to win the F.A. Cup. In his first season in charge at Stamford Bridge, Chelsea end the long wait – it's their first major trophy for 26 years.

(Photograph by *Eddie Keogh*)

CONTENTS

THE FOREIGNERS TAKE OVER

By Albert Sewell

As the world moves on, the football world moves fastest of all, with radical changes that, collectively, could not have been envisaged when the F.A. Premier League kicked off five years ago.

Nothing has been more startling than the influx of foreign personalities. Until 1978, they were banned from English football by the PFA, and in the last season of the old Football League Championship, the 22 clubs between them fielded only 28 players from abroad.

Now it is the **League of Nations**. By mid-July, the foreign contingent preparing to line up in the Premiership this season stood at 115 with more deals pending.

Foreign teachers, too, figure prominently in the take-over. **Ruud Gullit**, in his first season in charge of Chelsea, went into the records as the first foreign coach to win the F.A. Cup, and Arsenal have placed their revolution in the hands of Frenchman **Arsene Wenger**.

Two engaging characters bringing high ambitions and fresh tactical thinking to our game. From Gullit, who speaks five languages, some new vocabulary, too. At different stages of the season, he described Chelsea's football as "sloppy", "spooky", even "sexy."

The playing lists of those two clubs show the widest investment in foreign talent, with 13 overseas players on the books of Chelsea and 12 at Highbury.

It will be worth checking how many – or how few – Englishmen are on the field at the Chelsea-Arsenal game on September 21. For the good of youth schemes at the club level, the need might soon arise to limit the number of foreigners in a Premiership line-up to, say, five – as in Italy.

Colin Hutchinson, Chelsea's chief executive, who has had the dealings of all Gullit's foreign signings, says: "It would be nice to bring in one or two English players, but the market is against it. We were quoted £5m. for a goalkeeper in England, so we bought Dutch International Ed de Goey for £2m. instead. Rightly or wrongly, the best-value signings can still be made abroad, and until Bosman applies domestically to out-of-contract players, there will be no reduction in foreign signings."

What you don't buy from mercenaries is loyalty. Jürgen Klinsmann stayed one year at Tottenham, Juninho has left Middlesbrough after two.

Gianfranco Zola joined Chelsea in November and ended the season as the third successive foreign player to win the Footballer of the Year award, after Klinsmann and the now-retired Eric Cantona.

Down the league, three Spaniards helped **Wigan** win the Third Division and Walsall's new manager is a former Danish International, Jan Sorensen.

Not so many years ago, English clubs flocked to Scotland for star imports. Thanks to the foreign invasion, that seam has practically dried up, and there is less Scottish presence in England's top division than ever before.

Scottish clubs themselves go abroad these days to make big signings. Last season's two top Player of the Year awards up there went to Brian Laudrup and Paulo di Canio.

Crisis club **Celtic** have "gone foreign" and given Dutch coach **Wim Jansen** the job of halting Rangers. In terms of a two-club monopoly, Scotland has the weakest domestic league in Europe.

Rangers having equalled Celtic's record of nine titles in a row, it is hard not to see them making it ten. Ibrox imports are at a record level, and when they reported for new-season training Rangers staff-list contained more non-Scottish players than Scots.

The F.A. Premiership is threatened by the sort of domination that afflicts

Scottish football, **Manchester United** having equalled the record of four Championship successes in five seasons that was achieved by Aston Villa at the turn of the century, by Arsenal in the Thirties, and Liverpool twice in the Eighties. Can they now equal Liverpool's five Championship successes in six (1978-84)?

Their eleventh Championship triumph was a masterpiece of strategy by **Alex Ferguson**, stop-watch and all. At the outset, he said they would concentrate in the first half of the season on reaching the knock-out stage of the European Cup and then, if necessary, make up ground in the Premier League.

After a dozen games, United were 8 points behind leaders Newcastle and had just lost three in a row: 0-5 at Newcastle, 3-6 at Southampton and 1-2 at home to Chelsea. But from the end of January, they led the field and finished Champions by 7 points. That was not all: United's reserves, A and B teams won their leagues, too.

Their predominance, with a team of big signings and cost-nothing youngsters, is not Alex Ferguson's problem. The challenge is to Newcastle, Arsenal, Liverpool and the rest to topple them.

In persuading **Kenny Dalglish** back into management after Kevin Keegan pulled out in January, **Newcastle** acquired a man with the finest of championship pedigrees. It may be significant that they finished the season with four clean sheets in a row. With another ex-Celtic man at his side in Tommy Burns, Newcastle could well improve on their runners-up position of the last two seasons in the continued search of their first title since 1927.

It will be fascinating to see what **Arsenal** do in Wenger's first full campaign, and what **Liverpool** come up with after standing still for two seasons. They could be ready for serious business after Roy Evans strengthened his squad with the capture of Oyvind Leonhardsen and the bid to bring Paul Ince back into English football will, if successful, restore the missing steel to Liverpool's midfield. Given the armband, he would drive them harder still.

The story of **Middlesbrough** could not have been pre-scripted with any credibility. With the little Brazilian Juninho in his second season by other costly imports Ravanelli and Emerson, Boro' took their success-starved fans where they had never been before – to the two domestic Cup finals. They lost both, and were relegated by the 3 points they were docked for not turning up at Blackburn in December, when hit by injuries.

In the event, they could have sent a scratch team, been beaten by a record score, and still be in the Premier League. Their decision to call off the game has to go down as the costliest in football history, and the battle for top status begins again minus their best talent, following Juninho's inevitable departure to Atletico Madrid for £12m.

With the upheaval at Newcastle and relegation for Sunderland a year after promotion, it was some season in the North-east. So different in the North-west, where all the divisions were won by clubs in and around Manchester: United, Bolton, Bury, Wigan – and Macclesfield earning League status as Conference champions.

Five titles made it an unprecedented clean sweep for one area. Previously, Lancashire won all four divisions of the Football League in 1972-73 via Liverpool, Burnley, Bolton and Southport.

The season started with **Leicester City** favourites to go straight down from the Premier Division. Instead, Martin O'Neill took them into Europe as Coca-Cola Cup winners and to a creditable ninth place in the table.

Nottingham, meanwhile, suffered the relegation of both **Forest** and **County** in the same season for the first time in the 105 years the city has had two league clubs.

Amid all the high finance, Stock Market quotations and few players worth their £1m. and more a year, the successes of Leicester, Barnsley (now about to give Premiership giants a culture shock at Oakwell) and Chesterfield (who reached the

F.A. Cup semi-finals for the first time) showed there is still a touch of romance about the Great Game.

Attendances reached their highest League level for 17 years but the pattern may not be maintained this season. Chelsea's spectacular redevelopment means that Stamford Bridge is still three-sided, rebuilding goes on at Liverpool and Tottenham, and the loss through relegation of Sunderland, Middlesbrough and Forest will be felt.

Four of our oldest clubs have moved to new locations this summer – none of them before time: Sunderland, Bolton, Derby and Stoke.

So in seven years, no fewer than ten new League grounds have opened. In addition, there is a nationwide monument to Hillsborough in the transformation of so many of the football's traditional homes to venues worthy of the age.

The **European Cup** is now swollen to a record entry of 55 clubs. Pandering to football's never-ending greed, UEFA has allowed in the runners-up from the top eight European countries. So it is now the "European Champions and Runners-up League," and those who fail at the preliminary stage get a second chance in the UEFA Cup.

Thus has the status of the European Cup been devalued. It will serve UEFA right if the 1998 Final is between clubs who failed to win their domestic leagues last season.

On the **International front**, everything now focuses on getting to France 98. **England**'s first season under **Glenn Hoddle** ended with them strongly placed to reach at least the play-offs as group runners-up. In a "practice run", they won this summer's Tournoi de France, but the most important of Hoddle's nine victories was away to Poland.

There is the intriguing possibility that, if they make it, England could meet **Terry Venables'** Socceroos in France 98. He has started with 11 straight wins as **Australia**'s coach and is within a November play-off of qualifying.

Scotland resume in September as leaders of Group 4, but with Craig Brown still looking for goals. They scored only 12 in last season's ten Internationals – one of them a penalty, one an own goal.

Mick McCarthy's **Republic of Ireland** still have all to play for, too as they scrap with Macedonia and Lithuania for second place in their group.

To end back at the beginning, on the theme of the growing foreign influence on British football: **Wimbledon**, that model of good housekeeping under Sam Hammam, are changing from Lebanese to Norwegian ownership, with Sam staying in charge of day-to-day affairs.

And **Fulham**, having gone up a division, have moved upmarket, too, with Harrods chief Mohamed Al Fayed buying the club. He has big ambitions both on the field and for the development of Craven Cottage which, in terms of location on the banks of the Thames, is the most appealing of all London's grounds.

The compilation of this 111th. Edition of **football's oldest Annual** is a personal fifteenth involvement and I am again indebted to the help of many. Notably **Chris Hull** at the Football League; **David Barber** of the Football Association; **David Thomson** from the Scottish League; **David Prole** for his ever-welcome thoughts; **Rob McCarthy** and colleagues at Hayters; to clubs, leagues and correspondents; and, at the production end, **Richard Hawke** and **Chris Leggett**. Thank you, everyone.

REAL FOREIGN STARS WELL WORTH IT

By Alex Montgomery

News of the World Chief Football Reporter

Only the most insular of little Englanders would argue that the Premier League has not been better, more exciting and more spectacular for the foreign stars now in our midst. They are mercenaries, here for the cash, but we knew that and they themselves have never tried to hide the fact.

The truth is most of them have not only offered value for money but, contrary to the opinion of some, have opened the minds of players and coaches, young and not so young, to new ideas on how the game can be approached and played.

Have Chelsea's home-reared players not improved with Zola as one of their outstanding role models – a man to study and hopefully emulate? If just a little piece of Juninho's magic falls on one of the young Middlesbrough players he worked with last term, then there will be benefits from even their heartbreak season.

It is the same wherever England's top imports have landed, be it Eric Cantona at Manchester United or Dennis Bergkamp at Arsenal. Where that class of player has been performing, there has to have been a raising of the awareness factor of the others in the squad.

There have been problems off the pitch and on it, none more clearly highlighted than at Middlesbrough where manager Bryan Robson gambled so much cash and credibility on buying Fabrizio Ravanelli and Emerson as well as Juninho.

He was left on his own to pick up the pieces, with the Brazilian Emerson collecting his money, certainly in the final weeks, without offering too much in return and therefore breaking the mercenaries' first law of survival: always give value for money.

Middlesbrough's experience, bad as it has been, is still not dire enough to support the argument that top players are not worth the money they cost in transfer fees and their wages, of £20,000 a week and more.

The problem with English football is there are not enough Zolas or Juninhos or Bergkamps, but too many second or even third-class imports. These are the ones who, honest and workmanlike though they may be, have neither the class nor style to add anything to the learning curve. They are token players – every team has to have one, two, or three or even more.

The big attraction is they come cheap, if not always cheerful. They represent the single greatest threat to the nurturing of our own youngsters. English football has shown encouraging signs of returning to the days when you found, then brought on your own talent.

Arsenal, under Frenchman Arsene Wenger, have mostly chosen to ignore the established big-money stars from round the world and bought instead younger players who didn't break the bank and who admittedly may not fulfil their potential.

The analysts claim the English market has reached its dizzy top level and that those who have already laid out fortunes on super signings will have their fingers burned as the sell-on price drops in the season ahead.

But if the money men are going to lose, at least a little, then this financial gamble has been a considerable winner for an English game that needed the infusion of new blood, now gratefully received.

HOWARD'S WAY – FOR THIRD TIME

When Everton appointed 51-year-old **Howard Kendall** as Joe Royle's successor in June, he became manager of the club for the third time. He was previously in charge from 1981-87 and again from 1990-93. During his first spell he took Everton to two Championships (1985, 1987), the F.A. Cup in 1984 and the Cup-Winners' Cup in 1985. Kendall originally arrived at Goodison Park as a player from Preston in 1967.

FOOTBALLER OF THE YEAR

(Original award by the Football Writers' Association to the "player who, by precept and example, on the field and off, shall be considered to have done most for football")

1948 Stanley Matthews (Blackpool); **1949** Johnny Carey (Man. Utd.); **1950** Joe Mercer (Arsenal); **1951** Harry Johnston (Blackpool); **1952** Billy Wright (Wolves); **1953** Nat Lofthouse (Bolton); **1954** Tom Finney (Preston); **1955** Don Revie (Man. City); **1956** Bert Trautmann (Man. City); **1957** Tom Finney (Preston); **1958** Danny Blanchflower (Tottenham); **1959** Syd Owen (Luton); **1960** Bill Slater (Wolves); **1961** Danny Blanchflower (Tottenham); **1962** Jimmy Adamson (Burnley); **1963** Stanley Matthews (Stoke); **1964** Bobby Moore (West Ham); **1965** Bobby Collins (Leeds).

1966 Bobby Charlton (Man. Utd.); **1967** Jack Charlton (Leeds); **1968** George Best (Man. Utd.); **1969** Tony Book (Man. City) & Dave Mackay (Derby) – shared; **1970** Billy Bremner (Leeds); **1971** Frank McLintock (Arsenal); **1972** Gordon Banks (Stoke); **1973** Pat Jennings (Tottenham); **1974** Ian Callaghan (Liverpool); **1975** Alan Mullery (Fulham); **1976** Kevin Keegan (Liverpool); **1977** Emlyn Hughes (Liverpool); **1978** Kenny Burns (Nott'm F.); **1979** Kenny Dalglish (Liverpool); **1980** Terry McDermott (Liverpool); **1981** Frans Thijssen (Ipswich); **1982** Steve Perryman (Tottenham).

1983 Kenny Dalglish (Liverpool); **1984** Ian Rush (Liverpool); **1985** Neville Southall (Everton); **1986** Gary Lineker (Everton); **1987** Clive Allen (Tottenham); **1988** John Barnes (Liverpool); **1989** Steve Nicol (Liverpool); Special award to the Liverpool players for the compassion shown to bereaved families after the Hillsborough Disaster; **1990** John Barnes (Liverpool); **1991** Gordon Strachan (Leeds); **1992** Gary Lineker (Tottenham); **1993** Chris Waddle (Sheff. Wed.); **1994** Alan Shearer (Blackburn); **1995** Jurgen Klinsmann (Tottenham); **1996** Eric Cantona (Man. Utd.); **1997** Gianfranco Zola (Chelsea).

● Zola, 50th winner of the award, was presented with his trophy by Sir Stanley Matthews, first Footballer of the Year in 1948.

P.F.A. AWARDS

Player of the Year: 1974 Norman Hunter (Leeds); **1975** Colin Todd (Derby); **1976** Pat Jennings (Tottenham); **1977** Andy Gray (Aston Villa); **1978** Peter Shilton (Nott'm F.); **1979** Liam Brady (Arsenal); **1980** Terry McDermott (Liverpool); **1981** John Wark (Ipswich); **1982** Kevin Keegan (Southampton); **1983** Kenny Dalglish (Liverpool); **1984** Ian Rush (Liverpool); **1985** Peter Reid (Everton); **1986** Gary Lineker (Everton); **1987** Clive Allen (Tottenham); **1988** John Barnes (Liverpool); **1989** Mark Hughes (Man. Utd.); **1990** David Platt (Aston Villa); **1991** Mark Hughes (Man. Utd.); **1992** Gary Pallister (Man. Utd.); **1993** Paul McGrath (Aston Villa); **1994** Eric Cantona (Man. Utd.); **1995** Alan Shearer (Blackburn); **1996** Les Ferdinand (Newcastle); **1997** Alan Shearer (Newcastle).

Young Player of the Year: 1974 Kevin Beattie (Ipswich); **1975** Mervyn Day (West Ham); **1976** Peter Barnes (Man. City); **1977** Andy Gray (Aston Villa); **1978** Tony Woodcock (Nott'm F.); **1979** Cyrille Regis (W.B.A.); **1980** Glenn Hoddle (Tottenham); **1981** Gary Shaw (Aston Villa); **1982** Steve Moran (Southampton); **1983** Ian Rush (Liverpool); **1984** Paul Walsh (Luton); **1985** Mark Hughes (Man. Utd.); **1986** Tony Cottee (West Ham); **1987** Tony Adams (Arsenal); **1988** Paul Gascoigne (Newcastle); **1989** Paul Merson (Arsenal); **1990** Matthew Le Tissier (Southampton); **1991** Lee Sharpe (Man. Utd.); **1992** Ryan Giggs (Man. Utd.); **1993** Ryan Giggs (Man. Utd.); **1994** Andy Cole (Newcastle); **1995** Robbie Fowler (Liverpool); **1996** Robbie Fowler (Liverpool); **1997** David Beckham (Man. Utd.).

Merit Awards: 1974 Bobby Charlton & Cliff Lloyd; **1975** Denis Law; **1976** George Eastham; **1977** Jack Taylor; **1978** Bill Shankly; **1979** Tom Finney; **1980** Sir Matt

Busby; **1981** John Trollope; **1982** Joe Mercer; **1983** Bob Paisley; **1984** Bill Nicholson; **1985** Ron Greenwood; **1986** England 1966 World Cup-winning team; **1987** Sir Stanley Matthews; **1988** Billy Bonds; **1989** Nat Lofthouse; **1990** Peter Shilton; **1991** Tommy Hutchison; **1992** Brian Clough; **1993** Man. Utd., 1968 European Champions; Eusebio (Benfica & Portugal); **1994** Billy Bingham; **1995** Gordon Strachan; **1996** Pele; **1997** Peter Beardsley.

MANAGER OF THE YEAR (1)

1966 Jock Stein (Celtic); **1967** Jock Stein (Celtic); **1968** Matt Busby (Man. Utd.); **1969** Don Revie (Leeds); **1970** Don Revie (Leeds); **1971** Bertie Mee (Arsenal); **1972** Don Revie (Leeds); **1973** Bill Shankly (Liverpool); **1974** Jack Charlton (Middlesbrough); **1975** Ron Saunders (Aston Villa); **1976** Bob Paisley (Liverpool); **1977** Bob Paisley (Liverpool); **1978** Brian Clough (Nott'm F.); **1979** Bob Paisley (Liverpool); **1980** Bob Paisley (Liverpool); **1981** Ron Saunders (Aston Villa); **1982** Bob Paisley (Liverpool); **1983** Bob Paisley (Liverpool); **1984** Joe Fagan (Liverpool); **1985** Howard Kendall (Everton); **1986** Kenny Dalglish (Liverpool); **1987** Howard Kendall (Everton); **1988** Kenny Dalglish (Liverpool); **1989** George Graham (Arsenal); **1990** Kenny Dalglish (Liverpool); **1991** George Graham (Arsenal); **1992** Howard Wilkinson (Leeds); **1993** Alex Ferguson (Man. Utd.); **1994** Alex Ferguson (Man. Utd.); **1995** Kenny Dalglish (Blackburn); **1996** Alex Ferguson (Man. Utd.); **1997** Alex Ferguson (Man. Utd.).

MANAGER OF THE YEAR (2)

(As chosen by the League Managers' Association and awarded to "the manager who has made best use of the resources available to him")

1993 Dave Bassett (Sheff. United); **1994** Joe Kinnear (Wimbledon); **1995** Frank Clark (Nott'm. Forest); **1996** Peter Reid (Sunderland); **1997** Danny Wilson (Barnsley).

SCOTTISH FOOTBALL WRITERS' ASSOCIATION

Player of the Year: 1965 Billy McNeill (Celtic); **1966** John Greig (Rangers); **1967** Ronnie Simpson (Celtic); **1968** Gordon Wallace (Raith); **1969** Bobby Murdoch (Celtic); **1970** Pat Stanton (Hibernian); **1971** Martin Buchan (Aberdeen); **1972** David Smith (Rangers); **1973** George Connelly (Celtic); **1974** World Cup Squad; **1975** Sandy Jardine (Rangers); **1976** John Greig (Rangers); **1977** Danny McGrain (Celtic); **1978** Derek Johnstone (Rangers); **1979** Andy Ritchie (Morton); **1980** Gordon Strachan (Aberdeen); **1981** Alan Rough (Partick Thistle); **1982** Paul Sturrock (Dundee Utd.); **1983** Charlie Nicholas (Celtic); **1984** Willie Miller (Aberdeen); **1985** Hamish McAlpine (Dundee Utd.); **1986** Sandy Jardine (Hearts); **1987** Brian McClair (Celtic); **1988** Paul McStay (Celtic); **1989** Richard Gough (Rangers); **1990** Alex McLeish (Aberdeen); **1991** Maurice Malpas (Dundee Utd.); **1992** Ally McCoist (Rangers); **1993** Andy Goram (Rangers); **1994** Mark Hateley (Rangers); **1995** Brian Laudrup (Rangers); **1996** Paul Gascoigne (Rangers); **1997** Brian Laudrup (Rangers).

SCOTTISH P.F.A. AWARDS

Player of the Year: 1978 Derek Johnstone (Rangers); **1979** Paul Hegarty (Dundee Utd.); **1980** Davie Provan (Celtic); **1981** Mark McGee (Aberdeen); **1982** Sandy Clarke (Airdrieonians); **1983** Charlie Nicholas (Celtic); **1984** Willie Miller (Aberdeen); **1985** Jim Duffy (Morton); **1986** Richard Gough (Dundee Utd.); **1987** Brian McClair (Celtic); **1988** Paul McStay (Celtic); **1989** Theo Snelders (Aberdeen); **1990** Jim Bett (Aberdeen); **1991** Paul Elliott (Celtic); **1992** Ally McCoist (Rangers); **1993** Andy Goram (Rangers); **1994** Mark Hateley (Rangers); **1995**

Brian Laudrup (Rangers); **1996** Paul Gascoigne (Rangers); **1997** Paulo di Canio (Celtic).

Young Player of Year: 1978 Graeme Payne (Dundee Utd.); **1979** Ray Stewart (Dundee Utd.); **1980** John McDonald (Rangers); **1981** Charlie Nicholas (Celtic); **1982** Frank McAvennie (St. Mirren); **1983** Paul McStay (Celtic); **1984** John Robertson (Hearts); **1985** Craig Levein (Hearts); **1986** Craig Levein (Hearts); **1987** Robert Fleck (Rangers); **1988** John Collins (Hibernian); **1989** Billy McKinlay (Dundee Utd.); **1990** Scott Crabbe (Hearts); **1991** Eoin Jess (Aberdeen); **1992** Philip O'Donnell (Motherwell); **1993** Eoin Jess (Aberdeen); **1994** Phil O'Donnell (Motherwell); **1995** Charlie Miller (Rangers); **1996** Jackie McNamara (Celtic); **1997** Robbie Winters (Dundee Utd.).

SCOTTISH MANAGER OF THE YEAR

1987 Jim McLean (Dundee Utd.); **1988** Billy McNeill (Celtic); **1989** Graeme Souness (Rangers); **1990** Andy Roxburgh (Scotland); **1991** Alex Totten (St. Johnstone); **1992** Walter Smith (Rangers); **1993** Walter Smith (Rangers); **1994** Walter Smith (Rangers); **1995** Jimmy Nicholl (Raith); **1996** Walter Smith (Rangers); **1997** Walter Smith (Rangers).

EUROPEAN FOOTBALLER OF THE YEAR
(Poll conducted by *France Football*)

1956 Stanley Matthews (Blackpool); **1957** Alfredo di Stefano (Real Madrid); **1958** Raymond Kopa (Real Madrid); **1959** Alfredo di Stefano (Real Madrid); **1960** Luis Suarez (Barcelona); **1961** Omar Sivori (Juventus); **1962** Josef Masopust (Dukla Prague); **1963** Lev Yashin (Moscow Dynamo); **1964** Denis Law (Man. Utd.); **1965** Eusebio (Benfica); **1966** Bobby Charlton (Man. Utd.); **1967** Florian Albert (Ferencvaros); **1968** George Best (Man. Utd.); **1969** Gianni Rivera (AC Milan).

1970 Gerd Muller (Bayern Munich); **1971** Johan Cruyff (Ajax); **1972** Franz Beckenbauer (Bayern Munich); **1973** Johan Cruyff (Barcelona); **1974** Johan Cruyff (Barcelona); **1975** Oleg Blokhin (Dynamo Kiev); **1976** Franz Beckenbauer (Bayern Munich); **1977** Allan Simonsen (Borussia Moenchengladbach); **1978** Kevin Keegan (SV Hamburg); **1979** Kevin Keegan (SV Hamburg); **1980** Karl-Heinz Rummenigge (Bayern Munich); **1981** Karl-Heinz Rummenigge (Bayern Munich); **1982** Paolo Rossi (Juventus); **1983** Michel Platini (Juventus).

1984 Michel Platini (Juventus); **1985** Michel Platini (Juventus); **1986** Igor Belanov (Dynamo Kiev); **1987** Ruud Gullit (AC Milan); **1988** Marco Van Basten (AC Milan); **1989** Marco Van Basten (AC Milan); **1990** Lothar Matthaus (Inter Milan); **1991** Jean-Pierre Papin (Marseille); **1992** Marco Van Basten (AC Milan); **1993** Roberto Baggio (Juventus); **1994** Hristo Stoichkov (Barcelona); **1995** George Weah (AC Milan); **1996** Matthias Sammer (Borussia Dortmund).

ENGLAND IN TOP SEVEN

Glenn Hoddle's World Cup results, plus triumph in this summer's Tournoi de France, lifted **England** from 13th to 7th place in FIFA's world rankings. Brazil are top, and the other countries ranked above England in the June listing were Spain, Germany, Denmark, France and Romania.

Scotland (22nd) and the **Rep. of Ireland** (40th) also moved up. **Northern Ireland** were 63rd, with **Wales** bottom of the Home Countries at 85th.

'EVER-ABSENT' GIGGS

When **Ryan Giggs** withdrew through injury from **Wales'** match against the Rep. of Ireland in Cardiff on Feb. 11, he maintained a 5-year absence from friendly Internationals. He was also absent against Scotland on May 27, and has missed every friendly since becoming Wales' youngest player in 1991.

LEAGUE CLUB MANAGERS

Figure in brackets = number of managerial changes at club since war.
Date present manager took over shown on right.
Dario Gradi, appointed by Crewe in June 1983, is currently the longest serving one-club manager.

F.A. CARLING PREMIERSHIP

Arsenal (11)	Arsene Wenger	October 1996
Aston Villa (15)	Brian Little	November 1994
Barnsley (11)	Danny Wilson	June 1994
Blackburn Rovers (19)	Roy Hodgson	July 1997
Bolton Wanderers (16)	Colin Todd	January 1996
Chelsea (16)	Ruud Gullit (player-manager)	May 1996
Coventry City (21)	Gordon Strachan	November 1996
Crystal Palace (23)	Steve Coppell	February 1997
Derby County (14)	Jim Smith	June 1995
Everton (14)	Howard Kendall	June 1997
Leeds United (16)	George Graham	September 1996
Leicester City (15)	Martin O'Neill	December 1995
Liverpool (9)	Roy Evans	January 1994
Manchester United (8)	Alex Ferguson	November 1986
Newcastle United (16)	Kenny Dalglish	January 1997
Sheffield Wednesday (15)	David Pleat	June 1995
Southampton (11)	Dave Jones	June 1997
Tottenham Hotspur (13)	Gerry Francis	November 1994
West Ham United (7)	Harry Redknapp	August 1994
Wimbledon (7)	Joe Kinnear	March 1992

(Number of Wimbledon changes is since club elected to Football League in 1977).

NATIONWIDE LEAGUE – FIRST DIVISION

Birmingham City (20)	Trevor Francis	May 1996
Bradford City (22)	Chris Kamara	November 1995
Bury (19)	Stan Ternent	September 1995
Charlton Athletic (12)	Alan Curbishley	July 1991
Crewe Alexandra (17)	Dario Gradi	June 1983
Huddersfield Town (16)	Brian Horton	June 1995
Ipswich Town (11)	George Burley	December 1994
Manchester City (22)	Frank Clark	December 1996
Middlesbrough (15)	Bryan Robson	May 1994
Norwich City (18)	Mike Walker	June 1996
Nottingham Forest (8)	Dave Bassett	May 1997
Oxford United (11)	Denis Smith	September 1993
Portsmouth (16)	Terry Fenwick	February 1995
Port Vale (16)	John Rudge	March 1984
Q.P.R. (18)	Stewart Houston	September 1996
Reading (13)	Terry Bullivant	June 1997
Sheffield United (15)	Nigel Spackman (caretaker)	June 1997
Stockport County (27)	Gary Megson	July 1997
Stoke City (14)	Chic Bates	July 1997
Sunderland (17)	Peter Reid	March 1995
Swindon Town (15)	Steve McMahon	November 1994
Tranmere Rovers (13)	John Aldridge (player-manager)	April 1996
W.B.A. (22)	Ray Harford	February 1997
Wolverhampton W. (16)	Mark McGhee	December 1995

SECOND DIVISION

Blackpool (20)	Nigel Worthington	July 1997
Bournemouth (17)	Mel Machin	September 1994
Brentford (18)	David Webb	May 1993
Bristol City (15)	John Ward	March 1997
Bristol Rovers (16)	Ian Holloway (player-manager)	May 1996
Burnley (18)	Chris Waddle (player-manager)	July 1997
Carlisle United (22)	Mervyn Day	January 1996
Chesterfield (13)	John Duncan	February 1993
Fulham (18)	Micky Adams	February 1996
Gillingham (15)	Tony Pulis	July 1995
Grimsby Town (23)	Alan Buckley	May 1997
Luton Town (15)	Lennie Lawrence	December 1995
Millwall (19)	Billy Bonds	May 1997
Northampton Town (20)	Ian Atkins	January 1995
Oldham Athletic (16)	Neil Warnock	February 1997
Plymouth Argyle (23)	Mick Jones	February 1997
Preston North End (19)	Gary Peters	December 1994
Southend United (21)	Alvin Martin	July 1997
Walsall (25)	Jan Sorensen	June 1997
Watford (21)	Graham Taylor	May 1997
Wigan Athletic (11)	John Deehan	October 1995
Wrexham (16)	Brian Flynn	November 1989
Wycombe Wanderers (2)	John Gregory	October 1996
York City (16)	Alan Little	March 1993

(Number of Wycombe changes is since club elected to Football League in 1993).

THIRD DIVISION

Barnet (6)	John Still	June 1997
Brighton & H.A. (19)	Steve Gritt	December 1996
Cambridge United (11)	Roy McFarland	November 1996
Cardiff City (20)	Russell Osman	November 1996
Chester City (16)	Kevin Ratcliffe	April 1995
Colchester United (17)	Steve Wignall	January 1995
Darlington (26)	David Hodgson	November 1996
Doncaster Rovers (25)	Kerry Dixon (player-manager)	August 1996
Exeter City (21)	Peter Fox (player-manager)	June 1995
Hartlepool United (24)	Mick Tait (player-manager)	November 1996
Hull City (17)	Mark Hateley (player-manager)	July 1997
Leyton Orient (18)	Tommy Taylor	November 1996
Lincoln City (18)	John Beck	October 1995
Macclesfield Town (–)	Sammy McIlroy	June 1993
Mansfield Town (19)	Steve Parkin (player-manager)	August 1996
Notts County (22)	Sam Allardyce	January 1997
Peterborough United (20)	Barry Fry	May 1996
Rochdale (23)	Graham Barrow	May 1996
Rotherham United (18)	Ronnie Moore	May 1997
Scarborough (8)	Mick Wadsworth	June 1996
Scunthorpe United (21)	Brian Laws	February 1997
Shrewsbury Town (15)	Jake King	May 1997
Swansea City (19)	Jan Molby (player-manager)	February 1996
Torquay United (24)	Kevin Hodges (player-coach)	June 1996

(Number of changes at following clubs is since elected to Football League: Barnet 1991; Cambridge 1970; Peterborough 1960; Wigan 1978; Macclesfield new to League 1997).

CHANGES FOR SEASON 1997-98

Starting this season, a goal can be scored direct from the kick-off (previously the ball was not in play until it had travelled the distance of its circumference).

That was one of the amendments to the Laws of the Game – effective world-wide from July 1 – made when the International Board met in Belfast on March 1. Other points from the 111th annual conference and FIFA's subsequent Instructions to Referees:

- An indirect free-kick to be awarded if a goalkeeper handles the ball direct from a throw-in by his own team.
- Goalkeeper facing a penalty-kick can now move about but must remain on his line until the ball is kicked.
- A goal may now be scored direct from a goal kick.
- At start of play, team winning the toss to decide which goal they will attack, their opponents to kick-off (previously, team winning the toss had choice).
- Players to be reminded that they should not wear anything that is dangerous to themselves or other players ("including any kind of jewellery").
- Thermal shorts must be the same colour as the player's strip.

With women's football in mind, "unsporting behaviour" replaces "ungentlemanly conduct" as a cautionable offence.

- Using "offensive, insulting or abusive language" replaces "foul or abusive language" as a sending-off offence.
- Four-step rule for goalkeepers to be enforced.
- Crackdown on goalkeepers who waste time by holding on to the ball – now to be permitted only 5 or 6 seconds between receiving the ball and playing it.

FIFA unanimously rejected a proposal to introduce television replays to help referees make decisions over controversial incidents. General secretary Sepp Blatter said: "We were anxious that television does not take over by controlling the referee. We have to accept that football is composed of human beings, human frailties, mistakes and errors."

No more replays in the Coca-Cola Cup: The Football League decided (June 15) that ties in the one-leg third, fourth, fifth rounds and Final will be decided on the day on penalties if level after extra time.

All seven Premiership clubs playing in Europe this season are exempt until the third round of the Coca-Cola Cup.

Wendy steps up: Wendy Toms, 33, a ParcelForce manager from Poole, Dorset, becomes the Premiership's first woman assistant-referee this season. She spent the last three seasons "on line" in the Nationwide League, and as Conference referee.

Blank dates: To assist World Cup preparations, there will be no Premiership fixtures on the following Saturdays: August 16, September 6, October 11, November 15, March 21.

There will be no Scottish Premier Division matches on August 9, September 6 and October 11.

The 1998 **UEFA Cup Final** becomes a single match (neutral venue) and ends the competition's long tradition as a two-leg decider.

F.A. SCRAP PENALTY POINTS

The Football Association have scrapped the disciplinary points system that has operated since the early Seventies and, starting this season, players can earn "remission" for good behaviour.

Out go suspensions for players reaching 21, 33 or 45 penalty points, and in the Premiership, Nationwide League and F.A. Cup a player will be banned, under the new threshold, after five cautions with further suspension if reaching eight or 11 bookings and then after every additional three.

As previously, suspensions take effect 14 days after the last offence.

If following suspension a player stays out of trouble for five complete matches (without being substituted), he can apply to have his last yellow card deleted from his record.

The red-card rule for dismissals is unchanged, with suspension from one to three games, depending on the severity of the offence.

The 15-page memorandum sent to clubs by the F.A. on July 15 drew attention to stringent new punishments for assaults by players on match officials.

They range from 182 days' suspension, with £100 fine, for "common assault"; sine die suspension of not less than five years for "assaults causing bodily harm"; and permanent suspension for "assaults causing serious bodily harm".

THE BOSMAN RULING

After five years of legal wrangling, a 30-year-old midfield player Jean-Marc Bosman, little known outside Belgium when the case began, won a ruling in the European Court of Justice (Dec. 15, 1995) that shook the football world.

It gave out-of-contract players within the EC the right to become free agents, bringing footballers into line with other EU workers, and became effective in the 1996 summer. Bosman, the rebel with a cause, said of the ruling: "It is very positive. It is superb."

But there were warnings. Martin Edwards, chairman of Manchester United, commercially Britain's most successful club, said: "I think the new regulations will make it a paradise for stars and their agents. We might lose an expensively-signed player for nothing; we can bring in a new man for nothing, as well. It must be a serious concern for football that a lot less money will circulate. It will affect the smaller, selling clubs and their schools of excellence in producing players."

As a further sequel to the Bosman ruling, UEFA was required (Feb. 1996) to scrap its restriction on the "3 plus 2" system which limited a club, domestically or in European competition, to fielding three foreign players and two "assimilated players" in any one side.

It meant that managers and coaches no longer had to juggle their teams in Europe and leave out some of their best players. A club could now field an entirely foreign eleven.

The judgment affected only players with contracts at an end. Players still under contract could be transferred as normal for whatever fee the clubs agreed.

However, when a player gets to the end of his contract, his club must negotiate with him as the equal of any other club that is interested.

The implications for the smaller clubs, who survive by selling, could be serious as they will be deprived of vital transfer income. The top clubs with strong squads and effective commercial operations could expect to become stronger.

The first British player to take advantage of the Bosman verdict was Scottish International **John Collins** who, at the end of his contract with Celtic, joined Monaco in July 1996. He agreed a 3-year deal with the French club, reportedly worth £20,000 a week (plus signing-on fee), while Celtic received nothing.

At the same time, Motherwell lost Scottish International **Paul Lambert** "free" to Borussia Dortmund. Similarly last season, Liverpool paid no fee for £2m.-rated defender **Bjorne Tore Kvarme** from Norwegian club Rosenborg.

Among players who have moved without fee under Bosman this summer: **Gustavo Poyet** (Real Zaragoza to Chelsea), **Scott Booth** (Aberdeen to Borussia Dortmund), **Scott Minto** (Chelsea to Benfica) and two signings by Motherwell from Austrian club Vfb Modling – **Franz Resch** and **Mario Dorner**.

The loss of **David Connolly**, 20-year-old Rep. of Ireland striker, to Feyenoord (July 1) without recouping a fee provided an example of a small club, Watford in this case, suffering through Bosman. His value if he had joined an English club would have been at least £2m.

SOCCER'S TV JACKPOT

Season 1997-98 marks the start of the biggest TV deal in British sport. It brings Premiership clubs £743m. over four years.

The Premier League will receive £670m. from **Sky** for exclusive live match coverage until the year 2001, while **BBC TV** will pay £73m. to show recorded highlights over the same period.

Screenwise, but at vastly increased cost, it is the same Sky/BBC arrangement that completed the fifth season of its previous contract in 1996-97. It means that until the next century Premier League football will be shown live only on satellite TV.

For terrestrial viewers, the BBC beat off strong competition from ITV to preserve *Match of the Day* (born August 1964) in highlights form until 2001.

But from this season, BBC TV lose live coverage of the F.A. Cup, dating back to 1938. They were priced out by **ITV** when the Football Association agreed a £130m. four-year package with Sky (£55m.), ITV (£60m.) and BBC (£15m.).

Sky will screen F.A. Cup matches, including replays, live from first round to semi-finals. ITV will show the Final exclusively live from 1998 after earlier-round live coverage on Sunday afternoons and replay highlights in midweek. BBC will preserve their Road to Wembley with Saturday night highlights through the rounds.

England matches will continue to be shown live on Sky, with ITV annexing highlights from BBC.

Sky's take-over of live football is further demonstrated by the £125m. deal which the Football League completed with them via the five-year contract beginning last season. Up to 60 matches from Divisions 1, 2 and 3, plus Coca-Cola Cup-ties and all three end-of-season play-off finals, are live on BSkyB.

With the new TV double deal fully in place in 1997-98, Premier League and Football League clubs benefit by some £200m. a year.

ITV have also bought the rights to continue to show the European Champions' League live until the year 2001, thus warding off the threat of pay-per-view channels. Man. United and Newcastle are both in the Champions' League this season.

This is how football on TV has developed since the first live transmission of the Cup Final in 1938:

1964   First Match of the Day (BBC2, Liverpool 3, Arsenal 2).

1968   First Cup Final live in colour.

1979   BBC nearly lose Match of the Day, win High Court appeal against ITV's originally-accepted £5m. offer for exclusive contract for football coverage on TV. The BBC/ITV "cartel" continues with £9.2m. deal (for highlights) over 4 years.

1983   First contract for *live* TV coverage of League football (5 matches on BBC, Friday nights; 5 Sunday afternoon games on ITV). Cost of £5.2m. for 2-year deal split equally between TV companies.

1985   Soccer and TV in deadlock over new contract. Coverage blacked out from start of season until January 1986. Football then accepts £1.3m. for second half of season, including 11 live matches in League and Cups.

1986   BBC and ITV agree 2-year, £6.2m. contract (split equally) – each company to show 7 live League matches per season, plus League Cup semi-finals and Final.

1988   Satellite TV enters the bidding . . . end of BBC/ITV cartel. ITV sign League/League Cup contract (£44m. over 4 years, 21 live matches per season) . . . BBC/BSkyB deal is with the F.A. (£30m. over 5 years for F.A. Cup and England matches, live and recorded).

1992*   Sky's the limit as new Premier League completes £304m. deal with BSkyB and BBC for next 5 seasons. ITV agree 4-year, £24m. contract with the newly-formed Football League for League and League Cup coverage, live and recorded. Channel 4 brings Italian football to British screens (Sunday live).

1995   Sky begin £10.5m., 4-year deal to screen Scottish League matches live in midweek – 17 per season, starting with Rangers v Celtic (1-1) on Jan. 4.

1997   In new 4-year deal, Sky pay £670m. for live Premier League coverage and BBC TV £73m. for recorded highlights. F.A. agree new £130m. TV contract for F.A. Cup/England matches: ITV £60m., Sky £55m., BBC £15m. (Cup-Saturday night highlights only).

European club competitions: Season-by-season contracts, live coverage in selected rounds since 1991: **1991-92** BBC – UEFA Cup (plus E.Cup Final); ITV – European Cup, Cup-Winners' Cup; **1992-93** BBC – CWC; ITV – EC, UEFA Cup; **1993-94** BBC – UEFA Cup; ITV – EC, CWC; **1994-95** BBC – UEFA Cup; ITV – EC, CWC; **1995-96** BBC – UEFA Cup; ITV –EC; **1996-97** BBC – UEFA Cup; ITV – EC, CWC.

LIVE ON SKY IN 1997-98

(League matches unless stated)

AUGUST: Sun 3: Hibernian v Celtic. Man. Utd. v Chelsea *(Charity Shield, Wembley)*. **Mon 4:** Rangers v Hearts. **Sun 10:** Sheff. Utd. v Sunderland; Tottenham v Man. Utd.. **Mon 11:** Arsenal v Coventry. **Tue 12:** QPR v Wolves *(Coca-Cola Cup)*. **Fri 15:** Nott'm. F. v Norwich. **Mon 17:** Ipswich v Middlesbrough; Dundee Utd. v Hibernian. **Mon 18:** Luton v Southend. **Fri 22:** Man. City v Tranmere. **Sun 24:** WBA v Wolves; Barnsley v Chelsea. **Mon 25:** Blackburn v Sheff. W.. **Fri 29:** Stockport v Birmingham. **Sun 31:** Crewe v Port Vale; Liverpool v Newcastle.

SEPTEMBER: Mon 1: Bolton v Everton. **Sun 7:** Oxford Utd. v Wolves. **Mon 8:** QPR v Portsmouth. **Wed 10:** England v Moldova *(World Cup, Wembley)*. **Fri 12:** Bury v Man. City. **Sun 14:** Birmingham v Sunderland; Blackburn v Leeds. **Fri 19:** Brentford v Wycombe. **Sun 21:** Charlton v Bradford; Chelsea v Arsenal. **Mon 22:** Liverpool v Aston Villa. **Fri 26:** Norwich v Ipswich. **Sun 28:** Sunderland v Middlesbrough; Blackburn v Coventry.

OCTOBER: Fri 3: Huddersfield v Nott'm. F. **Sun 5:** Middlesbrough v Sheff. Utd.; Liverpool v Chelsea. **Sat 11:** Italy v England *(World Cup, Rome)*. **Sun 12:** Stoke v Port Vale. **Mon 13:** Birmingham v Wolves. **Fri 17:** Carlisle v Preston. **Sun 19:** Charlton v Stoke; Tottenham v Sheff. W. **Mon 20:** Barnsley v Coventry. **Fri 24:** Reading v Nott'm. F. **Sun 26:** QPR v Man. City; Arsenal v Aston Villa. **Mon 27:** Leicester v West Ham. **Fri 31:** Portsmouth v Swindon.

NOVEMBER: Sun 2: Cardiff v Swansea; Everton v Southampton. **Mon 3:** West Ham v Crystal Palace. **Fri 7:** Man. City v Huddersfield. **Sun 9:** Ipswich v Sheff. Utd.; Arsenal v Man. Utd. **Mon 10:** Leicester v Wimbledon. **Fri 21:** Fulham v Gillingham. **Sun 23:** WBA v Birmingham; Leeds v West Ham. **Mon 24:** Tottenham v Crystal Palace. **Fri 28:** Charlton v Swindon. **Sun 30:** Arsenal v Liverpool.

DECEMBER: Mon 1: Bolton v Newcastle. **Sat 6:** Liverpool v Man. Utd. **Sun 7:** Wimbledon v Southampton. **Mon 8:** Sheff. W. v Barnsley. **Fri 12:** Oxford v QPR. **Sun 14:** Wolves v Nott'm. F.; Bolton v Derby. **Mon 15:** Man. Utd. v Aston Villa. **Sun 21:** Newcastle v Man. Utd. **Mon 22:** Wimbledon v Arsenal. **Fri 26:** Reading v WBA; Aston Villa v Tottenham. **Sun 28:** Newcastle v Liverpool. **Mon 29:** Southampton v Chelsea.

JERSEY'S TITLE

Hosts **Jersey** won football "gold" in the seventh staging of the Island Games. The multi-sport tournament, held every two years, is restricted to islands around the world with a population of less than 125,000. A record twenty entered this summer, and in the soccer Final played at Springfield Stadium, St Helier, on July 4, Jersey beat Ynys Mon (formerly Anglesey) 1-0 after extra time.

BARNSLEY JOIN THE ELITE

Barnsley's arrival in the top flight for the first time in their history demonstrates to an increasingly cash-dominated game that it is still possible to reach the heights with minimum outlay.

Manager Danny Wilson's squad, assembled for a modest £830,000 stamped their Premiership passport with the season's 22nd win, at home to Bradford City on April 26.

"The party will go on all summer," declared chairman John Dennis, a wholesale greengrocer who has supported the club for 40 years including the dark 1960s, when his father Ernest rescued Barnsley from bankruptcy.

Celebrity followers like cricket umpire Dickie Bird and journalist/television personality Michael Parkinson rejoiced, and now the cream of English football prepares to welcome the most unlikely addition to their ranks since Wimbledon.

The Barnsley side included Paul Wilkinson and John Hendrie, rejects from Middlesbrough who spent heavily on replacements Juninho and Ravanelli. At season's end, the clubs passed each other on football's escalator.

Neil Redfearn, the midfielder who arrived at Oakwell via Nottingham Forest, Bolton, Lincoln, Doncaster, Crystal Palace, Watford and Oldham, finished top scorer with 19 goals, 17 of them in the League.

The cut-price team from an area blighted by pit closures brought Barnsley their greatest achievement since the 1912 FA Cup win as a Second Division club.

Danny Wilson looks back to look forward to 1997-98: "Wimbledon have proved an inspiration to us all, showing you don't need a huge budget to survive and even thrive in the Premiership."

The Barnsley of old produced legends like Danny Blanchflower, Tommy Taylor and "Skinner" Normanton. The team of 1997 prepares to test itself at the highest level, against the giants from Manchester, Merseyside and London.

FACTFILE

Founded: 1887.

Entered Football League: 1898 (Div.2).

Previous name: Barnsley St Peters 1887-97.

Nickname: "Tykes".

Ground: Oakwell.

Modern Capacity: 19,000 (Record att: 40,255 v Stoke F.A. Cup 5, 15.2.36)

Record League Wins: 9-0 v Loughborough, Div.2, 28.1.1899; 9-0 v Accrington, Div.3 North 3.2 34.

Record League defeat: 0-9 v Notts Co. Div.2, 19.11.1927.

Highest League scorer in season: Cecil McCormack, 33, Div.2.

Most League goals for club in career: Ernest Hine 123, 1921-26.

Most capped player: Gerry Taggart (N. Ireland) 42 (To 12.5.97).

Most League appearances: Barry Murphy, 514, 1962-78.

Record fee received: £1.5m from Nott'm. Forest for Carl Tiler, May 1991.

Record fee paid: £310,000 to Celtic for Andy Payton, Nov 1993.

Honours: Div. Three North Champions 1933-34, 1938-39, 1954-55. FA Cup: Winners 1912. Promoted to top division for first time 1997.

WELCOME, MACCLESFIELD

When the German national team decided to use Macclesfield's renovated Moss Rose ground as their training headquarters during Euro '96 it suggested it was going to be a season with a difference at the Cheshire club. And when they clinched the Vauxhall Conference title, with a run of 16 victories in their last 19 matches, some ten months later, the Macclesfield fans knew football had truly come home.

In November the Silkmen trailed runaway-leaders Kidderminster by 15 points but the club's incredible run, culminating in a 4-1 win over Kettering Town, brought them the title and long-overdue Football League status. On the run-in Peter Davenport, ex-Man. United and England, scored in each of the last four games.

Sammy McIlroy, the former Northern Ireland and Manchester United midfielder who has been in charge of Macclesfield since 1993, rated promotion as the biggest achievement of his career:

"I've played in World Cups and FA Cup Finals at Wembley but this has to be my greatest success and proudest moment.

"The players remained disciplined and stuck to their task all season. We have been promoted on merit. Now let's hope we can all take this club further," he added.

Macclesfield clinched the championship five points clear of Kidderminster and finally secured the promotion which eluded them two seasons earlier, when they won the title but were denied promotion because the Moss Rose ground did not then meet the criteria set out by the Football League.

McIlroy, his team and Macclesfield fans dedicated their Conference effort to Arthur Jones, the club's chairman who committed suicide in September.

Jones was a life-long Macclesfield Town supporter and he invested £300,000 of his own money in the club, a large part of which paid for the ground improvements which ensured the Silkmen would not miss out on promotion a second time.

"This season was for him," said McIlroy. "It has been a crusade for him and he will always be in our memory."

FACTFILE

Year formed: 1875.

Nickname: Silkmen.

Ground: Moss Rose, London Road, Macclesfield, Cheshire SK10 3JH.

Telephone: 01625 264686.

Colours: Royal blue shirts, white shorts.

Honours: Conference winners 1995, 1997; F.A. Trophy winners 1970, 1996.

Manager: Sammy McIlroy (since June 1993).

CONFERENCE CLEAN UP

All 14 **GM Vauxhall Conference** clubs in last season's F.A. Cup first qualifying round were drawn away, and all went through.

HUMBERSIDE ACE

At every match in the 51 years Hull City have played at Boothferry Park, **Fred Kettener** has sold programmes. In appreciation of his work for City over five decades, the club presented him with an engraved decanter. It all started when Fred, returning home in 1946 after five years as a prisoner-of-war, went along to the newly-opened Boothferry Park to see if they wanted any help on match days.

TEN-GOAL WONDERS

In the history of the League football in England, beginning in 1888, there have been 61 instances of a club scoring **TEN** goals or more in a match. The old Second Division produced 20 of these double-figure scores (but only three of them since 1919).

There have been none in the past nine seasons, and none so far in the Premiership:

Date	Div.	Result			
Nov. 7, 1987	2	Manchester City	10	Huddersfield Town	1
Sept. 5, 1987	3	Gillingham	10	Chesterfield	0
Jan. 25, 1964	4	Doncaster Rovers	10	Darlington	0
Dec. 26, 1963	1	Fulham	10	Ipswich Town	1
Dec. 26, 1962	4	Oldham Athletic	11	Southport	0
Mar. 3, 1962	4	Wrexham	10	Hartlepools United	1
Nov. 14, 1959	2	Aston Villa	11	Charlton Athletic	1
Apr. 4, 1959	4	Hartlepools United	10	Barrow	1
Oct. 11, 1958	1	Tottenham Hotspur	10	Everton	4
Jan. 19, 1952	3N	Oldham Athletic	11	Chester	2
Sept. 29, 1951	3N	Lincoln City	11	Crewe Alexandra	1
Jan. 15, 1949	3S	Notts County	11	Newport County	1
Oct. 5, 1946	2	* Newcastle United	13	Newport County	0
Sept. 4, 1946	3S	Reading	10	Crystal Palace	2
Jan. 14, 1939	3N	Hull City	11	Carlisle United	1
Apr. 15, 1938	1	Wolves	10	Leicester City	1
Jan. 13, 1938	3N	Hull City	10	Southport	1
Feb. 4, 1937	1	Stoke City	10	W.B.A.	3
Apr. 13, 1936	3S	Luton Town	12	Bristol Rovers	0
Feb. 1, 1936	3N	Chester	12	York City	0
Dec. 26, 1935	3N	† Tranmere Rovers	13	Oldham Athletic	4
May 5, 1934	3N	Barrow	12	Gateshead	1
Jan. 6, 1934	3N	* Stockport County	13	Halifax Town	0
Nov. 18, 1933	1	Middlesbrough	10	Sheffield United	3
Sept. 2, 1933	3S	Luton Town	10	Torquay United	2
Sept. 7, 1931	3S	Fulham	10	Torquay United	2
Dec. 26, 1930	3N	Hull City	10	Halifax Town	0
Dec. 13, 1930	1	Huddersfield Town	10	Blackpool	1
Apr. 10, 1930	3S	Newport County	10	Merthyr Tydfil	0
Mar. 15, 1930	3S	Norwich City	10	Coventry City	2
Mar. 6, 1929	3N	South Shields	10	Rotherham United	1
Jan. 19, 1929	1	Sheffield United	10	Burnley	0
Oct. 20, 1928	1	Leicester City	10	Portsmouth	0
Aug. 25, 1928	3N	Bradford City	11	Rotherham United	1
Jan. 7, 1928	3N	Tranmere Rovers	11	Durham City	1
Nov. 5, 1927	3S	Northampton Town	10	Walsall	0
Jan. 1, 1926	1	Sheffield United	11	Cardiff City	2
Aug. 29, 1925	1	Aston Villa	10	Burnley	0
Dec. 27, 1919	2	Hull City	10	Wolves	3
Jan. 6, 1915	1	Birmingham	11	Glossop	1
Oct. 5, 1912	1	Aston Villa	10	Sheffield Wednesday	0
Apr. 21, 1909	1	Nottingham Forest	12	Leicester Fosse	0
Apr. 11, 1903	2	Small Heath	12	Doncaster Rovers	0
Jan. 17, 1903	2	Chesterfield	10	Glossop	0
Mar. 2, 1901	2	Small Heath	10	Blackpool	0
Mar. 12, 1900	2	Woolwich Arsenal	12	Loughborough Town	0
Apr. 1, 1899	2	Loughborough Town	10	Darwen	0
Mar. 4, 1899	2	Walsall	10	Darwen	0
Feb. 18, 1899	2	Manchester City	10	Darwen	0
Dec. 26, 1896	2	Darwen	10	Walsall	0

Feb. 18, 1896	2	Liverpool	10	Rotherham Town	1
Jan. 13, 1896	2	Darwen	10	Rotherham Town	2
Mar. 23, 1895	2	Manchester City	11	Lincoln City	3
Feb. 26, 1895	2	Notts County	10	Burslem Port Vale	0
Mar. 17, 1894	2	Small Heath	10	Ardwick	2
Dec. 17, 1892	2	Small Heath	12	Walsall Town Swifts	0
Dec. 10, 1892	2	Burslem Port Vale	0	Sheffield United	10
Oct. 15, 1892	1	Newton Heath	10	Wolves	1
Apr. 4, 1892	1	W.B.A.	12	Darwen	0
Mar. 12, 1892	1	Aston Villa	12	Accrington	2
Sept. 14, 1889	1	Preston North End	10	Stoke	0

*Joint record Football League win (13-0)
†Highest Football League aggregate (17 goals)

(Small Heath later became Birmingham, Ardwick became Man. City, Newton Heath became Man. United)

QUOTE-UNQUOTE

Manager JIMMY NICHOLL after Raith's victory over Celtic in the 1995 Scottish Coca-Cola Cup Final: "This would bring a tear to a glass eye."

DAVID PLEAT (Sheff. Wed.) "Managers suffer agonies, standing by the dugout and making all kinds of signals, yelling advice and encouragement. But it makes next to no difference. We all know inside that once the whistle blows, there is nothing we can do. Yet we still urge them to run faster, jump higher, kick harder."

ALAN SHEARER on becoming the world's first £15m. footballer: "The money won't change me. After all, I'm a sheet-metal worker's son from Newcastle."

JOHN MOTSON: "If I hadn't been a commentator, I think I would have been a taxi driver. It's a similar sort of 'knowledge' really – names, places, attention to detail."

VICKI OYSTON, Blackpool's acting chairman, asked by then-manager Sam Ellis (as she travelled on the team bus for the first time) whether she might be embarrassed by industrial language: "Don't worry, I'll try not to use any."

ROY EVANS, Liverpool manager: "I always enjoy the summer. You can't lose any matches."

JOE HARVEY on team balance (in his days as Newcastle manager): "It's no good putting up your umbrella if your wellies are leaking."

SCOTLAND PLAYER, responding to manager Craig Brown's suggestion that the squad might enjoy a visit to the Parthenon while training in Athens: "I didn't know the discos were open at this time of day, boss."

PHILIPPE ALBERT (Newcastle) on criticism of a midfield performance: "I read an article which said I was like a fish outside the water."

HARRY REDKNAPP, West Ham manager, on the new breed of club administrator, the Director of Football: "They have no pressure, all the answers – and it's the manager who gets the boot."

RICK PARRY, moving from Premier League chief executive to a similar post with Liverpool: "God gave me two ears and one mouth, and I have attempted to use them in that ratio."

JOHN MOTSON (Cup Final Grandstand) after Roberto di Matteo's goal for Chelsea in 42 seconds: "Anybody late to their seats would have missed that, wouldn't they, Trevor?"

NEW HOMES OF SOCCER

As more clubs leave 19th-century grounds for homes worthy of the approaching millennium, supporter-continuity of grandfather, father and son all watching "their team" in the same old surroundings is bull-dozed into history.

Four of the oldest League clubs – Bolton, Derby, Stoke and Sunderland – have moved to pastures new for season 1997-98 after playing collectively for 422 years at Burnden Park, the Baseball Ground, the Victoria Ground and Roker Park respectively.

Bolton Wanderers are back in the Premiership, this time with prospects of staying after a £22m. takeover. They have left Burnden after 102 years for the 25,000, all-seat, state-of-the art Reebok Stadium six miles away at Horwich. Their new ground, costing £30m., is constructed on the site of what was once a wild-life retreat. The East stand is named after "Mr. Bolton" himself, their former player, manager and now president, **Nat Lofthouse**.

Derby County, after a satisfactory first season back in the top class, have moved a mile from the Baseball Ground, their home since 1895, to Pride Park, which has a capacity of 30,000. It cost £16m., and while the new pitch settles, the old home will be used for reserve and youth matches.

In the Potteries, **Stoke City** leave the historic Victoria Ground, the oldest in League football, after 119 years. Their £15m. Britannia Stadium complex at Trentham Lakes is half a mile away, and the main approach is Stanley Matthews Way. Nice touch, that. It seats 28,000, incorporates a sports centre for the community and has parking space for 2,000 cars.

The Roker Roar is no more. **Sunderland's** 99-year tenure of their only League headquarters ended on a sad note with relegation a year after they won the First Division. If only more money had been invested in the team. Their 42,000-capacity, £17.25m. home at Monkwearmouth is half a mile from Roker, which is to become a housing estate and the contents of which were auctioned in June.

Chelsea continue to build a spectacular £100m. new home without leaving their old one. Stamford Bridge is again three-sided this season while a new West stand is built. The reconstructed South end, formerly the Shed, is ready for business, and behind it, on Fulham Road, the Chelsea Village Hotel is due for completion in November.

It will have 160 bedrooms, four restaurants, conference centre, shops, offices, banqueting facilities and an apartment block. Atop it all, in his penthouse suite, **Ken Bates** will be more than ever the hands-on chairman.

Oxford United's departure from the Manor Ground draws closer. Their new £16m. stadium at Minchery Farm will hold 15,000 all-seated, with accommodation also for 2,000 cars.

Reading are playing their last season at Elm Park, and **Blackpool** have plans for a 40,000 all-seat super stadium.

Brighton's 95 years at the Goldstone Ground ended after last-day survival in the Third Division. But their future, as both a League club and in terms of location, was shrouded in obscurity. Well into July, it was undecided whether they would take a temporary home this season at Gillingham or Millwall.

The Football League introduced **Stadia Achievement Awards** in 1995, and four more clubs were recognised in April for their dedication and hard work in improving spectator facilities during the previous 12 months.

The Design and Innovation categories were won by **Sheffield United** and **Bradford City** for the imagination shown in redeveloping their grounds, while the **Most Progress** awards were won by Second Division clubs **Burnley** and **Wycombe Wanderers**.

FULHAM TAKE-OVER

Mohamed Al Fayed, 64-year-old, Egyptian-born owner of Harrods, went shopping himself in May, and bought Fulham Football Club for £30m. It was an eventful month for Fulham – they won promotion to the Second Division and Jimmy Hill resigned as chairman.

ATTENDANCES 1996-97
(Official Figures)

League attendances last season (Premiership and Nationwide League) totalled 22,791,527 and were the **highest for 17 years** – since 24,623,975 in 1979-80.

Premier League crowds, at an aggregate of 10,804,762, were up by 335,656 (an increase of 3.2%) and **Nationwide League** gates, totalling 11,986,765, showed an increase of 611,456.

In addition, the **play-offs** in Divs. 1, 2 and 3 were watched by 309,085 spectators.

The **ten best-supported clubs in the Premier League** were: **1** Man. United, average 55,081; **2** Liverpool 39,777; **3** Arsenal 37,821; **4** Newcastle 36,466; **5** Everton 36,186; **6** Aston Villa 36,027; **7** Leeds 32,109; **8** Tottenham 31,067; **9** Middlesbrough 29,848; **10** Chelsea 27,001. The first nine in that list finished in the same order the previous season.

In **Div. 1**, the top average attendance last season was **Man. City's** 26,753; in **Div. 2**, **Bristol City's** 10,802; and in **Div. 3**, **Fulham's** 6,644.

LEAGUE CROWDS SINCE 1980

	Total	Div. One	Div. Two	Div. Three	Div. Four
1979-80	24,623,975	12,163,002	6,112,025	3,999,328	2,349,620
1980-81	21,907,569	11,392,894	5,175,442	3,637,854	1,701,379
1981-82	20,006,961	10,420,793	4,750,463	2,836,915	1,998,790
1982-83	18,766,158	9,295,613	4,974,937	2,943,568	1,552,040
1983-84	18,358,631	8,711,448	5,359,757	2,729,942	1,557,484
1984-85	17,849,835	9,761,404	4,030,823	2,667,008	1,390,600
1985-86	16,498,868	9,037,854	3,555,343	2,495,991	1,409,680
1986-87	17,383,032	9,144,676	4,168,131	2,354,784	1,715,441
1987-88	17,968,887	8,094,571	5,350,754	2,751,275	1,772,287
1988-89	18,477,565	7,809,993	5,827,805	3,048,700	1,791,067
1989-90	19,466,826	7,887,658	6,884,439	2,803,551	1,891,178
1990-91	19,541,341	8,618,790	6,297,733	2,847,813	1,777,086
1991-92	20,487,273	9,989,160	5,809,787	2,993 352	1,694,974

New format	Total	Premier	Div. One	Div. Two	Div. Three
1992-93	20,657,327	9,759,809	5,874,017	3,483,073	1,540,428
1993-94	21,693,889	10,655,059	6,487,104	2,972,702	1,579,024
1994-95	21,856,223	11,213,371	6,044,293	3,037,752	1,560,807
1995-96	21,844,416	10,469,118	6,566,349	2,843,652	1,965,308
1996-97	22,791,527	10,804,762	6,804,606	3,332,451	1,849,708

Note: All-time record Football League attendance aggregate: 41,271,414 in season 1948-49 (88 clubs).

LOWEST CROWDS – BUT ON THE UP

Wimbledon have had the lowest single-match home attendances in all five seasons of the Premier League, but the figure has gone up each time: 3,039 in 1992-3; 4,739 in 1993-4; 5,268 in 1994-5; 6,352 in 1995-6; 7,979 in 1996-7.

TOP FIVE DO IT AGAIN

Led by **Manchester Utd.**, the top five in the Premiership's final table last May were the same clubs who filled those places the previous season, though not in the same order. That had never happened before in the 109 years of League football.

F.A. CARLING PREMIERSHIP RESULTS 1996-97

	Arsenal	Aston Villa	Blackburn Rovers	Chelsea	Coventry City	Derby County	Everton	Leeds United	Leicester City	Liverpool	Manchester Utd.	Middlesbrough	Newcastle Utd.	Nott'm Forest
Arsenal	–	2-2	1-1	3-3	0-0	2-2	3-1	3-0	2-0	1-2	1-2	2-0	0-1	2-0
Aston Villa	2-2	–	1-0	0-2	2-1	2-0	3-1	2-0	1-3	1-0	0-0	1-0	2-2	2-0
Blackburn Rovers	0-2	0-2	–	1-1	4-0	1-2	1-1	0-1	2-4	3-0	2-3	0-0	1-0	1-1
Chelsea	0-3	1-1	1-1	–	2-0	3-1	2-2	0-0	2-1	1-0	1-1	1-0	1-1	1-1
Coventry City	1-1	1-2	0-0	3-1	–	1-2	0-0	2-1	0-0	0-1	0-2	3-0	2-1	0-3
Derby County	1-3	2-1	0-0	3-2	2-1	–	0-1	3-3	2-0	0-1	1-1	2-1	0-1	0-0
Everton	0-2	0-1	0-2	1-2	1-1	1-0	–	0-0	1-1	1-1	0-2	1-2	2-0	2-0
Leeds United	0-0	0-0	0-0	2-0	1-3	0-0	1-0	–	3-0	0-2	0-4	1-1	0-1	2-0
Leicester City	0-2	1-0	1-1	1-3	0-2	4-2	1-2	1-0	–	0-3	2-2	1-3	2-0	2-2
Liverpool	2-0	3-0	0-0	5-1	1-2	2-1	1-1	4-0	1-1	–	1-3	5-1	4-3	4-2
Manchester Utd.	1-0	0-0	2-2	1-2	3-1	2-3	2-2	1-0	3-1	1-0	–	0-0	0-0	4-1
Middlesbrough	0-2	3-2	2-1	1-0	4-0	6-1	4-2	0-0	0-2	3-3	2-2	–	0-1	1-1
Newcastle Utd.	1-2	4-3	2-1	3-1	4-0	3-1	4-1	3-0	4-3	1-1	5-0	3-1	–	5-0
Nott'm Forest	2-1	0-2	2-2	2-0	0-1	1-1	0-1	1-0	0-0	1-1	0-4	1-1	0-0	–
Sheffield Wed.	0-0	2-1	1-1	0-2	0-0	0-0	2-1	2-2	1-1	1-1	3-1	1-1	2-0	
Southampton	0-2	0-1	2-0	0-0	2-2	3-1	2-2	0-2	2-2	0-1	6-3	4-0	2-2	2-2
Sunderland	1-0	1-0	0-0	3-0	1-0	2-0	3-0	0-1	0-0	1-2	2-1	2-2	1-2	1-1
Tottenham H.	0-0	1-0	2-1	1-2	1-2	1-1	0-0	1-0	1-2	0-2	1-2	1-0	1-2	0-1
West Ham Utd.	1-2	0-2	2-1	3-2	1-1	1-1	2-2	0-2	1-0	1-2	2-2	0-0	0-0	0-1
Wimbledon	2-2	0-2	1-0	0-1	2-2	1-1	4-0	2-0	1-3	2-1	0-3	1-1	1-1	1-0

Read across for home results, down for away

Sheffield Wed.	Southampton	Sunderland	Tottenham H.	West Ham Utd.	Wimbledon	
4-1	3-1	2-0	3-1	2-0	0-1	Arsenal
0-1	1-0	1-0	1-1	0-0	5-0	Aston Villa
4-1	2-1	1-0	0-2	2-1	3-1	Blackburn Rovers
2-2	1-0	6-2	3-1	3-1	2-4	Chelsea
0-0	1-1	2-2	1-2	1-3	1-1	Coventry City
2-2	1-1	1-0	4-2	1-0	0-2	Derby County
2-0	7-1	1-3	1-0	2-1	1-3	Everton
0-2	0-0	3-0	0-0	1-0	1-0	Leeds United
1-0	2-1	1-1	1-1	0-1	1-0	Leicester City
0-1	2-1	0-0	2-1	0-0	1-1	Liverpool
2-0	2-1	5-0	2-0	2-0	2-1	Manchester Utd.
4-2	0-1	0-1	0-3	4-1	0-0	Middlesbrough
1-2	0-1	1-1	7-1	1-1	2-0	Newcastle Utd.
0-3	1-3	1-4	2-1	0-2	1-1	Nott'm Forest
–	1-1	2-1	2-1	0-0	3-1	Sheffield Wed.
2-3	–	3-0	0-1	2-0	0-0	Southampton
1-1	0-1	–	0-4	0-0	1-3	Sunderland
1-0	3-1	2-0	–	1-0	1-0	Tottenham H.
5-1	2-1	2-0	4-3	–	0-2	West Ham Utd.
4-2	3-1	1-0	1-0	1-1	–	Wimbledon

NATIONWIDE LEAGUE
RESULTS 1996-97

FIRST DIVISION

	Barnsley	Birmingham City	Bolton Wanderers	Bradford City	Charlton Athletic	Crystal Palace	Grimsby Town	Huddersfield Town	Ipswich Town	Manchester City	Norwich City	Oldham Athletic	Oxford United	Portsmouth
Barnsley	–	0-1	2-2	2-0	4-0	0-0	1-3	3-1	1-2	2-0	3-1	2-0	0-0	3-2
Birmingham City	0-0	–	3-1	3-0	0-0	1-0	0-0	1-0	1-0	2-0	2-3	0-0	2-0	0-3
Bolton Wanderers	2-2	2-1	–	2-1	4-1	2-2	6-1	2-0	1-2	1-0	3-1	3-1	4-0	2-0
Bradford City	2-2	0-2	2-4	–	1-0	0-4	3-4	1-1	2-1	1-3	0-2	0-3	2-0	3-1
Charlton Athletic	2-2	2-1	3-3	0-2	–	2-1	1-2	1-1	1-1	4-4	1-0	2-0	2-1	
Crystal Palace	1-1	0-1	1-1	3-1	1-0	–	3-0	1-1	0-0	3-1	2-0	3-1	2-2	1-2
Grimsby Town	2-3	1-2	1-2	1-1	2-0	2-1	–	2-2	2-1	1-1	1-4	0-3	0-2	0-1
Huddersfield Town	0-0	3-0	1-2	3-3	2-0	1-1	2-0	–	2-0	1-1	2-0	3-2	1-0	1-3
Ipswich Town	1-1	1-1	0-1	3-2	2-1	3-1	1-1	1-3	–	1-0	2-0	4-0	2-1	1-1
Manchester City	1-2	1-0	1-2	3-2	2-1	1-1	3-1	0-0	1-0	–	2-1	1-0	2-3	1-1
Norwich City	1-1	0-1	0-1	2-0	1-2	1-1	2-1	2-0	3-1	0-0	–	2-0	1-1	1-0
Oldham Athletic	0-1	2-2	0-0	1-2	1-1	0-1	0-3	1-2	3-3	2-1	3-0	–	2-1	0-0
Oxford United	5-1	0-0	0-0	2-0	0-2	1-4	3-2	1-0	3-1	1-4	0-1	3-1	–	2-0
Portsmouth	4-2	1-1	0-3	3-1	2-0	2-2	1-0	3-1	0-1	2-1	0-1	1-0	2-1	–
Port Vale	1-3	3-0	1-1	1-1	2-0	0-2	1-1	0-0	2-2	0-2	6-1	3-2	2-0	0-2
Q.P.R.	3-1	1-1	1-2	1-0	1-2	0-1	3-0	2-0	0-1	2-2	3-2	0-1	2-1	2-1
Reading	1-2	0-0	3-2	0-0	2-2	1-6	1-1	4-1	1-0	2-0	2-1	2-0	2-0	0-0
Sheffield Utd.	0-1	4-4	1-1	3-0	3-0	3-0	3-1	3-1	1-3	2-0	2-3	2-2	3-1	1-0
Southend Utd.	1-2	1-1	5-2	1-1	0-2	2-1	1-0	1-2	0-0	2-3	1-1	1-1	2-2	2-1
Stoke City	1-0	1-0	1-2	1-0	1-0	2-2	3-1	3-2	0-1	2-1	1-2	2-1	2-1	3-1
Swindon Town	3-0	3-1	2-2	1-1	1-0	0-2	3-3	6-0	0-4	2-0	0-3	1-0	1-0	0-1
Tranmere Rovers	1-1	1-0	2-2	3-0	4-0	1-3	3-2	1-1	3-0	1-1	3-1	1-1	0-0	4-3
W.B.A.	1-2	2-0	2-2	0-0	1-2	1-0	2-0	1-1	0-0	1-3	5-1	1-1	3-3	0-2
Wolves	3-3	1-2	1-2	1-0	1-0	0-3	1-1	0-0	0-0	3-0	3-2	0-1	3-1	0-1

Read across for home results, down for away

Port Vale	Q.P.R.	Reading	Sheffield Utd.	Southend Utd.	Stoke City	Swindon Town	Tranmere Rovers	W.B.A.	Wolves	
1-0	1-3	3-0	2-0	3-0	3-0	1-1	3-0	2-0	1-3	Barnsley
1-2	0-0	4-1	1-1	2-1	3-1	1-0	0-0	2-3	1-2	Birmingham City
4-2	2-1	2-1	2-2	3-1	1-1	7-0	1-0	1-0	3-0	Bolton Wanderers
1-0	3-0	0-0	1-2	0-0	1-0	2-1	1-0	1-1	2-1	Bradford City
1-3	2-1	1-0	0-0	2-0	1-2	2-0	3-1	1-1	0-0	Charlton Athletic
1-1	3-0	3-2	0-1	6-1	2-0	1-2	0-1	0-0	2-3	Crystal Palace
1-1	2-0	2-0	2-4	4-0	1-1	2-1	0-0	1-1	1-3	Grimsby Town
0-1	1-2	1-0	2-1	0-0	2-1	0-0	0-1	0-0	0-2	Huddersfield Town
2-1	2-0	5-2	3-1	1-1	1-1	3-2	0-2	5-0	0-0	Ipswich Town
0-1	0-3	3-2	0-0	3-0	2-0	3-0	1-2	3-2	0-1	Manchester City
1-1	1-1	1-1	1-1	0-0	2-0	2-0	1-1	2-4	1-0	Norwich City
3-0	0-2	1-1	0-2	0-0	1-2	5-1	1-2	1-1	3-2	Oldham Athletic
0-2	2-3	2-1	4-1	5-0	4-1	2-0	2-1	1-0	1-1	Oxford United
1-1	1-2	1-0	1-1	1-0	1-0	0-1	1-3	4-0	0-2	Portsmouth
–	4-4	1-0	0-0	2-1	1-1	1-0	2-1	2-2	1-2	Port Vale
1-2	–	0-2	1-0	4-0	1-1	1-1	2-0	0-2	2-2	Q.P.R.
0-1	2-1	–	1-0	3-2	2-2	2-0	2-0	2-2	2-1	Reading
3-0	1-1	2-0	–	3-0	1-0	2-0	0-0	1-2	2-3	Sheffield Utd.
0-0	0-1	2-1	3-2	–	2-1	1-3	1-1	2-3	1-1	Southend Utd.
2-0	0-0	1-1	0-4	1-2	–	2-0	2-0	2-1	1-0	Stoke City
1-1	1-1	3-1	2-1	0-0	1-0	–	2-1	2-3	1-2	Swindon Town
2-0	2-3	2-2	1-1	3-0	0-0	2-1	–	2-3	0-2	Tranmere Rovers
1-1	4-1	3-2	1-2	4-0	0-2	1-2	1-2	–	2-4	W.B.A.
0-1	1-1	0-1	1-2	4-1	2-0	1-0	3-2	2-0	–	Wolves

SECOND DIVISION

	Blackpool	Bournemouth	Brentford	Bristol City	Bristol Rovers	Burnley	Bury	Chesterfield	Crewe Alexandra	Gillingham	Luton Town	Millwall	Notts County	Peterborough Utd.
Blackpool	–	1-1	1-0	1-0	3-2	1-3	2-0	0-1	1-2	2-0	0-0	3-0	1-0	5-1
Bournemouth	0-0	–	2-1	0-2	1-0	0-0	1-1	3-0	0-1	2-2	3-2	1-1	0-1	1-2
Brentford	1-1	1-0	–	0-0	0-0	0-3	0-2	1-0	0-2	2-0	3-2	0-0	2-0	0-1
Bristol City	0-1	0-1	1-2	–	1-1	2-1	1-0	2-0	3-0	0-1	5-0	1-1	4-0	2-0
Bristol Rovers	0-0	3-2	2-1	1-2	–	1-2	4-3	2-0	2-0	0-0	3-2	1-0	1-0	1-0
Burnley	2-0	1-0	1-2	2-3	2-2	–	3-1	0-0	2-0	5-1	0-2	1-0	1-0	5-0
Bury	1-0	2-1	1-1	4-0	2-1	1-0	–	1-0	1-0	3-0	0-0	2-0	2-0	1-0
Chesterfield	0-0	1-1	0-2	1-1	1-0	0-0	1-2	–	1-0	2-2	1-1	1-0	1-0	2-1
Crewe Alexandra	3-2	2-0	2-0	1-2	1-0	1-1	2-0	1-2	–	3-2	0-0	0-0	3-0	1-1
Gillingham	2-3	1-1	1-2	3-2	2-1	1-0	2-2	0-1	2-1	–	1-2	2-3	1-0	2-1
Luton Town	1-0	2-0	1-0	2-2	2-1	1-2	0-0	0-1	6-0	2-1	–	0-2	2-0	3-0
Millwall	2-1	0-1	0-0	0-2	2-0	2-1	1-0	2-1	2-0	0-2	0-1	–	1-0	0-2
Notts County	1-1	0-2	1-1	2-0	1-1	1-1	1-0	0-1	0-0	0-1	1-1	1-2	–	0-0
Peterborough Utd.	0-0	3-1	0-1	3-1	1-2	3-2	1-2	1-1	2-2	0-1	0-1	3-3	1-3	–
Plymouth Argyle	0-1	0-0	1-4	0-0	0-1	0-0	2-0	0-3	1-0	2-0	3-3	0-0	0-0	1-1
Preston North End	3-0	0-1	1-0	0-2	0-0	1-1	3-1	0-1	1-1	1-0	3-2	2-1	2-0	3-4
Rotherham United	1-2	1-0	0-1	2-2	0-0	1-0	1-1	0-1	1-4	1-2	0-3	0-0	2-2	2-0
Shrewsbury T.	1-3	1-1	0-3	1-0	2-0	2-1	1-1	2-0	0-1	1-2	0-3	1-1	2-1	2-2
Stockport County	1-0	0-1	1-2	1-1	1-0	1-0	2-1	1-0	1-0	2-1	1-1	5-1	0-0	0-0
Walsall	1-1	2-1	1-0	2-0	1-0	1-3	3-1	1-1	1-0	1-0	3-2	2-1	3-1	4-0
Watford	2-2	0-1	2-0	3-0	1-0	2-2	0-0	0-2	0-1	0-0	1-1	0-2	0-0	0-0
Wrexham	2-1	0-2	0-2	2-1	1-0	0-0	1-1	3-2	1-1	2-1	3-3	3-3	3-3	1-1
Wycombe W.	1-0	1-1	0-1	2-0	2-0	5-0	0-1	1-0	2-0	1-1	0-1	1-0	1-0	2-0
York City	1-0	1-2	2-4	0-3	2-2	1-0	0-2	0-0	1-1	2-3	1-1	3-2	1-2	1-0

Read across for home results, down for away

Plymouth Argyle	Preston North End	Rotherham United	Shrewsbury Town	Stockport County	Walsall	Watford	Wrexham	Wycombe W.	York City	
2-2	2-1	4-1	1-1	2-1	2-1	1-1	3-3	0-0	3-0	Blackpool
1-0	2-0	1-1	0-0	0-0	0-1	1-2	2-1	2-1	1-1	Bournemouth
3-2	0-0	4-2	0-0	2-2	1-1	1-1	2-0	0-0	3-3	Brentford
3-1	2-1	0-2	3-2	1-1	4-1	1-1	2-1	3-0	2-0	Bristol City
2-0	1-0	1-2	2-0	1-1	0-1	0-1	2-0	3-4	1-1	Bristol Rovers
2-1	1-2	3-3	1-3	5-2	2-1	4-1	2-0	2-1	1-2	Burnley
1-0	3-0	3-1	2-0	0-0	2-1	1-1	0-0	2-0	4-1	Bury
1-2	2-1	1-1	2-1	0-1	1-0	0-0	0-0	4-2	2-0	Chesterfield
3-0	1-0	1-0	5-1	1-0	1-0	0-2	3-1	3-0	0-1	Crewe Alexandra
4-1	1-1	3-1	2-0	1-0	2-0	3-1	1-2	1-0	0-1	Gillingham
2-2	5-1	1-0	2-0	1-1	3-1	0-0	0-0	0-0	2-0	Luton Town
0-0	3-2	2-0	2-1	3-4	1-0	0-1	1-1	2-1	1-1	Millwall
2-1	2-1	0-0	1-2	1-2	2-0	2-3	0-0	1-2	0-1	Notts County
0-0	2-0	6-2	2-2	0-2	0-1	2-1	0-1	6-3	2-2	Peterborough Utd.
–	2-1	1-0	2-2	0-0	2-0	0-0	0-1	0-0	2-1	Plymouth Argyle
1-1	–	0-0	2-1	1-0	2-0	1-1	2-1	2-1	1-0	Preston North End
1-2	0-1	–	1-2	0-0	1-2	0-0	0-0	2-1	0-2	Rotherham United
2-3	0-2	0-2	–	3-2	2-2	1-0	0-1	1-1	2-0	Shrewsbury Town
3-1	1-0	0-0	3-1	–	2-0	1-0	0-2	2-1	2-1	Stockport County
0-1	1-0	1-1	2-2	1-1	–	1-1	0-1	2-2	1-1	Walsall
0-2	1-0	2-0	2-0	1-0	1-0	–	1-1	1-0	4-0	Watford
4-4	1-0	1-0	2-1	2-3	1-2	3-1	–	1-0	0-0	Wrexham
2-1	0-1	4-2	3-0	0-2	0-2	0-0	0-0	–	3-1	Wycombe W.
1-1	3-1	2-1	0-0	1-2	0-2	1-2	1-0	2-0	–	York City

THIRD DIVISION

	Barnet	Brighton & H.A.	Cambridge United	Cardiff City	Carlisle United	Chester City	Colchester United	Darlington	Doncaster Rovers	Exeter City	Fulham	Hartlepool United	Hereford United	Hull City
Barnet	–	3-0	2-1	3-1	0-0	1-2	2-4	0-0	3-0	3-0	2-2	1-0	2-3	1-0
Brighton & H.A.	1-0	–	1-2	2-0	1-3	2-1	1-1	2-3	1-0	1-0	0-0	5-0	0-1	3-0
Cambridge United	1-0	1-1	–	0-2	1-3	2-2	1-0	5-2	0-1	3-2	0-1	1-0	0-1	1-0
Cardiff City	1-2	1-0	0-0	–	2-0	1-0	1-2	2-0	0-2	2-1	1-2	2-0	2-0	2-0
Carlisle United	2-1	2-1	3-0	0-2	–	3-1	3-0	1-0	0-0	2-0	1-2	1-0	2-3	0-0
Chester City	1-0	2-1	1-1	0-1	1-1	–	1-2	2-1	6-0	2-1	1-1	0-0	1-3	0-0
Colchester United	1-0	2-0	2-2	1-1	1-1	0-0	–	0-3	2-2	1-0	2-1	0-2	1-1	1-1
Darlington	0-1	2-0	2-0	2-1	2-1	1-1	1-1	–	0-3	0-1	0-2	1-2	1-0	1-0
Doncaster Rovers	1-1	3-0	2-1	3-3	0-1	0-1	0-0	3-2	–	1-2	0-2	0-1	1-0	0-0
Exeter City	1-1	2-1	0-1	2-0	2-1	1-5	0-3	3-2	1-1	–	0-1	2-0	1-1	0-0
Fulham	2-0	2-0	3-0	1-4	1-0	1-1	3-1	6-0	3-1	1-1	–	1-0	1-0	2-0
Hartlepool United	4-0	2-3	0-2	2-3	1-2	2-0	1-0	1-2	2-4	1-1	2-1	–	2-1	1-1
Hereford Town	1-1	1-1	0-1	1-1	2-3	1-2	1-0	1-1	1-0	1-2	0-0	0-1	–	0-1
Hull City	0-0	3-0	1-3	1-1	0-1	1-0	1-2	3-2	3-1	2-0	0-3	1-0	1-1	–
Leyton Orient	0-1	2-0	1-1	3-0	2-1	0-0	1-1	0-0	2-1	1-1	0-2	2-0	2-1	1-1
Lincoln City	1-0	2-1	1-1	2-0	1-1	0-0	3-2	2-0	3-2	2-3	2-0	2-1	3-3	0-1
Mansfield Town	0-0	1-1	1-0	1-3	0-0	0-2	1-1	2-1	2-0	0-1	0-0	1-0	3-1	1-0
Northampton Town	2-0	3-0	1-2	4-0	1-1	5-1	2-1	3-1	2-0	4-1	0-1	3-0	1-0	2-1
Rochdale	1-1	3-0	3-0	1-0	2-2	0-1	0-0	2-0	2-1	2-0	1-2	1-3	0-0	1-2
Scarborough	1-1	1-1	1-0	0-0	1-1	0-0	1-1	4-1	2-1	3-4	0-2	2-4	1-1	3-2
Scunthorpe United	1-2	1-0	3-2	0-1	0-0	0-2	2-1	3-2	1-2	4-1	1-4	2-1	5-1	2-2
Swansea City	3-0	1-0	3-1	0-1	2-1	1-1	1-1	2-0	3-1	1-2	2-2	4-0	0-0	
Torquay United	1-2	2-1	0-1	2-0	1-2	0-0	0-2	1-1	1-0	2-0	3-1	0-1	2-1	1-1
Wigan Athletic	2-0	1-0	1-1	0-1	1-0	4-2	1-0	3-2	4-1	2-0	1-1	2-2	4-1	1-2

Read across for home results, down for away

Leyton Orient	Lincoln City	Mansfield Town	Northampton Town	Rochdale	Scarborough	Scunthorpe United	Swansea City	Torquay United	Wigan Athletic	
0-0	1-0	1-1	1-1	3-2	1-3	1-1	0-1	0-0	1-1	Barnet
4-4	1-3	1-1	2-1	3-0	3-2	1-1	3-2	2-2	1-0	Brighton & H.A.
2-0	1-3	2-1	0-0	2-2	2-1	0-2	2-1	2-0	1-1	Cambridge United
3-0	1-3	1-2	2-2	2-1	1-1	0-0	1-3	2-0	0-2	Cardiff City
1-0	1-0	1-1	2-1	3-2	1-0	3-2	4-1	5-1	0-3	Carlisle United
0-1	4-1	1-0	2-1	0-0	1-0	1-0	2-0	0-0	1-1	Chester City
2-1	7-1	2-1	0-0	1-0	1-3	1-1	3-1	2-0	3-1	Colchester United
1-1	5-2	2-4	3-1	1-1	1-1	2-0	4-1	2-3	3-1	Darlington
2-1	1-3	0-0	·1-2	3-0	1-2	1-1	0-1	2-1	2-0	Doncaster Rovers
3-2	3-3	0-0	0-1	0-0	2-2	0-1	1-2	1-1	0-1	Exeter City
1-1	1-2	1-2	0-1	1-1	4-0	2-1	2-1	1-2	1-1	Fulham
3-1	2-1	2-2	0-2	1-2	1-0	0-1	1-1	1-1	1-1	Hartlepool United
2-0	1-1	0-1	1-2	3-0	2-2	3-2	0-1	1-1	3-1	Hereford United
3-1	2-1	1-1	1-1	1-1	0-2	0-2	1-1	2-0	1-1	Hull City
–	2-3	2-1	2-1	2-1	0-1	0-1	1-0	1-0	1-2	Leyton Orient
1-1	–	0-0	1-1	0-2	1-1	2-0	4-0	1-2	1-3	Lincoln City
0-2	2-2	–	1-0	0-0	2-0	2-0	0-0	1-2	0-1	Mansfield Town
0-1	1-1	3-0	–	2-2	1-0	1-0	1-2	1-1	0-1	Northampton Town
1-0	2-0	0-1	1-1	–	3-3	1-2	2-3	2-1	3-1	Rochdale
2-1	0-2	2-1	1-1	2-2	–	3-2	0-1	3-1	3-1	Scarborough
1-2	2-0	0-2	2-1	2-2	0-2	–	1-0	1-0	2-3	Scunthorpe United
1-0	1-2	3-2	1-0	2-1	1-2	1-1	–	2-0	2-1	Swansea City
0-0	2-1	1-2	1-2	0-1	1-0	1-2	2-0	–	0-3	Torquay United
5-1	1-0	2-0	2-1	0-1	7-1	3-0	3-2	3-2	–	Wigan Athletic

FINAL TABLES 1996-97
F.A. CARLING PREMIERSHIP

	P	W	D	L	F	A	W	D	L	F	A	Pts	GD
		HOME					**AWAY**						
1 Man. Utd.	38	12	5	2	38	17	9	7	3	38	27	75	+32
2 Newcastle Utd.	38	13	3	3	54	20	6	8	5	19	20	68	+33
3 Arsenal	38	10	5	4	36	18	9	6	4	26	14	68	+30
4 Liverpool	38	10	6	3	38	19	9	5	5	24	18	68	+25
5 Aston Villa	38	11	5	3	27	13	6	5	8	20	21	61	+13
6 Chelsea	38	9	8	2	33	24	7	3	9	25	33	59	+3
7 Sheffield Wed.	38	8	10	1	25	16	6	5	8	25	35	57	−1
8 Wimbledon	38	9	6	4	28	21	6	5	8	21	25	56	+3
9 Leicester City	38	7	5	7	22	26	5	6	8	24	28	47	−8
10 Tottenham H	38	8	4	7	19	17	5	3	11	25	34	46	−7
11 Leeds Utd.	38	7	5	7	15	13	4	6	9	13	25	46	−10
12 Derby Co.	38	8	6	5	25	22	3	7	9	20	36	46	−13
13 Blackburn Rov. ...	38	8	4	7	28	23	1	11	7	14	20	42	−1
14 West Ham Utd. ...	38	7	6	6	27	25	3	6	10	12	23	42	−9
15 Everton	38	7	4	8	24	22	3	8	8	20	35	42	−13
16 Southampton	38	6	7	6	32	24	4	4	11	18	32	41	−6
17 Coventry City	38	4	8	7	19	23	5	6	8	19	31	41	−16
18 Sunderland	38	7	6	6	20	18	3	4	12	15	35	40	−18
19 *Middlesbrough	38	8	5	6	34	25	2	7	10	17	35	39	−9
20 Nott'm Forest	38	3	9	7	15	27	3	7	9	16	32	34	−28

(*Middlesbrough deducted three points for failing to fulfil fixture at Blackburn on December 21) (Positions of clubs level on points decided on goal difference; if still level, on goals scored)

Man. United and Newcastle qualify for Champions' League; Arsenal, Liverpool, Aston Villa and Leicester (Coca-Cola Cup Winners) for UEFA Cup; Chelsea for Cup-Winners' Cup.

Prize Money: 1 £2,114,300; **2** £2,008,585; **3** £1,902,870; **4** £1,797,155; **5** £1,691,440; **6** £1,585,725; **7** £1,480,010; **8** £1,374,295; **9** £1,268,580; **10** £1,162,865; **11** £1,057,150; **12** £951,435; **13** £845,720; **14** £740,005; **15** £634,290; **16** £528,575; **17** £422,860; **18** £317,145; **19** £211,430; **20** £105,715.

Biggest Win: Everton 7, Southampton 1; Newcastle 7, Tottenham 1.

Highest Attendance: 55,314 (Man. United v Wimbledon).

Lowest Attendance: 7,979 (Wimbledon v Leeds).

Top League Scorer: 25 Alan Shearer (Newcastle).

Top Scorers, all Competitions: 31 Fowler (Liverpool), Ravanelli (Middlesbrough).

Carling Manager of Year (£7,500): Alex Ferguson (Man. Utd.).

Carling Player of Year (£2,500): Juninho (Middlesbrough).

Football Writers' Footballer of Year: Gianfranco Zola (Chelsea).

PFA Player of Year: Alan Shearer (Newcastle).

PFA Young Player of Year: David Beckham (Man. United).

PFA Divisional Team of Season: Seaman (Arsenal); G. Neville (Man. Utd.), Bjornebye (Liverpool), Adams (Arsenal), M.Wright (Liverpool), Batty (Newcastle), Keane (Man. U.), Beckham (Man. U.), McManaman (Liverpool), Shearer (Newcastle), I.Wright (Arsenal).

Fair Play Award: Liverpool (third successive year).

Best Behaved Supporters Award: Nottingham Forest.

Premier League Groundsman of Year: Steve Patrick (Blackburn).

NATIONWIDE FOOTBALL LEAGUE
FIRST DIVISION

		HOME					AWAY						
	P	W	D	L	F	A	W	D	L	F	A	Pts	Gls
1 Bolton Wand.	46	18	4	1	60	20	10	10	3	40	33	98	100
2 Barnsley	46	14	4	5	43	19	8	10	5	33	36	80	76
3 Wolves	46	10	5	8	31	24	12	5	6	37	27	76	68
4 Ipswich Town	46	13	7	3	44	23	7	7	9	24	27	74	68
5 Sheff. Utd.	46	13	5	5	46	23	7	8	8	29	29	73	75
6 *Crystal Palace	46	10	7	6	39	22	9	7	7	39	26	71	78
7 Portsmouth	46	12	4	7	32	24	8	4	11	27	29	68	59
8 Port Vale	46	9	9	5	36	28	8	7	8	22	27	67	58
9 Q.P.R.	46	10	5	8	33	25	8	7	8	31	35	66	64
10 Birmingham City	46	11	7	5	30	18	6	8	9	22	30	66	52
11 Tranmere Rov.	46	10	9	4	42	27	7	5	11	21	29	65	63
12 Stoke City	46	15	3	5	34	22	3	7	13	17	35	64	51
13 Norwich City	46	9	10	4	28	18	8	2	13	35	50	63	63
14 Man. City	46	12	4	7	34	25	5	6	12	25	35	61	59
15 Charlton Ath.	46	11	8	4	36	28	5	3	15	16	38	59	52
16 West Brom.	46	7	7	9	37	33	7	8	8	31	39	57	68
17 Oxford Utd.	46	14	3	6	44	26	2	6	15	20	42	57	64
18 Reading	46	13	7	3	37	24	2	5	16	21	43	57	58
19 Swindon Town	46	11	6	6	36	27	4	3	16	16	44	54	52
20 Huddersfield T.	46	10	7	6	28	20	3	8	12	20	41	54	48
21 Bradford City	46	10	5	8	29	32	2	7	14	18	40	48	47
22 Grimsby Town	46	7	7	9	31	34	4	6	13	29	47	46	60
23 Oldham Ath.	46	6	8	9	30	30	4	5	14	21	36	43	51
24 Southend Utd.	46	7	9	7	32	32	1	6	16	10	54	39	42

(*Also promoted via play-offs)
(Positions of clubs level on points decided on goals scored)

Prize Money – Champions: Bolton £50,000; runners-up: Barnsley £25,000.
Biggest Win: Bolton 7, Swindon 1.
Highest Attendance: 30,729 (Man. City v Oldham).
Lowest Attendance: 3,305 (Southend v Grimsby).
Top League Scorer: 24 John McGinlay (Bolton).
Top Scorer, all Competitions: 30 John McGinlay (Bolton).
First Division Manager of Year: Colin Todd (Bolton).
Managers' Manager of Year: Danny Wilson (Barnsley).
PFA Divisional Team of Season: A. Kelly (Sheff. U.); Eaden (Barnsley), Taggart (Bolton), Froggatt (Wolves), Kinkladze (Man. City), Richards (Wolves), Sheron (Stoke), Eadie (Norwich), Sinclair (Q.P.R.), Thompson (Bolton), McGinlay (Bolton).
Fair Play Award: Bolton.
First Division Groundsman of Year: Mike Phillips (Grimsby).

SECOND DIVISION

		HOME						AWAY						
	P	W	D	L	F	A	W	D	L	F	A	Pts	Gls
1 Bury	46	18	5	0	39	7	6	7	10	23	31	84	62
2 Stockport Co.	46	15	5	3	31	14	8	8	7	28	27	82	59
3 Luton Town	46	13	7	3	38	14	8	8	7	33	31	78	71
4 Brentford	46	8	11	4	26	22	12	3	8	30	21	74	56
5 Bristol City	46	14	4	5	43	18	7	6	10	26	33	73	69
6 *Crewe Alex.	46	15	4	4	38	15	7	3	13	18	32	73	56
7 Blackpool	46	13	7	3	41	21	5	8	10	19	26	69	60
8 Wrexham	46	11	9	3	37	28	6	9	8	17	22	69	54
9 Burnley	46	14	3	6	48	27	5	8	10	23	28	68	71
10 Chesterfield	46	10	9	4	25	18	8	5	10	17	21	68	42
11 Gillingham	46	13	3	7	37	25	6	7	10	23	34	67	60
12 Walsall	46	12	8	3	35	21	7	2	14	19	32	67	54
13 Watford	46	10	8	5	24	14	6	11	6	21	24	67	45
14 Millwall	46	12	4	7	27	22	4	9	10	23	33	61	50
15 Preston N.E.	46	14	5	4	33	19	4	2	17	16	36	61	49
16 Bournemouth	46	8	9	6	24	20	7	6	10	19	25	60	43
17 Bristol Rovers	46	13	4	6	34	22	2	7	14	13	28	56	47
18 Wycombe Wand. .	46	13	4	6	31	14	2	6	15	20	42	55	51
19 Plymouth Arg.	46	7	11	5	19	18	5	7	11	28	40	54	47
20 York City	46	8	6	9	27	31	5	7	11	20	37	52	47
21 Peterborough Utd. .	46	7	7	9	38	34	4	7	12	17	39	47	55
22 Shrewsbury T.	46	8	6	9	27	32	3	7	13	22	42	46	49
23 Rotherham Utd.	46	4	7	12	24	27	3	7	13	22	41	35	39
24 Notts Co.	46	4	9	10	20	25	3	5	15	13	34	35	33

(*Also promoted via play-offs)
(Positions of clubs level on points decided on goals scored)

Prize Money – Champions: Bury £25,000; runners-up: Stockport £10,000.
Biggest Win: Peterborough 6, Rotherham 2.
Highest Attendance: 18,674 (Bristol C. v Bristol R.).
Lowest Attendance: 1,610 (Shrewsbury v Bournemouth).
Top League Scorer: 28 Tony Thorpe (Luton).
Top Scorer, all Competitions: 32 Tony Thorpe (Luton).
Second Division Manager of Year: David Jones (Stockport).
PFA Divisional Team of Season: Miller (Watford); Parkinson (Burnley), Eyres (Burnley), Murphy (Crewe), Flynn (Stockport), Davis (Luton), Whalley (Crewe), Marsden (Stockport), Asaba (Brentford), B.Hughes (Wrexham), Thorpe (Luton).
Fair Play Award: Luton.
Second Division Groundsman of Year: John Huxley (Crewe).

THIRD DIVISION

		HOME					AWAY						
	P	W	D	L	F	A	W	D	L	F	A	Pts	Gls
1 Wigan Ath.	46	17	3	3	53	21	9	6	8	31	30	87	84
2 Fulham	46	13	5	5	41	20	12	7	4	31	18	87	72
3 Carlisle Utd.	46	16	3	4	41	21	8	9	6	26	23	84	67
4 *Northampton T. ...	46	14	4	5	43	17	6	8	9	24	27	72	67
5 Swansea City	46	13	5	5	37	20	8	3	12	25	38	71	62
6 Chester City	46	11	8	4	30	16	7	8	8	25	27	70	55
7 Cardiff City	46	11	4	8	30	23	9	5	9	26	31	69	56
8 Colchester Utd.	46	11	9	3	36	23	6	8	9	26	28	68	62
9 Lincoln City	46	10	8	5	35	25	8	4	11	35	44	66	70
10 Cambridge Utd. ...	46	11	5	7	30	27	7	6	10	23	32	65	53
11 Mansfield Town ...	46	9	8	6	21	17	7	8	8	26	28	64	47
12 Scarborough	46	9	9	5	36	31	7	6	10	29	37	63	65
13 Scunthorpe Utd. ..	46	11	3	9	36	33	7	6	10	23	29	63	59
14 Rochdale	46	10	6	7	34	24	4	10	9	24	34	58	58
15 Barnet	46	9	9	5	32	23	5	7	11	14	28	58	46
16 Leyton Orient	46	11	6	6	28	20	4	6	13	22	38	57	50
17 Hull City	46	9	8	6	29	26	4	10	9	15	24	57	44
18 Darlington	46	11	5	7	37	28	3	5	15	27	50	52	64
19 Doncaster Rov.	46	9	7	7	29	23	5	3	15	23	43	52	52
20 Hartlepool Utd.	46	8	6	9	33	32	6	3	14	20	34	51	53
21 Torquay Utd.	46	9	4	10	24	24	7	1	22	38	50	46
22 Exeter City	46	6	9	8	25	30	6	3	14	23	43	48	48
23 †Brighton & H.A. ..	46	12	6	5	41	27	1	4	18	12	43	47	53
24 Hereford Utd.	46	6	8	9	26	25	5	6	12	24	40	47	50

(† Brighton deducted two points after pitch invasion at home
to Lincoln on October 1.)
(*Also promoted via play-offs)
(Hereford relegated to GM Vauxhall Conference)
(Positions of clubs level on points decided on goals scored)

Prize Money – Champions: Wigan £25,000; runners-up: Fulham £10,000;
third-place: Carlisle £5,000.
Biggest Win: Colchester 7, Lincoln 1; Wigan 7, Scarborough 1.
Highest Attendance: 11,479 (Fulham v Northampton).
Lowest Attendance: 1,030 (Doncaster v Northampton).
Top League Scorer: 31 Graeme Jones (Wigan).
Top Scorer, all Competitions: 33 Graeme Jones (Wigan).
Third Division Manager of Year: Micky Adams (Fulham).
PFA Divisional Team of Season: Caig (Carlisle); Hendon (Leyton O), Molby
(Swansea), Archdeacon (Carlisle), Martinez (Wigan), Walling (Carlisle),
Craddock (Cambridge), Aspinall (Carlisle), Ainsworth (Lincoln), G.Jones
(Wigan), Conroy (Fulham).
Fair Play Award: Wigan.
Third Division Groundsman of Year: Mark Harrison (Hull City).

NATIONWIDE LEAGUE PLAY-OFFS 1997

All three Wembley play-off Finals were settled by a single goal, two of them in the last seconds.

In the Third Division decider against Swansea, John Frain's 20-yard free-kick, three minutes into stoppage time, turned **Northampton Town's** first Wembley appearance into a day of carnival for the 33,000 who followed them. The crowd of 46,804 was the highest for a bottom-division play-off.

Earlier in the season Brentford were strongly placed for automatic promotion from Div.2. But they lost form, finished fourth and were decidedly second best to the young **Crewe** team at Wembley. Shaun Smith's goal brought deserved reward to Dario Gradi, who has been in charge at Gresty Road for 14 years and is contracted until 2006.

Another youthful side triumphed in the First Division play-offs, with Steve Coppell's **Crystal Palace** beating Sheffield United by a goal in the last ten seconds. David Hopkin flighted it into the top corner from 25 yards to compensate Palace for the previous year's play-off defeat.

SEMI-FINALS

(1st legs Sunday, May 11; 2nd legs Wednesday, May 14)

Div. 1: Crystal Palace 3, Wolves 1; Wolves 2, Crystal Palace 1 (**Palace** won 4-3 on agg.).
Sheff. United 1, Ipswich 1; Ipswich 2, Sheff. United 2 aet (**Sheff. United** won on away goals).

Div. 2: Bristol City 1, Brentford 2; Brentford 2, Bristol City 1 (**Brentford** won 4-2 on agg.).
Crewe 2, Luton 1; Luton 2, Crewe 2 (**Crewe** won 4-3 on agg.).

Div. 3: Cardiff 0, Northampton 1; Northampton 3, Cardiff 2 (**Northampton** won 4-2 on agg.).
Chester 0, Swansea 0; Swansea 3, Chester 0 (**Swansea** won 3-0 on agg.).

FINALS – AT WEMBLEY

Div. 3: Sat., May 24 – **Northampton** 1 (Frain 90), **Swansea** 0. Att: 46,804.
Northampton: Woodman; Sampson, Rennie (Peer 40), Warburton, Clarkson, Hunter, Parris, Frain, Lee, Gayle (White 77), Grayson. Sub not used: Gibb. **Manager**: Ian Atkins.
Swansea: Freestone; Penney, Edwards, Walker, Moreira, Ampadu, Molby, Coates, Torpey, Heggs, Thomas (Brown 83). Subs not used: Chapple, Lacey. **Player-manager**: Jan Molby.
Referee: T. Heilbron (Newton Aycliffe, Durham). **Half-time**: 0-0.

Div. 2: Sun., May 25 – **Brentford** 0, **Crewe Alexandra** 1 (S. Smith 34). **Att**: 34,149.
Brentford: Dearden; Hurdle (Ashby 75), Hutchings, Bates, Anderson, Bent (Canham 45), P. Smith, Statham, Asaba, Taylor, McGhee. Sub not used: Fernandez. **Sent off**: Statham. **Manager**: David Webb.
Crewe: Kearton; Unsworth, Westwood, Macauley, S. Smith, Little, Murphy (Johnson 86), Charnock (Lightfoot 88), Whalley, Adebola, Rivers (Garvey 70). **Manager**: Dario Gradi.
Referee: U. Rennie (Sheffield). **Half-time**: 0-1.

Div. 1: Mon., May 26 – **Crystal Palace** 1 (Hopkin 90), **Sheffield United** 0. Att: 64,383.
Crystal P: Nash; Tuttle, Edworthy, Linighan, Muscat, Roberts, Rodger, Gordon, Hopkin, Dyer, Shipperley. Subs not used: Houghton, McKenzie, Veart. **Manager**: Steve Coppell.
Sheff. Utd: Tracey; Holdsworth, Tiler, Nilsen, Spackman (Walker 90), White, Hutchinson (Sandford 45), Ward, Whitehouse, Fjortoft, Katchouro (Taylor 25). **Manager**: Howard Kendall.
Referee: N. Barry (Scunthorpe). **Half-time**: 0-0.

PLAY-OFF FINALS – HOME & AWAY

1987　**Divs 1/2: Charlton** beat Leeds 2-1 in replay (Birmingham) after 1-1 agg (1-0h, 0-1a). Charlton remained in Div.1. Losing semi-finalists: Ipswich and Oldham.

Divs 2/3: Swindon beat Gillingham 2-0 in replay (Crystal P.) after 2-2 agg (0-1a, 2-1h). Swindon promoted to Div.2. Losing semi-finalists: Sunderland and Wigan; Sunderland relegated to Div.3.

Divs 3/4: Aldershot beat Wolves 3-0 on agg (2-0h, 1-0a) and promoted to Div.3. Losing semi-finalists: Bolton and Colchester; Bolton relegated to Div.4.

1988　**Divs 1/2: Middlesbrough** beat Chelsea 2-1 on agg (2-0h, 0-1a) and promoted to Div.1; Chelsea relegated to Div.2. Losing semi-finalists: Blackburn and Bradford C.

Divs 2/3: Walsall beat Bristol City 4-0 in replay (h) after 3-3 agg (3-1a, 0-2h) and promoted to Div.2. Losing semi-finalists: Sheff. Utd. and Notts Co; Sheff. Utd. relegated to Div.3.

Divs 3/4: Swansea beat Torquay 5-4 on agg (2-1h, 3-3a) and promoted to Div.3. Losing semi-finalists: Rotherham and Scunthorpe; Rotherham relegated to Div.4.

1989　**Div.2: Crystal Palace** beat Blackburn 4-3 on agg (1-3a, 3-0h). Losing semi-finalists: Watford and Swindon.

Div.3: Port Vale beat Bristol R. 2-1 on agg (1-1a, 1-0h). Losing semi-finalists: Fulham and Preston.

Div.4: Leyton O. beat Wrexham 2-1 on agg (0-0a, 2-1h). Losing semi-finalists: Scarborough and Scunthorpe.

PLAY-OFF FINALS AT WEMBLEY

1990　**Div.2: Swindon** 1, Sunderland 0 (att: 72,873). Swindon promoted, then demoted for financial irregularities; Sunderland promoted. Losing semi-finalists: Blackburn and Newcastle.

Div.3: Notts Co. 2, Tranmere 0 (att: 29,252). Losing semi-finalists: Bolton and Bury.

Div.4: Cambridge Utd. 1, Chesterfield 0 (att: 26,404). Losing semi-finalists: Maidstone and Stockport.

1991　**Div.2: Notts Co.** 3, Brighton 1 (att: 59,940). Losing semi-finalists: Middlesbrough and Millwall.

Div.3: Tranmere 1, Bolton 0 (att: 30,217). Losing semi-finalists: Brentford and Bury.

Div.4: Torquay 2, Blackpool 2 – Torquay won 5-4 on pens (att: 21,615). Losing semi-finalists: Burnley and Scunthorpe.

1992　**Div.2: Blackburn** 1, Leicester 0 (att: 68,147). Losing semi-finalists: Derby and Cambridge Utd.

Div.3: Peterborough 2, Stockport 1 (att: 35,087). Losing semi-finalists: Huddersfield and Stoke.

Div.4: Blackpool 1, Scunthorpe 1 – Blackpool won 4-3 on pens (att: 22,741). Losing semi-finalists: Barnet and Crewe.

1993　**Div.1: Swindon** 4, Leicester 3 (att: 73,802). Losing semi-finalists: Portsmouth and Tranmere.

Div.2: W.B.A. 3, Port Vale 0 (att: 53,471). Losing semi-finalists: Stockport and Swansea.

Div.3: York 1, Crewe 1 – York won 5-3 on pens (att: 22,416). Losing semi-finalists: Bury and Walsall.

1994　**Div.1: Leicester** 2, Derby 1 (att: 73,671). Losing semi-finalists: Millwall and Tranmere.

Div.2: Burnley 2, Stockport 1 (att: 44,806). Losing semi-finalists: Plymouth and York.

Div.3: Wycombe 4, Preston 2 (att: 40,109). Losing semi-finalists: Carlisle and Torquay.

1995 **Div.1: Bolton** 4, Reading 3 (att: 64,107). Losing semi-finalists: Tranmere and Wolves.
Div.2: Huddersfield 2, Bristol R. 1 (att: 59,175). Losing semi-finalists: Brentford and Crewe.
Div.3: Chesterfield 2, Bury 0 (att: 22,814). Losing semi-finalists: Mansfield and Preston.

1996 **Div.1: Leicester** 2, Crystal Palace 1, aet (att: 73,573). Losing semi-finalists: Charlton and Stoke.
Div.2: Bradford City 2, Notts County 0 (att: 39,972). Losing semi-finalists: Blackpool and Crewe.
Div.3: Plymouth 1, Darlington 0 (att: 43,431). Losing semi-finalists: Colchester and Hereford.

1997 **Div.1: Crystal Palace** 1, Sheffield United 0, (att: 64,383). Losing semi-finalists: Ipswich and Wolves.
Div.2: Crewe Alexandra 1, Brentford 0 (att: 34,149). Losing semi-finalists: Bristol City and Luton.
Div.3: Northampton 1, Swansea 0 (att: 46,804). Losing semi-finalists: Cardiff and Chester.

HISTORY OF THE PLAY-OFFS

Play-off matches were introduced by the Football League to decide final promotion and relegation issues at the end of season 1986-87.

A similar series styled "Test Matches" had operated between Divisions 1 and 2 for six seasons from 1893-98, and was abolished when both divisions were increased from 16 to 18 clubs.

Eighty-eight years later, the play-offs were back in vogue. In the first three seasons (1987-88-89), the Finals were played home-and-away, and since they were made one-off matches in 1990, they have featured regularly in Wembley's spring calendar.

Through the years, these have been the ups and downs of the play-offs:

1987 Initially, the 12 clubs involved comprised the one that finished directly above those relegated in Divisions 1, 2 and 3 and the three who followed the sides automatically promoted in each section. Two of the home-and-away Finals went to neutral-ground replays, in which **Charlton** clung to First Division status by denying Leeds promotion while **Swindon** beat Gillingham to complete their climb from Fourth Division to Second in successive seasons. Via the play-offs, **Sunderland** fell into Div.3 and **Bolton** into Div.4, both for the first time. **Aldershot** went up after finishing only sixth in Div.4; in their Final, they beat Wolves, who had finished nine points higher and missed automatic promotion by one point.

1988 Chelsea were relegated from the First Division after losing on aggregate to Middlesbrough, who had finished third in Div.2. So Boro', managed by Bruce Rioch, completed the rise from Third Division to First in successive seasons, only two years after their very existence had been threatened by the bailiffs. Also promoted via the play-offs were **Walsall** from Div.3 and **Swansea** from Div.4. Relegated, besides Chelsea, were **Sheffield United** (to Div.3) and **Rotherham** to Div.4.

1989 After two seasons of promotion-relegation play-offs, the system was changed to involve the four clubs who had just missed automatic promotion in Divs. 2, 3 and 4. That format has remained. Steve Coppell's **Crystal Palace**, third in Div.2, returned to the top flight after eight years, beating Blackburn 4-3 on aggregate after extra time. Similarly, **Port Vale** confirmed third place in Div.3 with promotion via the play-offs. For **Leyton Orient**, promotion seemed out of the question in Div.4 when they stood 15th. on March 1. But eight wins and a draw in the last nine home games swept them to sixth in the final table, and two more home victories in the play-offs completed their season in triumph.

1990 The play-off Finals now moved to Wembley over three days of Spring Holiday week-end. On successive afternoons, **Cambridge United** won promotion from Div.4 and **Notts County** from Div.3. Then, on Bank Holiday Monday, the biggest crowd for years at a Football League fixture (72,873) saw Ossie Ardiles' **Swindon Town** beat Sunderland 1-0 to reach the First Division for the first time. A few weeks later, however, Wembley losers **Sunderland** were promoted instead, by default; Swindon were found guilty of "financial irregularities" and stayed in Div.2.

1991 Again, the season's biggest League crowd (59,940) gathered at Wembley for the First Division Final in which **Notts County** (having missed promotion by one point) still fulfilled their ambition, beating Brighton 3-1. In successive years, County had climbed from Third Division to First via the play-offs – the first club to achieve double promotion by this route. Bolton were denied automatic promotion in Div.3 on goal difference, and lost at Wembley to an extra-time goal by **Tranmere**. The Fourth Division Final made history, with Blackpool beaten 5-4 on penalties by **Torquay** – first instance of promotion being decided by a shoot-out. In the table, Blackpool had finished seven points ahead of Torquay.

1992 Wembley that Spring Bank Holiday was the turning point in the history of **Blackburn Rovers**. Bolstered by Kenny Dalglish's return to management and owner Jack Walker's millions, they beat Leicester 1-0 by Mike Newell's 45th-minute penalty to achieve their objective – a place in the new Premier League. Newell, who also missed a second-half penalty, had recovered from a broken leg just in time for the play-offs. In the Div.4 Final **Blackpool** (denied by penalties the previous year) this time won a shoot-out 4-3 against Scunthorpe, who were unlucky in the play-offs for the fourth time in five years. **Peterborough** climbed out of the Third Division for the first time, beating Stockport 2-1 at Wembley.

1993 The crowd of 73,802 at Wembley to see **Swindon** beat Leicester 4-3 in the First Division Final was 11,000 bigger than that for the F.A. Cup Final replay between Arsenal and Sheffield Wednesday. Leicester rallied from three down to 3-3 before Paul Bodin's late penalty wiped away Swindon's bitter memories of three years earlier, when they were denied promotion after winning at Wembley. In the Third Division Final, **York** beat Crewe 5-3 in a shoot-out after a 1-1 draw, and in the Div.2 decider, **West Bromwich Albion** beat Port Vale 3-0. That was tough on Vale, who had finished third in the table with 89 points – the highest total never to earn promotion in any division. They had beaten Albion twice in the League, too.

1994 Wembley's record turn-out of 158,586 spectators at the three Finals started with a crowd of 40,109 to see Martin O'Neill's **Wycombe Wanderers** beat Preston 4-2. They thus climbed from Conference to Second Division with successive promotions. **Burnley's** 2-1 victory in the Second Division Final was marred by the sending-off of two Stockport players, and in the First Division decider **Leicester** came from behind to beat Derby and end the worst Wembley record of any club. They had lost on all six previous appearances there – four times in the F.A. Cup Final and in the play-offs of 1992 and 1993.

1995 Two months after losing the Coca-Cola Cup Final to Liverpool, Bruce Rioch's **Bolton** were back at Wembley for the First Division play-off Final. From two goals down to Reading in front of a crowd of 64,107, they returned to the top company after 15 years, winning 4-3 with two extra-time goals. **Huddersfield** ended the first season at their new £15m. home with promotion to the First Division via a 2-1 victory against Bristol Rovers – manager Neil Warnock's third play-off success (after two with Notts County). Of the three clubs who missed automatic promotion by one place, only **Chesterfield** achieved it in the play-offs, comfortably beating Bury 2-0.

1996 Under new manager **Martin O'Neill** (a Wembley play-off winner with Wycombe in 1994), **Leicester City** returned to the Premier League a year after leaving it. They had finished fifth in the table, but in the Final came from behind to beat third-placed Crystal Palace by Steve Claridge's shot in the last seconds of extra time. In the Second Division **Bradford City** came sixth, 9 points behind Blackpool (3rd), but beat them (from two down in the semi-final first leg) and then clinched promotion by 2-0 v Notts County at Wembley. It was City's greatest day since they won the Cup in 1911. **Plymouth Argyle** beat Darlington in the Third Division Final to earn promotion a year after being relegated. It was manager **Neil Warnock's** fourth play-off triumph in seven seasons after two with Notts County (1990 and 1991) and a third with Huddersfield in 1995.

RECORDS OF ALL CLUBS IN PLAY-OFFS

In eleven seasons of modern play-offs, no fewer than 66 clubs have participated in them.

Here are the play-off records of all the clubs who have been involved (W = Final winners; L = Final losers):

Aldershot	1	1987 (W)
Barnet	1	1992
Blackburn	4	1988, 89 (L), 90, 92 (W)
Blackpool	3	1991 (L), 92 (W), 96
Bolton	4	1987, 90, 91 (L), 95 (W)
Bradford C.	2	1988, 96 (W)
Brentford	3	1991, 95, 97 (L)
Brighton	1	1991 (L)
Bristol C.	2	1988 (L), 97
Bristol R.	2	1989 (L), 95
Burnley	2	1991, 94 (W)
Bury	4	1990, 91, 93, 95 (L)
Cambridge U.	2	1990 (W), 92
Cardiff	1	1997
Carlisle	1	1994
Charlton	2	1987 (W), 96
Chelsea	1	1988 (L)
Chester	1	1997
Chesterfield	2	1990 (L), 95 (W)
Colchester	2	1987, 96
Crewe	5	1992, 93 (L), 95, 96, 97 (W)
Crystal P.	3	1989 (W), 96 (L), 97 (W)
Darlington	1	1996 (L)
Derby	2	1992, 94 (L)
Fulham	1	1989
Gillingham	1	1987 (L)
Hereford	1	1996

Huddersfield	2	1992, 95 (W)
Ipswich	2	1987, 97
Leeds	1	1987 (L)
Leicester	4	1992 (L), 93 (L), 94 (W), 96 (W)
Leyton O.	1	1989 (W)
Luton	1	1997
Maidstone	1	1990
Mansfield	1	1995
Mid'bro'	2	1988 (W), 91
Millwall	2	1991, 94
Newcastle	1	1990
Northampton	1	1997 (W)
Notts Co.	4	1988, 90 (W), 91 (W), 96 (L)
Oldham	1	1987
Peterborough	1	1992 (W)
Plymouth	2	1994, 96 (W)
Portsmouth	1	1993
Port Vale	2	1989 (W), 93 (L)
Preston	3	1989, 94 (L), 95
Reading	1	1995 (L)
Rotherham	1	1988
Scarborough	1	1989
Scunthorpe	4	1988, 89, 91, 92 (L)
Sheff. Utd.	2	1988, 97 (L)
Stockport	4	1990, 92 (L), 93, 94 (L)
Stoke	2	1992, 96
Sunderland	2	1987, 90 (L)
Swansea	3	1988 (W), 93, 97 (L)

Swindon	4 1987 (W), 89, 90 (W), 93 (W)	W.B.A.	1 1993 (W)
		Wigan	1 1987
		Wolves	3 1987 (L), 95, 97
Torquay	3 1988 (L), 91 (W), 94	Wrexham	1 1989 (L)
Tranmere	5 1990 (L), 91 (W), 93, 94, 95	Wycombe	1 1994 (W)
Walsall	2 1988 (W), 93	York	2 1993 (W), 94
Watford	1 1989		

PLAY-OFF CROWDS YEAR BY YEAR

The rights and wrongs of the play-offs have been argued ever since they were introduced, but their popularity is beyond question.

Clubs have frequently reported season-best crowds at the home-and-away semi-finals, and over 11 seasons the 177 play-off matches have been watched by 3,233,399 spectators.

Of that number, 1,123,000 have watched the Finals in the eight seasons they have been staged at Wembley, including a record 158,586 at the three matches there in May 1994.

Year	Matches	Agg. Att.
1987	20	310,000
1988	19	305,817
1989	18	234,393
1990	15	291,428
1991	15	266,442
1992	15	277,684
1993	15	319,907
1994	15	314,817
1995	15	295,317
1996	15	308,515
1997	15	309,085
	177	3,233,399

QUOTE-UNQUOTE

DES LYNAM, with a touch of solemnity as he closed BBC TV's last live Cup Final transmission: "That ends another piece of history as far as the F.A. Cup is concerned."

COLIN HENDRY, Blackburn and Scotland defender: "My only vice? Ten pounds on me to score the first goal – every game."

BILL SHANKLY to Liverpool captain Tommy Smith: "You know, Smithy, you could cause a riot in a cemetery."

BRIAN CLOUGH: "At Derby I told Roy McFarland to get his b-hair cut. That's coaching at top level."

KARREN BRADY, managing director of Birmingham: "Footballers are only interested in drinking, clothes and the size of their willies."

JOE KINNEAR on what he preaches at Wimbledon: "I teach them what Bill Nicholson taught me when I was at Spurs: never give in, never settle for second best, never be in awe of anybody. The players I have bought, to go with six home-grown boys, have all been hungry. I don't want players with full bellies."

OTHER COMPETITIONS 1996-97

AUTO WINDSCREENS SHIELD FINAL

CARLISLE UNITED 0, COLCHESTER UNITED 0
(After extra time: Carlisle won 4-3 on pens.)
Wembley (45,077), Sunday, April 20, 1997

Carlisle: Caig; Delap, Walling, Varty, Pounewatchy, Archdeacon, Hayward (Capt.), Conway, Aspinall, Smart (Thomas 23, Jansen 95), Peacock. **Booked**: Conway, Aspinall, Hayward. **Manager**: Mervyn Day.

Colchester: Emberson; Dunne, Greene, Cawley, Gibbs (Fry 105), Abrahams (Duguid 90), Gregory (Locke 85), Whitton, Wilkins (Capt.), Sale, Adcock. **Booked**: Greene, Gregory, Cawley, Dunne, Gibbs. **Manager**: Steve Wignall.

Referee: J. Kirkby (Sheffield).

Penalty shoot-out (Colchester first): Wilkins 1-0, Conway 1-1, Adcock 2-1, Archdeacon saved, Greene 3-1, Walling 3-2, Duguid saved, Aspinall 3-3, Cawley saved, Hayward 3-4.

● With promotion to Div. 2 already won, Carlisle completed a double with their first success at Wembley. The 45,000 crowd included 25,000 from Carlisle.

FINALS – RESULTS

Associated Members' Cup
1984   (Hull) Bournemouth 2, Hull City 1.
Freight Rover Trophy
1985   (Wembley) Wigan Athletic 3, Brentford 1.
1986   (Wembley) Bristol City 3, Bolton Wanderers 0.
1987   (Wembley) Mansfield Town 1, Bristol City 1 (aet; Mansfield won 5-4 on pens.).
Sherpa Van Trophy
1988   (Wembley) Wolverhampton Wanderers 2, Burnley 0.
1989   (Wembley) Bolton Wanderers 4, Torquay United 1.
Leyland Daf Cup
1990   (Wembley) Tranmere Rovers 2, Bristol Rovers 1.
1991   (Wembley) Birmingham City 3, Tranmere Rovers 2.
Autoglass Trophy
1992   (Wembley) Stoke City 1, Stockport County 0.
1993   (Wembley) Port Vale 2, Stockport County 1.
1994   (Wembley) Huddersfield Town 1, Swansea City 1 (aet; Swansea won 3-1 on pens.).
Auto Windscreens Shield
1995   (Wembley) Birmingham City 1, Carlisle United 0 (Birmingham won in sudden-death overtime).
1996   (Wembley) Rotherham United 2, Shrewsbury Town 1.

OTHER LEAGUE CLUBS' CUP COMPETITIONS
(Discontinued after 1992)

FINALS – AT WEMBLEY

Full Members' Cup
1985-86   Chelsea 5, Manchester City 4.
1986-87   Blackburn Rovers 1, Charlton Athletic 0.
Simod Cup
1987-88   Reading 4, Luton Town 1.
1988-89   Nottingham Forest 4, Everton 3.
Zenith Data Systems Cup
1989-90   Chelsea 1, Middlesbrough 0.
1990-91   Crystal Palace 4, Everton 1.
1991-92   Nottingham Forest 3, Southampton 2.
Anglo-Italian Cup
(* Home club)
1970   *Napoli 0, Swindon Town 3.
1971   *Bologna 1, Blackpool 2 (aet).
1972   *AS Roma 3, Blackpool 1.
1973   *Fiorentina 1, Newcastle United 2.
1993   Derby County 1, Cremonese 3 (at Wembley).
1994   Notts County 0, Brescia 1 (at Wembley).
1995   Ascoli 1, Notts County 2 (at Wembley).
1996   Port Vale 2, Genoa 5 (at Wembley).

F.A. CHALLENGE VASE FINALS
(At Wembley)

1975   Hoddesdon Town 2, Epsom & Ewell 1
1976   Billericay Town 1, Stamford 0*
1977   Billericay Town 2, Sheffield 1 (replay Nottingham, after a 1-1 draw at Wembley)
1978   Blue Star 2, Barton Rovers 1
1979   Billericay Town 4, Almondsbury Greenway 1
1980   Stamford 2, Guisborough Town 0
1981   Whickham 3, Willenhall Town 2*
1982   Forest Green Rovers 3, Rainworth Miners' Welfare 0
1983   V.S. Rugby 1, Halesowen Town 0
1984   Stansted 3, Stamford 2
1985   Halesowen Town 3, Fleetwood Town 1
1986   Halesowen Town 3, Southall 0
1987   St. Helens Town 3, Warrington Town 2
1988   Colne Dynamoes 1, Emley 0*
1989   Tamworth 3, Sudbury Town 0 (replay Peterborough, after a 1-1 draw at Wembley)
1990   Yeading 1, Bridlington 0 (replay Leeds, after 0-0 draw at Wembley)
1991   Guiseley 3, Gresley Rovers 1 (replay Bramall Lane, Sheffield, after a 4-4 draw at Wembley)
1992   Wimborne Town 5, Guiseley 3
1993   Bridlington Town 1, Tiverton Town 0
1994   Diss Town 2, Taunton Town 1*
1995   Arlesey Town 2, Oxford City 1
1996   Brigg Town 3, Clitheroe 0
1997   Whitby Town 3, North Ferriby United 0

(Sponsors: Carlsberg since 1995; * After extra time)

F.A. CHALLENGE TROPHY FINALS
(At Wembley)

1970   Macclesfield Town 2, Telford United 0
1971   Telford United 3, Hillingdon Borough 2
1972   Stafford Rangers 3, Barnet 0
1973   Scarborough 2, Wigan Athletic 1*
1974   Morecambe 2, Dartford 1
1975   Matlock Town 4, Scarborough 0
1976   Scarborough 3, Stafford Rangers 2*
1977   Scarborough 2, Dagenham 1
1978   Altrincham 3, Leatherhead 1
1979   Stafford Rangers 2, Kettering Town 0
1980   Dagenham 2, Mossley 1
1981   Bishop's Stortford 1, Sutton United 0
1982   Enfield 1, Altrincham 0*
1983   Telford United 2, Northwich Victoria 1
1984   Northwich Victoria 2, Bangor City 1 (replay Stoke, after a 1-1 draw at Wembley)
1985   Wealdstone 2, Boston United 1
1986   Altrincham 1, Runcorn 0
1987   Kidderminster Harriers 2, Burton Albion 1 (replay W.B.A., after a 0-0 draw at Wembley)
1988   Enfield 3, Telford United 2 (replay W.B.A., after a 0-0 draw at Wembley)
1989   Telford United 1, Macclesfield Town 0*
1990   Barrow 3, Leek Town 0
1991   Wycombe Wanderers 2, Kidderminster Harriers 1
1992   Colchester United 3, Witton Albion 1
1993   Wycombe Wanderers 4, Runcorn 1
1994   Woking 2, Runcorn 1
1995   Woking 2, Kidderminster 1
1996   Macclesfield Town 3, Northwich Victoria 1
1997   Woking 1, Dagenham & Redbridge 0*

(Sponsors: Umbro since 1995; * After extra time)

F.A. YOUTH CUP WINNERS

Year	Winners	Runners-up	Aggregate
1953	Manchester United	Wolves	9-3
1954	Manchester United	Wolves	5-4
1955	Manchester United	W.B.A.	7-1
1956	Manchester United	Chesterfield	4-3
1957	Manchester United	West Ham United	8-2
1958	Wolves	Chelsea	7-6
1959	Blackburn Rovers	West Ham United	2-1
1960	Chelsea	Preston North End	5-2
1961	Chelsea	Everton	5-3
1962	Newcastle United	Wolves	2-1
1963	West Ham United	Liverpool	6-5
1964	Manchester United	Swindon Town	5-2
1965	Everton	Arsenal	3-2
1966	Arsenal	Sunderland	5-3
1967	Sunderland	Birmingham City	2-0
1968	Burnley	Coventry City	3-2
1969	Sunderland	W.B.A.	6-3
1970	Tottenham Hotspur	Coventry City	4-3
1971	Arsenal	Cardiff City	2-0

1972	Aston Villa	Liverpool	5-2
1973	Ipswich Town	Bristol City	4-1
1974	Tottenham Hotspur	Huddersfield Town	2-1
1975	Ipswich Town	West Ham United	5-1
1976	W.B.A.	Wolves	5-0
1977	Crystal Palace	Everton	1-0
1978	Crystal Palace	Aston Villa	*1-0
1979	Millwall	Manchester City	2-0
1980	Aston Villa	Manchester City	3-2
1981	West Ham United	Tottenham Hotspur	2-1
1982	Watford	Manchester United	7-6
1983	Norwich City	Everton	6-5
1984	Everton	Stoke City	4-2
1985	Newcastle United	Watford	4-1
1986	Manchester City	Manchester United	3-1
1987	Coventry City	Charlton Athletic	2-1
1988	Arsenal	Doncaster Rovers	6-1
1989	Watford	Manchester City	2-1
1990	Tottenham Hotspur	Middlesbrough	3-2
1991	Millwall	Sheffield Wednesday	3-0
1992	Manchester United	Crystal Palace	6-3
1993	Leeds United	Manchester United	4-1
1994	Arsenal	Millwall	5-3
1995	Manchester United	Tottenham	†2-2
1996	Liverpool	West Ham United	4-1
1997	Leeds United	Crystal Palace	3-1

(* One match only; † Man. U. won 4-3 on pens.)

F.A. SUNDAY CUP FINAL

April 27 (at Mansfield): Marston Sports 1, Northwood 0.

WELSH CUP FINAL

May 18 (at Ninian Park, Cardiff):
Barry Town 2, Cwmbran Town 1
● Barry completed an historic hat-trick, having won the League of Wales, and League of Wales Cup.

SCOTTISH B & Q CUP FINALS
(For clubs outside Premier Division)

1990-91 Dundee 3, Ayr United 2 (at Motherwell)
1991-92 Hamilton Academical 1, Ayr United 0 (at Motherwell)
1992-93 Hamilton Academical 3, Morton 2 (at St. Mirren)
1993-94 Falkirk 3, St. Mirren 0 (at Motherwell)
1994-95 Airdrieonians 3, Dundee 2 (at McDiarmid Park, Perth)

SCOTTISH LEAGUE CHALLENGE CUP FINAL

1995-96 Dundee United 0, Stenhousemuir 0 (aet); Stenhousemuir won 5-4 on pens (at St. Johnstone).
1996-97 Stranraer 1, St. Johnstone 0 (at Broadwood Stadium, Cumbernauld – first trophy in Stranraer's 126-year history).

F.A. CHARITY SHIELD
(SPONSORS: LITTLEWOODS POOLS)

MANCHESTER UNITED 4, NEWCASTLE UNITED 0

Wembley (73,214), Sunday, August 11, 1996

Man. United: Schmeichel; Irwin (G. Neville 45), May, Pallister, P. Neville, Beckham, Keane, Butt (Poborsky 41), Giggs, Cantona (Capt.), Scholes (Cruyff 66). **Scorers**: Cantona (25), Butt (30), Beckham (86), Keane (88). **Booked**: Keane, Cantona.

Newcastle: Srnicek; Watson, Peacock, Albert, Beresford, Beardsley (Capt.) (Asprilla 66), Batty, Lee, Ginola (Gillespie 77), Shearer, Ferdinand. **Booked**: Albert.

Referee: P. Durkin (Portland). **Half-time**: 2-0.
Man of Match: Cantona (Man. United).

● United won the Shield for the third time in 4 seasons and the ninth time (outright) in all.

SHIELD HISTORY: The Charity Shield fixture began in 1908, and has been played every year since, except in war-time. It has mostly featured League Champions against F.A. Cup winners.

CHARITY SHIELD RESULTS

Year	Winners	Runners-up	Score
1908	Manchester United	Q.P.R.	4-0
			(after 1-1 draw)
1909	Newcastle United	Northampton Town	2-0
1910	Brighton & H.A.	Aston Villa	1-0
1911	Manchester United	Swindon Town	8-4
1912	Blackburn Rovers	Q.P.R.	2-1
1913	Professionals	Amateurs	7-2
1920	West Bromwich Albion	Tottenham Hotspur	2-0
1921	Tottenham Hotspur	Burnley	2-0
1922	Huddersfield Town	Liverpool	1-0
1923	Professionals	Amateurs	2-0
1924	Professionals	Amateurs	3-1
1925	Amateurs	Professionals	6-1
1926	Amateurs	Professionals	6-3
1927	Cardiff City	Corinthians	2-1
1928	Everton	Blackburn Rovers	2-1
1929	Professionals	Amateurs	3-0
1930	Arsenal	Sheffield Wednesday	2-1
1931	Arsenal	West Bromwich Albion	1-0
1932	Everton	Newcastle United	5-3
1933	Arsenal	Everton	3-0
1934	Arsenal	Manchester City	4-0
1935	Sheffield Wednesday	Arsenal	1-0
1936	Sunderland	Arsenal	2-1
1937	Manchester City	Sunderland	2-0
1938	Arsenal	Preston North End	2-1
1948	Arsenal	Manchester United	4-3
1949	Portsmouth	Wolverhampton W.	*1-1
1950	England World Cup XI	F.A. Canadian Tour Team	4-2
1951	Tottenham Hotspur	Newcastle United	2-1

1952	Manchester United	Newcastle United	4-2
1953	Arsenal	Blackpool	3-1
1954	Wolverhampton W.	West Bromwich Albion	*4-4
1955	Chelsea	Newcastle United	3-0
1956	Manchester United	Manchester City	1-0
1957	Manchester United	Aston Villa	4-0
1958	Bolton Wanderers	Wolverhampton W.	4-1
1959	Wolverhampton W.	Nottingham Forest	3-1
1960	Burnley	Wolverhampton W.	*2-2
1961	Tottenham Hotspur	F.A. XI	3-2
1962	Tottenham Hotspur	Ipswich Town	5-1
1963	Everton	Manchester United	4-0
1964	Liverpool	West Ham United	*2-2
1965	Manchester United	Liverpool	*2-2
1966	Liverpool	Everton	1-0
1967	Manchester United	Tottenham Hotspur	*3-3
1968	Manchester City	West Bromwich Albion	6-1
1969	Leeds United	Manchester City	2-1
1970	Everton	Chelsea	2-1
1971	Leicester City	Liverpool	1-0
1972	Manchester City	Aston Villa	1-0
1973	Burnley	Manchester City	1-0
1974	Liverpool	Leeds United	1-1

(Liverpool won 6-5 on penalties)

1975	Derby County	West Ham United	2-0
1976	Liverpool	Southampton	1-0
1977	Liverpool	Manchester United	*0-0
1978	Nottingham Forest	Ipswich Town	5-0
1979	Liverpool	Arsenal	3-1
1980	Liverpool	West Ham United	1-0
1981	Aston Villa	Tottenham Hotspur	*2-2
1982	Liverpool	Tottenham Hotspur	1-0
1983	Manchester United	Liverpool	2-0
1984	Everton	Liverpool	1-0
1985	Everton	Manchester United	2-0
1986	Everton	Liverpool	*1-1
1987	Everton	Coventry City	1-0
1988	Liverpool	Wimbledon	2-1
1989	Liverpool	Arsenal	1-0
1990	Liverpool	Manchester United	*1-1
1991	Arsenal	Tottenham Hotspur	*0-0
1992	Leeds United	Liverpool	4-3
1993	Manchester United	Arsenal	1-1

(Man. United won 5-4 on penalties)

1994	Manchester United	Blackburn Rovers	2-0
1995	Everton	Blackburn Rovers	1-0
1996	Manchester United	Newcastle United	4-0

(Fixture played at Wembley since 1974. *Trophy shared)

WILF HONOURED

Doyen of Middlesbrough, 78-year-old **Wilf Mannion** was made a Freeman of the Borough of Redcar & Cleveland last September.

SALUTE TO SHANKLY

Bill Shankly, late, great manager of Liverpool, is to be honoured this season with the unveiling of a bronze statue behind the Kop end at Anfield. The inscription: "Shankly – He made the people happy."

HONOURS LIST

F.A. PREMIER LEAGUE

	First	Pts.	Second	Pts.	Third	Pts.
1992-3a	Man. Utd.	84	Aston Villa	74	Norwich	72
1993-4a	Man. Utd.	92	Blackburn	84	Newcastle	77
1994-5a	Blackburn	89	Man. Utd.	88	Nott'm Forest	77
1995-6b	Man. Utd.	82	Newcastle	78	Liverpool	71
1996-7b	Man. Utd.	75	Newcastle	68	Arsenal	68

Maximum points: a, 126; b, 114.

FOOTBALL LEAGUE
NEW FIRST DIVISION

1992-3	Newcastle	96	West Ham	88	††Portsmouth	88
1993-4	Crystal Palace	90	Nott'm Forest	83	††Millwall	74
1994-5	Middlesbrough	82	††Reading	79	Bolton	77
1995-6	Sunderland	83	Derby	79	††Crystal Palace	75
1996-7	Bolton	98	Barnsley	80	††Wolves	76

Maximum points: 138. ††Not promoted after play-offs.

NEW SECOND DIVISION

1992-3	Stoke	93	Bolton	90	††Port Vale	89
1993-4	Reading	89	Port Vale	88	††Plymouth	85
1994-5	Birmingham	89	††Brentford	85	††Crewe	83
1995-6	Swindon	92	Oxford Utd.	83	††Blackpool	82
1996-7	Bury	84	Stockport	82	††Luton	78

Maximum points: 138. †† Not promoted after play-offs.

NEW THIRD DIVISION

1992-3a	Cardiff	83	Wrexham	80	Barnet	79
1993-4a	Shrewsbury	79	Chester	74	Crewe	73
1994-5a	Carlisle	91	Walsall	83	Chesterfield	81
1995-6b	Preston	86	Gillingham	83	Bury	79
1996-7b	Wigan	87	Fulham	87	Carlisle	84

Maximum points: a, 126; b, 138.

FOOTBALL LEAGUE

1888-89a	Preston	40	Aston Villa	29	Wolves	28
1889-90a	Preston	33	Everton	31	Blackburn	27
1890-1a	Everton	29	Preston	27	Notts County	26
1891-2b	Sunderland	42	Preston	37	Bolton	36

ORIGINAL FIRST DIVISION

1892-3c	Sunderland	48	Preston	37	Everton	36
1893-4c	Aston Villa	44	Sunderland	38	Derby	36
1894-5c	Sunderland	47	Everton	42	Aston Villa	39
1895-6c	Aston Villa	45	Derby	41	Everton	39
1896-7c	Aston Villa	47	Sheff. Utd.	36	Derby	36
1897-8c	Sheff. Utd.	42	Sunderland	39	Wolves	35

Year			
1898-9d	Aston Villa 45	Liverpool 43	Burnley 39
1899-1900d	Aston Villa 50	Sheff. Utd. 48	Sunderland 41
1900-1d	Liverpool 45	Sunderland 43	Notts County 40
1901-2d	Sunderland 44	Everton 41	Newcastle 37
1902-3d	The Wednesday ... 42	Aston Villa 41	Sunderland 41
1903-4d	The Wednesday ... 47	Man. City 44	Everton 43
1904-5d	Newcastle 48	Everton 47	Man. City 46
1905-6e	Liverpool 51	Preston 47	The Wednesday ... 44
1906-7e	Newcastle 51	Bristol City 48	Everton 45
1907-8e	Man. Utd. 52	Aston Villa 43	Man. City 43
1908-9e	Newcastle 53	Everton 46	Sunderland 44
1909-10e	Aston Villa 53	Liverpool 48	Blackburn 45
1910-11e	Man. Utd. 52	Aston Villa 51	Sunderland 45
1911-12e	Blackburn 49	Everton 46	Newcastle 44
1912-13e	Sunderland 54	Aston Villa 50	Sheff. Wed. 49
1913-14e	Blackburn 51	Aston Villa 44	Middlesbrough ... 43
1914-15e	Everton 46	Oldham 45	Blackburn 43
1919-20f	W.B.A. 60	Burnley 51	Chelsea 49
1920-1f	Burnley 59	Man. City 54	Bolton 52
1921-2f	Liverpool 57	Tottenham 51	Burnley 49
1922-3f	Liverpool 60	Sunderland 54	Huddersfield 53
1923-4f	*Huddersfield 57	Cardiff 57	Sunderland 53
1924-5f	Huddersfield 58	W.B.A. 56	Bolton 55
1925-6f	Huddersfield 57	Arsenal 52	Sunderland 48
1926-7f	Newcastle 56	Huddersfield 51	Sunderland 49
1927-8f	Everton 53	Huddersfield 51	Leicester City 48
1928-9f	Sheff. Wed. 52	Leicester City 51	Aston Villa 50
1929-30f	Sheff. Wed. 60	Derby 50	Man. City 47
1930-1f	Arsenal 66	Aston Villa 59	Sheff. Wed. 52
1931-2f	Everton 56	Arsenal 54	Sheff. Wed. 50
1932-3f	Arsenal 58	Aston Villa 54	Sheff. Wed. 51
1933-4f	Arsenal 59	Huddersfield 56	Tottenham 49
1934-5f	Arsenal 58	Sunderland 54	Sheff. Wed. 49
1935-6f	Sunderland 56	Derby 48	Huddersfield 48
1936-7f	Man. City 57	Charlton 54	Arsenal 52
1937-8f	Arsenal 52	Wolves 51	Preston 49
1938-9f	Everton 59	Wolves 55	Charlton 50
1946-7f	Liverpool 57	Man. Utd. 56	Wolves 56
1947-8f	Arsenal 59	Man. Utd. 52	Burnley 52
1948-9f	Portsmouth 58	Man. Utd. 53	Derby 53
1949-50f	*Portsmouth 53	Wolves 53	Sunderland 52
1950-1f	Tottenham 60	Man. Utd. 56	Blackpool 50
1951-2f	Man. Utd. 57	Tottenham 53	Arsenal 53
1952-3f	*Arsenal 54	Preston 54	Wolves 51
1953-4f	Wolves 57	W.B.A. 53	Huddersfield 51
1954-5f	Chelsea 52	Wolves 48	Portsmouth 48
1955-6f	Man. Utd. 60	Blackpool 49	Wolves 49
1956-7f	Man. Utd. 64	Tottenham 56	Preston 56
1957-8f	Wolves 64	Preston 59	Tottenham 51
1958-9f	Wolves 61	Man. Utd. 55	Arsenal 50
1959-60f	Burnley 55	Wolves 54	Tottenham 53
1960-1f	Tottenham 66	Sheff. Wed. 58	Wolves 57
1961-2f	Ipswich 56	Burnley 53	Tottenham 52
1962-3f	Everton 61	Tottenham 55	Burnley 54
1963-4f	Liverpool 57	Man. Utd. 53	Everton 52
1964-5f	*Man. Utd. 61	Leeds 61	Chelsea 56
1965-6f	Liverpool 61	Leeds 55	Burnley 55
1966-7f	Man. Utd. 60	Nott'm Forest 56	Tottenham 56
1967-8f	Man. City 58	Man. Utd. 56	Liverpool 55
1968-9f	Leeds 67	Liverpool 61	Everton 57
1969-70f	Everton 66	Leeds 57	Chelsea 55

47

	First	Pts.	Second	Pts.	Third	Pts.
1970-1f	Arsenal	65	Leeds	64	Tottenham	52
1971-2f	Derby	58	Leeds	57	Liverpool	57
1972-3f	Liverpool	60	Arsenal	57	Leeds	53
1973-4f	Leeds	62	Liverpool	57	Derby	48
1974-5f	Derby	53	Liverpool	51	Ipswich	51
1975-6f	Liverpool	60	Q.P.R.	59	Man. Utd.	56
1976-7f	Liverpool	57	Man. City	56	Ipswich	52
1977-8f	Nott'm Forest	64	Liverpool	57	Everton	55
1978-9f	Liverpool	68	Nott'm Forest	60	W.B.A.	59
1979-80f	Liverpool	60	Man. Utd.	58	Ipswich	53
1980-1f	Aston Villa	60	Ipswich	56	Arsenal	53
1981-2g	Liverpool	87	Ipswich	83	Man. Utd.	78
1982-3g	Liverpool	82	Watford	71	Man. Utd.	70
1983-4g	Liverpool	80	Southampton	77	Nott'm Forest	74
1984-5g	Everton	90	Liverpool	77	Tottenham	77
1985-6g	Liverpool	88	Everton	86	West Ham	84
1986-7g	Everton	86	Liverpool	77	Tottenham	71
1987-8h	Liverpool	90	Man. Utd.	81	Nott'm Forest	73
1988-9j	†Arsenal	76	Liverpool	76	Nott'm Forest	64
1989-90j	Liverpool	79	Aston Villa	70	Tottenham	63
1990-1j	Arsenal	83	Liverpool	76	Crystal Palace	69
1991-2g	Leeds	82	Man. Utd.	78	Sheff. Wed.	75

Maximum points: a, 44; b, 52; c, 60; d, 68; e, 76; f, 84; g, 126; h, 120; j, 114.
*Won on goal average. †Won on goal diff. No comp. 1915-19 – 1939-46 (war-time)

ORIGINAL SECOND DIVISION

	First	Pts.	Second	Pts.	Third	Pts.
1892-3a	Small Heath	36	Sheff. Utd.	35	Darwen	30
1893-4b	Liverpool	50	Small Heath	42	Notts County	39
1894-5c	Bury	48	Notts County	39	Newton Heath	38
1895-6c	*Liverpool	46	Man. City	46	Grimsby	42
1896-7c	Notts County	42	Newton Heath	39	Grimsby	38
1897-8c	Burnley	48	Newcastle	45	Man. City	39
1898-9d	Man. City	52	Glossop	46	Leicester Fosse	45
1899-1900d	The Wednesday	54	Bolton	52	Small Heath	46
1900-1d	Grimsby	49	Small Heath	48	Burnley	44
1901-2d	W.B.A.	55	Middlesbrough	51	Preston	42
1902-3d	Man. City	54	Small Heath	51	Woolwich Arsenal	48
1903-4d	Preston	50	Woolwich Arsenal	49	Man. Utd.	48
1904-5d	Liverpool	58	Bolton	56	Man. Utd.	53
1905-6e	Bristol City	66	Man. Utd.	62	Chelsea	53
1906-7e	Nott'm Forest	60	Chelsea	57	Leicester Fosse	48
1907-8e	Bradford City	54	Leicester Fosse	52	Oldham	50
1908-9e	Bolton	52	Tottenham	51	W.B.A.	51
1909-10e	Man. City	54	Oldham	53	Hull	53
1910-11e	W.B.A.	53	Bolton	51	Chelsea	49
1911-12e	*Derby	54	Chelsea	54	Burnley	52
1912-13e	Preston	53	Burnley	50	Birmingham	46
1913-14e	Notts County	53	Bradford P.A.	49	Woolwich Arsenal	49
1914-15e	Derby	53	Preston	50	Barnsley	47
1919-20f	Tottenham	70	Huddersfield	64	Birmingham	56
1920-1f	*Birmingham	58	Cardiff	58	Bristol City	51
1921-2f	Nott'm Forest	56	Stoke	52	Barnsley	52
1922-3f	Notts County	53	West Ham	51	Leicester City	51
1923-4f	Leeds	54	Bury	51	Derby	51
1924-5f	Leicester City	59	Man. Utd.	57	Derby	55
1925-6f	Sheff. Wed.	60	Derby	57	Chelsea	52

1926-7f	Middlesbrough ... 62	Portsmouth 54	Man. City 54
1927-8f	Man. City 59	Leeds 57	Chelsea 54
1928-9f	Middlesbrough 55	Grimsby 53	Bradford City 48
1929-30f	Blackpool 58	Chelsea 55	Oldham 53
1930-1f	Everton 61	W.B.A. 54	Tottenham 51
1931-2f	Wolves 56	Leeds 54	Stoke 52
1932-3f	Stoke 56	Tottenham 55	Fulham 50
1933-4f	Grimsby 59	Preston 52	Bolton 51
1934-5f	Brentford 61	Bolton 56	West Ham 56
1935-6f	Man. Utd. 56	Charlton 55	Sheff. Utd. 52
1936-7f	Leicester City 56	Blackpool 55	Bury 52
1937-8f	Aston Villa 57	Man. Utd. 53	Sheff. Utd. 53
1938-9f	Blackburn 55	Sheff. Utd. 54	Sheff. Wed. 53
1946-7f	Man. City 62	Burnley 58	Birmingham 55
1947-8f	Birmingham 59	Newcastle 56	Southampton 52
1948-9f	Fulham 57	W.B.A. 56	Southampton 55
1949-50f	Tottenham 61	Sheff. Wed. 52	Sheff. Utd. 52
1950-1f	Preston 57	Man. City 52	Cardiff 50
1951-2f	Sheff. Wed. 53	Cardiff 51	Birmingham 51
1952-3f	Sheff. Utd. 60	Huddersfield 58	Luton 52
1953-4f	*Leicester City 56	Everton 56	Blackburn 55
1954-5f	*Birmingham 54	Luton 54	Rotherham 54
1955-6f	Sheff. Wed. 55	Leeds 52	Liverpool 48
1956-7f	Leicester City 61	Nott'm Forest 54	Liverpool 53
1957-8f	West Ham 57	Blackburn 56	Charlton 55
1958-9f	Sheff. Wed. 62	Fulham 60	Sheff. Utd. 53
1959-60f	Aston Villa 59	Cardiff 58	Liverpool 50
1960-1f	Ipswich 59	Sheff. Utd. 58	Liverpool 52
1961-2f	Liverpool 62	Leyton Orient 54	Sunderland 53
1962-3f	Stoke 53	Chelsea 52	Sunderland 52
1963-4f	Leeds 63	Sunderland 61	Preston 56
1964-5f	Newcastle 57	Northampton 56	Bolton 50
1965-6f	Man. City 59	Southampton 54	Coventry 53
1966-7f	Coventry 59	Wolves 58	Carlisle 52
1967-8f	Ipswich 59	Q.P.R. 58	Blackpool 58
1968-9f	Derby 63	Crystal Palace 56	Charlton 50
1969-70f	Huddersfield 60	Blackpool 53	Leicester City 51
1970-1f	Leicester City 59	Sheff. Utd. 56	Cardiff 53
1971-2f	Norwich 57	Birmingham 56	Millwall 55
1972-3f	Burnley 62	Q.P.R. 61	Aston Villa 60
1973-4f	Middlesbrough 65	Luton 50	Carlisle 49
1974-5f	Man. Utd. 61	Aston Villa 58	Norwich 53
1975-6f	Sunderland 56	Bristol City 53	W.B.A. 53
1976-7f	Wolves 57	Chelsea 55	Nott'm Forest 52
1977-8f	Bolton 58	Southampton 57	Tottenham 56
1978-9f	Crystal Palace 57	Brighton 56	Stoke 56
1979-80f	Leicester City 55	Sunderland 54	Birmingham 53
1980-1f	West Ham 66	Notts County 53	Swansea 50
1981-2g	Luton 88	Watford 80	Norwich 71
1982-3g	Q.P.R. 85	Wolves 75	Leicester City 70
1983-4g	†Chelsea 88	Sheff. Wed. 88	Newcastle 80
1984-5g	Oxford 84	Birmingham 82	Man. City 74
1985-6g	Norwich 84	Charlton 77	Wimbledon 76
1986-7g	Derby 84	Portsmouth 78	†† Oldham 75
1987-8h	Millwall 82	Aston Villa 78	Middlesbrough 78
1988-9j	Chelsea 99	Man. City 82	Crystal Palace 81
1989-90j	†Leeds 85	Sheff. Utd. 85	†† Newcastle 80
1990-1j	Oldham 88	West Ham 87	Sheff. Wed. 82
1991-2g	Ipswich 84	Middlesbrough 80	†† Derby 78

Maximum points: *a*, 44; *b*, 56; *c*, 60; *d*, 68; *e*, 76; *f*, 84; *g*, 126; *h*, 132; *j*, 138.
* Won on goal average. † Won on goal difference. †† Not promoted after play-offs.

THIRD DIVISION 1958-92

	First	Pts.	Second	Pts.	Third	Pts.
1958-9	Plymouth	62	Hull	61	Brentford	57
1959-60	Southampton	61	Norwich	59	Shrewsbury	52
1960-1	Bury	68	Walsall	62	Q.P.R.	60
1961-2	Portsmouth	65	Grimsby	62	Bournemouth	59
1962-3	Northampton	62	Swindon	58	Port Vale	54
1963-4	*Coventry	60	Crystal Palace	60	Watford	58
1964-5	Carlisle	60	Bristol City	60	Mansfield	59
1965-6	Hull	69	Millwall	65	Q.P.R.	57
1966-7	Q.P.R.	67	Middlesbrough	55	Watford	54
1967-8	Oxford	57	Bury	56	Shrewsbury	55
1968-9	*Watford	64	Swindon	64	Luton	61
1969-70	Orient	62	Luton	60	Bristol Rovers	56
1970-1	Preston	61	Fulham	60	Halifax	56
1971-2	Aston Villa	70	Brighton	65	Bournemouth	62
1972-3	Bolton	61	Notts County	57	Blackburn	55
1973-4	Oldham	62	Bristol Rovers	61	York	61
1974-5	Blackburn	60	Plymouth	59	Charlton	55
1975-6	Hereford	63	Cardiff	57	Millwall	56
1976-7	Mansfield	64	Brighton	61	Crystal Palace	59
1977-8	Wrexham	61	Cambridge	58	Preston	56
1978-9	Shrewsbury	61	Watford	60	Swansea	60
1979-80	Grimsby	62	Blackburn	59	Sheff. Wed.	58
1980-1	Rotherham	61	Barnsley	59	Charlton	59
†1981-2	*Burnley	80	Carlisle	80	Fulham	78
†1982-3	Portsmouth	91	Cardiff	86	Huddersfield	82
†1983-4	Oxford	95	Wimbledon	87	Sheff. Utd.	83
†1984-5	Bradford City	94	Millwall	90	Hull	87
†1985-6	Reading	94	Plymouth	87	Derby	84
†1986-7	Bournemouth	97	Middlesbrough	94	Swindon	87
†1987-8	Sunderland	93	Brighton	84	Walsall	82
†1988-9	Wolves	92	Sheff. Utd.	84	Port Vale	84
†1989-90	Bristol Rovers	93	Bristol City	91	Notts County	87
†1990-1	Cambridge	86	Southend	85	Grimsby	83
† 1991-2	Brentford	82	Birmingham	81	†† Huddersfield	78

* Won on goal average. † Maximum points 138 (previously 92).
†† Not promoted after play-offs.

FOURTH DIVISION 1958-92

	First	Pts.	Second	Pts.	Third	Pts.	Fourth	Pts.
1958-9	Port Vale	64	Coventry	60	York	60	Shrewsbury	58
1959-60	Walsall	65	Notts County	60	Torquay	60	Watford	57
1960-1	Peterborough	66	Crystal Palace	64	Northampton	60	Bradford P.A.	60
1961-2	Millwall	56	Colchester	55	Wrexham	53	Carlisle	52
1962-3	Brentford	62	Oldham	59	Crewe	59	Mansfield	57
1963-4	*Gillingham	60	Carlisle	60	Workington	59	Exeter	58
1964-5	Brighton	63	Millwall	62	York	62	Oxford	61
1965-6	*Doncaster	59	Darlington	59	Torquay	58	Colchester	56
1966-7	Stockport	64	Southport	59	Barrow	59	Tranmere	58
1967-8	Luton	66	Barnsley	61	Hartlepool	60	Crewe	58
1968-9	Doncaster	59	Halifax	57	Rochdale	56	Bradford City	56
1969-70	Chesterfield	64	Wrexham	61	Swansea	60	Port Vale	59
1970-1	Notts County	69	Bournemouth	60	Oldham	59	York	56
1971-2	Grimsby	63	Southend	60	Brentford	59	Scunthorpe	57
1972-3	Southport	62	Hereford	58	Cambridge	57	Aldershot	56
1973-4	Peterborough	65	Gillingham	62	Colchester	60	Bury	59
1974-5	Mansfield	68	Shrewsbury	62	Rotherham	58	Chester	57
1975-6	Lincoln	74	Northampton	68	Reading	60	Tranmere	58

50

1976-7	Cambridge 65	Exeter 62	Colchester 59	Bradford City .. 59
1977-8	Watford 71	Southend 60	Swansea 56	Brentford 59
1978-9	Reading 65	Grimsby 61	Wimbledon 61	Barnsley 61
1979-80	Huddersfield 66	Walsall 64	Newport 61	Portsmouth 60
1980-1	Southend 67	Lincoln 65	Doncaster 56	Wimbledon 55
†1981-2	Sheff. Utd. 96	Bradford City 91	Wigan 91	Bournemouth .. 88
†1982-3	Wimbledon 98	Hull 90	Port Vale 88	Scunthorpe 83
1983-4	York 101	Doncaster 85	Reading 82	Bristol City 82
1984-5	Chesterfield 91	Blackpool 86	Darlington 85	Bury 84
1985-6	Swindon 102	Chester 84	Mansfield 81	Port Vale 79
1986-7	Northampton 99	Preston 90	Southend 80	††Wolves 79
1987-8	Wolves 90	Cardiff 85	Bolton 78	††Scunthorpe .. 77
†1988-9	Rotherham 82	Tranmere 80	Crewe 78	††Scunthorpe .. 77
†1989-90	Exeter 89	Grimsby 79	Southend 75	††Stockport 74
†1990-1	Darlington 83	Stockport 82	Hartlepool 82	Peterborough .. 80
1991-2a	Burnley 83	Rotherham 77	Mansfield 77	Blackpool 76

* Won on goal average.   Maximum points: †, 138; a, 126; previously 92.
†† Not promoted after play-offs.

THIRD DIVISION – SOUTH 1920-58

	First	Pts.	Second	Pts.	Third	Pts.
1920-1a	Crystal Palace	59	Southampton	54	Q.P.R.	53
1921-2a	*Southampton	61	Plymouth	61	Portsmouth	53
1922-3a	Bristol City	59	Plymouth	53	Swansea	53
1923-4a	Portsmouth	59	Plymouth	55	Millwall	54
1924-5a	Swansea	57	Plymouth	56	Bristol City	53
1925-6a	Reading	57	Plymouth	56	Millwall	53
1926-7a	Bristol City	62	Plymouth	60	Millwall	56
1927-8a	Millwall	65	Northampton	55	Plymouth	53
1928-9a	*Charlton	54	Crystal Palace	54	Northampton	52
1929-30a	Plymouth	68	Brentford	61	Q.P.R.	51
1930-31a	Notts County	59	Crystal Palace	51	Brentford	50
1931-2a	Fulham	57	Reading	55	Southend	53
1932-3a	Brentford	62	Exeter	58	Norwich	57
1933-4a	Norwich	61	Coventry	54	Reading	54
1934-5a	Charlton	61	Reading	53	Coventry	51
1935-6a	Coventry	57	Luton	56	Reading	54
1936-7a	Luton	58	Notts County	56	Brighton	53
1937-8a	Millwall	56	Bristol City	55	Q.P.R.	53
1938-9a	Newport	55	Crystal Palace	52	Brighton	49
1946-7a	Cardiff	66	Q.P.R.	57	Bristol City	51
1947-8a	Q.P.R.	61	Bournemouth	57	Walsall	51
1948-9a	Swansea	62	Reading	55	Bournemouth	52
1949-50a	Notts County	58	Northampton	51	Southend	51
1950-1d	Nott'm Forest	70	Norwich	64	Reading	57
1951-2d	Plymouth	66	Reading	61	Norwich	61
1952-3d	Bristol Rovers	64	Millwall	62	Northampton	62
1953-4d	Ipswich	64	Brighton	61	Bristol City	56
1954-5d	Bristol City	70	Leyton Orient	61	Southampton	59
1955-6d	Leyton Orient	66	Brighton	65	Ipswich	64
1956-7d	*Ipswich	59	Torquay	59	Colchester	58
1957-8d	Brighton	60	Brentford	58	Plymouth	58

THIRD DIVISION – NORTH 1921-58

	First	Pts.	Second	Pts.	Third	Pts.
1921-2b	Stockport	56	Darlington	50	Grimsby	50
1922-3b	Nelson	51	Bradford P.A.	47	Walsall	46
1923-4b	Wolves	63	Rochdale	62	Chesterfield	54

Maximum points: a, 84; b, 76; c, 80; d, 92. * Won on goal average.

CHAMPIONSHIP WINNERS

F.A. PREMIER LEAGUE
Man. Utd. 4
Blackburn 1

FOOTBALL LEAGUE
DIV.1 (NEW)
Bolton 1
Crystal Palace 1
Middlesbrough 1
Newcastle 1
Sunderland 1

DIV.1 (ORIGINAL)
Liverpool 18
Arsenal 10
Everton 9
Aston Villa 7
Man. Utd. 7
Sunderland 6
Newcastle 4
Sheff. Wed. 4
Huddersfield 3
Leeds 3
Wolves 3
Blackburn 2
Burnley 2
Derby 2
Man. City 2
Portsmouth 2
Preston 2

Tottenham 2
Chelsea 1
Ipswich 1
Nott'm Forest 1
Sheff. Utd. 1
W.B.A. 1

DIV.2 (NEW)
Birmingham 1
Bury 1
Reading 1
Stoke 1
Swindon 1

DIV.2 (ORIGINAL)
Leicester City 6
Man. City 6
Sheff. Wed. 5
Birmingham 4
Derby 4
Liverpool 4
Ipswich 3
Leeds 3
Middlesbrough 3
Notts County 3
Preston 3
Aston Villa 2
Bolton 2
Burnley 2
Chelsea 2
Grimsby 2

Man. Utd. 2
Norwich 2
Nott'm Forest 2
Stoke 2
Tottenham 2
W.B.A. 2
West Ham 2
Wolves 2
Blackburn 1
Blackpool 1
Bradford City 1
Brentford 1
Bristol City 1
Bury 1
Coventry 1
Crystal Palace 1
Everton 1
Fulham 1
Huddersfield 1
Luton 1
Millwall 1
Newcastle 1
Oldham 1
Oxford 1
Q.P.R. 1
Sheff. Utd. 1
Sunderland 1

APPLICATIONS FOR RE-ELECTION
(System discontinued 1987)

14 Hartlepool	5 Gillingham	2 Aberdare	2 Watford
12 Halifax	5 Lincoln	2 Ashington	1 Blackpool
11 Barrow	5 New Brighton	2 Bournemouth	1 Brighton
11 Southport	4 Bradford P.A.	2 Brentford	1 Bristol Rovers
10 Crewe	4 Northampton	2 Colchester	1 Cambridge
10 Newport	4 Norwich	2 Durham C.	1 Cardiff
10 Rochdale	3 Aldershot	2 Gateshead	1 Carlisle
8 Darlington	3 Bradford City	2 Grimsby	1 Charlton
8 Exeter	3 Crystal P.	2 Millwall	1 Mansfield
7 Chester	3 Doncaster	2 Nelson	1 Port Vale
7 Walsall	3 Hereford	2 Oldham	1 Preston
7 Workington	3 Merthyr Tyd.	2 Q.P.R.	1 Shrewsbury
7 York	3 Swindon	2 Rotherham	1 Swansea
6 Stockport	3 Torquay	2 Scunthorpe	1 Thames
5 Accrington	3 Tranmere	2 Southend	1 Wrexham

RELEGATED CLUBS (To 1992)

1892-3	In Test matches, Darwen and Sheff. Utd. won promotion in place of Accrington and Notts County.
1893-4	Tests, Liverpool and Small Heath won promotion. Darwen and Newton Heath relegated.
1894-5	After Tests, Bury promoted, Liverpool relegated.
1895-6	After Tests, Liverpool promoted, Small Heath relegated.
1896-7	After Tests, Notts County promoted, Burnley relegated.
1897-8	Test system abolished after success of Burnley and Stoke, League extended. Blackburn and Newcastle elected to First Division. Automatic promotion and relegation introduced.

FIRST DIVISION TO SECOND DIVISION

1898-9	Bolton, Sheff. Wed.	1923-4	Chelsea, Middlesbrough
1899-1900	Burnley, Glossop	1924-5	Preston, Nott'm Forest
1900-1	Preston, W.B.A.	1925-6	Man. City, Notts County
1901-2	Small Heath, Man. City	1926-7	Leeds, W.B.A.
1902-3	Grimsby, Bolton	1927-8	Tottenham, Middlesbrough
1903-4	Liverpool, W.B.A.	1928-9	Bury, Cardiff
1904-5	League extended. Bury and Notts County, two bottom clubs in First Division, re-elected.	1929-30	Burnley, Everton
		1930-1	Leeds, Man. Utd.
		1931-2	Grimsby, West Ham
		1932-3	Bolton, Blackpool
1905-6	Nott'm Forest, Wolves	1933-4	Newcastle, Sheff. Utd.
1906-7	Derby, Stoke	1934-5	Leicester City, Tottenham
1907-8	Bolton, Birmingham	1935-6	Aston Villa, Blackburn
1908-9	Man. City, Leicester Fosse	1936-7	Man. Utd., Sheff. Wed.
1909-10	Bolton, Chelsea	1937-8	Man. City, W.B.A.
1910-11	Bristol City, Nott'm Forest	1938-9	Birmingham, Leicester City
1911-12	Preston, Bury	1946-7	Brentford, Leeds
1912-13	Notts County, Woolwich Arsenal	1947-8	Blackburn, Grimsby
		1948-9	Preston, Sheff. Utd.
1913-14	Preston, Derby	1949-50	Man. City, Birmingham
1914-15	Tottenham, *Chelsea	1950-1	Sheff. Wed., Everton
1919-20	Notts County, Sheff. Wed.	1951-2	Huddersfield, Fulham
1920-1	Derby, Bradford P.A.	1952-3	Stoke, Derby
1921-2	Bradford City, Man. Utd.	1953-4	Middlesbrough, Liverpool
1922-3	Stoke, Oldham	1954-5	Leicester City, Sheff. Wed.

1955-6 Huddersfield, Sheff. Utd.	1978-9 Q.P.R., Birmingham, Chelsea
1956-7 Charlton, Cardiff	
1957-8 Sheff. Wed., Sunderland	1979-80 Bristol City, Derby, Bolton
1958-9 Portsmouth, Aston Villa	
1959-60 Luton, Leeds	1980-1 Norwich, Leicester City, Crystal Palace
1960-61 Preston, Newcastle	
1961-2 Chelsea, Cardiff	1981-2 Leeds, Wolves, Middlesbrough
1962-3 Man. City, Leyton Orient	
1963-4 Bolton, Ipswich	1982-3 Man. City, Swansea, Brighton
1964-5 Wolves, Birmingham	
1965-6 Northampton, Blackburn	1983-4 Birmingham, Notts County, Wolves
1966-7 Aston Villa, Blackpool	
1967-8 Fulham, Sheff. Utd.	1984-5 Norwich, Sunderland, Stoke
1968-9 Leicester City, Q.P.R.	
1969-70 Sheff. Wed., Sunderland	1985-6 Ipswich, Birmingham, W.B.A.
1970-1 Burnley, Blackpool	
1971-2 Nott'm Forest, Huddersfield	1986-7 Leicester City, Man. City, Aston Villa
1972-3 W.B.A., Crystal Palace	
1973-4 Norwich, Man. Utd., Southampton	1987-8 Chelsea**, Portsmouth, Watford, Oxford
1974-5 Chelsea, Luton, Carlisle	1988-9 Middlesbrough, West Ham, Newcastle
1975-6 Sheff. Utd., Burnley, Wolves	1989-90 Sheff. Wed., Charlton, Millwall
1976-7 Tottenham, Stoke, Sunderland	1990-1 Sunderland, Derby
1977-8 Leicester City, West Ham, Newcastle	1991-2 Luton, Notts County, West Ham

* Subsequently re-elected to First Division when League extended after the war.
** Relegated after play-offs.

SECOND DIVISION TO THIRD DIVISION

1920-1 Stockport	1955-6 Plymouth, Hull
1921-2 Bradford City, Bristol City	1956-7 Port Vale, Bury
1922-3 Rotherham, Wolves	1957-8 Doncaster, Notts County
1923-4 Nelson, Bristol City	1958-9 Barnsley, Grimsby
1924-5 Crystal Palace, Coventry	1959-60 Bristol City, Hull
1925-6 Stoke, Stockport	1960-1 Lincoln, Portsmouth
1926-7 Darlington, Bradford City	1961-2 Brighton, Bristol Rovers
1927-8 Fulham, South Shields	1962-3 Walsall, Luton
1928-9 Port Vale, Clapton Orient	1963-4 Grimsby, Scunthorpe
1929-30 Hull, Notts County	1964-5 Swindon, Swansea
1930-1 Reading, Cardiff	1965-6 Middlesbrough, Leyton Orient
1931-2 Barnsley, Bristol City	
1932-3 Chesterfield, Charlton	1966-7 Northampton, Bury
1933-4 Millwall, Lincoln	1967-8 Plymouth, Rotherham
1934-5 Oldham, Notts County	1968-9 Fulham, Bury
1935-6 Port Vale, Hull	1969-70 Preston, Aston Villa
1936-7 Doncaster, Bradford City	1970-1 Blackburn, Bolton
1937-8 Barnsley, Stockport	1971-2 Charlton, Watford
1938-9 Norwich, Tranmere	1972-3 Huddersfield, Brighton
1946-7 Swansea, Newport	1973-4 Crystal Palace, Preston, Swindon
1947-8 Doncaster, Millwall	
1948-9 Nott'm Forest, Lincoln	1974-5 Millwall, Cardiff, Sheff. Wed.
1949-50 Plymouth, Bradford P.A.	
1950-1 Grimsby, Chesterfield	1975-6 Portsmouth, Oxford, York
1951-2 Coventry, Q.P.R.	
1952-3 Southampton, Barnsley	1976-7 Carlisle, Plymouth, Hereford
1953-4 Brentford, Oldham	
1954-5 Ipswich, Derby	1977-8 Hull, Mansfield, Blackpool

1978-9	Sheff. Utd., Millwall, Blackburn	1986-7	Sunderland**, Grimsby, Brighton
1979-80	Fulham, Burnley, Charlton	1987-8	Sheff. Utd.**, Reading, Huddersfield
1980-1	Preston, Bristol City, Bristol Rovers	1988-9	Shrewsbury, Birmingham, Walsall
1981-2	Cardiff, Wrexham, Orient	1989-90	Bournemouth, Bradford City, Stoke
1982-3	Rotherham, Burnley, Bolton	1990-1	W.B.A., Hull
1983-4	Derby, Swansea, Cambridge	1991-2	Plymouth, Brighton, Port Vale
1984-5	Notts County, Cardiff, Wolves		
1985-6	Carlisle, Middlesbrough, Fulham		

** Relegated after play-offs.

THIRD DIVISION TO FOURTH DIVISION

1958-9	Rochdale, Notts County, Doncaster, Stockport	1975-6	Aldershot, Colchester, Southend, Halifax
1959-60	Accrington, Wrexham, Mansfield, York	1976-7	Reading, Northampton, Grimsby, York
1960-1	Chesterfield, Colchester, Bradford City, Tranmere	1977-8	Port Vale, Bradford City, Hereford, Portsmouth
1961-2	Newport, Brentford, Lincoln, Torquay	1978-9	Peterborough, Walsall, Tranmere, Lincoln
1962-3	Bradford P.A., Brighton, Carlisle, Halifax	1979-80	Bury, Southend, Mansfield, Wimbledon
1963-4	Millwall, Crewe, Wrexham, Notts County	1980-1	Sheff. Utd., Colchester, Blackpool, Hull
1964-5	Luton, Port Vale, Colchester, Barnsley	1981-2	Wimbledon, Swindon, Bristol City, Chester
1965-6	Southend, Exeter, Brentford, York	1982-3	Reading, Wrexham, Doncaster, Chesterfield
1966-7	Doncaster, Workington, Darlington, Swansea	1983-4	Scunthorpe, Southend, Port Vale, Exeter
1967-8	Scunthorpe, Colchester, Grimsby, Peterborough (demoted)	1984-5	Burnley, Orient, Preston, Cambridge
1968-9	Oldham, Crewe, Hartlepool, Northampton	1985-6	Lincoln, Cardiff, Wolves, Swansea
1969-70	Bournemouth, Southport, Barrow, Stockport	1986-7	Bolton**, Carlisle, Darlington, Newport
1970-1	Gillingham, Doncaster, Bury, Reading	1987-8	Doncaster, York, Grimsby, Rotherham**
1971-2	Mansfield, Barnsley, Torquay, Bradford City	1988-9	Southend, Chesterfield, Gillingham, Aldershot
1972-3	Scunthorpe, Swansea, Brentford, Rotherham	1989-90	Cardiff, Northampton, Blackpool, Walsall
1973-4	Cambridge, Shrewsbury, Rochdale, Southport	1990-1	Crewe, Rotherham, Mansfield
1974-5	Bournemouth, Watford, Tranmere, Huddersfield	1991-2	Bury, Shrewsbury, Torquay, Darlington

** Relegated after plays-offs.

DEMOTED FROM FOURTH DIVISION TO GM VAUXHALL CONFERENCE

1987	Lincoln	1990	Colchester
1988	Newport	1991	No demotion
1989	Darlington	1992	No demotion

DEMOTED FROM THIRD DIVISION TO
GM VAUXHALL CONFERENCE

1993	Halifax	1996	No demotion
1994	No demotion	1997	Hereford
1995	No demotion		

RELEGATED CLUBS (Since 1993)

1993

Premier League to Div. 1: Crystal Palace, Middlesbrough, Nott'm Forest
Div. 1 to Div. 2: Brentford, Cambridge, Bristol Rovers
Div. 2 to Div. 3: Preston, Mansfield, Wigan, Chester

1994

Premier League to Div. 1: Sheffield Utd., Oldham, Swindon
Div. 1 to Div. 2: Birmingham, Oxford, Peterborough
Div. 2 to Div. 3: Fulham, Exeter, Hartlepool, Barnet

1995

Premier League to Div. 1: Crystal Palace, Norwich, Leicester, Ipswich
Div. 1 to Div. 2: Swindon, Burnley, Bristol City, Notts Co.
Div. 2 to Div. 3: Cambridge, Plymouth, Cardiff, Chester, Leyton Orient

1996

Premier League to Div. 1: Manchester City, Q.P.R., Bolton
Div. 1 to Div. 2: Millwall, Watford, Luton
Div. 2 to Div. 3: Carlisle, Swansea, Brighton, Hull

1997

Premier League to Div. 1: Sunderland, Middlesbrough, Nott'm Forest
Div. 1 to Div. 2: Grimsby, Oldham, Southend
Div. 2 to Div. 3: Peterborough, Shrewsbury, Rotherham, Notts Co.

QUOTE-UNQUOTE

GLENN HODDLE, after Liverpool pulled Robbie Fowler out of England's last five matches last season to have a nasal operation that could have waited: "I don't get mad . . . I get even."

PETER SCHMEICHEL, on the eve of Man. United's European Cup semi-final against Borussia Dortmund: "This United team would have beaten the old United that won the European Cup ten-nil."

ALAN SUGAR, chairman of Tottenham (Feb. 1997): "I think, when we look back, this season will be seen as the year of the mercenary. It will be interesting to see how many of these foreign mercenaries are still here in August."

SAM HAMMAM, Wimbledon owner, under fixture pressure last season: "We use every stumbling block as a stepping stone."

F.A. CUP 1996-97

First Round – November 16

Ashford T. v Dagenham & Red.	2-2
Blackpool v Wigan	1-0
Boreham W. v Rushden & Diam.	1-1
Boston Utd. v Morecambe	3-0
Brentford v Bournemouth	2-0
Bristol Rov. v Exeter	1-2
Bromley v Enfield	1-3
Burnley v Lincoln	2-1
Cambridge Utd. v Welling	3-0
Cardiff v Hendon	2-0
Carlisle v Shepshed Dyn.	6-0
Chester v Stalybridge	3-0
Chesterfield v Bury	1-0
Colchester v Wycombe	1-2
Colwyn Bay v Wrexham	1-1
Crewe v Kidderminster	4-1
Farnborough v Barnet	2-2
Gillingham v Hereford	1-0
Hartlepool v York	0-0
Hednesford v Southport	2-1
Leton Orient v Merthyr T.	2-1
Macclesfield v Rochdale	0-2
Mansfield v Consett	4-0
Newcastle T. v Notts County (at Stoke)	0-2
Northampton v Watford	0-1
Northwich v Walsall	2-2
Peterborough v Cheltenham	0-0
Plymouth v Fulham	5-0
Preston v Altrincham	4-1
Runcorn v Darlington	1-4
Scunthorpe v Rotherham	4-1
Shrewsbury v Scarborough	1-1
Stevenage v Hayes	2-2
Stockport v Doncaster	2-1
Sudbury T. v Brighton	0-0
Swansea v Bristol City	1-1
Torquay v Luton	0-1
Whitby T. v Hull	0-0
Wisbech v St Albans	1-2
Woking v Millwall	2-2

Replays

Barnet v Farnborough	1-0

Brighton v Sudbury T.	*1-1
(Sudbury T. won 4-3 on pens.)	
Bristol City v Swansea	1-0
Cheltenham v Peterborough	*1-3
Dagenham & Red. v Ashford T.	*1-1
(Ashford T. won 4-3 on pens.)	
Hayes v Stevenage	0-2
Hull v Whitby T.	*8-4
Millwall v Woking	0-1
Rushden & Dia. v Boreham W.	2-3
Scarborough v Shrewsbury	1-0
Wrexham v Colwyn Bay	2-0
York v Hartlepool	3-0
Walsall v Northwich	3-1

Second Round – December 7

Barnet v Wycombe	3-3
Blackpool v Hednesford	0-1
Bristol City v St Albans	9-2
Cambridge Utd v Woking	0-2
Cardiff v Gillingham	0-2
Carlisle v Darlington	1-0
Chester v Boston Utd.	1-0
Chesterfield v Scarborough	2-0
Enfield v Peterborough	1-1
Hull v Crewe	1-5
Leyton Orient v Stevenage	1-2
Luton v Boreham W.	2-1
Mansfield v Stockport	0-3
Notts County v Rochdale	3-1
Plymouth v Exeter	4-1
Preston v York	2-3
Sudbury T. v Brentford (at Colchester)	1-3
Walsall v Burnley	1-1
Watford v Ashford T.	5-0
Wrexham v Scunthorpe	2-2

Replays

Burnley v Walsall	*1-1
(Burnley won 4-2 on pens.)	
Peterborough v Enfield	4-1
Scunthorpe v Wrexham	*2-3
Wycombe v Barnet	3-2

(* After extra time.)

HOOLIGAN HOTLINE

If you have any information, any time, about any person involved in football hooliganism, the **National Criminal Intelligence Service** await your call on free-phone number 0800-515495.

THE F.A. CUP GOES BACK TO CHELSEA AFTER 27-YEAR WAIT

THIRD ROUND (January 4)	FOURTH ROUND (January 25)	FIFTH ROUND (February 15)	SIXTH ROUND (March 8)	SEMI-FINALS (April 13)	FINAL (May 17)
*Chelsea 3					
W.B.A. 0	*Chelsea 4				
Liverpool 1	Liverpool 2	Chelsea .... 2:†1			
Burnley 0					
*Leicester 2	*Leicester 2	*Leicester 2:0	Chelsea 4		
Southend 0	Norwich 1				
Norwich 1				Chelsea 3	
Sheff. Utd. 0					
*Arsenal 1:2	*Arsenal 0	*Leeds 2			
Sunderland .. 1:0	Leeds 1				
*Crystal Palace 2:0		Portsmouth 3	*Portsmouth 1		
Leeds 2:1					
*Reading 0	*Reading 0				Chelsea 2
Southampton .. 1	Portsmouth 3				
*Portsmouth 2					
Wolves 1					
*Everton 3	*Everton 2	*Bradford 0			
Swindon 0	Bradford 3				
*Wycombe 0		Sheff. Wed. 0	*Sheff. Wed. 0		
Bradford 2					
*Carlisle 3	*Carlisle 3			Wimbledon 0	
Tranmere 0	Sheff. Wed. 2				
*Sheff. Wed. 7					
Grimsby 1					
*Huddersfield .. 1:1	*Q.P.R. 3	Q.P.R. 1			
Q.P.R. 1:2	Barnsley 2				
*Barnsley 2		*Wimbledon 2	Wimbledon 2		
Oldham 2					
Man Utd. 1:0	Man Utd. 1:0				
Tottenham 0	*Wimbledon 1:1				
*Crewe 1:0					
Wimbledon 1:2					

(at Highbury)

(at Wembley – Att: 79,160)

58

FA CUP FINAL STAGES 1996-97

*Chesterfield 2
Bristol City 0
*Luton 1:2
Bolton 1:6
*Charlton 1:1
Newcastle 1:2
*Nott'm Forest 3
Ipswich 1:2
*Birmingham A2
Stevenage 0
*Stoke 1
Stockport 0
*Plymouth 2
Peterborough 2
*Wrexham 1:1
West Ham 1:0
*Gillingham B0
Derby 3
*Aston Villa 1
Notts County 0:3
*Blackburn 1
Port Vale 1
*Coventry 2
Woking 1:2
*Brentford 1:1
Man. City 3
*Watford 1
Oxford Utd. 2
*Hednesford 1
York 2
*Middlesbrough 6

Chesterfield 3
*Bolton 2
*Newcastle 1
Nott'm Forest 0
*Birmingham 1
Stockport 1
*Peterborough 2
Wrexham 4
*Derby 3
Aston Villa 1
*Blackburn 1
Coventry 2
*Man. City 3
Watford 1
Hednesford 2
Middlesbrough .. C3

*Chesterfield 1
Nott'm Forest 0
*Birmingham 1
Wrexham 3
*Derby 3
Coventry 2
*Man. City 0
Middlesbrough .. 2

Chesterfield ...... †3:0
Wrexham 0
*Derby 0
Middlesbrough .. 3:3

Chesterfield 1
(at Old Trafford;
replay at
Hillsborough)

Middlesbrough 1

(* Drawn at home. †After extra time. A – Tie switched from Stevenage. B – First match abandoned, 66 mins (0-0) – frost.
C – Tie switched from Hednesford. Dates shown as scheduled for main round – subject to TV variations and postponements.)

F.A. CUP FINAL TEAMS 1900-97

1900 **BURY** – Thompson; Darrock, Davidson, Pray, Leeming, Ross, Richards, Wood, McLuckie, Sagar, Plant.
SOUTHAMPTON – Robinson; Meehan, Durber, Meston, Chadwick, Petrie, Turner, Yates, Farrell, Wood, Milward.
Scorers: Bury – McLuckie 2, Wood, Plant.

1901 **TOTTENHAM HOTSPUR** – Clawley; Erentz, Tait, Norris, Hughes, Jones, Smith, Cameron, Brown, Copeland, Kirwan.
SHEFFIELD UNITED – Foulke; Thickett, Boyle, Johnson, Morren, Needham, Bennett, Field, Hedley, Priest, Lipsham.
Scorers: (first match) Tottenham – Brown 2, Sheff. Utd. – Bennett, Priest.
Scorers: (second match) Tottenham – Cameron, Smith, Brown, Sheff. Utd. – Priest.

1902 **SHEFFIELD UNITED** – Foulke; Thickett, Boyle, Needham, Wilkinson, Johnson, Barnes, Common, Hedley, Priest, Lipsham. (Bennett injured in first match and Barnes took his place in the replay).
SOUTHAMPTON – Robinson; C. B. Fry, Molyneux, Bowman, Lee, A. Turner, Wood, Brown, Chadwick, J. Turner, Metson.
Scorers: (first match) Sheff. Utd. – Common, Southampton – Wood.
Scorers: (second match) Sheff. Utd. – Hedley, Barnes, Southampton – Brown.

1903 **BURY** – Monteith; Lindsey, McEwan, Johnson, Thorpe, Ross, Richards, Wood, Sagar, Leeming, Plant.
DERBY COUNTY – Fryer; Methven, Morris, Warren, Goodall (A.), May, Warrington, York, Boag, Richards, Davis.
Scorers: Bury – Ross, Sagar, Leeming 2, Wood, Plant.

1904 **MANCHESTER CITY** – Hillman; McMahon, Burgess, Frost, Hynde, S. B. Ashworth, Meredith, Livingstone, Gillespie, Turnbull (A.), Booth.
BOLTON WANDERERS – D. Davies; Brown, Struthers, Clifford, Greenhalgh, Freebairn, Stokes, Marsh, Yenson, White, Taylor.
Scorer: Man. City – Meredith.

1905 **ASTON VILLA** – George; Spencer, Miles, Pearson, Leake, Windmill, Brawn, Garratty, Hampton, Bache, Hall.
NEWCASTLE UNITED – Lawrence; McCombie, Carr, Gardner, Aitken, McWilliam, Rutherford, Howie, Appleyard, Veitch, Gosnell.
Scorer: Aston Villa – Hampton 2.

1906 **EVERTON** – Scott; Balmer (W.), Crelly, Makepeace, Taylor, Abbott, Sharp, Bolton, Young, Settle, H. P. Hardman.
NEWCASTLE UNITED – Lawrence; McCombie, Carr, Gardner, Aitken, McWilliam, Rutherford, Howie, Veitch, Orr, Gosnell.
Scorer: Everton – Young.

1907 **SHEFFIELD WEDNESDAY** – Lyall; Layton, Burton, Brittleton, Crawshaw, Bartlett, Chapman, Bradshaw, Wilson, Stewart, Simpson.
EVERTON – Scott; Balmer (W.), Balmer (R.), Makepeace, Taylor, Abbott, Sharp, Bolton, Young, Settle, H. P. Hardman.
Scorers: Sheff. Wed. – Stewart, Simpson, Everton – Sharp.

1908 **WOLVERHAMPTON WANDERERS** – Lunn; Jones, Collins, Rev. K. R. G. Hunt, Wooldridge, Bishop, Harrison, Shelton, Hedley, Radford, Pedley.
NEWCASTLE UNITED – Lawrence; McCracken, Pudan, Gardner, Veitch, McWilliam, Rutherford, Howie, Appleyard, Speedie, Wilson.
Scorers: Wolves – Rev. K. R. G. Hunt, Hedley, Harrison, Newcastle – Howie.

1909 **MANCHESTER UNITED** – Moger; Stacey, Hayes, Duckworth, Roberts, Bell, Meredith, Halse, Turnbull (J.), Turnbull (A.), Wall.

BRISTOL CITY – Clay; Annan, Cottle, Hanlin, Wedlock, Spear, Staniforth, Hardy, Gilligan, Burton, Hilton.
Scorer: Man. Utd. – Turnbull (A.).

1910 **NEWCASTLE UNITED** – Lawrence; McCracken, Carr, Veitch, Low, McWilliam, Rutherford, Howie, Shepherd, Higgins, Wilson. (Whitson was injured in first match and Carr took his place in the replay).
BARNSLEY – Mearns; Downs, Ness, Glendinning, Boyle, Utley, Bartrop, Gadsby, Lillycrop, Tufnell, Forman.
Scorers: (first match) Newcastle – Rutherford, Barnsley – Tufnell.
Scorer: (second match) Newcastle – Shepherd 2 (1 pen.).

1911 **BRADFORD CITY** – Mellors; Campbell, Taylor, Robinson, Torrance, McDonald, Logan, Spiers, O'Rourke, Devine, Thompson. (Gildea played centre half in the first match).
NEWCASTLE UNITED – Lawrence; McCracken, Whitson, Veitch, Low, Willis, Rutherford, Jobey, Stewart, Higgins, Wilson.
Scorer: Bradford – Spiers.

1912 **BARNSLEY** – Cooper; Downs, Taylor, Glendinning, Bratley, Utley, Bartrop, Tufnell, Lillycrop, Travers, Moore.
WEST BROMWICH ALBION – Pearson; Cook, Pennington, Baddeley, Buck, McNeal, Jephcott, Wright, Pailor, Bower, Shearman.
Scorer: Barnsley – Tufnell.

1913 **ASTON VILLA** – Hardy; Lyons, Weston, Barber, Harrop, Leach, Wallace, Halse, Hampton, Stephenson (C.), Bache.
SUNDERLAND – Butler; Gladwin, Ness, Cuggy, Thompson, Low, Mordue, Buchan, Richardson, Holley, Martin.
Scorer: Aston Villa – Barber.

1914 **BURNLEY** – Sewell; Bamford, Taylor, Halley, Boyle, Watson, Nesbit, Lindley, Freeman, Hodgson, Mosscrop.
LIVERPOOL – Campbell; Longworth, Pursell, Fairfoul, Ferguson, McKinlay, Sheldon, Metcalfe, Miller, Lacey, Nicholl.
Scorer: Burnley – Freeman.

1915 **SHEFFIELD UNITED** – Gough; Cook, English, Sturgess, Brelsford, Utley, Simmons, Fazackerley, Kitchen, Masterman, Evans.
CHELSEA – Molyneux; Bettridge, Harrow, Taylor, Logan, Walker, Ford, Halse, Thompson, Croal, McNeil.
Scorers: Sheff. Utd. – Simmons, Fazackerley, Kitchen.

1920 **ASTON VILLA** – Hardy; Smart, Weston, Ducat, Barson, Moss, Wallace, Kirton, Walker, Stephenson (C.), Dorrell.
HUDDERSFIELD TOWN – Mutch; Wood, Bullock, Slade, Wilson, Watson, Richardson, Mann, Taylor, Swan, Islip.
Scorer: Aston Villa – Kirton.

1921 **TOTTENHAM HOTSPUR** – Hunter; Clay, McDonald, Smith, Walters, Grimsdell; Banks, Seed, Cantrell, Bliss, Dimmock.
WOLVERHAMPTON WANDERERS – George; Woodward, Marshall, Gregory, Hodnett, Riley, Lea, Burrill, Edmonds, Potts, Brooks.
Scorer: Tottenham – Dimmock.

1922 **HUDDERSFIELD TOWN** – Mutch; Wood, Wadsworth, Slade, Wilson, Watson, Richardson, Mann, Islip, Stephenson, Smith (W.H.).
PRESTON NORTH END – J. F. Mitchell; Hamilton, Doolan, Duxbury, McCall, Williamson, Rawlings, Jefferis, Roberts, Woodhouse, Quinn.
Scorer: Huddersfield – Smith (pen.).

1923 **BOLTON WANDERERS** – Pym; Hawarth, Finney, Nuttall, Seddon, Jennings, Butler, Jack, Smith (J. R.), Smith (J.), Vizard.
WEST HAM UNITED – Hufton; Henderson, Young, Bishop, Kay, Tresadern, Richards, Brown, Watson (V.), Moore, Ruffell.
Scorers: Bolton – Jack, Smith (J. R.).

1924 **NEWCASTLE UNITED** – Bradley; Hampson, Hudspeth, Mooney, Spencer, Gibson, Low, Cowan, Harris, McDonald, Seymour.

ASTON VILLA – Jackson; Smart, Mort, Moss, Dr. V. E. Milne, Blackburn, York, Kirton, Capewell, Walker, Dorrell.
Scorers: Newcastle – Harris, Seymour.

1925 **SHEFFIELD UNITED** – Sutcliffe; Cook, Milton, Pantling, King, Green, Mercer, Boyle, Johnson, Gillespie, Tunstall.
CARDIFF CITY – Farquharson; Nelson, Blair, Wake, Keenor, Hardy, Davies (W.), Gill, Nicholson, Beadles, Evans (J.).
Scorer: Sheff. Utd. – Tunstall.

1926 **BOLTON WANDERERS** – Pym; Haworth, Greenhalgh, Nuttall, Seddon, Jennings, Butler, Jack, Smith (J. R.), Smith (J.), Vizard.
MANCHESTER CITY – Goodchild; Cookson, McCloy, Pringle, Cowan, McMullan, Austin, Browell, Roberts, Johnson, Hicks.
Scorer: Bolton – Jack.

1927 **CARDIFF CITY** – Farquharson; Nelson, Watson, Keenor, Sloan, Hardy, Curtis, Irving, Ferguson, Davies (L.), McLachlan.
ARSENAL – Lewis; Parker, Kennedy, Baker, Butler, John, Hulme, Buchan, Brain, Blyth, Hoar.
Scorer: Cardiff – Ferguson.

1928 **BLACKBURN ROVERS** – Crawford; Hutton, Jones, Healless, Rankin, Campbell, Thornwell, Puddefoot, Roscamp, McLean, Rigby.
HUDDERSFIELD TOWN – Mercer; Goodall, Barkas, Redfern, Wilson, Steele, Jackson (A.), Kelly, Brown, Stephenson, Smith (W.H.).
Scorers: Blackburn – Roscamp 2, McLean, Huddersfield – Jackson.

1929 **BOLTON WANDERERS** – Pym; Haworth, Finney, Kean, Seddon, Nuttall, Butler, McClelland, Blackmore, Gibson, Cook (W.).
PORTSMOUTH – Gilfillan; Mackie, Bell, Nichol, McIlwaine, Thackeray, Forward, Smith (J.), Weddle, Watson, Cook (F.).
Scorers: Bolton – Butler, Blackmore.

1930 **ARSENAL** – Preedy; Parker, Hapgood, Baker, Seddon, John, Hulme, Jack, Lambert, James, Bastin.
HUDDERSFIELD TOWN – Turner; Goodall, Spence, Naylor, Wilson, Campbell, Jackson (A.), Kelly, Davies, Raw, Smith (W. H.).
Scorers: Arsenal – James, Lambert.

1931 **WEST BROMWICH ALBION** – Pearson; Shaw, Trentham, Magee, Richardson (W.), Edwards, Glidden, Carter, Richardson (W. G.), Sandford, Wood.
BIRMINGHAM – Hibbs; Liddell, Barkas, Cringan, Morrall, Leslie, Briggs, Crosbie, Bradford, Gregg, Curtis.
Scorers: W.B.A. – Richardson (W. G.) 2, Birmingham – Bradford.

1932 **NEWCASTLE UNITED** – McInroy; Nelson, Fairhurst, McKenzie, Davidson, Weaver, Boyd, Richardson, Allen, McMenemy, Lang.
ARSENAL – Moss; Parker, Hapgood, Jones (C.), Roberts, Male, Hulme, Jack, Lambert, Bastin, John.
Scorers: Newcastle – Allen 2, Arsenal – John.

1933 **EVERTON** – Sagar; Cook, Cresswell, Britton, White, Thomson, Geldard, Dunn, Dean, Johnson, Stein.
MANCHESTER CITY – Langford; Cann, Dale, Busby, Cowan, Bray, Toseland, Marshall, Herd, McMullan, Brook.
Scorers: Everton – Stein, Dean, Dunn.

1934 **MANCHESTER CITY** – Swift; Barnett, Dale, Busby, Cowan, Bray, Toseland, Marshall, Tilson, Herd, Brook.
PORTSMOUTH – Gilfillan; Mackie, Smith (W.), Nichol, Allen, Thackeray, Worrall, Smith (J.), Weddle, Easson, Rutherford.
Scorers: Man. City – Tilson 2, Portsmouth – Rutherford.

1935 **SHEFFIELD WEDNESDAY** – Brown; Nibloe, Catlin, Sharp, Millership, Burrows, Hooper, Surtees, Palethorpe, Starling, Rimmer.
WEST BROMWICH ALBION – Pearson; Shaw, Trentham, Murphy, Richardson (W.), Edwards, Glidden, Carter, Richardson (W. G.), Sandford, Boyes.

Scorers: Sheff. Wed. – Rimmer 2, Palethorpe, Hooper, W.B.A. – Boyes, Sandford.

1936   **ARSENAL** – Wilson; Male, Hapgood, Crayston, Roberts, Copping, Hulme, Bowden, Drake, James, Bastin.
SHEFFIELD UNITED – Smith; Hooper, Wilkinson, Jackson, Johnson, McPherson, Barton, Barclay, Dodds, Pickering, Williams.
Scorer: Arsenal – Drake.

1937   **SUNDERLAND** – Mapson; Gorman, Hall, Thompson, Johnston, McNab, Duns, Carter, Gurney, Gallacher, Burbanks.
PRESTON NORTH END – Burns; Gallimore, Beattie (A.), Shankly, Tremelling, Milne, Dougal, Beresford, O'Donnell (F.), Fagan, O'Donnell (H).
Scorers: Sunderland – Gurney, Carter, Burbanks, Preston – O'Donnell (F.).

1938   **PRESTON NORTH END** – Holdcroft; Gallimore, Beattie (A.), Shankly, Smith, Batey, Watmough, Mutch, Maxwell, Beattie (R.), O'Donnell (H.).
HUDDERSFIELD TOWN – Hesford; Craig, Mountford, Willingham, Young, Boot, Hulme, Isaac, McFadyen, Barclay, Beasley.
Scorer: Preston – Mutch (pen.).

1939   **PORTSMOUTH** – Walker; Morgan, Rochford, Guthrie, Rowe, Wharton, Worrall, McAlinden, Anderson, Barlow, Parker.
WOLVERHAMPTON WANDERERS – Scott; Morris, Taylor, Galley, Cullis, Gardiner, Burton, McIntosh, Westcott, Dorsett, Maguire.
Scorers: Portsmouth – Parker 2, Barlow, Anderson, Wolves – Dorsett.

1946   **DERBY COUNTY** – Woodley; Nicholas, Howe, Bullions, Leuty, Musson, Harrison, Carter, Stamps, Doherty, Duncan.
CHARLTON ATHLETIC – Bartram; Phipps, Shreeve, Turner (H.), Oakes, Johnson, Fell, Brown, A. A. Turner, Welsh, Duffy.
Scorers: Derby – Turner (H.) (o.g.), Doherty, Stamps 2, Charlton – Turner (H.).

1947   **CHARLTON ATHLETIC** – Bartram; Croker (P.), Shreeve, Johnson, Phipps, Whittaker, Hurst, Dawson, Robinson (W.), Welsh, Duffy.
BURNLEY – Strong; Woodruff, Mather, Attwell, Brown, Bray, Chew, Morris, Harrison, Potts, F. P. Kippax.
Scorer: Charlton – Duffy.

1948   **MANCHESTER UNITED** – Crompton; Carey, Aston, Anderson, Chilton, Cockburn, Delaney, Morris, Rowley, Pearson, Mitten.
BLACKPOOL – Robinson; Shimwell, Crosland, Johnston, Hayward, Kelly, Matthews, Munro, Mortensen, Dick, Rickett.
Scorers: Man. Utd. – Rowley 2, Pearson, Anderson, Blackpool – Shimwell (pen.), Mortensen.

1949   **WOLVERHAMPTON WANDERERS** – Williams; Pritchard, Springthorpe, Crook (W.), Shorthouse, Wright, Hancocks, Smyth, Pye, Dunn, Mullen.
LEICESTER CITY – Bradley; Jelly, Scott, Harrison (W.), Plummer, King, Griffiths, Lee, Harrison (J.), Chisholm, Adam.
Scorers: Wolves – Pye 2, Smyth, Leicester – Griffiths.

1950   **ARSENAL** – Swindin; Scott, Barnes, Forbes, Compton (L.), Mercer, Cox, Logie, Goring, Lewis, Compton (D.).
LIVERPOOL – Sidlow; Lambert, Spicer, Taylor, Hughes, Jones, Payne, Baron, Stubbins, Fagan, Liddell.
Scorer: Arsenal – Lewis 2.

1951   **NEWCASTLE UNITED** – Fairbrother; Cowell, Corbett, Harvey, Brennan, Crowe, Walker, Taylor, Milburn, Robledo (G.), Mitchell.
BLACKPOOL – Farm; Shimwell, Garrett, Johnston, Hayward, Kelly, Matthews, Mudie, Mortensen, W. J. Slater, Perry.
Scorer: Newcastle – Milburn 2.

1952   **NEWCASTLE UNITED** – Simpson; Cowell, McMichael, Harvey, Brennan, Robledo (E.), Walker, Foulkes, Milburn, Robledo (G.), Mitchell.
ARSENAL – Swindin; Barnes, Smith (L.), Forbes, Daniel, Mercer, Cox, Logie, Holton, Lishman, Roper.
Scorer: Newcastle – Robledo (G.).

1953   **BLACKPOOL** – Farm; Shimwell, Garrett, Fenton, Johnston, Robinson, Matthews, Taylor, Mortensen, Mudie, Perry.
BOLTON WANDERERS – Hanson; Ball, Banks (R.), Wheeler, Barrass, Bell, Holden, Moir, Lofthouse, Hassall, Langton.
Scorers: Blackpool – Mortensen 3, Perry, Bolton – Lofthouse, Moir, Bell.

1954   **WEST BROMWICH ALBION** – Sanders; Kennedy, Millard, Dudley, Dugdale, Barlow, Griffin, Ryan, Allen, Nicholls, Lee.
PRESTON NORTH END – Thompson; Cunningham, Walton, Docherty, Marston, Forbes, Finney, Foster, Wayman, Baxter, Morrison.
Scorers: W.B.A. – Allen 2 (1 pen.), Griffin, Preston – Morrison, Wayman.

1955   **NEWCASTLE UNITED** – Simpson; Cowell, Batty, Scoular, Stokoe, Casey, White, Milburn, Keeble, Hannah, Mitchell.
MANCHESTER CITY – Trautmann; Meadows, Little, Barnes, Ewing, Paul, Spurdle, Hayes, Revie, Johnstone, Fagan.
Scorers: Newcastle – Milburn, Mitchell, Hannah, Man. City – Johnstone.

1956   **MANCHESTER CITY** – Trautmann; Leivers, Little, Barnes, Ewing, Paul, Johnstone, Hayes, Revie, Dyson, Clarke.
BIRMINGHAM CITY – Merrick; Hall, Green, Newman, Smith, Boyd, Astall, Kinsey, Brown, Murphy, Govan.
Scorers: Man. City – Hayes, Dyson, Johnstone, Birmingham – Kinsey.

1957   **ASTON VILLA** – Sims; Lynn, Aldis, Crowther, Dugdale, Saward, Smith, Sewell, Myerscough, Dixon, McParland.
MANCHESTER UNITED – Wood; Foulkes, Byrne, Colman, Blanchflower, Edwards, Berry, Whelan, Taylor (T.), Charlton, Pegg.
Scorers: Aston Villa – McParland 2, Man. Utd. – Taylor.

1958   **BOLTON WANDERERS** – Hopkinson; Hartle, Banks (T.), Hennin, Higgins, Edwards, Birch, Stevens, Lofthouse, Parry, Holden.
MANCHESTER UNITED – Gregg; Foulkes, Greaves, Goodwin, Cope, Crowther, Dawson, Taylor (E.), Charlton, Viollet, Webster.
Scorer: Bolton – Lofthouse 2.

1959   **NOTTINGHAM FOREST** – Thomson; Whare, McDonald, Whitefoot, McKinlay, Burkitt, Dwight, Quigley, Wilson, Gray, Imlach.
LUTON TOWN – Baynham; McNally, Hawkes, Groves, Owen, Pacey, Bingham, Brown, Morton, Cummins, Gregory.
Scorers: Nott'm. Forest – Dwight, Wilson, Luton – Pacey.

1960   **WOLVERHAMPTON WANDERERS** – Finlayson; Showell, Harris, Clamp, Slater, Flowers, Deeley, Stobart, Murray, Broadbent, Horne.
BLACKBURN ROVERS – Leyland; Bray, Whelan, Clayton, Woods, McGrath, Bimpson, Dobing, Dougan, Douglas, MacLeod.
Scorers: Wolves – McGrath (o.g.), Deeley 2.

1961   **TOTTENHAM HOTSPUR** – Brown; Baker, Henry, Blanchflower, Norman, Mackay, Jones, White, Smith, Allen, Dyson.
LEICESTER CITY – Banks; Chalmers, Norman, McLintock, King, Appleton, Riley, Walsh, McIlmoyle, Keyworth, Cheesebrough.
Scorers: Tottenham – Smith, Dyson.

1962   **TOTTENHAM HOTSPUR** – Brown; Baker, Henry, Blanchflower, Norman, Mackay, Medwin, White, Smith, Greaves, Jones.

BURNLEY – Blacklaw; Angus, Elder, Adamson, Cummings, Miller, Connelly, McIlroy, Pointer, Robson, Harris.
Scorers: Tottenham – Greaves, Smith, Blanchflower (pen.), Burnley – Robson.

1963   **MANCHESTER UNITED** – Gaskell; Dunne, Cantwell, Crerand, Foulkes, Setters, Giles, Quixall, Herd, Law, Charlton.
LEICESTER CITY – Banks; Sjoberg, Norman, McLintock, King, Appleton, Riley, Cross, Keyworth, Gibson, Stringfellow.
Scorers: Man. Utd. – Law, Herd 2, Leicester – Keyworth.

1964   **WEST HAM UNITED** – Standen; Bond, Burkett, Bovington, Brown, Moore, Brabrook, Boyce, Byrne, Hurst, Sissons.
PRESTON NORTH END – Kelly; Ross, Smith, Lawton, Singleton, Kendall, Wilson, Ashworth, Dawson, Spavin, Holden.
Scorers: West Ham – Sissons, Hurst, Boyce, Preston – Holden, Dawson.

1965   **LIVERPOOL** – Lawrence; Lawler, Byrne, Strong, Yeats, Stevenson, Callaghan, Hunt, St. John, Smith, Thompson.
LEEDS UNITED – Sprake; Reaney, Bell, Bremner, Charlton, Hunter, Giles, Storrie, Peacock, Collins, Johanneson.
Scorers: Liverpool – Hunt, St. John, Leeds – Bremner.

1966   **EVERTON** – West; Wright, Wilson, Gabriel, Labone, Harris, Scott, Trebilcock, Young, Harvey, Temple.
SHEFFIELD WEDNESDAY – Springett; Smith, Megson, Eustace, Ellis, Young, Pugh, Fantham, McCalliog, Ford, Quinn.
Scorers: Everton – Trebilcock 2, Temple, Sheff. Wed. – McCalliog, Ford.

1967   **TOTTENHAM HOTSPUR** – Jennings; Kinnear, Knowles, Mullery, England, Mackay, Robertson, Greaves, Gilzean, Venables, Saul.
CHELSEA – Bonetti; Harris (A.), McCreadie, Hollins, Hinton, Harris (R.), Cooke, Baldwin, Hateley, Tambling, Boyle.
Scorers: Tottenham – Robertson, Saul, Chelsea – Tambling.

1968   **WEST BROMWICH ALBION** – Osborne; Fraser, Williams, Brown, Talbut, Kaye (Clarke), Lovett, Collard, Astle, Hope, Clark.
EVERTON – West; Wright, Wilson, Kendall, Labone, Harvey, Husband, Ball, Royle, Hurst, Morrissey.
Scorer: W.B.A. – Astle.

1969   **MANCHESTER CITY** – Dowd; Book, Pardoe, Doyle, Booth, Oakes, Summerbee, Bell, Lee, Young, Coleman.
LEICESTER CITY – Shilton; Rodrigues, Nish, Roberts, Woollett, Cross, Fern, Gibson, Lochhead, Clarke, Glover (Manley).
Scorer: Man. City – Young.

1970   **CHELSEA** – Bonetti; Webb, McCreadie, Hollins, Dempsey, Harris (R.) (Hinton), Baldwin, Houseman, Osgood, Hutchinson, Cooke.
LEEDS UNITED – Sprake; Madeley, Cooper, Bremner, Charlton, Hunter, Lorimer, Clarke, Jones, Giles, Gray.
Scorers: Chelsea – Houseman, Hutchinson, Leeds – Charlton, Jones.
Replay: CHELSEA – Bonetti; Harris (R.), McCreadie, Hollins, Dempsey, Webb, Baldwin, Cooke, Osgood (Hinton), Hutchinson, Houseman.
LEEDS UNITED – Harvey; Madeley, Cooper, Bremner, Charlton, Hunter, Lorimer, Clarke, Jones, Giles, Gray.
Scorers: Chelsea – Osgood, Webb, Leeds – Jones.

1971   **ARSENAL** – Wilson; Rice, McNab, Storey (Kelly), McLintock, Simpson, Armstrong, Graham, Radford, Kennedy, George.
LIVERPOOL – Clemence; Lawler, Lindsay, Smith, Lloyd, Hughes, Callaghan, Evans (Thompson), Heighway, Toshack, Hall.
Scorers: Arsenal – Kelly, George, Liverpool – Heighway.

1972   **LEEDS UNITED** – Harvey; Reaney, Madeley, Bremner, Charlton, Hunter, Lorimer, Clarke, Jones, Giles, Gray.

ARSENAL – Barnett; Rice, McNab, Storey, McLintock, Simpson, Armstrong, Ball, Radford (Kennedy), George, Graham.
Scorer: Leeds – Clarke.

1973 **SUNDERLAND** – Montgomery; Malone, Guthrie, Horswill, Watson, Pitt, Kerr, Hughes, Halom, Porterfield, Tueart.
LEEDS UNITED – Harvey; Reaney, Cherry, Bremner, Madeley, Hunter, Lorimer, Clarke, Jones, Giles, Gray (Yorath).
Scorer: Sunderland – Porterfield.

1974 **LIVERPOOL** – Clemence; Smith, Lindsay, Thompson, Cormack, Hughes, Keegan, Hall, Heighway, Toshack, Callaghan.
NEWCASTLE UNITED – McFaul; Clark, Kennedy, McDermott, Howard, Moncur, Smith (Gibb), Cassidy, Macdonald, Tudor, Hibbitt.
Scorers: Liverpool – Keegan (2), Heighway.

1975 **WEST HAM UNITED** – Day; McDowell, Lampard, Bonds, Taylor (T.), Lock, Jennings, Paddon, Taylor (A.), Brooking, Holland.
FULHAM – Mellor; Cutbush, Fraser, Mullery, Lacy, Moore, Mitchell, Conway, Busby, Slough, Barrett.
Scorer: West Ham – Taylor (A.) 2.

1976 **SOUTHAMPTON** – Turner; Rodrigues, Peach, Holmes, Blyth, Steele, Gilchrist, Channon, Osgood, McCalliog, Stokes.
MANCHESTER UNITED – Stepney; Forsyth, Houston, Daly, Greenhoff (B.), Buchan, Coppell, McIlroy, Pearson, Macari, Hill (McCreery).
Scorer: Southampton – Stokes.

1977 **MANCHESTER UNITED** – Stepney; Nicholl, Albiston, McIlroy, Greenhoff (B.), Buchan, Coppell, Greenhoff (J.), Pearson, Macari, Hill (McCreery).
LIVERPOOL – Clemence; Neal, Jones, Smith, Kennedy, Hughes, Keegan, Case, Heighway, McDermott, Johnson (Callaghan).
Scorers: Man. Utd. – Pearson, Greenhoff (J.), Liverpool – Case.

1978 **IPSWICH TOWN** – Cooper; Burley, Mills, Talbot, Hunter, Beattie, Osborne (Lambert), Wark, Mariner, Geddis, Woods.
ARSENAL – Jennings; Rice, Nelson, Price, O'Leary, Young, Brady (Rix), Sunderland, Macdonald, Stapleton, Hudson.
Scorer: Ipswich – Osborne.

1979 **ARSENAL** – Jennings; Rice, Nelson, Talbot, O'Leary, Young, Brady, Sunderland, Stapleton, Price (Walford), Rix.
MANCHESTER UNITED – Bailey; Nicholl, Albiston, McIlroy, McQueen, Buchan, Coppell, Greenhoff (J.), Jordan, Macari, Thomas.
Scorers: Arsenal – Talbot, Stapleton, Sunderland, Man. Utd. – McQueen, McIlroy.

1980 **WEST HAM UNITED** – Parkes; Stewart, Lampard, Bonds, Martin, Devonshire, Allen, Pearson, Cross, Brooking, Pike.
ARSENAL – Jennings; Rice, Devine (Nelson), Talbot, O'Leary, Young, Brady, Sunderland, Stapleton, Price, Rix.
Scorer: West Ham – Brooking.

1981 **TOTTENHAM HOTSPUR** – Aleksic; Hughton, Miller, Roberts, Perryman, Villa (Brooke), Ardiles, Archibald, Galvin, Hoddle, Crooks.
MANCHESTER CITY – Corrigan; Ranson, McDonald, Reid, Power, Caton, Bennett, Gow, Mackenzie, Hutchison (Henry), Reeves.
Scorer: Tottenham – Hutchison (o.g.), Man. City – Hutchison.
Replay: TOTTENHAM HOTSPUR – Aleksic; Hughton, Miller, Roberts, Perryman, Villa, Ardiles, Archibald, Galvin, Hoddle, Crooks.
MANCHESTER CITY – Corrigan; Ranson, McDonald (Tueart), Reid, Power, Caton, Bennett, Gow, Mackenzie, Hutchison, Reeves.
Scorers: Tottenham – Villa 2, Crooks, Man. City – Mackenzie, Reeves (pen.).

1982   **TOTTENHAM HOTSPUR** – Clemence; Hughton, Miller, Price, Hazard (Brooke), Perryman, Roberts, Archibald, Galvin, Hoddle, Crooks.
QUEENS PARK RANGERS – Hucker; Fenwick, Gillard, Waddock, Hazell, Roeder, Currie, Flanagan, Allen (Micklewhite), Stainrod, Gregory.
Scorers: Tottenham – Hoddle, Q.P.R. – Fenwick.
Replay: TOTTENHAM HOTSPUR – Clemence; Hughton, Miller, Price, Hazard (Brooke), Perryman, Roberts, Archibald, Galvin, Hoddle, Crooks.
QUEENS PARK RANGERS – Hucker; Fenwick, Gillard, Waddock, Hazell, Neill, Currie, Flanagan, Micklewhite (Burke), Stainrod, Gregory.
Scorer: Tottenham – Hoddle (pen.).

1983   **MANCHESTER UNITED** – Bailey; Duxbury, Albiston, Wilkins, Moran, McQueen, Robson, Muhren, Stapleton, Whiteside, Davies.
BRIGHTON & HOVE ALBION – Moseley; Ramsey (Ryan), Pearce, Grealish, Gatting, Stevens, Case, Howlett, Robinson, Smith, Smillie.
Scorers: Man. Utd. – Stapleton, Wilkins, Brighton – Smith, Stevens.
Replay: MANCHESTER UNITED – Bailey; Duxbury, Albiston, Wilkins, Moran, McQueen, Robson, Muhren, Stapleton, Whiteside, Davies.
BRIGHTON & HOVE ALBION – Moseley; Gatting, Pearce, Grealish, Foster, Stevens, Case, Howlett (Ryan), Robinson, Smith, Smillie.
Scorers: Man. Utd. – Robson 2, Whiteside, Muhren (pen.).

1984   **EVERTON** – Southall; Stevens, Bailey, Ratcliffe, Mountfield, Reid, Steven, Heath, Sharp, Gray, Richardson.
WATFORD – Sherwood; Bardsley, Price (Atkinson), Taylor, Terry, Sinnott, Callaghan, Johnston, Reilly, Jackett, Barnes.
Scorers: Everton – Sharp, Gray.

1985   **MANCHESTER UNITED** – Bailey; Gidman, Albiston (Duxbury), Whiteside, McGrath, Moran, Robson, Strachan, Hughes, Stapleton, Olsen.
EVERTON – Southall; Stevens, Van den Hauwe, Ratcliffe, Mountfield, Reid, Steven, Sharp, Gray, Bracewell, Sheedy.
Scorer: Man. Utd. – Whiteside.
Sent off: Moran.

1986   **LIVERPOOL** – Grobbelaar; Lawrenson, Beglin, Nicol, Whelan, Hansen, Dalglish, Johnston, Rush, Molby, MacDonald.
EVERTON – Mimms; Stevens (Heath), Van den Hauwe, Ratcliffe, Mountfield, Reid, Steven, Lineker, Sharp, Bracewell, Sheedy.
Scorers: Liverpool – Rush 2, Johnston, Everton – Lineker.

1987   **COVENTRY CITY** – Ogrizovic; Phillips, Downs, McGrath, Kilcline (Rodger), Peake, Bennett, Gynn, Regis, Houchen, Pickering.
TOTTENHAM HOTSPUR – Clemence; Hughton (Claesen), Thomas (M.), Hodge, Gough, Mabbutt, Allen (C.), Allen (P.), Waddle, Hoddle, Ardiles (Stevens).
Scorers: Coventry – Bennett, Houchen, Mabbutt (o.g.), Tottenham – Allen (C.), Mabbutt.

1988   **WIMBLEDON** – Beasant; Goodyear, Phelan, Jones, Young, Thorn, Gibson (Scales), Cork (Cunningham), Fashanu, Sanchez, Wise.
LIVERPOOL – Grobbelaar; Gillespie, Ablett, Nicol, Spackman (Molby), Hansen, Beardsley, Aldridge (Johnston), Houghton, Barnes, McMahon.
Scorer: Wimbledon – Sanchez.

1989   **LIVERPOOL** – Grobbelaar; Ablett, Staunton (Venison), Nicol, Whelan, Hansen, Beardsley, Aldridge (Rush), Houghton, Barnes, McMahon.
EVERTON – Southall; McDonald, Van den Hauwe, Ratcliffe, Watson, Bracewell (McCall), Nevin, Steven, Sharp, Cottee, Sheedy (Wilson).
Scorers: Liverpool – Aldridge, Rush 2, Everton – McCall 2.

1990   **MANCHESTER UNITED** – Leighton; Ince, Martin (Blackmore), Bruce, Phelan, Pallister (Robins), Robson, Webb, McClair, Hughes, Wallace.
CRYSTAL PALACE – Martyn; Pemberton, Shaw, Gray (Madden), O'Reilly, Thorn, Barber (Wright), Thomas, Bright, Salako, Pardew.
Scorers: Man. Utd. – Robson, Hughes 2, Crystal Palace – O'Reilly, Wright 2.
Replay: MANCHESTER UNITED – Sealey; Ince, Martin, Bruce, Phelan, Pallister, Robson, Webb, McClair, Hughes, Wallace.
CRYSTAL PALACE – Martyn; Pemberton, Shaw, Gray, O'Reilly, Thorn, Barber (Wright), Thomas, Bright, Salako (Madden), Pardew.
Scorer: Man. Utd. – Martin.

1991   **TOTTENHAM HOTSPUR** – Thorstvedt; Edinburgh, Van den Hauwe, Sedgley, Howells, Mabbutt, Stewart, Gascoigne (Nayim), Samways (Walsh), Lineker, Allen.
NOTTINGHAM FOREST – Crossley; Charles, Pearce, Walker, Chettle, Keane, Crosby, Parker, Clough, Glover (Laws), Woan (Hodge).
Scorers: Tottenham – Stewart, Walker (o.g.), Nott'm. Forest – Pearce.

1992   **LIVERPOOL** – Grobbelaar; Jones (R.), Burrows, Nicol, Molby, Wright, Saunders, Houghton, Rush (I.), McManaman, Thomas.
SUNDERLAND – Norman; Owers, Ball, Bennett, Rogan, Rush (D.) (Hardyman), Bracewell, Davenport, Armstrong (Hawke), Byrne, Atkinson.
Scorers: Liverpool – Thomas, Rush (I.).

1993   **ARSENAL** – Seaman; Dixon, Winterburn, Linighan, Adams, Parlour (Smith), Davis, Merson, Jensen, Wright (O'Leary), Campbell.
SHEFFIELD WEDNESDAY – Woods; Nilsson, Worthington, Palmer, Hirst, Anderson (Hyde), Waddle (Bart-Williams), Warhurst, Bright, Sheridan, Harkes.
Scorers: Arsenal – Wright, Sheff. Wed. – Hirst.
Replay:ARSENAL – Seaman; Dixon, Winterburn, Linighan, Adams, Davis, Jensen, Merson, Smith, Wright (O'Leary), Campbell.
SHEFFIELD WEDNESDAY – Woods; Nilsson (Bart-Williams), Worthington, Palmer, Hirst, Wilson (Hyde), Waddle, Warhurst, Bright, Sheridan, Harkes.
Scorers: Arsenal – Wright, Linighan, Sheff. Wed. – Waddle.

1994   **MANCHESTER UNITED** – Schmeichel; Parker, Bruce, Pallister, Irwin (Sharpe), Kanchelskis (McClair), Keane, Ince, Giggs, Cantona, Hughes.
CHELSEA – Kharine; Clarke, Johnsen, Kjeldbjerg, Sinclair, Burley (Hoddle), Newton, Wise, Peacock, Stein (Cascarino), Spencer.
Scorers: Man. Utd. – Cantona 2 (2 pens.), Hughes, McClair.

1995   **EVERTON** – Southall; Jackson, Watson, Unsworth, Ablett, Horne, Parkinson, Hinchcliffe, Stuart, Limpar (Amokachi), Rideout (Ferguson).
MANCHESTER UNITED – Schmeichel; Neville (G.), Bruce (Giggs), Pallister, Irwin, Butt, Keane, Ince, Sharpe (Scholes), McClair, Hughes.
Scorer: Everton – Rideout.

1996   **MANCHESTER UNITED** – Schmeichel; Irwin, May, Pallister, Neville (P.), Beckham (Neville, G.), Keane, Butt, Giggs, Cantona, Cole (Scholes).
LIVERPOOL – James; McAteer, Scales, Wright, Babb, Jones (Thomas), McManaman, Redknapp, Barnes, Collymore (Rush), Fowler.
Scorer: Man. Utd. – Cantona.

1997   **CHELSEA** – Grodas; Sinclair, Lebouef, Clarke, Minto, Petrescu, Di Matteo, Newton, Wise, Zola (Vialli), Hughes (M.).
Scorers: Di Matteo, Newton.
MIDDLESBROUGH – Roberts; Blackmore, Pearson, Festa, Fleming, Stamp, Emerson, Mustoe (Vickers), Hignett, (Kinder), Juninho, Ravanelli, (Beck).

F.A. CUP FINALS –
COMPLETE RESULTS

AT KENNINGTON OVAL

1872   The Wanderers beat Royal Engineers (1-0)

AT LILLIE BRIDGE, LONDON

1873   The Wanderers beat Oxford University (2-1)

AT KENNINGTON OVAL

1874	Oxford University beat Royal Engineers (2-0)
1875	Royal Engineers beat Old Etonians (2-0 after a 1-1 draw)
1876	The Wanderers beat Old Etonians (3-0 after a 0-0 draw)
1877††	The Wanderers beat Oxford University (2-1)
1878*	The Wanderers beat Royal Engineers (3-1)
1879	Old Etonians beat Clapham Rovers (1-0)
1880	Clapham Rovers beat Oxford University (1-0)
1881	Old Carthusians beat Old Etonians (3-0)
1882	Old Etonians beat Blackburn Rovers (1-0)
1883††	Blackburn Olympic beat Old Etonians (2-1)
1884	Blackburn Rovers beat Queen's Park (Glasgow) (2-1)
1885	Blackburn Rovers beat Queen's Park (Glasgow) (2-0)
1886†*a*	Blackburn Rovers beat West Bromwich Albion (2-0 after a 0-0 draw)
1887	Aston Villa beat West Bromwich Albion (2-0)
1888	West Bromwich Albion beat Preston North End (2-1)
1889	Preston North End beat Wolverhampton Wanderers (3-0)
1890	Blackburn Rovers beat Sheffield Wednesday (6-1)
1891	Blackburn Rovers beat Notts County (3-1)
1892	West Bromwich Albion beat Aston Villa (3-0)

AT FALLOWFIELD, MANCHESTER

1893   Wolverhampton Wanderers beat Everton (1-0)

AT GOODISON PARK, LIVERPOOL

1894   Notts County beat Bolton Wanderers (4-1)

AT CRYSTAL PALACE

1895	Aston Villa beat West Bromwich Albion (1-0)
1896	Sheffield Wednesday beat Wolverhampton Wanderers (2-1)
1897	Aston Villa beat Everton (3-2)
1898	Nottingham Forest beat Derby County (3-1)
1899	Sheffield United beat Derby County (4-1)
1900	Bury beat Southampton (4-0)
1901†††	Tottenham Hotspur beat Sheffield United (3-1 after a 2-2 draw)
1902	Sheffield United beat Southampton (2-1 after a 1-1 draw)
1903	Bury beat Derby County (6-0)
1904	Manchester City beat Bolton Wanderers (1-0)
1905	Aston Villa beat Newcastle United (2-0)
1906	Everton beat Newcastle United (1-0)
1907	Sheffield Wednesday beat Everton (2-1)
1908	Wolverhampton Wanderers beat Newcastle United (3-1)
1909	Manchester United beat Bristol City (1-0)

1910**	Newcastle United beat Barnsley (2-0 after a 1-1 draw)
1911b	Bradford City beat Newcastle United (1-0 after a 0-0 draw)
1912c	Barnsley beat West Bromwich Albion (1-0 after a 0-0 draw)
1913	Aston Villa beat Sunderland (1-0)
1914	Burnley beat Liverpool (1-0)

AT OLD TRAFFORD, MANCHESTER

| 1915 | Sheffield United beat Chelsea (3-0) |

AT STAMFORD BRIDGE, LONDON

1920††	Aston Villa beat Huddersfield Town (1-0)
1921	Tottenham Hotspur beat Wolverhampton Wanderers (1-0)
1922	Huddersfield Town beat Preston North End (1-0)

AT WEMBLEY

1923	Bolton Wanderers beat West Ham United (2-0)
1924	Newcastle United beat Aston Villa (2-0)
1925	Sheffield United beat Cardiff City (1-0)
1926	Bolton Wanderers beat Manchester City (1-0)
1927	Cardiff City beat Arsenal (1-0)
1928	Blackburn Rovers beat Huddersfield Town (3-1)
1929	Bolton Wanderers beat Portsmouth (2-0)
1930	Arsenal beat Huddersfield Town (2-0)
1931	West Bromwich Albion beat Birmingham (2-1)
1932	Newcastle United beat Arsenal (2-1)
1933	Everton beat Manchester City (3-0)
1934	Manchester City beat Portsmouth (2-1)
1935	Sheffield Wednesday beat West Bromwich Albion (4-2)
1936	Arsenal beat Sheffield United (1-0)
1937	Sunderland beat Preston North End (3-1)
1938††	Preston North End beat Huddersfield Town (1-0)
1939	Portsmouth beat Wolverhampton Wanderers (4-1)
1946††	Derby County beat Charlton Athletic (4-1)
1947††	Charlton Athletic beat Burnley (1-0)
1948	Manchester United beat Blackpool (4-2)
1949	Wolverhampton Wanderers beat Leicester City (3-1)
1950	Arsenal beat Liverpool (2-0)
1951	Newcastle United beat Blackpool (2-0)
1952	Newcastle United beat Arsenal (1-0)
1953	Blackpool beat Bolton Wanderers (4-3)
1954	West Bromwich Albion beat Preston North End (3-2)
1955	Newcastle United beat Manchester City (3-1)
1956	Manchester City beat Birmingham City (3-1)
1957	Aston Villa beat Manchester United (2-1)
1958	Bolton Wanderers beat Manchester United (2-0)
1959	Nottingham Forest beat Luton Town (2-1)
1960	Wolverhampton Wanderers beat Blackburn Rovers (3-0)
1961	Tottenham Hotspur beat Leicester City (2-0)
1962	Tottenham Hotspur beat Burnley (3-1)
1963	Manchester United beat Leicester City (3-1)
1964	West Ham United beat Preston North End (3-2)
1965††	Liverpool beat Leeds United (2-1)
1966	Everton beat Sheffield Wednesday (3-2)
1967	Tottenham Hotspur beat Chelsea (2-1)
1968††	West Bromwich Albion beat Everton (1-0)
1969	Manchester City beat Leicester City (1-0)
1970††•	Chelsea beat Leeds United (2-1 after a 2-2 draw)
1971††	Arsenal beat Liverpool (2-1)

1972	Leeds United beat Arsenal (1-0)
1973	Sunderland beat Leeds United (1-0)
1974	Liverpool beat Newcastle United (3-0)
1975	West Ham United beat Fulham (2-0)
1976	Southampton beat Manchester United (1-0)
1977	Manchester United beat Liverpool (2-1)
1978	Ipswich Town beat Arsenal (1-0)
1979	Arsenal beat Manchester United (3-2)
1980	West Ham United beat Arsenal (1-0)
1981	Tottenham Hotspur beat Manchester City (3-2 after a 1-1 draw)
1982	Tottenham Hotspur beat Queens Park Rangers (1-0 after a 1-1 draw)
1983	Manchester United beat Brighton & H.A. (4-0 after a 2-2 draw)
1984	Everton beat Watford (2-0)
1985††	Manchester United beat Everton (1-0)
1986	Liverpool beat Everton (3-1)
1987††	Coventry City beat Tottenham Hotspur (3-2)
1988	Wimbledon beat Liverpool (1-0)
1989††	Liverpool beat Everton (3-2)
1990	Manchester United beat Crystal Palace (1-0 after a 3-3 draw)
1991††	Tottenham Hotspur beat Nottingham Forest (2-1)
1992	Liverpool beat Sunderland (2-0)
1993††	Arsenal beat Sheffield Wednesday (2-1 after a 1-1 draw)
1994	Manchester United beat Chelsea (4-0)
1995	Everton beat Manchester United (1-0)
1996	Manchester United beat Liverpool (1-0)
1997	Chelsea beat Middlesbrough (2-0)

†† After extra time. * Won outright but restored to the Association. *a* Replayed at Baseball Ground, Derby. † A special trophy was awarded for the third consecutive win. ††† Replayed at Burnden Park, Bolton. ** Replayed at Goodison Park, Liverpool. *b* Replayed at Old Trafford, Manchester, new trophy provided. *c* Replayed at Bramall Lane, Sheffield. • Replayed at Old Trafford.
(All replays since 1981 played at Wembley.)

1997 F.A. CUP FINAL
(Competition sponsored by Littlewoods)

CHELSEA 2 (Di Matteo 42 sec., Newton 83 mins), MIDDLESBROUGH 0

Wembley, Saturday, May 17. **Attendance**: 79,160. **Receipts**: Est. £2,400,000

Chelsea (blue shirts): Grodas; Sinclair, Leboeuf, Clarke, Minto, Petrescu, Di Matteo, Newton, Wise (Capt.), Zola (Vialli 88), M. Hughes. **Subs not used:** Myers, Hitchcock (gk). **Booked:** Newton, Di Matteo, Leboeuf. **Coach:** Ruud Gullit.

Middlesbrough (red shirts): Roberts; Blackmore, Pearson (Capt.) Festa, Fleming, Stamp, Emerson, Mustoe (Vickers 28), Hignett (Kinder 74), Juninho, Ravanelli (Beck 23). **Booked:** Festa. **Manager:** Bryan Robson.

Referee: S. Lodge (Barnsley). **Half-time**: 1-0. **Kick-off**: 3.0 (BBC TV).

Guests of Honour: The Duke and Duchess of Kent.

Conditions: Hot and sunny, pitch excellent.

The fastest goal in Wembley's Cup Final history – timed on BBC TV's clock at 42 seconds – launched Chelsea's second F.A. Cup success. For Middlesbrough, failure added to a disastrous spring which had already brought defeat in the Coca-Cola Cup Final and relegation.

Bryan Robson gambled on an unfit player and lost. Fabrizio Ravanelli's hamstring succumbed after 23 minutes, and Boro' were struggling from the opening seconds, when their defence held off as Roberto Di Matteo advanced from ten yards inside his own half and dipped a 30-yard shot over Ben Roberts. In its timing, the goal eclipsed Jack Milburn's 45-second effort for Newcastle (1955) as Wembley's fastest goal.

Although the balance of possession was heavily in Chelsea's favour, Boro' delayed the second goal, a rarity from Eddie Newton, until 7 minutes from the end.

In personnel, this was the "least English Cup Final" on record, with 13 players from 8 other countries among the 22 who started. Italy contributed 4 (2 to each side), and 3 of the 4 substitutes used were foreign. Crowning it all, Ruud Gullit, the one Dutchman on the scene, was the first foreign coach/manager of an F.A. Cup-winning team. In his first season in charge, too.

For Boro', caught offside 16 times, this was anything but a showpiece occasion. No club has won the Cup in a season of relegation, and in just a month they had lost the first two major Finals in their history. On top of relegation, their fans were resigned to the break-up of the side with the expected departure of foreigners Ravanelli, Emerson and the delightful Juninho.

In contrast, as "Blue is the Colour" chorused round Wembley, Chelsea supporters revelled in the club's first real success since the F.A. Cup and Cup-Winners' Cup were won at the start of the Seventies.

Chelsea were 11-10 favourites on the day, but you could have had any price about their winning the Cup when they trailed 0-2 at half-time at home to Liverpool in Round 4.

Mark Hughes became the latest player to appear in 5 F.A. Cup Finals at Wembley and the first this century to collect 4 winner's medals (his first 3 with Man. United).

Ticket prices were as in 1996, ranging from £17 to £115 in the Olympic Gallery. The programme again cost £6.

Officials' fees: Referee £350, assistants each £150 plus medals all round.

BBC TV had an 11m. audience for their last live F.A. Cup Final broadcast. It switches to ITV in 1998.

HOW THEY REACHED THE FINAL

CHELSEA

3rd Round: W 3-0 home to W.B.A. (Wise, Burley, Zola).
4th Round: W 4-2 home to Liverpool (M. Hughes, Zola, Vialli 2).
5th Round: D 2-2 away to Leicester (Di Matteo, M. Hughes).
Replay: W 1-0 home to Leicester, aet (Lebouef pen.).
6th Round: W 4-1 away to Portsmouth (M. Hughes, Wise 2, Zola).
Semi-final (Highbury): W 3-0 v Wimbledon (M. Hughes 2, Zola).

MIBBLESBROUGH

3rd Round: W 6-0 home to Chester (Ravanelli 2, Hignett, Cox, Beck, Stamp).
4th Round: W 3-2 home to Hednesford (switched from Hednesford) (Opponent og, Fjortoft, Ravanelli).
5th Round: W 1-0 away to Man. City (Juninho).
6th Round: W 2-0 away to Derby (Juninho, Ravanelli).
Semi-final (Old Trafford): D 3-3 v Chesterfield, aet (Ravanelli, Hignett pen., Festa).
Replay (Hillsborough): W 3-0 v Chesterfield (Beck, Ravanelli, Emerson).

SUMMARY OF F.A. CUP WINS

Manchester United 9	Arsenal 6	Everton 5
Tottenham Hotspur 8	Blackburn Rovers 6	Liverpool 5
Aston Villa 7	Newcastle United 6	The Wanderers 5

W.B.A 5	Preston North End 2	Derby County 1
Bolton Wanderers 4	Sunderland 2	Huddersfield Town 1
Manchester City 4	Barnsley 1	Ipswich Town 1
Sheffield United 4	Blackburn Olympic 1	Leeds United 1
Wolves 4	Blackpool 1	Notts County 1
Sheffield Wednesday . 3	Bradford City 1	Old Carthusians 1
West Ham United 3	Burnley 1	Oxford University 1
Bury 2	Cardiff City 1	Portsmouth 1
Chelsea 2	Charlton Athletic 1	Royal Engineers 1
Nottingham Forest 2	Clapham Rovers 1	Southampton 1
Old Etonians 2	Coventry City 1	Wimbledon 1

APPEARANCES IN FINALS
(Figures do not include replays)

Manchester United . 14	*The Wanderers 5	Clapham Rovers 2
Arsenal 12	Derby County 4	Notts County 2
Everton 12	Leeds United 4	Queen's Park (Glas.) .. 2
Liverpool 11	Leicester City 4	*Blackburn Olympic 1
Newcastle United 11	Oxford University 4	*Bradford City 1
W.B.A. 10	Royal Engineers 4	Brighton & H.A. 1
Aston Villa 9	Sunderland 4	Bristol City 1
Tottenham Hotspur .. 9	West Ham United 4	*Coventry City 1
Blackburn Rovers 8	Blackpool 3	Crystal Palace 1
Manchester City 8	Burnley 3	Fulham 1
Wolves 8	Nottingham Forest 3	*Ipswich Town 1
Bolton Wanderers 7	Portsmouth 3	Luton Town 1
Preston North End ... 7	Southampton 3	Middlesbrough 1
Old Etonians 6	Barnsley 2	*Old Carthusians 1
Sheffield United 6	Birmingham City 2	Queens Park Rangers 1
Sheffield Wednesday . 6	*Bury 2	Watford 1
Chelsea 5	Cardiff City 2	*Wimbledon 1
Huddersfield Town 5	Charlton Athletic 2	(* Denotes undefeated)

APPEARANCES IN SEMI-FINALS
(Figures do not include replays)

Everton 23, Man. Utd. 21, Liverpool 20, W.B.A. 19, Arsenal 18, Aston Villa 18, Blackburn Rovers 16, Sheffield Wed. 16, Tottenham H. 15, Chelsea 13, Derby Co. 13, Newcastle Utd. 13, Wolves 13, Bolton W. 12, Nott'm Forest 12, Sheffield Utd. 11, Sunderland 11, Man. City 10, Preston N.E. 10, Southampton 10, Birmingham City 9, Burnley 9, Leeds Utd. 8, Huddersfield Town 7, Leicester City 7, Old Etonians 6, Oxford University 6, West Ham United 6, Fulham 5, Notts County 5, Portsmouth 5, The Wanderers 5, Luton Town 4, Queen's Park (Glasgow) 4, Royal Engineers 4, Blackpool 3, Cardiff City 3, Clapham Rovers 3, *Crystal Palace 3, Ipswich Town 3, Millwall 3, Norwich City 3, Old Carthusians 3, Oldham Athletic 3, Stoke City 3, The Swifts 3, Watford 3, Barnsley 2, Blackburn Olympic 2, Bristol City 2, Bury 2, Charlton Athletic 2, Grimsby Town 2, Swansea Town 2, Swindon Town 2, Wimbledon 2, Bradford City 1, Brighton & H.A. 1, Cambridge University 1, Chesterfield 1, Coventry City 1, Crewe Alexandra 1, Darwen 1, Derby Junction 1, Hull City 1, Marlow 1, Middlesbrough 1, Old Harrovians 1, Orient 1, Plymouth Argyle 1, Port Vale 1, Q.P.R. 1, Rangers (Glasgow) 1, Reading 1, Shropshire Wanderers 1, York City 1.
(*A previous and different Crystal Palace club also reached the semi-final in season 1871-72)

WEMBLEY'S F.A. CUP FINALS – THE TOP MEN

Year	Winners	Manager	Captain	Referee
1923	Bolton Wanderers	Charles Foweraker	Joe Smith	D.H. Asson (West Bromwich)
1924	Newcastle United	No manager	Frank Hudspeth	W.E. Russell (Swindon)
1925	Sheffield United	John Nicholson	Billy Gillespie	G.N. Watson (Nottingham)
1926	Bolton Wanderers	Charles Foweraker	Joe Smith	I. Baker (Crewe)
1927	Cardiff City	Fred Stewart	Fred Keenor	W.F. Bunnell (Preston)
1928	Blackburn Rovers	Bob Crompton	Harry Healless	T.G. Bryan (Willenhall)
1929	Bolton Wanderers	Charles Foweraker	Jimmy Seddon	A. Josephs (South Shields)
1930	Arsenal	Herbert Chapman	Tom Parker	T. Crew (Leicester)
1931	West Bromwich Albion	Fred Everiss	Tommy Glidden	A.H. Kingscott (Long Eaton)
1932	Newcastle United	Andy Cunningham	Jimmy Nelson	W.P. Harper (Stourbridge)
1933	Everton	No manager	W.R. ('Dixie') Dean	E. Wood (Sheffield)
1934	Manchester City	Wilf Wild	Sam Cowan	S.F. Rous (Watford)
1935	Sheffield Wednesday	Billy Walker	Ronnie Starling	A.E. Fogg (Bolton)
1936	Arsenal	George Allison	Alex James	H. Nattrass (Seaham, Co. Durham)
1937	Sunderland	Johnny Cochrane	Raich Carter	G. Rudd (Kenton, Middlesex)
1938	Preston North End	No manager	Tom Smith	T. Thompson (Lemington-on-Tyne)
1939	Portsmouth	Jack Tinn	Jimmy Guthrie	E.D. Smith (Whitehaven)
1946	Derby County	Stuart McMillan	Jack Nicholas	A.J. Jewell (London)
1947	Charlton Athletic	Jimmy Seed	Don Welsh	J.M. Wiltshire (Sherborne)
1948	Manchester United	Matt Busby	Johnny Carey	C.J. Barrick (Northampton)
1949	Wolves	Stan Cullis	Billy Wright	R.A. Mortimer (Huddersfield)
1950	Arsenal	Tom Whittaker	Joe Mercer	H. Pearce (Luton)
1951	Newcastle United	Stan Seymour (Snr.)	Joe Harvey	W. Ling (Stapleford, Cambs.)

Year	Winners	Manager	Captain	Referee
1952	Newcastle United	Stan Seymour (Snr.)	Joe Harvey	A.E. Ellis (Halifax)
1953	Blackpool	Joe Smith	Harry Johnston	B.M. Griffiths (Newport, Mon.)
1954	West Bromwich Albion	Vic Buckingham	Len Millard	A.W. Luty (Leeds)
1955	Newcastle United	Dugald Livingstone	Jimmy Scoular	R.J. Leafe (Nottingham)
1956	Manchester City	Les McDowall	Roy Paul	A. Bond (Fulham)
1957	Aston Villa	Eric Houghton	Johnny Dixon	F. Coultas (Hull)
1958	Bolton Wanderers	Bill Ridding	Nat Lofthouse	J. Sherlock (Sheffield)
1959	Nottingham Forest	Billy Walker	Jack Burkitt	J.H. Clough (Bolton)
1960	Wolves	Stan Cullis	Bill Slater	K. Howley (Middlesbrough)
1961	Tottenham Hotspur	Bill Nicholson	Danny Blanchflower	J. Kelly (Chorley)
1962	Tottenham Hotspur	Bill Nicholson	Danny Blanchflower	J. Finney (Hereford)
1963	Manchester United	Matt Busby	Noel Cantwell	K.G. Aston (Ilford, Essex)
1964	West Ham United	Ron Greenwood	Bobby Moore	A. Holland (Barnsley)
1965	Liverpool	Bill Shankly	Ron Yeats	W. Clements (West Bromwich)
1966	Everton	Harry Catterick	Brian Labone	J.F. Taylor (Wolverhampton)
1967	Tottenham Hotspur	Bill Nicholson	Dave Mackay	K. Dagnall (Bolton)
1968	West Bromwich Albion	Alan Ashman	Graham Williams	L. Callaghan (Merthyr Tydfil)
1969	Manchester City	Joe Mercer	Tony Book	G. McCabe (Sheffield)
1970	Chelsea (Rep. Old Trafford)	Dave Sexton	Ron Harris	E. Jennings (Stourbridge)
1971	Arsenal	Bertie Mee	Frank McLintock	N. Burtenshaw (Gt. Yarmouth)
1972	Leeds United	Don Revie	Billy Bremner	D. Smith (Gloucester)
1973	Sunderland	Bob Stokoe	Bobby Kerr	K. Burns (Stourbridge)
1974	Liverpool	Bill Shankly	Emlyn Hughes	C.G. Kew (Amersham)
1975	West Ham United	John Lyall	Billy Bonds	P. Partridge (Durham)
1976	Southampton	Lawrie McMenemy	Peter Rodrigues	C. Thomas (Treorchy)

Year	Winners	Manager	Captain	Referee
1977	Manchester United	Tommy Docherty	Martin Buchan	R. Matthewson (Bolton)
1978	Ipswich Town	Bobby Robson	Mick Mills	D.R.G. Nippard (Bournemouth)
1979	Arsenal	Terry Neill	Pat Rice	R. Challis (Tonbridge)
1980	West Ham United	John Lyall	Billy Bonds	G. Courtney (Spennymoor)
1981	Tottenham Hotspur	Keith Burkinshaw	Steve Perryman	K. Hackett (Sheffield)
1982	Tottenham Hotspur	Keith Burkinshaw	Steve Perryman	C. White (Harrow)
1983	Manchester United	Ron Atkinson	Bryan Robson	A. Grey (Gt. Yarmouth)
1984	Everton	Howard Kendall	Kevin Ratcliffe	J. Hunting (Leicester)
1985	Manchester United	Ron Atkinson	Bryan Robson	P. Willis (Co. Durham)
1986	Liverpool	Kenny Dalglish	Alan Hansen	A. Robinson (Waterlooville)
1987	Coventry City	John Sillett (Coach)	Brian Kilcline	N. Midgley (Salford)
1988	Wimbledon	Bobby Gould	Dave Beasant	B. Hill (Kettering)
1989	Liverpool	Kenny Dalglish	Ronnie Whelan	J. Worrall (Warrington)
1990	Manchester United	Alex Ferguson	Bryan Robson	A. Gunn (Sussex)
1991	Tottenham Hotspur	Terry Venables	Gary Mabbutt	R. Milford (Bristol)
1992	Liverpool	Graeme Souness	Mark Wright	P. Don (Middlesex)
1993	Arsenal	George Graham	Tony Adams	K. Barratt (Coventry)
1994	Manchester United	Alex Ferguson	Steve Bruce	D. Elleray (Harrow)
1995	Everton	Joe Royle	Dave Watson	G. Ashby (Worcester)
1996	Manchester United	Alex Ferguson	Eric Cantona	D. Gallagher (Banbury)
1997	Chelsea	Ruud Gullit	Dennis Wise	S. Lodge (Barnsley)

76

NATIONAL REFEREES 1997-98

From a list of 68 National List referees (6 of them newcomers), a panel of 19 will take charge of Premier League matches this season. Eight of them are on the FIFA list.

Match fees – Premier League and FA Cup (from 3rd. Round): referees £375 (previously £350); assistant-referees (formerly linesmen) £165 (£150). Nationwide Football League: referees £185 (£175); assistant-referees £90 (£87.50).

▲ ALCOCK, Paul (Redhill, Surrey)
▲ ASHBY, Gerald (Worcester)
BAILEY, Mike (Impington, Cambs.)
BAINES, Steve (Chesterfield)
▲ BARBER, Graham (Pyrford, Surrey)
▲ BARRY, Neale (Scunthorpe)
BATES, Tony (Stoke-on-Trent)
BENNETT, Steve (Redhill, Surrey)
▲ BODENHAM, Martin (East Looe, Cornwall)
BRANDWOOD, John (Lichfield, Staffs)
▲ BURGE, Keith (Tonypandy)
BURNS, Bill (Scarborough)
BUTLER, Alan (Sutton-in-Ashfield)
CAIN, George (Bootle)
CODDINGTON, Brian (Sheffield)
★ CRICK, David (Worcester Park, Surrey)
DANSON, Paul (Leicester)
▲ DEAN, Mike (Eastham, Wirral)
†▲ DUNN, Steve (Bristol)
†▲ DURKIN, Paul (Portland, Dorset)
D'URSO, Andy (Billericay, Essex)
†▲ ELLERAY, David (Harrow-on-the-Hill)
FINCH, Carl (Bury St Edmunds)
FLETCHER, Mike (Warley, W. Midlands)
FOY, Chris (St Helens)
FRANKLAND, Graham (Middlesbrough)
FURNANDIZ, Roger (Doncaster)
†▲ GALLAGHER, Dermot (Banbury, Oxon)
★ HALL, Andy (Birmingham)
HALSEY, Mark (Welwyn Garden City, Herts.)
HARRIS, Rob (Oxford)

HEILBRON, Terry (Newton Aycliffe)
★ JONES, Mike (Chester)
†▲ JONES, Peter (Loughborough)
JONES, Trevor (Barrow-in-Furness)
KIRKBY, John (Sheffield)
KNIGHT, Barry (Orpington)
LAWS, David (Whitley Bay)
LAWS, Graham (Whitley Bay)
LEACH, Ken (Wolverhampton)
LEAKE, Tony (Darwen, Lancs.)
†▲ LODGE, Steve (Barnsley)
LOMAS, Eddie (Manchester)
LYNCH, Kevin (Knaresborough)
MATHIESON, Scott (Stockport)
★ MESSIAS, Matt (York)
ORR, David (Iver, Bucks.)
PEARSON, Roy (Peterlee, Durham)
PIERCE, Mike (Portsmouth)
★ PIKE, Mike (Barrow-in-Furness)
†▲ POLL, Graham (Tring, Herts.)
PUGH, David (Wirral)
▲ REED, Mike (Birmingham)
REJER, Paul (Tipton, W. Midlands)
▲ RENNIE, Uriah (Sheffield)
RICHARDS, Phil (Preston)
▲ RILEY, Mike (Leeds)
ROBINSON, John (Hull)
SINGH, Gurnam (Wolverhampton)
STRETTON, Fraser (Nottingham)
★ STYLES, Robert (Waterlooville, Hants.)
TAYLOR, Paul (Cheshunt, Herts.)
WILEY, Alan (Burntwood, Staffs.)
WILKES, Clive (Gloucester)
†▲ WILKIE, Alan (Chester-le-Street)
†▲ WILLARD, Gary (Worthing)
†▲ WINTER, Jeff (Stockton-on-Tees)
WOLSTENHOLME, Eddie (Blackburn)

(† FIFA list; ▲ Premier League; ★ First season)

BROTHERS-IN-CHARGE

For the first time in Football League history, brothers figured on the panel of National Referees last season. **Graham Laws**, 34-year-old police officer joined 38-year-old **David** on the list. They come from Whitley Bay.

LEICESTER GO INTO EUROPE AS COCA-COLA CUP WINNERS

SECOND ROUND	THIRD ROUND	FOURTH ROUND	FIFTH ROUND	SEMI-FINALS	FINAL
Leicester 2:2	Leicester 2	*Leicester 2	Leicester 1	Leicester 0:†1	Leicester
*Scarborough 0:1	*York 0	Man Utd. 0			
York 1:3					
*Everton 1:2					
Bye●					
Q.P.R. 2:1	*Man Utd. 2				
*Swindon 1:3	Swindon 1				
*Fulham 1:2					
Ipswich 1:4	*Ipswich 4	*Ipswich 1	*Ipswich 2		
Crystal Palace 3:4	Crystal Palace 1				
*Bury 1:0					
Gillingham 1:1†1	*Gillingham 2:1	Gillingham 0			
*Barnsley 1:0					
*Coventry 1:1	Coventry 1:1				
Birmingham 2:0					Leicester 1:1
*Bristol City 0:1					
Bolton 0:1‡3	*Bolton 2	*Bolton 6	*Bolton 0		
*Blackpool 4:1	Chelsea 1				
Chelsea 1:3					
*Preston 1:0					
Tottenham 1:2	*Tottenham 2	Tottenham 1			
Sunderland 2:1	Sunderland 1				
*Watford 0:0					
*Wimbledon 1:1	*Wimbledon 1	*Wimbledon 1	Wimbledon 2	Wimbledon 0:1	
Portsmouth 0:1					
*Luton 1:1	Luton 1				
Derby 0:2					
*Leeds 2:2	*Leeds 1	Aston Villa 0			
Darlington 2:0	Aston Villa 2				
Bye●					

(at Wembley – Sunday, April 6 1997. Att: 76,757) (replay Hillsborough Wednesday, April 16 1997. Att: 39,428)

Round 1

*Stockport	2:5
Sheffield Utd	1:2
*Brentford	1:0
Blackburn	2:2
*Barnet	1:0
West Ham	1:1
*Nott'm Forest	1:1
Wycombe	0:1
*Port Vale	1:2
Carlisle	0:2
*Sheffield Wed.	1:0
Oxford	0:2
*Lincoln	4:1
Man. City	1:0
*Southampton	2:4
Peterborough	0:1
*Stoke	1:2
Northampton	0:1
Bye ●	
*Charlton	4:1
Burnley	1:1
Bye ●	
*Oldham	2:1
Tranmere	2:0
Bye ●	
*Newcastle	1
*Huddersfield	1:2
Colchester	1
Hereford	0:0
*Middlesbrough	7:3

Round 2

Stockport	1
*Blackburn	0
*West Ham	4
Nott'm Forest	0
*Port Vale	0:0
Oxford	0:2
Lincoln	2:1
*Southampton	2:3
Stoke	1:2
Arsenal	1:5
*Charlton	1:1
Liverpool	1:4
Oldham	0
Newcastle	1
Huddersfield	1
*Middlesbrough	5

Round 3

Stockport	1:2
*West Ham	1:1
*Oxford	1:2
Southampton	1:3
Arsenal	2
*Liverpool	4
Newcastle	1
*Middlesbrough	3

Round 4

Stockport	2:2
Southampton	2:1
Liverpool	1
*Middlesbrough	2

Semi-finals

*Stockport	0:1
Middlesbrough	2:0

Final

Middlesbrough . 1†:0

(* Drawn at home: in 2nd round and semi-finals; team drawn at home in first leg. † After extra time. ● Given a bye into the 3rd round because of European Competitions.)

79

COCA-COLA CUP 1996-97

First Round (Two Legs)

Barnet 6 Exeter 0 (2-0h, 4-0a); Barnsley 3 Rochdale 2 (2-0h, 1-2a); Blackpool 3, Scunthorpe 2 (2-0h, 1-2a); Birmingham 3 Brighton 0 (2-0h, 1-0a); Brentford 1 Plymouth 0 (1-0h, 0-0a); Bristol City 4 Torquay 3 (1-0h, 3-3a); Burnley 5 Mansfield 0 (2-0h, 3-0a); Bury 2 Notts County 1 (1-0h, 1-1a);

Carlisle 4 Chester 1 (1-0h, 3-1a); Colchester 5 W.B.A. 4 (2-3h, 3-1a); Darlington 2 Rotherham 0 (1-0h, 1-0a); Fulham 3 Southend 2 (1-2h 2-0a); Gillingham 3 Swansea 0 (2-0h, 1-0a); Hereford 4 Cambridge 1 (3-0h, 1-1a); Huddersfield 5 Wrexham 1 (3-0h, 2-1a); Ipswich 5 Bournemouth 1 (3-0h 2-1a);

Lincoln 5 Hartlepool 4 (3-2h, 2-2a); Luton 4 Bristol Rovers 2 (3-0h, 1-2a); Northampton 2 Cardiff 1 (2-0h, 0-1a); Oldham 1 Grimsby 1†* (0-1h, 1-0a, Oldham won 6-5 on pens.); Oxford 4 Norwich 3† (1-1h, 3-2a); Peterborough 2 Millwall 1 (2-0h, 0-1a); Portsmouth 2 Leyton Orient 1 (2-0h, 0-1a); Port Vale 6 Crewe 1 (1-0h, 5-1a); Preston 7 Wigan 6† (4-4h, 3-2a);

Scarborough 5 Hull 4 (3-2h, 2-2a); Sheffield Utd 5 Bradford City 1 (3-0h, 2-1a); Stockport 4 Chesterfield 2 (2-1h, 2-1a); Swindon 2 Wolves 1 (2-0h, 0-1a); Tranmere 3 Shrewsbury 1 (1-1h, 2-0a); Watford 2 Walsall 1 (2-0h, 0-1a); Wycombe 3 Reading 1 (2-0h, 1-1a); York 3 Doncaster 1 (2-0h, 1-1a).

(† After extra time)

LEAGUE CUP FINALS

1961*	Aston Villa beat Rotherham United 3-2 on agg. (0-2a, 3-0h)
1962	Norwich City beat Rochdale 4-0 on agg. (3-0a, 1-0h)
1963	Birmingham City beat Aston Villa 3-1 on agg. (3-1h, 0-0a)
1964	Leicester City beat Stoke City 4-3 on agg. (1-1a, 3-2h)
1965	Chelsea beat Leicester City 3-2 on agg. (3-2h, 0-0a)
1966	West Bromwich Albion beat West Ham United 5-3 on agg. (1-2a, 4-1h)

AT WEMBLEY

1967	Queens Park Rangers beat West Bromwich Albion (3-2)
1968	Leeds United beat Arsenal (1-0)
1969*	Swindon Town beat Arsenal (3-1)
1970*	Manchester City beat West Bromwich Albion (2-1)
1971	Tottenham Hotspur beat Aston Villa (2-0)
1972	Stoke City beat Chelsea (2-1)
1973	Tottenham Hotspur beat Norwich City (1-0)
1974	Wolverhampton Wanderers beat Manchester City (2-1)
1975	Aston Villa beat Norwich City (1-0)
1976	Manchester City beat Newcastle United (2-1)
1977†*	Aston Villa beat Everton (3-2 after 0-0 and 1-1 draws)
1978††	Nottingham Forest beat Liverpool (1-0 after 0-0 draw)
1979	Nottingham Forest beat Southampton (3-2)
1980	Wolverhampton Wanderers beat Nottingham Forest (1-0)
1981†††	Liverpool beat West Ham United (2-1 after 1-1 draw)

MILK CUP

1982*	Liverpool beat Tottenham Hotspur (3-1)
1983*	Liverpool beat Manchester United (2-1)
1984**	Liverpool beat Everton (1-0 after *0-0 draw)
1985	Norwich City beat Sunderland (1-0)
1986	Oxford United beat Queens Park Rangers (3-0)

1987	Arsenal beat Liverpool (2-1)
1988	Luton Town beat Arsenal (3-2)
1989	Nottingham Forest beat Luton Town (3-1)
1990	Nottingham Forest beat Oldham Athletic (1-0)

RUMBELOWS CUP

| 1991 | Sheffield Wednesday beat Manchester United (1-0) |
| 1992 | Manchester United beat Nottingham Forest (1-0) |

COCA-COLA CUP

1993	Arsenal beat Sheffield Wednesday (2-1)
1994	Aston Villa beat Manchester United (3-1)
1995	Liverpool beat Bolton Wanderers (2-1)
1996	Aston Villa beat Leeds United (3-0)
1997	★ Leicester City beat Middlesbrough (*1-0 after *1-1 draw)

* After extra time. † First replay at Hillsborough, second replay at Old Trafford. ††
Replayed at Old Trafford. ††† Replayed at Villa Park. ** Replayed at Maine Road.
★ Replay at Hillsborough

COCA-COLA (LEAGUE) CUP FINAL

LEICESTER CITY 1 (Heskey 118),
MIDDLESBROUGH 1 (Ravanelli 95), aet.

Wembley (76,757), Sunday, April 6, 1997. Kick-off: 3.0 (Sky live)

Leicester: Keller; Grayson, Prior, Walsh (Capt.), Whitlow (Robins 105), Kaamark,
Lennon, Izzit (Taylor 107), Parker, Heskey, Claridge. **Sub not used:** Poole (gk).
Booked: Kaamark, Grayson, Heskey.

Middlesbrough: Schwarzer; Cox, Pearson (Capt.), Festa, Fleming, Hignett,
Mustoe, Emerson, Juninho, Beck, Ravanelli. **Subs no used:** Vickers, Moore,
Blackmore. **Booked:** Beck, Juninho, Cox.

Referee: M. Bodenham (Looe, Cornwall). **Receipts:** £2,750,000.

Guest of Honour: Keith Wiseman, Chairman of Football Association.

REPLAY

LEICESTER CITY 1 (Claridge 100), **MIDDLESBROUGH 0**, aet.
Hillsborough (39,428), Wednesday, April 16, 1997. Kick-off 7.45 (Sky live)

Leicester: Keller; Grayson, Whitlow (Lawrence 109), Walsh (Capt.), Izzit, Lennon, Claridge (Robins 117), Parker, Heskey, Kaamark, Prior. **Sub not used:**
Poole (gk). **Booked:** Lennon, Prior, Izzet, Heskey. **Manager:** Martin O'Neill.

Middlesbrough: Roberts; Cox (Moore 105), Pearson (Capt.), Festa (Vickers 76),
Emerson, Kinder, Mustoe, Juninho, Ravanelli, Blackmore, Hignett (Beck 105).
Booked: Moore. **Manager:** Bryan Robson.

Referee: M. Bodenham (Looe, Cornwall).

Man of Match – Alan Hardaker Trophy: Emile Heskey (Leicester).

Prize money: Leicester £100,000, Middlesbrough £50,000.

In extra time at Wembley, Middlesbrough were within two minutes of winning the first major trophy in their history. In the replay at Hillsborough, 31-year-old Steve Claridge's extra-time shot earned Leicester the prize – a year after his last-minute strike had won the Wembley play-off final to take City into the Premier League.

So Leicester won the League Cup for the second time (previously in 1964). They enter Europe for a second time, too, having qualified for the Cup-Winners' Cup in 1961 as runners-up because Tottenham did the Double.

Manager Martin O'Neill said: "After promotion last season and winning the Coca-Cola Cup, this has to be the most unbelievable year in my career. Now we have to make sure we stay in the Premiership."

They did so comfortably, finishing ninth. But for Boro' a month of heart-break was in store, with relegation and defeat in the other domestic final awaiting them.

SUMMARY OF LEAGUE CUP WINNERS

Aston Villa 5	Tottenham Hotspur 2	Oxford United 1
Liverpool 5	Wolverhampton W. 2	Queens Park Rangers 1
Nottingham Forest 4	Birmingham City 1	Sheffield Wednesday . 1
Arsenal 2	Chelsea 1	Stoke City 1
Leicester City 2	Leeds United 1	Swindon Town 1
Manchester City 2	Luton Town 1	West Bromwich Albion 1
Norwich City 2	Manchester United 1	

LEAGUE CUP FINAL APPEARANCES
(Figures do not include replays)

7 Aston Villa, Liverpool; **6** Nott'm. F.; **5** Arsenal; **4** Man. Utd., Norwich; **3** Leicester, Man. C., Tottenham, W.B.A.; **2** Chelsea, Everton, Leeds, Luton, Q.P.R., Sheff. Wed., Stoke, West Ham, Wolves; **1** Birmingham, Bolton, Middlesbrough Newcastle, Oldham, Oxford, Rochdale, Rotherham, Southampton, Sunderland, Swindon.

LEAGUE CUP SEMI-FINAL APPEARANCES
(Figures do not include replays)

10 Aston Villa; **9** Liverpool; **8** Arsenal, Tottenham; **7** Man. Utd., West Ham; **6** Nott'm. F.; **5** Chelsea, Leeds, Man C., Norwich; **4** W.B.A.; **3** Birmingham, Burnley, Everton, Leicester, Mid'bro', Q.P.R., Sheff. Wed., Swindon, Wolves; **2** Blackburn, Bolton, Bristol C., Coventry, Crystal P., Ipswich, Luton, Oxford, Plymouth, Southampton, Stoke, Sunderland; **1** Blackpool, Bury, Cardiff, Carlisle, Chester, Derby, Huddersfield, Newcastle, Oldham, Peterboro', Rochdale, Rotherham, Shrewsbury, Stockport, Tranmere, Walsall, Watford, Wimbledon.

NO MORE COCA-COLA CUP REPLAYS

At the Football League AGM in June, it was agreed to discontinue replays in the Coca-Cola Cup. As a means of invigorating the competition, and to help ease fixture congestion, ties from the third round will be decided on the night via extra time and, if necessary, penalties. The semi-finals will continue over two legs.

Nottingham Forest were the first club to find themselves in the draw for the opening round in the season following relegation from the Premiership.

Forest, who face Doncaster in the two-legged first round, were included as part of a formula to produce 32 teams in the third round, when England's seven European representatives enter the competition.

Middlesbrough and Sunderland, both also relegated; are exempt from the first round through finishing last season in a higher position than Forest. They, and the 13 Premiership teams not involved in Europe, will enter at the second-round stage.

QUOTE-UNQUOTE

BOB LYNCH, manager of Liverpool Schools Under-14s, on Robbie Fowler: "He's got to be worth his weight in gold to Liverpool. He rings me every week and still calls me Sir."

ALAN GREEN, Radio 5 commentator: "I refuse to call linesmen referees' assistants. I just won't do it."

MICKY ADAMS, Fulham manager, after a goalless draw with Northampton: "It was a bit of a damp squid."

ALEX FERGUSON last Hogmanay: "People ask me when I'm going to quit. Good grief, I'd miss all that purgatory."

THE 1949 STANLEY MATTHEWS FOOTBALL ALBUM: "Billy Wright is a model professional. He is a teetotaller, does not smoke, goes to bed early and lives modestly in lodgings. After home games he goes to the theatre, and two evenings a week to the Technical College. He likes to spend other evenings quietly at home, listening to gramophone records of opera and classical music, and making rugs."

MARTIN O'NEILL, Leicester manager, on teenage striker Emile Heskey: "The future is up to him. He can be anything he wants – world-class or a Conference player."

GARY PALLISTER: "The ideal defender is an old head on young legs. Unfortunately, such a person does not exist."

FRANK CLARK on resigning as Nott'm. Forest manager (Dec. 19) amid ongoing talk of take-overs and consortiums: "I had to go. I felt like a turkey waiting for Christmas."

TOMMY DOCHERTY: "I played with the legendary Tom Finney – he earned £14 a week. Today we have players who are on £8,000 a week for sitting on the subs' bench and can't even play properly."

TONY PARKES, as Blackburn's caretaker for the third time: "It's easy. You get the keys in the morning and open up for training. Then when it's over, you lock up and go home."

Referee **DAVID ELLERAY:** "I'd introduce a sin-bin for yellow-card offences. You should be punished in the game you're playing – like a sending off. Then the team you've offended against gains the advantage of your punishment and not your opponents in a couple of weeks. It would also improve the game because if a team already has one or two players in the sin-bin, they're going to be very careful."

LEEDS FANS' SING-ALONG after their ninth 0-0 draw under George Graham (at Chelsea, May 3): "We'll score again, don't know where, don't know when, but we know we'll score again some sunny day."

PUBLIC ADDRESS announcement at local Sussex cup final between Heath Pilgrims and Wivelsfield Green: "And the man of the match is . . . the streaker."

TERRY VENABLES, as Portsmouth chairman: "Because of the money the play-offs generate, I suppose I should be in favour, but I am totally opposed to the idea. They are a complete nonsense. You can finish a long way behind the team who come third and still gain promotion. One, two and three should go up – simple as that."

THE DUKE OF DEVONSHIRE, president of Chesterfield, on F.A. Cup semi-final Sunday against Middlesbrough: "I told them all – butler, chambermaids, everybody – to have the day off and go to the game. I even had to make my own lunch."

BELL'S SCOTTISH LEAGUE FINAL TABLES 1996-97

PREMIER DIVISION

	P	HOME					AWAY					Pts	GD
		W	D	L	F	A	W	D	L	F	A		
1 Rangers	36	13	2	3	44	16	12	3	3	41	17	80	+52
2 Celtic	36	14	2	2	48	9	9	4	5	30	23	75	+46
3 Dundee Utd.	36	10	4	4	21	10	7	5	6	25	23	60	+13
4 Hearts	36	8	6	4	27	20	6	4	8	19	23	52	+3
5 Dunfermline Ath.	36	8	4	6	32	30	4	5	9	20	35	45	-13
6 Aberdeen	36	6	8	4	25	19	4	6	8	20	35	44	-9
7 Kilmarnock	36	8	4	6	28	26	3	2	13	13	35	39	-20
8 Motherwell	36	5	5	8	24	25	4	6	8	20	30	38	-11
9 *Hibernian	36	6	4	8	18	25	3	7	8	20	30	38	-17
10 Raith Rovers	36	3	5	10	18	39	3	2	13	11	34	25	-44

(* Hibernian remain in Premier Division after winning play-off v Airdrie 5-2 on agg, 1-0h, 4-2a.)

FIRST DIVISION

	P	HOME					AWAY					Pts	GD
		W	D	L	F	A	W	D	L	F	A		
1 St. Johnstone	36	12	5	1	37	10	12	3	3	37	13	80	+51
2 Airdrie	36	6	7	5	26	19	9	8	1	30	15	60	+22
3 Dundee	36	10	3	5	26	14	5	10	3	21	19	58	+14
4 St. Mirren	36	12	0	6	28	21	5	7	6	20	20	58	+7
5 Falkirk	36	8	7	3	28	20	7	2	9	14	19	54	+3
6 Partick Thistle	36	6	8	4	24	21	6	4	8	25	27	48	+1
7 Stirling Albion	36	8	3	7	27	25	4	7	7	27	36	46	-7
8 Greenock Morton	36	6	7	5	20	19	6	2	10	22	22	45	+1
9 Clydebank	36	6	4	8	19	24	1	3	14	12	35	28	-28
10 East Fife	36	1	5	12	15	48	1	3	14	13	44	14	-64

SECOND DIVISION

	P	HOME					AWAY					Pts	GD
		W	D	L	F	A	W	D	L	F	A		
1 Ayr United	36	12	3	3	32	16	11	5	2	29	17	77	+28
2 Hamilton Acad.	36	11	5	2	47	17	11	3	4	28	11	74	+47
3 Livingston	36	11	3	4	32	18	7	7	4	24	20	64	+18
4 Clyde	36	8	4	6	21	18	6	6	6	21	21	52	+3
5 Queen of South	36	8	3	7	27	27	5	5	8	28	30	47	-2
6 Stenhousemuir	36	4	6	8	19	23	7	5	6	30	20	44	+6
7 Brechin City	36	5	7	6	18	22	5	4	9	18	27	41	-13
8 Stranraer	36	6	5	7	17	18	3	4	11	12	33	38	-22
9 Dumbarton	36	2	7	9	21	35	7	1	10	23	31	35	-22
10 Berwick Rangers	36	4	4	10	15	36	0	7	11	17	39	23	-43

THIRD DIVISION

		HOME					AWAY						
	P	W	D	L	F	A	W	D	L	F	A	Pts	GD
1 Inverness C.T.	36	13	3	2	37	19	10	4	4	33	18	76	+33
2 Forfar Athletic	36	10	5	3	35	19	9	5	4	39	26	67	+29
3 Ross County	36	10	4	4	33	22	10	3	5	25	19	67	+17
4 Alloa	36	9	4	5	24	21	7	3	8	26	26	55	+3
5 Albion Rovers	36	8	4	6	27	22	5	6	7	23	25	49	+3
6 Montrose	36	6	5	7	19	27	6	2	10	27	35	43	−16
7 Cowdenbeath	36	6	6	6	22	23	4	3	11	16	28	39	−13
8 Queen's Park	36	7	3	8	27	29	2	6	10	19	30	36	−13
9 East Stirling	36	6	4	8	21	29	2	5	11	15	29	33	−22
10 Arbroath	36	4	6	8	18	25	2	7	9	13	27	31	−21

SCOTTISH HONOURS LIST

PREMIER DIVISION

	First	Pts.	Second	Pts.	Third	Pts.
1975-6	Rangers	54	Celtic	48	Hibernian	43
1976-7	Celtic	55	Rangers	46	Aberdeen	43
1977-8	Rangers	55	Aberdeen	53	Dundee Utd	40
1978-9	Celtic	48	Rangers	45	Dundee Utd	44
1979-80	Aberdeen	48	Celtic	47	St. Mirren	42
1980-81	Celtic	56	Aberdeen	49	Rangers	44
1981-2	Celtic	55	Aberdeen	53	Rangers	43
1982-3	Dundee Utd	56	Celtic	55	Aberdeen	55
1983-4	Aberdeen	57	Celtic	50	Dundee Utd	47
1984-5	Aberdeen	59	Celtic	52	Dundee Utd	47
1985-6	*Celtic	50	Hearts	50	Dundee Utd	47
1986-7	Rangers	69	Celtic	63	Dundee Utd.	60
1987-8	Celtic	72	Hearts	62	Rangers	60
1988-9	Rangers	56	Aberdeen	50	Celtic	46
1989-90	Rangers	51	Aberdeen	44	Hearts	44
1990-1	Rangers	55	Aberdeen	53	Celtic	41
1991-2	Rangers	72	Hearts	63	Celtic	62
1992-3	Rangers	73	Aberdeen	64	Celtic	60
1993-4	Rangers	58	Aberdeen	55	Motherwell	54
1994-5	Rangers	69	Motherwell	54	Hibernian	53
1995-6	Rangers	87	Celtic	83	Aberdeen	55
1996-7	Rangers	80	Celtic	75	Dundee Utd	60

Maximum points: 72 except 1986-8, 1991-4 (88) and 1994-7 (108).
* Won on goal difference.

FIRST DIVISION
(Scottish Championship until 1975-76)

	First	Pts.	Second	Pts.	Third	Pts.
1890-1a	††Dumbarton	29	Rangers	29	Celtic	24
1891-2b	Dumbarton	37	Celtic	35	Hearts	30
1892-3a	Celtic	29	Rangers	28	St Mirren	23
1893-4a	Celtic	29	Hearts	26	St Bernard's	22
1894-5a	Hearts	31	Celtic	26	Rangers	21
1895-6a	Celtic	30	Rangers	26	Hibernian	24
1896-7a	Hearts	28	Hibernian	26	Rangers	25
1897-8a	Celtic	33	Rangers	29	Hibernian	22

Season	Champion	Pts	Runner-up	Pts	Third	Pts
1898-9a	Rangers	36	Hearts	26	Celtic	24
1899-1900a	Rangers	32	Celtic	25	Hibernian	24
1900-1c	Rangers	35	Celtic	29	Hibernian	25
1901-2a	Rangers	28	Celtic	26	Hearts	22
1902-3b	Hibernian	37	Dundee	31	Rangers	29
1903-4d	Third Lanark	43	Hearts	39	Rangers	38
1904-5a	†Celtic	41	Rangers	41	Third Lanark	35
1905-6a	Celtic	46	Hearts	39	Rangers	38
1906-7f	Celtic	55	Dundee	48	Rangers	45
1907-8f	Celtic	55	Falkirk	51	Rangers	50
1908-9f	Celtic	51	Dundee	50	Clyde	48
1909-10f	Celtic	54	Falkirk	52	Rangers	49
1910-11f	Rangers	52	Aberdeen	48	Falkirk	44
1911-12f	Rangers	51	Celtic	45	Clyde	42
1912-13f	Rangers	53	Celtic	49	Hearts	41
1913-14g	Celtic	65	Rangers	59	Hearts	54
1914-15g	Celtic	65	Hearts	61	Rangers	50
1915-16g	Celtic	67	Rangers	56	Morton	51
1916-17g	Celtic	64	Morton	54	Rangers	53
1917-18f	Rangers	56	Celtic	55	Kilmarnock	43
1918-19f	Celtic	58	Rangers	57	Morton	47
1919-20h	Rangers	71	Celtic	68	Motherwell	57
1920-1h	Rangers	76	Celtic	66	Hearts	56
1921-2h	Celtic	67	Rangers	66	Raith	56
1922-3g	Rangers	55	Airdrieonians	50	Celtic	40
1923-4g	Rangers	59	Airdrieonians	50	Celtic	41
1924-5g	Rangers	60	Airdrieonians	57	Hibernian	52
1925-6g	Celtic	58	Airdrieonians	50	Hearts	50
1926-7g	Rangers	56	Motherwell	51	Celtic	49
1927-8g	Rangers	60	Celtic	55	Motherwell	55
1928-9g	Rangers	67	Celtic	51	Motherwell	50
1929-30g	Rangers	60	Motherwell	55	Aberdeen	53
1930-1g	Rangers	60	Celtic	58	Motherwell	56
1931-2g	Motherwell	66	Rangers	61	Celtic	48
1932-3g	Rangers	62	Motherwell	59	Hearts	50
1933-4g	Rangers	66	Motherwell	62	Celtic	47
1934-5g	Rangers	55	Celtic	52	Hearts	50
1935-6g	Celtic	68	Rangers	61	Aberdeen	61
1936-7g	Rangers	61	Aberdeen	54	Celtic	52
1937-8g	Celtic	61	Hearts	58	Rangers	49
1938-9f	Rangers	59	Celtic	48	Aberdeen	46
1946-7f	Rangers	46	Hibernian	44	Aberdeen	39
1947-8g	Hibernian	48	Rangers	46	Partick	46
1948-9i	Rangers	46	Dundee	45	Hibernian	39
1949-50i	Rangers	50	Hibernian	49	Hearts	43
1950-1i	Hibernian	48	Rangers	38	Dundee	38
1951-2i	Hibernian	45	Rangers	41	East Fife	37
1952-3i	*Rangers	43	Hibernian	43	East Fife	39
1953-4i	Celtic	43	Hearts	38	Partick	35
1954-5f	Aberdeen	49	Celtic	46	Rangers	41
1955-6f	Rangers	52	Aberdeen	46	Hearts	45
1956-7f	Rangers	55	Hearts	53	Kilmarnock	42
1957-8f	Hearts	62	Rangers	49	Celtic	46
1958-9f	Rangers	50	Hearts	48	Motherwell	44
1959-60f	Hearts	54	Kilmarnock	50	Rangers	42
1960-1f	Rangers	51	Kilmarnock	50	Third Lanark	42
1961-2f	Dundee	54	Rangers	51	Celtic	46
1962-3f	Rangers	57	Kilmarnock	48	Partick	46
1963-4f	Rangers	55	Kilmarnock	49	Celtic	47
1964-5f	*Kilmarnock	50	Hearts	50	Dunfermline	49
1965-6f	Celtic	57	Rangers	55	Kilmarnock	45

1966-7f	Celtic	58	Rangers	55	Clyde	46
1967-8f	Celtic	63	Rangers	61	Hibernian	45
1968-9f	Celtic	54	Rangers	49	Dunfermline	45
1969-70f	Celtic	57	Rangers	45	Hibernian	44
1970-1f	Celtic	56	Aberdeen	54	St Johnstone	44
1971-2f	Celtic	60	Aberdeen	50	Rangers	44
1972-3f	Celtic	57	Rangers	56	Hibernian	45
1973-4f	Celtic	53	Hibernian	49	Rangers	48
1974-5f	Rangers	56	Hibernian	49	Celtic	45

* Won on goal average. †Won on deciding match. ††Title shared.
Competition suspended 1940-46 (Second World War).

SCOTTISH CHAMPIONSHIP WINS

Rangers	*47	Hibernian	4	Kilmarnock	1
Celtic	35	Dumbarton	*2	Motherwell	1
Aberdeen	4	Dundee	1	Third Lanark	1
Hearts	4	Dundee Utd.	1	(* Incl. 1 shared)

FIRST DIVISION
(Since formation of Premier Division)

	First	Pts.	Second	Pts.	Third	Pts.
1975-6d	Partick	41	Kilmarnock	35	Montrose	30
1976-7j	St. Mirren	62	Clydebank	58	Dundee	51
1977-8j	*Morton	58	Hearts	58	Dundee	57
1978-9j	Dundee	55	Kilmarnock	54	Clydebank	54
1979-80j	Hearts	53	Airdrieonians	51	Ayr	44
1980-1j	Hibernian	57	Dundee	52	St. Johnstone	51
1981-2j	Motherwell	61	Kilmarnock	51	Hearts	50
1982-3j	St. Johnstone	55	Hearts	54	Clydebank	50
1983-4j	Morton	54	Dumbarton	51	Partick	46
1984-5j	Motherwell	50	Clydebank	48	Falkirk	45
1985-6j	Hamilton	56	Falkirk	45	Kilmarnock	44
1986-7k	Morton	57	Dunfermline	56	Dumbarton	53
1987-8k	Hamilton	56	Meadowbank	52	Clydebank	49
1988-9j	Dunfermline	54	Falkirk	52	Clydebank	48
1989-90j	St. Johnstone	58	Airdrieonians	54	Clydebank	44
1990-1j	Falkirk	54	Airdrieonians	53	Dundee	52
1991-2k	Dundee	58	Partick	57	Hamilton	57
1992-3k	Raith	65	Kilmarnock	54	Dunfermline	52
1993-4k	Falkirk	66	Dunfermline	65	Airdrieonians	54
1994-5l	Raith	69	Dunfermline	68	Dundee	68
1995-6l	Dunfermline	71	Dundee Utd.	67	Greenock Morton	62
1996-7l	St. Johnstone	80	Airdrieonians	60	Dundee	58

Maximum points: a, 36; b, 44; c, 40; d, 52; e, 60; f, 68; g, 76; h, 84; i, 60; j, 78;
k, 88; l, 108. * Won on goal difference.

SECOND DIVISION

	First	Pts.	Second	Pts.	Third	Pts.
1921-2a	Alloa	60	Cowdenbeath	47	Armadale	45
1922-3a	Queen's Park	57	Clydebank	52	St. Johnstone	50
1923-4a	St. Johnstone	56	Cowdenbeath	55	Bathgate	44
1924-5a	Dundee Utd.	50	Clydebank	48	Clyde	47
1925-6a	Dunfermline	59	Clyde	53	Ayr	52
1926-7a	Bo'ness	56	Raith	49	Clydebank	45

Year	First	Pts	Second	Pts	Third	Pts
1927-8a	Ayr	54	Third Lanark	45	King's Park	44
1928-9b	Dundee Utd.	51	Morton	50	Arbroath	47
1929-30a	*Leith Athletic	57	East Fife	50	Albion	54
1930-1a	Third Lanark	61	Dundee Utd.	50	Dunfermline	47
1931-2a	*East Stirling	55	St. Johnstone	55	Stenhousemuir	46
1932-3c	Hibernian	55	Queen of South	49	Dunfermline	47
1933-4c	Albion	45	Dunfermline	44	Arbroath	44
1934-5c	Third Lanark	52	Arbroath	50	St. Bernard's	47
1935-6c	Falkirk	59	St. Mirren	52	Morton	48
1936-7c	Ayr	54	Morton	51	St. Bernard's	48
1937-8c	Raith	59	Albion	48	Airdrieonians	47
1938-9c	Cowdenbeath	60	Alloa	48	East Fife	48
1946-7d	Dundee Utd.	45	Airdrieonians	42	East Fife	31
1947-8e	East Fife	53	Albion	42	Hamilton	40
1948-9e	*Raith	42	Stirling	42	Airdrieonians	41
1949-50e	Morton	47	Airdrieonians	44	St. Johnstone	36
1950-1e	*Queen of South	45	Stirling	44	Ayr	36
1951-2e	Clyde	44	Falkirk	43	Ayr	39
1952-3e	Stirling	44	Hamilton	43	Queen's Park	37
1953-4e	Motherwell	45	Kilmarnock	42	Third Lanark	36
1954-5e	Airdrieonians	46	Dunfermline	42	Hamilton	39
1955-6b	Queen's Park	54	Ayr	51	St. Johnstone	49
1956-7b	Clyde	64	Third Lanark	51	Cowdenbeath	45
1957-8b	Stirling	55	Dunfermline	53	Arbroath	47
1958-9b	Ayr	60	Arbroath	51	Stenhousemuir	46
1959-60b	St. Johnstone	53	Dundee Utd.	50	Queen of South	49
1960-1b	Stirling	55	Falkirk	54	Stenhousemuir	50
1961-2b	Clyde	54	Queen of South	53	Morton	44
1962-3b	St. Johnstone	55	East Stirling	49	Morton	48
1963-4b	Morton	67	Clyde	53	Arbroath	46
1964-5b	Stirling	59	Hamilton	50	Queen of South	45
1965-6b	Ayr	53	Airdrieonians	50	Queen of South	47
1966-7b	Morton	69	Raith	58	Arbroath	57
1967-8b	St. Mirren	62	Arbroath	53	East Fife	49
1968-9b	Motherwell	64	Ayr	53	East Fife	48
1969-70b	Falkirk	56	Cowdenbeath	55	Queen of South	50
1970-1b	Partick	56	East Fife	51	Arbroath	46
1971-2b	*Dumbarton	52	Arbroath	52	Stirling	50
1972-3b	Clyde	56	Dunfermline	52	Raith	47
1973-4b	Airdrieonians	60	Kilmarnock	58	Hamilton	55
1974-5b	Falkirk	54	Queen of South	53	Montrose	53

SECOND DIVISION (Modern)

Year	First	Pts.	Second	Pts.	Third	Pts.
1975-6d	*Clydebank	40	Raith	40	Alloa	35
1976-7f	Stirling	55	Alloa	51	Dunfermline	50
1977-8f	*Clyde	53	Raith	53	Dunfermline	48
1978-9f	Berwick	54	Dunfermline	52	Falkirk	50
1979-80f	Falkirk	50	East Stirling	49	Forfar	46
1980-1f	Queen's Park	50	Queen of South	46	Cowdenbeath	45
1981-2f	Clyde	59	Alloa	50	Arbroath	50
1982-3f	Brechin	55	Meadowbank	54	Arbroath	49
1983-4f	Forfar	63	East Fife	47	Berwick	43
1984-5f	Montrose	53	Alloa	50	Dunfermline	49
1985-6f	Dunfermline	57	Queen of South	55	Meadowbank	49
1986-7f	Meadowbank	55	Raith	52	Stirling	52
1987-8f	Ayr	61	St. Johnstone	59	Queen's Park	51
1988-9f	Albion	50	Alloa	45	Brechin	43
1989-90f	Brechin	49	Kilmarnock	48	Stirling	47
1990-1f	Stirling	54	Montrose	46	Cowdenbeath	45

1991-2f	Dumbarton 52	Cowdenbeath 51	Alloa 50
1992-3f	Clyde 54	Brechin 53	Stranraer 53
1993-4f	Stranraer 56	Berwick 48	Stenhousemuir ... 47
1994-5g	Greenock Morton .. 64	Dumbarton 60	Stirling 58
1995-6g	Stirling 81	East Fife 67	Berwick 60
1996-7g	Ayr 77	Hamilton 74	Livingstone 64

Maximum points: *a*, 76; *b*, 72; *c*, 68; *d*, 52; *e*, 60; *f*, 78; *g*, 108.
* Won on goal average.

THIRD DIVISION (Modern)

	First .... Pts.	Second .... Pts.	Third .... Pts.
1994-5	Forfar 80	Montrose 67	Ross County 60
1995-6	Livingston 72	Brechin 63	Caledonian Th. 57
1996-7	Inverness Cal.T. .. 76	Forfar 67	Ross County 77

Maximum points: 108.

RELEGATED FROM PREMIER DIVISION

1975-6	Dundee, St. Johnstone	1986-7	Clydebank, Hamilton
1976-7	Kilmarnock, Hearts	1987-8	Falkirk, Dunfermline, Morton
1977-8	Ayr, Clydebank	1988-9	Hamilton
1978-9	Hearts, Motherwell	1989-90	Dundee
1979-80	Dundee, Hibernian	1990-1	No relegation
1980-1	Kilmarnock, Hearts	1991-2	St. Mirren, Dunfermline
1981-2	Partick, Airdrieonians	1992-3	Falkirk, Airdrieonians
1982-3	Morton, Kilmarnock	1993-4	St. J'stone, Raith, Dundee
1983-4	St. Johnstone, Motherwell	1994-5	Dundee Utd.
1984-5	Dumbarton, Morton	1995-6	Falkirk, Partick Thistle
1985-6	No relegation	1996-7	Raith

RELEGATED FROM FIRST DIVISION

1975-6	Dunfermline, Clyde	1987-8	East Fife, Dumbarton
1976-7	Raith, Falkirk	1988-9	Kilmarnock, Queen of South
1977-8	Alloa, East Fife		
1978-9	Montrose, Queen of South	1989-90	Albion, Alloa
1979-80	Arbroath, Clyde	1990-1	Clyde, Brechin
1980-1	Stirling, Berwick	1991-2	Montrose, Forfar
1981-2	East Stirling, Queen of South	1992-3	Meadowbank, Cowdenbeath
1982-3	Dunfermline, Queen's Park	1993-4	Dumbarton, Stirling Alb., Clyde, Morton, Brechin
1983-4	Raith, Alloa		
1984-5	Meadowbank, St. Johnstone	1994-5	Ayr, Stranraer
1985-6	Ayr, Alloa	1995-6	Hamilton, Dumbarton
1986-7	Brechin, Montrose	1996-7	Clydebank, East Fife

RELEGATED FROM SECOND DIVISION

1993-4	Alloa, Forfar, E. Stirling, Montrose, Queen's Park, Arbroath, Albion, Cowdenbeath	1994-5 Meadowbank, Brechin
		1995-6 Forfar, Montrose
		1996-7 Dumbarton, Berwick

The Association of Football Statisticians
(FORMED 1978)

Full details from: Ray Spiller,
22 Bretons, Basildon, Essex SS15 5BY

BELL'S SCOTTISH LEAGUE RESULTS 1996-97

PREMIER DIVISION

	Aberdeen	Celtic	Dundee Utd	Dunfermline Ath.	Hearts	Hibernian	Kilmarnock	Motherwell	Raith Rovers	Rangers
Aberdeen	–	2-2	3-3	3-0	4-0	0-2	3-0	0-0	1-0	0-3
	–	1-2	1-1	0-2	0-0	1-1	2-1	0-0	2-0	2-2
Celtic	1-0	–	1-0	5-1	2-2	5-0	6-0	1-0	4-1	0-1
	3-0	–	3-0	4-2	2-0	4-1	0-0	5-0	2-0	0-1
Dundee Utd	1-0	1-2	–	1-1	1-0	0-1	0-0	1-1	1-2	1-0
	4-0	1-0	–	2-1	1-0	0-0	2-0	2-0	2-1	0-1
Dunfermline Ath.	2-3	0-2	1-1	–	2-1	2-1	2-1	1-1	3-1	2-5
	3-0	2-2	1-3	–	2-3	1-1	3-1	3-1	2-0	0-3
Hearts	1-2	2-2	1-0	2-0	–	0-0	3-2	1-1	0-0	1-4
	0-0	1-2	1-2	1-1	–	1-0	2-0	4-1	3-2	0-1
Hibernian	0-1	0-4	1-1	0-0	1-3	–	1-2	2-0	1-0	2-1
	3-1	1-3	2-0	1-0	0-4	–	0-1	1-1	1-1	1-2
Kilmarnock	3-0	1-3	0-2	2-2	2-0	4-2	–	2-4	2-1	1-4
	1-1	2-0	2-3	2-1	1-0	1-1	–	1-0	0-1	1-1
Motherwell	2-2	2-1	1-3	2-3	0-2	1-1	1-0	–	0-1	0-1
	2-2	0-1	1-1	2-2	0-1	2-1	2-0	–	5-0	1-3
Raith Rovers	1-4	1-2	3-2	1-2	1-1	0-3	1-0	0-3	–	2-2
	2-2	1-1	0-1	0-1	1-2	1-1	2-1	1-5	–	0-6
Rangers	2-2	2-0	1-0	3-1	3-0	4-3	4-2	5-0	1-0	–
	4-0	3-1	0-2	4-0	0-0	3-1	1-2	0-2	4-0	–

Read across for home results, down for away

(Play-off: Hibernian 1, Airdrieonians 0; Airdrieonians 2, Hibernian 4. Hibernian win 5-2 on agg. and stay in Premier Division.)

FIRST DIVISION

	Airdrieonians	Clydebank	Dundee	East Fife	Falkirk	Greenock Morton	Partick Thistle	Stirling Albion	St. Johnstone	St. Mirren
Airdrieonians	–	3-1	0-0	0-0	0-1	1-2	4-4	3-1	0-1	2-2
	–	4-1	2-0	1-1	2-0	1-0	1-1	1-2	0-1	1-1
Clydebank	1-4	–	0-0	2-0	0-1	2-1	1-3	1-0	2-1	2-1
	1-1	–	0-0	0-4	1-2	0-1	4-1	1-2	1-1	0-1
Dundee	0-1	2-1	–	2-0	2-0	2-1	0-2	1-1	0-1	0-1
	2-1	1-0	–	6-0	0-2	1-0	1-1	4-2	0-0	2-0
East Fife	0-4	1-1	1-7	–	3-1	0-3	1-3	2-2	1-4	0-4
	0-0	1-2	1-1	–	0-2	1-4	0-2	1-3	2-2	0-3
Falkirk	1-1	2-0	0-1	2-1	–	0-0	1-0	5-2	2-0	1-0
	0-3	1-1	1-1	3-1	–	3-0	2-1	2-2	1-4	1-1
Greenock Morton	1-1	3-0	0-0	0-0	1-0	–	1-0	3-2	0-2	1-3
	1-1	2-2	1-1	2-0	0-2	–	1-3	1-1	0-1	2-0
Partick Thistle	0-0	1-0	0-0	6-0	3-0	0-0	–	1-1	0-4	1-1
	1-2	3-1	2-2	3-1	2-1	0-3	–	1-1	0-4	0-0
Stirling Albion	0-1	2-0	1-1	2-1	1-0	1-3	1-2	–	1-3	1-1
	1-2	4-2	0-1	4-1	0-0	4-3	2-0	–	1-4	1-0
St. Johnstone	1-1	2-0	0-1	3-0	0-0	1-0	2-0	5-0	–	4-0
	2-2	1-0	7-2	3-2	3-1	1-0	0-0	1-1	–	1-0
St. Mirren	2-3	1-0	0-1	4-1	0-1	1-0	3-2	2-1	0-3	–
	1-2	1-0	3-2	1-0	1-0	3-1	2-0	1-3	2-1	–

Read across for home results, down for away

(Play-off: Partick Thistle 1, Dundee Utd. 1; Dundee Utd. 2, Partick Thistle 1. After extra time; Dundee Utd. win 3-2 on agg., promoted to Premier Division).

SECOND DIVISION

	Ayr United	Berwick Rangers	Brechin City	Clyde	Dumbarton	Hamilton Acad.	Livingston	Queen of South	Stenhousemuir	Stranraer
Ayr United	–	6-0	1-0	2-4	1-4	1-1	1-0	1-0	1-2	2-0
	–	2-0	2-0	3-1	1-1	1-0	1-0	2-2	2-1	2-0
Berwick Rangers	1-2	–	0-0	1-5	3-1	0-2	1-2	2-2	0-6	1-2
	0-2	–	1-0	0-2	0-3	0-5	1-1	1-1	1-0	2-0
Brechin City	1-1	3-2	–	1-2	2-1	0-2	0-0	3-3	0-0	0-2
	1-1	3-1	–	2-1	0-3	0-1	1-0	0-1	1-1	0-0
Clyde	2-3	2-1	1-0	–	0-1	1-1	2-0	0-2	0-4	1-0
	1-1	0-0	1-1	–	2-1	0-1	0-1	2-1	3-0	3-0
Dumbarton	1-3	1-0	1-1	2-2	–	1-3	2-4	1-2	1-1	1-1
	1-1	2-2	1-2	2-0	–	0-3	2-3	0-3	0-2	2-2
Hamilton Acad.	1-2	4-2	5-1	2-0	2-0	–	3-3	2-2	0-2	4-0
	1-1	4-1	4-0	4-0	4-0	–	0-0	4-1	1-1	2-1
Livingston	1-0	2-1	2-1	0-0	5-0	1-0	–	3-1	2-1	2-0
	2-1	2-2	2-3	0-0	1-2	1-2	–	2-1	1-3	3-0
Queen of South	1-2	2-1	1-5	0-2	2-1	1-1	2-2	–	1-0	3-2
	1-3	2-0	2-1	0-1	4-0	1-0	1-2	–	2-3	1-1
Stenhousemuir	1-2	1-1	0-0	0-0	0-1	0-1	0-0	2-1	–	0-1
	1-2	1-1	3-1	1-1	1-4	3-1	1-3	0-3	–	4-0
Stranraer	0-1	1-1	0-1	0-0	2-0	0-3	1-2	2-1	2-2	–
	0-1	1-1	0-1	1-0	1-0	0-1	1-1	3-1	2-1	–

Read across for home results, down for away

THIRD DIVISION

	Albion Rovers	Alloa	Arbroath	Cowdenbeath	East Stirling	Forfar Ath.	Inverness Cal. Th.	Montrose	Queen's Park	Ross County
Albion Rovers	–	1-1	1-0	2-0	4-3	2-0	0-0	1-2	1-1	0-2
	–	3-0	1-2	4-0	1-1	1-3	0-3	2-1	1-1	1-2
Alloa	2-0	–	1-1	1-1	1-0	3-4	0-2	3-1	2-1	1-3
	2-0	–	0-2	1-0	1-1	0-3	1-0	1-0	3-1	1-1
Arbroath	1-3	0-2	–	0-1	0-0	1-1	1-4	1-2	1-0	3-1
	1-2	1-2	–	1-0	1-2	3-3	0-0	1-1	0-0	2-1
Cowdenbeath	1-1	2-0	2-2	–	1-0	1-3	3-4	1-0	1-1	0-1
	0-0	2-1	1-1	–	2-0	1-2	2-1	0-1	1-4	0-1
East Stirling	0-1	2-2	0-0	1-0	–	2-1	0-0	1-3	2-1	0-1
	1-4	0-3	3-0	2-2	–	0-3	0-3	4-2	1-0	2-3
Forfar Athletic	0-0	1-1	1-1	2-5	3-0	–	3-1	3-1	2-2	0-2
	3-1	1-0	1-1	3-0	1-0	–	2-0	5-3	4-0	0-1
Inverness Cal.Th.	1-1	1-0	2-0	1-3	2-0	1-1	–	2-0	2-2	2-0
	4-1	3-1	4-1	2-1	3-2	0-4	–	3-2	1-0	3-0
Montrose	2-1	1-2	0-0	0-2	1-0	4-1	2-2	–	3-2	2-1
	0-4	2-3	1-0	0-0	0-2	0-4	0-2	–	1-1	0-0
Queen's Park	1-1	2-1	3-1	1-0	3-3	1-4	2-3	0-2	–	0-3
	0-0	0-4	3-1	2-1	3-0	4-0	1-2	0-1	–	1-2
Ross County	3-2	1-2	2-0	1-0	1-1	1-1	1-3	4-4	1-2	–
	3-1	3-1	1-0	4-0	1-0	1-1	0-3	3-1	2-0	–

Read across for home results, down for away

KILMARNOCK AVENGE 1957 SCOTTISH CUP FINAL DEFEAT

THIRD ROUND	FOURTH ROUND	FIFTH ROUND	SEMI-FINALS	FINAL
*Falkirk .... 1:2 Berwick 1:1	*Falkirk 2	*Falkirk 2	Falkirk 1:1	
*Dunfermline ..... 4 Ross County 0	Dunfermline 1			
*Brechin .... 3 Alloa 0	*Brechin 1	Raith 0	(both matches at Ibrox)	Falkirk 0
*Airdrie .... 1 Raith 4	Raith 2			
*Rangers .... 2 St Johnstone 0	*Rangers 3	Rangers 0	Celtic 1:0	
*Queens Park ..... 1 East Fife 3	East Fife 0			(at Ibrox Saturday, May 24)
*Hibernian ..... 2:B0 Aberdeen 2:0	Hibernian ..... 1:0 *	Celtic 2		
Celtic .... 5 *Clydebank 0	*Celtic 1:2			
*Stirling Albion .. 0 Dundee Utd. 2	Dundee Utd 1:1	*Dundee Utd 4	Dundee Utd 0:0	
*Hearts .... 5 Cowdenbeath 0	*Hearts 1:0			

94

*Inverness C.T. 1
Hamilton 3

*Hamilton 1:0

*Partick 0
Motherwell 2

Motherwell 1:2

Gr. Morton 2:4
*Arbroath 2:0

*Gr. Morton 2:1

*Dundee 3
Queen of South 1

Dundee 2:0

*Clyde 3
St Mirren 1

*Clyde 0

*East Stirling 0
Kilmarnock 2

Kilmarnock 1

Kilmarnock 1

(both matches
at Easter Road)

Kilmarnock 0:1

*Gr. Morton 2

Kilmarnock 5

FIRST ROUND: Albion 0, Forfar 0; Alloa 3, Hawick 1; Elgin City 0, Whitehill Wel. 3; Huntly 1, Clyde 1. **Replays:** Forfar 4, Albion 0; Clyde 3, Huntly 2†.

SECOND ROUND: Berwick 2, Peterhead 1; Queens Park 2, Gala Fairydean 1; Ayr 0, Clyde 2, East Stirling 4, Brora Rangers 3; Spartans 0, Arbroath 0; Whitehill 2, Queen of the South 3; Brechin 2, Livingston 1; Cowdenbeath 1, Dumbarton 0; Forfar 0, Alloa 1; Ross County 3, Montrose 0; Strenhousemuir 1, Hamilton 2; Stranraer 1, Inverness C.T. 1. **Replays:** Arbroath 3, Spartans 0; Inverness C.T. 0, Stranraer A0. (* Drawn at home. † After extra time. A – Inverness Caledonian Thistle won 4-3 on pens. B – Hibernian won 5-3 on pens.).

TENNENTS SCOTTISH F.A. CUP FINAL
KILMARNOCK 1 (Wright 21), FALKIRK 0
Ibrox Park (48,953), Saturday, May 24, 1997

Kilmarnock: Lekovic; McGowan (Capt.), Montgomerie, McGowne, Kerr, Holt, Reilly, Bagan (Mitchell 88), Wright (Henry 77), McIntyre (Brown 83), Burke. **Booked:** Kerr, Wright. **Manager:** Bobby Williamson.

Falkirk: Nelson; McGowan (Capt.), James, Gray, Seaton, McAllister, McKenzie, Oliver, Hagen, McGillen (Fellner 63), Crabbe (Craig 77). **Subs not used:** Mathers. **Booked:** Gray, Craig. **Manager:** Alex Totten.

Referee: H. Dallas (Motherwell). **Half-time:** 1-0.

SCOTTISH F.A. CUP FINALS

1874	Queen's Park beat Clydesdale (2-0)
1875	Queen's Park beat Renton (3-0)
1876	Queen's Park beat Third Lanark (2-0 after 1-1 draw)
1877	Vale of Leven beat Rangers (3-2 after 0-0, 1-1 draws)
1878	Vale of Leven beat Third Lanark (1-0)
1879	Vale of Leven awarded Cup (Rangers withdrew after 1-1 draw)
1880	Queen's Park beat Thornliebank (3-0)
1881	Queen's Park beat Dumbarton (3-1)
1882	Queen's Park beat Dumbarton (4-1 after 2-2 draw)
1883	Dumbarton beat Vale of Leven (2-1 after 2-2 draw)
1884	Queen's Park awarded Cup (Vale of Leven withdrew from Final)
1885	Renton beat Vale of Leven (3-1 after 0-0 draw)
1886	Queen's Park beat Renton (3-1)
1887	Hibernian beat Dumbarton (2-1)
1888	Renton beat Cambuslang (6-1)
1889	Third Lanark beat Celtic (2-1)
1890	Queen's Park beat Vale of Leven (2-1 after 1-1 draw)
1891	Hearts beat Dumbarton (1-0)
1892	Celtic beat Queen's Park (5-1)
1893	Queen's Park beat Celtic (2-1)
1894	Rangers beat Celtic (3-1)
1895	St. Bernard's beat Renton (2-1)
1896	Hearts beat Hibernian (3-1)
1897	Rangers beat Dumbarton (5-1)
1898	Rangers beat Kilmarnock (2-0)
1899	Celtic beat Rangers (2-0)
1900	Celtic beat Queen's Park (4-3)
1901	Hearts beat Celtic (4-3)
1902	Hibernian beat Celtic (1-0)
1903	Rangers beat Hearts (2-0 after 0-0, 1-1 draws)
1904	Celtic beat Rangers (3-2)
1905	Third Lanark beat Rangers (3-1 after 0-0 draw)
1906	Hearts beat Third Lanark (1-0)
1907	Celtic beat Hearts (3-0)
1908	Celtic beat St. Mirren (5-1)
1909	Cup withheld because of riot after two drawn games in Final between Celtic and Rangers (2-2, 1-1)
1910	Dundee beat Clyde (2-1 after 2-2, 0-0 draws)
1911	Celtic beat Hamilton Academical (2-0 after 0-0 draw)
1912	Celtic beat Clyde (2-0)
1913	Falkirk beat Raith Rovers (2-0)
1914	Celtic beat Hibernian (4-1 after 0-0 draw)
1915-19	No competition (World War 1)
1920	Kilmarnock beat Albion Rovers (3-2)
1921	Partick Thistle beat Rangers (1-0)
1922	Morton beat Rangers (1-0)
1923	Celtic beat Hibernian (1-0)
1924	Airdrieonians beat Hibernian (2-0)
1925	Celtic beat Dundee (2-1)
1926	St. Mirren beat Celtic (2-0)
1927	Celtic beat East Fife (3-1)
1928	Rangers beat Celtic (4-0)
1929	Kilmarnock beat Rangers (2-0)
1930	Rangers beat Partick Thistle (2-1 after 0-0 draw)
1931	Celtic beat Motherwell (4-2 after 2-2 draw)
1932	Rangers beat Kilmarnock (3-0 after 1-1 draw)
1933	Celtic beat Motherwell (1-0)
1934	Rangers beat St. Mirren (5-0)
1935	Rangers beat Hamilton Academical (2-1)
1936	Rangers beat Third Lanark (1-0)

1937	Celtic beat Aberdeen (2-1)
1938	East Fife beat Kilmarnock (4-2 after 1-1 draw)
1939	Clyde beat Motherwell (4-0)
1940-6	No competition (World War 2)
1947	Aberdeen beat Hibernian (2-1)
1948†	Rangers beat Morton (1-0 after 1-1 draw)
1949	Rangers beat Clyde (4-1)
1950	Rangers beat East Fife (3-0)
1951	Celtic beat Motherwell (1-0)
1952	Motherwell beat Dundee (4-0)
1953	Rangers beat Aberdeen (1-0 after 1-1 draw)
1954	Celtic beat Aberdeen (2-1)
1955	Clyde beat Celtic (1-0 after 1-1 draw)
1956	Hearts beat Celtic (3-1)
1957†	Falkirk beat Kilmarnock (2-1 after 1-1 draw)
1958	Clyde beat Hibernian (1-0)
1959	St. Mirren beat Aberdeen (3-1)
1960	Rangers beat Kilmarnock (2-0)
1961	Dunfermline Athletic beat Celtic (2-0 after 0-0 draw)
1962	Rangers beat St. Mirren (2-0)
1963	Rangers beat Celtic (3-0 after 1-1 draw)
1964	Rangers beat Dundee (3-1)
1965	Celtic beat Dunfermline Athletic (3-2)
1966	Rangers beat Celtic (1-0 after 0-0 draw)
1967	Celtic beat Aberdeen (2-0)
1968	Dunfermline Athletic beat Hearts (3-1)
1969	Celtic beat Rangers (4-0)
1970	Aberdeen beat Celtic (3-1)
1971	Celtic beat Rangers (2-1 after 1-1 draw)
1972	Celtic beat Hibernian (6-1)
1973	Rangers beat Celtic (3-2)
1974	Celtic beat Dundee United (3-0)
1975	Celtic beat Airdrieonians (3-1)
1976	Rangers beat Hearts (3-1)
1977	Celtic beat Rangers (1-0)
1978	Rangers beat Aberdeen (2-1)
1979†	Rangers beat Hibernian (3-2 after two 0-0 draws)
1980†	Celtic beat Rangers (1-0)
1981	Rangers beat Dundee United (4-1 after 0-0 draw)
1982†	Aberdeen beat Rangers (4-1)
1983†	Aberdeen beat Rangers (1-0)
1984†	Aberdeen beat Celtic (2-1)
1985	Celtic beat Dundee United (2-1)
1986	Aberdeen beat Hearts (3-0)
1987†	St. Mirren beat Dundee United (1-0)
1988	Celtic beat Dundee United (2-1)
1989	Celtic beat Rangers (1-0)
1990†	Aberdeen beat Celtic (9-8 on pens. after 0-0 draw)
1991†	Motherwell beat Dundee United (4-3)
1992	Rangers beat Airdrieonians (2-1)
1993	Rangers beat Aberdeen (2-1)
1994	Dundee United beat Rangers (1-0)
1995	Celtic beat Airdrieonians (1-0)
1996	Rangers beat Hearts (5-1)
1997	Kilmarnock beat Falkirk (1-0)

(† After extra time; Cup sponsored by Tennents since season 1989-90)

SUMMARY OF SCOTTISH F.A. CUP WINNERS

Celtic 30, Rangers 27, Queen's Park 10, Aberdeen 7, Hearts 5, Clyde 3, Kilmarnock 3, St. Mirren 3, Vale of Leven 3, Dunfermline Ath. 2, Falkirk 2, Hibernian 2, Motherwell 2, Renton 2, Third Lanark 2, Airdrieonians 1, Dumbarton 1, Dundee 1, Dundee United 1, East Fife 1, Morton 1, Partick Thistle 1, St. Bernard's 1.

RANGERS' 20th SCOTTISH LEAGUE CUP TRIUMPH

SECOND ROUND	THIRD ROUND	FOURTH ROUND	SEMI-FINALS	FINAL
Rangers 3				
*Clydebank A0	*Rangers 3			
*Kilmarnock 0	Ayr United 1	*Rangers 4		
Ayr United 1			Rangers 6	
*Falkirk 2	*Albion Rovers 0			
Albion Rovers 3	Hibernian 2	Hibernian 0	(at Celtic Park)	
*Brechin 2				Rangers 4
Hibernian 2				
*Stranraer 1	*Dunfermline 3			
Dunfermline 3	St. Mirren 1	*Dunfermline 2	Dunfermline 1	
*St Mirren 4				
Berwick 0				
*Partick 3	*Partick 1	Partick 0		
Forfar 0	Airdrie 0			
*Airdrie ...... †2				
Raith 2				
*Stirling 1	*Dundee Utd. ...... †2	*Dundee 2		
Dundee Utd. 2	Dundee 2		Dundee 1	
*Dundee 2				
Dumbarton 1	Dundee D2			
*Gr. Morton ...... E†1	*Gr. Morton ...... †3	Aberdeen 1		
Hamilton 1				

(at Celtic Park Sunday, November 24)

98

*Queen's Park 0
Aberdeen 2

Aberdeen 7

Hearts 3

*East Stirling .....†1
Alloa B1

*Alloa B1

Celtic ....†0
(at Easter Road)

*Clyde 1
Celtic 3

Celtic 5

*East Fife 1
St. Johnstone 5

*St Johnstone ...†1

*Hearts 1

Hearts 3

Stenhousemuir 1
*Hearts 3

Hearts 3

Celtic 3
*Hearts 3

FIRST ROUND: Albion 4, Arbroath 0; Brechin 3, Montrose 0; Clyde 1, Inverness CT 0†; Cowdenbeath 1, Forfar 2†; East Stirling 1, Alloa 3†; Queens Park 3, Ross County 1†; Stranraer 2, Queen of the South 0.

(* Drawn at home. † After extra time. A – played at Partick Thistle. B – played at Firhill Park. C – Hearts won 5-4 on pens. D – Dundee won 4-2 on pens. E – Morton won 4-3 on pens.).

SCOTTISH LEAGUE (COCA-COLA) CUP FINAL

HEARTS 3 (Fulton 44, Robertson 59, Weir 90), **RANGERS 4** (McCoist 11, 27; Gascoigne 64, 66)

Celtic Park (48,559), Sunday, November 24, 1996

Hearts: Rousset; Weir, Pointon, MacKay (Capt.) Ritchie, Bruno Paille (Beckford), Fulton, Robertson, Cameron, McCann. **Sub not used:** Goss, McManus. **Booked:** Bruno, Ritchie. **Manager:** Jim Jefferies.

Rangers: Goram; Cleland (Robertson), Moore, Gough (Capt.), Petric, Bjorklund, Miller, Gascoigne, McCoist, Albertz, Laudrup. **Subs not used:** Van Vossen, Snelders (gk). **Booked:** Laudrup, Petric, Miller, Moore, Bjorklund **Manager:** Walter Smith.

Referee: H Dallas (Motherwell). **Half-time:** 1-2.

SCOTTISH LEAGUE CUP FINALS

1946	Aberdeen beat Rangers (3-2)
1947	Rangers beat Aberdeen (4-0)
1948	East Fife beat Falkirk (4-1 after 0-0 draw)
1949	Rangers beat Raith Rovers (2-0)
1950	East Fife beat Dunfermline Athletic (3-0)
1951	Motherwell beat Hibernian (3-0)
1952	Dundee beat Rangers (3-2)
1953	Dundee beat Kilmarnock (2-0)
1954	East Fife beat Partick Thistle (3-2)
1955	Hearts beat Motherwell (4-2)
1956	Aberdeen beat St. Mirren (2-1)
1957	Celtic beat Partick Thistle (3-0 after 0-0 draw)
1958	Celtic beat Rangers (7-1)
1959	Hearts beat Partick Thistle (5-1)
1960	Hearts beat Third Lanark (2-1)
1961	Rangers beat Kilmarnock (2-0)
1962	Rangers beat Hearts (3-1 after 1-1 draw)
1963	Hearts beat Kilmarnock (1-0)
1964	Rangers beat Morton (5-0)
1965	Rangers beat Celtic (2-1)
1966	Celtic beat Rangers (2-1)
1967	Celtic beat Rangers (1-0)
1968	Celtic beat Dundee (5-3)
1969	Celtic beat Hibernian (6-2)
1970	Celtic beat St. Johnstone (1-0)
1971	Rangers beat Celtic (1-0)
1972	Partick Thistle beat Celtic (4-1)
1973	Hibernian beat Celtic (2-1)
1974	Dundee beat Celtic (1-0)
1975	Celtic beat Hibernian (6-3)
1976	Rangers beat Celtic (1-0)
1977†	Aberdeen beat Celtic (2-1)
1978†	Rangers beat Celtic (2-1)
1979	Rangers beat Aberdeen (2-1)
1980	Dundee United beat Aberdeen (3-0 after 0-0 draw)
1981	Dundee United beat Dundee (3-0)
1982	Rangers beat Dundee United (2-1)
1983	Celtic beat Rangers (2-1)
1984†	Rangers beat Celtic (3-2)
1985	Rangers beat Dundee United (1-0)
1986	Aberdeen beat Hibernian (3-0)
1987	Rangers beat Celtic (2-1)
1988†	Rangers beat Aberdeen (5-3 on pens. after 3-3 draw)
1989	Rangers beat Aberdeen (3-2)
1990†	Aberdeen beat Rangers (2-1)
1991†	Rangers beat Celtic (2-1)
1992	Hibernian beat Dunfermline Athletic (2-0)
1993†	Rangers beat Aberdeen (2-1)
1994	Rangers beat Hibernian (2-1)
1995	Raith Rovers beat Celtic (6-5 on pens. after 2-2 draw)
1996	Aberdeen beat Dundee (2-0)
1997	Rangers beat Hearts (4-3)

(† After extra time; Skol Cup 1985-93, Coca-Cola Cup 1995-97)

SUMMARY OF SCOTTISH LEAGUE CUP WINNERS

Rangers	20	Dundee	3	Motherwell	1
Celtic	9	East Fife	3	Partick Thistle	1
Aberdeen	6	Dundee United	2	Raith Rovers	1
Hearts	4	Hibernian	2		

WELSH CUP FINALS
1878-1997

1878 **Wrexham 1** Druids 0	1938 **Shrewsbury 2** Swansea 0
1879 **Newtown 2** Wrexham 1	1939 **South Liverpool 2** Cardiff City 1
1880 **Druids 2** Ruthin 1	1940 **Wellington 4** Swansea 0
1881 **Druids 2** Newtown 0	1947 **Chester 5** Merthyr 1
1882 **Druids 2** Northwich 1	1948 **Lovells 3** Shrewsbury 0
1883 **Wrexham 1** Druids 0	1949 **Merthyr 2** Swansea 0
1884 **Oswestry 3** Druids 2	1950 **Swansea 4** Wrexham 1
1885 **Druids 2** Oswestry 0	1951 **Merthyr 3** Cardiff City 2
1886 **Druids 5** Newtown 1	1952 **Rhyl 4** Merthyr 3
1887 **Chirk 4** Davenham 2	1953 **Rhyl 2** Chester 1
1888 **Chirk 5** Newtown 0	1954 **Flint 2** Chester 1
1889 **Bangor 2** Northwich 1	1955 **Barry 4** Chester 3
1890 **Chirk 1** Wrexham 0	1956 **Cardiff City 3** Swansea 2
1891 **Shrewsbury 5** Wrexham 2	1957 **Wrexham 2** Swansea 1
1892 **Chirk 2** Westminster 1	1958 **Wrexham 2** Chester 0
1893 **Wrexham 2** Chirk 1	1959 **Cardiff City 2** Lovells 0
1894 **Chirk 2** Westminster 0	1960 **Wrexham 1** Cardiff City 0
1895 **Newtown 3** Wrexham 2	1961 **Swansea 3** Bangor 1
1896 **Bangor 3** Wrexham 1	1962 **Bangor 3** Wrexham 1
1897 **Wrexham 2** Newtown 0	1963 **Borough** v Newport 2-1, 0-0
1898 **Druids 2** Wrexham 1	1964 **Cardiff City 2** Bangor 0
1899 **Druids 1** Wrexham 0	1965 **Cardiff City 3** Wrexham 0
1900 **Aberwystwyth 3** Druids 0	1966 **Swansea 2** Chester 1
1901 **Oswestry 1** Druids 0	1967 **Cardiff City** v Wrexham 2-2, 2-1
1902 **Wellington 1** Wrexham 0	1968 **Cardiff City** v Hereford 2-0, 4-1
1903 **Wrexham 8** Aberaman 0	1969 **Cardiff City** v Swansea 3-1, 2-0
1904 **Druids 3** Aberdare 0	1970 **Cardiff City** v Chester 1-0, 4-0
1905 **Wrexham 3** Aberdare 0	1971 **Cardiff City** v Wrexham 1-0, 3-1
1906 **Wellington 3** Whitchurch 2	1972 **Wrexham** v Cardiff City 2-1, 1-1
1907 **Oswestry 2** Whitchurch 0	1973 **Cardiff City** v Bangor 0-1, 5-0
1908 **Chester 3** Connah's Quay 1	1974 **Cardiff C.** v Stourbridge 1-0, 1-0
1909 **Wrexham 1** Chester 0	1975 **Wrexham** v Cardiff City 2-1, 3-1
1910 **Wrexham 2** Chester 0	1976 **Cardiff City** v Hereford 3-3, 3-2
1911 **Wrexham 6** Connah's Quay 1	1977 **Shr'sbury** v Cardiff City 1-2, 3-0
1912 **Cardiff City 3** Pontypridd 0	1978 **Wrexham** v Bangor 2-1, 1-0
1913 **Swansea 1** Pontypridd 0	1979 **Shrewsbury** v Wrexham 1-1, 1-0
1914 **Wrexham 3** Llanelli 0	1980 **Newport Co.** v Shr'sbury 2-1, 3-0
1915 **Wrexham 1** Swansea 0	1981 **Swansea** v Hereford 1-0, 1-1
1920 **Cardiff City 2** Wrexham 1	1982 **Swansea** v Cardiff 0-0, 2-1
1921 **Wrexham 3** Pontypridd 1	1983 **Swansea** v Wrexham 2-1, 2-0
1922 **Cardiff City 2** Ton Pentre 0	1984 **Shrewsbury** v Wrexham 2-0, 0-0
1923 **Cardiff City 3** Aberdare 2	1985 **Shrewsbury** v Bangor 3-1, 2-0
1924 **Wrexham 1** Merthyr 0	1986 **Wrexham 2** K'minster 1
1925 **Wrexham 3** Flint 1	1987 **Merthyr 1** Newport County 0
1926 **Ebbw Vale 3** Swansea 2	1988 **Cardiff City 2** Wrexham 0
1927 **Cardiff City 2** Rhyl 0	1989 **Swansea 5** K'minster 0
1928 **Cardiff City 2** Bangor 0	1990 **Hereford 2** Wrexham 1
1929 **Connah's Quay 3** Cardiff City 0	1991 **Swansea 2** Wrexham 0
1930 **Cardiff City 4** Rhyl 2	1992 **Cardiff City 1** Hednesford 0
1931 **Wrexham 7** Shrewsbury 0	1993 **Cardiff City 5** Rhyl 0
1932 **Swansea 2** Wrexham 0	1994 **Barry Town 2** Cardiff City 1
1933 **Chester 2** Wrexham 0	1995 **Wrexham 2** Cardiff City 1
1934 **Bristol City 3** Tranmere 0	1996 **Liansantffraid 3** Barry Town 3
1935 **Tranmere 1** Chester 0	(Liansantffraid won 3-2 on pens).
1936 **Crewe 2** Chester 0	1997 **Barry Town 2** Cwmbran 1
1937 **Crewe 3** Rhyl 1	

IRISH F.A. CUP WINNERS

Year	Winner	Year	Winner	Year	Winner	Year	Winner
1881	Moyola Park	1911	Shelbourne	1940	Ballymena	1969	Ards
1882	Queen's Island	1912	Linfield	1941	Celtic	1970	Linfield
1883	Cliftonville	1913	Linfield	1942	Linfield	1971	Distillery
1884	Distillery	1914	Glentoran	1943	Celtic	1972	Coleraine
1885	Distillery	1915	Linfield	1944	Celtic	1973	Glentoran
1886	Distillery	1916	Linfield	1945	Linfield	1974	Ards
1887	Ulster	1917	Glentoran	1946	Linfield	1975	Coleraine
1888	Cliftonville	1918	Celtic	1947	Celtic	1976	Carrick Rgrs.
1889	Distillery	1919	Linfield	1948	Linfield	1977	Coleraine
1890	Gordon H.	1920	Shelbourne	1949	Derry City	1978	Linfield
1891	Linfield	1921	Glentoran	1950	Linfield	1979	Cliftonville
1892	Linfield	1922	Linfield	1951	Glentoran	1980	Linfield
1893	Linfield	1923	Linfield	1952	Ards	1981	Ballymena Utd.
1894	Distillery	1924	Queen's Island	1953	Linfield	1982	Linfield
1895	Linfield	1925	Distillery	1954	Derry City	1983	Glentoran
1896	Distillery	1926	Celtic	1955	Dundela	1984	Ballymena Utd.
1897	Cliftonville	1927	Ards	1956	Distillery	1985	Glentoran
1898	Linfield	1928	Willowfield	1957	Glenavon	1986	Glentoran
1899	Linfield	1929	Ballymena	1958	Ballymena	1987	Glentoran
1900	Cliftonville	1930	Linfield	1959	Glenavon	1988	Glentoran
1901	Cliftonville	1931	Linfield	1960	Linfield	1989	Ballymena Utd.
1902	Linfield	1932	Glentoran	1961	Glenavon	1990	Glentoran
1903	Distillery	1933	Glentoran	1962	Linfield	1991	Portadown
1904	Linfield	1934	Linfield	1963	Linfield	1992	Glenavon
1905	Distillery	1935	Glentoran	1964	Derry City	1993	Bangor
1906	Shelbourne	1936	Linfield	1965	Coleraine	1994	Linfield
1907	Cliftonville	1937	Celtic	1966	Glentoran	1995	Linfield
1908	Bohemians	1938	Celtic	1967	Crusaders	1996	Glentoran
1909	Cliftonville	1939	Linfield	1968	Crusaders	1997	Glenavon
1910	Distillery						

IRISH LEAGUE CHAMPIONS

Year	Champion	Year	Champion	Year	Champion	Year	Champion
1891	Linfield	1915	Celtic	1951	Glentoran	1976	Crusaders
1892	Linfield	1916	Celtic	1952	Glenavon	1977	Glentoran
1893	Linfield	1921	Glentoran	1953	Glentoran	1978	Linfield
1894	Glentoran	1922	Linfield	1954	Linfield	1979	Linfield
1895	Linfield	1923	Linfield	1955	Linfield	1980	Linfield
1896	Distillery	1924	Queen's Island	1956	Linfield	1981	Glentoran
1897	Glentoran	1925	Glentoran	1957	Glenavon	1982	Linfield
1898	Linfield	1926	Celtic	1958	Ards	1983	Linfield
1899	Distillery	1927	Celtic	1959	Linfield	1984	Linfield
1900	Celtic	1928	Celtic	1960	Glenavon	1985	Linfield
1901	Distillery	1929	Celtic	1961	Linfield	1986	Linfield
1902	Linfield	1930	Linfield	1962	Linfield	1987	Linfield
1903	Distillery	1931	Glentoran	1963	Distillery	1988	Glentoran
1904	Linfield	1932	Linfield	1964	Glentoran	1989	Linfield
1905	Glentoran	1933	Celtic	1965	Derry City	1990	Portadown
1906	Cliftonville	1934	Linfield	1966	Linfield	1991	Portadown
1907	Linfield	1935	Linfield	1967	Glentoran	1992	Glentoran
1908	Linfield	1936	Celtic	1968	Glentoran	1993	Linfield
1909	Linfield	1937	Celtic	1969	Linfield	1994	Linfield
1910	Cliftonville	1938	Celtic	1970	Glentoran	1995	Crusaders
1911	Linfield	1939	Celtic	1971	Linfield	1996	Portadown
1912	Glentoran	1940	Celtic	1972	Glentoran	1997	Crusaders
1913	Glentoran	1948	Celtic	1973	Crusaders		
1914	Linfield	1949	Linfield	1974	Coleraine		
		1950	Linfield	1975	Linfield		

REPUBLIC OF IRELAND: All-time Winners

Season	League	FAI Cup
1921-22	St.James' Gate	St.James' Gate
1922-23	Shamrock R.	Alton United
1923-24	Bohemians	Athlone Town
1924-25	Shamrock R.	Shamrock R.
1925-26	Shelbourne	Fordsons
1926-27	Shamrock R.	Drumcondra
1927-28	Bohemians	Bohemians
1928-29	Shelbourne	Shamrock R.
1929-30	Bohemians	Shamrock R.
1930-31	Shelbourne	Shamrock R.
1931-32	Shamrock R.	Shamrock R.
1932-33	Shamrock R.	Shamrock R.
1933-34	Bohemians	Cork
1934-35	Dolphin	Bohemians
1935-36	Bohemians	Shamrock R.
1936-37	Sligo Rovers	Waterford
1937-38	Shamrock R.	St.James' Gate
1938-39	Shamrock R.	Shelbourne
1939-40	St.James' Gate	Shamrock R.
1940-41	Cork United	Cork United
1941-42	Cork United	Dundalk
1942-43	Cork United	Drumcondra
1943-44	Shelbourne	Shamrock R.
1944-45	Cork United	Shamrock R.
1945-46	Cork United	Drumcondra
1946-47	Shelbourne	Cork United
1947-48	Drumcondra	Shamrock R.
1948-49	Drumcondra	Dundalk
1949-50	Cork Athletic	Transport
1950-51	Cork Athletic	Cork Athletic
1951-52	St.Patrick's Ath.	Dundalk
1952-53	Shelbourne	Cork Athletic
1953-54	Shamrock R.	Drumcondra
1954-55	St.Patrick's Ath.	Shamrock R.
1955-56	St.Patrick's Ath.	Shamrock R.
1956-57	Shamrock R.	Drumcondra
1957-58	Drumcondra	Dundalk
1958-59	Shamrock R.	St.Patrick's Ath.
1959-60	Limerick	Shelbourne
1960-61	Drumcondra	St.Patrick's Ath.
1961-62	Shelbourne	Shamrock R.
1962-63	Dundalk	Shelbourne
1963-64	Shamrock R.	Shamrock R.
1964-65	Drumcondra	Shamrock R.
1965-66	Waterford	Shamrock R.
1966-67	Dundalk	Shamrock R.
1967-68	Waterford	Shamrock R.
1968-69	Waterford	Shamrock R.
1969-70	Waterford	Bohemians
1970-71	Cork Hibs.	Limerick
1971-72	Waterford	Cork Hibs.
1972-73	Waterford	Cork Hibs.
1973-74	Cork Celtic	Finn Harps
1974-75	Bohemians	Home Farm
1975-76	Dundalk	Bohemians
1976-77	Sligo Rovers	Dundalk
1977-78	Bohemians	Shamrock R.
1978-79	Dundalk	Dundalk
1979-80	Limerick United	Waterford
1980-81	Athlone Town	Dundalk
1981-82	Dundalk	Limerick United
1982-83	Athlone Town	Sligo Rovers
1983-84	Shamrock R.	Univ. Cllge. Dublin
1984-85	Shamrock R.	Shamrock R.
1985-86	Shamrock R.	Shamrock R.
1986-87	Shamrock R.	Shamrock R.
1987-88	Dundalk	Dundalk
1988-89	Derry City	Derry City
1989-90	St.Patrick's Ath.	Bray Wanderers
1990-91	Dundalk	Galway United
1991-92	Shelbourne	Bohemians
1992-93	Cork City	Shelbourne
1993-94	Shamrock R.	Sligo Rovers
1994-95	Dundalk	Derry City
1995-96	St. Patrick's Ath.	Shelbourne
1996-97	Derry City	Shelbourne

IRISH FOOTBALL 1996-97

FAI HARP LAGER NATIONAL LEAGUE

PREMIER DIVISION

	P	W	D	L	F	A	Pts
Derry City	33	19	10	4	58	27	67
Bohemians	33	16	9	8	43	32	57
Shelbourne	33	15	9	9	52	36	54
Cork City	33	15	9	9	38	24	54
St. Patrick's Ath.	33	13	14	6	45	33	53
Sligo Rovers	33	12	11	10	43	43	47
Shamrock Rovers	33	10	13	10	43	46	43
U.C.D.	33	12	7	14	34	39	43
Finn Harps	33	10	9	14	41	43	39
Dundalk	33	9	9	15	32	50	30
Bray Wanderers	33	5	8	20	30	59	23
Home Farm/Everton	33	3	10	20	27	53	19

Top Scorer: 16 Tony Cousins (Shamrock Rovers) and Stephen Geoghegan (Shelbourne); **Player of the Year:** Peter Hutton (Derry City); **Young Player of the Year:** Gary Beckett (Derry City); **Personality of the Year:** Peter Tutton (Derry City).

FIRST DIVISION

	P	W	D	L	F	A	Pts
Kilkenny City	27	15	10	2	47	20	55
Drogheda Utd.	27	12	8	7	44	27	44
Waterford Utd.	27	12	8	7	41	28	44
Athlone Town	27	10	7	10	40	39	37
Cobh Ramblers	27	9	8	10	34	28	35
Galway Utd.	27	9	8	10	33	38	35
Longford Town	27	7	13	7	31	38	34
Monaghan Utd.	27	7	9	11	30	46	30
St. Francis	27	7	7	13	29	33	28
Limerick F.C.	27	4	8	15	23	55	20

Top Scorer: 13 Tony Izzi (Cobh Ramblers); **Player of the Year:** Paul Cashin (Kilkenny City).

FAI HARP LAGER CUP FINAL
(Dalymount Park, Dublin, May 4)

SHELBOURNE 2 (Campbell, S. Geoghegan), **Derry City 0**

Shelbourne: Gough; Vaudequin (Costello) D. Geoghegan, Campbell, Neville, Scully, Flood, O'Rourke, Sheridan, S. Geoghegan, Rutherford (Baker).

Derry City: Devine; Boyle (Semple), Dunne, Hutton, Curran, Dykes, Hargan, Hegarty, Coyle, Beckett, Keddy.

Referee: D. O'Hanlan (Waterford)

BORD FAI LEAGUE CUP FINAL

1st leg, Terryland Park, December 17: Galway Utd. 3 (Herrick, Killeen, Brennan), **Cork City 1** (Caulfield)

2nd leg, Turner's Cross, January 1: Cork City 1 (O'Connell), **Galway Utd. 1** (Coleman). **Galway Utd. won 4-2 on aggregate.**

SMIRNOFF IRISH LEAGUE

PREMIER DIVISION

	P	W	D	L	F	A	Pts
Crusaders	28	12	10	6	39	26	46
Coleraine	28	10	13	5	37	31	43
Glentoran	28	10	11	7	36	30	41
Portadown	28	10	8	10	35	32	38
Linfield	28	10	8	10	35	33	38
Glenavon	28	8	11	9	35	34	35
Cliftonville	28	7	9	12	23	38	30
Ards	28	5	10	13	33	49	25

● Ards not relegated. Premier Division extended to ten clubs for 1997-98, with Ballymena and Omagh both promoted from the First Division.

Top Scorer: 15 Gary Haylock (Portadown); **Player of the Year:** Stephen Baxter (Crusaders); **Young Player of the Year:** Andy Kirk (Glentoran); **Manager of the Year:** Roy Walker (Crusaders).

FIRST DIVISION

	P	W	D	L	F	A	Pts
Ballymena	28	21	2	5	4	17	65
Omagh	28	15	5	8	40	39	50
Bangor	28	15	4	9	42	29	49
Ballyclare	28	11	4	13	44	42	37
Newry Town	28	10	5	13	32	35	35
Distillery	28	10	4	14	31	37	34
Larne	28	9	5	14	34	48	32
Carrick Rangers	28	5	3	20	25	50	18

Top Scorers: 14 David Rainey (Ballyclare) and Ciaran Feehan (Ballymena).

BASS IRISH CUP FINAL

(Windsor Park, Belfast, May 3)

GLENTORAN 1 (Grant), CLIFTONVILLE 0

Glenavon: O'Neill; Caffrey, Glendenning, Doherty, Byrne, Swyft, Johnston, McCoy (Murphy), Ferguson, Grant, Gregg (Williamson).

Cliftonville: Reece; Hill (Strang), Flynn, Tabb, Davy, O'Neill, McCann, Collins, Small (Toland), Stokes, Donnelly.

Referee: H. Barr (Bangor).

BASS IRISH CUP 1997-98

Sept. 27	First Round	Feb. 21	Sixth Round
Oct. 18	Second Round	Mar. 14	Seventh Round
Nov. 22	Third Round	Apr. 3/4	Semi-finals
Dec. 6	Fourth Round	May 2	Final
Jan. 24	Fifth Round		

MAN OF MANY A MILLION WORDS

Malcolm Brodie has reported every Northern Ireland match since 1944, home and away. He has covered every Irish Cup Final in that period, and the last 11 World Cup final series, from Switzerland in 1954 ("I would have been in Brazil in 1950, but I had just got married").

He has been at Wembley for all but three F.A. Cup Finals since the war – he was abroad with Northern Ireland in 1953, 1994 and 1997. He has missed only two of 50 Football Writers' Association dinners, again when on International duty.

Malcolm joined the *Belfast Telegraph* in 1942 and was Sports Editor from 1950-91. Now 70 ("I feel 45"), he continues freelance to pour out his words on Irish football in various directions, and is the *News of the World's* correspondent in Belfast.

He has written ten books, including histories of the Irish F.A., the Irish League, the Belfast Telegraph, and of the Linfield, Glentoran and Glenavon clubs. Since 1964, he has produced the Northern Ireland Soccer Yearbook, from which all profits go to charity.

In 1978, the Queen added an E to his initials to make him an MBE for his extraordinary services to journalism. To have seen Malcolm Brodie operate since we were in Sweden together at the 1958 World Cup is to have observed a true professional at work. France 98 beckons one of the best of colleagues, too.

Albert Sewell

£2½m. THAT'S GONE OUT THE GAME

Reported settlements in **top ten pay-offs to departed managers:** 1 **Ossie Ardiles**, sacked by Tottenham, Nov. 1994, **£500,000**; 2 **Bruce Rioch**, sacked by Arsenal, Aug. 1996, **£400,000**; 3 **Keith Burkinshaw**, sacked by WBA, Oct. 1994, **£300,000**; 4 **Graham Taylor**, resigned at Wolves, Nov. 1995, **£250,000**; 5 **Terry Butcher**, sacked by Coventry, Jan. 1992, **£214,000**; 6 **Mike Walker**, sacked by Everton, Nov. 1994, **£200,000**; 7 **Ron Atkinson**, sacked by Aston Villa, Nov. 1994, **£200,000**; 8 **Roy McFarland**, sacked by Bolton, Jan. 1996, **£200,000**; 9 **Joe Royle**, left Everton, Mar. 1997, **£200,000**; 10 **Barry Fry**, sacked by Birmingham, May 1996, **£150,000**.

HULL CITY BOUGHT OUT

David Lloyd, British David Cup tennis captain, and business partner **Tim Wilby** completed the £2.5m. take-over of Third Division **Hull City** from the Needler family in June. They plan a £30m., 25,000 all-seat stadium, to be shared with Rugby League club Hull Sharks.

OTHER LEAGUES 1996-97

GM VAUXHALL CONFERENCE

		P	W	D	L	F	A	GD	Pts
1	Macclesfield Town	42	27	9	6	80	30	+50	90
2	Kidderminster Harriers	42	26	7	9	84	42	+42	85
3	Stevenage Borough	42	24	10	8	87	53	+34	82
4	Morecambe	42	19	9	14	69	56	+13	66
5	Woking	42	18	10	14	71	63	+8	64
6	Northwich Victoria	42	17	12	13	61	54	+7	63
7	Farnborough Town	42	16	13	13	58	53	+5	61
8	Hednesford Town	42	16	12	14	52	50	+2	60
9	Telford United	42	16	10	16	46	56	-10	58
10	Gateshead	42	15	11	16	59	63	-4	56
11	Southport	42	15	10	17	51	61	-10	55
12	Rushden & Diamonds	42	14	11	17	61	63	-2	53
13	Stalybridge Celtic	42	14	10	18	53	58	-5	52
14	Kettering Town	42	14	9	19	53	62	-9	51
15	Hayes	42	12	14	16	54	55	-1	50
16	Slough Town	42	12	14	16	62	65	-3	50
17	Dover Athletic	42	12	14	16	57	68	-11	50
18	Welling United	42	13	9	20	50	60	-10	48
19	Halifax Town	42	12	12	18	55	74	-19	48
20	Bath City	42	12	11	19	53	80	-27	47
21	Bromsgrove Rovers	42	12	5	25	41	67	-26	41
22	Altrincham	42	9	12	21	49	73	-24	39

● Macclesfield Town promoted to Football League.

CONFERENCE AWARDS

Prize money – Champions: Macclesfield £10,000; Kidderminster (runners-up) £5,000; Stevenage Borough (third) £3,000.
Manager of Year: Sammy McIlroy (Macclesfield)
Player of Year: Lee Hughes (Kidderminster)
Goalscorer of Year: Lee Hughes (Kidderminster – 30 goals)
Relegated: Bath, Bromsgrove (both to Dr. Martens League), Altrincham (to Unibond League).
Promoted to Conference: Yeovil Town (ICIS League), Cheltenham Town (Dr. Martens League) and Leek Town (Unibond League). They are joined as new members by Hereford United (relegated from Football League).

GM VAUXHALL CONFERENCE CHAMPIONS

1979-80	Altrincham	**1988-89**	* Maidstone United
1980-81	Altrincham	**1989-90**	* Darlington
1981-82	Runcorn	**1990-91**	* Barnet
1982-83	Enfield	**1991-92**	* Colchester United
1983-84	Maidstone United	**1992-93**	* Wycombe Wanderers
1984-85	Wealdstone	**1993-94**	Kidderminster H.
1985-86	Enfield	**1994-95**	Macclesfield Town
1986-87	* Scarborough	**1995-96**	Stevenage Borough
1987-88	* Lincoln City	**1996-97**	* Macclesfield Town

(* Promoted to Football League)

Conference – Record Attendance: 9,432, Lincoln City v Wycombe, May 2, 1988.

PONTIN'S LEAGUE

DIVISION ONE

		P	W	D	L	F	A	Pts
1	Manchester United	24	15	6	3	55	24	51
2	Blackburn Rovers	24	13	4	7	28	23	43
3	Sheffield Wednesday	24	12	4	8	42	32	40
4	Stoke City	24	11	2	11	34	37	35
5	Leeds United	24	10	4	10	29	34	34
6	Derby County	24	9	6	9	41	32	33
7	Birmingham City	24	8	7	9	34	31	31
8	Nottingham Forest	24	9	4	11	33	45	31
9	Tranmere Rovers	24	9	3	12	48	48	30
10	Everton	24	8	6	10	31	42	30
11	Liverpool	24	8	5	11	32	39	29
12	Bolton Wdrs	24	7	5	12	31	38	26
13	Oldham Athletic	24	5	8	11	27	40	23

DIVISION TWO

		P	W	D	L	F	A	Pts
1	Preston North End	24	16	6	2	41	14	54
2	Aston Villa	24	16	4	4	62	25	52
3	Notts County	24	12	5	7	38	35	41
4	Middlesbrough	24	10	8	6	42	36	38
5	Wolverhampton Wdrs	24	11	5	8	37	32	38
6	Leicester City	24	11	3	10	37	42	36
7	Sunderland	24	9	8	7	47	37	35
8	Huddersfield Town	24	8	5	11	32	39	29
9	Port Vale	24	7	6	11	30	37	27
10	Coventry City	24	6	8	10	22	25	26
11	West Bromwich Albion	24	6	6	12	21	36	24
12	Sheffield United	24	7	3	14	26	44	24
13	Blackpool	24	1	5	18	12	46	8

DIVISION THREE

		P	W	D	L	F	A	Pts
1	Grimsby Town	24	15	5	4	54	29	50
2	Manchester City	24	14	6	4	43	26	48
3	York City	24	13	6	5	41	30	45
4	Wrexham	24	13	5	6	51	30	44
6	Barnsley	24	12	5	7	53	39	41
6	Shrewsbury Town	24	10	5	9	42	38	35
7	Rotherham United	24	10	4	10	29	30	34
8	Burnley	24	9	5	10	46	41	32
9	Carlisle United	24	10	2	12	37	38	32
10	Stockport County	24	7	5	12	34	43	26
11	Bradford City	24	7	5	12	36	47	26
12	Hull City	24	7	4	13	27	45	25
13	Mansfield Town	24	0	1	23	29	86	1

		P	W	D	L	F	A	Pts
1	Rochdale	20	14	4	2	39	20	46
2	Lincoln City	20	11	7	2	35	20	40
3	Walsall	20	9	8	3	35	16	35
4	Doncaster Rovers	20	7	5	8	37	35	26
5	Bury	20	6	7	7	20	25	25
6	Chesterfield	20	7	4	9	25	31	25
7	Wigan Athletic	20	6	5	9	24	33	23
8	Chester City	20	6	4	10	26	30	22
9	Scunthorpe United	20	6	4	10	29	35	22
10	Darlington	20	4	7	9	25	37	19
11	Scarborough	20	5	3	12	22	35	18

FOOTBALL COMBINATION
(Sponsors: Avon Insurance)

		P	W	D	L	F	A	Pts
1	Wimbledon	22	14	5	3	44	25	47
2	Portsmouth	22	14	2	6	40	23	44
3	Tottenham	22	13	4	5	50	26	43
4	Ipswich	22	12	5	5	41	18	41
5	Crystal Palace	22	10	6	6	37	32	36
6	Arsenal	22	10	5	7	49	30	35
7	Brighton	22	9	8	5	40	31	35
8	Luton	22	10	5	7	32	24	35
9	Swindon	22	9	5	8	37	35	32
10	Chelsea	22	9	5	8	31	35	32
11	Q.P.R.	22	9	4	9	37	37	31
12	Watford	22	7	8	7	28	32	29
13	Swansea	22	7	7	8	24	33	28
14	Charlton	22	7	6	9	30	38	27
15	Southampton	22	7	5	10	34	40	26
16	Bournemouth	22	7	5	10	34	43	26
17	Millwall	22	7	4	11	30	38	25
18	Bristol City	22	6	5	11	38	37	23
19	Oxford	22	6	5	11	37	40	23
20	West Ham	22	6	4	12	29	45	22
21	Bristol Rovers	22	6	4	12	22	42	22
22	Cardiff	22	4	7	11	17	42	19
23	Norwich	22	4	6	12	32	47	18

SOUTH-EAST COUNTIES LEAGUE

DIVISION ONE

		P	W	D	L	F	A	Pts
1	Norwich City	30	20	6	4	66	26	46
2	Chelsea	30	19	4	7	61	41	42
3	West Ham United	30	16	7	7	74	31	39
4	Arsenal	30	14	7	9	51	38	35
5	Tottenham Hotspur	30	14	6	10	46	31	34
6	Watford	30	16	2	12	60	50	34
7	Queens Park Rangers	30	14	5	11	53	44	33
8	Gillingham	30	12	9	9	50	47	33
9	Ipswich Town	30	11	8	11	57	62	30
10	Portsmouth	30	11	4	15	45	54	26
11	Millwall	30	10	6	14	47	64	26
12	Cambridge United	30	7	8	15	34	55	22
13	Charlton Athletic	30	6	9	15	46	66	21
14	Southend United	30	7	7	16	38	62	21
15	Fulham	30	8	5	17	36	65	21
16	Leyton Orient	30	3	11	16	35	63	17

Div. 2 winners: Luton Town, **runners-up** Crystal Palace.

HOW JOHNNY HAYNES MADE HISTORY

Related to the sky-high wages paid to today's stars – with many Premier League players on upwards of £10,000 a week and £20,000 not uncommon – this extract from the *BBC GRANDSTAND BOOK OF SPORT*, published in 1962, tells of the deal that took footballers on the first step towards Millionaires' Row.

Only the previous Saturday (April 15, 1961) Johnny Haynes, one of the most creative inside-forwards of any era, had captained England to their record victory against Scotland, 9-3 at Wembley. Now, as 26-year-old Haynes prepared for Fulham's First Division home match against Blackburn Rovers two telegrams were handed to the club's comedian-chairman Tommy Trinder.

The first, from AC Milan said: "We will pay £100,000 for Haynes." The second, from AS Roma, informed Fulham that their representative was on his way to London to outbid any offer by Milan. Trinder said: "We don't want to lose Johnny, but the decision is up to him."

Haynes would earn enormous money in Italy, whereas in England players were restricted to the maximum £20 a week. He had been with Fulham eleven years since he left school. The England side was built round him and the passes he threaded through defences from 20 and 30 yards, but a move abroad might write off his International career.

Johnny went home after Fulham's 1-1 draw with Blackburn to weigh it all up. Next morning, he rang Trinder, who invited him over for a cup of tea. The business part of their chat lasted three minutes.

Trinder asked Fulham's star player what he wanted to stay in England. Haynes didn't know. Trinder suggested a figure – and that was how Johnny Haynes became Britain's first £100-a-week footballer. As he accepted, he said: "I never wanted to go to Italy, anyway."

Haynes's first-class career continued for nine more seasons. He made 594 League appearances (146 goals) for his only club and was capped 56 times by England. Now 62, he lives in Edinburgh, occasionally watches Heart of Midlothian, and sometimes travels to London to visit his old home at Craven Cottage.

UNIBOND LEAGUE

PREMIER DIVISION

	P	W	D	L	F	A	GD	Pts
1 Leek Town	44	28	9	7	71	35	+36	93
2 Bishop Auckland	44	23	14	7	88	43	+45	83
3 Hyde United	44	22	16	6	93	46	+47	82
4 Emley	44	23	12	9	89	54	+35	81
5 Barrow	44	23	11	10	71	45	+26	80
6 Boston United	44	23	10	11	74	47	+27	79
7 Blyth Spartans	44	22	11	11	74	49	+25	77
8 Marine	44	20	15	9	53	37	+16	75
9 Guiseley	44	20	11	13	63	54	+9	71
10 Gainsborough Trinity	44	18	12	14	65	46	+19	66
11 Accrington Stanley	44	18	12	14	77	70	+7	66
12 Runcorn	44	15	15	14	63	62	+1	60
13 Chorley	44	16	9	19	69	66	+3	57
14 Winsford United	44	13	14	17	50	56	-6	53
15 Knowsley United	44	12	14	18	58	79	-21	49
16 Colwyn Bay	44	11	13	20	60	76	-16	46
17 Lancaster City	44	12	9	23	48	75	-27	45
18 Frickley Athletic	44	12	8	24	62	91	-29	44
19 Spennymoor United	44	10	10	24	52	68	-16	40
20 Bamber Bridge	44	11	7	26	59	99	-40	40
21 Alfreton Town	44	8	13	23	45	83	-38	37
22 Witton Albion	44	5	14	25	41	91	-50	29
23 Buxton	44	5	12	27	33	86	-53	27

(Knowsley: –1 point deducted)
First Div. – 1 Radcliffe Borough: 2 Leigh.

LEAGUE OF WALES

	P	W	D	L	F	A	GD	Pts
1 Barry Town	40	33	6	1	128	26	+102	105
2 Inter Cable-tel	40	26	6	8	80	31	+49	84
3 Ebbw Vale	40	23	9	8	87	40	+47	78
4 Caernarfon Town	40	23	9	8	81	58	+23	78
5 Newton	40	22	5	13	74	49	+25	71
6 Llansantffraid	40	19	12	9	78	54	+24	69
7 Conway United	40	20	8	12	66	44	+22	68
8 Bangor City	40	20	5	15	82	62	+20	65
9 Cwmbran Town	40	19	8	13	71	61	+10	65
10 CPD Porthmadog	40	18	8	14	64	60	+4	62
11 Connah's Quay Nomads	40	16	9	15	62	64	-2	57
12 Cemaes Bay	40	13	10	17	62	72	-10	49
13 Aberystwyth Town	40	13	8	19	67	82	-15	47
14 Caersws	40	11	9	20	53	77	-24	42
15 Flint Town Utd	40	11	8	21	48	76	-28	41
16 Carmarthen Town	40	11	7	22	41	79	-38	40
17 Welshpool	40	10	9	21	50	80	-30	39
18 Ton Pentre	40	12	3	25	59	99	-40	39
19 Rhyl	40	10	8	22	51	71	-20	38
20 Holywell Town	40	7	8	25	52	81	-29	29
21 Briton Ferry Athletic	40	5	1	34	39	129	-90	16

FEDERATION BREWERY NORTHERN LEAGUE

DIVISION ONE

	P	W	D	L	F	A	GD	Pts
1 Whitby Town	38	32	3	3	130	36	+94	99
2 Billingham Synthonia	38	28	6	4	109	46	+63	90
3 Bedlington Terriers	38	28	5	5	113	37	+76	86
4 Durham City	38	19	11	8	69	50	+19	68
5 Crook Town	38	19	9	10	88	56	+32	66
6 Morpeth Town	38	20	6	12	73	56	+17	66
7 Guisborough Town	38	17	9	12	68	54	+14	60
8 Tow Law Town	38	14	11	13	76	70	+6	53
9 South Shields	38	13	11	14	52	63	-11	50
10 Murton	38	15	5	18	58	81	-23	50
11 Consett	38	12	11	15	66	59	+7	47
12 Dunston FB	38	12	10	16	64	70	-6	46
13 Shildon	38	13	7	18	73	87	-14	46
14 Easington	38	12	8	18	56	74	-18	44
15 RTM Newcastle	38	13	3	22	66	87	-21	42
16 Seaham Red Star	38	7	14	17	50	83	-33	35
17 Stockton	38	8	10	20	71	106	-35	34
18 Chester-le-St Town	38	7	12	19	53	86	-33	33
19 Whickham	38	5	6	27	38	98	-60	21
20 West Auckland	38	6	3	29	43	117	-74	18

(3 points deducted: Bedlington and W. Auckland)
Div. 2 – 1 Northallerton; 2 Billingham Town; 3 Jarrow Roofing.

CARLING NORTH WEST LEAGUE

DIVISION ONE

	P	W	D	L	F	A	GD	Pts
1 Trafford	42	29	7	6	99	38	+61	94
2 Newcastle Town	42	27	7	8	71	31	+40	88
3 Clitheroe	42	23	14	5	75	36	+39	83
4 Penrith	42	23	10	9	75	49	+26	79
5 Burscough	42	22	9	11	68	48	+20	75
6 Eastwood Hanley	42	20	10	12	64	51	+13	70
7 Mossley	42	20	8	14	79	58	+21	68
8 Blackpool Rovers	42	17	16	9	70	47	+23	67
9 Prescot Cables	42	17	11	14	68	60	+8	62
10 Vauxhall GM	42	14	15	13	70	69	+1	57
11 Nantwich Town	42	14	11	17	74	74	0	53
12 Glossop North End	42	14	11	17	56	67	-11	53
13 Bootle	42	15	8	19	61	73	-12	53
14 St Helens Town	42	14	6	22	65	79	-14	48
15 Atherton Collieries	42	12	9	21	63	85	-22	45
16 Kidsgrove Athletic	42	10	14	18	53	73	-20	44
17 Rossendale United	42	11	9	22	51	76	-25	42
18 Chadderton	42	10	11	21	49	80	-31	41
19 Holker Old Boys	42	10	9	23	60	80	-20	39
20 Maine Road	42	9	11	22	44	80	-36	38
21 Darwen	42	9	10	23	49	81	-32	37
22 Salford City	42	8	12	22	53	82	-29	36

Div. 2 – 1 Ramsbottom Utd; 2 Haslingden

DR. MARTENS LEAGUE

PREMIER DIVISION

	P	W	D	L	F	A	GD	Pts
1 Gresley Rovers	42	25	10	7	75	40	+35	85
2 Cheltenham Town	42	21	11	10	76	44	+32	74
3 Gloucester City	42	21	10	11	81	56	+25	73
4 Halesowen Town	42	21	10	11	77	54	+23	73
5 King's Lynn	42	20	8	14	65	61	+4	68
6 Burton Albion	42	18	12	12	70	53	+17	66
7 Nuneaton Borough	42	19	9	14	61	52	+9	66
8 Sittingbourne	42	19	7	16	76	65	+11	64
9 Merthyr Tydfil	42	17	7	18	69	61	+8	60
10 Worcester City	42	15	14	13	52	50	+2	59
11 Atherstone United	42	15	13	14	46	47	-1	58
12 Salisbury City	42	15	13	14	57	66	-9	58
13 Sudbury Town	42	16	7	19	72	72	0	55
14 Gravesend & Northfleet	42	16	7	19	63	73	-10	55
15 Dorchester Town	42	14	9	19	62	66	-4	51
16 Hastings Town	42	12	15	15	49	60	-11	51
17 Crawley Town	42	13	8	21	49	67	-18	47
18 Cambridge City	42	11	13	18	57	65	-8	46
19 Ashford Town	42	9	18	15	53	79	-26	45
20 Baldock Town	42	11	8	23	52	90	-38	41
21 Newport AFC	42	9	13	20	49	70	-20	40
22 Chelmsford City	42	6	14	22	49	70	-21	32

Midland Div. – 1 Tamworth, 2 Rothwell Town.
Southern Div. – 1 Forest Green Rovers, 2 St. Leonards.

ICIS LEAGUE

PREMIER DIVISION

	P	W	D	L	F	A	GD	Pts
1 Yeovil Town	42	31	8	3	83	34	+49	101
2 Enfield	42	28	11	3	91	29	+62	95
3 Sutton United	42	18	13	11	87	70	+17	67
4 Dagenham & Redbridge	42	18	11	13	57	43	+14	65
5 Yeading	42	17	14	11	58	47	+11	65
6 St Albans City	42	18	11	13	65	55	+10	65
7 Aylesbury United	42	18	11	13	64	54	+10	65
8 Purfleet	42	17	11	14	67	63	+4	62
9 Heybridge Swifts	42	16	14	12	62	62	0	62
10 Boreham Wood	42	15	13	14	56	52	+4	58
11 Kingstonian	42	16	8	18	79	79	0	56
12 Dulwich Hamlet	42	14	13	15	57	57	0	55
13 Carshalton Athletic	42	14	11	17	51	56	-5	53
14 Hitchin Town	42	15	7	20	67	73	-6	52
15 Oxford City	42	14	10	18	67	83	-16	52
16 Hendon	42	13	12	17	53	59	-6	51
17 Harrow Borough	42	12	14	16	58	62	-4	50
18 Bromley	42	13	9	20	67	72	-5	48
19 Bishop's Stortford	42	10	13	19	43	64	-21	43
20 Staines Town	42	10	8	24	46	71	-25	38
21 Grays Athletic	42	8	9	25	43	79	-36	33
22 Chertsey Town	42	8	7	27	41	98	-57	31

Div. 1 – Chesham United; 2 Basingstoke Town; 3 Walton & Hersham.

114

JEWSON WESSEX LEAGUE

FIRST DIVISION

	P	W	D	L	F	A	GD	Pts
1 AFC Lymington	40	35	5	0	112	22	+90	110
2 Wimborne Town	40	26	7	7	97	42	+55	85
3 Thatcham Tn	40	26	5	9	91	45	+46	79
4 Ryde	40	25	4	11	77	50	+27	79
5 Bemerton HH	40	23	9	8	69	45	+24	78
6 Andover	40	19	12	9	80	42	+38	69
7 Eastleigh	40	19	8	13	71	56	+15	65
8 Downton	40	18	7	15	72	70	+2	61
9 Cowes Sports	40	15	14	11	65	55	+10	59
10 Portsmouth RN	40	16	4	20	65	66	-1	51
11 Gosport Borough	40	15	5	20	56	66	-10	50
12 Aerostructures	40	13	9	18	45	66	-21	48
13 Bournemouth	40	14	5	21	50	72	-22	47
14 Brockenhurst	40	13	7	20	54	73	-19	46
15 Whitchurch Utd	40	12	7	21	58	81	-23	43
16 Christchurch	40	13	4	23	49	72	-23	43
17 East Cowes Vics	40	10	7	23	53	72	-19	37
18 Romsey Town	40	10	7	23	52	94	-42	37
19 BAT Sports	40	8	9	23	43	74	-31	33
20 AFC Totton	40	8	8	24	54	87	-33	32
21 Petersfield Town	40	8	5	27	42	92	-50	29

(4 points deducted: Thatcham; 1 point deducted: Portsmouth RN.)

JEWSON EASTERN COUNTIES

PREMIER DIVISION

	P	W	D	L	F	A	GD	Pts
1 Wroxham	44	34	7	3	141	37	+104	109
2 Wisbech Town	44	32	8	4	133	34	+99	104
3 Harwich & Parkeston	44	32	8	4	81	41	+40	104
4 Diss Town	44	29	4	11	87	51	+36	91
5 Great Yarmouth	44	26	7	11	86	54	+32	85
6 Gorleston	44	26	5	13	101	54	+47	83
7 Bury Town	44	23	10	11	97	75	+22	79
8 Newmarket Town	44	23	8	13	84	56	+28	77
9 Lowestoft Town	44	22	9	13	74	62	+12	75
10 Stowmarket Town	44	22	4	18	64	59	+5	70
11 Tiptree United	44	19	8	17	87	79	+8	65
12 Halstead Town	44	17	12	15	82	87	-5	63
13 Soham Town Rangers	44	15	13	16	78	80	-2	58
14 Fakenham Town	44	15	11	18	62	72	-10	56
15 Warboys Town	44	15	10	19	70	82	-12	55
16 Woodbridge Town	44	12	12	20	61	100	-39	48
17 Sudbury Wanderers	44	13	5	26	56	103	-47	44
18 Felixstowe P&T	44	11	6	27	49	106	-57	39
19 Watton United	44	10	6	28	46	96	-50	36
20 Sudbury Town Res	44	7	7	30	43	156	-113	28
21 Clacton Town	44	7	5	32	47	90	-43	26
22 Hadleigh United	44	5	8	31	41	128	-87	23
23 March Town Utd	44	5	3	36	25	133	-108	18

Div. 1 – 1 Ely City, 2 Histon.

115

HIGHLAND LEAGUE

		Home			Away					
	P	W	D	L	W	D	L	F	A	Pts
1 Huntly	31	11	3	1	12	1	2	86	26	73
2 Keith	30	12	0	3	9	3	3	76	36	66
3 Peterhead	30	9	3	3	8	4	3	77	30	58
4 Lossiemouth	30	10	2	3	8	2	5	66	31	58
5 Clachnacuddin	30	10	4	1	6	1	8	59	46	53
6 Fraserburgh	30	8	3	4	7	4	4	56	38	52
7 Cove Rovers	30	8	1	6	7	4	4	84	47	50
8 Deveronvale	30	10	2	3	6	0	9	55	54	50
9 Elgin City	30	8	3	6	6	1	7	64	66	43
10 Wick Academy	30	4	5	6	5	3	7	41	46	35
11 Rothes	30	5	3	7	4	5	6	44	52	35
12 Forres Mechanics	30	6	2	7	2	3	10	40	60	29
13 Buckie Thistle	30	4	1	10	4	3	8	41	55	28
14 Brora Rangers	30	3	6	6	2	4	9	43	88	25
15 Nairn County	30	2	2	11	2	1	12	21	93	15
16 Fort William	30	1	1	13	1	2	12	31	116	9

ESSEX SENIOR LEAGUE

PREMIER DIVISION

	P	W	D	L	F	A	GD	Pts
1 Ford United	28	21	6	1	91	24	+67	69
2 Great Wakering Rvrs	28	20	6	2	67	19	+48	66
3 Concord Rangers	28	19	5	4	106	31	+75	62
4 Stansted	28	19	2	7	53	37	+16	59
5 Burnham Ramblers	28	13	6	9	62	40	+22	45
6 Brentwood	28	11	10	7	46	34	+12	43
7 Hullbridge Sports	28	13	4	11	52	42	+10	43
8 Ilford	28	11	3	14	36	40	-4	36
9 Basildon Utd	28	11	5	12	39	52	-13	35
10 Saffron Walden T	28	8	8	12	40	39	+1	32
11 Southend Manor	28	8	5	15	32	42	-10	29
12 Bowers United	28	8	4	16	32	77	-45	28
13 East Ham United	28	7	3	18	29	61	-32	24
14 Sawbridgeworth T	28	3	3	22	17	69	-52	12
15 Eton Manor	28	1	4	23	13	108	-95	7

(3 points deducted: Basildon)

F.A. WOMEN'S PREMIER LEAGUE

NATIONAL DIVISION

	P	W	D	L	F	A	GD	Pts
1 Arsenal	18	16	1	1	65	9	+56	49
2 Doncaster Belles	18	13	2	3	44	15	+29	41
3 Croydon	18	9	4	5	39	26	+13	31
4 Liverpool	18	9	3	6	30	16	–14	30
5 Millwall Lionesses	18	7	6	5	25	19	+1	27
6 Everton	18	8	3	7	36	36	+0	27
7 Wembley	18	6	4	8	26	27	–1	22
8 Tranmere Rovers	18	3	3	12	23	48	–25	12
9 Southampton Saints	18	3	0	15	16	61	–45	9
10 Ilkeston Town	18	1	4	13	14	56	–42	7

SOUTHERN DIVISION

	P	W	D	L	F	A	GD	Pts
1 Berkhamsted Town	18	14	2	2	57	16	+41	44
2 Brighton & Hove Albion	18	13	2	3	59	33	+26	41
3 Whitehawk	18	12	1	5	39	17	+22	37
4 Wimbledon	18	10	2	6	66	28	+38	32
5 Three Bridges	18	7	5	6	36	28	+8	26
6 Langford	18	7	5	6	28	33	–5	26
7 Ipswich Town	18	5	4	9	24	26	–2	19
8 Leyton Orient	18	3	4	11	27	50	–23	13
9 Town & Country	18	2	3	13	18	65	–47	9
10 Oxford United	18	2	2	14	17	75	–58	8

NORTHERN DIVISION

	P	W	D	L	F	A	GD	Pts
1 Bradford City	16	15	0	1	56	13	+43	45
2 Aston Villa	16	12	1	3	50	15	+35	37
3 Blyth Spartans Kestrels	16	9	2	5	40	25	+15	29
4 Huddersfield Town	16	8	3	5	37	32	+5	27
5 Wolverhampton Wand.	16	7	1	8	30	29	+1	22
6 Sheffield Wednesday	16	4	4	8	25	36	–11	16
7 Garswood Saints	16	3	5	8	26	29	–3	14
8 Stourport Swifts	16	3	2	11	22	60	–38	11
9 Notts County	16	0	4	12	21	68	–47	4

F.A. WOMEN'S CUP FINAL

(Sponsored by UK Living)

Sunday, May 4 (at West Ham – att: 3,500)

Millwall Lionesses 1, Wembley 0

WOMEN'S WORLD CHAMPIONSHIP 1997-98

Sept. 25	Germany v England
Oct. 30	England v Holland
Mar. 8	England v Germany
May 14	England v Norway
May 23	Holland v England

EUROPEAN CUP FINALS

1956	Real Madrid 4, Rheims 3 (Paris)
1957	Real Madrid 2, Fiorentina 0 (Madrid)
1958†	Real Madrid 3, AC Milan 2 (Brussels)
1959	Real Madrid 2, Rheims 0 (Stuttgart)
1960	Real Madrid 7, Eintracht Frankfurt 3 (Glasgow)
1961	Benfica 3, Barcelona 2 (Berne)
1962	Benfica 5, Real Madrid 3 (Amsterdam)
1963	AC Milan 2, Benfica 1 (Wembley)
1964	Inter Milan 3, Real Madrid 1 (Vienna)
1965	Inter Milan 1, Benfica 0 (Milan)
1966	Real Madrid 2, Partizan Belgrade 1 (Brussels)
1967	Celtic 2, Inter Milan 1 (Lisbon)
1968†	Manchester United 4, Benfica 1 (Wembley)
1969	AC Milan 4, Ajax 1 (Madrid)
1970†	Feyenoord 2, Celtic 1 (Milan)
1971	Ajax 2, Panathinaikos 0 (Wembley)
1972	Ajax 2, Inter Milan 0 (Rotterdam)
1973	Ajax 1, Juventus 0 (Belgrade)
1974	Bayern Munich 4, Atletico Madrid 0 (replay Brussels, after a 1-1 draw, Brussels)
1975	Bayern Munich 2, Leeds United 0 (Paris)
1976	Bayern Munich 1, St. Etienne 0 (Glasgow)
1977	Liverpool 3, Borussia Moenchengladbach 1 (Rome)
1978	Liverpool 1, Brugge 0 (Wembley)
1979	Nottingham Forest 1, Malmo 0 (Munich)
1980	Nottingham Forest 1, Hamburg 0 (Madrid)
1981	Liverpool 1, Real Madrid 0 (Paris)
1982	Aston Villa 1, Bayern Munich 0 (Rotterdam)
1983	SV Hamburg 1, Juventus 0 (Athens)
1984†	Liverpool 1, AS Roma 1 (Liverpool won 4-2 on penalties) (Rome)
1985	Juventus 1, Liverpool 0 (Brussels)
1986†	Steaua Bucharest 0, Barcelona 0 (Steaua won 2-0 on penalties) (Seville)
1987	Porto 2, Bayern Munich 1 (Vienna)
1988†	PSV Eindhoven 0, Benfica 0 (PSV won 6-5 on penalties) (Stuttgart)
1989	AC Milan 4, Steaua Bucharest 0 (Barcelona)
1990	AC Milan 1, Benfica 0 (Vienna)
1991†	Red Star Belgrade 0, Marseille 0 (Red Star won 5-3 on penalties) (Bari)
1992	Barcelona 1, Sampdoria 0 (Wembley)
1993	Marseille 1, AC Milan 0 (Munich)
1994	AC Milan 4, Barcelona 0 (Athens)
1995	Ajax 1, AC Milan 0 (Vienna)
1996†	Juventus 1, Ajax 1 (Juventus won 4-2 on penalties) (Rome)
1997	Borussia Dortmund 3, Juventus 1 (Munich)

(† After extra time)

EUROPEAN CUP FINAL

BORUSSIA DORTMUND 3, JUVENTUS 1
Olympic Stadium, Munich (55,500), Wednesday, May 28, 1997

Bor. Dortmund: Klos; Reuter, Kohler, Sammer (Capt.), Kree, Lambert, Sousa, Moller (Zorc 89), Heinrich, Riedle (Herrlich 67), Chapuisat (Ricken 70). **Scorers:** Riedle (29,34), Ricken (71).

Juventus: Peruzzi (Capt.); Porrini (Del Pierro 45), Ferrara, Montero, Juliano, Di Livio, Deschamps, Zidane, Jugovic, Boksic (Tacchinardi 87), Vieri (Amoruso 71).
Scorer: Del Piero (64).

Referee: S. Puhl (Hungary). **Half-time:** 2-0

CUP-WINNERS' CUP FINALS

1961	Fiorentina beat Rangers 4-1 on agg. (2-0 a, 2-1 h: Glasgow first leg, Florence second leg)
1962	Atletico Madrid beat Fiorentina 3-0 (replay Stuttgart, after a 1-1 draw, Glasgow)
1963	Tottenham Hotspur beat Atletico Madrid 5-1 (Rotterdam)
1964	Sporting Lisbon beat MTK Budapest 1-0 (replay Antwerp, after a 3-3 draw, Brussels)
1965	West Ham United beat Munich 1860 2-0 (Wembley)
1966†	Borussia Dortmund beat Liverpool 2-1 (Glasgow)
1967†	Bayern Munich beat Rangers 1-0 (Nuremberg)
1968	AC Milan beat SV Hamburg 2-0 (Rotterdam)
1969	Slovan Bratislava beat Barcelona 3-2 (Basle)
1970	Manchester City beat Gornik Zabrze 2-1 (Vienna)
1971†	Chelsea beat Real Madrid 2-1 (replay Athens, after a 1-1 draw, Athens)
1972	Rangers beat Moscow Dynamo 3-2 (Barcelona)
1973	AC Milan beat Leeds United 1-0 (Salonika)
1974	Magdeburg beat AC Milan 2-0 (Rotterdam)
1975	Dynamo Kiev beat Ferencvaros 3-0 (Basle)
1976	Anderlecht beat West Ham United 4-2 (Brussels)
1977	SV Hamburg beat Anderlecht 2-0 (Amsterdam)
1978	Anderlecht beat Austria WAC 4-0 (Paris)
1979†	Barcelona beat Fortuna Dusseldorf 4-3 (Basle)
1980†	Valencia beat Arsenal 5-4 on penalties after a 0-0 draw (Brussels)
1981	Dynamo Tbilisi beat Carl Zeiss Jena 2-1 (Dusseldorf)
1982	Barcelona beat Standard Liege 2-1 (Barcelona)
1983†	Aberdeen beat Real Madrid 2-1 (Gothenburg)
1984	Juventus beat Porto 2-1 (Basle)
1985	Everton beat Rapid Vienna 3-1 (Rotterdam)
1986	Dynamo Kiev beat Atletico Madrid 3-0 (Lyon)
1987	Ajax beat Lokomotiv Leipzig 1-0 (Athens)
1988	Mechelen beat Ajax 1-0 (Strasbourg)
1989	Barcelona beat Sampdoria 2-0 (Berne)
1990	Sampdoria beat Anderlecht 2-0 (Gothenburg)
1991	Manchester United beat Barcelona 2-1 (Rotterdam)
1992	Werder Bremen beat Monaco 2-0 (Lisbon)
1993	Parma beat Royal Antwerp 3-1 (Wembley)
1994	Arsenal beat Parma 1-0 (Copenhagen)
1995†	Real Zaragoza beat Arsenal 2-1 (Paris)
1996	Paris St. Germain beat Rapid Vienna 1-0 (Brussels)
1997	Barcelona beat Paris St. Germain 1-0 (Rotterdam)

(† After extra time)

CUP-WINNERS' CUP FINAL

BARCELONA 1, PARIS ST. GERMAIN 0
Feyenoord Stadium, Rotterdam (50,000), Wednesday, May 14, 1997

Barcelona: Vitor Baia; Sergi, Fernando Couto, Abelardo, Ferrer, Guardiola, Popescu (Amor 45), Luis Figo, De La Pena (Stoichkov 84), Luis Enrique (Pizzi 88), Ronaldo. **Scorer:** Ronaldo pen. (38).

Paris SG: Lama; Domi, Fournier (Algerino 58), N'Gotty, Le Guen, Leroy, Cauet, Guerin (Dely Valdes 68), Leonardo, Rai, Loko (Pouget 77).

Referee: M. Merk (Germany).

UEFA CUP FINALS

1972	Tottenham Hotspur beat Wolverhampton Wanderers 3-2 on agg. (2-1a, 1-1h)
1973	Liverpool beat Borussia Moenchengladbach 3-2 on agg. (3-0h, 0-2a)
1974	Feyenoord beat Tottenham Hotspur 4-2 on agg. (2-2a, 2-0h)
1975	Borussia Moenchengladbach beat Twente Enschede 5-1 on agg. (0-0h, 5-1a)
1976	Liverpool beat Brugge 4-3 on agg. (3-2h, 1-1a)
1977	Juventus beat Atletico Bilbao on away goals after 2-2 agg. (1-0h, 1-2a)
1978	PSV Eindhoven beat Bastia 3-0 on agg. (0-0a, 3-0h)
1979	Borussia Moenchengladbach beat Red Star Belgrade 2-1 on agg. (1-1a, 1-0h)
1980	Eintracht Frankfurt beat Borussia Moenchengladbach on away goals after 3-3 agg. (2-3a, 1-0h)
1981	Ipswich Town beat AZ 67 Alkmaar 5-4 on agg. (3-0h, 2-4a)
1982	IFK Gothenburg beat SV Hamburg 4-0 on agg. (1-0h, 3-0a)
1983	Anderlecht beat Benfica 2-1 on agg. (1-0h, 1-1a)
1984	Tottenham Hotspur beat Anderlecht 4-3 on penalties after 2-2 agg. (1-1a, 1-1h)
1985	Real Madrid beat Videoton 3-1 on agg. (3-0a, 0-1h)
1986	Real Madrid beat Cologne 5-3 on agg. (5-1h, 0-2a)
1987	IFK Gothenburg beat Dundee United 2-1 on agg. (1-0h, 1-1a)
1988	Bayer Leverkusen beat Espanol 3-2 on penalties after 3-3 agg. (0-3a, 3-0h)
1989	Napoli beat VfB Stuttgart 5-4 on agg. (2-1h, 3-3a)
1990	Juventus beat Fiorentina 3-1 on agg. (3-1h, 0-0a)
1991	Inter Milan beat AS Roma 2-1 on agg. (2-0h, 0-1a)
1992	Ajax beat Torino on away goals after 2-2 agg. (2-2a, 0-0h)
1993	Juventus beat Borussia Dortmund 6-1 on agg. (3-1a, 3-0h)
1994	Inter Milan beat Salzburg 2-0 on agg. (1-0a, 1-0h)
1995	Parma beat Juventus 2-1 on agg. (1-0h, 1-1a)
1996	Bayern Munich beat Bordeaux 5-1 on agg. (2-0h, 3-1a)
1997	FC Schalke beat Inter Milan 4-1 on penalties after 1-1 agg. (1-0h, 0-1a)

FAIRS CUP FINALS

(As UEFA Cup previously known)

1958	Barcelona beat London 8-2 on agg. (2-2a, 6-0h)
1960	Barcelona beat Birmingham 4-1 on agg. (0-0a, 4-1h)
1961	AS Roma beat Birmingham City 4-2 on agg. (2-2a, 2-0h)
1962	Valencia beat Barcelona 7-3 on agg. (6-2h, 1-1a)
1963	Valencia beat Dynamo Zagreb 4-1 on agg. (2-1a, 2-0h)
1964	Real Zaragoza beat Valencia 2-1 (Barcelona)
1965	Ferencvaros beat Juventus 1-0 (Turin)
1966	Barcelona beat Real Zaragoza 4-3 on agg. (0-1h, 4-2a)
1967	Dynamo Zagreb beat Leeds United 2-0 on agg. (2-0h, 0-0a)
1968	Leeds United beat Ferencvaros 1-0 on agg. (1-0h, 0-0a)
1969	Newcastle United beat Ujpest Dozsa 6-2 on agg. (3-0h, 3-2a)
1970	Arsenal beat Anderlecht 4-3 on agg. (1-3a, 3-0h)
1971	Leeds United beat Juventus on away goals after 3-3 agg. (2-2a, 1-1h)

UEFA CUP FINAL
(Schalke won 4-1 on pens. after 1-1 agg.)

First Leg, Wednesday, May 7, 1997
SCHALKE 1, INTER MILAN 0 (Att: 56,824)

Schalke: Lehmann; Thon (Capt.), de Kock, Linke, Eigenrauch, Nemec, Muller, Anderbrugge, Buskens (Max 67), Wilmots, Latal. **Scorer:** Wilmots (70).

Inter Milan: Pagliuca; Bergomi (Capt.), Paganin, Fresi (Berti 61) Pistone, Zanetti, Sforza, Galante, Winter, Zamorano, Ganz.

Referee: M. Batta (France).

Second Leg, Wednesday, May 21, 1997
INTER MILAN 1, SCHALKE 0, AET (Att: 83,347)

Inter Milan: Pagliuca; Bergomi (Capt.) (Angloma 71), Paganin, Fresi, Pistone, Zanetti (Berti 119), Sforza (Winter 81), Ince, Djorkaeff, Zamorano, Ganz. **Scorer:** Zamorano (85). **Sent off:** Fresi (89).

Schalke: Lehmann; Thon (capt.), de Kock, Linke (Helde 111), Muller (Anderbrugge 96), Nemec, Buskens, Eigenrauch, Latal (Held 96), Wilmots, Max.

Referee: J-G. Aranda (Spain).

Penalty Shoot-out (Schalke first): Anderbrugge 1-0, Zamorano saved, Thon 2-0, Djorkaeff 2-1, Max 3-1, Winter Missed, Wilmots (4-1).

BRITISH AND IRISH CLUBS IN EUROPE 1996-97

EUROPEAN CUP

Qualifying Round: Rangers beat Aliana Vladikavkaz (Russia) 10-3 (3-1h, 7-2a).

Champions' League (Gp. B): Juventus 1, **Man. Utd.** 0; **Man. Utd.** 2, Rapid Vienna 0; Fenerbahce 0, **Man. Utd.** 2; **Man. Utd.** 0, Fenerbahce 1; **Man. Utd.** 0, Juventus 1; Rapid Vienna 0, **Man. Utd.** 2. **Man. Utd.** finished 2nd. to Juventus in group, qualified for knock-out stage.

Quarter-final: Man. Utd. beat Porto 4-0 (4-0h, 0-0a). **Semi-final: Man. Utd.** lost 0-2 v Bor. Dortmund (0-1a, 0-1h).

Champions' League (Gp. A): Grasshopper, Zur. 3, **Rangers** 0; **Rangers** 1, Auxerre 2; Ajax 4, **Rangers** 1; **Rangers** 0 Ajax 1; **Rangers** 2, Grasshopper, Zur. 1; Auxerre 2, **Rangers** 1. **Rangers** finished bottom of group.

CUP-WINNERS' CUP

Qualifying round: Red Star Belgrade beat **Hearts** on away goal (0-0h, 1-1a); Sporting Prague beat **Glentoran** 10-1 (2-1a, 8-0h); Ruch Chorzow (Pol.) beat **Llansantffraid** (Wales) 6-1 (1-1a, 5-0h); FK Brann (Nor.) beat **Shelbourne** 5-2 (3-1a, 2-1h).

First Round: Liverpool beat MyPa 47 (Fin.) 4-1 (1-0a, 3-1h).

Second Round: Liverpool beat Sion (Switz.) 8-4 (2-1a, 6-3h).

Quarter-final: Liverpool beat Brann (Nor.) 4-1 (1-1a, 3-0h).

Semi-final: Paris SG beat **Liverpool** 3-2 (3-0h, 0-2a).

UEFA CUP

Preliminary Round: Barry Town (Wales) beat Dinaburg, Latvia 2-1 (0-0h, 2-1a); Vojvodina (Yugos.) beat **Portadown** (N. Ireland) 5-1 (1-0a, 4-1h); Vilnius (Lith.) beat **Crusaders** (N. Ireland) 3-2 (2-1h, 1-2a); Dynamo Minsk (Belarus) beat **Bohemians** (Rep. of Ireland) on away goal (1-1a, 0-0h); Slovan Bratislava (Slovakia) beat **St. Patrick's Ath.** (Rep. of Ireland) 5-3 (4-3a, 1-0h); Skonto (Latvia) beat **Newtown** (Wales) 7-1 (4-1a, 3-0h).

Qualifying round: Aberdeen beat Vilnius (Lith.) 5-4 (4-1a, 1-3h); **Celtic** beat Kosice (Slovakia) 1-0 (0-0a, 1-0h).

First Round: Newcastle beat Halmstads (Sweden) 5-2 (4-0h, 1-2a); Helsingborgs (Sweden) beat **Aston Villa** on away goal (1-1a, 0-0h); Bor. M'Gladbach beat **Arsenal** 6-4 (3-2a, 3-2h); Aberdeen beat **Barry Town** 6-4 (3-1h, 3-3a); Hamburg beat **Celtic** 4-0 (2-0a, 2-0h).

Second Round: Newcastle beat Ferencvaros (Hungary) 6-3 (2-3a, 4-0h); Brondby (Denmark) beat **Aberdeen** 2-0 (0-0h, 2-0a).

Third Round: Newcastle beat Metz (France) 3-1 (1-1a, 2-0h).

Quarter-final: Monaco beat **Newcastle** 4-0 (1-0a, 3-0h).

EUROPEAN TROPHY WINNERS – SUMMARY

European Cup (42 competitions, 21 different winners): **6** Real Madrid; **5** AC Milan; **4** Ajax Amsterdam, Liverpool; **3** Bayern Munich; **2** Benfica, Inter Milan, Juventus, Nott'm. Forest; **1** Aston Villa, Barcelona, Celtic, Feyenoord, Hamburg SV, Man. United, Marseille, PSV Eindhoven, FC Porto, Red Star Belgrade, Steaua Bucharest, Borussia Dortmund.

Cup-Winners' Cup (37 competitions, 31 different winners): **4** Barcelona; **2** Anderlecht, Dynamo Kiev, AC Milan; **1** Aberdeen, Ajax Amsterdam, Arsenal, Atletico Madrid, Bayern Munich, Borussia Dortmund, Chelsea, Dynamo Tbilisi, Everton, Fiorentina, Hamburg SV, Juventus, Magdeburg, Man. City, Man. United, Mechelen, Paris St. Germain, Parma, Rangers, Real Zaragoza, Sampdoria, Slovan Bratislava, Sporting Lisbon, Tottenham, Valencia, Werder Bremen, West Ham.

UEFA Cup (orig. Fairs Cup) (39 competitions, 27 different winners): **3** Barcelona, Juventus; **2** Borussia Moenchengladbach, IFK Gothenburg, Inter Milan, Leeds, Liverpool, Real Madrid, Tottenham, Valencia; **1** Ajax Amsterdam, Anderlecht, Arsenal, Bayer Leverkusen, Bayern Munich, Dynamo Zagreb, Eintracht Frankfurt, PSV Eindhoven, Ferencvaros, Feyenoord, Ipswich, Napoli, Newcastle, Parma, Real Zaragoza, AS Roma, FC Schalke.

● Four clubs have won all three trophies – Barcelona, Bayern Munich, Juventus and Ajax.

EUROPE'S TOP CLUBS 1996-97
(Source: *World Soccer*)

Country	Champions	P	W	D	L	F	A	Pts
Austria	Salzburg	34	19	11	4	53	22	68
Belgium	Lierse	34	21	10	3	70	38	73
Bulgaria	CSKA Sofia	30	22	5	3	65	19	71
Croatia	FC Croatia Zagreb	30	26	3	1	90	23	81
Czech Rep.	Sparta Prague	30	19	8	3	61	20	65
England	Manchester United	38	21	12	5	76	44	75
Finland	Jazz Pori	27	13	8	6	47	33	47
France	Monaco	38	23	10	5	69	30	79
Germany	Bayern Munich	34	20	11	3	68	34	71
Greece	Olympiakos Athens	34	26	6	2	72	14	84
Holland	PSV Eindhoven	34	24	5	5	90	26	77
Hungary	MTK Budapest	34	26	7	1	87	25	85
Italy	Juventus	34	17	14	3	51	24	65
N. Ireland	Crusaders	28	12	10	6	39	26	46
Norway	Rosenborg Trondheim	26	18	5	3	82	26	59
Poland	Widzew Lodz	34	25	6	3	74	21	81
Portugal	Porto	33	26	4	3	77	24	82
Rep. Ireland	Derry City	33	19	10	4	58	27	67
Romania	Sparta Bucharest	34	23	4	7	86	40	73
Russia	Spartak Moscow	34	21	9	4	70	34	72*
Scotland	Rangers	36	25	5	6	85	33	80
Slovakia	Kosice	30	21	7	2	61	19	70
Spain	Real Madrid	42	27	11	4	85	36	92
Sweden	IFK Gothenburg	26	17	5	4	61	23	56
Switzerland	Sion	14	9	3	2	18	10	49†
Turkey	Galatasaray	34	25	7	2	90	30	82
Wales	Barry Town	40	33	6	1	129	26	105
Yugoslavia	Partizan Belgrade	33	26	6	1	88	17	84

Other champions: Albania: competition suspended owing to civil strife. **Armenia**: Pyounic Yerevan. **Cyprus**: Anorthosis Famagusta. **Estonia**: Lantana Tallinn. **Faroe Islands**: GI. **Georgia**: Dynamo Tbilisi. **Iceland**: IA Akranes. **Israel**: Betar Jerusalem. **Latvia**: Skonto Riga. **Lithuania**: Kareda Siauliai. **Luxemboug**: Jeunesse Esch. **Macedonia**: Sileks Kratovo. **Malta**: Valetta. **Moldova**: Constructoral Chisinau. **San Marino**: Folgore. **Slovenia**: Maribor Branik. **Ukraine**: Dynamo Kiev.

† after play-offs
* incl. bonus points.

FIFA World Player of the Year

1991	Lothar Matthaus (Inter Milan and Germany)
1992	Marco van Basten (AC Milan and Holland)
1993	Roberto Baggio (Juventus and Italy)
1994	Romario (Barcelona and Brazil)
1995	George Weah (Milan and Liberia)
1996	Ronaldo (Barcelona and Brazil)

WORLD CLUB CUP 1996 FINAL

(Sponsored by Toyota)

JUVENTUS (Italy) 1, RIVER PLATE (Argentina) 0

Tokyo (48,305), Tuesday, November 26, 1996

Juventus: Peruzzi; Ferrara, Porrini, Torricelli, Montero, Di Livio, Deschamps, Jugovic, Zidane (Tacchinardi 86), Del Piero, Boksic. **Scorer:** Del Piero (82).
Coach: Marcello Lippi.

River Plate: Banano; Diaz, Berizzo, Ayala, Sorin, Astrada, Montserrat, Berti (Gancedo 75), Ortega, Francescoli, Cruz (Salas 84). **Coach:** Ramon Diaz.

Referee: Marcio Rezende de Freitas (Brazil).
Man of Match: Alessandro del Piero (Juventus).

COMPLETE RESULTS

(Played as a single match in Tokyo since 1980)

Year	Winners	Runners-up	Score		
1960	Real Madrid (Spa.)	Penarol (Uru.)	0-0	5-1	
1961	Penarol (Uru.)	Benfica (Por.)	0-1	2-1	5-0
1962	Santos (Bra.)	Benfica (Por.)	3-2	5-2	
1963	Santos (Bra.)	AC Milan (Ita.)	2-4	4-2	1-0
1964	Inter Milan (Ita.)	Independiente (Arg.)	0-1	2-0	1-0
1965	Inter Milan (Ita.)	Independiente (Arg.)	3-0	0-0	
1966	Penarol (Uru.)	Real Madrid (Spa.)	2-0	2-0	
1967	Racing (Arg.)	Celtic (Sco.)	0-1	2-1	1-0
1968	Estudiantes (Arg.)	Manchester Utd. (Eng.)	1-0	1-1	
1969	AC Milan (Ita.)	Estudiantes (Arg.)	3-0	1-2	
1970	Feyenoord (Hol.)	Estudiantes (Arg.)	2-2	1-0	
1971	Nacional (Uru.)	Panathanaikos (Gre.)*	1-1	2-1	
1972	Ajax (Hol.)	Independiente (Arg.)	1-1	3-0	
1973	Independiente (Arg.)	Juventus (Ita.)*	1-0		
1974	Atletico Madrid (Spa.)*	Independiente (Arg.)	0-1	2-0	
1975	Not played				
1976	Bayern Munich (W.Ger.)	Cruzeiro (Bra.)	2-0	0-0	
1977	Boca Juniors (Arg.)	Borussia Mönchengladbach (W.Ger.)*	2-2	3-0	
1978	Not played				
1979	Olimpia Asuncion (Par.)	Malmö (Swe.)*	1-0	2-1	
1980	Nacional (Arg.)	Nottingham Forest (Eng.)	1-0		
1981	Flamengo (Bra.)	Liverpool (Eng.)	3-0		
1982	Penarol (Uru.)	Aston Villa (Eng.)	2-0		
1983	Porto Alegre (Bra.)	SV Hamburg (W.Ger.)	2-1		
1984	Independiente (Arg.)	Liverpool (Eng.)	1-0		
1985	Juventus (Ita.)	Argentinos Juniors (Arg.)	2-2 (aet)		
	(Juventus won 4-2 on penalties)				
1986	River Plate (Arg.)	Steaua Bucharest (Rum.)	1-0		
1987	Porto (Por.)	Penarol (Uru.)	2-1 (aet)		
1988	Nacional (Uru.)	PSV Eindhoven (Hol.)	1-1 (aet)		
	(Nacional won 7-6 on penalties)				
1989	AC Milan (Ita.)	Nacional (Col.)	1-0 (aet)		
1990	AC Milan (Ita.)	Olimpia Asuncion (Par.)	3-0		
1991	Red Star (Yug.)	Colo Colo (Chi.)	3-0		
1992	Sao Paulo (Bra.)	Barcelona (Spa.)	2-1		
1993	Sao Paulo (Bra.)	AC Milan (Ita.)	3-2		
1994	Velez Sarsfield (Arg.)	AC Milan (Ita.)	2-0		
1995	Ajax (Hol.)	Gremio (Bra.)	0-0 (aet)		
	(Ajax won 4-3 on penalties)				
1996	Juventus (Ita.)	River Plate (Arg.)	1-0		

* European Cup runners-up.
Summary: 35 contests; South America 20 wins, Europe 15 wins.

WORLD CUP – FRANCE 98

France will host the finals of the 16th. World Cup in 1998 with a **record assembly** of 32 nations (previously 24). The tournament will be staged over 33 days, starting June 10, with a programme of 64 matches (12 more than at US 94) at ten venues: Stade de France, Paris; Parc des Princes, Paris; Montpellier; Toulouse; Bordeaux; Lens; Marseilles; St Etienne; Lyon; Nantes.

The **official logo** chosen by the French organisers takes the form of a football rising sun-like over part of the globe, and the **tournament mascot** will be a cockerel, named Footix.

Draw for the finals will be held in the open air at the Stade Velodrome in Marseille on December 4.

The **Final** will take place on July 12 at the £223m., 80,000 all-seat Stade de France at St Denis, just north of Paris.

FIFA was founded in Paris in 1904, and France now presents the World Cup for the second time (previously in 1938). President of the organising committee is **Michel Platini**, former captain and coach of France.

FIFA estimate that it will cost £273m to stage France 98 – some £96m more than the budget for US 94.

At the end of the 1998 World Cup **Joao Havelange**, FIFA's 80-year-old Brazilian president, will retire after 24 years as head of football's governing body. Strongest contender to succeed him is Sweden's Lennart Johansson, UEFA president and FIFA vice-president.

THE FINALS

GROUP MATCHES

June 10	Paris Stade de France (Gp A); Montpellier (A)
June 11	Toulouse (B); Bordeaux (B)
June 12	Lens (C); Marseille (D); Montpellier (C)
June 13	Paris Stade de France (E); Lyon (E); Nantes (D)
June 14	Lens (H); St Etienne (F); Toulouse (H)
June 15	Paris Parc des Princes (F); Lyon (G) Marseille (G)
June 16	Bordeaux (A); Nantes (A)
June 17	St Etienne (B); Montepellier (B)
June 18	Paris Stade de France (C); Toulouse (C)
June 19	Paris Parc des Princes (D); St Etienne (D)
June 20	Marseille (E); Bordeaux (E); Nantes (H)
June 21	Paris Parc des Princes (H); Lens (F); Lyon (F)
June 22	Montpellier (G); Toulouse (G)
June 23	Paris Stade de France (B); St Etienne (A); Marseille (A); Nantes (B)
June 24	Lens (D); Lyon (C); Toulouse (D); Bordeaux (C)
June 25	Paris Parc des Princes (E); Montpellier (F); Nantes (F); St Etienne (E)
June 26	Paris Stade de France (G); Lens (G); Lyon (H); Bordeaux (H)

2ND ROUND

June 27	Paris Parc des Princes; Marseille
June 28	Paris Stade de France; Lens
June 29	Montpellier; Toulouse
June 30	St Etienne; Bordeaux

QUARTER-FINALS

July 3	Paris Stade de France; Nantes
July 4	Lyon; Marseille

SEMI-FINALS

July 7   Marseille
July 8   Paris Stade de France

3RD PLACE PLAY-OFF

July 11   Paris Parc des Princes

FINAL

July 12   Paris Stade de France

BETTING (Ladbrokes, July 97): 4-1 Brazil; 5-1 France; 6-1 Germany; 7-1 Italy; 9-1 Holland; 12-1 England, Spain; 16-1 Argentina; 25-1 Colombia, Nigeria, Russia; 33-1 Norway, Portugal, Yugoslavia; 40-1 Bulgaria, Croatia, Denmark, Romania; 66-1 Scotland; 80-1 Belgium, Cameroon; 250-1 Rep. Of Ireland.

World Cup 2002: FIFA decided (June 1, 1996) that the tournament will be **jointly hosted** for the first time – by Japan and South Korea. It is expected that the tournament will open in SEOUL, with the Final in TOKYO.

World Cup 2006: Nine countries have shown interest in staging the tournament: Germany, England, Russia, South Africa, Morocco, Egypt, Argentina, Brazil and Australia. Applications will not officially be invited until France 98 is completed.

QUALIFYING ROUND

The draw took place in Paris on Tuesday, December 12, 1995, with a record 171 entries (excluding hosts France and holders Brazil) from FIFA's 193 members. Bermuda and the Bahamas later withdrew for financial reasons.

Europe's entry was split into 9 groups, in which the first seeds were Denmark, Italy, Norway, Sweden, Russia, Spain, Holland, Romania and Germany.

First of the 639 matches scheduled in the World Cup 98 qualifying round took place in the Caribbean Zone on March 10, 1996: Dominica v Antigua (3-3).

The European qualifying groups started with 3 matches on April 24: Greece 2, Slovenia 0; Yugoslavia 3, Faroe Islands 1; Macedonia 3, Liechtenstein 0.

Wales played the first qualifying match among the **British countries** on June 2, winning 5-0 away to San Marino.

QUALIFYING ROUND
EUROPE

From 49 entries, 14 to qualify plus France as hosts. The nine group winners and the best runner-up go through automatically, with the other eight runners-up drawn into pairs for play-offs (home and away, Oct 29 & Nov 15). The winners qualify for the Finals.

When teams finish level on points for first place, the placings will be determined by: 1, goal difference; 2, goals scored; 3, goal difference in two matches between themselves; 4, play-off at a neutral venue.

To determine the best runner-up in each of the nine groups, only matches against first, third and fourth-placed finishers in each group will be taken into account. Where teams finish level on points their position will be decided by: 1, goal difference; 2, goals scored; 3, away goals; 4, play-off on neutral ground (Oct 19).

Situation as at start of season 1997-98:-

GROUP 1

Greece 2, Slovenia 0; Greece 3, Bosnia 0; Slovenia 0, Denmark 2; Denmark 2, Greece 1; Bosnia 1, Croatia 4; Slovenia 1, Bosnia 2; Croatia 1, Greece 1; Croatia 1, Denmark 1; Croatia 3, Slovenia 3; Bosnia 0, Greece 1; Denmark 4, Slovenia 0; Greece 0, Croatia 1; Denmark 2, Bosnia 0.

	P	W	D	L	F	A	Pts
Denmark	5	4	1	0	11	2	13
Greece	6	3	1	2	8	4	10
Croatia	5	2	3	0	10	6	9
Bosnia	5	1	0	4	3	11	3
Slovenia	5	0	1	4	4	13	1

To play: Aug. 20 Bosnia v Denmark; Sept. 6 Croatia v Bosnia, Slovenia v Greece; Sept. 10 Denmark v Croatia, Bosnia v Slovenia; Oct. 11 Greece v Denmark, Slovenia v Croatia.

GROUP 2

Moldova 0, England 3; Moldova 1, Italy 3; England 2, Poland 1; Italy 1, Georgia 2; Georgia 0, England 2; Poland 2, Moldova 1; England 0, Italy 1; Italy 3, Moldova 0; Poland 0, Italy 0; England 2, Georgia 0; Italy 3, Poland 0; Poland 0, England 2; Georgia 2, Moldova 1; Poland 4, Georgia 1.

	P	W	D	L	F	A	Pts
Italy	6	5	1	0	11	1	16
England	6	5	0	1	11	2	15
Poland	6	2	1	3	7	9	7
Georgia	5	1	0	4	3	9	3
Moldova	5	0	0	5	2	13	0

To play: Sept. 10 England v Moldova, Georgia v Italy; Sept. 24 Moldova v Georgia; Oct. 7 Moldova v Poland; Oct. 11 Italy v England, Georgia v Poland.

GROUP 3

Norway 5, Azerbaijan 0; Azerbaijan 1, Switzerland 0; Hungary 1, Finland 0; Finland 2, Switzerland 3; Norway 3, Hungary 0; Switzerland 0, Norway 1; Azerbaijan 0, Hungary 3; Azerbaijan 1, Finland 2; Norway 1, Finland 1; Switzerland 1, Hungary 0; Finland 2, Azerbaijan 0; Hungary 1, Norway 1.

	P	W	D	L	F	A	Pts
Norway	5	3	2	0	11	2	11
Finland	5	2	1	2	8	6	7
Hungary	5	2	1	2	5	5	7
Switzerland	4	2	0	2	4	4	6
Azerbaijan	5	1	0	4	2	13	3

To play: Aug. 20 Finland v Norway, Hungary v Switzerland; Sept. 6 Switzerland v Finland, Azerbaijan v Norway; Sept. 10 Hungary v Azerbaijan, Norway v Switzerland; Oct. 11 Finland v Hungary, Switzerland v Azerbaijan.

GROUP 4

Sweden 5, Belarus 1; Austria 0, Scotland 0; Belarus 1, Estonia 0; Latvia 1, Sweden 2; Estonia 1, Belarus 0; Latvia 0, Scotland 2; Sweden 0, Austria 1; Belarus 1, Latvia 1; Estonia v Scotland (Oct. 9) postponed; Austria 2, Latvia 1; Scotland 1, Sweden 0; Estonia 0, Scotland 0 (in Monaco); Scotland 2, Estonia 0; Scotland 2, Austria 0; Austria 2, Estonia 0; Sweden 2, Scotland 1; Latvia 2, Belarus 0; Estonia 1, Latvia 1; Estonia 2, Sweden 3; Latvia 1, Austria 3; Belarus 0, Scotland 1.

	P	W	D	L	F	A	Pts
Scotland	8	5	2	1	9	2	17
Austria	6	4	1	1	8	4	13
Sweden	6	4	0	2	12	7	12
Latvia	7	2	1	4	9	11	7
Estonia	7	1	1	5	4	11	4
Belarus	6	1	1	4	3	10	4

To play: Aug. 20 Estonia v Austria, Belarus v Sweden; Sept. 6 Scotland v Belarus, Austria v Sweden, Latvia v Estonia; Sept. 10 Sweden v Latvia, Belarus v Austria; Oct. 11 Scotland v Latvia, Sweden v Estonia, Austria v Belarus.

GROUP 5

Israel 2, Bulgaria 1; Russia 4, Cyprus 0; Luxembourg 1, Bulgaria 2; Israel 1, Russia 1; Cyprus 2, Israel 0; Luxembourg 0, Russia 4; Cyprus 1, Bulgaria 3; Israel 1, Luxembourg 0; Cyprus 1, Russia 1; Luxembourg 0, Israel 3; Bulgaria 4, Cyprus 1; Israel 2, Cyprus 0; Russia 3, Luxembourg 0; Bulgaria 4, Luxembourg 0; Russia 2, Israel 0.

127

	P	W	D	L	F	A	Pts
Russia	6	4	2	0	15	2	14
Israel	7	4	1	2	9	6	13
Bulgaria	5	4	0	1	14	5	12
Cyprus	6	1	1	4	5	14	4
Luxembourg	6	0	0	6	1	17	0

To play: Aug. 20 Bulgaria v Israel; Sept. 7 Luxembourg v Cyprus; Sept. 10 Bulgaria v Russia; Oct. 11 Russia v Bulgaria, Cyprus v Luxembourg.

	P	W	D	L	F	A	Pts
Holland	6	5	0	1	23	3	15
Belgium	6	5	0	1	16	6	15
Turkey	5	2	1	2	10	5	7
Wales	6	2	1	3	14	12	7
San Marino	7	0	0	7	0	37	0

To play: Aug. 20 Turkey v Wales; Sept. 6 Holland v Belgium; Sept. 10 San Marino v Turkey; Oct. 11 Belgium v Wales, Holland v Turkey.

GROUP 6

Yugoslavia 3, Faroe Isles 1; Yugoslavia 6, Malta 0; Faroe Isles 1, Slovakia 2; Faroe Isles 2, Spain 6; Czech Republic 6, Malta 0; Slovakia 6, Malta 0; Faroe Isles 1, Yugoslavia 8; Czech. Rep. 0, Spain 0; Slovakia 3, Faroe Isles 0; Yugoslavia 1, Czech. Rep. 0; Spain 4, Slovakia 1; Spain 2, Yugoslavia 0; Malta 0, Spain 3; Spain 4, Malta 0; Malta 0, Slovakia 2; Czech. Rep. 1, Yugoslavia 2; Malta 1, Faroe Isles 2; Yugoslavia 1, Spain 1; Spain 1, Czech. Rep. 0; Yugoslavia 2, Slovakia 0; Faroe Isles 2, Malta 1.

	P	W	D	L	F	A	Pts
Spain	8	6	2	0	21	4	20
Yugoslavia	8	6	1	1	23	6	19
Slovakia	6	4	0	2	14	7	12
Faroe Isles	7	2	0	5	9	24	6
Czech Rep	5	1	1	3	7	4	4
Malta	8	0	0	8	2	31	0

To play: Aug. 20 Czech. Rep. v Faroe Isles; Sept. 6 Faroe Isles v Czech. Rep.; Sept. 10 Slovakia v Yugoslavia; Sept. 24 Malta v Czech. Rep., Slovakia v Spain; Oct. 11 Malta v Yugoslavia, Spain v Faroe Isles, Czech. Rep. v Slovakia.

GROUP 7

San Marino 0, Wales 5; Belgium 2, Turkey 1; Wales 6, San Marino 0; Wales 1, Holland 3; San Marino 0, Belgium 3; Holland 7, Wales 1; Turkey 7, San Marino 0; Belgium 0, Holland 3; Wales 0, Turkey 0; Holland 4, San Marino 0; Wales 1, Belgium 2; Turkey 1, Holland 0; Turkey 1, Belgium 3; San Marino 0, Holland 6; Belgium 6, San Marino 0.

GROUP 8

Macedonia 3, Liechtenstein 0; Iceland 1, Macedonia 1; Liechtenstein 0, Rep. of Ireland 5; Romania 3, Lithuania 0; Lithuania 2, Iceland 0; Iceland 0, Romania 4; Rep. of Ireland 3, Macedonia 0; Lithuania 2, Liechtenstein 1; Liechtenstein 1, Macedonia 11; Rep. of Ireland 0, Iceland 0; Macedonia 0, Romania 3; Romania 8, Liechtenstein 0; Lithuania 0, Romania 1; Macedonia 3, Rep. of Ireland 2; Liechtenstein 0, Lithuania 2; Romania 1, Rep. of Ireland 0; Rep. of Ireland 5, Liechtenstein 0; Macedonia 1, Iceland 0; Iceland 1 v Lithuania 0.

	P	W	D	L	F	A	Pts
Romania	6	6	0	0	20	0	18
Macedonia	7	4	1	2	19	10	13
Rep. of Ireland	6	3	1	2	15	4	10
Lithuania	6	3	1	2	6	5	10
Iceland	6	0	3	3	1	8	3
Liechtenstein	7	0	0	7	2	36	0

To play: Aug. 19 Liechtenstein v Iceland; Aug. 20 Rep. of Ireland v Lithuania, Romania v Macedonia; Sept. 6 Iceland v Rep. of Ireland, Liechtenstein v Romania, Lithuania v Macedonia; Sept. 10 Lithuania v Rep. of Ireland, Romania v Iceland; Oct. 11 Iceland v Liechtenstein, Macedonia v Lithuania, Rep. of Ireland v Romania.

GROUP 9

N. Ireland 0, Ukraine 1; Armenia 1, Portugal 0; N. Ireland 1, Armenia 1; Ukraine 2, Portugal 1; Albania 0, Portugal 3; Armenia 1, Germany 5; Albania 1, Armenia 1; Germany 1, N. Ireland 1; Portugal 1, Ukraine 0; N. Ireland 2, Albania 0; Portugal 1, Germany 0; Albania 0, Ukraine 1; N.

Ireland 0, Portugal 0; Albania 2, Germany 3; Ukraine 2, N. Ireland 1; Germany 2, Ukraine 0; Armenia 0, N. Ireland 0; Ukraine 1, Armenia 1; Portugal 2, Albania 0; Ukraine 0, Germany 0.

	P	W	D	L	F	A	Pts
Ukraine	8	4	2	2	7	6	14
Germany	6	3	3	0	11	4	12
Portugal	7	3	3	1	7	2	12
N. Ireland	7	1	4	2	5	5	7
Armenia	6	0	5	1	4	8	5
Albania	6	0	1	5	3	12	1

To play: Aug. 20 N. Ireland v Germany, Portugal v Armenia, Ukraine v Albania; Sept. 6 Germany v Portugal, Armenia v Albania; Sept. 10 Albania v N. Ireland, Germany v Armenia; Oct. 11 Germany v Albania, Portugal v N. Ireland, Armenia v Ukraine.

SOUTH AMERICA

Five countries qualify – Brazil as World Champions plus top 4 from 72-match, round robin, home-and-away tournament which ends on November 16. Positions after matches played on July 6:

	P	W	D	L	F	A	Pts
Paraguay	11	7	2	2	16	8	23
Argentina	12	6	4	2	18	11	22
Colombia	12	5	3	4	17	14	18
Chile	11	4	4	3	22	14	16
Peru	12	4	4	4	13	15	16
Ecuador	12	4	3	5	16	14	15
Bolivia	11	3	5	3	16	12	14
Uruguay	11	4	2	5	11	15	14
Venezuela	12	0	3	9	8	34	3

CONCACAF

NORTH-CENTRAL AMERICA/CARIBBEAN

Top three countries qualify from six in final qualifying round played on league system: Mexico, USA, Costa Rica, Jamaica, Canada, El Salvador. There was an original entry of 30 countries.

AFRICA

Africa provided the first 3 countries to play their way to France 98. Olympic Champions Nigeria qualified as Group 1 winners on June 7, followed the next day by Tunisia (Group 2) and Morocco (Group 5).

In Group 3 South Africa, champions of Africa, were then within one win of reaching the World Cup Finals for the first time, with Cameroon favourites to win Group 4.

From an entry of 36 countries, 20 advanced to the second round – 5 leagues of 4, from which the winners qualify.

ASIA

From 36 entries, 3 or 4 countries to qualify. First of the ten first round group winners to reach Round 2 were Saudi Arabia, United Arab Emirates, South Korea and Qatar.

Second round comprises two groups of 5, with countries meeting in one-off matches. The group winners qualify for France 98; runners-up to meet in play-off – winner to qualify, loser to play-off v Oceania Group winner.

OCEANIA

Ten countries entered – 1 to play-off for place in Finals. The second round comprised 2 sections of 3 – Group 1: Australia (coached by Terry Venables), Tahiti, Solomon Islands; Group 2: Fiji, New Zealand, Papua New Guinea.

Australia won two-leg play-off against New Zealand and will meet Asia's fourth-place team for place at France 98.

WORLD CUP SUMMARIES 1930-94

1930 in Uruguay

WINNERS: Uruguay. RUNNERS-UP: Argentina. THIRD: U.S.A.

Other countries taking part: Belgium, Bolivia, Brazil, Chile, France, Mexico, Paraguay, Peru, Rumania, Yugoslavia. **Total entries**: 13.
Venue: All matches played in Montevideo.
Top scorer: Stabile (Argentina) 8 goals.
Final (30.7.30): **Uruguay 4** (Dorado 12, Cea 55, Iriarte 64, Castro 89),
Argentina 2 (Peucelle 29, Stabile 35). **Att**: 90,000.
Uruguay: Ballesteros; Nasazzi (Capt.), Mascheroni, Andrade, Fernandez, Gestido, Dorado, Scarone, Castro, Cea, Iriarte.
Argentina: Botasso; Della Torre, Paternoster, Evaristo (J.), Monti, Suarez, Peucelle, Varallo, Stabile, Ferreira (Capt.), Evaristo (M.).
Referee: Langenus (Belgium). **Half-time**: 1-2.

1934 in Italy

WINNERS: Italy. RUNNERS-UP: Czechoslovakia. THIRD: Germany.

Other countries in finals: Argentina, Austria, Belgium, Brazil, Egypt, France, Holland, Hungary, Romania, Spain, Sweden, Switzerland, U.S.A. **Total entries**: 29 (16 qualifiers).
Venues: Bologna, Florence, Genoa, Milan, Naples, Rome, Trieste, Turin.
Top scorers: Conen (Germany), Nejedly (Czechoslovakia), Schiavio (Italy), each 4 goals.
Final (Rome, 10.6.34): **Italy 2** (Orsi 82, Schiavio 97), **Czechoslovakia 1** (Puc 70), **after extra time. Att**: 50,000.
Italy: Combi (Capt.); Monzeglio, Allemandi, Ferraris, Monti, Bertolini, Guaita, Meazza, Schiavio, Ferrari, Orsi.
Czechoslovakia: Planicka (Capt.); Zenisek, Ctyroky, Kostalek, Cambal, Krcil, Junek, Svoboda, Sobotka, Nejedly, Puc.
Referee: Eklind (Sweden). **Half-time**: 0-0. **90 mins**: 1-1.

1938 in France

WINNERS: Italy. RUNNERS-UP: Hungary. THIRD: Brazil.

Other countries in finals: Belgium, Cuba, Czechoslovakia, Dutch East Indies, France, Germany, Holland, Norway, Poland, Rumania, Sweden, Switzerland.
Total entries: 25 (15 qualifiers).
Venues: Antibes, Bordeaux, Le Havre, Lille, Marseilles, Paris, Reims, Strasbourg, Toulouse.
Top scorer: Leonidas (Brazil) 8 goals.

Final (Paris, 19.6.38): **Italy 4** (Colaussi 6, 36, Piola 15, 81), **Hungary 2** (Titkos 7, Sarosi 65). **Att:** 45,000.
Italy: Olivieri; Foni, Rava, Serantoni, Andreolo, Locatelli, Biavati, Meazza (Capt.), Piola, Ferrari, Colaussi.
Hungary: Szabo; Polgar, Biro, Szalay, Szucs, Lazar, Sas, Vincze, Sarosi (Capt.), Szengeller, Titkos.
Referee: Capdeville (France). **Half-time:** 3-1.

1950 in Brazil

WINNERS: Uruguay. RUNNERS-UP: Brazil. THIRD: Sweden.

Other countries in finals: Bolivia, Chile, England, Italy, Mexico, Paraguay, Spain, Switzerland, U.S.A., Yugoslavia. **Total entries:** 29 (13 qualifiers).
Venues: Belo Horizonte, Curitiba, Porto Alegre, Recife, Rio de Janeiro, Sao Paulo.
Top scorer: Ademir (Brazil) 7 goals.
Deciding Match (Rio de Janeiro, 16.7.50): **Uruguay 2** (Schiaffino 64, Ghiggia 79), **Brazil 1** (Friaca 47). **Att:** 199,850.
(For the only time, the World Cup was decided on a final pool system, in which the winners of the four qualifying groups met in a six-match series. So, unlike previous and subsequent tournaments, there was no official Final as such, but Uruguay v Brazil was the deciding final match in the final pool).
Uruguay: Maspoli; Gonzales, Tejera, Gambetta, Varela (Capt.), Andrade, Ghiggia, Perez, Miguez, Schiaffino, Moran.
Brazil: Barbosa; Augusto (Capt.), Juvenal, Bauer, Danilo, Bigode, Friaca, Zizinho, Ademir, Jair, Chico.
Referee: Reader (England). **Half-time:** 0-0.

1954 in Switzerland

WINNERS: West Germany. RUNNERS-UP: Hungary. THIRD: Austria.

Other countries in finals: Belgium, Brazil, Czechoslovakia, England, France, Italy, Korea, Mexico, Scotland, Switzerland, Turkey, Uruguay, Yugoslavia. **Total entries:** 35 (16 qualifiers).
Venues: Basle, Berne, Geneva, Lausanne, Lugano, Zurich.
Top scorer: Kocsis (Hungary) 11 goals.
Final (Berne, 4.7.54): **West Germany 3** (Morlock 12, Rahn 17, 84), **Hungary 2** (Puskas 4, Czibor 9). **Att:** 60,000.
West Germany: Turek; Posipal, Kohlmeyer, Eckel, Liebrich, Mai, Rahn, Morlock, Walter (O.), Walter (F.) (Capt.), Schaefer.
Hungary: Grosics; Buzansky, Lantos, Bozsik, Lorant, Zakarias, Czibor, Kocsis, Hidegkuti, Puskas (Capt.), Toth (J.).
Referee: Ling (England). **Half-time:** 2-2.

1958 in Sweden

WINNERS: Brazil. RUNNERS-UP: Sweden. THIRD: France.

Other countries in finals: Argentina, Austria, Czechoslovakia, England, Hungary, Mexico, Northern Ireland, Paraguay, Scotland, Soviet Union, Wales, West Germany, Yugoslavia. **Total entries:** 47 (16 qualifiers).
Venues: Boras, Eskilstuna, Gothenburg, Halmstad, Helsingborg, Malmo, Norrkoping, Orebro, Sandviken, Stockholm, Vasteras.
Top scorer: Fontaine (France) 13 goals.

Final (Stockholm, 29.6.58): **Brazil 5** (Vava 10, 32, Pele 55, 88, Zagalo 76), **Sweden 2** (Liedholm 4, Simonsson 83). **Att**: 49,737.
Brazil: Gilmar; Santos (D.), Santos (N.), Zito, Bellini (Capt.), Orlando, Garrincha, Didi, Vava, Pele, Zagalo.
Sweden: Svensson; Bergmark, Axbom, Boerjesson, Gustavsson, Parling, Hamrin, Gren, Simonsson, Liedholm (Capt.), Skoglund.
Referee: Guigue (France). **Half-time**: 2-1.

1962 in Chile

WINNERS: Brazil. RUNNERS-UP: Czechoslovakia. THIRD: Chile.

Other countries in finals: Argentina, Bulgaria, Colombia, England, Hungary, Italy, Mexico, Soviet Union, Spain, Switzerland, Uruguay, West Germany, Yugoslavia. **Total entries**: 53 (16 qualifiers).
Venues: Arica, Rancagua, Santiago, Vina del Mar.
Top scorers: Albert (Hungary), Garrincha (Brazil), Ivanov (Russia), Jerkovic (Yugoslavia), Sanchez (Chile), Vava (Brazil), each 4 goals.
Final (Santiago, 17.6.62): **Brazil 3** (Amarildo 17, Zito 69, Vava 77), **Czechoslovakia 1** (Masopust 16). **Att**: 68,679.
Brazil: Gilmar; Santos (D.), Mauro (Capt.), Zozimo, Santos (N.), Zito, Didi, Garrincha, Vava, Amarildo, Zagalo.
Czechoslovakia: Schroiff; Tichy, Novak, Pluskal, Popluhar, Masopust (Capt.), Pospichal, Scherer, Kvasnak, Kadraba, Jelinek.
Referee: Latychev (Soviet Union). **Half-time**: 1-1.

1966 in England

WINNERS: England. RUNNERS-UP: West Germany. THIRD: Portugal.

Other countries in finals: Argentina, Brazil, Bulgaria, Chile, France, Hungary, Italy, Mexico, North Korea, Soviet Union, Spain, Switzerland, Uruguay. **Total entries**: 53 (16 qualifiers).
Venues: Birmingham (Villa Park), Liverpool (Goodison Park), London (Wembley and White City), Manchester (Old Trafford), Middlesbrough, Sheffield (Hillsborough), Sunderland.
Top scorer: Eusebio (Portugal) 9 goals.
Final (Wembley, 30.7.66): **England 4** (Hurst 19, 100, 120, Peters 78), **West Germany 2** (Haller 13, Weber 89), **after extra time. Att**: 93,802.
England: Banks; Cohen, Wilson, Stiles, Charlton (J.), Moore (Capt.), Ball, Hurst, Hunt, Charlton (R.), Peters.
West Germany: Tilkowski; Hottges, Schnellinger, Beckenbauer, Schulz, Weber, Haller, Held, Seeler (Capt.), Overath, Emmerich.
Referee: Dienst (Switzerland). **Half-time**: 1-1. **90 mins**: 2-2.

1970 in Mexico

WINNERS: Brazil. RUNNERS-UP: Italy. THIRD: West Germany.

Other countries in finals: Belgium, Bulgaria, Czechoslovakia, El Salvador, England, Israel, Mexico, Morocco, Peru, Romania, Soviet Union, Sweden, Uruguay. **Total entries**: 68 (16 qualifiers).
Venues: Guadalajara, Leon, Mexico City, Puebla, Toluca.
Top scorer: Muller (West Germany) 10 goals.
Final (Mexico City, 21.6.70): **Brazil 4** (Pele 18, Gerson 66, Jairzinho 71, Carlos Alberto 87), **Italy 1** (Boninsegna 38). **Att**: 107,412.

Brazil: Felix; Carlos Alberto (Capt.), Brito, Piazza, Everaldo, Clodoaldo, Gerson, Jairzinho, Tostao, Pele, Rivelino.
Italy: Albertosi; Burgnich, Facchetti (Capt.), Cera, Rosato, Bertini (Juliano 72), Domenghini, De Sisti, Mazzola, Boninsegna (Rivera 84), Riva.
Referee: Glockner (East Germany). **Half-time**: 1-1.

1974 in West Germany

WINNERS: West Germany. RUNNERS-UP: Holland. THIRD: Poland.

Other countries in finals: Argentina, Australia, Brazil, Bulgaria, Chile, East Germany, Haiti, Italy, Scotland, Sweden, Uruguay, Yugoslavia, Zaire. **Total entries**: 98 (16 qualifiers).
Venues: Berlin, Dortmund, Dusseldorf, Frankfurt, Gelsenkirchen, Hamburg, Hanover, Munich, Stuttgart.
Top scorer: Lato (Poland) 7 goals
Final (Munich, 7.7.74): **West Germany 2** (Breitner 25 pen., Muller 43), **Holland 1** (Neeskens 2 pen.). **Att**: 77,833.
West Germany: Maier; Vogts, Schwarzenbeck, Beckenbauer (Capt.), Breitner, Bonhof, Hoeness, Overath, Grabowski, Muller, Holzenbein.
Holland: Jongbloed; Suurbier, Rijsbergen (De Jong 69), Haan, Krol, Jansen, Van Hanegem, Neeskens, Rep, Cruyff (Capt.), Rensenbrink (Van der Kerkhof (R.) 46).
Referee: Taylor (England). **Half-time**: 2-1.

1978 in Argentina

WINNERS: Argentina. RUNNERS-UP: Holland. THIRD: Brazil.

Other countries in finals: Austria, France, Hungary, Iran, Italy, Mexico, Peru, Poland, Scotland, Spain, Sweden, Tunisia, West Germany. **Total entries**: 102 (16 qualifiers).
Venues: Buenos Aires, Cordoba, Mar del Plata, Mendoza, Rosario.
Top scorer: Kempes (Argentina) 6 goals.
Final (Buenos Aires, 25.6.78): **Argentina 3** (Kempes 38, 104, Bertoni 115), **Holland 1** (Nanninga 82), **after extra time. Att**: 77,000.
Argentina: Fillol; Passarella (Capt.), Olguin, Galvan, Tarantini, Ardiles (Larrosa 66), Gallego, Ortiz (Houseman 74), Bertoni, Luque, Kempes.
Holland: Jongbloed; Krol (Capt.), Poortvliet, Brandts, Jansen (Suurbier 73), Haan, Neeskens, Van der Kerkhof (W.), Rep (Nanninga 58), Van der Kerkhof (R.), Rensenbrink.
Referee: Gonella (Italy). **Half-time**: 1-0. **90 mins**: 1-1.

1982 in Spain

WINNERS: Italy. RUNNERS-UP: West Germany. THIRD: Poland.

Other countries in finals: Algeria, Argentina, Austria, Belgium, Brazil, Cameroon, Chile, Czechoslovakia, El Salvador, England, France, Honduras, Hungary, Kuwait, New Zealand, Northern Ireland, Peru, Scotland, Soviet Union, Spain, Yugoslavia. **Total entries**: 109 (24 qualifiers).
Venues: Alicante, Barcelona, Bilbao, Coruna, Elche, Gijon, Madrid, Malaga, Oviedo, Seville, Valencia, Valladolid, Vigo, Zaragoza.
Top scorer: Rossi (Italy) 6 goals.
Final (Madrid, 11.7.82): **Italy 3** (Rossi 57, Tardelli 69, Altobelli 81), **West Germany 1** (Breitner 84). **Att**: 90,089.

Italy: Zoff (Capt.); Bergomi, Scirea, Collovati, Cabrini, Oriali, Gentile, Tardelli, Conti, Rossi, Graziani (Altobelli 18 – Causio 88).
West Germany: Schumacher; Kaltz, Stielike, Forster (K-H.), Forster (B.), Dremmler (Hrubesch 63), Breitner, Briegel, Rummenigge (Capt.) (Muller 70), Fischer, Littbarski.
Referee: Coelho (Brazil). **Half-time:** 0-0.

1986 in Mexico

WINNERS: Argentina. RUNNERS-UP: West Germany. THIRD: France.

Other countries in finals: Algeria, Belgium, Brazil, Bulgaria, Canada, Denmark, England, Hungary, Iraq, Italy, Mexico, Morocco, Northern Ireland, Paraguay, Poland, Portugal, Scotland, South Korea, Soviet Union, Spain, Uruguay. **Total entries:** 118 (24 qualifiers).
Venues: Guadalajara, Irapuato, Leon, Mexico City, Monterrey, Nezahualcoyotl, Puebla, Queretaro, Toluca.
Top scorer: Lineker (England) 6 goals.
Final (Mexico City, 29.6.86): **Argentina 3** (Brown 23, Valdano 56, Burruchaga 85), **West Germany 2** (Rummenigge 74, Voller 82). **Att:** 115,026.
Argentina: Pumpido; Cuciuffo, Brown, Ruggeri, Olarticoechea, Batista, Giusti, Maradona (Capt.), Burruchaga (Trobbiani 89), Enrique, Valdano.
West Germany: Schumacher; Berthold, K-H.Forster, Jakobs, Brehme, Briegel, Eder, Matthaus, Magath (Hoeness 62), Allofs (Voller 45), Rummenigge (Capt.).
Referee: Filho (Brazil). **Half-time:** 1-0.

1990 in Italy

WINNERS: West Germany. RUNNERS-UP: Argentina. THIRD: Italy.

Other countries in finals: Austria, Belgium, Brazil, Cameroon, Colombia, Costa Rica, Czechoslovakia, Egypt, England, Holland, Rep. of Ireland, Romania, Scotland, Spain, South Korea, Soviet Union, Sweden, United Arab Emirates, U.S.A., Uruguay, Yugoslavia. **Total entries:** 103 (24 qualifiers).
Venues: Bari, Bologna, Cagliari, Florence, Genoa, Milan, Naples, Palermo, Rome, Turin, Udine, Verona.
Top scorer: Schillaci (Italy) 6 goals.
Final (Rome, 8.7.90): **Argentina 0, West Germany 1** (Brehme 85 pen.). **Att:** 73,603.
Argentina: Goycochea; Ruggeri (Monzon 45), Simon, Serrizuela, Lorenzo, Basualdo, Troglio, Burruchaga (Calderon 53), Sensini, Maradona (Capt.), Dezotti.
Sent off: Monzon (65), Dezotti (86) – first players ever to be sent off in World Cup Final.
West Germany: Illgner; Berthold (Reuter 75), Buchwald, Augenthaler, Kohler, Brehme, Matthaus (Capt.), Littbarski, Hassler, Klinsmann, Voller.
Referee: Codesal (Mexico). **Half-time:** 0-0.

1994 in U.S.A.

WINNERS: Brazil. RUNNERS-UP: Italy. THIRD: Sweden.

Other countries in finals: Argentina, Belgium, Bolivia, Bulgaria, Cameroon, Colombia, Germany, Greece, Holland, Mexico, Morocco, Nigeria, Norway, Rep. of Ireland, Romania, Russia, Saudi Arabia, South Korea, Spain, Switzerland, U.S.A. **Total entries:** 144 (24 qualifiers).
Venues: Boston, Chicago, Dallas, Detroit, Los Angeles, New York, Orlando, San

Francisco, Washington.
Top scorers: Salenko (Russia), Stoichkov (Bulgaria), each 6 goals.
Final (Los Angeles, 17.7.94): **Brazil 0, Italy 0**, after extra time; **Brazil** won 3-2 on pens. **Att**: 94,194.
Brazil: Taffarel; Jorginho (Cafu 21), Aldair, Marcio Santos, Branco, Mazinho, Mauro Silva, Dunga (Capt.), Zinho (Viola 105), Romario, Bebeto.
Italy: Pagliuca; Mussi (Apolloni 35), Baresi (Capt.), Maldini, Benarrivo, Berti, Albertini, D. Baggio (Evani 95), Donadoni, R. Baggio, Massaro.
Referee: Puhl (Hungary).

WORLD CUP FINALS 1-2-3

Year	Venue	Winners	Runners-up	Score	Third
1930	Montevideo	Uruguay	Argentina	4-2	–
1934	Rome	*Italy	Czech'kia	2-1	Germany
1938	Paris	Italy	Hungary	4-2	Brazil
•1950	Rio de Janeiro	Uruguay	Brazil	2-1	–
1954	Berne	Germany	Hungary	3-2	Austria
1958	Stockholm	Brazil	Sweden	5-2	France
1962	Santiago	Brazil	Czech'kia	3-1	Chile
1966	Wembley	*England	W. Germany	4-2	Portugal
1970	Mexico City	Brazil	Italy	4-1	W. Germany
1974	Munich	W. Germany	Holland	2-1	Poland
1978	Buenos Aires	*Argentina	Holland	3-1	Brazil
1982	Madrid	Italy	W. Germany	3-1	Poland
1986	Mexico City	Argentina	W. Germany	3-2	France
1990	Rome	W. Germany	Argentina	1-0	Italy
1994	Los Angeles	†Brazil	Italy	0-0	Sweden

(•Finals on pool basis; *After extra time; †3-2 on penalties, after extra time)

World Champions: 4 – Brazil; 3 – Italy, West Germany; 2 – Argentina, Uruguay; 1 – England.
Next Finals: 1998 in France, 2002 Japan and South Korea joint hosts.

WORLD CUP-WINNING MANAGERS/COACHES

1930 Uruguay, Alberto Supicci; **1934** Italy, Vittorio Pozzo; **1938** Italy, Vittorio Pozzo; **1950** Uruguay, Juan Lopez; **1954** West Germany, Sepp Herberger; **1958** Brazil, Vicente Feola; **1962** Brazil, Aimore Moreira; **1966** England, Alf Ramsey; **1970** Brazil, Mario Zagalo; **1974** West Germany, Helmut Schoen; **1978** Argentina, Cesar Luis Menotti; **1982** Italy, Enzo Bearzot; **1986** Argentina, Carlos Bilardo; **1990** West Germany, Franz Beckenbauer; **1994** Brazil, Carlos Alberto Parreira.

● No World Cup-winning team has had a foreign manager/coach.

BIGGEST WORLD CUP WINS
(Source: *World Soccer*)

Score	Opponents	Date	Venue	Stage
17-0	*Iran v Maldives	2.06.97	Damascus	qual
13-0	New Zealand v Fiji	16.08.81	Auckland	qual
13-0	Australia v Solomon Is.	11.06.97	Sydney	qual
12-0	West Germany v Cyprus	21.05.70	Essen	qual
12-0	Syria v Maldives	8.06.97	Tehran	qual
11-0	Mexico v St. Vincent	6.12.92	Mexico City	qual

11-1	Hungary v Greece	25.03.38	Budapest	qual
11-1	Trinidad v Antigua	10.11.74	Port of Spain	qual
11-1	*Macedonia v Liechtenstein	9.11.96	Eschen	qual
11-3	Honduras v St. Vincent	17.11.96	Honduras	qual
10-0	*Soviet Union v Finland	15.08.58	Helsinki	qual
10-0	Australia v Fiji	14.08.82	Melbourne	qual
10-0	Norway v San Marino	9.09.92	Oslo	qual
10-0	*Japan v Macao	22.06.97	Tokyo	qual
10-0	Japan v Macao	25.03.97	Muscat, Oman	qual
10-1	Hungary v El Salvador	15.06.82	Elche	finals
10-1	Kuwait v Macao	3.05.93	Kuala Lumpur	qual
9-0	Spain v Portugal	11.03.34	Madrid	qual
9-0	Hungary v South Korea	17.06.54	Zurich	finals
9-0	*England v Luxembourg	19.10.62	Luxembourg	qual
9-0	Holland v Norway	1.11.74	Rotterdam	qual
9-0	Romania v Finland	14.10.74	Bucharest	qual
9-0	Yugoslavia v Zaire	18.06.74	Gelsenkirchen	finals
9-0	Austria v Malta	30.04.78	Salzburg	qual
9-0	East Germany v Malta	29.10.78	Potsdam	qual
9-0	South Korea v Nepal	25.05.90	Seoul	qual

(* = away team)

WORLD CUP TWICE STOLEN

Four months before the 1966 World Cup Finals in England the World Cup itself, the gold Jules Rimet Trophy, insured for £30,000, was stolen while on exhibition in London. One week later, March 27, the Cup, undamaged and wrapped in a copy of the *News of the World*, was found in the front garden of his home at Norwood, London, by a man and his dog. The finder obtained rewards exceeding £5,000; the dog, Pickles, became famous overnight.

To commemorate their third triumph in 1970, Brazil were given the Jules Rimet Trophy to keep permanently, and it was replaced for competition by the F.I.F.A. World Cup. But, on December 19, 1983, the original cup vanished from the Brazilian Confederation offices. Two men were arrested, but the Jules Rimet Cup was never seen again; it had been melted down. A replica, valued at £25,000 and made in West Germany, was presented to Brazil at a ceremony in Frankfurt in March 1984.

WORLD CUP 'FIRSTS'

First World Cup match on artificial turf: Canada v U.S.A. (Vancouver, September 24, 1976); **first World Cup match staged indoors**: U.S.A. v Canada (Seattle, October 20, 1976). First **World Cup Finals match** indoors: U.S.A. v Switzerland (Detroit, June 18, 1994).

WALTER SMITH HONOURED

Rangers manager **Walter Smith** capped the club's record-equalling ninth successive Championship success with the award of the **OBE** for his services to football in the Queen's Birthday Honours in June.

PREMIER LEAGUE'S NEW BOSS

Peter Leaver QC (52), deputy High Court judge, was appointed (Feb. 27) chief executive of the F.A. Premier League. He replaced Rick Parry, who left at the end of the season to become Liverpool's chief executive.

EUROPEAN CHAMPIONSHIP

It was announced last October that the Euro 1996 Finals in England made a record profit of £56m. It was to be distributed (a) to the 16 competing countries and (b) to UEFA's "special fund" dedicated to the development of the game in the emerging nations of Eastern Europe.

The Football Association were to receive £3.75m. as reward for England's progress to the semi-finals, plus a "surplus" of £500,000 and a further £750,000 towards the cost of staging the tournament. Scotland received £2.5m.

The eight host stadiums shared £5m. for ground hire. Germany received £6m. as winners.

History: After the World Cup, the European Championship is football's most prestigious tournament. It was launched in 1958 and the trophy is the Henri Delaunay Cup, named after its French founder.

Later known as the Nations Cup and, since 1966, as the European Championship, the tournament spans two years, with the Final exactly midway between one World Cup and the next. Eight different countries have won the ten Finals, with Germany successful on three occasions.

Year	Venue	Winners		Runners-up	
1960	Paris	*U.S.S.R.	2	Yugoslavia	1
1964	Madrid	Spain	2	U.S.S.R.	1
1968	Rome	Italy	2	Yugoslavia	0
		(replay, after 1-1 draw)			
1972	Brussels	West Germany	3	U.S.S.R.	0
1976	Belgrade	*Czechoslovakia	2	West Germany	2
		(Czechoslovakia won 5-3 on penalties)			
1980	Rome	West Germany	2	Belgium	1
1984	Paris	France	2	Spain	0
1988	Munich	Holland	2	U.S.S.R.	0
1992	Gothenburg	Denmark	2	Germany	0
1996	London	†Germany	2	Czech Republic	1

(*After extra time; †decided in overtime)

● **Record scorer** in European Championship final series: **Michel Platini** with 9 goals when he captained France to victory in 1984. He scored in every match.

● The Finals in 2000 will be hosted jointly for the first time. Holland and Belgium were the only applicants by the deadline in September 1994.

QUOTE-UNQUOTE

BILL SHANKLY: "If you've got three Scots in your team, you've a chance of winning something. Any more and you've got trouble."

JIMMY HILL on retiring as Fulham chairman: "I've had ten years and the club has progressed, especially now with promotion and the freehold of Craven Cottage secure. I feel I have repaid football for the pleasure it has given me. I need freedom from all the responsibility of finance and performance and to have more time with my family."

BOBBY ROBSON (Barcelona): "Football is my drug. No matter how long you've been in it, you don't lose the edge, the excitement, the adrenalin, the little electric shocks. Football isn't a game – not to me. It's my life, my hobby too."

GLENN HODDLE, on being England coach: "The more I find out about the job, the more I realise that club management is no apprenticeship for it."

BRITISH AND IRISH INTERNATIONALS 1996-97

Note: In the senior Internationals that follow, * = new cap.

WORLD CUP QUALIFYING ROUND

AUSTRIA 0, SCOTLAND 0
Vienna (29,500), Saturday, August 31, 1996

Austria: Konsel; Schopp, Schottel, Pfeffer, Feiersinger, Marasek, Ramusch (Ogris 76), Kuhbauer, Polster (Sabitzer 68), Herzog, Heraf.

Scotland: Goram (Rangers); Burley (Chelsea), Boyd (Celtic), Calderwood (Tottenham), Hendry (Blackburn), T. McKinlay (Celtic), D. Ferguson (Everton), McCall (Rangers), McCoist (Rangers) (Durie, Rangers, 75), G. McAllister (Coventry, Capt), Collins (Monaco). **Booked:** McAllister, Ferguson.

Referee: M. Piraux (Belgium).

WALES 6, SAN MARINO 0
National Stadium, Cardiff (15,150), Saturday, August 31, 1996

Wales: Southall (Everton) (Roberts, QPR, 71); M. Bowen (West Ham), Pembridge (Sheff. Wed.), Browning (Bristol Rovers), Melville (Sunderland), Coleman (Blackburn) (Taylor, Sheff. Utd., 80), Horne (Birmingham, Capt), Robinson (Charlton) (Speed, Everton, 77), Saunders (Nott'm. Forest), M. Hughes (Chelsea), Giggs (Man. Utd.). **Scorers:** Saunders (2,75), Hughes (25,54), Melville (33), Robinson (45). **Booked:** Giggs.

San Marino: Muccioli; Valentini, L. Gasperoni (Matteoni 66), Guerra, Gobbi, Genari, B. Gasperoni, Bacciocchi (Francini 43), Mazza (Pasalini 79), Pier Manzaroli, Montagna. **Booked:** Muccioli, L. Gasperoni, B. Gasperoni. **Sent off:** Pier Manzaroli.

Referee: A. Hamer (Luxembourg). **Half-time:** 4-0.

- 6-0 equalled Wales' record score in World Cup.

NORTHERN IRELAND 0, UKRAINE 1
Windsor Park, Belfast (9,358), Saturday, August 31, 1996

Northern Ireland: Fettis (Nott'm. Forest); Griffin (St Johnstone) (M. O'Neill, Coventry, 78), Rowland (West Ham) (Magilton, Southampton, 84), Hill (Leicester), Morrow (Arsenal), Lomas (Man. City), Gillespie (Newcastle), Lennon (Leicester), Dowie (West Ham, Capt), P. Gray (Nancy), Hughes (West Ham). **Booked:** Lomas, O'Neill.

Ukraine: Shovkovskyi; Luzhnyi (Parfenov 69), Golovko, Bezhenar, Skrypnyk, Orbu, Popov, Kalitvintsev (Kriventsov 73), Luchkevych (Rebrov 45), Maximov, Leonenko. **Scorer:** Rebrov (79). **Booked:** Leonenko.

Referee: A. Sars (France). **Half-time:** 0-0.

LIECHTENSTEIN 0, REPUBLIC OF IRELAND 5
Eschen (3,900), Saturday, August 31, 1996

Liechtenstein: Heeb; Hefti, Stocklasa, Hilti, Hasler, Hanselmann (Telser 82), Quaderer, Zech, H. Schadler (Klaunzer 78), Frick, F. Schadler. **Booked:** Stocklasa.

Rep. of Ireland: Given (Blackburn); Irwin (Man. Utd.), Harte (Leeds), Kenna (Blackburn), Breen (Birmingham), Staunton (Aston Villa), Townsend (Aston Villa, Capt) (Cascarino, Nancy, 83), Houghton (Crystal Palace), Quinn (Sunderland), McLoughlin (Portsmouth), K. O'Neill (Norwich) (Moore, Middlesbrough, 72). **Scorers:** Townsend (5), O'Neill (7), Quinn (11,61), Harte (19).

Referee: S. Shmolik (Belarus). **Half-time:** 0-4.

● Rep. of Ireland's record away score.

MOLDOVA 0, ENGLAND 3
Kishinev (9,500), Sunday, September 1, 1996

Moldova: Romanenco; Secu, Nani, Testimitanu, Gaidamasiuc, Epureanu, Curteanu, Belous (Sischin 58), Clescenco, Mitereu (Rebeja 61), Popovici. **Booked:** Clescenco.

England: Seaman (Arsenal); G. Neville (Man. Utd.), Pearce (Nott'm Forest), Ince (Inter Milan), Pallister (Man. Utd.), Southgate (Aston Villa), *Beckham (Man. Utd.), *Hinchcliffe (Everton), Gascoigne (Rangers) (Batty, Newcastle, 80), Shearer (Newcastle, Capt), Barmby (Middlesbrough) (Le Tissier, Southampton, 80). **Scorers:** Barmby (24), Gascoigne (25), Shearer (61). **Booked:** Pearce, Ince.

Referee: I. Koho (Finland). **Half-time:** 0-2.

LATVIA 0, SCOTLAND 2
Riga (9,500), Saturday, October 5, 1996

Latvia: Karavajevs; Troickis, Astafievs, Zemlinskis, Shevljakovs, Stephanov, V. Ivanovs, Bledidelis, Rimkus, Babicevs (Stolsers 45), Pahars. **Booked:** Stepanov.

Scotland: Goram (Rangers); Burley (Chelsea), Boyd (Celtic), Calderwood (Tottenham), Whyte (Middlesbrough), T. McKinlay (Celtic) (*McNamara, Celtic, 80), Spencer (Chelsea) (*Dodds, Aberdeen, 59), McCall (Rangers) (Lambert, Bor. Dortmund, 45), Jackson (Hibernian), G. McAllister (Coventry, Capt), Collins (Monaco). **Scorers:** Collins (18), Jackson (78). **Booked:** Collins, McAllister.

Referee: J. Ulrich (Czech Republic). **Half-time:** 0-0.

WALES 1, HOLLAND 3
National Stadium, Cardiff (25,000), Saturday, October 5, 1996

Wales: Southall (Everton); Melville (Sunderland), M. Bowen (West Ham), Symons (Man. City), Robinson (Charlton), Browning (Bristol Rovers) (Jenkins, Huddersfield, 83), Horne (Birmingham, Capt), Pembridge (Sheff. Wed.) (Legg, Birmingham, 65), Speed (Everton), Saunders (Nott'm Forest), M. Hughes (Chelsea). **Scorer:** Saunders (17). **Booked:** Speed, Hughes.

Holland: Van der Saar; Vierklau (Van Hooijdonk 70), Valckx, F. de Boer, Bogarde, Jonk, Winter, Seedorf, Cocu, Cruyff (Makaay 45), R. de Boer (Van Bronckhorst 89). **Scorers:** Van Hooijdonk (72, 75), R. de Boer (79). **Booked:** Valckx.

Referee: A. Lopez Nieto (Spain). **Half-time:** 1-0.

NORTHERN IRELAND 1, ARMENIA 1
Windsor Park, Belfast (8,357), Saturday, October 5, 1996

Northern Ireland: Fettis (Nott'm Forest); *Nolan (Sheff. Wed.), Hill (Leicester), Hunter (Reading), Rowland (West Ham), Gillespie (Newcastle) (M. O'Neill, Coventry, 80), Lomas (Man. City), Hughes (West Ham), Lennon (Leicester) (Magilton, Southampton, 60), Dowie (West Ham, Capt), P. Gray (Nancy) (McMahon, Stoke, 60). **Scorer:** Lennon (30). **Booked:** Hill, Hunter, Dowie, Gillespie.

Armenia: Berezovski; Hovespian, Soukiasyan, Vardanyan, Khachatryan, Oganesyan, Petrossyan (Avetissyan 82) Tonoyan (Minassyan 55), Mkhitaryan, Assadouryan, Mikaelyan (Ter-Petrossyan 70). **Scorer:** Assadouryan (8). **Booked:** Khachatryan, Petrossyan, Tonoyan.

Referee: K. Danilovski (Macedonia). **Half-time:** 1-1.

ENGLAND 2, POLAND 1
Wembley (74,663), Wednesday, October 9, 1996

England: Seaman (Arsenal); G. Neville (Man. Utd.), Pearce (Nott'm Forest), Ince (Inter Milan), Southgate (Aston Villa) (Pallister, Man. Utd., 51), Beckham (Man. Utd.), Gascoigne (Rangers), McManaman (Liverpool), Hinchcliffe (Everton), Ferdinand (Newcastle), Shearer (Newcastle, Capt). **Scorers:** Shearer (24, 38).

Poland: Wozniak; Wojtala, Zielinski, Joswiak, Hajto, Michalski, Waldoch, Baluszynski, Nowak, Warzycha (Saganowski 75), Citko. **Scorer:** Citko (7). **Booked:** Hajto.

Referee: H. Krug (Germany). **Half-time:** 2-1.

ESTONIA v SCOTLAND
Tallinin, Wednesday, October 9, 1996

No match. Estonia refused to turn up after FIFA advanced the kick-off by four hours to 3 p.m. because of a potential floodlight problem. The home side were at lunch in their training camp 60 miles away when Yugoslav referee Miroslav Radoman blew his whistle to start the "game". Billy Dodds passed the ball to John Collins and within three seconds proceedings were abandoned.

The match was ordered to be played on neutral ground (Monaco) on February 11.

Scotland awarded caps to the 11 players who lined up in Tallinin: Goram; McNamara, Boyd, Calderwood, T. McKinlay, Lambert, Collins (Capt), Burley, Jackson, Dodds, McGinlay.

REPUBLIC OF IRELAND 3, MACEDONIA 0
Landsdowne Road, Dublin (31,600), Wednesday, October 9, 1996

Rep. of Ireland: A. Kelly (Sheff. Utd.); Irwin (Man. Utd.), Harte (Leeds) (Moore, Middlesbrough, 85), Kenna (Blackburn), Breen (Birmingham), Staunton (Aston Villa), Townsend (Aston Villa, Capt), McLoughlin (Portsmouth) (O'Brien, Tranmere, 88), K. O'Neill (Norwich) (Aldridge, Tranmere, 72), McAteer (Liverpool), Cascarino (Marseille). **Scorers:** McAteer (8), Cascarino (46, 70). **Booked:** Harte, McLoughlin.

Macedonia: Celeski; Nikoloski, Sedloski, Jovanovski, Milosavov, Gosev, Milosevski (Zaharievski 60), Ciric, Beganovic (Sakiri 73), T. Micevski, Hristov. **Booked:** T. Micevski.

Referee: K. Fisker (Denmark). **Half-time:** 1-0.

140

GEORGIA 0, ENGLAND 2

Tbilisi (48,000), Saturday, November 9, 1996

Georgia: Ziodze; Lobjanidze, Tskhadadze, Shelia, Gogichaishvili, Nemsadze, Jamarauli, Kinkladze, Kobiashvili (Ghudushauri 67), Arveladze (Gogrichiani 52), Ketsbaia. **Booked:** Lobjanidze.

England: Seaman (Arsenal); Southgate (Aston Villa), Adams (Arsenal, Capt), Campbell (Tottenham), Hinchcliffe (Everton), Beckham (Man. Utd.), Ince (Inter Milan), Gascoigne (Rangers), Batty (Newcastle), Sheringham (Tottenham), Ferdinand (Newcastle) (Wright, Arsenal, 81). **Scorers:** Sheringham (15), Ferdinand (37). **Booked:** Beckham.

Referee: J. Monteiro (Portugal). **Half-time:** 0-2.

HOLLAND 7, WALES 1

Eindhoven (25,000), Saturday, November 9, 1996

Holland: Van der Saar; Reiziger, Stam, F. de Boer, Numan, Seedorf (Van Hooijdonk 68), Winter, Jonk (van Bronckhorst 81), Cocu, Bergkamp, R. de Boer (Overmars 57). **Scorers:** Bergkamp (22, 72, 78), R. de Boer (33), Jonk (34), F. de Boer (45), Cocu (61).

Wales: Southall (Everton); M. Bowen (West Ham), Pembridge (Sheff. Wed.), Melville (Sunderland), Symons (Man. City), V. Jones (Wimbledon, Capt), J. Bowen (Birmingham) (Robinson, Charlton, 58), Speed (Everton), Neilson (Southampton), Saunders (Nott'm. Forest), Hartson (Arsenal) (Taylor, Sheff. Utd., 67). **Scorer:** Saunders (40). **Booked:** Jones, Melville.

Referee: V. Melo Oereira (Portugal). **Half-time:** 4-1.

• Wales' worst ever World Cup defeat was their heaviest loss for 66 years.

GERMANY 1, NORTHERN IRELAND 1

Nuremberg (40,718), Saturday, November 9, 1996

Germany: Kopke; Strunz, Reuter, Kohler, Babbel, Tarnat, Hassler, Keilts (Palsack 62), Moller, Klinsmann, Bobic (Bierhof 70). **Scorer:** Moller (40). **Booked:** Kohler, Strunz, Reuter.

Northern Ireland: Wright (Nott'm. Forest); Hill (Leicester), Nolan (Sheff. Wed.), Hunter (Reading), Taggart (Bolton), Horlock (Swindon), Morrow (Arsenal), Lennon (Leicester) (Rogan, Millwall, 85), Lomas (Man. City), Hughes (West Ham), Dowie (West Ham, Capt) (P. Gray, Nancy, 76). **Scorer:** Taggart (38). **Booked:** Horlock, Hughes, Wright.

Referee: A. Cakar (Turkey). **Half-time:** 1-1.

SCOTLAND 1, SWEDEN 0

Ibrox (46,738), Sunday, November 10, 1996

Scotland: Leighton (Hibernian); Calderwood (Tottenham), Hendry (Blackburn, Capt), Boyd (Celtic), McNamara (Celtic) (Lambert, Bor. Dortmund, 45), Burley (Chelsea), W. McKinlay (Blackburn), Collins (Monaco), T. McKinlay (Celtic), McGinlay (Bolton) (McCoist, Rangers, 84), Jackson (Hibernian) (Gallacher, Blackburn, 78). **Scorer:** McGinlay (8). **Booked:** Calderwood.

Sweden: Ravelli; Nilsson, P. Andersson, Bjorklund, Sundgren, Alexandersson (Larsson 67), Thern, Schwarz, Zetterberg (Andersson 70), Blomqvist, Dahlin.

Referee: J. Aranda (Spain). **Half-time:** 1-0.

REPUBLIC OF IRELAND 0, ICELAND 0
Lansdowne Road, Dublin (33,869), Sunday, November 10, 1996

Rep. of Ireland: A. Kelly (Sheff. Utd.); Irwin (Man. Utd.) (Harte, Leeds 64), Breen (Birmingham), Keane (Man. Utd.), Babb (Liverpool), Kenna (Blackburn) (Cunningham, Wimbledon, 64), McAteer (Liverpool), McLoughlin (Portsmouth), Townsend (Aston Villa, Capt), Cascarino (Marseille), D. Kelly (Sunderland) (Moore, Middlesbrough, 79). **Booked:** Breen, D. Kelly.

Iceland: B. Kristinsson; Birgisson, Adolfsson, Jonsson, L. Sigurdsson, Gylfason, H. Gudjonsson (Thordarson 85), Sverrison, R. Kristinsson (Gretarsson 70), H. Sigurdsson, T. Gudjonsson. **Booked:** Sverrison, R. Kristinsson, Gretarsson.

Referee: S. Ormandjiev (Bulgaria).

WALES 0, TURKEY 0
National Stadium, Cardiff (14,206), Saturday, December 14, 1996

Wales: Southall (Everton); Jenkins (Huddersfield), Melville (Sunderland), Speed (Everton), *Page (Watford), Pembridge (Sheff. Wed.), V. Jones (Wimbledon), Horne (Birmingham, Capt), Giggs (Man. Utd.), Saunders (Nott'm Forest) (Hartson, Arsenal, 81), M. Hughes (Chelsea). **Booked:** Jenkins, Pembridge, Melville.

Turkey: Engin; Alpay, Ogun, Bulent, Ilker (Saffet 88), Kemalettin (Tolunay 88), Tugay, Abdullah, Recep, Arif (Oktay 70), Hakan. **Booked:** Recep.

Referee: A. Hazu (Romania).

NORTHERN IRELAND 2, ALBANIA 0
Windsor Park, Belfast (7,935), Saturday, December 14, 1996

Northern Ireland: Wright (Nott'm Forest); Nolan (Sheff. Wed.), Taggart (Bolton), Hill (Leicester), Hunter (Reading), Horlock (Swindon), Morrow (Arsenal) (McMahon, Stoke, 72), Lomas (Man. City), Lennon (Leicester), Hughes (West Ham), Dowie (West Ham, Capt), (J. Quinn, Blackpool, 90). **Scorer:** Dowie (12, 21). **Booked:** Horlock, Hughes.

Albania: Nallbani; Dede (Tole 34), Shulku, R. Vata, Malko, Kola, Haxhi (Fraholli 37), Fakaj, F. Vata, Rraklli, Paco. **Booked:** Shulku.

Referee: A. Georgiou (Cyprus). **Half-time:** 2-0.

ESTONIA 0, SCOTLAND 0
Monaco (4,000), Tuesday, February 11, 1997

Estonia: Poom; Kirs, Hohlov-Simson, Lemsalu, U. Rooba, Reim, Leetma (Oper 76), M. Rooba (Pari 67), Alonen, Kristal, Zelinski. **Booked:** Alonen, Zelinski.

Scotland: Goram (Rangers); Calderwood (Tottenham), Hendry (Blackburn), Boyd (Celtic), McNamara (Celtic) (T. McKinlay, Celtic, 75), McStay (Celtic) (I. Ferguson, Rangers, 63), G. McAllister (Coventry, Capt), Collins (Monaco), Gallacher (Black-

burn), McGinlay (Bolton) (McCoist, Rangers, 73), D. Ferguson (Everton).
Booked: Collins, McNamara, McAllister.

Referee: M. Radoman (Yugoslavia).

ENGLAND 0, ITALY 1
Wembley (75,055), Wednesday, February 12, 1997

England: Walker (Tottenham); G. Neville (Man. Utd.), Campbell (Tottenham), Pearce (Nott'm Forest), Beckham (Man. Utd.), Ince (Inter Milan), Batty (Newcastle) (Wright, Arsenal, 87), Le Saux (Blackburn), McManaman (Liverpool) (Merson, Arsenal, 76), Le Tissier (Southampton) (Ferdinand, Newcastle, 60), Shearer (Newcastle, Capt).

Italy: Peruzzi; Ferrera, Costacurta, Cannavaro, Di Livio, Di Matteo, Albertini, D. Baggio, Maldini, Zola (Fuser 90), Casiraghi (Ravanelli 76). **Scorer:** Zola (18).

Referee: S. Puhl (Hungary). **Half-time:** 0-1.

- England's first World Cup defeat on home soil.

SCOTLAND 2, ESTONIA 0
Rugby Park, Kilmarnock (17,996), Saturday, March 29, 1997

Scotland: Leighton (Hibernian); Burley (Chelsea), Boyd (Celtic), T. McKinlay (Celtic), Gemmill (Nott'm Forest), McStay (Celtic), Jackson (Hiberbnian) (McGinlay, Bolton, 83), G. McAllister (Coventry, Capt), Gallacher (Blackburn). **Scorers:** Boyd (25), Meet og (52).

Estonia: Poom; Lemsalu, Kirs, Hohlov-Simson, Zelinski (Arbeter 81), Meet, Pari (M. Rooba 55), Kristal, Reim, Oper, Viikmae (Leetma 72). **Booked:** Hohlov-Simson, Zelinski.

Referee: B. Heynemann (Germany). **Half-time:** 1-0.

WALES 1, BELGIUM 2
Cardiff Arms Park (15,000), Saturday, March 29, 1997

Wales: Southall (Everton); Blackmore (Middlesbrough), Page (Watford), Speed (Everton), Symons (Man. City), Pembridge (Sheff. Wed.), Horne (Birmingham, Capt), V. Jones (Wimbledon), Giggs (Man. Utd.), M. Hughes (Chelsea), Saunders (Nott'm Forest) (Hartson, West Ham, 62). **Scorer:** Speed (67). **Booked:** Hughes, Page, Horne.

Belgium: De Wilde; Crasson, De Roover, Van Meir, Smidts, Van Kerckhoven, Van der Elst, Staelens, Lemoine, Oliveira-Barroso (Scifo 79), L. M'Penza (M. M'Penza 62). **Scorers:** Crasson (24), Staelens (45). **Booked:** L. M'Penza.

Referee: C. Faellstrom (Sweden). **Half-time:** 0-2.

NORTHERN IRELAND 0, PORTUGAL 0
Windsor Park, Belfast (9,392), Saturday, March 29, 1997

Northern Ireland: Wright (Man. City); Hill (Leicester), Taggart (Bolton), Morrow (Arsenal), Gillespie (Newcastle), Lomas (Man. City), Lennon (Leicester), Magilton (Southampton), Nolan (Sheff. Wed.), Dowie (West Ham, Capt), J. Quinn (Blackpool) McMahon, Stoke, 63). **Booked:** Quinn.

Portugal: Baia; Santos, Couto (Martins 63), Costa, Dimas (Cadete 63), Oceano, Sousa, Conceicao, Rui Costa, Figo, Pinto. **Booked:** Oceano, Couto, Martins, Figo.

Referee: G. Cesari (Italy).

MACEDONIA 3, REPUBLIC OF IRELAND 2
Skopje (8,000), Wednesday, April 2, 1997

Macedonia: Celeski; Milosavov, Stojkovski, Markovski, Nikolovski, Sedloski, Gosev, Glavevski (Micevski 87), Hristov (Beganovic 79), Sainovski (Georgievski 82), Sakiri. **Scorers:** Stojkovski (28, 44 pens), Hristov (59). **Booked:** Milosavov, Celeski. **Sent off:** Stojkovski (90).

Rep. of Ireland: A. Kelly (Sheff. Utd.); Irwin (Man. Utd.), Phelan (Everton) (Harte, Leeds, 56), McAteer (Liverpool), Breen (Coventry), Keane (Man. Utd.), Townsend (Aston Villa, Capt), McLoughlin (Portsmouth), Cascarino (Nancy) (K. O'Neill, Norwich, 45) (D. Kelly, Sunderland, 75), Goodman (Wimbledon), Staunton (Aston Villa). **Scorers:** McLoughlin (8), D. Kelly (78). **Booked:** Keane, McLoughlin, Phelan. **Sent off:** McAteer (90).

Referee: A. Trentalange (Italy). **Half-time:** 2-1.

SCOTLAND 2, AUSTRIA 0
Celtic Park (43,295), Wednesday, April 2, 1997

Scotland: Leighton (Hibernian); Calderwood (Tottenham), Hendry (Blackburn), Boyd (Celtic), Lambert (Bor. Dortmund), Burley (Chelsea), G. McAllister (Coventry, Capt) (McStay, Celtic, 88), Collins (Monaco), T. McKinlay (Celtic), Gallacher (Blackburn) (McCoist, Rangers, 86), Jackson (Hibernian) (McGinlay, Bolton, 73). **Scorer:** Gallacher (24, 77). **Booked:** Collins.

Austria: Konsel; Feiersinger, Schottel (Kogler 45), Pfeffer, Schopp, Heraf, Stoger (Vastic 67), Aigner (Ogris 81), Wetl, Herzog, Polster. **Booked:** Schottel.

Referee: N. Levnikov (Russia). **Half-time:** 1-0.

UKRAINE 2, NORTHERN IRELAND 1
Kiev (70,000), Wednesday, April 2, 1997

Ukraine: Shovkovski; Luzhnyi, Bezhenar, Golovko, Skrypnyk, Mikhailenko, Kardash, Kalitvintsev, Kosovski (Orbu 72), Shevchenko, Rebrov. **Scorers:** Kosovski (3), Shevchenko (70). **Booked:** Luzhnyi, Golovko.

Northern Ireland: Wright (Man. City, Capt); Nolan (Sheff. Wed.), Hill (Leicester), Morrow (QPR), Taggart (Bolton), Horlock (Man. City), Gillespie (Newcastle) (McMahon, stoke, 81), Lennon (Leicester) (J. Quinn, Blackpool, 75), Lomas (Man. City), Hughes (West Ham), Dowie (West Ham). **Scorer:** Dowie (14 pen). **Booked:** Hughes, Gillespie.

Referee: V. Kronde (Czech Republic). **Half-time:** 1-1.

ENGLAND 2, GEORGIA 0
Wembley (71,208), Wednesday, April 30, 1997

England: Seaman (Arsenal); G. Neville (Man. Utd.), Adams (Arsenal) (Southgate, Aston Villa, 87), Campbell (Tottenham), Beckham (Man. Utd.), Ince (Inter Milan)

(Redknapp, Liverpool, 77), Batty (Newcastle), Le Saux (Blackburn), Lee (Newcastle), Sheringham (Tottenham), Shearer (Newcastle, Capt). **Scorers:** Sheringham (43), Shearer (90). **Booked:** Le Saux, Lee.

Georgia: Zoidze; Tskhadadze, Chikhradze, Sheqiladze, Shelia, Machaviariani (Gogrichiani 32) (A. Arveladze 76), Jamarauli, Nemsadze, Ketsbaia, Kinkladze (Gakhokidze 61), S. Arveladze. **Booked:** Nemsadze, Kinkladze, Gogrichiani, Shelia.

Referee: R. Harrel (France). **Half-time:** 1-0.

SWEDEN 2, SCOTLAND 1
Gothenberg (40,000), Wednesday, April 30, 1997

Sweden: Ravelli; Sundgren, Bjorklund, P. Andersson, Kamark, Thern, Zetterberg, Schwarz (Mild 17), K. Andersson, Dahlin, A. Andersson. **Scorer:** K. Andersson (43, 63). **Booked:** Bjorklund, Dahlin, Zetterberg.

Scotland: Leighton (Hibernian); Calderwood (Tottenham), Hendry (Blackburn), Boyd (Celtic), Burley (Chelsea), G. McAllister (Coventry, Capt), Lambert (Bor. Dortmund), Collins (Monaco), T. McKinlay (Celtic) (Gemmill, Nott'm Forest, 67), Jackson (Hibernian) (Durie, Rangers, 65), Gallacher (Blackburn). **Scorer:** Gallacher (83). **Booked:** Calderwood.

Referee: P. Collina (Italy). **Half-time:** 1-0.

ROMANIA 1, REPUBLIC OF IRELAND 0
Bucharest (25,000), Wednesday, April 30, 1997

Romania: Stelea; Dobos, Prodan, Filipescu, Petrescu, Gica Popescu (Rotariu 72), Munteanu, Selymes, Hagi (Craioveanu 87), Ilie (Gabriel Popescu 84), Moldovan. **Scorer:** Ilie (32). **Booked:** Filipescu, Hagi, Stelea, Munteanu, Moldovan.

Rep. of Ireland: A. Kelly (Sheff. Utd.); Irwin (Man. Utd.) (Kenna, Blackburn, 45), Cunningham (Wimbledon), Harte (Leeds) (Goodman, Wimbledon, 74), Staunton (Aston Villa), Houghton (Crystal Palace), Keane (Man. Utd.), Townsend (Aston Villa, Capt), G. Kelly (Leeds), Connolly (Watford) (Cascarino, Nancy, 74), Kennedy (Liverpool). **Booked:** Irwin, Cunningham, Kennedy.

Referee: M. Van der Ende (Holland). **Half-time:** 1-0.

- Roy Keane penalty (47 mins) – saved.

ARMENIA 0, NORTHERN IRELAND 0
Yerevan (10,000), Wednesday, April 30, 1997

Armenia: Berezovsky; Yepiskoposyan (Minasyan 87), Sukiasyan, Ter-Zakarian, Hovsepyan, Khachatryan, Avalyan (Avetisyan 75), Mkhitaryan, Mikaelyan, Assadourian, Petrosyan. **Booked:** Khachatryan, Mkhitaryan, Sukiasyan.

Northern Ireland: Fettis (Nott'm Forest); *Jenkins (Chester), Taggart (Bolton), Hill (Leicester), Morrow (QPR), McCarthy (Port Vale) (Mulryne, Man. Utd., 71), Lomas (West Ham), Lennon (Leicester), Horlock (Man. City), Dowie (West Ham, Capt), J. Quinn (Blackpool) (McMahon, Stoke, 59). **Booked:** Lomas, Lennon, Dowie.

Referee: K. Nielsen (Sweden).

REPUBLIC OF IRELAND 5, LIECHTENSTEIN 0
Lansdowne Road, Dublin (28,575), Wednesday, May 21, 1997

Rep. of Ireland: Given (Blackburn); Kenna (Blackburn), Cunningham (Wimbledon), Harte (Leeds), Staunton (Aston Villa), Keane (Man. Utd.), Townsend (Aston Villa, Capt), Houghton (Crystal Palace) (Cascarino, Nancy, 53), G. Kelly (Leeds), Connolly (Watford) (Goodman, Wimbledon, 78), Kennedy (Liverpool) (Fleming, Middlesbrough, 63). **Scorers:** Connolly (29, 34, 40), Cascarino (60, 77). **Booked:** Kennedy, Kenna, G. Kelly.

Liechtenstein: Heeb, Stocklasa, Hefti, Hanselmann (Ackermann 80), D. Telser (Verling 63), C. Frick, Hasler, M. Frick (Ospelt 45), Schadler, Klaunzer, D. Frick. **Booked:** Veeling. **Sent off:** C. Frick (27).

Referee: A. Boutenko (Russia). **Half-time:** 3-0.

POLAND 0, ENGLAND 2
Katowice (35,000), Saturday, May 31, 1997

Poland: Wozniak; Joswiak, Zielinski, Kaluzny, Ledwon, Bukalski (Swierczewski 45), Waldoch, Nowak (Kucharski 57), Majak, Dembinski, Juskowiak (Adamczyk 51). **Booked:** Joswiak, Majak, Kaluzny.

England: Seaman (Arsenal); G. Neville (Man. Utd.), Campbell (Tottenham), Southgate (Aston Villa), Beckham (Man. Utd.) (P. Neville, Man. Utd., 89), Le Saux (Blackburn), Ince (Inter Milan), Gascoigne (Rangers) (Batty, Newcastle, 17), Lee (Newcastle), Sheringham (Tottenham), Shearer (Newcastle, Capt). **Scorers:** Shearer (6), Sheringham (90). **Booked:** Ince, Batty.

Referee: U. Meier (Switzerland). **Half-time:** 1-0.

BELARUS 0, SCOTLAND 1
Minsk (12,000), Sunday, June 8, 1997

Belarus: Satsounkevitch; Lavrik, Yakimovich, Otrovsky, Shtanyuk, Gerassimets, Gourenko, Dovnar (Belkevitch 60), Orlovski (Balachov 64), Romatchenko, Khlebossolov (Makovski 63).

Scotland: Leighton (Hibernian), Burley (Chelsea), Boyd (Celtic), Dailly (Derby), Hopkin (Crystal Palace) (Gemmill, Nott'm Forest, 67), Lambert (Bor. Dortmund), G. McAllister (Coventry, Capt), Jackson (Hibernian) (Dodds, Aberdeen, 87), T. McKinlay (Celtic) (B. McAllister, Wimbledon, 84), Gallacher (Blackburn), Durie (Rangers). **Scorer:** McAllister (49 pen). **Booked:** Hopkin, Durie.

Referee: A. Caker (Turkey). **Half-time:** 0-0.

FRIENDLY INTERNATIONALS

ITALY 2, NORTHERN IRELAND 0
Palermo (30,866), Wednesday, January 22, 1997

Italy: Peruzzi, Ferrara, Maldini, Costacurta (Cannavaro 71), Di Livio (Eranio 78), Carboni, D. Baggio, Albertini, Di Matteo (Fuser 57), Zola (Del Piero 62), Casiraghi (Ravanelli 57). **Scorers:** Zola (8), Del Piero (88).

Northern Ireland: Wright (Nott'm Forest); Griffin (St. Johnstone), Morrow (Arsenal), Hunter (Reading), Taggart (Bolton), Hughes (West Ham) (Rowland, West Ham, 69), Lomas (West Ham), Horlock (Swindon), Quinn (Blackpool) (O'Boyle, St. Johnstone, 59), Worthington (Stoke), McCarthy (Port Vale) (Dennison, Wolves, 81).

Referee: L. Frohlich (Germany). **Half-time:** 1-0.

NORTHERN IRELAND 3, BELGIUM 0
Windsor Park, Belfast (7,126), Tuesday, February 11, 1997

Northern Ireland: Wright (Nott'm. Forest); Morrow (Arsenal), Lomas (Man. City), Gillespie (Newcastle), Lennon (Leicester) (Worthington, Stoke, 69), Magilton (Southampton), Hunter (Reading) (Griffin, St. Johnstone, 45), McMahon (Stoke) (*Mulryne, Man. Utd., 45), Taggart (Bolton), Horlock (Swindon) (*Whitley, Man. City, 81), J. Quinn (Blackpool) (O'Boyle, St. Johnstone, 59). **Scorers:** Quinn (14), Magilton (62 pen), Mulryne (88).

Belgium: De Wilde; Medved, De Roover, Staelens, Albert, Van der Elst, Verheyen (Pierre 71), Wilmots (Jbari 81), Nilis (L. M'Penza 45), Scifo (Lemoine 77), Van Kerckhoven (Schepens 86).

Referee: J. Rowbotham (Scotland). **Half-time:** 1-0.

WALES 0, REPUBLIC OF IRELAND 0
National Stadium, Cardiff (7,200), Tuesday, February 11, 1997

Wales: *Crossley (Nott'm. Forest); Speed (Everton), *Ready (QPR) Symons (Man. City), Pembridge (Sheff. Wed.), Horne (Birmingham Capt), Legg (Birmingham), V. Jones (Wimbledon) (Hughes, Luton, 75), Robinson (Charlton) (M. Bowen, West Ham, 62), M. Hughes (Chelsea) (Savage, Crewe, 88), Hartson (Arsenal) (Taylor, Sheff. Utd., 69).

Rep. Of Ireland: *Branagan (Bolton); Harte (Leeds), Staunton (Aston Villa, Capt), McLoughlin (Portsmouth) (G. Kelly, Leeds, 52), Cascarino (Nancy), McAteer (Liverpool), Keane (Man. Utd.) (D. Kelly, Sunderland, 74), Cunningham (Wimbledon), McGrath (Derby), Phelan (Everton), *Goodman (Wimbledon).

Referee: W. Young (Scotland).

ENGLAND 2, MEXICO 0
Wembley (48,076), Saturday, March 29, 1997

England: *James (Liverpool); Keown (Arsenal), Southgate (Aston Villa), Pearce (Nott'm. Forest), Lee (Newcastle), Ince (Inter Milan, Capt), Batty (Newcastle) (Redknapp, Liverpool, 54), Le Saux (Blackburn), Sheringham (Tottenham) (Wright, Arsenal, 37), McManaman (Liverpool) (Butt, Man. Utd., 68), Fowler (Liverpool). **Scorers:** Sheringham (20 pen), Fowler (55).

Mexico: Rios (Pineda 60); Pardo, Suarez, Davino, Alfaro, Coyote (R. Ramirez 66), Aspe, Ramirez, Galindo (Bernal 56), Hermosillo (Pelaez 45), Zague (Hernandez 45). **Booked:** Aspe Coyote.

Referee: V. Pelo Pereira (Portugal). **Half-time:** 1-0.

ENGLAND 2, SOUTH AFRICA 1
Old Trafford (52,676), Saturday, May 24, 1997

England: Martyn (Leeds); Keown (Arsenal), Southgate (Aston Villa), Pearce (Nott'm. Forest, Capt), P. Neville (Man. Utd.), Gascoigne (Rangers) (Campbell, Tottenham, 90), Redknapp (Liverpool) (Batty, Newcastle, 56), Le Saux (Blackburn) (Beckham, Man. Utd., 69), Lee (Newcastle) (*Butt, Man. Utd., 80), Sheringham (Tottenham) (*Scholes, Man. Utd., 64), Wright (Arsenal). **Scorers:** Lee (20), Wright (76).

South Africa: Arendse; Fish, Tovey, Radebe, Motaung, Tinkler (Buthelezi 85), Moshoeu, Moeti, Khumalo (Mkhalele 77), Masinga (Bartlett 85), Augustine (Sikhosana 54). **Scorer:** Masinga (43). **Booked:** Buthelezi.

Referee: A. Frisk (Sweden). **Half-time:** 1-1.

SCOTLAND 0, WALES 1
Rugby Park Kilmarnock (9,013), Tuesday, May 27, 1997

Scotland: *Sullivan (Wimbledon) (Leighton, Hibernian, 80); Boyd (Celtic), *B. McAllister (Wimbleton), T. McKinlay (Celtic), G. McAllister (Coventry, Capt), Gemmill (Nott'm. Forest), Jackson (Hibernian) (Spencer, QPR, 45), Gallacher (Blackburn) (*Donnelly, Celtic, 80) Dodds (Aberdeen), *Weir (Hearts), *Dailly (Derby) (McNamara, Celtic, 75).

Wales: Marriott (Wrexham) (*Jones, Stockport, 45); Speed (Everton) Jenkins (Huddersfield), Symons (Man. City), *Trollope (Derby), Pembridge (Sheff. Wed), page (Watford), Savage (Crewe), Robinson (Charlton) (Browning, Huddersfield, 88), Saunders (Nott'm Forest) (*L. Jones, Liverpool, 80), Hartson (West Ham) (*Haworth, Cardiff, 71). **Scorer:** Hartson (46).

Referee: A. Snoddy (Northern Ireland). **Half-time:** 0-0.

THAILAND 0, NORTHERN IRELAND 0
Bangkok (15,000), Wednesday, May 21, 1997

Thailand: Kampian; Tinnakorn, Krisada, Jirasirackote, Promrut, Chalermsan, Kijmonckolsak, Jaturapattararong, Damkong-Ongtrakul, Daorung, Piyapong.

Northern Ireland: Davison (Bradford C.) (*Carroll, Wigan, 45); Jenkins (Chester) (Whitley, Man. C., 45), Hill (Leicester), McGibbon (Man. Utd.), Griffin (St. Johnstone), McCarthy (Port Vale) (McMahon, Stoke, 45), Lomas (West Ham), Lennon (Leicester), Horlock (Man. C.), Mulryne (Man. Utd.) (J. Quinn, Blackpool, 45), Dowie (West Ham, Capt) (*Robinson, Bournemouth, 63).

Referee: P. Hanlumyavna (Thailand).

MALTA 2, SCOTLAND 3
Valletta (3,500), Sunday, June 1, 1997

Malta: Muscat; Attard (Turner 66) Brincatt, Debono, Chetcuti, Carabott, Vella (Giglio 75), Zammit, Saliba, Suda (Sultana 45), Agius. **Scorers:** Suda (17), Sultana (57).

Scotland: Leighton (Hibernian); Dailly (Derby), Boyd (Celtic), B. McAllister (Wimbledon) (Weir, Hearts, 45), Burley (Chelsea), G. McAllister (Coventry, Capt), *Hopkin (Crystal Palace) (Gemmill, Nott'm. Forest, 60), Collins (Monaco) (Donnelly, Celtic, 84), T. McKinlay (Celtic), Jackson (Hibernian), Gallacher (Blackburn) (Durie, Rangers, 60). **Scorers:** Dailly (4), Jackson (44), (81).

Referee: S. Braschi (Italy). **Half-time:** 1-2.

TOURNOI DE FRANCE (Winners: England)

ENGLAND 2, ITALY 0
Nantes (25,000), Wednesday, June 4, 1997

England: Flowers (Blackburn); Keown (Arsenal), Southgate (Aston Villa), Pearce (Nott'm. Forest), P. Neville (Man. Utd.), Beckham (Man. Utd.), Scholes (Man. Utd.), Ince (Inter Milan, Capt), Le Saux (Blackburn) (G. Neville, Man. Utd., 45), Sheringham (Tottenham) (Gascoigne, Rangers, 78), Wright (Arsenal) (Cole, Man. Utd., 76). **Scorers:** Wright (26), Scholes (43). **Booked:** Beckham, Scholes, Gascoigne, Ince.

Italy: Peruzzi; Ferrara (Nesta 45), Costacurta, Cannavaro, Di Livio (Maini 45), D. Baggio, Albertini, Di Matteo (Fuser 17), Bennarivo, Zola, Casiragi. **Booked:** Cannavaro, Costacurta.

Referee: G. Benko (Austria). **Half-time:** 2-0.

FRANCE 0, ENGLAND 1
Montpellier (25,000), Saturday, June 7, 1997

France: Barthez; Thuram, Blanc, Ngotty, Laigle (Lizarazu 81), Deschamps, Vieira, Keller, Djorkaeff, Dugarry (Zidane 73), Quedec (Loko 62).

England: Seaman (Arsenal); G. Neville (Man. Utd.), Southgate (Aston Villa), Campbell (Tottenham), P. Neville (Man. Utd.), Beckham (Man. Utd.) (Lee, Newcastle, 73), Batty (Newcastle) (Ince, Inter Milan, 45), Le Saux (Blackburn), Gascoigne (Rangers), Shearer (Newcastle, Capt), Wright (Arsenal) (Sheringham, Tottenham, 78). **Scorer:** Shearer (86). **Booked:** Beckham, Batty, Le Saux.

Referee: S. Belqola (Morocco). **Half-time:** 0-0.

ENGLAND 0, BRAZIL 1
Parc des Princes, Paris (33,000), Tuesday, June 10, 1997

England: Seaman (Arsenal); Keown (Arsenal) (G. Neville, Man. Utd., 19), Southgate (Aston Villa), Campbell (Tottenham), P. Neville (Man. Utd.), Gascoigne (Rangers), Le Saux (Blackburn), Ince (Inter Milan), Scholes (Man. Utd.) (Lee, Newcastle, 74), Shearer (Newcastle, Capt), Sheringham (Tottenham) (Wright, Arsenal, 74). **Booked:** Shearer, Scholes, Campbell.

Brazil: Taffarel; Celio Silva, Aldair, Cafu, Flavio Conceicao, Dunga, Roberto Carlos, Leonardo (Ze Roberto 82), Denilson (Djalminha 20), Ronaldo, Romario. **Scorer:** Romario (61). **Booked:** Ronaldo, Dunga, Ceilo Silva.

Referee: J. Toro Rendon (Colombia). **Half-time:** 0-0.

Other results: France 1, Brazil 1; Brazil 3, Italy 3; France 2, Italy 2.

149

FINAL TABLE

	P	W	D	L	F	A	Pts
England	3	2	0	1	3	1	6
Brazil	3	1	2	0	5	4	5
France	3	0	2	1	3	4	2
Italy	3	0	2	1	5	7	2

EUROPEAN U-21 CHAMP – QUAL. ROUND

AUSTRIA 4, SCOTLAND 0
Amstetten (800), Friday, August 30, 1906

Scotland: Meldrum (Kilmarnock); Shields (Rangers), Bonar (Raith), Browne (Raith), McConnell (Clyde) (McMillan, Motherwell) Ritchie (Hearts), Thomas (Hearts) (Hartley, Millwall), Harper (Hibernian), Hamilton (Dundee) (Gillies, Hamilton), Miller (Rangers, Capt), Glass (Aberdeen).

Scorers – Austria: Brenner (5), Stieglmair (42), Brunmayr (43, 56). **Half-time:** 3-0.

WALES 4, SAN MARINO 0
Barry (1,800), Friday, August 30, 1996

Wales: Williams (Blackburn); Blaney (West Ham), Brace (Wrexham), Young (Cardiff) (Oster, Grimsby, 61), Jarman (Cardiff) (Hughes, Aston Villa, 78), Edwards (Swansea), Bellamy (Norwich), Robinson (Wolves), Hartson (Arsenal, Capt), Thomas (Blackburn), Rowlands (Man. City).

Scorers – Wales: Hartson (12, 56, 83), Young (24). **Half-time:** 2-0.

MOLDOVA 0, ENGLAND 2
Kishinev (900), Saturday, August 31, 1996

England: Day (Crystal Palace); Scimeca (Aston Villa), Duberry (Chelsea), Thatcher (Wimbledon, Capt), Newton (Charlton), Potter (Southampton), Ford (Leeds), Bowyer (Leeds), Holland (Newcastle), Dyer (Crystal Palace), Eadie (Norwich) (Moore, Tranmere, 70).

Scorers – England: Dyer (39), Eadie (53). **Half-time:** 0-1.

WALES 0, HOLLAND 2
Nimian Park, Cardiff (767), Friday, October 4, 1996

Wales: Williams (Blackburn); Brace (Wrexham), Young (Cardiff) (Oster, Grimsby, 52), Jarman (Cardiff), Edwards (Swansea), Robinson (Wolves), Hartson (Arsenal) (Roberts, Porthmadog, 69), Thomas (Blackburn), Rowlands (Man. City), Hughes (Aston Villa), Coates (Swansea). **Sent off:** Coates (83).

Scorers – Holland: Bruggink (52), Fuchs (83 pen). **Half-time:** 0-0.

LATVIA 0, SCOTLAND 0
Riga (500), Sunday, October 6, 1996

Scotland: Meldrum (Kilmarnock); Shields (Rangers), Bonar (Raith) (Anthony, Celtic), Ritchie (Hearts), Harper (Hibernian) (Teale, Clydebank), Hamilton (Dundee), Miller (Rangers, Capt), Gillies (St Mirren) (McCulloch, Motherwell), Naysmith (Hearts), Rowson (Aberdeen), Dods (Hibernian).

ENGLAND 0, POLAND 0
Wolverhampton (3,183), Tuesday, October 8, 1996

England: Marshall (Norwich); Scimeca (Aston Villa), Thatcher (Wimbledon, Capt), Duberry (Chelsea), Newton (Charlton), Holland (Newcastle) (Morris, Chelsea, 71), Butt (Man. Utd.), Humphreys (Sheff. Wed.) (Thompson, Liverpool, 45), Hall (Coventry), Heskey (Leicester) (Branch, Everton, 71), Scowcroft (Ipswich).

REPUBLIC OF IRELAND 4, MACEDONIA 0
Dalymount Park, Dublin (2,300), Tuesday, October 8, 1996

Rep. of Ireland: Murphy (Wimbledon); Carr (Tottenham), Kennedy (Liverpool), Worrell (Blackburn), Coll (Bournemouth), Darcy (Tottenham), O'Toole (Coventry), Finnan (Birmingham), Foley (Wolves) (Crowe, Wolves, 45), O'Halloran (Middlesbrough), Farrelly (Aston Villa) (Mahon, Tranmere, 89).

Scorers – Rep. of Ireland: Foley (32), Carr (72), Kennedy (86, 88). **Half-time:** 1-0.

ESTONIA 0, SCOTLAND 1
Tallinin (500), Tuesday, October 8, 1996

Scotland: Meldrum (Kilmarnock); Ritchie (Hearts), Hamilton (Dundee) (Anthony, Celtic), Miller (Rangers, Capt) (Bonar, Raith), Gillies (St. Mirren) (Hetherston, St Mirren), Naysmith (Hearts), Rowson (Aberdeen), Dods (Hibernian), McCulloch (Motherwell), Teale (Clydebank), McCluskey (St Johnstone).

Scorer – Scotland: Hamilton (31). **Half-time:** 0-1.

GEORGIA 0, ENGLAND 1
Batumi (4,000), Friday, November 8, 1996

England: Day (Crystal Palace); Scimeca (Aston Villa), Duberry (Chelsea), Newton (Charlton) (Rose, Arsenal, 69), Dyer (Crystal Palace), Eadie (Norwich) (Hall, Coventry, 69), Butt (Man. Utd., Capt), Scowcroft (Ipswich), Thompson (Liverpool), Carbon (Derby), P. Neville (Man. Utd.).

Scorer – England: Duberry (81). **Half-time:** 0-0.

HOLLAND 0, WALES 1
Breda (8,809), Friday, November 8, 1996

Wales: Mountain (Cardiff); Blaney (West Ham), Young (Cardiff), Jarman (Cardiff), Edwards (Swansea), Robinson (Wolves), Thomas (Blackburn), Hughes (Aston Villa), Roberts (Liverpool), Ramasut (Bristol Rovers) (Rowlands, Man. City, 78), Haworth (Cardiff) (Williams, Caernafon, 63).

Scorer – Wales: Haworth (7). **Half-time:** 0-1.

REPUBLIC OF IRELAND 0, ICELAND 1
Dalymount Park, Dublin (1,975), Saturday, November 9, 1996

Rep. of Ireland: Murphy (Wimbledon); Carr (Tottenham), Kennedy (Liverpool), Worrell (Blackburn), Darcy (Tottenham), O'Toole (Coventry), Finnan (Birmingham), Foley (Wolves), O'Halloran (Middlesbrough) (Scully, Crystal Palace, 58), Farrelly (Aston Villa), Boland (Coventry) (Mahon, Tranmere, 58).

Scorer – Iceland: Gudjonsson (61). **Half-time:** 0-0.

SCOTLAND 1, SWEDEN 4
Dundee (3,878), Saturday, November 9, 1996

Scotland: Meldrum (Kilmarnock); Bonar (Raith) (McCulloch, Motherwell), Ritchie (Hearts), Harper (Hamilton), Hamilton (Dundee), Gillies (St Mirren), Naysmith (Hearts), Rowson (Aberdeen), Dods (Hibernian), Boyack (Rangers), Jupp (Wimbledon).

Scorers – Scotland: Johannesson (40 og). **Sweden:** Lantz (55), Ljunberg (69, 77), Petterson (49). **Half-time:** 1-0.

WALES 0, TURKEY 3
Ebbw Vale (700), Friday, December 13, 1996

Wales: Mountain (Cardiff); Blaney (West Ham) (Rowlands, Man. City, 64), Roberts (Liverpool), Edwards (Swansea, Capt), Bellamy (Norwich), Robinson (Wolves) (Coates, Swansea, 57), Thomas (Blackburn) (Williams, Caernafon, 80), Oster (Grismby), Hughes (Aston Villa), Haworth (Cardiff), Partridge (West Ham).

Scorers – Turkey: Aykut (29, 80), Topraktepe (73). **Half-time:** 0-1.

ENGLAND 1, ITALY 0
Ashton Gate, Bristol (13,850), Wednesday, February 12, 1997

England: Marshall (Norwich); Scimeca (Aston Villa, Capt), Rufus (Charlton), Carbon (Derby), Rose (Arsenal), Bowyer (Leeds) (Carragher, Liverpool, 15), Murray (QPR), Hughes (Arsenal), Hall (Coventry), Heskey (Leicester) (Scowcroft, Ipswich, 90) Eadie (Norwich) (Huckerby, Coventry, 61).

Scorer – England: Eadie (51). **Half-time:** 0-0.

WALES 1, BELGIUM 0
Swansea (1,025), Friday, March 28, 1997

Wales: Williams (Blackburn); Jarman (Cardiff), Edwards (Swansea, Capt), Bellamy (Norwich) Robinson (Wolves), Thomas (Blackburn), Oster (Grimsby), Hughes (Aston Villa), Roberts (Liverpool), Haworth (Cardiff), Ramasut (Bristol Rovers) (Young, Cardiff, 90).

Scorer – Wales: Haworth (20). **Half-time:** 1-0.

SCOTLAND 4, ESTONIA 0
Stirling (3,223), Friday, March 28, 1997

Scotland: McKenzie (Hearts); Anderson (Aberdeen), Glass (Aberdeen) (Naysmith, Hearts), Locke (Hearts), Ritchie (Hearts), McCluskey (St Johnstone), Bagan (Kilmarnock) (McCulloch, Motherwell), Gillies (St Mirren), Hamilton (Hearts), Harper (Hibernian) (Young, Aberdeen), Burke (Kilmarnock).

Scorers – Scotland: Harper (23), Glass (35), Hamilton (47), Anderson (70). **Half-time:** 2-0.

SCOTLAND 1, AUSTRIA 2
Motherwell (4,079), Tuesday, April 1, 1997

Scotland: Meldrum (Kilmarnock); Anderson (Aberdeen), Naysmith (Hearts), Locke (Hearts), Ritchie (Hearts), McCluskey (St Johnstone), Harper (Hibernian), Gillies (St Mirren), Hamilton (Hearts), Glass (Aberdeen), Burke (Kilmarnock).

Scorers – Scotland: Hamilton (64). **Austria:** Aukhauser (32), McCluskey (41 og). **Half-time:** 0-2.

ENGLAND 0, GEORGIA 0
Charlton (12,714), Tuesday, April 29, 1997

England: Wright (Ipswich); Oakley (Southampton), Broomes (Blackburn) (Granville, Chelsea, 45), Ferdinand (West Ham), Hall (Coventry), Carragher (Liverpool), Bowyer (Leeds, Capt), Hughes (Arsenal), Eadie (Norwich) (Morris, Chelsea, 70), Scowcroft (Ipswich), Heskey (Leicester) (Huckerby, Coventry, 45).

SWEDEN 2, SCOTLAND 1
Trollhattan (2,200), Tuesday, April 29, 1997

Scotland: Germaine (West Brom); Hamilton (Dundee), McMillan (Motherwell), Rowson (Aberdeen, Capt), Dods (Hibernian), McCulloch (Motherwell) (O'Neill, Clyde), McCluskey (St Johnstone), Anderson (Aberdeen), Young (Aberdeen) (Bagan, Kilmarnock), C. Davidson (St Johnstone), M. Buchan (Aberdeen).

Scorers – Sweden: Mellberg (38), Jonsson (86). **Scotland:** Hamilton (18). **Half-time:** 1-1.

ROMANIA 1, REPUBLIC OF IRELAND 0
Bucharest (7,820), Tuesday, April 29, 1997

Rep. of Ireland: Murphy (Wimbledon); Worrall (Blackburn), Kilbane (Preston), Quinn (Crystal Palace), Coll (Bournemouth) (Foley, Wolves, 82), Maher (Tottenham) (Inman, Peterborough, 45), Finnan (Notts County), Boland (Coventry), Delap (Carlisle), Fenn (Tottenham), Farrelly (Aston Villa).

Scorer – Romania: Frasineanu (15). **Half-time:** 1-0.

POLAND 1, ENGLAND 1
Katowice (2,500), Friday, May 30, 1997

England: Wright (Ipswich); Moses (Barnsley), Carragher (Liverpool), Hall (Coventry), Hamilton (Newcastle), Murray (QPR), Quashie (QPR), Hughes (Arsenal), Granville (Chelsea), Heskey (Leicester) (Huckerby, Coventry, 67), Bradbury (Portsmouth).

Scorers – Poland: Dubicki (66). **England:** Heskey (35). **Half-time:** 0-1.

UEFA U-21 CHAMP. QUAL.								UEFA U-21 CHAMP. QUAL.							
Group 2								**Group 4**							
	P	W	D	L	F	A	Pts		P	W	D	L	F	A	Pts
England	6	3	3	0	5	1	12	Belarus	6	5	1	0	13	3	16
Italy	6	3	2	1	17	3	11	Sweden	5	4	0	1	13	6	12
Poland	5	0	4	1	4	6	4	Austria	5	3	1	1	14	6	10
Moldova	4	1	0	3	3	12	3	Scotland	8	2	1	5	8	13	7
Georgia	3	0	1	2	0	7	1	Latvia	6	1	2	3	1	7	5
								Estonia	6	0	1	5	3	17	1

OTHER U-21 INTERNATIONAL

ENGLAND 0, SWITZERLAND 0
Swindon (10,167), Tuesday, April 1, 1997

England: Day (Crystal Palace) (Roberts, Middlesbrough, 62); Broomes (Blackburn), Ferdinand (West Ham) (Morris, Chelsea, 54), Carbon (Derby) (Briscoe, Sheff. Wed., 46), Holland (Birmingham), Carragher (Liverpool), Bowyer (Leeds, Capt), Hughes (Arsenal), Hall (Coventry), Huckerby (Coventry) (Moore, Nott'm Forest, 84), Humphreys (Sheff. Wed.) (Bridges, Sunderland, 66).

ENGLAND'S RECORD
England's first international was a 0-0 draw against Scotland in Glasgow, on the West of Scotland cricket ground, Partick, on November 30, 1872. Now, 125 years on, their complete International record, at the start of 1997-98, is:

P	W	D	L	F	A
736	420	174	142	1701	768

BRITISH AND IRISH INTERNATIONAL RESULTS

Note: In the results that follow, W.C. = World Cup, E.C. = European Championship. For Ireland, read Northern Ireland from 1921.

ENGLAND v. SCOTLAND

Played 108; England 44; Scotland 40; drawn 24. Goals: England 190, Scotland 168.

Year	Venue	E	S	Year	Venue	E	S
1872	Glasgow	0	0	1931	Glasgow	0	2
1873	The Oval	4	2	1932	Wembley	3	0
1874	Glasgow	1	2	1933	Glasgow	1	2
1875	The Oval	2	2	1934	Wembley	3	0
1876	Glasgow	0	3	1935	Glasgow	0	2
1877	The Oval	1	3	1936	Wembley	1	1
1878	Glasgow	2	7	1937	Glasgow	1	3
1879	The Oval	5	4	1938	Wembley	0	1
1880	Glasgow	4	5	1939	Glasgow	2	1
1881	The Oval	1	6	1947	Wembley	1	1
1882	Glasgow	1	5	1948	Glasgow	2	0
1883	Sheffield	2	3	1949	Wembley	1	3
1884	Glasgow	0	1	1950	Glasgow (W.C.)	1	0
1885	The Oval	1	1	1951	Wembley	2	3
1886	Glasgow	1	1	1952	Glasgow	2	1
1887	Blackburn	2	3	1953	Wembley	2	2
1888	Glasgow	5	0	1954	Glasgow (W.C.)	4	2
1889	The Oval	2	3	1955	Wembley	7	2
1890	Glasgow	1	1	1956	Glasgow	1	1
1891	Blackburn	2	1	1957	Wembley	2	1
1892	Glasgow	4	1	1958	Glasgow	4	0
1893	Richmond	5	2	1959	Wembley	1	0
1894	Glasgow	2	2	1960	Glasgow	1	1
1895	Goodison Park	3	0	1961	Wembley	9	3
1896	Glasgow	1	2	1962	Glasgow	0	2
1897	Crystal Palace	1	2	1963	Wembley	1	2
1898	Glasgow	3	1	1964	Glasgow	0	1
1899	Birmingham	2	1	1965	Wembley	2	2
1900	Glasgow	1	4	1966	Glasgow	4	3
1901	Crystal Palace	2	2	1967	Wembley (E.C.)	2	3
1902	Birmingham	2	2	1968	Glasgow (E.C.)	1	1
1903	Sheffield	1	2	1969	Wembley	4	1
1904	Glasgow	1	0	1970	Glasgow	0	0
1905	Crystal Palace	1	0	1971	Wembley	3	1
1906	Glasgow	1	2	1972	Glasgow	1	0
1907	Newcastle	1	1	1973	Glasgow	5	0
1908	Glasgow	1	1	1973	Wembley	1	0
1909	Crystal Palace	2	0	1974	Glasgow	0	2
1910	Glasgow	0	2	1975	Wembley	5	1
1911	Goodison Park	1	1	1976	Glasgow	1	2
1912	Glasgow	1	1	1977	Wembley	1	2
1913	Stamford Bridge	1	0	1978	Glasgow	1	0
1914	Glasgow	1	3	1979	Wembley	3	1
1920	Sheffield	5	4	1980	Glasgow	2	0
1921	Glasgow	0	3	1981	Wembley	0	1
1922	Birmingham	0	1	1982	Glasgow	1	0
1923	Glasgow	2	2	1983	Wembley	2	0
1924	Wembley	1	1	1984	Glasgow	1	1
1925	Glasgow	0	2	1985	Glasgow	0	1
1926	Manchester	0	1	1986	Wembley	2	1
1927	Glasgow	2	1	1987	Glasgow	0	0
1928	Wembley	1	5	1988	Glasgow	1	0
1929	Glasgow	0	1	1989	Glasgow	2	0
1930	Wembley	5	2	1996	Wembley (E.C.)	2	0

ENGLAND v. WALES

Played 97; England won 62; Wales 14; drawn 21. Goals: England 239, Wales 90.

Year	Venue	E	W	Year	Venue	E	W
1879	The Oval	2	1	1932	Wrexham	0	0
1880	Wrexham	3	2	1933	Newcastle	1	2
1881	Blackburn	0	1	1934	Cardiff	4	0
1882	Wrexham	3	5	1935	Wolverhampton	1	2
1883	The Oval	5	0	1936	Cardiff	1	2
1884	Wrexham	4	0	1937	Middlesbrough	2	1
1885	Blackburn	1	1	1938	Cardiff	2	4
1886	Wrexham	3	1	1946	Manchester	3	0
1887	The Oval	4	0	1947	Cardiff	3	0
1888	Crewe	5	1	1948	Villa Park	1	0
1889	Stoke	4	1	1949	Cardiff (W.C.)	4	1
1890	Wrexham	3	1	1950	Sunderland	4	2
1891	Sunderland	4	1	1951	Cardiff	1	1
1892	Wrexham	2	0	1952	Wembley	5	2
1893	Stoke	6	0	1953	Cardiff (W.C.)	4	1
1894	Wrexham	5	1	1954	Wembley	3	2
1895	London	1	1	1955	Cardiff	1	2
1896	Cardiff	9	1	1956	Wembley	3	1
1897	Sheffield	4	0	1957	Cardiff	4	0
1898	Wrexham	3	0	1958	Birmingham	2	2
1899	Bristol	4	0	1959	Cardiff	1	1
1900	Cardiff	1	1	1960	Wembley	5	1
1901	Newcastle	6	0	1961	Cardiff	1	1
1902	Wrexham	0	0	1962	Wembley	4	0
1903	Portsmouth	2	1	1963	Cardiff	4	0
1904	Wrexham	2	2	1964	Wembley	2	1
1905	Anfield	3	1	1965	Cardiff	0	0
1906	Cardiff	1	0	1966	Wembley (E.C.)	5	1
1907	Fulham	1	1	1967	Cardiff (E.C.)	3	0
1908	Wrexham	7	1	1969	Wembley	2	1
1909	Nottingham	2	0	1970	Cardiff	1	1
1910	Cardiff	1	0	1971	Wembley	0	0
1911	Millwall	3	0	1972	Cardiff	3	0
1912	Wrexham	2	0	1972	Cardiff (W.C.)	1	0
1913	Bristol	4	3	1973	Wembley (W.C.)	1	1
1914	Cardiff	2	0	1973	Wembley	3	0
1920	Highbury	1	2	1974	Cardiff	2	0
1921	Cardiff	0	0	1975	Wembley	2	2
1922	Anfield	1	0	1976	Wrexham	2	1
1923	Cardiff	2	2	1976	Cardiff	1	0
1924	Blackburn	1	2	1977	Wembley	0	1
1925	Swansea	2	1	1978	Cardiff	3	1
1926	Selhurst Park	1	3	1979	Wembley	0	0
1927	Wrexham	3	3	1980	Wrexham	1	4
1927	Burnley	1	2	1981	Wembley	0	0
1928	Swansea	3	2	1982	Cardiff	1	0
1929	Stamford Bridge	6	0	1983	Wembley	2	1
1930	Wrexham	4	0	1984	Wrexham	0	1
1931	Anfield	3	1				

ENGLAND v. IRELAND

Played 96; England won 74; Ireland 6; drawn 16. Goals: England 319, Ireland 80.

		E	I			E	I
1882	Belfast	13	0	1935	Belfast	3	1
1883	Aigburth, Liverpool	7	0	1936	Stoke	3	1
1884	Belfast	8	1	1937	Belfast	5	1
1885	Manchester	4	0	1938	Manchester	7	0
1886	Belfast	6	1	1946	Belfast	7	2
1887	Sheffield	7	0	1947	Goodison Park	2	2
1888	Belfast	5	1	1948	Belfast	6	2
1889	Goodison Park	6	1	1949	Manchester (W.C.)	9	2
1890	Belfast	9	1	1950	Belfast	4	1
1891	Wolverhampton	6	1	1951	Birmingham	2	0
1892	Belfast	2	0	1952	Belfast	2	2
1893	Birmingham	6	1	1953	Goodison Park (W.C.)	3	1
1894	Belfast	2	2	1954	Belfast	2	0
1895	Derby	9	0	1955	Wembley	3	0
1896	Belfast	2	0	1956	Belfast	1	1
1897	Nottingham	6	0	1957	Wembley	2	3
1898	Belfast	3	2	1958	Belfast	3	3
1899	Sunderland	13	2	1959	Wembley	2	1
1900	Dublin	2	0	1960	Belfast	5	2
1901	Southampton	3	0	1961	Wembley	1	1
1902	Belfast	1	0	1962	Belfast	3	1
1903	Wolverhampton	4	0	1963	Wembley	8	3
1904	Belfast	3	1	1964	Belfast	4	3
1905	Middlesbrough	1	1	1965	Wembley	2	1
1906	Belfast	5	0	1966	Belfast (E.C.)	2	0
1907	Goodison Park	1	0	1967	Wembley (E.C.)	2	0
1908	Belfast	3	1	1969	Belfast	3	1
1909	Bradford (Park Ave)	4	0	1970	Wembley	3	1
1910	Belfast	1	1	1971	Belfast	1	0
1911	Derby	2	1	1972	Wembley	0	1
1912	Dublin	6	1	1973	*Goodison Park	2	1
1913	Belfast	1	2	1974	Wembley	1	0
1914	Middlesbrough	0	3	1975	Belfast	0	0
1919	Belfast	1	1	1976	Wembley	4	0
1920	Sunderland	2	0	1977	Belfast	2	1
1921	Belfast	1	1	1978	Wembley	1	0
1922	West Bromwich	2	0	1979	Wembley (E.C.)	4	0
1923	Belfast	1	2	1979	Belfast	2	0
1924	Goodison Park	3	1	1979	Belfast (E.C.)	5	1
1925	Belfast	0	0	1980	Wembley	1	1
1926	Anfield	3	3	1982	Wembley	4	0
1927	Belfast	0	2	1983	Belfast	0	0
1928	Goodison Park	2	1	1984	Wembley	1	0
1929	Belfast	3	0	1985	Belfast (W.C.)	1	0
1930	Sheffield	5	1	1985	Wembley (W.C.)	0	0
1931	Belfast	6	2	1986	Wembley (E.C.)	3	0
1932	Blackpool	1	0	1987	Belfast (E.C.)	2	0
1933	Belfast	3	0				
1935	Goodison Park	2	1				

(* Switched from Belfast because of political situation in N. Ireland)

157

SCOTLAND v. WALES

Played 102; Scotland won 60; Wales 19; drawn 23. Goals: Scotland 238, Wales 113.

Year	Venue	S	W	Year	Venue	S	W
1876	Glasgow	4	0	1932	Wrexham	3	2
1877	Wrexham	2	0	1933	Edinburgh	2	5
1878	Glasgow	9	0	1934	Cardiff	2	3
1879	Wrexham	3	0	1935	Aberdeen	3	2
1880	Glasgow	5	1	1936	Cardiff	1	1
1881	Wrexham	5	1	1937	Dundee	1	2
1882	Glasgow	5	0	1938	Cardiff	1	2
1883	Wrexham	4	1	1939	Edinburgh	3	2
1884	Glasgow	4	1	1946	Wrexham	1	3
1885	Wrexham	8	1	1947	Glasgow	1	2
1886	Glasgow	4	1	1948	Cardiff (W.C.)	3	1
1887	Wrexham	2	0	1949	Glasgow	2	0
1888	Edinburgh	5	1	1950	Cardiff	3	1
1889	Wrexham	0	0	1951	Glasgow	0	1
1890	Paisley	5	0	1952	Cardiff (W.C.)	2	1
1891	Wrexham	4	3	1953	Glasgow	3	3
1892	Edinburgh	6	1	1954	Cardiff	1	0
1893	Wrexham	8	0	1955	Glasgow	2	0
1894	Kilmarnock	5	2	1956	Cardiff	2	2
1895	Wrexham	2	2	1957	Glasgow	1	1
1896	Dundee	4	0	1958	Cardiff	3	0
1897	Wrexham	2	2	1959	Glasgow	1	1
1898	Motherwell	5	2	1960	Cardiff	0	2
1899	Wrexham	6	0	1961	Glasgow	2	0
1900	Aberdeen	5	2	1962	Cardiff	3	2
1901	Wrexham	1	1	1963	Glasgow	2	1
1902	Greenock	5	1	1964	Cardiff	2	3
1903	Cardiff	1	0	1965	Glasgow (E.C.)	4	1
1904	Dundee	1	1	1966	Cardiff (E.C.)	1	1
1905	Wrexham	1	3	1967	Glasgow	3	2
1906	Edinburgh	0	2	1969	Wrexham	5	3
1907	Wrexham	0	1	1970	Glasgow	0	0
1908	Dundee	2	1	1971	Cardiff	0	0
1909	Wrexham	2	3	1972	Glasgow	1	0
1910	Kilmarnock	1	0	1973	Wrexham	2	0
1911	Cardiff	2	2	1974	Glasgow	2	0
1912	Tynecastle	1	0	1975	Cardiff	2	2
1913	Wrexham	0	0	1976	Glasgow	3	1
1914	Glasgow	0	0	1977	Glasgow (W.C.)	1	0
1920	Cardiff	1	1	1977	Wrexham	0	0
1921	Aberdeen	2	1	1977	Anfield (W.C.)	2	0
1922	Wrexham	1	2	1978	Glasgow	1	1
1923	Paisley	2	0	1979	Cardiff	0	3
1924	Cardiff	0	2	1980	Glasgow	1	0
1925	Tynecastle	3	1	1981	Swansea	0	2
1926	Cardiff	3	0	1982	Glasgow	1	0
1927	Glasgow	3	0	1983	Cardiff	2	0
1928	Wrexham	2	2	1984	Glasgow	2	1
1929	Glasgow	4	2	1985	Glasgow (W.C.)	0	1
1930	Cardiff	4	2	1985	Cardiff (W.C.)	1	1
1931	Glasgow	1	1	1997	Kilmarnock	0	1

SCOTLAND v. IRELAND

Played 92; Scotland won 61; Ireland 15; drawn 16. Goals: Scotland 254, Ireland 81.

Year	Venue	S	I		Year	Venue	S	I
1884	Belfast	5	0		1935	Belfast	1	2
1885	Glasgow	8	2		1936	Edinburgh	2	1
1886	Belfast	7	2		1937	Belfast	3	1
1887	Belfast	4	1		1938	Aberdeen	1	1
1888	Belfast	10	2		1939	Belfast	2	0
1889	Glasgow	7	0		1946	Glasgow	0	0
1890	Belfast	4	1		1947	Belfast	0	2
1891	Glasgow	2	1		1948	Glasgow	3	2
1892	Belfast	3	2		1949	Belfast	8	2
1893	Glasgow	6	1		1950	Glasgow	6	1
1894	Belfast	2	1		1951	Belfast	3	0
1895	Glasgow	3	1		1952	Glasgow	1	1
1896	Belfast	3	3		1953	Belfast	3	1
1897	Glasgow	5	1		1954	Glasgow	2	2
1898	Belfast	3	0		1955	Belfast	1	2
1899	Glasgow	9	1		1956	Glasgow	1	0
1900	Belfast	3	0		1957	Belfast	1	1
1901	Glasgow	11	0		1958	Glasgow	2	2
1902	Belfast	5	1		1959	Belfast	4	0
1903	Glasgow	0	2		1960	Glasgow	5	1
1904	Dublin	1	1		1961	Belfast	6	1
1905	Glasgow	4	0		1962	Glasgow	5	1
1906	Dublin	1	0		1963	Belfast	1	2
1907	Glasgow	3	0		1964	Glasgow	3	2
1908	Dublin	5	0		1965	Belfast	2	3
1909	Glasgow	5	0		1966	Glasgow	2	1
1910	Belfast	0	1		1967	Belfast	0	1
1911	Glasgow	2	0		1969	Glasgow	1	1
1912	Belfast	4	1		1970	Belfast	1	0
1913	Dublin	2	1		1971	Glasgow	0	1
1914	Belfast	1	1		1972	Glasgow	2	0
1920	Glasgow	3	0		1973	Glasgow	1	2
1921	Belfast	2	0		1974	Glasgow	0	1
1922	Glasgow	2	1		1975	Glasgow	3	0
1923	Belfast	1	0		1976	Glasgow	3	0
1924	Glasgow	2	0		1977	Glasgow	3	0
1925	Belfast	3	0		1978	Glasgow	1	1
1926	Glasgow	4	0		1979	Glasgow	1	0
1927	Belfast	2	0		1980	Belfast	0	1
1928	Glasgow	0	1		1981	Glasgow (W.C.)	1	1
1929	Belfast	7	3		1981	Glasgow	2	0
1930	Glasgow	3	1		1981	Belfast (W.C.)	0	0
1931	Belfast	0	0		1982	Belfast	1	1
1932	Glasgow	3	1		1983	Glasgow	0	0
1933	Belfast	4	0		1984	Belfast	0	2
1934	Glasgow	1	2		1992	Glasgow	1	0

WALES v. IRELAND

Played 90; Wales won 42; Ireland 27; drawn 21. Goals: Wales 182, Ireland 127.

Year	Venue	W	I
1882	Wrexham	7	1
1883	Belfast	1	1
1884	Wrexham	6	0
1885	Belfast	8	2
1886	Wrexham	5	0
1887	Belfast	1	4
1888	Wrexham	11	0
1889	Belfast	3	1
1890	Shrewsbury	5	2
1891	Belfast	2	7
1892	Bangor	1	1
1893	Belfast	3	4
1894	Swansea	4	1
1895	Belfast	2	2
1896	Wrexham	6	1
1897	Belfast	3	4
1898	Llandudno	0	1
1899	Belfast	0	1
1900	Llandudno	2	0
1901	Belfast	1	0
1902	Cardiff	0	3
1903	Belfast	0	2
1904	Bangor	0	1
1905	Belfast	2	2
1906	Wrexham	4	4
1907	Belfast	3	2
1908	Aberdare	0	1
1909	Belfast	3	2
1910	Wrexham	4	1
1911	Belfast	2	1
1912	Cardiff	2	3
1913	Belfast	1	0
1914	Wrexham	1	2
1920	Belfast	2	2
1921	Swansea	2	1
1922	Belfast	1	1
1923	Wrexham	0	3
1924	Belfast	1	0
1925	Wrexham	0	0
1926	Belfast	0	3
1927	Cardiff	2	2
1928	Belfast	2	1
1929	Wrexham	2	2
1930	Belfast	0	7
1931	Wrexham	3	2
1932	Belfast	0	4
1933	Wrexham	4	1
1934	Belfast	1	1
1935	Wrexham	3	1
1936	Belfast	2	3
1937	Wrexham	4	1
1938	Belfast	0	1
1939	Wrexham	3	1
1947	Belfast	1	2
1948	Wrexham	2	0
1949	Belfast	2	0
1950	Wrexham (W.C.)	0	0
1951	Belfast	2	1
1952	Swansea	3	0
1953	Belfast	3	2
1954	Wrexham (W.C.)	1	2
1955	Belfast	3	2
1956	Cardiff	1	1
1957	Belfast	0	0
1958	Cardiff	1	1
1959	Belfast	1	4
1960	Wrexham	3	2
1961	Belfast	5	1
1962	Cardiff	4	0
1963	Belfast	4	1
1964	Swansea	2	3
1965	Belfast	5	0
1966	Cardiff	1	4
1967	Belfast (E.C.)	0	0
1968	Wrexham (E.C.)	2	0
1969	Belfast	0	0
1970	Swansea	1	0
1971	Belfast	0	1
1972	Wrexham	0	0
1973	*Goodison Park	0	1
1974	Wrexham	1	0
1975	Belfast	0	1
1976	Swansea	1	0
1977	Belfast	1	1
1978	Wrexham	1	0
1979	Belfast	1	1
1980	Cardiff	0	1
1982	Wrexham	3	0
1983	Belfast	1	0
1984	Swansea	1	1

(* Switched from Belfast because of political situation in N. Ireland)

OTHER BRITISH INTERNATIONAL RESULTS

ENGLAND

v. ALBANIA

		E	A				E	A
1989	Tirana (W.C.)	2	0	1989	Wembley (W.C.)		5	0

v. ARGENTINA

		E	A				E	A
1951	Wembley	2	1	1977	Buenos Aires		1	1
1953	* Buenos Aires	0	0	1980	Wembley		3	1
1962	Rancagua (W.C.)	3	1	1986	Mexico City (W.C.)		1	2
1964	Rio de Janeiro	0	1	1991	Wembley		2	2
1966	Wembley (W.C.)	1	0	(* Abandoned after 21 mins. – rain)				
1974	Wembley	2	2					

v. AUSTRALIA

		E	A				E	A
1980	Sydney	2	1	1983	Melbourne		1	1
1983	Sydney	0	0	1991	Sydney		1	0
1983	Brisbane	1	0					

v. AUSTRIA

		E	A				E	A
1908	Vienna	6	1	1958	Boras (W.C.)		2	2
1908	Vienna	11	1	1961	Vienna		1	3
1909	Vienna	8	1	1962	Wembley		3	1
1930	Vienna	0	0	1965	Wembley		2	3
1932	Stamford Bridge	4	3	1967	Vienna		1	0
1936	Vienna	1	2	1973	Wembley		7	0
1951	Wembley	2	2	1979	Vienna		3	4
1952	Vienna	3	2					

v. BELGIUM

		E	B				E	B
1921	Brussels	2	0	1936	Brussels		2	3
1923	Highbury	6	1	1947	Brussels		5	2
1923	Antwerp	2	2	1950	Brussels		4	1
1924	West Bromwich	4	0	1952	Wembley		5	0
1926	Antwerp	5	3	1954	Basle (W.C.)		4	4
1927	Brussels	9	1	1964	Wembley		2	2
1928	Antwerp	3	1	1970	Brussels		3	1
1929	Brussels	5	1	1980	Turin (E.C.)		1	1
1931	Brussels	4	1	1990	Bologna (W.C.)		1	0

v. BOHEMIA

		E	B
1908	Prague	4	0

v. BRAZIL

		E	B			E	B
1956	Wembley	4	2	1978	Wembley	1	1
1958	Gothenburg (W.C.)	0	0	1981	Wembley	0	1
1959	Rio de Janeiro	0	2	1984	Rio de Janeiro	2	0
1962	Vina del Mar (W.C.)	1	3	1987	Wembley	1	1
1963	Wembley	1	1	1990	Wembley	1	0
1964	Rio de Janeiro	1	5	1992	Wembley	1	1
1969	Rio de Janeiro	1	2	1993	Washington	1	1
1970	Guadalajara (W.C.)	0	1	1995	Wembley	1	3
1976	Los Angeles	0	1	1997	Paris	0	1
1977	Rio de Janeiro	0	0				

v. BULGARIA

		E	B			E	B
1962	Rancagua (W.C.)	0	0	1979	Sofia (E.C.)	3	0
1968	Wembley	1	1	1979	Wembley (E.C.)	2	0
1974	Sofia	1	0	1996	Wembley	1	0

v. CAMEROON

		E	C			E	C
1990	Naples (W.C.)	3	2	1991	Wembley	2	0

v. CANADA

		E	C
1986	Vancouver	1	0

v. CHILE

		E	C			E	C
1950	Rio de Janeiro (W.C.)	2	0	1984	Santiago	0	0
1953	Santiago	2	1	1989	Wembley	0	0

v. CHINA

		E	C
1996	Beijing	3	0

v. C.I.S. (formerly Soviet Union)

		E	C
1992	Moscow	2	2

v. COLOMBIA

		E	C			E	C
1970	Bogota	4	0	1995	Wembley	0	0
1988	Wembley	1	1				

v. CROATIA

		E	C
1995	Wembley	0	0

v. CYPRUS

		E	C			E	C
1975	Wembley (E.C.)	5	0	1975	Limassol (E.C.)	1	0

v. CZECHOSLOVAKIA

		E	C				E	C
1934	Prague	1	2	1975	* Bratislava (E.C.)		1	2
1937	Tottenham	5	4	1978	Wembley (E.C.)		1	0
1963	Bratislava	4	2	1982	Bilbao (W.C.)		2	0
1966	Wembley	0	0	1990	Wembley		4	2
1970	Guadalajara (W.C.)	1	0	1992	Prague		2	2
1973	Prague	1	1	(* Aband. 0-0, 17 mins. prev. day –			
1974	Wembley (E.C.)	3	0	fog)			

v. DENMARK

		E	D			E	D
1948	Copenhagen	0	0	1982	Copenhagen (E.C.)	2	2
1955	Copenhagen	5	1	1983	Wembley (E.C.)	0	1
1956	W'hampton (W.C.)	5	2	1988	Wembley	1	0
1957	Copenhagen (W.C.)	4	1	1989	Copenhagen	1	1
1966	Copenhagen	2	0	1990	Wembley	1	0
1978	Copenhagen (E.C.)	4	3	1992	Malmo (E.C.)	0	0
1979	Wembley (E.C.)	1	0	1994	Wembley	1	0

v. EAST GERMANY

		E	EG			E	EG
1963	Leipzig	2	1	1974	Leipzig	1	1
1970	Wembley	3	1	1984	Wembley	1	0

v. ECUADOR

		E	Ec
1970	Quito	2	0

v. EGYPT

		E	Eg			E	Eg
1986	Cairo	4	0	1990	Cagliari (W.C.)	1	0

v. F.I.F.A.

		E	F			E	F
1938	Highbury	3	0	1963	Wembley	2	1
1953	Wembley	4	4				

v. FINLAND

		E	F			E	F
1937	Helsinki	8	0	1982	Helsinki	4	1
1956	Helsinki	5	1	1984	Wembley (W.C.)	5	0
1966	Helsinki	3	0	1985	Helsinki (W.C.)	1	1
1976	Helsinki (W.C.)	4	1	1992	Helsinki	2	1
1976	Wembley (W.C.)	2	1				

v. FRANCE

		E	F			E	F
1923	Paris	4	1	1929	Paris	4	1
1924	Paris	3	1	1931	Paris	2	5
1925	Paris	3	2	1933	Tottenham	4	1
1927	Paris	6	0	1938	Paris	4	2
1928	Paris	5	1	1947	Highbury	3	0

		E	F			E	F
1949	Paris	3	1	1969	Wembley	5	0
1951	Highbury	2	2	1982	Bilbao (W.C.)	3	1
1955	Paris	0	1	1984	Paris	0	2
1957	Wembley	4	0	1992	Wembley	2	0
1962	Sheffield (E.C.)	1	1	1992	Malmo (E.C.)	0	0
1963	Paris (E.C.)	2	5	1997	Montpellier	1	0
1966	Wembley (W.C.)	2	0				

v. GEORGIA

		E	G			E	G
1996	Tbilisi (W.C.)	2	0	1997	Wembley (W.C.)	2	0

v. GERMANY/WEST GERMANY

		E	G			E	G
1930	Berlin	3	3	1975	Wembley	2	0
1935	Tottenham	3	0	1978	Munich	1	2
1938	Berlin	6	3	1982	Madrid (W.C.)	0	0
1954	Wembley	3	1	1982	Wembley	1	2
1956	Berlin	3	1	1985	Mexico City	3	0
1965	Nuremberg	1	0	1987	Dusseldorf	1	3
1966	Wembley	1	0	1990	* Turin (W.C.)	1	1
1966	Wembley (W.C.F.)	4	2	1991	Wembley	0	1
1968	Hanover	0	1	1993	Detroit	1	2
1970	Leon (W.C.)	2	3	1996	† Wembley (E.C.)	1	1
1972	Wembley (E.C.)	1	3	(* England lost 3-4 on pens.)			
1972	Berlin (E.C.)	0	0	(†England lost 5-6 on pens.)			

v. GREECE

		E	G			E	G
1971	Wembley (E.C.)	3	0	1983	Wembley (E.C.)	0	0
1971	Athens (E.C.)	2	0	1989	Athens	2	1
1982	Salonika (E.C.)	3	0	1994	Wembley	5	0

v. HOLLAND

		E	H			E	H
1935	Amsterdam	1	0	1988	Wembley	2	2
1946	Huddersfield	8	2	1988	Dusseldorf (E.C.)	1	3
1964	Amsterdam	1	1	1990	Cagliari (W.C.)	0	0
1969	Amsterdam	1	0	1993	Wembley (W.C.)	2	2
1970	Wembley	0	0	1993	Rotterdam (W.C.)	0	2
1977	Wembley	0	2	1996	Wembley (E.C.)	4	1
1982	Wembley	2	0				

v. HUNGARY

		E	H			E	H
1908	Budapest	7	0	1978	Wembley	4	1
1909	Budapest	4	2	1981	Budapest (W.C.)	3	1
1909	Budapest	8	2	1981	Wembley (W.C.)	1	0
1934	Budapest	1	2	1983	Wembley (E.C.)	2	0
1936	Highbury	6	2	1983	Budapest (E.C.)	3	0
1953	Wembley	3	6	1988	Budapest	0	0
1954	Budapest	1	7	1990	Wembley	1	0
1960	Budapest	0	2	1992	Budapest	1	0
1962	Rancagua (W.C.)	1	2	1996	Wembley	3	0
1965	Wembley	1	0				

164

v. ICELAND

		E	I
1982	Reykjavik	1	1

v. REPUBLIC OF IRELAND

		E	RofI			E	RofI
1946	Dublin	1	0	1985	Wembley	2	1
1950	Goodison Park	0	2	1988	Stuttgart (E.C.)	0	1
1957	Wembley (W.C.)	5	1	1990	Cagliari (W.C.)	1	1
1957	Dublin (W.C.)	1	1	1990	Dublin (E.C.)	1	1
1964	Dublin	3	1	1991	Wembley (E.C.)	1	1
1977	Wembley	1	1	1995	* Dublin	0	1
1978	Dublin (E.C.)	1	1	(* Abandoned 27 mins. – crowd riot)			
1980	Wembley (E.C.)	2	0				

v. ISRAEL

		E	I			E	I
1986	Tel Aviv	2	1	1988	Tel Aviv	0	0

v. ITALY

		E	I			E	I
1933	Rome	1	1	1976	New York	3	2
1934	Highbury	3	2	1976	Rome (W.C.)	0	2
1939	Milan	2	2	1977	Wembley (W.C.)	2	0
1948	Turin	4	0	1980	Turin (E.C.)	0	1
1949	Tottenham	2	0	1985	Mexico City	1	2
1952	Florence	1	1	1989	Wembley	0	0
1959	Wembley	2	2	1990	Bari (W.C.)	1	2
1961	Rome	3	2	1996	Wembley (W.C.)	0	1
1973	Turin	0	2	1997	Nantes	2	0
1973	Wembley	0	1				

v. JAPAN

		E	J
1995	Wembley	2	1

v. KUWAIT

		E	K
1982	Bilbao (W.C.)	1	0

v. LUXEMBOURG

		E	L			E	L
1927	Luxembourg	5	2	1977	Luxembourg (W.C.)	2	0
1960	Luxembourg (W.C.)	9	0	1982	Wembley (E.C.)	9	0
1961	Highbury (W.C.)	4	1	1983	Luxembourg (E.C.)	4	0
1977	Wembley (W.C.)	5	0				

v. MALAYSIA

		E	M
1991	Kuala Lumpur	4	2

v. MALTA

		E	M				E	M
1971	Valletta (E.C.)	1	0	1971	Wembley (E.C.)	5	0

v. MEXICO

		E	M				E	M
1959	Mexico City	1	2	1985	Mexico City	0	1
1961	Wembley	8	0	1986	Los Angeles	3	0
1966	Wembley (W.C.)	2	0	1997	Wembley	2	0
1969	Mexico City	0	0				

v. MOLDOVA

		E	M
1996	Kishinev	3	0

v. MOROCCO

		E	M
1986	Monterrey (W.C.)	0	0

v. NEW ZEALAND

		E	NZ				E	NZ
1991	Auckland	1	0	1991	Wellington	2	0

v. NIGERIA

		E	N
1994	Wembley	1	0

v. NORWAY

		E	N				E	N
1937	Oslo	6	0	1981	Oslo (W.C.)	1	2
1938	Newcastle	4	0	1992	Wembley (W.C.)	1	1
1949	Oslo	4	1	1993	Oslo (W.C.)	0	2
1966	Oslo	6	1	1994	Wembley	0	0
1980	Wembley (W.C.)	4	0	1995	Oslo	0	0

v. PARAGUAY

		E	P
1986	Mexico City (W.C.)	3	0

v. PERU

		E	P				E	P
1959	Lima	1	4	1961	Lima	4	0

v. POLAND

		E	P				E	P
1966	Goodison Park	1	1	1990	Wembley (E.C.)	2	0
1966	Chorzow	1	0	1991	Poznan (E.C.)	1	1
1973	Chorzow (W.C.)	0	2	1993	Chorzow (W.C.)	1	1
1973	Wembley (W.C.)	1	1	1993	Wembley (W.C.)	3	0
1986	Monterrey (W.C.)	3	0	1996	Wembley (W.C.)	2	1
1989	Wembley (W.C.)	3	0	1997	Katowice (W.C.)	2	0
1989	Katowice (W.C.)	0	0				

v. PORTUGAL

		E	P				E	P
1947	Lisbon	10	0	1964	Sao Paulo		1	1
1950	Lisbon	5	3	1966	Wembley (W.C.)		2	1
1951	Goodison Park	5	2	1969	Wembley		1	0
1955	Oporto	1	3	1974	Lisbon		0	0
1958	Wembley	2	1	1974	Wembley (E.C.)		0	0
1961	Lisbon (W.C.)	1	1	1975	Lisbon (E.C.)		1	1
1961	Wembley (W.C.)	2	0	1986	Monterrey (W.C.)		0	1
1964	Lisbon	4	3	1995	Wembley		1	1

v. ROMANIA

		E	R			E	R
1939	Bucharest	2	0	1981	Wembley (W.C.)	0	0
1968	Bucharest	0	0	1985	Bucharest (W.C.)	0	0
1969	Wembley	1	1	1985	Wembley (W.C.)	1	1
1970	Guadalajara (W.C.)	1	0	1994	Wembley	1	1
1980	Bucharest (W.C.)	1	2				

v. SAN MARINO

		E	SM			E	SM
1993	Wembley (W.C.)	6	0	1994	Bologna (W.C.)	7	1

v. SAUDI ARABIA

		E	SA
1988	Riyadh	1	1

v. SOUTH AFRICA

		E	SA
1997	Old Trafford	2	1

v. SOVIET UNION (see also C.I.S.)

		E	SU			E	SU
1958	Moscow	1	1	1973	Moscow	2	1
1958	Gothenburg (W.C.)	2	2	1984	Wembley	0	2
1958	Gothenburg (W.C.)	0	1	1986	Tbilisi	1	0
1958	Wembley	5	0	1988	Frankfurt (E.C.)	1	3
1967	Wembley	2	2	1991	Wembley	3	1
1968	Rome (E.C.)	2	0				

v. SPAIN

		E	S			E	S
1929	Madrid	3	4	1968	Madrid (E.C.)	2	1
1931	Highbury	7	1	1980	Barcelona	2	0
1950	Rio de Janeiro (W.C.)	0	1	1980	Naples (E.C.)	2	1
1955	Madrid	1	1	1981	Wembley	1	2
1955	Wembley	4	1	1982	Madrid (W.C.)	0	0
1960	Madrid	0	3	1987	Madrid	4	2
1960	Wembley	4	2	1992	Santander	0	1
1965	Madrid	2	0	1996 *	Wembley (E.C.)	0	0
1967	Wembley	2	0	(*England won 4-2 on pens.)			
1968	Wembley (E.C.)	1	0				

v. SWEDEN

		E	S			E	S
1923	Stockholm	4	2	1968	Wembley	3	1
1923	Stockholm	3	1	1979	Stockholm	0	0
1937	Stockholm	4	0	1986	Stockholm	0	1
1948	Highbury	4	2	1988	Wembley (W.C.)	0	0
1949	Stockholm	1	3	1989	Stockholm (W.C.)	0	0
1956	Stockholm	0	0	1992	Stockholm (E.C.)	1	2
1959	Wembley	2	3	1995	Elland Road	3	3
1965	Gothenburg	2	1				

v. SWITZERLAND

		E	S			E	S
1933	Berne	4	0	1971	Wembley (E.C.)	1	1
1938	Zurich	1	2	1975	Basle	2	1
1947	Zurich	0	1	1977	Wembley	0	0
1949	Highbury	6	0	1980	Wembley (W.C.)	2	1
1952	Zurich	3	0	1981	Basle (W.C.)	1	2
1954	Berne (W.C.)	2	0	1988	Lausanne	1	0
1962	Wembley	3	1	1995	Wembley	3	1
1963	Basle	8	1	1996	Wembley (E.C.)	1	1
1971	Basle (E.C.)	3	2				

v. TUNISIA

		E	T
1990	Tunis	1	1

v. TURKEY

		E	T			E	T
1984	Istanbul (W.C.)	8	0	1991	Izmir (E.C.)	1	0
1985	Wembley (W.C.)	5	0	1992	Wembley (E.C.)	1	0
1987	Izmir (E.C.)	0	0	1992	Wembley (W.C.)	4	0
1987	Wembley (E.C.)	8	0	1993	Izmir (W.C.)	2	0

v. URUGUAY

		E	U			E	U
1953	Montevideo	1	2	1977	Montevideo	0	0
1954	Basle (W.C.)	2	4	1984	Montevideo	0	2
1964	Wembley	2	1	1990	Wembley	1	2
1966	Wembley (W.C.)	0	0	1995	Wembley	0	0
1969	Montevideo	2	1				

v. U.S.A.

		E	USA			E	USA
1950	Belo H. (W.C.)	0	1	1985	Los Angeles	5	0
1953	New York	6	3	1993	Boston	0	2
1959	Los Angeles	8	1	1994	Wembley	2	0
1964	New York	10	0				

v. YUGOSLAVIA

		E	Y			E	Y
1939	Belgrade	1	2	1958	Belgrade	0	5
1950	Highbury	2	2	1960	Wembley	3	3
1954	Belgrade	0	1	1965	Belgrade	1	1
1956	Wembley	3	0	1966	Wembley	2	0

		E	Y			E	Y
1968	Florence (E.C.)	0	1	1986	Wembley (E.C.)	2	0
1972	Wembley	1	1	1987	Belgrade (E.C.)	4	1
1974	Belgrade	2	2	1989	Wembley	2	1

ENGLAND "B" TEAM RESULTS

(England score shown first)

1949	Finland (A)	4	0	1979	Austria (A)	1	0
1949	Holland (A)	4	0	1979	N. Zealand (H)	4	1
1950	Italy (A)	0	5	1980	U.S.A. (H)	1	0
1950	Holland (H)	1	0	1980	Spain (H)	1	0
1950	Holland (A)	0	3	1980	Australia (H)	1	0
1950	Luxembourg (A)	2	1	1981	Spain (A)	2	3
1950	Switzerland (H)	5	0	1984	N. Zealand (H)	2	0
1952	Holland (A)	1	0	1987	Malta (A)	2	0
1952	France (A)	1	7	1989	Switzerland (A)	2	0
1953	Scotland (A)	2	2	1989	Iceland (A)	2	0
1954	Scotland (H)	1	1	1989	Norway (A)	1	0
1954	Germany (A)	4	0	1989	Italy (H)	1	1
1954	Yugoslavia (A)	1	2	1989	Yugoslavia (H)	2	1
1954	Switzerland (A)	0	2	1990	Rep. of Ireland (A)	1	4
1955	Germany (H)	1	1	1990	Czechoslovakia (H)	2	0
1955	Yugoslavia (H)	5	1	1990	Algeria (A)	0	0
1956	Switzerland (H)	4	1	1991	Wales (A)	1	0
1956	Scotland (A)	2	2	1991	Iceland (A)	1	0
1957	Scotland (H)	4	1	1991	Switzerland (H)	2	1
1978	W. Germany (A)	2	1	1991	Spanish XI (A)	1	0
1978	Czechoslovakia (A)	1	0	1992	France (A)	3	0
1978	Singapore (A)	8	0	1992	Czechoslovakia (A)	1	0
1978	Malaysia (A)	1	1	1992	C.I.S. (A)	1	1
1978	N. Zealand (A)	4	0	1994	N. Ireland (H)	4	2
1978	N. Zealand (A)	3	1	1995	Rep. of Ireland (H)	2	0
1978	N. Zealand (A)	4	0				

GREAT BRITAIN v. REST OF EUROPE
(F.I.F.A.)

		GB	RofE			GB	RofE
1947	Glasgow	6	1	1955	Belfast	1	4

SCOTLAND

v. ARGENTINA

		S	A			S	A
1977	Buenos Aires	1	1	1990	Glasgow	1	0
1979	Glasgow	1	3				

v. AUSTRALIA

		S	A			S	A
1985	* Glasgow (W.C.)	2	0	1996	Glasgow	1	0
1985	* Melbourne (W.C.)	0	0				

(* World Cup play-off)

v. AUSTRIA

		S	A			S	A
1931	Vienna	0	5	1963	* Glasgow	4	1
1933	Glasgow	2	2	1968	Glasgow (W.C.)	2	1
1937	Vienna	1	1	1969	Vienna (W.C.)	0	2
1950	Glasgow	0	1	1978	Vienna (E.C.)	2	3
1951	Vienna	0	4	1979	Glasgow (E.C.)	1	1
1954	Zurich (W.C.)	0	1	1994	Vienna	2	1
1955	Vienna	4	1	1996	Vienna (W.C.)	0	0
1956	Glasgow	1	1	1997	Glasgow (W.C.)	2	0
1960	Vienna	1	4	(* Abandoned after 79 minutes)			

v. BELARUS

		S	B
1997	Minsk (W.C.)	1	0

v. BELGIUM

		S	B			S	B
1947	Brussels	1	2	1979	Brussels (E.C.)	0	2
1948	Glasgow	2	0	1979	Glasgow (E.C.)	1	3
1951	Brussels	5	0	1982	Brussels (E.C.)	2	3
1971	Liege (E.C.)	0	3	1983	Glasgow (E.C.)	1	1
1971	Aberdeen (E.C.)	1	0	1987	Brussels (E.C.)	1	4
1974	Brugge	1	2	1987	Glasgow (E.C.)	2	0

v. BRAZIL

		S	B			S	B
1966	Glasgow	1	1	1977	Rio de Janeiro	0	2
1972	Rio de Janeiro	0	1	1982	Seville (W.C.)	1	4
1973	Glasgow	0	1	1987	Glasgow	0	2
1974	Frankfurt (W.C.)	0	0	1990	Turin (W.C.)	0	1

v. BULGARIA

		S	B			S	B
1978	Glasgow	2	1	1990	Sofia (E.C.)	1	1
1986	Glasgow (E.C.)	0	0	1991	Glasgow (E.C.)	1	1
1987	Sofia (E.C.)	1	0				

v. CANADA

		S	C			S	C
1983	Vancouver	2	0	1983	Toronto	2	0
1983	Edmonton	3	0	1992	Toronto	3	1

v. CHILE

		S	C			S	C
1977	Santiago	4	2	1989	Glasgow	2	0

v. C.I.S. (formerly Soviet Union)

		S	C
1992	Norrkoping (E.C.)	3	0

v. COLOMBIA

		S	C			S	C
1988	Glasgow	0	0	1996	Miami	0	1

v. COSTA RICA

		S	C
1990	Genoa (W.C.)	0	1

v. CYPRUS

		S	C			S	C
1968	Nicosia (W.C.)	5	0	1989	Limassol (W.C.)	3	2
1969	Glasgow (W.C.)	8	0	1989	Glasgow (W.C.)	2	1

v. CZECHOSLOVAKIA

		S	C			S	C
1937	Prague	3	1	1972	Porto Alegre	0	0
1937	Glasgow	5	0	1973	Glasgow (W.C.)	2	1
1961	Bratislava (W.C.)	0	4	1973	Bratislava (W.C.)	0	1
1961	Glasgow (W.C.)	3	2	1976	Prague (W.C.)	0	2
1961	* Brussels (W.C.)	2	4	1977	Glasgow (W.C.)	3	1

(* World Cup play-off)

v. DENMARK

		S	D			S	D
1951	Glasgow	3	1	1972	Glasgow (W.C.)	2	0
1952	Copenhagen	2	1	1975	Copenhagen (E.C.)	1	0
1968	Copenhagen	1	0	1975	Glasgow (E.C.)	3	1
1970	Glasgow (E.C.)	1	0	1986	Neza (W.C.)	0	1
1971	Copenhagen (E.C.)	0	1	1996	Copenhagen	0	2
1972	Copenhagen (W.C.)	4	1				

v. EAST GERMANY

		S	EG			S	EG
1974	Glasgow	3	0	1983	Halle (E.C.)	1	2
1977	East Berlin	0	1	1986	Glasgow	0	0
1982	Glasgow (E.C.)	2	0	1990	Glasgow	0	1

v. ECUADOR

		S	E
1995	Toyama, Japan	2	1

v. EGYPT

		S	E
1990	Aberdeen	1	3

v. ESTONIA

		S	E			S	E
1993	Tallinn (W.C.)	3	0	1997	Monaco (W.C.)	0	0
1993	Aberdeen	3	1	1997	Kilmarnock (W.C.)	2	0
1996	Tallinn (W.C.)	* No result					

(* Estonia absent)

171

v. FAROE ISLANDS

		S	F			S	F
1994	Glasgow (E.C.)	5	1	1995	Toftir (E.C.)	2	0

v. FINLAND

		S	F			S	F
1954	Helsinki	2	1	1992	Glasgow	1	1
1964	Glasgow (W.C.)	3	1	1994	Helsinki (E.C.)	2	0
1965	Helsinki (W.C.)	2	1	1995	Glasgow (E.C.)	1	0
1976	Glasgow	6	0				

v. FRANCE

		S	F			S	F
1930	Paris	2	0	1951	Glasgow	1	0
1932	Paris	3	1	1958	Orebro (W.C.)	1	2
1948	Paris	0	3	1984	Marseilles	0	2
1949	Glasgow	2	0	1989	Glasgow (W.C.)	2	0
1950	Paris	1	0	1990	Paris (W.C.)	0	3

v. GERMANY/WEST GERMANY

		S	G			S	G
1929	Berlin	1	1	1969	Hamburg (W.C.)	2	3
1936	Glasgow	2	0	1973	Glasgow	1	1
1957	Stuttgart	3	1	1974	Frankfurt	1	2
1959	Glasgow	3	2	1986	Queretaro (W.C.)	1	2
1964	Hanover	2	2	1992	Norrkoping (E.C.)	0	2
1969	Glasgow (W.C.)	1	1	1993	Glasgow	0	1

v. GREECE

		S	G			S	G
1994	Athens (E.C.)	0	1	1995	Glasgow	1	0

v. HOLLAND

		S	H			S	H
1929	Amsterdam	2	0	1982	Glasgow	2	1
1938	Amsterdam	3	1	1986	Eindhoven	0	0
1959	Amsterdam	2	1	1992	Gothenburg (E.C.)	0	1
1966	Glasgow	0	3	1994	Glasgow	0	1
1968	Amsterdam	0	0	1994	Utrecht	1	3
1971	Amsterdam	1	2	1996	Birmingham (E.C.)	0	0
1978	Mendoza (W.C.)	3	2				

v. HUNGARY

		S	H			S	H
1938	Glasgow	3	1	1960	Budapest	3	3
1955	Glasgow	2	4	1980	Budapest	1	3
1955	Budapest	1	3	1987	Glasgow	2	0
1958	Glasgow	1	1				

v. ICELAND

		S	I			S	I
1984	Glasgow (W.C.)	3	0	1985	Reykjavik (W.C)	1	0

v. IRAN

		S	I
1978	Cordoba (W.C.)	1	1

v. REPUBLIC OF IRELAND

		S	R of I			S	R of I
1961	Glasgow (W.C.)	4	1	1969	Dublin	1	1
1961	Dublin (W.C.)	3	0	1986	Dublin (E.C.)	0	0
1963	Dublin	0	1	1987	Glasgow (E.C.)	0	1

v. ISRAEL

		S	I			S	I
1981	Tel Aviv (W.C.)	1	0	1986	Tel Aviv	1	0
1981	Glasgow (W.C.)	3	1				

v. ITALY

		S	I			S	I
1931	Rome	0	3	1988	Perugia	0	2
1965	Glasgow (W.C.)	1	0	1992	Glasgow (W.C.)	0	0
1965	Naples (W.C.)	0	3	1993	Rome (W.C.)	1	3

v. JAPAN

		S	J
1995	Hiroshima	0	0

v. LATVIA

		S	L
1996	Riga (W.C.)	2	0

v. LUXEMBOURG

		S	L			S	L
1947	Luxembourg	6	0	1987	Esch (E.C.)	0	0
1986	Glasgow (E.C.)	3	0				

v. MALTA

		S	M			S	M
1988	Valletta	1	1	1993	Valletta (W.C.)	2	0
1990	Valletta	2	1	1997	Valletta	3	2
1993	Glasgow (W.C.)	3	0				

v. NEW ZEALAND

		S	NZ
1982	Malaga (W.C.)	5	2

v. NORWAY

		S	N			S	N
1929	Bergen	7	3	1978	Glasgow (E.C.)	3	2
1954	Glasgow	1	0	1979	Oslo (E.C.)	4	0
1954	Oslo	1	1	1988	Oslo (W.C.)	2	1
1963	Bergen	3	4	1989	Glasgow (W.C.)	1	1
1963	Glasgow	6	1	1992	Oslo	0	0
1974	Oslo	2	1				

173

v. PARAGUAY

		S	P
1958	Norrkoping (W.C.)	2	3

v. PERU

		S	P			S	P
1972	Glasgow	2	0	1979	Glasgow	1	1
1978	Cordoba (W.C.)	1	3				

v. POLAND

		S	P			S	P
1958	Warsaw	2	1	1965	Glasgow (W.C.)	1	2
1960	Glasgow	2	3	1980	Poznan	0	1
1965	Chorzow (W.C.)	1	1	1990	Glasgow	1	1

v. PORTUGAL

		S	P			S	P
1950	Lisbon	2	2	1978	Lisbon (E.C.)	0	1
1955	Glasgow	3	0	1980	Glasgow (E.C.)	4	1
1959	Lisbon	0	1	1980	Glasgow (W.C.)	0	0
1966	Glasgow	0	1	1981	Lisbon (W.C.)	1	2
1971	Lisbon (E.C.)	0	2	1992	Glasgow (W.C.)	0	0
1971	Glasgow (E.C.)	2	1	1993	Lisbon (W.C.)	0	5
1975	Glasgow	1	0				

v. ROMANIA

		S	R			S	R
1975	Bucharest (E.C.)	1	1	1990	Glasgow (E.C.)	2	1
1975	Glasgow (E.C.)	1	1	1991	Bucharest (E.C.)	0	1
1986	Glasgow	3	0				

v. RUSSIA

		S	R			S	R
1994	Glasgow (E.C.)	1	1	1995	Moscow (E.C.)	0	0

v. SAN MARINO

		S	SM			S	SM
1991	Serravalle (E.C.)	2	0	1995	Serravalle (E.C.)	2	0
1991	Glasgow (E.C.)	4	0	1995	Glasgow (E.C.)	5	0

v. SAUDI ARABIA

		S	SA
1988	Riyadh	2	2

v. SOVIET UNION (see also C.I.S. and RUSSIA)

		S	SU			S	SU
1967	Glasgow	0	2	1982	Malaga (W.C.)	2	2
1971	Moscow	0	1	1991	Glasgow	0	1

v. SPAIN

		S	Sp			S	Sp
1957	Glasgow (W.C.)	4	2	1975	Valencia (E.C.)	1	1
1957	Madrid (W.C.)	1	4	1982	Valencia	0	3
1963	Madrid	6	2	1985	Glasgow (W.C.)	3	1
1965	Glasgow	0	0	1985	Seville (W.C.)	0	1
1975	Glasgow (E.C.)	1	2	1988	Madrid	0	0

v. SWEDEN

		S	Swe			S	Swe
1952	Stockholm	1	3	1981	Glasgow (W.C.)	2	0
1953	Glasgow	1	2	1990	Genoa (W.C.)	2	1
1975	Gothenburg	1	1	1995	Solna	0	2
1977	Glasgow	3	1	1996	Glasgow (W.C.)	1	0
1980	Stockholm (W.C.)	1	0	1997	Gothenburg (W.C.)	1	2

v. SWITZERLAND

		S	Sw			S	Sw
1931	Geneva	3	2	1982	Berne (E.C.)	0	2
1948	Berne	1	2	1983	Glasgow (E.C.)	2	2
1950	Glasgow	3	1	1990	Glasgow (E.C.)	2	1
1957	Basle (W.C.)	2	1	1991	Berne (E.C.)	2	2
1957	Glasgow (W.C.)	3	2	1992	Berne (W.C.)	1	3
1973	Berne	0	1	1993	Aberdeen (W.C.)	1	1
1976	Glasgow	1	0	1996	Birmingham (E.C.)	1	0

v. TURKEY

		S	T
1960	Ankara	2	4

v. U.S.A.

		S	USA			S	USA
1952	Glasgow	6	0	1996	Connecticut	1	2
1992	Denver	1	0				

v. URUGUAY

		S	U			S	U
1954	Basle (W.C.)	0	7	1983	Glasgow	2	0
1962	Glasgow	2	3	1986	Neza (W.C.)	0	0

v. YUGOSLAVIA

		S	Y			S	Y
1955	Belgrade	2	2	1974	Frankfurt (W.C.)	1	1
1956	Glasgow	2	0	1984	Glasgow	6	1
1958	Vaasteras (W.C.)	1	1	1988	Glasgow (W.C.)	1	1
1972	Belo Horizonte	2	2	1989	Zagreb (W.C.)	1	3

v. ZAIRE

		S	Z
1974	Dortmund (W.C.)	2	0

WALES

v. ALBANIA

		W	A			W	A
1994	Cardiff (E.C.)	2	0	1995	Tirana (E.C.)	1	1

v. ARGENTINA

		W	A
1992	Gifu (Japan)	0	1

v. AUSTRIA

		W	A			W	A
1954	Vienna	0	2	1975	Wrexham (E.C.)	1	0
1955	Wrexham	1	2	1992	Vienna	1	1
1975	Vienna (E.C.)	1	2				

v. BELGIUM

		W	B			W	B
1949	Liege	1	3	1992	Brussels (W.C.)	0	2
1949	Cardiff	5	1	1993	Cardiff (W.C.)	2	0
1990	Cardiff (E.C.)	3	1	1997	Cardiff (W.C.)	1	2
1991	Brussels (E.C.)	1	1				

v. BRAZIL

		W	B			W	B
1958	Gothenburg (W.C.)	0	1	1966	Belo Horizonte	0	1
1962	Rio de Janeiro	1	3	1983	Cardiff	1	1
1962	Sao Paulo	1	3	1991	Cardiff	1	0
1966	Rio de Janeiro	1	3				

v. BULGARIA

		W	B			W	B
1983	Wrexham (E.C.)	1	0	1994	Cardiff (E.C.)	0	3
1983	Sofia (E.C.)	0	1	1995	Sofia (E.C.)	1	3

v. CANADA

		W	C			W	C
1986	Toronto	0	2	1986	Vancouver	3	0

v. CHILE

		W	C
1966	Santiago	0	2

v. COSTA RICA

		W	C
1990	Cardiff	1	0

v. CYPRUS

		W	C			W	C
1992	Limassol (W.C.)	1	0	1993	Cardiff (W.C.)	2	0

v. CZECHOSLOVAKIA (see also R.C.S.)

		W	C			W	C
1957	Cardiff (W.C.)	1	0	1977	Prague (W.C.)	0	1
1957	Prague (W.C.)	0	2	1980	Cardiff (W.C.)	1	0
1971	Swansea (E.C.)	1	3	1981	Prague (W.C.)	0	2
1971	Prague (E.C.)	0	1	1987	Wrexham (E.C.)	1	1
1977	Wrexham (W.C.)	3	0	1987	Prague (E.C.)	0	2

v. DENMARK

		W	D			W	D
1964	Copenhagen (W.C.)	0	1	1987	Copenhagen (E.C.)	0	1
1965	Wrexham (W.C.)	4	2	1990	Copenhagen	0	1
1987	Cardiff (E.C.)	1	0				

v. EAST GERMANY

		W	EG			W	EG
1957	Leipzig (W.C.)	1	2	1969	Dresden (W.C.)	1	2
1957	Cardiff (W.C.)	4	1	1969	Cardiff (W.C.)	1	3

v. ESTONIA

		W	E
1994	Tallinn	2	1

v. FAROE ISLANDS

		W	Fi			W	Fi
1992	Cardiff (W.C.)	6	0	1993	Toftir (W.C.)	3	0

v. FINLAND

		W	F			W	F
1971	Helsinki (E.C.)	1	0	1987	Wrexham (E.C.)	4	0
1971	Swansea (E.C.)	3	0	1988	Swansea (W.C.)	2	2
1986	Helsinki (E.C.)	1	1	1989	Helsinki (W.C.)	0	1

v. FRANCE

		W	F			W	F
1933	Paris	1	1	1953	Paris	1	6
1939	Paris	1	2	1982	Toulouse	1	0

v. GEORGIA

		W	G			W	G
1994	Tbilisi (E.C.)	0	5	1995	Cardiff (E.C.)	0	1

v. GERMANY/WEST GERMANY

		W	G			W	G
1991	Cardiff (E.C.)	1	0	1989	Cardiff (W.C.)	0	0
1968	Cardiff	1	1	1989	Cologne (W.C.)	1	2
1969	Frankfurt	1	1	1991	Cardiff (E.C.)	1	0
1977	Cardiff	0	2	1991	Nuremberg (E.C.)	1	4
1977	Dortmund	1	1	1995	Dusseldorf (E.C.)	1	1
1979	Wrexham (E.C.)	0	2	1995	Cardiff (E.C.)	1	2
1979	Cologne (E.C.)	1	5				

v. GREECE

		W	G				W	G
1964	Athens (W.C.)	0	2	1965	Cardiff (W.C.)		4	1

v. HOLLAND

		W	H				W	H
1988	Amsterdam (W.C.)	0	1	1996	Cardiff (W.C.)		1	3
1989	Wrexham (W.C.)	1	2	1996	Eindhoven (W.C.)		1	7
1992	Utrecht	0	4					

v. HUNGARY

		W	H				W	H
1958	Sanviken (W.C.)	1	1	1963	Cardiff (E.C.)		1	1
1958	Stockholm (W.C.)	2	1	1974	Cardiff (E.C.)		2	0
1961	Budapest	2	3	1975	Budapest (E.C.)		2	1
1963	Budapest (E.C.)	1	3	1986	Cardiff		0	3

v. ICELAND

		W	I				W	I
1980	Reykjavik (W.C.)	4	0	1984	Cardiff (W.C.)		2	1
1981	Swansea (W.C.)	2	2	1991	Cardiff		1	0
1984	Reykjavik (W.C.)	0	1					

v. IRAN

		W	I
1978	Teheran	1	0

v. REPUBLIC OF IRELAND

		W	RI				W	RI
1960	Dublin	3	2	1991	Wrexham		0	3
1979	Swansea	2	1	1992	Dublin		1	0
1981	Dublin	3	1	1993	Dublin		1	2
1986	Dublin	1	0	1997	Cardiff		0	0
1990	Dublin	0	1					

v. ISRAEL

		W	I				W	I
1958	Tel Aviv (W.C.)	2	0	1984	Tel Aviv		0	0
1958	Cardiff (W.C.)	2	0	1989	Tel Aviv		3	3

v. ITALY

		W	I				W	I
1965	Florence	1	4	1988	Brescia		1	0
1968	Cardiff (W.C.)	0	1	1996	Terni		0	3
1969	Rome (W.C.)	1	4					

v. JAPAN

		W	J
1992	Matsuyama	1	0

v. KUWAIT

		W	K			W	K
1977	Wrexham	0	0	1977	Kuwait	0	0

v. LUXEMBOURG

		W	L			W	L
1974	Swansea (E.C.)	5	0	1990	Luxembourg (E.C.)	1	0
1975	Luxembourg (E.C.)	3	1	1991	Luxembourg (E.C.)	1	0

v. MALTA

		W	M			W	M
1978	Wrexham (E.C.)	7	0	1988	Valletta	3	2
1979	Valletta (E.C.)	2	0				

v. MEXICO

		W	M			W	M
1958	Stockholm (W.C.)	1	1	1962	Mexico City	1	2

v. MOLDOVA

		W	M			W	M
1994	Kishinev (E.C.)	2	3	1995	Cardiff (E.C.)	1	0

v. NORWAY

		W	N			W	N
1982	Swansea (E.C.)	1	0	1985	Wrexham	1	1
1983	Oslo (E.C.)	0	0	1985	Bergen	2	4
1984	Trondheim	0	1	1994	Cardiff	1	3

v. POLAND

		W	P			W	P
1973	Cardiff (W.C.)	2	0	1991	Radom	0	0
1973	Katowice (W.C.)	0	3				

v. PORTUGAL

		W	P			W	P
1949	Lisbon	2	3	1951	Cardiff	2	1

v. R.C.S. (formerly Czechoslovakia)

		W	RCS			W	RCS
1993	Ostrava (W.C.)	1	1	1993	Cardiff (W.C.)	2	2

v. REST OF UNITED KINGDOM

		W	R of UK			W	R of UK
1951	Cardiff	3	2	1969	Cardiff	0	1

v. ROMANIA

		W	R			W	R
1970	Cardiff (E.C.)	0	0	1992	Bucharest (W.C.)	1	5
1971	Bucharest (E.C.)	0	2	1993	Cardiff (W.C.)	1	2
1983	Wrexham	5	0				

v. SAN MARINO

		W	SM			W	SM
1996	Serravalle (W.C.)	5	0	1996	Cardiff (W.C.)	6	0

v. SAUDI ARABIA

		W	SA
1986	Dahran	2	1

v. SOVIET UNION

		W	SU			W	SU
1965	Moscow (W.C.)	1	2	1981	Tbilisi (W.C.)	0	3
1965	Cardiff (W.C.)	2	1	1987	Swansea	0	0
1981	Wrexham (W.C.)	0	0				

v. SPAIN

		W	S			W	S
1961	Cardiff (W.C.)	1	2	1984	Seville (W.C.)	0	3
1961	Madrid (W.C.)	1	1	1985	Wrexham (W.C.)	3	0
1982	Valencia	1	1				

v. SWEDEN

		W	S			W	S
1958	Stockholm (W.C.)	0	0	1990	Stockholm	2	4
1988	Stockholm	1	4	1994	Wrexham	0	2
1989	Wrexham	0	2				

v. SWITZERLAND

		W	S			W	S
1949	Berne	0	4	1996	Lugano	0	2
1951	Wrexham	3	2				

v. TURKEY

		W	T			W	T
1978	Wrexham (E.C.)	1	0	1981	Ankara (W.C.)	1	0
1979	Izmir (E.C.)	0	1	1996	Cardiff (W.C.)	0	0
1980	Cardiff (W.C.)	4	0				

v. URUGUAY

		W	U
1986	Wrexham	0	0

v. YUGOSLAVIA

		W	Y			W	Y
1953	Belgrade	2	5	1982	Titograd (E.C.)	4	4
1954	Cardiff	1	3	1983	Cardiff (E.C.)	1	1
1976	Zagreb (E.C.)	0	2	1988	Swansea	1	2
1976	Cardiff (E.C.)	1	1				

NORTHERN IRELAND

v. ALBANIA

		NI	A			NI	A
1965	Belfast (W.C.)	4	1	1992	Belfast (W.C.)	3	0
1965	Tirana (W.C.)	1	1	1993	Tirana (W.C.)	2	1
1983	Tirana (E.C.)	0	0	1996	Belfast (W.C.)	2	0
1983	Belfast (E.C.)	1	0				

v. ALGERIA

		NI	A
1986	Guadalajara (W.C.)	1	1

v. ARGENTINA

		NI	A
1958	Halmstad (W.C.)	1	3

v. ARMENIA

		NI	A			NI	A
1996	Belfast (W.C.)	1	1	1997	Yerevan (W.C.)	0	0

v. AUSTRALIA

		NI	A			NI	A
1980	Sydney	2	1	1980	Adelaide	2	1
1980	Melbourne	1	1				

v. AUSTRIA

		NI	A			NI	A
1982	Madrid (W.C.)	2	2	1991	Belfast (E.C.)	2	1
1982	Vienna (E.C.)	0	2	1994	Vienna (E.C.)	2	1
1983	Belfast (E.C.)	3	1	1995	Belfast (E.C.)	5	3
1990	Vienna (E.C.)	0	0				

v. BELGIUM

		NI	B			NI	B
1976	Liege (W.C.)	0	2	1997	Belfast (W.C.)	3	0
1977	Belfast (W.C.)	3	0				

v. BRAZIL

		NI	B
1986	Guadalajara (W.C.)	0	3

v. BULGARIA

		NI	B			NI	B
1972	Sofia (W.C.)	0	3	1978	Sofia (E.C.)	2	0
1973	Sheffield (W.C.)	0	0	1979	Belfast (E.C.)	2	0

v. CANADA

		NI	C
1995	Edmonton	0	2

v. CHILE

		NI	C				NI	C
1989	Belfast	0	1	1995	Edmonton, Canada	0	2	

v. COLOMBIA

		NI	C
1994	Boston (USA)	0	2

v. CYPRUS

		NI	C				NI	C
1971	Nicosia (E.C.)	3	0	1973	Nicosia (W.C.)	0	1	
1971	Belfast (E.C.)	5	0	1973	Fulham (W.C.)	3	0	

v. CZECHOSLOVAKIA

		NI	C				NI	C
1958	Halmstad (W.C.)	1	0	1958	Malmo (W.C.)	2	1	

v. DENMARK

		NI	D				NI	D
1978	Belfast (E.C.)	2	1	1991	Odense (E.C.)	1	2	
1979	Copenhagen (E.C.)	0	4	1992	Belfast (W.C.)	0	1	
1986	Belfast	1	1	1993	Copenhagen (W.C.)	0	1	
1990	Belfast (E.C.)	1	1					

v. FAROE ISLANDS

		NI	FI				NI	FI
1991	Belfast (E.C.)	1	1	1991	Landskrona, Sw. (E.C.)	5	0	

v. FINLAND

		NI	F				NI	F
1984	Pori (W.C.)	0	1	1984	Belfast (W.C.)	2	1	

v. FRANCE

		NI	F				NI	F
1951	Belfast	2	2	1982	Madrid (W.C.)	1	4	
1952	Paris	1	3	1986	Paris	0	0	
1958	Norrkoping (W.C.)	0	4	1988	Belfast	0	0	
1982	Paris	0	4					

v. GERMANY/WEST GERMANY

		NI	G				NI	G
1958	Malmo (W.C.)	2	2	1982	Belfast (E.C.)	1	0	
1960	Belfast (W.C.)	3	4	1983	Hamburg (E.C.)	1	0	
1961	Berlin (W.C.)	1	2	1992	Bremen	1	1	
1966	Belfast	0	2	1996	Belfast	1	1	
1977	Cologne	0	5	1997	Nuremberg (W.C.)	1	1	

v. GREECE

		NI	G				NI	G
1961	Athens (W.C.)	1	2	1988	Athens	2	3	
1961	Belfast (W.C.)	2	0					

v. HOLLAND

		NI	H			NI	H
1962	Rotterdam	0	4	1976	Rotterdam (W.C.)	2	2
1965	Belfast (W.C.)	2	1	1977	Belfast (W.C.)	0	1
1965	Rotterdam (W.C.)	0	0				

v. HONDURAS

		NI	H
1982	Zaragoza (W.C.)	1	1

v. HUNGARY

		NI	H			NI	H
1988	Budapest (W.C.)	0	1	1989	Belfast (W.C.)	1	2

v. ICELAND

		NI	I			NI	I
1977	Reykjavik (W.C.)	0	1	1977	Belfast (W.C.)	2	0

v. REPUBLIC OF IRELAND

		NI	RI			NI	RI
1978	Dublin (E.C.)	0	0	1993	Dublin (W.C.)	0	3
1979	Belfast (E.C.)	1	0	1993	Belfast (W.C.)	1	1
1988	Belfast (W.C.)	0	0	1994	Belfast (E.C.)	0	4
1989	Dublin (W.C.)	0	3	1995	Dublin (E.C.)	1	1

v. ISRAEL

		NI	I			NI	I
1968	Jaffa	3	2	1981	Belfast (W.C.)	1	0
1976	Tel Aviv	1	1	1984	Belfast	3	0
1980	Tel Aviv (W.C.)	0	0	1987	Tel Aviv	1	1

v. ITALY

		NI	I			NI	I
1957	Rome (W.C.)	0	1	1961	Bologna	2	3
1957	Belfast	2	2	1997	Palermo	0	2
1958	Belfast (W.C.)	2	1				

v. LATVIA

		NI	L			NI	L
1993	Riga (W.C.)	2	1	1995	Riga (E.C.)	1	0
1993	Belfast (W.C.)	2	0	1995	Belfast (E.C.)	1	2

v. LIECHTENSTEIN

		NI	L			NI	L
1994	Belfast (E.C.)	4	1	1995	Eschen (E.C.)	4	0

v. LITHUANIA

		NI	L			NI	L
1992	Belfast (W.C.)	2	2	1993	Vilnius (W.C.)	1	0

v. MALTA

		NI	M				NI	M
1988	Belfast (W.C.)	3	0	1989	Valletta (W.C.)		2	0

v. MEXICO

		NI	M				NI	M
1966	Belfast	4	1	1994	Miami		0	3

v. MOROCCO

		NI	M
1986	Belfast	2	1

v. NORWAY

		NI	N				NI	N
1974	Oslo (E.C.)	1	2	1990	Belfast		2	3
1975	Belfast (E.C.)	3	0	1996	Belfast		0	2

v. POLAND

		NI	P				NI	P
1962	Katowice (E.C.)	2	0	1988	Belfast		1	1
1962	Belfast (E.C.)	2	0	1991	Belfast		3	1

v. PORTUGAL

		NI	P				NI	P
1957	Lisbon (W.C.)	1	1	1981	Belfast (W.C.)		1	0
1957	Belfast (W.C.)	3	0	1994	Belfast (E.C.)		1	2
1973	Coventry (W.C.)	1	1	1995	Oporto (E.C.)		1	1
1973	Lisbon (W.C.)	1	1	1997	Belfast (W.C.)		0	0
1980	Lisbon (W.C.)	0	1					

v. ROMANIA

		NI	R				NI	R
1984	Belfast (W.C.)	3	2	1994	Belfast		2	0
1985	Bucharest (W.C.)	1	0					

v. SOVIET UNION

		NI	SU				NI	SU
1969	Belfast (W.C.)	0	0	1971	Moscow (E.C.)		0	1
1969	Moscow (W.C.)	0	2	1971	Belfast (E.C.)		1	1

v. SPAIN

		NI	S				NI	S
1958	Madrid	2	6	1985	Palma, Majorca		0	0
1963	Bilbao	1	1	1986	Guadalajara (W.C.)		1	2
1963	Belfast	0	1	1988	Seville (W.C.)		0	4
1970	Seville (E.C.)	0	3	1989	Belfast (W.C.)		0	2
1972	Hull (E.C.)	1	1	1992	Belfast (W.C.)		0	0
1982	Valencia (W.C.)	1	0	1993	Seville (W.C.)		1	3

v. SWEDEN

		NI	S				NI	S
1974	Solna (E.C.)	2	0	1981	Stockholm (W.C.)		0	1
1975	Belfast (E.C.)	1	2	1996	Belfast		1	2
1980	Belfast (W.C.)	3	0					

v. SWITZERLAND

		NI	S				NI	S
1964	Belfast (W.C.)	1	0	1964	Lausanne (W.C.)		1	2

v. THAILAND

		NI	T
1997	Bangkok	0	0

v. TURKEY

		NI	T				NI	T
1968	Belfast (W.C.)	4	1	1985	Belfast (W.C.)		2	0
1968	Istanbul (W.C.)	3	0	1985	Izmir (W.C.)		0	0
1983	Belfast (E.C.)	2	1	1986	Izmir (E.C.)		0	0
1983	Ankara (E.C.)	0	1	1987	Belfast (E.C.)		1	0

v. UKRAINE

		NI	U				NI	U
1996	Belfast (W.C.)	0	1	1997	Kiev (W.C.)		1	2

v. URUGUAY

		NI	U				NI	U
1964	Belfast	3	0	1990	Belfast		1	0

v. YUGOSLAVIA

		NI	Y				NI	Y
1975	Belfast (E.C.)	1	0	1987	Sarajevo (E.C.)		0	3
1975	Belgrade (E.C.)	0	1	1990	Belfast (E.C.)		0	2
1982	Zaragoza (W.C.)	0	0	1991	Belgrade (E.C.)		1	4
1987	Belfast (E.C.)	1	2					

REPUBLIC OF IRELAND

v. ALBANIA

		R of I	A				R of I	A
1992	Dublin (W.C.)	2	0	1993	Tirana (W.C.)		2	1

v. ARGENTINA

		R of I	A				R of I	A
1951	Dublin	0	1	1980	Dublin		0	1
1979	* Dublin	0	0	(* Not regarded as full Int.)				

185

v. AUSTRIA

		R of I	A			R of I	A
1952	Vienna	0	6	1966	Vienna	0	1
1953	Dublin	4	0	1968	Dublin	2	2
1958	Vienna	1	3	1971	Dublin (E.C.)	1	4
1962	Dublin	2	3	1971	Linz (E.C.)	0	6
1963	Vienna (E.C.)	0	0	1995	Dublin (E.C.)	1	3
1963	Dublin (E.C.)	3	2	1995	Vienna (E.C.)	1	3

v. BELGIUM

		R of I	B			R of I	B
1928	Liege	4	2	1965	Dublin	0	2
1929	Dublin	4	0	1966	Liege	3	2
1930	Brussels	3	1	1980	Dublin (W.C.)	1	1
1934	Dublin (W.C.)	4	4	1981	Brussels (W.C.)	0	1
1949	Dublin	0	2	1986	Brussels (E.C.)	2	2
1950	Brussels	1	5	1987	Dublin (E.C.)	0	0

v. BOLIVIA

		R of I	B			R of I	B
1994	Dublin	1	0	1996	New Jersey	3	0

v. BRAZIL

		R of I	B			R of I	B
1974	Rio de Janeiro	1	2	1987	Dublin	1	0
1982	Uberlandia	0	7				

v. BULGARIA

		R of I	B			R of I	B
1977	Sofia (W.C.)	1	2	1979	Dublin (E.C.)	3	0
1977	Dublin (W.C.)	0	0	1987	Sofia (E.C.)	1	2
1979	Sofia (E.C.)	0	1	1987	Dublin (E.C.)	2	0

v. CHILE

		R of I	C			R of I	C
1960	Dublin	2	0	1982	Santiago	0	1
1972	Recife	1	2	1991	Dublin	1	1
1974	Santiago	2	1				

v. CROATIA

		R of I	C
1996	Dublin	2	2

v. CYPRUS

		R of I	C			R of I	C
1980	Nicosia (W.C.)	3	2	1980	Dublin (W.C.)	6	0

v. CZECHOSLOVAKIA/CZECH REPUBLIC

		R of I	C			R of I	C
1938	Prague	2	2	1961	Dublin (W.C.)	1	3
1959	Dublin (E.C.)	2	0	1961	Prague (W.C.)	1	7
1959	Bratislava (E.C.)	0	4	1967	Dublin (E.C.)	0	2

Year	Venue	R of I	C		Year	Venue	R of I	C
1967	Prague (E.C.)	2	1		1981	Dublin	3	1
1969	Dublin (W.C.)	1	2		1986	Reykjavik	1	0
1969	Prague (W.C.)	0	3		1994	Dublin	1	3
1979	Prague	1	4		1996	Prague	0	2

v. DENMARK

Year	Venue	R of I	D		Year	Venue	R of I	D
1956	Dublin (W.C.)	2	1		1979	Dublin (E.C.)	2	0
1957	Copenhagen (W.C.)	2	0		1984	Copenhagen (W.C.)	0	3
1968	*Dublin (W.C.)	1	1		1985	Dublin (W.C.)	1	4
1969	Copenhagen (W.C.)	0	2		1992	Copenhagen (W.C.)	0	0
1969	Dublin (W.C.)	1	1		1993	Copenhagen (W.C.)	1	1
1978	Copenhagen (E.C.)	3	3		(* Abandoned after 51 mins. – fog)			

v. ECUADOR

Year	Venue	R of I	E
1972	Natal	3	2

v. EGYPT

Year	Venue	R of I	E
1990	Palermo (W.C.)	0	0

v. ENGLAND (See England results)

v. FINLAND

Year	Venue	R of I	F		Year	Venue	R of I	F
1949	Dublin (W.C.)	3	0		1990	Dublin	1	1
1949	Helsinki (W.C.)	1	1					

v. FRANCE

Year	Venue	R of I	F		Year	Venue	R of I	F
1937	Paris	2	0		1976	Paris (W.C.)	0	2
1952	Dublin	1	1		1977	Dublin (W.C.)	1	0
1953	Dublin (W.C.)	3	5		1980	Paris (W.C.)	0	2
1953	Paris (W.C.)	0	1		1981	Dublin (W.C.)	3	2
1972	Dublin (W.C.)	2	1		1989	Dublin	0	0
1973	Paris (W.C.)	1	1					

v. GERMANY/WEST GERMANY

Year	Venue	R of I	G		Year	Venue	R of I	G
1935	Dortmund	1	3		1960	Dusseldorf	1	0
1936	Dublin	5	2		1966	Dublin	0	4
1939	Bremen	1	1		1970	Berlin	1	2
1951	Dublin	3	2		1979	Dublin	1	3
1952	Cologne	0	3		1981	Bremen	0	3
1955	Hamburg	1	2		1989	Dublin	1	1
1956	Dublin	3	0		1994	Hanover	2	0

v. HOLLAND

Year	Venue	R of I	H		Year	Venue	R of I	H
1932	Amsterdam	2	0		1935	Dublin	3	5
1934	Amsterdam	2	5		1955	Dublin	1	0

	R of I	H			R of I	H
1956	Rotterdam 4	1		1990	Palermo (W.C.) 1	1
1980	Dublin (W.C.) 2	1		1994	Tilburg 1	0
1981	Rotterdam (W.C.) 2	2		1994	Orlando (W.C.) 0	2
1982	Rotterdam (E.C.) 1	2		1995	*Liverpool (E.C.) 0	2
1983	Dublin (E.C.) 2	3		1996	Rotterdam 1	3
1988	G'kirchen (E.C.) 0	1		(*Qual. Round play-off)		

v. HUNGARY

	R of I	H			R of I	H
1934	Dublin 2	4		1969	Dublin (W.C.) 1	2
1936	Budapest 3	3		1969	Budapest (W.C.) 0	4
1936	Dublin 2	3		1989	Budapest (W.C.) 0	0
1939	Cork 2	2		1989	Dublin (W.C.) 2	0
1939	Budapest 2	2		1992	Gyor 2	1

v. ICELAND

	R of I	I			R of I	I
1962	Dublin (E.C.) 4	2		1983	Reykjavik (E.C.) 3	0
1962	Reykjavik (E.C.) 1	1		1986	Reykjavik 2	1
1982	Dublin (E.C.) 2	0		1996	Dublin (W.C.) 0	0

v. IRAN

	R of I	I
1972	Recife 2	1

v. ISRAEL

	R of I	I			R of I	I
1984	Tel Aviv 0	3		1987	Dublin 5	0
1985	Tel Aviv 0	0				

v. ITALY

	R of I	I			R of I	I
1926	Turin 0	3		1985	Dublin 1	2
1927	Dublin 1	2		1990	Rome (W.C.) 0	1
1970	Florence (E.C.) 0	3		1992	Boston (U.S.A.) 0	2
1971	Dublin (E.C.) 1	2		1994	New York (W.C.) 1	0

v. LATVIA

	R of I	L			R of I	L
1992	Dublin (W.C.) 4	0		1994	Riga (E.C.) 3	0
1993	Riga (W.C.) 2	0		1995	Dublin (E.C.) 2	1

v. LIECHTENSTEIN

	R of I	L			R of I	L
1994	Dublin (E.C.) 4	0		1996	Eschen (W.C.) 5	0
1995	Eschen (E.C.) 0	0		1997	Dublin (W.C.) 5	0

v. LITHUANIA

	R of I	L			R of I	L
1993	Vilnius (W.C.) 1	0		1993	Dublin (W.C.) 2	0

v. LUXEMBOURG

		R of I	L			R of I	L
1936	Luxembourg	5	1	1987	Luxembourg (E.C.)	2	0
1953	Dublin (W.C.)	4	0	1987	Luxembourg (E.C.)	2	1
1954	Luxembourg (W.C.)	1	0				

v. MACEDONIA

		R of I	M			R of I	M
1996	Dublin (W.C.)	3	0	1997	Skopje (W.C.)	2	3

v. MALTA

		R of I	M			R of I	M
1983	Valletta (E.C.)	1	0	1989	Valletta (W.C.)	2	0
1983	Dublin (E.C.)	8	0	1990	Valletta	3	0
1989	Dublin (W.C.)	2	0				

v. MEXICO

		R of I	M			R of I	M
1984	Dublin	0	0	1996	New Jersey	2	2
1994	Orlando (W.C.)	1	2				

v. MOROCCO

		R of I	M
1990	Dublin	1	0

v. NORTHERN IRELAND (See N. Ireland results)

v. NORWAY

		R of I	N			R of I	N
1937	Oslo (W.C.)	2	3	1973	Oslo	1	1
1937	Dublin (W.C.)	3	3	1976	Dublin	3	0
1950	Dublin	2	2	1978	Oslo	0	0
1951	Oslo	3	2	1984	Oslo (W.C.)	0	1
1954	Dublin	2	1	1985	Dublin (W.C.)	0	0
1955	Oslo	3	1	1988	Oslo	0	0
1960	Dublin	3	1	1994	New York (W.C.)	0	0
1964	Oslo	4	1				

v. POLAND

		R of I	P			R of I	P
1938	Warsaw	0	6	1973	Dublin	1	0
1938	Dublin	3	2	1976	Poznan	2	0
1958	Katowice	2	2	1977	Dublin	0	0
1958	Dublin	2	2	1978	Lodz	0	3
1964	Cracow	1	3	1981	Bydgoscz	0	3
1964	Dublin	3	2	1984	Dublin	0	0
1968	Dublin	2	2	1986	Warsaw	0	1
1968	Katowice	0	1	1988	Dublin	3	1
1970	Dublin	1	2	1991	Dublin (E.C.)	0	0
1970	Poznan	0	2	1991	Poznan (E.C.)	3	3
1973	Wroclaw	0	2				

v. PORTUGAL

Year	Venue	R of I	P		Year	Venue	R of I	P
1946	Lisbon	1	3		1992	Boston(U.S.A.)	2	0
1947	Dublin	0	2		1995	Dublin (E.C.)	1	0
1948	Lisbon	1	0		1995	Lisbon (E.C.)	0	3
1949	Dublin	1	0		1996	Dublin	0	1
1972	Recife	1	2					

v. ROMANIA

Year	Venue	R of I	R		Year	Venue	R of I	R
1988	Dublin	2	0		1997	Bucharest (W.C.)	0	1
1990	* Genoa	0	0					

(* Rep. won 5-4 on pens.)

v. RUSSIA (See also Soviet Union)

Year	Venue	R of I	R		Year	Venue	R of I	R
1994	Dublin	0	0		1996	Dublin	0	2

v. SCOTLAND

Year	Venue	R of I	S		Year	Venue	R of I	S
1961	Glasgow (W.C.)	1	4		1969	Dublin	1	1
1961	Dublin (W.C.)	0	3		1986	Dublin (E.C.)	0	0
1963	Dublin	1	0		1987	Glasgow (E.C.)	1	0

v. SOVIET UNION (See also Russia)

Year	Venue	R of I	SU		Year	Venue	R of I	SU
1972	Dublin (W.C.)	1	2		1984	Dublin (W.C.)	1	0
1973	Moscow (W.C.)	0	1		1985	Moscow (W.C.)	0	2
1974	Dublin (E.C.)	3	0		1988	Hanover (E.C.)	1	1
1975	Kiev (E.C.)	1	2		1990	Dublin	1	0

v. SPAIN

Year	Venue	R of I	S		Year	Venue	R of I	S
1931	Barcelona	1	1		1965	Paris (W.C.)	0	1
1931	Dublin	0	5		1966	Dublin (E.C.)	0	0
1946	Madrid	1	0		1966	Valencia (E.C.)	0	2
1947	Dublin	3	2		1977	Dublin	0	1
1948	Barcelona	1	2		1982	Dublin (E.C.)	3	3
1949	Dublin	1	4		1983	Zaragoza (E.C.)	0	2
1952	Madrid	0	6		1985	Cork	0	0
1955	Dublin	2	2		1988	Seville (W.C.)	0	2
1964	Seville (E.C.)	1	5		1989	Dublin (W.C.)	1	0
1964	Dublin (E.C.)	0	2		1992	Seville (W.C.)	0	0
1965	Dublin (W.C.)	1	0		1993	Dublin (W.C.)	1	3
1965	Seville (W.C.)	1	4					

v. SWEDEN

Year	Venue	R of I	S		Year	Venue	R of I	S
1949	Stockholm (W.C.)	1	3		1960	Malmo	1	4
1949	Dublin (W.C.)	1	3		1970	Dublin (E.C.)	1	1
1959	Dublin	3	2		1970	Malmo (E.C.)	0	1

v. SWITZERLAND

Year	Venue	R of I	S
1935	Basle	0	1
1936	Dublin	1	0
1937	Berne	1	0
1938	Dublin	4	0
1948	Dublin	0	1
1975	Dublin (E.C.)	2	1
1975	Berne (E.C.)	0	1
1980	Dublin	2	0
1985	Dublin (W.C.)	3	0
1985	Berne (W.C.)	0	0
1992	Dublin	2	1

v. TRINIDAD & TOBAGO

Year	Venue	R of I	T&T
1982	Port of Spain	1	2

v. TUNISIA

Year	Venue	R of I	T
1988	Dublin	4	0

v. TURKEY

Year	Venue	R of I	T
1966	Dublin (E.C.)	2	1
1967	Ankara (E.C.)	1	2
1974	Izmir (E.C.)	1	1
1975	Dublin (E.C.)	4	0
1976	Ankara	3	3
1978	Dublin	4	2
1990	Izmir	0	0
1990	Dublin (E.C.)	5	0
1991	Istanbul (E.C.)	3	1

v. URUGUAY

Year	Venue	R of I	U
1974	Montevideo	0	2
1986	Dublin	1	1

v. U.S.A.

Year	Venue	R of I	USA
1979	Dublin	3	2
1991	Boston	1	1
1992	Dublin	4	1
1992	Washington	1	3
1996	Boston	1	2

v. WALES

Year	Venue	R of I	W
1960	Dublin	2	3
1979	Swansea	1	2
1981	Dublin	1	3
1986	Dublin	0	1
1990	Dublin	1	0
1991	Wrexham	3	0
1992	Dublin	0	1
1993	Dublin	2	1
1997	Cardiff	0	0

v. YUGOSLAVIA

Year	Venue	R of I	Y
1955	Dublin	1	4
1988	Dublin	2	0

BRITISH CHAMPIONSHIP

WINNERS OF THE TITLE – COMPLETE RECORD

	Pts.		Pts.		Pts.
1883-84 Scotland	6	1919-20 Wales	4	Ireland	3
1884-85 Scotland	5	1920-21 Scotland	6	1956-57 England	5
1885-86 England	5	1921-22 Scotland	4	1957-58 England	4
Scotland	5	1922-23 Scotland	4	Ireland	4
1886-87 Scotland	6	1923-24 Wales	6	1958-59 Ireland	4
1887-88 England	6	1924-25 Scotland	6	England	4
1888-89 Scotland	5	1925-26 Scotland	6	1959-60 England	4
1889-90 Scotland	5	1926-27 Scotland	4	Scotland	4
England	5	England	4	Wales	4
1890-91 England	6	1927-28 Wales	5	1960-61 England	6
1891-92 England	6	1928-29 Scotland	6	1961-62 Scotland	6
1892-93 England	6	1929-30 England	6	1962-63 Scotland	6
1893-94 Scotland	5	1930-31 Scotland	4	1963-64 England	4
1894-95 England	5	England	4	Scotland	4
1895-96 Scotland	5	1931-32 England	6	Ireland	4
1896-97 Scotland	5	1932-33 Wales	5	1964-65 England	5
1897-98 England	6	1933-34 Wales	5	1965-66 England	5
1898-99 England	6	1934-35 England	4	1966-67 Scotland	5
1899-1900 Scotland	6	Scotland	4	1967-68 England	5
1900-01 England	6	1935-36 Scotland	4	1968-69 England	6
1901-02 Scotland	5	1936-37 Wales	6	1969-70 England	4
1902-03 England	4	1937-38 England	4	Scotland	4
Ireland	4	1938-39 England	4	Wales	4
Scotland	4	Scotland	4	1970-71 England	5
1903-04 England	5	Wales	4	1971-72 England	4
1904-05 England	5			Scotland	4
1905-06 England	4	1939-46 No contest		1972-73 England	6
Scotland	4	1946-47 England	5	1973-74 Scotland	4
1906-07 Wales	5	1947-48 England	5	England	4
1907-08 Scotland	5	1948-49 Scotland	6	1974-75 England	4
England	5	1949-50 England	6	1975-76 Scotland	6
1908-09 England	6	1950-51 Scotland	6	1976-77 Scotland	5
1909-10 Scotland	4	1951-52 Wales	5	1977-78 England	6
1910-11 England	5	England	5	1978-79 England	5
1911-12 England	5	1952-53 England	4	1979-80 Ireland	5
Scotland	5	Scotland	4	1980-81 Declared Void †	
1912-13 England	4	1953-54 England	6	1981-82 England	6
1913-14 Ireland	5	1954-55 England	6	1982-83 England	5
1915-19 No contest		1955-56 England	3	1983-84 Ireland	3
		Scotland	3		
		Wales	3		

* Title shared when countries finished level on points until 1983-84, when goal difference was used for the first and only time. The competition was discontinued after that season.

† Because of political unrest in Ireland.

INTERNATIONAL APPEARANCES SINCE THE WAR (1946-97)

(As at start of season 1997-8. Year shown = season, ie. 1997 = season 1996-7. *Also a pre-war International player. Totals include appearances as substitute).

ENGLAND

A'Court, A. (Liverpool, 1958-9) 5
Adams, T. (Arsenal, 1987-97) 47
Allen, A. (Stoke, 1960) 3
Allen, C. (Q.P.R., Tottenham, 1984-8) 5
Allen, R. (W.B.A., 1952-5) 5
Anderson, S. (Sunderland, 1962) ... 2
Anderson, V. (Nott'm F., Arsenal, Man. Utd., 1979-88) 30
Anderton, D. (Tottenham, 1994-6) . 16
Angus, J. (Burnley, 1961) 1
Armfield, J. (Blackpool, 1959-66) .. 43
Armstrong, D. (Middlesbrough, Southampton, 1980-4) 3
Armstrong, K. (Chelsea, 1955) 1
Astall, G. (Birmingham, 1956) 2
Astle, J. (W.B.A., 1969-70) 5
Aston, J. (Man. Utd., 1949-51) 17
Atyeo, J. (Bristol City, 1956-7) 6

Bailey, G. (Man. Utd., 1985) 2
Bailey, M. (Charlton, 1964-5) 2
Baily, E. (Tottenham, 1950-3) 9
Baker, J. (Hibernian, Arsenal, 1960-6) 8
Ball, A. (Blackpool, Everton, Arsenal, 1965-75) 72
Banks, G. (Leicester, Stoke, 1963-72) 73
Banks, T. (Bolton, 1958-9) 6
Bardsley, D. (Q.P.R., 1993) 2
Barham, M. (Norwich, 1983) 2
Barlow, R. (W.B.A., 1955) 1
Barmby, N. (Tottenham, Middlesbrough, 1995-7) 10
Barnes, J. (Watford, Liverpool, 1983-96) 79
Barnes, P. (Man. City, W.B.A., Leeds, 1978-82) 22

Barrass, M. (Bolton, 1952-3) 3
Barrett, E. (Oldham, Aston Villa, 1991-3) 3
Barton, W. (Wimbledon, Newcastle, 1995) 3
Batty, D. (Leeds, Blackburn, Newcastle, 1991-7) 25
Baynham, R. (Luton, 1956) 3
Beardsley, P. (Newcastle, Liverpool, Newcastle, 1986-96) 59
Beasant, D. (Chelsea, 1990) 2
Beattie, K. (Ipswich, 1975-8) 9
Beckham, D. (Man. Utd., 1997) 9
Bell, C. (Man. City, 1968-76) 48
Bentley, R. (Chelsea, 1949-55) 12
Berry, J. (Man. Utd., 1953-6) 4
Birtles, G. (Nott'm F., 1980-1) 3
Blissett, L. (Watford, AC Milan, 1983-4) 14
Blockley, J. (Arsenal, 1973) 1
Blunstone, F. (Chelsea, 1955-7) 5
Bonetti, P. (Chelsea, 1966-70) 7
Bould, S. (Arsenal, 1994) 2
Bowles, S. (Q.P.R., 1974-7) 5
Boyer, P. (Norwich, 1976) 1
Brabrook, P. (Chelsea, 1958-60) 3
Bracewell, P. (Everton, 1985-6) 3
Bradford, G. (Bristol Rovers, 1956) . 1
Bradley, W. (Man. Utd., 1959) 3
Bridges, B. (Chelsea, 1965-6) 4
Broadbent, P. (Wolves, 1958-60) 7
Broadis, I. (Man. City, Newcastle, 1952-4) 14
Brooking, T. (West Ham, 1974-82) 47
Brooks, J. (Tottenham, 1957) 3
Brown, A. (W.B.A., 1971) 1
Brown, K. (West Ham, 1960) 1
Bull, S. (Wolves, 1989-91) 13
Butcher, T. (Ipswich, Rangers, 1980-90) 77
Butt, N. (Man. Utd., 1997) 2

193

194

NORTHERN IRELAND

198

SCOTLAND

WALES

REPUBLIC OF IRELAND

212

213

INTERNATIONAL GOALSCORERS 1946-97
(As at start of season 1997-8)

ENGLAND

Charlton, R	49	Macdonald	6	Bradley	2
Lineker	48	Mullen	6	Broadbent	2
Greaves	44	Rowley	6	Brooks	2
Finney	30	Waddle	6	Cowans	2
Lofthouse	30	Anderton	5	Eastham	2
Platt	28	Atyeo	5	Froggatt, J	2
Robson, B	26	Baily	5	Froggatt, R	2
Hurst	24	Brooking	5	Haines	2
Mortensen	23	Carter	5	Hancocks	2
Channon	21	Edwards	5	Hunter	2
Keegan	21	Ferdinand	5	Ince	2
Peters	20	Hitchens	5	Lee, R	2
Haynes	18	Latchford	5	Lee, S	2
Hunt, R	18	Neal	5	Moore	2
Lawton	16	Pearce	5	Perry	2
Shearer	16	Pearson, Stan	5	Pointer	2
Taylor, T	16	Pearson, Stuart	5	Royle	2
Woodcock	16	Pickering, F	5	Smith, A	2
Chivers	13	Adams	4	Stone	2
Mariner	13	Barnes, P	4	Taylor, P	2
Smith, R	13	Bull	4	Tueart	2
Francis, T	12	Dixon, K	4	Wignall	2
Barnes, J	11	Hassall	4	Worthington	2
Douglas	11	Revie	4	A'Court	1
Mannion	11	Robson, R	4	Astall	1
Clarke, A	10	Steven	4	Beattie	1
Flowers, R	10	Watson, Dave (Sunderland)	4	Bowles	1
Lee, F	10	Webb	4	Bradford	1
Milburn	10	Baker	3	Bridges	1
Wilshaw	10	Barmby	3	Chamberlain	1
Beardsley	9	Blissett	3	Crawford	1
Bell	9	Butcher	3	Dixon, L	1
Bentley	9	Currie	3	Fowler	1
Gascoigne	9	Elliott	3	Goddard	1
Hateley	9	Francis, G	3	Hirst	1
Ball	8	Grainger	3	Hughes, E	1
Broadis	8	Kennedy, R	3	Kay	1
Byrne, J	8	McDermott	3	Keown	1
Hoddle	8	Matthews, S	3	Kidd	1
Kevan	8	Morris	3	Langton	1
Sheringham	8	O'Grady	3	Lawler	1
Connelly	7	Peacock	3	Lee, J	1
Coppell	7	Ramsey	3	Le Saux	1
Paine	7	Sewell	3	Mabbutt	1
Wright, I	7	Wilkins	3	Marsh	1
Charlton, J	6	Wright, W	3	Medley	1
Johnson	6	Allen, R	2	Melia	1
		Anderson	2	Merson	1
				Mullery	1

Nicholas	5	Shearer, D	2
O'Hare	5	Aitken, R	1
Scott, A	5	Bannon	1
Strachan	5	Bett	1
Young, A	5	Bone	1
Archibald	4	Boyd	1
Caldow	4	Brazil	1
Hamilton	4	Buckley	1
Hartford	4	Burns	1
Herd, D.	4	Calderwood	1
Johnstone, J	4	Campbell, R	1
Lorimer	4	Combe	1
Mackay, D	4	Conn	1
Mason	4	Craig	1
McGinlay	4	Crawford	1
McKinlay, W.	4	Curran	1
McLaren	4	Dailly	1
Smith, G	4	Davidson	1
Souness	4	Docherty	1
Baxter	3	Dodds	1
Bremner, W	3	Duncan, M	1
Chalmers	3	Fernie	1
Gibson	3	Gray, F	1
Graham, G	3	Gemmell, T	1
Gray, E	3	Henderson, J	1
Greig	3	Hendry	1
Jackson, D	3	Howie	1
Lennox	3	Hughes, J	1
MacDougall	3	Hunter, W	1
McInally, A	3	Hutchison	1
McNeill	3	Jackson, C	1
McPhail	3	Jardine	1
Morris	3	Jess	1
Robertson, J (1991-5)	3	Johnstone, L	1
Sturrock	3	Linwood	1
White	3	Mackay, G	1
Baird, S	2	MacLeod	1
Bauld	2	McAvennie	1
Flavell	2	McCall	1
Fleming	2	McCalliog	1
Graham, A	2	McKenzie	1
Harper	2	McKimmie	1
Hewie	2	McKinnon	1
Holton	2	McLean	1
Houliston	2	McLintock	1
Johnstone, D.	2	Miller, W	1
McClair	2	Mitchell	1
McGhee	2	Morgan	1
McMillan	2	Mulhall	1
Pettigrew	2	Murray, J	1
Ring	2	Narey	1
Robertson, A	2	Ormond	1

Orr	1
Parlane	1
Provan, D	1
Quinn	1
Sharp	1
Stewart, R	1
Thornton	1
Wallace, I	1
Weir, A	1

WALES

Rush	28
Allchurch, I	23
Ford	23
Saunders	20
Hughes, M	16
Charles, John	15
Jones, C	15
Toshack	13
James, L	10
Davies, Ron	9
Vernon	8
Flynn	7
Walsh, I	7
Charles, Mel	6
Curtis, A	6
Griffiths, A	6
James, R	6
Medwin	6
Clarke, R	5
Leek	5
Deacy	4
Edwards, I	4
Giggs	4
Tapscott	4
Thomas, M	4
Woosnam	4
Allen, M	3
Bodin	3
Bowen, M	3
Coleman	3
England	3
Palmer, D	3
Pembridge	3
Rees, R	3
Speed	3
Davies, G	2
Durban, A	2
Dwyer	2
Edwards, G	2
Giles, D	2

RECORDS SECTION

INDEX

GOALSCORING
(† Football League pre 1992-3. * Home team)

Highest: *Arbroath 36, Bon Accord (Aberdeen) 0, in **Scottish Cup** 1st Round, Sept. 12, 1885. On same day, also in Scottish Cup 1st Round, Dundee Harp beat Aberdeen Rovers 35-0.

Internationals: England 15, *France 0, in Paris, 1906 (Amateur); England 13 *Ireland 0, in Belfast, Feb. 18, 1882 (record in U.K.); *England 9, Scotland 3, at Wembley, Apr. 15, 1961; Biggest England win at Wembley: 9-0 v Luxembourg (E.Champ), Dec. 15, 1982.

Other record wins: Scotland: 11-0 v Ireland (Glasgow, Feb. 23, 1901); **Northern Ireland:** 7-0 v Wales (Belfast, Feb. 1, 1930); **Wales:** 11-0 v Ireland (Wrexham, Mar. 3, 1888); **Rep. of Ireland:** 8-0 v Malta (E. Champ., Dublin, Nov. 16, 1983).

Record International defeats: England: 1-7 v Hungary (Budapest, May 23, 1954); **Scotland:** 3-9 v England (Wembley, April 15, 1961); **Ireland:** 0-13 v England (Belfast, Feb. 18, 1882); **Wales:** 0-9 v Scotland (Glasgow, March 23, 1878); **Rep. of Ireland:** 0-7 v Brazil (Uberlandia, May 27, 1982).

World Cup: Qualifying round – Maldives 0, Iran 17 (June 2, 1997). **Finals – highest scorers:** Hungary 10, El Salvador 1 (Spain, June 15, 1982); Hungary 9, S. Korea 0 (Switzerland, June 17, 1954); Yugoslavia 9, Zaire 0 (W. Germany, June 18, 1974).

F.A. Cup: *Preston North End 26, Hyde 0, 1st Round, Oct. 15, 1887.

League Cup: *West Ham United 10, Bury 0 (2nd Round, 2nd Leg, Oct 25, 1983); *Liverpool 10, Fulham 0 (2nd Round, 1st Leg, Sept. 23, 1986). **Record Aggregates:** Liverpool 13, Fulham 2 (10-0h, 3-2a), Sept. 23-Oct. 7, 1986; West Ham 12, Bury 1 (2-1a, 10-0h), Oct. 4-25, 1983; Liverpool 11, Exeter 0 (5-0h, 6-0a), Oct 7-28, 1981.

F.A. Premier League (beginning 1992-3): *Manchester United 9, Ipswich 0, Mar. 4, 1995. **Record away win:** Nottingham Forest 7, *Sheff. Wednesday 1, Apr. 1, 1995.

† Football League (First Division): *Aston Villa 12, Accrington 2, Mar. 12, 1892; *Tottenham 10, Everton 4, Oct. 11, 1958 (highest 1st. Div. aggregate this century); *West Bromwich 12, Darwen 0, Apr. 4, 1892; *Nottingham Forest 12, Leicester Fosse 0, Apr. 21, 1909. **Record away wins:** Sunderland 9, *Newcastle United 1, Dec. 5, 1908; Wolves 9, *Cardiff City 1, Sept. 3, 1955.

New First Division (beginning 1992-3): *Bolton 7, Swindon 0, Mar. 8, 1997.

† Second Division: *Manchester City 11, Lincoln City 3, Mar. 23, 1895; *Newcastle United 13, Newport County 0, Oct. 5, 1946; *Small Heath 12, Walsall Town Swifts 0, Dec. 17, 1892; *Darwen 12, Walsall 0, Dec. 26, 1896; *Small Heath

12, Doncaster Rovers 0, Apr. 11, 1903. **Record away win:** Sheffield United 10, *Burslem Port Vale 0, Dec. 10, 1892.

New Second Division (beginning 1992-3): *Hartlepool 1, Plymouth 8, May 7, 1994.

† **Third Division:** *Gillingham 10, Chesterfield 0, Sept. 5, 1987; *Tranmere R. 9, Accrington Stanley 0, Apr. 18, 1959; *Brighton 9, Southend 1, Nov. 22, 1965; *Brentford 9, Wrexham 0, Oct. 15, 1963. **Record away win:** Fulham 8, *Halifax Town 0, Sept. 16, 1969.

New Third Division (beginning 1992-3): *Torquay 1, Scunthorpe 8, Oct. 28, 1995.

† **Third Division (North):** *Stockport County 13, Halifax Town 0 (still joint biggest win in F. League – see Div. 2) Jan. 6, 1934; *Tranmere Rovers 13, Oldham Athletic 4, Dec. 26, 1935. *(17 is highest Football League aggregate score)*. **Record away win:** Barnsley 9, *Accrington Stanley 0, Feb. 3, 1934.

† **Third Division (South):** *Luton Town 12, Bristol Rovers 0, Apr. 13, 1936; *Gillingham 9, Exeter City 4, Jan. 7, 1951. **Record away win:** Walsall 8, *Northampton Town 0, Apr. 8, 1947.

† **Fourth Division:** *Oldham Ath. 11, Southport 0, Dec. 26, 1962; *Hartlepool 10, Barrow 1, Apr. 4, 1959; *Wrexham 10, Hartlepool U. 1, Mar. 3, 1962. **Record away win:** Rotherham Utd. 8, *Crewe Alex. 1, Sept. 8, 1973.

Scottish Premier Division – Highest aggregate: 11 goals – Celtic 8, Hamilton 3, Jan. 3, 1987. **Other highest team scores:** Aberdeen 8, Motherwell 0 (Mar. 26, 1979); Kilmarnock 1, Rangers 8 (Sept. 6, 1980); Hamilton 0, Celtic 8 (Nov. 5, 1988).

Scottish League Div. 1: *Celtic 11, Dundee 0, Oct. 26, 1895. **Record away win:** Hibs 11, *Airdrie 1, Oct. 24, 1959.

Scottish League Div. 2: *Airdrieonians 15, Dundee Wanderers 1, Dec. 1, 1894.

Record British score this century: Stirling Albion 20, Selkirk 0 (Scottish Cup 1st. Round, Dec. 8, 1984). Winger Davie Thompson (7 goals) was one of 9 Stirling players to score.

FOOTBALL LEAGUE – BEST IN SEASON
(Before restructure in 1992)

Div.		Goals	Games
1	W.R. (Dixie) Dean, Everton, 1927-8	60	39
2	George Camsell, Middlesbrough, 1926-7	59	37
3(S)	Joe Payne, Luton Town, 1936-7	55	39
3(N)	Ted Harston, Mansfield Town, 1936-7	55	41
3	Derek Reeves, Southampton, 1959-60	39	46
4	Terry Bly, Peterborough U., 1960-1	52	46

(Since restructure in 1992)

Div.		Goals	Games
1	Guy Whittingham, Portsmouth, 1992-3	42	46
2	Jimmy Quinn, Reading, 1993-4	35	46
3	Graeme Jones, Wigan, 1996-7	31	40

F.A. PREMIER LEAGUE – BEST IN SEASON

Andy Cole **34 goals** (Newcastle – 40 games, 1993-4); Alan Shearer **34 goals** (Blackburn – 42 games, 1994-5).

FOOTBALL LEAGUE – BEST MATCH HAULS
(Before restructure in 1992)

Div.		Goals
1	Ted Drake (Arsenal), away to Aston V., Dec. 14, 1935	7
	James Ross (Preston N.E.) v Stoke, Oct 6, 1888	7
2	*Neville (Tim) Coleman (Stoke City) v. Lincoln, Feb. 23, 1957 .	7
	Tommy Briggs (Blackburn Rovers) v. Bristol Rovers, Feb. 5, 1955	7
3(S)	Joe Payne (Luton Town) v. Bristol Rovers, April 13, 1936	10
3(N)	Robert ('Bunny') Bell (Tranmere Rovers) v. Oldham Athletic, Dec. 26, 1935 – he also missed a penalty ...	9
3	Barrie Thomas (Scunthorpe Utd) v. Luton, April 24, 1965	5
	Keith East (Swindon Town) v. Mansfield, Nov. 20, 1965	5
	Steve Earle (Fulham) v. Halifax, Sept. 16, 1969	5
	Alf Wood (Shrewsbury Town) v. Blackburn Rov., Oct. 2, 1971 .	5
	Tony Caldwell (Bolton W.) v. Walsall, Sept 10, 1983	5
	Andy Jones (Port Vale) v. Newport Co., May 4, 1987	5
4	Bert Lister (Oldham Ath.) v. Southport, Dec. 26, 1962	6

* Scored from the wing

(Since restructure in 1992)

Div.	Goals
1	4 in match – John Durnin (Oxford v Luton, 1992-3); Guy Whittingham (Portsmouth v Bristol R. 1992-3); Craig Russell (Sunderland v Millwall, 1995-6).
2	5 in match – Paul Barnes (Burnley v Stockport, 1996-7).
3	5 in match – Tony Naylor (Crewe v Colchester, 1992-3); Steve Butler (Cambridge v Exeter, 1993-4).

F.A. PREMIER LEAGUE – BEST MATCH HAUL

5 goals in match: Andy Cole (Man. United v Ipswich, 1994-5).

SCOTTISH LEAGUE

Div.		Goals
1	Jimmy McGrory (Celtic) v. Dunfermline Athletic, Jan. 14, 1928	8
1	Owen McNally (Arthurlie) v. Armadale, Oct. 1, 1927	8
2	Jim Dyet (King's Park) v. Forfar Athletic, Jan. 2, 1930, on his debut for the club	8
2	John Calder (Morton) v. Raith Rovers, April 18, 1936	8
2	Norman Haywood (Raith Rovers) v. Brechin, Aug. 20, 1937	8
Prem.	Paul Sturrock (Dundee United) v. Morton, Nov. 20, 1984	5

SCOTTISH LEAGUE – BEST IN SEASON

Prem.	Brian McClair (Celtic, 1986-7)	35
1	William McFadyen (Motherwell, 1931-2)	53
2	*Jimmy Smith (Ayr, 1927-8 – 38 appearances)	66

(*British record)

CUP FOOTBALL

Scottish Cup: John Petrie (Arbroath) v. Bon Accord, at Arbroath, 1st Round, Sept. 12, 1885 .... **13**

F.A. Cup: Ted MacDougall (Bournemouth) v. Margate, 1st Round, Nov. 20, 1971 .... **9**

F.A. Cup Final: Billy Townley (Blackburn Rovers) v. Sheffield Wednesday, at Kennington Oval, 1890; Jimmy Logan (Notts County) v. Bolton Wanderers, at Everton, 1894; Stan Mortensen (Blackpool) v. Bolton Wanderers, at Wembley, 1953 .... **3**

League Cup: Frank Bunn (Oldham Athletic) v. Scarborough (3rd Round), Oct. 25, 1989 .... **6**

Scottish League Cup: Jim Fraser (Ayr) v. Dumbarton, Aug. 13, 1952 . **5**

Jim Forrest (Rangers) v. Stirling Albion, Aug. 17, 1966 .... **5**

Scottish Cup: Most goals in match since war: **10** by **Gerry Baker** (St. Mirren) in 15-0 win (1st Round) v Glasgow Univ., Jan 30, 1960; **9** by his brother **Joe Baker** (Hibernian) in 15-1 win (2nd. Round) v Peebles Rov., Feb. 11, 1961.

AGGREGATE LEAGUE SCORING RECORDS

Goals

* Arthur Rowley (1947-65, WBA, Fulham, Leicester, Shrewsbury) **434**

† Jimmy McGrory (1922-38, Celtic, Clydebank) **410**

Hughie Gallacher (1921-39, Airdrieonians, Newcastle, Chelsea, Derby, Notts County, Grimsby, Gateshead) **387**

William ('Dixie') Dean (1923-37, Tranmere, Everton, Notts County) **379**

Hugh Ferguson (1916-30, Motherwell, Cardiff City, Dundee) **362**

■Jimmy Greaves (1957-71, Chelsea, Tottenham, West Ham) **357**

Steve Bloomer (1892-1914, Derby County, Middlesbrough, Derby County) ... **352**

George Camsell (1923-39, Durham City, Middlesbrough) **348**

Dave Halliday (1920-35, St. Mirren, Dundee, Sunderland, Arsenal, Man. City, Clapton Orient) **338**

John Aldridge (1979-97, Newport, Oxford, Liverpool, Tranmere) **324**

John Atyeo (1951-66, Bristol City) **315**

Joe Smith (1908-29, Bolton, Stockport County) **315**

Victor Watson (1920-36, West Ham, Southampton) **312**

Harry Johnson (1919-36, Sheff. United, Mansfield) **309**

Bob McPhail (1920s–1930s, Airdrie, Rangers) **306**

(* **Rowley** scored 4 for WBA, 27 for Fulham, 251 for Leicester, 152 for Shrewsbury. ■ **Greaves's** 357 is record top-division total (he also scored 9 League goals for AC Milan). **Aldridge** also scored 33 League goals for Real Sociedad. † **McGrory** scored 397 for Celtic, 13 for Clydebank.)

Most League goals for one club: 349 – Dixie Dean (Everton 1925-37); **326 – George Camsell** (Middlesbrough 1925-39); **315 – John Atyeo** (Bristol City 1951-66); **306 – Vic Watson** (West Ham 1920-35); **291 – Steve Bloomer** (Derby 1892-1906, 1910-14); **259 – Arthur Chandler** (Leicester 1923-35); **255 – Nat Lofthouse** (Bolton 1946-61); **251 – Arthur Rowley** (Leicester 1950-58).

Over 500 Goals: Jimmy McGrory (Celtic, Clydebank and Scotland) scored a total of 550 goals in his first-class career (1922-38). ●

Over 1,000 goals: Brazil's **Pele** is reputedly the game's all-time highest scorer with 1,282 goals in 1,365 matches (1956-77), but many of them were scored in friendlies for his club, Santos. He scored his 1,000th goal, a penalty, against Vasco da Gama in the Maracana Stadium, Rio, on November 19, 1969. Pele (born Oct. 23, 1940) played regularly for Santos from the age of 16. During his career, he was sent off once. He played 95 'A' Internationals for Brazil and in their World Cup-winning teams in 1958 and 1970. ● Pele (Edson Arantes do Nascimento) subsequently Brazil's Minister for Sport. He never played at Wembley, apart from being filmed there scoring a goal for a commercial.

MOST LEAGUE GOALS IN SEASON: DEAN'S 60

W.R. ('Dixie') Dean, Everton centre-forward, created a League scoring record in 1927-8 with an aggregate of 60 in 39 First Division matches. He also scored three goals in F.A. Cup-ties, and 19 in representative games (total for the season 82).

George Camsell, of Middlesbrough, previously held the record with 59 goals in 37 Second Division matches in 1926-7, his total for the season being 75.

SHEARER'S RECORD 'FIRST'

Alan Shearer (Blackburn) is the first player to score more than 30 top-division goals in 3 successive seasons since the war: 31 in 1993-4, 34 in 1994-5, 31 in 1995-6. **David Halliday** (Sunderland) topped 30 First Div. goals in 4 consecutive seasons with totals of 38, 36, 36 and 49 from 1925-26 to 1928-29.

MOST GOALS IN A MATCH

TOP SCORE by a player in a first-class match is **13** in the Scottish Cup and **10** in the Football League.

October 6, 1888: James Ross for Preston N.E. (7-0 v. Stoke City) set a League record in its first season by scoring all 7

December 14, 1935: Ted Drake for Arsenal in 7-1 win away to Aston Villa (Div. 1). Scored six goals with his first six shots and in all equalled Ross's Football League record by scoring 7

February 5, 1955: Tommy Briggs for Blackburn Rovers v. Bristol Rovers set Second Division record during an 8-3 win by scoring 7

February 23, 1957: Neville ('Tim') Coleman for Stoke City v. Lincoln City (8-0) in Second Division set a record as a winger by scoring 7

December 26, 1935: Robert ('Bunny') Bell for Tranmere Rovers v. Oldham Athletic (Div. III North) beat Drake's 12-day-old record in a 13-4 win by scoring . 9

April 13, 1936: Joe Payne set the still-existing individual record on his debut as a centre-forward, for Luton Town v. Bristol Rovers (Div. III South). In a 12-0 win he scored 10

September 12, 1885: John Petrie set the all-time British individual record for a first-class match when, in Arbroath's 36-0 win against Bon Accord (Scottish Cup first round), he scored 13

OTHER BIG HAULS

Gerry Baker 10 for St. Mirren v. Glasgow University in Scottish Cup, January 30, 1960 (15-0).

Eric Gemmell for Oldham Athletic v. Chester in Third Division North (11-2), January 19, 1952, and **Albert Whitehurst** for Bradford City v. Tranmere Rovers (Third Division North) (8-0), March 6, 1929; both scored **seven**.

W.H. (Billy) Minter scored **seven** goals for St. Albans City in replayed F.A. Cup 4th Qualifying Round against Dulwich Hamlet, November 22, 1922. Dulwich won 8-7, and Minter's seven is still the most goals scored in one match by a player in a losing side.

Denis Law scored **seven** but finished a loser in Man. City's F.A. Cup 4th Round tie at Luton in 1961. The original match on January 28 was washed out (69 mins.) when City led 6-2 (Law 6). He scored a seventh when the game was played again, but Luton won 3-1.

Louis Page, England outside-left, when tried for the first time as centre-forward, accomplished the **double hat-trick** for Burnley in a First Division match against Birmingham, at St. Andrews, April 10, 1926. Burnley won 7-1.

Davie Wilson, Rangers outside-left, scored **six** goals from centre-forward at Falkirk in Scottish league, March 17, 1962. Result: 7-1.

Geoff Hurst was the last player to score **six** in a League match, in West Ham's 8-0 win v Sunderland (Div. 1) on October 19, 1968.

ALDRIDGE CLOSE TO ALL-TIME RECORD

Arthur Rowley is still English football's **top club scorer** with a total of 464 goals for WBA, Fulham, Leicester and Shrewsbury (1947-65). They comprised 434 in the League, 26 F.A. Cup, 4 League Cup.

Jimmy Greaves was second with a total of 420 goals for Chelsea, AC Milan, Tottenham and West Ham, made up of 366 League (incl. 9 for AC Milan), 35 F.A. Cup, 10 League Cup and 9 in Europe.

But **John Aldridge**, still scoring last season as Tranmere's 38-year-old player-manager, is only 5 short of Rowley's record. His total of 429 club goals for Newport, Oxford, Liverpool, Real Sociedad and Tranmere from 1979-97 comprises 357 League (incl. 33 for Real Soc.), 19 F.A. Cup, 44 League Cup, 7 Spanish Cup and 2 in Europe.

MOST GOALS IN INTERNATIONAL FOOTBALL
SEVEN by

Vivian Woodward for England v France in Amateur International in Paris, November 1, 1906. Result 15-0.

SIX by

Nat Lofthouse for Football League v. Irish League, at Wolverhampton, September 24, 1952. Result: 7-1.

Joe Bambrick for Ireland against Wales, in Belfast, February 1, 1930. Result: 7-0.

W.C. Jordan in Amateur International for England v. France, at Park Royal, March 23, 1908. Result 12-0.

Vivian Woodward for England v. Holland in Amateur International, at Chelsea, December 11, 1909. Result: 9-1.

FIVE by

Oliver Vaughton for England v Ireland (Belfast), February 18, 1882. Result: 13-0.

Steve Bloomer for England v. Wales (Cardiff) March 16, 1896. Result: 9-1.

Hughie Gallacher for Scotland against Ireland (Belfast), February 23, 1929. Result: 7-3.

Willie Hall for England v. Ireland, at Old Trafford, Manchester, November 16, 1938. Five in succession (first three in 3 mins. – fastest International hat-trick). Result: 7-0.

Malcolm Macdonald for England v. Cyprus (Wembley) April 16, 1975. Result: 5-0.

Hughie Gallacher for Scottish League against Irish League (Belfast) November 11, 1925. Result: 7-3.

Barney Battles for Scottish League against Irish League (Firhill Park, Glasgow) October 31, 1928. Result: 8-2.

Bobby Flavell for Scottish League against Irish League (Belfast) April 30, 1947. Result: 7-4.

Joe Bradford for Football League v. Irish League (Everton) September 25, 1929. Result: 7-2.

Albert Stubbins for Football League v. Irish League (Blackpool) October 18, 1950. Result: 6-3.

Brian Clough for Football League v. Irish League (Belfast) September 23, 1959. Result: 5-0.

INTERNATIONAL TOP SHOTS

		Goals	Games
England	– Bobby Charlton (1958-70)	49	106
N. Ireland	– Colin Clarke (1986-92)	13	38
Scotland	– Denis Law (1958-74)	30	55
	– Kenny Dalglish (1971-86)	30	102
Wales	– Ian Rush (1980-96)	28	73
Rep. of I.	– Frank Stapleton (1977-90)	20	71

ENGLAND'S TOP MARKSMEN
(As at start of season 1997-98)

	Goals	Games
Bobby Charlton (1958-70)	49	106
Gary Lineker (1984-92)	48	80
Jimmy Greaves (1959-67)	44	57
Tom Finney (1946-58)	30	76
Nat Lofthouse (1950-58)	30	33
Vivian Woodward (1903-11)	29	23
Steve Bloomer (1895-1907)	28	23
David Platt (1989-96)	27	62
Bryan Robson (1979-91)	26	90
Geoff Hurst (1966-72)	24	49
Stan Mortensen (1947-53)	23	25
Tommy Lawton (1938-48)	22	23
Mike Channon (1972-77)	21	46
Kevin Keegan (1972-82)	21	63
Martin Peters (1966-74)	20	67
George Camsell (1929-36)	18	9
"Dixie" Dean (1927-32)	18	16
Johnny Haynes (1954-62)	18	56
Roger Hunt (1962-69)	18	34
Tommy Taylor (1953-57)	16	19
Tony Woodcock (1978-86)	16	42
Alan Shearer (1992-97)	16	35

CONSECUTIVE GOALS FOR ENGLAND

Tinsley Lindley (Cambridge Univ.) scored in **NINE** consecutive Internationals for **England** in three seasons (March 1886-March 1888) – three games against each of Ireland, Wales and Scotland.

In modern times, **Paul Mariner** scored in six consecutive **England** appearances (7 goals) between November 1981 and June 1982.

'GOLDEN GOAL' DECIDERS

The Football League, in an experiment to avoid penalty shoot-outs, introduced a new "golden goal" system in the 1994-95 **Auto Windscreens Shield** to decide matches in the knock-out stages of the competition in which scores were level after 90 minutes. The first goal scored in overtime ended play.

Iain Dunn (Huddersfield) became the first player in British football to settle a match by this sudden-death method. His 107th-minute goal beat Lincoln 3-2 on Nov. 30, 1994, and to mark his "moment in history" he was presented with a golden football trophy.

The AWS Final of 1995 was decided when **Paul Tait** headed the only goal for Birmingham against Carlisle 13 minutes into overtime – the first time a match at Wembley had been decided by the "golden goal" formula.

First major International tournament match to be decided by sudden death was the final of the 1996 European Championship in which Germany beat Czech Rep. 2-1 by Oliver Bierhoff's goal in the 95th minute.

PREMIERSHIP TOP SHOTS (1992-97)

Alan Shearer	137	Eric Cantona	70
Les Ferdinand	101	Chris Sutton	59
Ian Wright	94	Peter Beardsley	58
Robbie Fowler	83	Dean Holdsworth	58
Matthew Le Tissier	79	(As at start of season 1997-98)	
Teddy Sheringham	76		
Andy Cole	73		

LEAGUE GOAL RECORDS

The highest goal-scoring aggregates in the Football League, Premier and Scottish League are as follows:

FOR

	Goals	Games	Club	Season
Prem.	82	42	Newcastle	1993-4
Div. 1	128	42	Aston Villa	1930-1
New Div. 1	100	46	Bolton	1996-7
Div. 2	122	42	Middlesbrough	1926-7
New Div. 2	88	46	W.B.A.	1992-3
	88	46	Plymouth	1993-4
Div. 3(S)	127	42	Millwall	1927-8
Div. 3(N)	128	42	Bradford City	1928-9
Div. 3	111	42	Q.P.R.	1961-2
New Div. 3	84	46	Wigan	1996-7
Div. 4	134	46	Peterborough Utd.	1960-1
Scot. Prem.	101	44	Rangers	1991-2
Scot. L. 1	132	34	Hearts	1957-8
Scot. L. 2	142	34	Raith Rovers	1937-8
Scot. L. 3 (Modern)	74	36	Forfar	1996-7

AGAINST

	Goals	Games	Club	Season
Prem.	100	42	Swindon	1993-4
Div. 1	125	42	Blackpool	1930-1
New Div. 1	87	46	Bristol R.	1992-3
Div. 2	141	34	Darwen	1898-9
New Div. 2	102	46	Chester	1992- 3
Div. 3(S)	135	42	Merthyr T.	1929-30
Div. 3(N)	136	42	Nelson	1927-8
Div. 3	123	46	Accrington S.	1959-60
New Div. 3	84	46	Torquay	1995-6
Div. 4	109	46	Hartlepool	1959-60
Scot. Prem.	100	36	Morton	1984-5
Scot. Prem.	100	44	Morton	1987-8
Scot. L. 1	137	38	Leith A.	1931-2
Scot. L. 2	146	38	Edinburgh C.	1931-2
Scot. L. 3 (Modern)	82	36	Albion Rovers	1994-5

BEST DEFENSIVE RECORDS
* Denotes under old offside law

Div.	Goals Agst.	Games	Club	Season
Prem.	28	42	Arsenal	1993-4
1	16	42	Liverpool	1978-9
1	*15	22	Preston N.E.	1888-9
New Div. 1	33	46	Sunderland	1995-6
2	18	28	Liverpool	1893-4
2	*22	34	Sheffield W.	1899-1900
2	24	42	Birmingham C.	1947-8
2	24	42	Crystal Palace	1978-9
New Div. 2	34	46	Stoke	1992-3
New Div. 2	34	46	Swindon	1995-6
3(S)	*21	42	Southampton	1921-2
3(S)	30	42	Cardiff City	1946-7
3(N)	*21	38	Stockport C.	1921-2

3(N)	21	46	Port Vale	1953-4
3	30	46	Middlesbrough	1986-7
New Div. 3	20	46	Gillingham	1995-6
4	25	46	Lincoln City	1980-1

SCOTTISH LEAGUE

Div.	Goals Agst.	Games	Club	Season
Prem.	19	36	Rangers	1989-90
1	*12	22	Dundee	1902-3
1	*14	38	Celtic	1913-14
2	20	38	Morton	1966-7
2	*29	38	Clydebank	1922-3
2	29	36	East Fife	1995-6
New Div. 3	21	36	Brechin	1995-6

TOP SCORERS (LEAGUE ONLY)

		Goals	Div.
1996-7	Graeme Jones (Wigan)	31	3
1995-6	Alan Shearer (Blackburn)	31	Prem.
1994-5	Alan Shearer (Blackburn)	34	Prem.
1993-4	Jimmy Quinn (Reading)	35	2
1992-3	Guy Whittingham (Portsmouth)	42	1
1991-2	Ian Wright (C. Palace 5, Arsenal 24)	29	1
1990-1	Teddy Sheringham (Millwall)	33	2
1989-90	Mick Quinn (Newcastle)	32	2
1988-9	Steve Bull (Wolves)	37	3
1987-8	Steve Bull (Wolves)	34	4
1986-7	Clive Allen (Tottenham Hotspur)	33	1
1985-6	Gary Lineker (Everton)	30	1
1984-5	Tommy Tynan (Plymouth)	31	3
	John Clayton (Tranmere)	31	4
1983-4	Trevor Senior (Reading)	36	4
1982-3	Luther Blissett (Watford)	27	1
1981-2	Keith Edwards (Hull 1, Sheff U 35)	36	4
1980-1	Tony Kellow (Exeter City)	25	3
1979-80	Clive Allen (Queens Park Rangers)	28	2
1978-9	Ross Jenkins (Watford)	29	3
1977-8	Steve Phillips (Brentford)	32	4
	Alan Curtis (Swansea)	32	4
1976-7	Peter Ward (Brighton)	32	3
1975-6	Dixie McNeil (Hereford)	35	3
1974-5	Dixie McNeil (Hereford)	31	3
1973-4	Brian Yeo (Gillingham)	31	4
1972-3	Bryan (Pop) Robson (West Ham United)	28	1
1971-2	Ted MacDougall (Bournemouth)	35	3
1970-1	Ted MacDougall (Bournemouth)	42	4
1969-70	Albert Kinsey (Wrexham)	27	4
1968-9	Jimmy Greaves (Tottenham Hotspur)	27	1
1967-8	George Best (Manchester United)	28	1
	Ron Davies (Southampton)	28	1
1966-7	Ron Davies (Southampton)	37	1
1965-6	Kevin Hector (Bradford P.A.)	44	4
1964-5	Alick Jeffrey (Doncaster Rovers)	36	4
1963-4	Hugh McIlmoyle (Carlisle United)	39	4
1962-3	Jimmy Greaves (Tottenham Hotspur)	37	1
1961-2	Roger Hunt (Liverpool)	41	2
1960-1	Terry Bly (Peterborough United)	52	4

100 LEAGUE GOALS

Bolton Wanderers, as First Div. Champions in 1996-7, reached exactly 100 goals, the first side to complete a century in League football for ten years – since 103 by Northampton T. (Div. 4 Champions) in 1986-7.

Last League Champions to reach **100** League goals: **Tottenham** (115 in 1960-1). Last century of goals in the top division: **111** by runners-up **Tottenham** in 1962-3.

In **1930-1**, the Championship top three all scored a century of League goals: 1 Arsenal (127), 2 Aston Villa (128), 3 Sheffield Wednesday (102).

100 GOALS AGAINST

Swindon Town, relegated with 100 goals against in 1993-4, were the first top-division club to concede a century of League goals since **Ipswich** (121) went down in 1964. Most goals conceded in the top division: 125 by **Blackpool** in 1930-31, but they avoided relegation.

MOST GOALS IN TOP DIV. ON ONE DAY

This record has stood since December 26, 1963, when **66 goals** were scored in the ten First Division matches played.

MOST F.A. PREMIER LEAGUE GOALS ON ONE DAY

47, in nine matches on May 8, 1993 (last day of season).

FEWEST FIRST DIV. GOALS ON ONE DAY

For full/near full programme: **Ten goals** all by home clubs, in ten matches on April 28, 1923 (day of Wembley's first F.A. Cup Final).

ONE-DAY GOAL FEAST

Most goals scored in the Football League on one day: **209 (44 matches)** on February 1, 1936.

SIX-OUT-OF-SIX HEADERS

When **Oxford United** beat Shrewsbury Town 6-0 (Div. 2) on April 23, 1996, all six goals were headers.

FIVE IN A MATCH

Latest players to score 5 goals in a top-division match: **Tony Woodcock** (for Arsenal in 6-2 win away to Aston Villa) and **Ian Rush** (Liverpool 6, Luton 0), both on October 29, 1983; **Andy Cole** (Man. United 9, Ipswich 0) on March 4, 1995.

ALL–ROUND MARKSMAN

Alan Cork scored in four divisions of the Football League, in the F.A. Premier League and F.A. Premiership in his 18-season career with Wimbledon, Sheff. United, and Fulham (1977-95).

MOST CUP GOALS

F.A. Cup – most goals in one season: 20 by J.D. Ross (Preston, runners-up 1887-8); 15 by Albert (Sandy) Brown (Tottenham, winners 1900-1).

Most F.A. Cup goals in individual careers: 48 by Henry Cursham (Notts Co. 1880-87); this century: 42 by Ian Rush (39 for Liverpool, 3 for Chester, 1979-96).

Denis Law was the previous highest F.A. Cup scorer this century with 41 goals for Huddersfield, Man. City and Man. United (1957-74).

Most F.A. Cup Final goals by individual: 5 by Ian Rush for Liverpool (2 in 1986, 2 in 1989, 1 in 1992).

HOTTEST CUP HOT-SHOT

Geoff Hurst scored 21 cup goals in season 1965-66: 11 League Cup, 4 F.A. Cup and 2 Cup-Winners' Cup for West Ham, and 4 in the World Cup for England.

SCORERS IN EVERY ROUND

Twelve players have scored in **every round** of the F.A. Cup in one season, from opening to Final inclusive: **Archie Hunter** (Aston Villa, winners 1887); **Albert (Sandy) Brown** (Tottenham, winners 1901); **Harry Hampton** (Aston Villa, winners 1905); **Harold Blackmore** (Bolton, winners 1929); **Ellis Rimmer** (Sheff. Wed., winners 1935); **Frank O'Donnell** (Preston, beaten 1937); **Stan Mortensen** (Blackpool, beaten 1948); **Jack Milburn** (Newcastle, winners 1951); **Nat Lofthouse** (Bolton, beaten 1953); **Charlie Wayman** (Preston, beaten 1954); **Jeff Astle** (W.B.A., winners 1968); **Peter Osgood** (Chelsea, winners 1970).

Blackmore and the next seven completed their "set" in the Final at Wembley; Osgood did so in the Final replay at Old Trafford.

Only player to score in every **Football League Cup** round possible in one season: **Tony Brown** for W.B.A., winners 1965-6, with 9 goals in 10 games (after bye in Round 1).

TEN IN A ROW

Dixie McNeill scored for Wrexham in **ten** successive F.A. Cup rounds (18 goals): 11 in Rounds 1-6, 1977-8; 3 in Rounds 3-4, 1978-9; 4 in Rounds 3-4, 1979-80.

Stan Mortensen (Blackpool) scored 25 goals in 16 F.A. Cup rounds out of 17 (1946-51).

SIX GOALS IN FA CUP PROPER

By **Duane Darby** for Hull City (8-4) v Whitby in 1st. Round replay on November 26, 1996.

George Best was the previous last player to score **six** in the F.A. Cup proper – when Man. United won 8-2 away to Northampton in the fifth round, on February 7, 1970. Others to achieve this feat: **George Hilsdon** (for Chelsea v. Worksop, 1907-8); **Ronnie Rooke** (for Fulham v. Bury, 1938-9); **Harold Atkinson** (for Tranmere v. Ashington, 1952-3); **Ted MacDougall** (for Bournemouth v Oxford City, 1970-1).

Denis Law scored all **six** for Manchester City at Luton (6-2) in an F.A. Cup 4th Round tie on January 28, 1961, but none of them counted – the match was abandoned because of a waterlogged pitch.

Tony Philliskirk scored **five** when Peterborough Utd. beat Kingstonian 9-1 in an F.A. Cup 1st Round replay on November 25, 1992, but had them wiped from the records. With the score at 3-0, the Kingstonian goalkeeper was concussed by a coin thrown from the crowd and unable to play on. The F.A. ordered the match to be replayed at Peterborough behind closed doors, and Kingstonian lost 1-0.

QUICKEST GOALS AND RAPID SCORING

Six seconds after kick-off by **Albert Mundy** for Aldershot v. Hartlepool, October 25, 1958; **Barrie Jones** for Newport County v. Torquay United, March 31, 1962; **Keith Smith** for Crystal Palace v. Derby County, December 12, 1964.

9.6 seconds by **John Hewitt** for Aberdeen at Motherwell, 3rd Round, January 23, 1982 (fastest goal in Scottish Cup history).

A goal in **4 seconds** was claimed by **Jim Fryatt**, for Bradford P.A. v. Tranmere (Div. 4, April 25, 1965), and by **Gerry Allen** for Whitstable Town v. Danson (Kent League, March 3,1989). Backed by filmed evidence, **Damian Mori** scored in 4 seconds for Adelaide City v Sydney United (Australian National League, December 6, 1995).

Colin Cowperthwaite reputedly scored in 3½ **seconds** for Barrow v. Kettering (Alliance Premier League) on December 8, 1979, but the timing was unofficial.

Phil Starbuck scored for Huddersfield only **3 seconds** after entering the field as 54th min. substitute at home to Wigan (Div. 2) on Easter Monday, April 12, 1993. A corner-kick was delayed, awaiting his arrival, and he scored with a header.

Malcolm Macdonald scored after **5 seconds** (officially timed) in Newcastle United's 7-3 win in a pre-season friendly at St. Johnstone on July 29, 1972. From the kick-off, the ball was passed to him, and Macdonald, spotting the goalkeeper off his line, smashed a shot over him and into the net.

Scored first kick: Billy Foulkes (Newcastle United) for Wales v. England at Cardiff, October 20, 1951, in his first International match.

Six goals in seven minutes in Preston's record 26-0 F.A. Cup 1st Round win v. Hyde, October 15, 1887.

Five in 20 minutes: Frank Keetley in Lincoln's 9-1 win over Halifax in Div. III (North), January 16, 1932; **Brian Dear** for West Ham United v. West Bromwich Albion (6-1, Div.1) April 16, 1965.

Four in five minutes: by **John McIntyre** for Blackburn Rovers v. Everton (Div. 1), September 16, 1922; **W.G. Richardson** for West Bromwich Albion v. West Ham United (Div. 1), November 7, 1931.

Three in three minutes: Billy Lane for Watford v. Clapton Orient (Div.3S), December 20, 1933; **Johnny Hartburn** for Leyton Orient v Shrewsbury (Div.3S), January 22, 1955; **Gary Roberts** for Brentford v. Newport, (Freight Rover Trophy, South Final), May 17, 1985; **Gary Shaw** for Shrewsbury v Bradford City (Div. 3), December 22, 1990.

Three in two minutes: Jimmy Scarth for Gillingham v. Leyton Orient (Div. 3S), November 1, 1952.

Arsenal scored six goals in 18 minutes (71-89 mins.) in 7-1 home win v. Sheffield Wednesday, February 15, 1992.

Sunderland scored eight goals in 28 minutes at Newcastle (9-1 Div 1), December 5, 1908.

Southend United scored all seven goals in 29 minutes in 7-0 win at home to Torquay (Leyland Daf Cup, Southern quarter-final), February 26, 1991. Score was 0-0 until 55th. minute.

Six goals in first 19 minutes by Tranmere when they beat Oldham 13-4 (Div. 3 North) on December 26, 1935.

Notts County scored six second-half goals in 12 minutes (Tommy Lawton 3, Jackie Sewell 3) when they beat Exeter 9-0 (Div. 3 South) at Meadow Lane on October 16, 1948.

Fastest International goal: 8.3 secs. by **Davide Gualtieri** for San Marino v England (World Cup qual., Bologna, November 17, 1993).

Fastest International hat-trick: 3½ minutes by **Willie Hall** for England v. N. Ireland at Old Trafford, Manchester, November 16, 1938. (Hall scored 5 in England's 7-0 win).

Fastest International goal by substitute: 5 seconds by Arsenal's **John Jensen** for Denmark v Belgium (Eur. Champ.), October 12, 1994.

Fastest England goals: 27 seconds by **Bryan Robson** v. France in World Cup at Bilbao, Spain on June 16, 1982; at Wembley: 38 seconds by **Bryan Robson** v Yugoslavia, December 13, 1989; 42 seconds by **Gary Lineker** v Malaysia in Kuala Lumpur, June 12, 1991.

Fastest F.A. Cup Final goals: 30 seconds by **John Devey**, for Aston Villa v

W.B.A., 1895; at Wembley: 42 seconds by **Roberto di Matteo**, for Chelsea v Middlesbrough, 1997.

Fastest F.A. Cup hat-tricks: In 3 minutes by **Billy Best** for Southend v Brentford (2nd. Round, December 7, 1968); 2 minutes 20 seconds by **Andy Locke** for Nantwich v Droylesden (1st. Qual. Round, September 9, 1995).

F.A. Premier League – fastest scoring: Four goals in 4 minutes, 44 seconds by Tottenham at home to Southampton on Sunday, February 7, 1993.

Fastest First Division hat-tricks since war: Graham Leggat, 3 goals in 3 minutes (first half) when Fulham beat Ipswich 10-1 on Boxing Day, 1963; **Nigel Clough**, 3 goals in 4 minutes (81, 82, 85 pen) when Nott'm Forest beat Q.P.R. 4-0 on Sunday, December 13, 1987.

F.A. Premier League – fastest hat-trick: 4½ minutes (26, 29, 31) by **Robbie Fowler** in Liverpool 3, Arsenal 0 on Sunday, August 28, 1994.

Fastest Premier League goals: 13 seconds by **Chris Sutton** for Blackburn at Everton, April 1, 1995; 13 seconds by **Dwight Yorke** for Aston Villa at Coventry, September 30, 1995.

Fastest Premier League goal by substitute: 13 seconds by Jamie Cureton for Norwich v Chelsea, December 10, 1994.

Fastest new-First Division goal: 10 seconds by **Keith O'Neill** for Norwich v Stoke, April 12, 1997.

Fastest Scottish hat-trick: 2½ mins. by **Ian St. John** for Motherwell away to Hibernian (Scottish League Cup), August 15, 1959.

Fastest all-time hat-trick: Reported at 1 min. 50 secs. by **Maglioni** for Independiente against Gimnasia de la Plata in Argentina, March 18, 1973.

Fastest own goals: 8 seconds by Pat Kruse of Torquay, for Cambridge United (Div. 4), January 3, 1977; in **First Division**, 16 seconds by Steve Bould (Arsenal) away to Sheff. Wed., February 17, 1990.

FASTEST GOALS IN WORLD CUP FINAL SERIES

15 secs. by **Vaclav Masek** for Czechoslovakia v Mexico (in Chile, 1962).
27 secs. by **Bryan Robson** for England v France (in Bilbao, Spain, 1982).

TOP MATCH SCORES SINCE WAR

By English clubs: **13-0** by Newcastle v Newport (Div. 2, Oct. 1946); **13-2** by Tottenham v Crewe (F.A. Cup 4th. Rd. replay, Feb. 1960); **13-0** by Chelsea v Jeunesse Hautcharage, Lux. (Cup-Winners' Cup 1st. Rd., 2nd. Leg, Sept. 1971).

By Scottish club: 20-0 by Stirling Albion v Selkirk (E. of Scotland League) in Scottish Cup 1st. Rd. (Dec. 1984). That is the highest score in British first-class football this century, since Preston beat Hyde 26-0 in F.A. Cup, Oct. 1887.

GOALS BY WINGERS

	Season	Matches	Goals
Football League	(Div. I)		
Cliff Bastin (Arsenal)	1932-3	42	33
Scottish League	(Div. I)		
Bob Ferrier (Motherwell)	1929-30	27	32
Scottish League	(Div. II)		
Ken Dawson (Falkirk)	1935-6	34	39

GOALS BY GOALKEEPERS

Goalkeepers who have scored with long clearances include:

Pat Jennings for Tottenham away to Man. United (goalkeeper Alex Stepney) in the F.A. Charity Shield on August 12, 1967.

Peter Shilton for Leicester at Southampton (goalkeeper Campbell Forsyth) on October 14, 1967 (Div. 1).

Ray Cashley for Bristol City at home to Hull (goalkeeper Jeff Wealands) on September 18, 1973 (Div. 2).

Steve Sherwood for Watford away to Coventry (goalkeeper Raddy Avramovic) on January 14, 1984 (Div. 1).

Steve Ogrizovic for Coventry away to Sheff. Wednesday (goalkeeper Martin Hodge) on October 25, 1986 (Div. 1).

Andy Goram for Hibernian at home to Morton (goalkeeper David Wylie) on May 7, 1988 (Scottish Premier Div.).

Andy McLean, on Irish League debut, for Cliftonville v. Linfield (goalkeeper George Dunlop) on August 20, 1988.

Alan Paterson for Glentoran against Linfield (goalkeeper George Dunlop) on November 30, 1989 (Roadferry Cup Final at The Oval, Belfast).

Ray Charles for East Fife at Stranraer (goalkeeper Bernard Duffy) on February 28, 1990 (Scottish Div. 2).

Iain Hesford scored Maidstone's winner (3-2 v Hereford, Div. 4, November 2, 1991) with long kick-out that went first bounce past Tony Elliott in opposite goal.

Chris Mackenzie for Hereford at home to Barnet (goalkeeper Mark Taylor) in Div. 3, August 12, 1995.

Aston Villa's Mark Bosnich scored the last goal (a penalty) when Australia beat Solomon Islands 13-0 in World Cup Oceania Zone qualifier in Sydney on June 11, 1997.

Most goals by a goalkeeper in a League season: 5 (all penalties) by Arthur Birch for Chesterfield (Div. 3 North), 1923-4.

Arthur Wilkie, Reading's goalkeeper at home to Halifax (Div. 3) on August 31, 1962, injured a hand, then played as a forward and scored twice in a 4-2 win.

Alex Stepney was Man. United's joint top scorer for two months in season 1973-4 with two penalties.

Alan Fettis, N. Ireland goalkeeper, scored twice for Hull in Div. 2 in season 1994-5: as a substitute in 3-1 home win v Oxford (Dec. 17) and, when selected outfield, with last-minute winner (2-1) at Blackpool on May 6.

Peter Schmeichel, Man. United's goalkeeper, headed an 89th minute equaliser (2-2) from Ryan Giggs' corner in the UEFA Cup 1st. Round, 2nd leg against Rotor Volgograd (Russia) on September 26, 1995, but United lost the tie on away goals.

In League matches for Swansea City, Roger Freestone scored with a penalty at Oxford (Div. 2, April 30, 1995) and, in 1995-6 (Div. 2) with penalties at home to Shrewsbury (August 12) and Chesterfield (August 26).

MOST SCORERS IN MATCH

Liverpool set a Football League record with EIGHT scorers when they beat Crystal Palace 9-0 (Div.1) on September 12, 1989. Their marksmen were: Steve Nicol (7 and 88 mins), Steve McMahon (16), Ian Rush (45), Gary Gillespie (56), Peter Beardsley (61), John Aldridge pen. (67), John Barnes (79) and Glenn Hysen (82).

Fifteen years earlier, Liverpool went one better with NINE different scorers when they achieved their record win, 11-0 at home to Stromsgodset (Norway) in the Cup-Winners' Cup 1st. round, 1st leg on September 17, 1974.

Eight players scored for Swansea City when they beat Sliema, Malta, 12-0 in the Cup-Winners' Cup 1st round, 1st leg on September 15, 1982.

Nine Stirling Albion players scored in the 20-0 win against Selkirk in the Scottish Cup 1st. Round on December 8, 1984.

LONG SCORING RUNS

The record in England is held by Bill Prendergast, who scored on 13 consecutive appearances for Chester (Div. 3, Sept.-Dec., 1938).

Dixie Dean scored in 12 consecutive games (23 goals) for Everton in Div. 2 in 1930-1.

Danish striker **Finn Dossing** scored in 15 consecutive matches (Scottish record) for Dundee United (Div. 1) in 1964-5.

In modern times, **John Aldridge** (Liverpool) scored in 10 successive First Division matches – the last game of season 1986-7 and the first nine in 1987-8.

Kevin Russell (Wrexham) scored in nine consecutive matches in Div. 4, March-May, 1988.

In the F.A. Premier League, **Mark Stein** scored in seven successive matches for Chelsea (Dec. 28, 1993-Feb. 5, 1994). **Alan Shearer** equalled the feat for Newcastle (Sept. 14-Nov. 30, 1996).

Ian Wright scored on 12 successive first-team appearances, including 7 Premiership, for Arsenal (Sept. 15-Nov. 23, 1994).

50-GOAL PLAYERS

With **52** goals for **Wolves** in 1987-8 (34 League, 12 Sherpa Van Trophy, 3 Littlewoods Cup, 3 F.A. Cup), **Steve Bull** became the first player to score 50 in a season for a League club since Terry Bly for 4th Division newcomers Peterborough United in 1960-1. Bly's 54 comprised 52 League goals and 2 in the F.A. Cup, and included 7 hat-tricks, still a post-war League record.

Bull was again the country's top scorer with 50 goals in season 1988-9: 37 League, 2 Littlewoods Cup and 11 Sherpa Van Trophy.

Between Bly and Bull, the highest individual scoring total for a season was 49 by two players: Ted MacDougall (Bournemouth 1970-1, 42 League, 7 F.A. Cup) and Clive Allen (Tottenham 1986-7, 33 League, 12 Littlewoods Cup, 4 F.A. Cup).

HOT SHOTS

Jimmy Greaves was First Division top scorer (League goals) six times in 11 seasons: 32 for Chelsea (1958-9), 41 for Chelsea (1960-1) and, for Tottenham, 37 in 1962-3, 35 in 1963-4, 29 in 1964-5 (joint top) and 27 in 1968-9.

Brian Clough (Middlesbrough) was the Second Division's leading scorer in three successive seasons: 40 goals in 1957-8, 42 in 1958-9 and 39 in 1959-60.

John Hickton (Middlesbrough) was top Div. 2 scorer three times in four seasons: 24 goals in 1967-8, 24 in 1969-70 and 25 in 1970-1.

MOST HAT-TRICKS

Nine by **George Camsell** (Middlesbrough) in Div. 2, 1926-7, is the record for one season. Most League hat-tricks in career: 37 by **Dixie Dean** for Tranmere and Everton (1924-38).

Most **top division** hat-tricks in a season since last war: 6 by **Jimmy Greaves** for Chelsea (1960-1). **Alan Shearer** scored 5 for Blackburn in the Premier League, season 1995-96.

Frank Osborne (Tottenham) scored three consecutive hat-tricks in Div. 1 in October-November 1925, against Liverpool (home), Leicester (away) and West Ham (home).

Tom Jennings (Leeds) scored hat-tricks in three successive First Div. matches (Sept-Oct, 1926): 3 goals v Arsenal, 4 at Liverpool, 4 v Blackburn.

Jack Balmer (Liverpool) scored hat-tricks in three successive First Div. matches (Nov. 1946): 3 goals v Portsmouth, 4 at Derby, 3 v Arsenal.

Gilbert Alsop scored hat-tricks in three successive matches for Walsall in Div. 3 South in April 1939: 3 goals at Swindon, 3 v Bristol City (home) and 4 v Swindon (home).

Alf Lythgoe scored hat-tricks in three successive games for Stockport (Div. 3 North) in March 1934: 3 v Darlington, 3 v Southport and 4 v Wrexham.

TRIPLE HAT-TRICKS

There have been at least three instances of **3 hat-tricks being scored** for **one team** in a Football League match:-

April 21, 1909: Enoch West, Billy Hooper and Arthur Spouncer scored 3 apiece for Nott'm. Forest (12-0 v Leicester Fosse, Div. 1).

March 3, 1962: Ron Barnes, Wyn Davies and Roy Ambler registered hat-tricks in Wrexham's 10-1 win against Hartlepool (Div. 4).

November 7, 1987: Tony Adcock, Paul Stewart and David White each scored 3 goals for Man. City in 10-1 win at home to Huddersfield (Div. 2).

For the first time in the Premiership, **three hat-tricks** were completed **on one day** (September 23, 1995): Tony Yeboah for Leeds at Wimbledon; Alan Shearer for Blackburn v Coventry; and Robbie Fowler with 4 goals for Liverpool v Bolton.

In the F.A. Cup, **Jack Carr**, **George Elliott** and **Walter Tinsley** each scored 3 in Middlesbrough's 9-3 first round win against Goole in Jan. 1915.

HAT-TRICKS v THREE 'KEEPERS

When West Ham beat Newcastle 8-1 (Div.1) at home on April 21, 1986 **Alvin Martin** scored 3 goals against different 'keepers: Martin Thomas injured a shoulder and was replaced, in turn, by outfield players Chris Hedworth and Peter Beardsley.

In 1948 **Jock Dodds** of Lincoln had done the same **against** West Ham, scoring past **Gregory**, **Moroney** and **Dick**. The Hammers lost 3-4.

David Herd (Man. United) scored against three Sunderland goalkeepers (Montgomery, Hurley and Parke) in 5-0 First Division home win on Nov. 26, 1966.

Brian Clark, of Bournemouth, scored against three Rotherham goalkeepers (McDonough, Gilbert and Leng twice) in 7-2 win at Rotherham (Div. 3) on Oct. 10, 1972.

On Oct. 16, 1993 (Div.3) **Chris Pike** (Hereford) scored a hat-trick against different goalkeepers. Opponents Colchester, beaten 5-0, had two 'keepers sent off for professional fouls.

TON UP – BOTH ENDS

Manchester City are the only club to **score and concede** a century of League goals in the same season. When fifth in the 1957-8 Championship, they scored 104 goals and gave away 100.

HALF AN OWN GOAL EACH

Chelsea's second goal in a 3-1 home win against Leicester City on December 18, 1954 was uniquely described as "shared own goal". Leicester defenders **Stan Milburn** and **Jack Froggatt**, both lunging at the ball in an attempt to clear, connected simultaneously and sent it rocketing into the net.

THE DAY IT RAINED GOALS

Saturday, February 1, 1936 has a permanent place in the Football League records, because on that afternoon the **44** matches played in the four divisions produced **209** goals – the most that have ever been scored on one day.

They piled up like this: 46 in Div.1; 46 in Div.2; 68 in Div.3 North; 49 in Div.3 South. Two matches in the Northern Section provided no fewer than 23 goals – Chester 12, York City 0, and Crewe Alexandra 5, Chesterfield 6.

There was only one 0-0 result (Aldershot v Bristol City, Div. 3 South).

● The previous record was set four years earlier on January 2, 1932, when 205 goals were scored in 43 League matches: 56 in Div.1, 49 in Div.2, 57 in Div.3 South and 43 in Div.3 North.

TOURNAMENT TOP SHOTS

Most individual goals in a World Cup Final series: 13 by **Just Fontaine** for France, in Sweden, 1958.

Most in European Championship Finals: 9 by **Michel Platini** for France, in France 1984.

MOST GOALS ON CLUB DEBUT

Jim Dyet scored **eight** goals for King's Park against Forfar Athletic (Jan. 2, 1930).

Len Shackleton scored **six** times in Newcastle United's 13-0 win v. Newport County (Div. 2, Oct. 5, 1946) in the week he joined them from Bradford Park Avenue.

MOST GOALS ON LEAGUE DEBUT

Five by **George Hilsdon**, for Chelsea (9-2) v Glossop, Div. 2 Sept. 1, 1906.

Alan Shearer, with three goals for Southampton (4-2) v Arsenal, April 9, 1988, became, at 17, the youngest player to score a First Division hat-trick on his full debut.

CLEAN-SHEET RECORDS

On the way to promotion from Div. 3 in season 1995-6, **Gillingham's** ever-present goalkeeper **Jim Stannard** set a new clean-sheet record. In 46 matches, he achieved 29 shut-outs (17 at home, 12 away), beating the 28 by Ray Clemence for Liverpool (42 matches in Div. 1, 1978-9) and the previous best in a 46-match programme of 28 by Port Vale (Div. 3 North, 1953-4). In conceding only 20 League goals in 1995-6, Gillingham created a defensive record for the lower divisions.

Chris Woods, Rangers' England goalkeeper, set a British record in season 1986-7 by going 1,196 minutes without conceding a goal. The sequence began in the UEFA Cup match against Borussia Moenchengladbach on Nov. 26, 1986 and ended when Rangers were sensationally beaten 1-0 at home by Hamilton in the Scottish Cup 3rd. Round on Jan. 31, 1987 with a 70th.-minute goal by Adrian Sprott.

The previous British record of 1,156 minutes without a goal conceded was held by Aberdeen goalkeeper **Bobby Clark** (season 1970-1).

There have been three instances of clubs keeping 11 consecutive clean sheets in the Football League: Coventry City (Div. 2, 1919-20), Millwall (Div. 3 South, 1925-6) and Reading (Div. 4, 1978-9). In that sequence, Reading goalkeeper Steve Death set the existing Football League shut-out record of 1,103 minutes.

Mark Leonard (Chesterfield) kept a clean sheet in 8 consecutive Div.3 away games (Jan-April 1994). Believed an away-match record in British football.

Sebastiano Rossi kept a clean sheet in 8 successive away matches for AC Milan (Nov. 1993-Apr. 1994).

A world record of 1,275 minutes without conceding a goal was set in 1990-1 by **Abel Resino**, the Atletico Madrid goalkeeper. He was finally beaten by Sporting Gijon's Enrique in Atletico's 3-1 win on March 19, 1991.

In International football, the record is held by **Dino Zoff** with a shut-out for Italy (Sept. 1972 to June 1974) lasting 1,142 minutes.

LOW SCORING

Fewest goals by any club in season in Football League: **24** by **Stoke City** (Div. 1, 42 matches, 1984-5); **24** by **Watford** (Div. 2, 42 matches, 1971-2). In 46-match programme, **27** by **Stockport County** (Div. 3, 1969-70).

Arsenal were the lowest Premier League scorers in its opening season

(1992-3) with 40 goals in 42 matches, but won both domestic cup competitions. In subsequent seasons the lowest Premier League scorers were **Ipswich** (35) in 1993-4, **Crystal Palace** (34) in 1994-5, **Man. City** (33) in 1995-6 and **Nott'm. Forest** setting the Premiership's new fewest-goals record with only 31 when relegated last season.

LONG TIME NO SCORE

Longest non-scoring sequences in Football League: 11 matches by **Coventry City** in 1919-20 (Div. 2); 11 matches by **Hartlepool United** in 1992-3 (Div. 2). After beating Crystal Palace 1-0 in the F.A. Cup 3rd round on Jan. 2, they went 13 games and 2 months without scoring (11 League, 1 F.A. Cup, 1 Autoglass Trophy). The sequence ended after 1,227 blank minutes with a 1-1 draw at Blackpool (League) on March 6.

In the **Premier League** (Oct.-Jan. season 1994-5) Crystal Palace failed to score in nine consecutive matches.

The British non-scoring record is held by Scottish club **Stirling Albion**: 14 consecutive matches (13 League, 1 Scottish Cup) and 1,292 minutes play, from Jan. 31, 1981 until Aug. 8, 1981 (when they lost 4-1 to Falkirk in the League Cup).

In season 1971-2, **Mansfield Town** did not score in any of their first nine home games in Div. 3.

F.A. CUP CLEAN SHEETS

Most consecutive F.A. Cup matches without conceding a goal: 12 by **Bradford City**. The sequence spanned 8 rounds, from 3rd. in 1910-11 to 4th. Round 3rd. replay in 1911-12, and included winning the Cup in 1911.

ATTENDANCES

GREATEST WORLD CROWDS

World Cup, Maracana Stadium, Rio de Janeiro, July 16, 1950. Final match (Brazil v. Uruguay) attendance 199,850; receipts £125,000.

Total attendance in three matches (including play-off) between Santos (Brazil) and AC Milan for the Inter-Continental Cup (World Club Championship) 1963, exceeded 375,000.

BRITISH RECORD CROWDS

Most to pay: 149,547, Scotland v. England, at Hampden Park, Glasgow, April 17, 1937. This was the first all-ticket match in Scotland (receipts £24,000).

At Scottish F.A. Cup Final: 146,433, Celtic v. Aberdeen, at Hampden Park, April 24, 1937. Estimated another 20,000 shut out.

For British club match (apart from a Cup Final): 143,470, Rangers v. Hibernian, at Hampden Park, March 27, 1948 (Scottish Cup semi-final).

F.A. Cup Final: 126,047, Bolton Wanderers v. West Ham United, at Wembley, April 28, 1923. Estimated 150,000 in stadium.

World Cup Qualifying Ties: 120,000, Cameroon v. Morocco, Yaounde, November 29, 1981; 107,580, Scotland v. Poland, Hampden Park, October 13, 1965.

European Cup: 135,826, Celtic v. Leeds United (semi-final) at Hampden Park, Glasgow, April 15, 1970.

European Cup Final: 127,621, Real Madrid v. Eintracht Frankfurt, at Hampden Park, Glasgow, May 18, 1960.

European Cup-Winners' Cup Final: 100,000, West Ham v. TSV Munich, at Wembley, May 19, 1965.

Scottish League: 118,567, Rangers v. Celtic, January 2, 1939.

Scottish League Cup Final: 107,609, Celtic v. Rangers, at Hampden Park, October 23, 1965.

Football League old format: First Div.: 83,260, Manchester United v. Arsenal, January 17, 1948 (at Maine Road); **Second Div.:** 70,302 Tottenham v Southampton, February 25, 1950; **Third Div. South:** 51,621, Cardiff City v. Bristol City, April 7, 1947; **Third Div. North:** 49,655, Hull City v. Rotherham United, December 25, 1948; **Third Div.:** 49,309, Sheff. Wed. v. Sheff. United, December 26, 1979; **Fourth Div.:** 37,774, Crystal Palace v. Millwall, March 31, 1961.

F.A. Premier League: 55,314, Manchester Utd. v. Wimbledon, January 29, 1997.

Football League – New Div. 1: 30,729, Manchester City v Oldham, March 8, 1997; **New Div. 2:** 18,674, Bristol City v Bristol Rovers, December 15, 1996; **New Div. 3:** 18,700, Preston N.E. v Exeter City, May 4, 1996.

In English Provinces: 84,569, Manchester City v. Stoke City (F.A. Cup 6th Round), March 3, 1934.

Record for Under-21 International: 25,863, England v. Rep. of Ireland at Newcastle, November 15, 1994.

Record for friendly match: 104,679, Rangers v. Eintract Frankfurt, at Hampden Park, Glasgow, October 17, 1961.

Record Football League aggregate (season): 41,271,414 (1948-9) – 88 clubs.

Record Football League aggregate (single day): 1,269,934, December 27, 1949.

Record average home League attendance for season: 57,758 by Man. United in 1967-8.

Long-ago League attendance aggregates: 10,929,000 in 1906-07 (40 clubs); 28,132,933 in 1937-8 (88 clubs).

Last 1m. crowd aggregate, League: 1,007,200, December 27, 1971.

Record Amateur match attendance: 100,000 for F.A. Amateur Cup Final, Pegasus v. Harwich & Parkeston at Wembley, April 11, 1953.

Record Cup-tie aggregate: 265,199, at two matches between Rangers and Morton, in the Scottish Cup Final, 1947-8.

Abandoned match attendance records: In England – 63,480 at Newcastle v. Swansea F.A. Cup 3rd round, Jan. 10, 1953, abandoned 8 mins (0-0), fog.

In Scotland: 94,596 at Scotland v. Austria (4-1), Hampden Park, May 8, 1963. Referee Jim Finney ended play (79 minutes) after Austria had two players sent off and one carried off.

What is still **Colchester United's** record crowd (19,072) was for the F.A. Cup 1st round tie v. Reading on Nov. 27, 1948, abandoned 35 minutes (0-0), fog.

SMALLEST CROWDS

Lowest post-war League attendance: 450 Rochdale v. Cambridge United (Div. 3, February 2, 1974).

Lowest First Division crowds since the war: 3,121 for Wimbledon v. Sheff. W., Oct. 2, 1991; 3,231 for Wimbledon v. Luton, Sept. 7, 1991; 3,270 for Wimbledon v. Coventry, Dec. 28, 1991; 3,496 for Wimbledon v. Luton, Feb. 14, 1990.

Lowest top-division crowd at a major ground since the war: 4,554 for Arsenal v Leeds United (May 5, 1966) – fixture clashed with live TV coverage of Cup-Winners' Cup Final (Liverpool v Borussia Dortmund).

Lowest Saturday post-war top-division crowd: 3,231 for Wimbledon v. Luton, Sept. 7, 1991 (Div. 1).

Lowest F.A. Premier League crowds: 3,039 for Wimbledon v Everton, Jan. 26, 1993 (smallest top-division attendance since war).

Lowest Football League crowds, new format – Div. 1: 3,086 Southend v Bristol City, February 10,1993; **Div. 2:** 1,077, Hartlepool v Cardiff, March 22, 1994; **Div. 3:** 1,030, Doncaster v Northampton, November 19, 1996.

Smallest League Cup attendance at top-division ground: 1,987 for Wimbledon v Bolton (2nd Round, 2nd Leg) Oct. 6, 1992.

Smallest Wembley crowds for England matches: 15,628 v Chile (Rous Cup, May 23, 1989 – affected by Tube strike); 20,038 v Colombia (Friendly, Sept. 6, 1995); 21,432 v Czech. (Friendly, Apr. 25, 1990); 21,142 v Japan (Umbro Cup, June 3, 1995); 23,600 v Wales (British Championship, Feb. 23, 1983); 23,659 v Greece (Friendly, May 17, 1994); 23,951 v. East Germany (Friendly, Sept. 12, 1984); 24,000 v. N. Ireland (British Championship, Apr. 4, 1984); 25,756 v.

Colombia (Rous Cup, May 24, 1988); 25,837 v Denmark (Friendly, Sept. 14, 1988).

Other smallest Int. crowds – N.Ireland: 2,500 v Chile (Belfast, May 26, 1989 – clashed with ITV live screening of Liverpool v Arsenal Championship decider); **Scotland:** 7,843 v N.Ireland (Hampden Park, May 6, 1969); **Wales:** 2,315 v N.Ireland (Wrexham, May 27, 1982).

Smallest attendance for any England match: 2,378 v San Marino (World Cup) at Bologna (Nov. 17, 1993). Tie clashed with Italy v Portugal (World Cup) shown live on Italian TV.

F.A. CUP CROWD RECORD (OUTSIDE FINAL)

The first F.A. Cup-tie shown on closed-circuit TV (5th. Round, Saturday, March 11, 1967, kick-off 7pm) drew a total of 105,000 spectators to Goodison Park and Anfield.

This is the biggest attendance for a single F.A. Cup match other than the Final. At Goodison, 64,851 watched the match "for real", while 40,149 saw the TV version on eight giant screens at Anfield. Everton beat Liverpool 1-0.

LOWEST SEMI-FINAL CROWD

The smallest F.A. Cup semi-final attendance since the war was 17,987 for Man. United v. Crystal Palace replay, at Villa Park on April 12, 1995. Palace supporters largely boycotted tie after a fan died in car-park clash outside pub in Walsall before first match. Previous lowest: 25,963 for Wimbledon v Luton, at Tottenham on April 9, 1988.

Lowest quarter-final crowd since the war: 8,735 for Chesterfield v Wrexham on March 9, 1997.

Smallest F.A. Cup 3rd. Round attendances, for matches between League clubs: 1,833 for Chester v Bournemouth (at Macclesfield) Jan. 5, 1991; 1,966 for Aldershot v Oxford Utd., Jan. 10, 1987.

PRE-WEMBLEY CUP FINAL CROWDS

At Crystal Palace

1895	42,560	1902	48,036	1908	74,967
1896	48,036	Replay	33,050	1909	67,651
1897	65,891	1903	64,000	1910	76,980
1898	62,017	1904	61,734	1911	69,098
1899	73,833	1905	101,117	1912	54,434
1900	68,945	1906	75,609	1913	120,028
1901	110,802	1907	84,584	1914	72,778

At Old Trafford

1915	50,000

At Stamford Bridge

1920	50,018	1921	72,805	1922	53,000

RECEIPTS RECORDS

Wembley Stadium underwent its first considerable alteration during 1962-3 in preparation for the World Cup in 1966. Higher admission fees at the 1963 F.A. Cup Final resulted in 100,000 spectators paying a record £89,000.

This is how Wembley's receipts record have risen since then:–

1968 F.A. Cup Final (Everton v W.B.A.)	£110,000
1968 European Cup Final (Man. United v Benfica)	£120,000

1976	F.A. Cup Final (Southampton v Man. United)	£420,000
1978	F.A. Cup Final (Ipswich v Arsenal)	£500,000
1981	England v Hungary (World Cup)	£671,000
1982	F.A. Cup Final (Tottenham v Q.P.R.)	£886,000
	(plus £605,000 for replay)	
1984	F.A. Cup Final (Everton v Watford)	£919,000
*1985	F.A. Cup Final (Man. United v Everton)	£1,100,000
1986	F.A. Cup Final (Liverpool v Everton)	£1,100,000
†1987	League Cup Final (Arsenal v Liverpool)	£1,000,000
1987	F.A. Cup Final (Coventry v Tottenham)	£1,286,737
1988	F.A. Cup Final (Wimbledon v Liverpool)	£1,422,814
1989	F.A. Cup Final (Liverpool v Everton)	£1,600,000
1990	League Cup Final (Nott'm Forest v Oldham)	£1,650,000
1990	F.A. Cup Final (Man. United v Crystal P. – first match)	£2,000,000
1991	League Cup Final (Man. United v Sheff. Wed.)	£2,000,000
1991	F.A. Cup Final (Nott'm F. v Tottenham)	£2,016,000
1992	F.A. Cup Final (Liverpool v Sunderland)	£2,548,174
1993	F.A. Cup Final (Arsenal v Sheff. W. – first match)	£2,818,000
	(Replay took receipts for both matches to £4,695,200)	
1994	F.A. Cup Final record (Man. United v Chelsea)	£2,962,167
1995	League Cup Final record (Liverpool v Bolton)	£2,600,000

(* Britain's first £1m. gate; †First £1m. gate for League Cup Final)

Record England match receipts: £1,500,000 (v. Brazil, Wembley, Sunday, May 17, 1992 - att: 53,428)

Record Friendly International receipts: £1,392,515 for England v Denmark at Wembley, March 9, 1994 (att: 71,970).

Note (July 1997): Receipts for 1996 European Champ. matches England v Germany (s-f) and Germany v Czech. Rep (Final) still not available from F.A. or UEFA.

EARLY CUP FINAL RECEIPTS

1885	Blackburn Rovers v Queens Park	£442
1913	Aston Villa v Sunderland	£9,406
1923	Bolton v West Ham, first Wembley Final	£27,776
1939	Portsmouth v Wolves	£29,000
1946	Derby v Charlton	£45,000

WORLD RECORD MATCH RECEIPTS

£4,300,000 for **World Cup Final**, Argentina v West Germany (Rome, July 8, 1990).

BRITISH CLUB MATCH RECORD RECEIPTS

£2,962,167 at the **1994 F.A. Cup Final**, Man. United v Chelsea.

INTERNATIONAL RECORDS

MOST APPEARANCES

Peter Shilton, England goalkeeper, then aged 40, retired from International football after the 1990 World Cup Finals with the then world record number of caps – 125. Previous record (119) was set by **Pat Jennings**, Northern Ireland's goalkeeper from 1964-86, who retired at 41 at the end of the 1986 World Cup in Mexico. Shilton's England career spanned 20 seasons from his debut against East Germany at Wembley on Nov. 25, 1970.

Four players have completed a century of appearances in full International matches for England. **Billy Wright** of Wolves, was the first, retiring in 1959 with a total of 105 caps.

Bobby Charlton, of Manchester United, beat Wright's record in the World Cup match against West Germany in Leon, Mexico, in June 1970 and **Bobby Moore,** of West Ham, overtook Charlton's 106 caps against Italy in Turin, in June 1973. Moore played 108 times for England, a record that stood until **Peter Shilton** reached 109 against Denmark in Copenhagen (June 7, 1989).

Kenny Dalglish became Scotland's first 100-cap International v. Romania (Hampden Park, March 26, 1986).

BRITAIN'S MOST-CAPPED PLAYERS
(As at start of season 1997-98)

England

Peter Shilton	125
Bobby Moore	108
Bobby Charlton	106
Billy Wright	105

Scotland

Kenny Dalglish	102
Jim Leighton	81
Alex McLeish	77
Paul McStay	76

Wales

Neville Southall	91
Peter Nicholas	73
Ian Rush	73
Joey Jones	72

N. Ireland

Pat Jennings	119
Mal Donaghy	91
Sammy McIlroy	88

Republic of Ireland

Paul McGrath	83
Pat Bonner	80
Liam Brady	72
Frank Stapleton	71

MOST CAPS IN ROW

Most consecutive International appearances: 70 by **Billy Wright**, for England from October 1951 to May 1959. He played 105 of England's first 108 post-war matches. **England captains most times: Billy Wright** and **Bobby Moore,** 90 each.

WORLD'S MOST-CAPPED PLAYERS

157 – Majid Abdullah (Saudi Arabia); 139 Thomas Ravelli (Sweden); 125 – Peter Shilton (England); 122 – Lothar Matthaus (Germany); 119 – Pat Jennings (N. Ireland); 117 – Heinz Hermann (Switzerland); 115 – Bjorn Nordqvist (Sweden); 112 – Dino Zoff (Italy); 111 — Hector Chumpitaz (Peru); 111 – Alain Geiger (Switzerland); 110 – Pele (Brazil); 110 – Andoni Zubizaretta (Spain); 109 – Oleg Blokhin (USSR); 108 – Bobby Moore (England); 108 – Ladislau Boloni (Romania); 108 – Park Kyung Hoon (S. Korea); 106 – Bobby Charlton (England); 105 – Billy Wright (England); 105 – Gregorz Lato (Poland); 104 – Thorbjorn Svenssen (Norway); 103 – Franz Beckenbauer (W. Germany); 102 – Kenny Dalglish

(Scotland); 102 – Kazimierz Deyna (Poland); 102 – Joachim Streich (E. Germany); 102 Morten Olsen (Denmark); 102 – Soon-Ho Choi (S. Korea); 100 – Jozsef Bozsik (Hungary); 100 – Djalma Santos (Brazil); 100 – Hans-Juergen Doerner (E. Germany); 100 – Gheorghe Hagi (Romania).

ENGLAND'S WORLD CUP-WINNERS

At Wembley, July 30, 1966, 4-2 v West Germany (2-2 after 90 mins), scorers Hurst 3, Peters. Team: Banks; Cohen, Wilson, Stiles, Charlton (J.), Moore (Captain), Ball, Hurst, Charlton (R.), Hunt, Peters. Manager **Alf Ramsey** fielded that same eleven in six successive matches (an England record): the World Cup quarter-final, semi-final and Final, and the first three games of the following season. England wore red shirts in the Final and Her Majesty the Queen presented the Cup to Bobby Moore. The players each received a £1,000 bonus, less tax. The match was shown live on TV (in black and white).

BRAZIL'S RECORD RUN

Brazil hold the record for the longest unbeaten sequence in International football: 37 matches (30W, 7D, goals 85-18) from December 1993 until they lost 2-0 to Mexico in the CONCACAF Gold Cup Final on January 21, 1996. The previous record of 32 matches undefeated was held by Hungary.

ALL-SEATED INTERNATIONALS

The first **all-seated crowd** (30,000) for a full International in Britain saw **Wales** and **West Germany** draw 0-0 at Cardiff Arms Park on May 31, 1989. The terraces were closed.

England's first all-seated International at Wembley was against Yugoslavia (2-1) on December 13, 1989 (attendance 34,796). The terracing behind the goals was closed for conversion to seating.

England's first **full-house all-seated** International at Wembley was for England v Brazil (1-0) on March 28, 1990, when a capacity 80,000 crowd paid record British receipts of £1,200,000.

FIRST BLACK CAPS

England's first black player was Nottingham Forest full-back **Viv Anderson** against Czechoslovakia at Wembley on November 29, 1978.

Aston Villa's **Ugo Ehiogu** was **England's** first black captain (U-21 v Holland at Portsmouth, April 27, 1993).

Paul Ince (Man. United) became the first black player to captain **England** in a full International (v U.S.A., Boston, June 9, 1993).

First black British International was **Eddie Parris** (Bradford Park Avenue) for Wales against N. Ireland in Belfast on December 5, 1931.

PLAYED FOR MORE THAN ONE COUNTRY

Multi-nationals in senior International football include: **Johnny Carey** (1938-53) – caps Rep. of Ireland 29, N. Ireland 7; **Ferenc Puskas** (1945-62) – caps Hungary 84, Spain 4; **Alfredo di Stefano** (1950-6) – caps Argentina 7, Spain 31; **Ladislav Kubala** (1948-58) – caps Hungary 3, Czechoslovakia 11, Spain 19, only player to win full Int. honours with 3 countries. Kubala also played in a fourth Int. team, scoring twice for FIFA v England at Wembley in 1953.

Johnny Carey, Peter Farrell, Tommy Eglington and **Alec Stevenson** played for N. Ireland and the Republic of Ireland in seasons directly after the last war,

Cecil Moore, capped by N. Ireland in 1949 when with Glentoran, played for USA v England in 1953.

John Reynolds (West Bromwich Albion) played for both England and Ireland in the 1890s.

Robert Evans (Sheffield United) had played 10 times for Wales when capped for England, in 1910-11. He was born in Chester of Welsh parents.

FATHER & SON SAME-DAY CAPS

Iceland made father-and-son Int. history when they beat Estonia 3-0 in Tallin. Arnor Gudjohnsen (35) started the match and was replaced (62 mins.) by his 17-year-old son Eidur.

LATEST HAT-TRICKS v ENGLAND

May 17, 1959, scorer **Juan Seminario** (Peru 4, England 1, Lima); June 15, 1988, scorer **Marco Van Basten** (Holland 3, England 1, European Championship, Dusseldorf).

NO-SAVE GOALKEEPERS

Chris Woods did not have one save to make when England beat San Marino 6-0 (World Cup) at Wembley on February 17, 1993. He touched the ball only six times throughout the match.

Gordon Banks had a similar no-save experience when England beat Malta 5-0 (European Championship) at Wembley on May 12, 1971. Malta did not force a goal-kick or corner, and the four times Banks touched the ball were all from back passes.

FIFA PIONEERS

FIFA, now with a membership of 198 countries, began in 1904 with seven founder nations: Belgium, Denmark, France, Holland, Spain, Sweden and Switzerland.

FIFA WORLD YOUTH CHAMPIONSHIP (U-20)
(Malaysia, June 16-July 5, 1997)

Favourites **Argentina** successfully defended their title and beat Uruguay 2-1 in the Final in Kuala Lumpur, for their third triumph (equalling Brazil's record) in the 11 tournaments. The **Rep. of Ireland** won the third-place play-off 2-1 v Ghana.

England were knocked out 2-1 by Argentina after first-round wins against Ivory Coast (2-1), United Arab Emirates (5-0) and Mexico (1-0). England's best placing in the competition was third in 1993. **Finals: 1977** (Tunis) Soviet Union 2, Mexico 2 (Soviet won 9-8 on pens.); **1979** (Tokyo) Argentina 3, Soviet Union 1; **1981** (Sydney) W. Germany 4, Qatar 0; **1983** (Mexico City) Brazil 1, Argentina 0; **1985** (Moscow) Brazil 1, Spain 0; **1987** (Santiago) Yugoslavia 1, W. Germany 1 (Yugoslavia won 5-4 on pens.); **1989** (Riyadh) Portugal 2, Nigeria 0; **1991** (Lisbon) Portugal 0, Brazil 0 (Portugal won 4-2 on pens.); **1993** (Sydney) Brazil, 2 Ghana 1; **1995** (Qatar) Argentina 2, Brazil 0; **1997** (Kuala Lumpur) Argentina 2, Uruguay 1.

FAMOUS CLUB FEATS

Home Runs: Sunderland were undefeated at home in Football League (Div. 1) in seasons 1891-2, 2-3, 4-5 and 5-6, losing only one home match in 1893-4. **Brentford** won all 21 home games in 1929-30 in the Third Division (South). Others have won all home games in a smaller programme.

Record Home Run: Liverpool went 85 competitive first-team games unbeaten at home between losing 2-3 to Birmingham on January 21, 1978 and 1-2 to Leicester on January 31, 1981. They comprised 63 in the League, 9 League Cup, 7 in European competition and 6 F.A. Cup.

Millwall were unbeaten at home in the League for 59 consecutive matches from 1964-67.

Third to First: Charlton Athletic, in 1936, became the first club to advance from the Third to First Division in successive seasons. **Queen's Park Rangers** were the second club to achieve the feat in 1968, and **Oxford United** did it in 1984 and 1985 as Champions of each division. **Derby County** (1987), **Middlesbrough** (1988), **Sheffield United** (1990) and **Notts County** (1991) were the latest to climb from Third Division to First in successive seasons.

Fourth to First: Northampton Town, in 1965 became the first club to rise from the Fourth to the First Division. **Swansea City** climbed from the Fourth Division to the First (three promotions in four seasons), 1977-8 to 1980-1. **Watford** did so in five seasons, 1977-8 to 1981-2. **Carlisle United** climbed from Fourth Division to First, 1973-74.

Non-League to First: When **Wimbledon** finished third in the Second Division in 1986, they completed the phenomenal rise from non-League football (Southern League) to the First Division in nine years. Two years later they won the F.A. Cup.

Tottenham Hotspur, in 1960-1, not only carried off the First Division Championship and the F.A. Cup for the first time this century but set up other records by opening with 11 successive wins, registering most First Division wins (31), most away wins in the League's history (16), and equalling Arsenal's First Division records of 66 points (33 away). They already held the Second Division record of 70 points (1919-20).

Arsenal repeated Tottenham's Double feat by winning the F.A. Cup and the League in 1970-1. **Liverpool** did the Double in 1985-6, **Manchester United** in 1993-4.

Manchester United's dual success again in 1995-6 made them the first English club to complete the Double **twice.**

Arsenal, in 1993, became the first club to win both English domestic cup competitions (F.A. Cup and League Cup) in the same season.

Preston North End, in season 1888-9, won the first League Championship without losing a match and the F.A. Cup without having a goal scored against them throughout the competition.

Bury, in 1903, also won the F.A. Cup without conceding a goal.

Everton won Div. 2, Div. 1 and the F.A. Cup in successive seasons, 1930-1, 1931-2, 1932-3.

Liverpool won the League Championship in 1964, the F.A. Cup in 1965 and the Championship again in 1966. In 1978 they became the first British club to win the European Cup in successive seasons. **Nott'm. Forest** repeated the feat in 1979 and 1980.

Liverpool won the League Championship six times in eight seasons (1976-83) under **Bob Paisley's** management. During his nine years in charge at Anfield – he succeeded Bill Shankly July 1974 – they won a total of 20 major prizes: 6 League titles, 3 European Cups, 3 League (Milk) Cups, 1 UEFA Cup, 1 European Super Cup and 6 F.A. Charity Shields (1 shared).

Triple Triumph: Liverpool are the only Football League club to win three major competitions in one season. In 1983-4 (their first under manager **Joe Fagan**) they were League Champions, League Cup winners and European Cup winners.

Arsenal supplied seven men (still a record) to the England team v. Italy at Highbury on November 14, 1935. They were: Frank Moss, George Male, Eddie

Hapgood, Wilf Copping, Ray Bowden, Ted Drake and Cliff Bastin. In addition, Arsenal's Tom Whittaker was England's trainer.

Since then, the most players from one club in an England team was six from **Liverpool** against Switzerland at Wembley in September 1977. The side also included a Liverpool old boy, Kevin Keegan (Hamburg).

COVENTRY UNIQUE

Coventry City are the only club to have played in the Premier League, all four previous divisions of the Football League and in both sections (North and South) of the old Third Division.

Grimsby Town were the other club to play in the four divisions of the Football League and its two Third Division sections.

FAMOUS UPS & DOWNS

Sunderland: Relegated in 1958 after maintaining First Division status since their election to the Football League in 1890. They dropped into Division 3 for the first time in 1987.

Aston Villa: Relegated with **Preston North End** to the Third Division in 1970.

Arsenal up: When the League was extended in 1919, Woolwich Arsenal (sixth in Division Two in 1914-15, last season before the war) were elected to Division One. Arsenal have been in Div. 1 ever since.

Spurs down: At the same meeting Chelsea (due for relegation) retained their place in Division One but the bottom club (Tottenham Hotspur) had to go down to Division Two.

Preston and Burnley down: Preston North End, the first League Champions in season 1888-9, dropped into the Fourth Division in 1985. So did Burnley, also among the League's original members in 1888. In 1986, Preston were required to apply for re-election.

Wolves' fall: Wolverhampton Wanderers, another of the Football League's original members, completed the fall from First Division to Fourth in successive seasons (1984-5-6).

Lincoln out: Lincoln City became the first club to suffer automatic demotion from the Football League when they finished bottom of Div. 4 in season 1986-7. They were replaced by Scarborough, champions of the GM Vauxhall Conference. Lincoln regained their place a year later.

Swindon up and down: In the 1990 play-offs, Swindon Town won promotion to the First Division for the first time, but remained in the Second Division because of financial irregularities.

MOST CHAMPIONSHIP WINS

Liverpool, by winning the First Division in 1976-7, established a record of 10 Championship victories. They have since increased the total to 18.

CHAMPIONS: FEWEST PLAYERS

Liverpool used only 14 players (five ever-present) when they won the League Championship in season 1965-6. **Aston Villa** also called on no more than 14 players to win the title in 1980-81, with seven ever-present.

MOST PLAYERS USED IN LEAGUE SEASON

46: By **Birmingham City** in 1995-6.

42: By **Coventry** and **Sheff. Wed.** (both 1919-20) and by **Hull City** (1946-7), in each case in a season following a break in League football because of war.

BEST OF CENTURY

Arsenal (1990-91) were the first League Champions this century to lose only once (38 matches). **Preston** were undefeated first Champions in 1888-9, but played only 22 matches.

LEAGUE HAT-TRICKS

Huddersfield Town created a record in 1925-6 by winning the League Championship for the third year in succession.

Arsenal equalled this League hat-trick in 1933-4-5, and **Liverpool** in 1982-3-4.

'SUPER DOUBLE' WINNERS

Since the war, there have been three instances of players appearing in and then managing F.A. Cup and Championship-winning teams:

Joe Mercer: Player in Arsenal Championship teams 1948, 1953 and in their 1950 F.A. Cup side; manager of Man. City when they won Championship 1968, F.A. Cup 1969.

Kenny Dalglish: Player in Liverpool Championship-winning teams 1979, 1980, 1982, 1983, 1984, player-manager 1986, 1988, 1990: player-manager when Liverpool won F.A. Cup (to complete Double) 1986; manager of Blackburn Rovers, Champions 1995.

George Graham: Played in Arsenal's Double-winning team in 1971, and as manager took them to Championship success in 1989 and 1991 and the F.A. Cup – League Cup double in 1993.

CHAMPIONS IN SUCCESSIVE SEASONS

Preston North End (1888-9, 1889-90).
Sunderland (1891-2, 1892-3).
Aston Villa (1895-6, 1896-7, 1898-9, 1899-1900).
Sheffield Wednesday (1902-3, 1903-4, 1928-9, 1929-30).
Liverpool (1921-2, 1922-3, 1975-6, 1976-7, 1978-9, 1979-80, 1981-2, 1982-3, 1983-4).
Portsmouth (1948-9, 1949-50).
Manchester United (1955-6, 1956-7, 1992-3, 1993-4, 1995-6, 1996-7).
Wolverhampton Wanderers (1957-8, 1958-9).

The Second Division Championship and League Championship were won in successive seasons by **Liverpool** (1905-6), **Everton** (1931-2), **Tottenham** (1950-1) and **Ipswich Town** (1961-2).

Oxford United became the first club to win the Third and Second Division Championships in successive years (1984, 1985).

Wolves are the only club to win the Fourth and Third Division Championships in successive years (1988, 1989).

BACK FIRST TIME

The following clubs won promotion the season after losing their position in the First Division of the League (*as Champions):

Sheffield Wednesday *1899-1900, *1951-2, *1955-6, *1958-9, 1990-1; **Bolton Wanderers** 1899-1900, *1908-9, 1910-11; **West Bromwich Albion** *1901-2; **Manchester City** *1902-3, *1909-10, 1950-1; **Burnley** *1897-8.

Small Heath 1902-3; **Liverpool** *1904-5; **Nottingham Forest** *1906-7; **Preston North End** *1912-13, 1914-15; **Notts County** *1913-14; **Derby County** *1914-15.

Tottenham Hotspur *1919-20, 1977-8; **Leeds United** 1927-8, 1931-2; **Mid-**

dlesbrough *1928-9; **Everton** *1930-1; **Manchester United** 1937-8, *1974-5; **Huddersfield Town** 1952-3.

Aston Villa *1959-60, 1987-8; **Chelsea** 1962-3; *1988-9; **Norwich City** 1974-5, 1981-2, *1985-6; **Wolverhampton Wanderers** 1976-7, 1982-3; **Birmingham City** 1979-80, 1984-5.

West Ham, relegated in 1992, won promotion to the **Premier League** in 1993; *Crystal Palace and **Nott'm. Forest** both returned to the Premiership in 1994, a year after relegation; so did **Leicester City** in 1996, and *Bolton Wanderers in 1997.

ORIGINAL TWELVE

The original 12 members of the Football League (formed in 1888) were: **Accrington, Aston Villa, Blackburn Rovers, Bolton Wanderers, Burnley, Derby County, Everton, Notts County, Preston North End, Stoke, West Bromwich Albion** and **Wolverhampton Wanderers.**

Results on the opening day (September 8, 1888): Bolton 3, Derby 6; Everton 2, Accrington 1; Preston 5, Burnley 2; Stoke 0, W.B.A. 2; Wolves 1, Aston Villa 1. Preston had the biggest first-day crowd: 6,000. Blackburn Rovers and Notts County did not play that day. They kicked off a week later (September 15) – Blackburn 5, Accrington 5; Everton 2, Notts County 1.

FASTEST CLIMB – FOURTH DIV. TO FIRST

Three promotions in four seasons by two clubs – **Swansea City:** 1978 third in Div.4; 1979 third in Div.3; 1981 third in Div.2; **Wimbledon:** 1983 Champions of Div.4; 1984 second in Div.3; 1986 third in Div.2.

MERSEYSIDE RECORD

Liverpool is the only city to have staged top-division football – through Everton or Liverpool – in **every season** since the League football began in 1888.

LEAGUE RECORDS

MOST POINTS IN A SEASON

The following records applied before the introduction of three points for a win in the Football League in 1981-2.

Lincoln City set a **Football League** record in season 1975-6 with 74 points from 46 games, (including 32 victories) in **Division 4.**
First Division: Liverpool (1978-9), 68 points from 42 matches.
Second Division: Tottenham Hotspur (1919-20), 70 points from 42 matches.
Third Division: Aston Villa (1971-2) 70 points from 46 matches.

Since 3 points for win (pre-Premier League):
First Division: Everton (1984-5) and Liverpool (1987-8) 90 points: **Second Division:** Chelsea (1988-9) 99 points; **Third Division:** Bournemouth (1986-7) 97 points; **Fourth Division:** Swindon Town (1985-6) 102 points – record for any division, beating York City's 101 points in 1983-4.

Since change of League format:
Premier League: Man. United (1993-4) 92 points; **First Division:** Bolton (1996-7) 98 points; **Second Division:** Stoke City (1992-3) 93 points; **Third Division:** Carlisle United (1994-5) 91 points.

Fewest Points: Doncaster Rovers, 8 points (of possible 68) in Second Division, 1904-5. Stirling Albion 6 points (of possible 60) in Scottish League Division A, 1954-5.

DOUBLE CHAMPIONS

Nine men have played in and later managed League Championship-winning teams:

Ted Drake	Player – Arsenal 1934, 1935, 1938. Manager – Chelsea 1955.
Bill Nicholson	Player – Tottenham 1951. Manager – Tottenham 1961.
Alf Ramsey	Player – Tottenham 1951. Manager – Ipswich 1962.
Joe Mercer	Player – Everton 1939, Arsenal 1948, 1953. Manager – Manchester City 1968.
Dave Mackay	Player – Tottenham 1961. Manager – Derby County 1975.
Bob Paisley	Player – Liverpool 1947. Manager – Liverpool 1976, 1977, 1979, 1980, 1982, 1983.
Howard Kendall	Player – Everton 1970. Manager – Everton 1985, 1987.
Kenny Dalglish	Player – Liverpool 1979, 1980, 1982, 1983, 1984. Player-Manager – Liverpool 1986, 1988, 1990. Manager – Blackburn 1995.
George Graham	Player – Arsenal 1971. Manager – Arsenal 1989, 1991.

MOST LEAGUE CHAMPIONSHIP MEDALS

Kenny Dalglish: 9 – 8 for Liverpool (5 as player, 1979-80-82-83-84; 3 as manager, 1986-88-90); 1 for Blackburn (as manager, 1995). As a player he also won 4 Scottish Championship medals with Celtic (1972-73-74-77). **Phil Neal:** 8 for Liverpool (1976-77-79-80-82-83-84-86); **Alan Hansen:** 8 for Liverpool (1979-80-82-83-84-86-88-90).

CANTONA'S FOUR-TIMER

Eric Cantona played in four successive Championship-winning teams: Marseille 1990-1, Leeds 1991-2, Man. United in 1992-3 and 1993-4.

ARRIVALS AND DEPARTURES

The following are the Football League arrivals and departures since 1923:

Year	In	Out
1923	Doncaster Rovers	Stalybridge Celtic
	New Brighton	
1927	Torquay Athletic	Aberdare Athletic
1928	Carlisle United	Durham City
1929	York City	Ashington
1930	Thames	Merthyr Tydfil
1931	Mansfield Town	Newport County
	Chester	Nelson
1932	Aldershot	Thames
	Newport County	Wigan Borough
1938	Ipswich Town	Gillingham
1950	Colchester United	
	Gillingham	
	Scunthorpe United	
	Shrewsbury Town	
1951	Workington	New Brighton
1960	Peterborough United	Gateshead
1962	Oxford United	Accrington Stanley (resigned)
1970	Cambridge United	Bradford P.A.

248

1972	Hereford United	Barrow
1977	Wimbledon	Workington
1978	Wigan Athletic	Southport
1987	Scarborough	Lincoln City
1988	Lincoln City	Newport County
1989	Maidstone United	Darlington
1990	Darlington	Colchester United
1991	Barnet	
1992	Colchester United	Aldershot, Maidstone (resigned)
1993	Wycombe W.	Halifax Town
1997	Macclesfield Town	Hereford United

Leeds City were expelled from Div. 2 in October, 1919; Port Vale took over their fixtures.

EXTENSIONS TO FOOTBALL LEAGUE

Clubs	Season	Clubs	Season
12 to 14	1891-2	+44 to 66	1920-1
*14 to 28	1892-3	† 66 to 86	1921-2
28 to 31	1893-4	86 to 88	1923-4
31 to 32	1894-5	88 to 92	1950-1
32 to 36	1898-9	92 to 93	1991-2
36 to 40	1905-6	(Reverted to 92 when Aldershot	
40 to 44	1919-20	closed, March 1992)	

* Second Division formed. + Third Division (South) formed from Southern League clubs. † Third Division (North) formed.
Football League reduced to 70 clubs and three divisions on the formation of the F.A. Premier League in 1992; increased to 72 season 1994-5, when Premier League reduced to 20 clubs.

RECORD RUNS

Nottingham Forest hold the record unbeaten sequence in the English League – 42 matches spanning the last 26 of season 1977-8 and the first 16 of 1978-9. The run began in November 1977 and ended on December 9, 1978 when Forest lost 0-2 at Liverpool. Their sequence comprised 21 wins and 21 draws.

Best debuts: Ipswich Town won the First Division at their first attempt in 1961-2. **Peterborough United** in their first season in the Football League (1960-1) not only won the Fourth Division but set a scoring record for the League of 134 goals. **Hereford United** were promoted from the Fourth Division in their first League season, 1972-3. **Wycombe Wanderers** were promoted from the Third Division (via the play-offs) in their first League season, 1993-4.

Record winning sequence: 14 consecutive League victories by three clubs (all in Second Division): **Manchester United** 1904-5, **Bristol City** 1905-6 and **Preston** 1950-1. Since then, **Reading** have gone closest to equalling this record with 13 successive League wins in Div. 3 from the start of season 1985-6.

Best starts in "old" First Division: 11 consecutive victories by **Tottenham** in 1960-1; 10 by **Manchester United** in 1985-6. **Newcastle** won their first 11 matches in the "new" First Division in 1992-3.

Longest unbeaten sequence (all competitions): 40 by **Nott'm. Forest**, March-December 1978. It comprised 21 wins, 19 draws in 29 League matches, 6 League Cup, 4 European Cup, 1 Charity Shield.

Longest unbeaten start to League season: 29 matches – **Leeds United**, Div. 1 1973-4 (19 wins, 10 draws, goals 51-16); **Liverpool**, Div. 1 1987-8 (22 wins, 7 draws, goals 67-13).

Most consecutive League matches unbeaten in a season: 30 **Burnley** (21 wins, 9 draws, goals 68-17), September 6, 1920 – March 25, 1921, Div. 1.

Longest winning sequence in Div. 1: 13 matches by **Tottenham** – last two of season 1959-60, first 11 of 1960-1.

Longest winning one-season sequences in Championship: 13 matches by **Preston N.E.** in 1891-2 (September 12–January 2); 13 by **Sunderland**, also in 1891-2 (November 14–April 2).

Premier League's record unbeaten run: 25 matches (15W, 10D) by Nott'm. Forest (Feb.-Nov. 1995). It ended with a 7-0 defeat at Blackburn.

Record Home-win sequences: Bradford Park Avenue won 25 successive home games in Div. 3 North – the last 18 in 1926-7 and the first 7 the following season. Longest run of home wins in the top division is 21 by **Liverpool** – the last 9 of 1971-2 and the first 12 of 1972-3.

WORST SEQUENCES

Cambridge United experienced the longest run without a win in Football League history in season 1983-4: 31 matches (21 lost, 10 drawn) between October 8 and April 23. They finished bottom of the Second Division.

Previous worst no-win League sequence was 30 by **Crewe Alexandra** (Div. 3 North) in season 1956-7.

Worst losing start to a League season: 12 consecutive defeats by **Manchester United** (Div. 1) in 1930-1.

Worst Premier League start: Swindon Town 15 matches without win (6 draws, 9 defeats), 1993-4.

Longest non-winning start to League season: 25 matches (4 draws, 21 defeats) by **Newport County**, Div. 4 (Aug. 15, 1970 – Jan. 9, 1971). Worst no-win League starts since then: 16 matches by **Burnley** (9 draws, 7 defeats in Div. 2, 1979-80); 16 by **Hull City** (10 draws, 6 defeats in Div. 2, 1989-90); 16 by **Sheffield United** (4 draws, 12 defeats in Div. 1, 1990-91).

Most consecutive League defeats: 18 by **Darwen** (Div. 1) 1898-9. **In modern times:** 15 by Walsall (Div. 2, 1988-9), longest such sequence since last War.

Most League defeats in season: 33 by **Rochdale** (Div. 3 North) 1931-2; by **Cambridge United** (Div. 3) 1984-5; by **Newport County** (Div. 4) 1987-8; by **Chester City** (Div. 2) 1992-3.

Most home League defeats in season: 18 by **Cambridge United** (Div. 3, 1984-5).

Away League defeats record: 24 in row by **Nelson** (Div. 3 North) – 3 in April 1930 followed by all 21 in season 1930-31. They then dropped out of League.

UNBEATEN LEAGUE SEASON

Only two clubs have completed a Football League season unbeaten: **Preston N.E.** (22 matches in 1888-9, the League's first season) and **Liverpool** (28 matches in Div. 2, 1893-4).

100 PER CENT HOME RECORDS

Five clubs have won every home League match in a season, four of them in the old Second Division: **Liverpool** (14) in 1893-4, **Bury** (15) in 1894-5, **Sheffield Wed.** (17) in 1899-1900 and **Birmingham** (17) in 1902-3.

The last club to do it was **Brentford**, who won all 21 home games in Div. 3 South in 1929-30.

Rotherham United just failed to equal that record in 1946-7. They won the first 20 home matches in Div. 3 North, then drew the last 3-3 v Rochdale.

WORST HOME RUN

Most consecutive home League defeats: 8 by **Rochdale** in Div. 3 North in season 1931-2.

Between November 1958 and October 1959 **Portsmouth** drew 2 and lost 14 out of 16 consecutive home games.

MOST AWAY WINS IN SEASON

Doncaster Rovers won 18 of their 21 away League fixtures as Div. 3 North Champions in 1946-7.

AWAY WINS RECORD

Most **consecutive away League wins**: **10 by Tottenham** (Div. 1) – 8 at start of 1960-1, after ending previous season with 2 away victories.

100 PER CENT HOME WINS ON ONE DAY

Div. 1 – All 11 home teams won on Feb. 13, 1926 and on Dec. 10, 1955. **Div. 2** – All 12 home teams won on Nov. 26, 1988.
In **Div. 3**, all 12 home teams won in the week-end programme of Oct. 18-19, 1968.

NO HOME WINS IN DIV. ON ONE DAY

Div. 1 – 8 away wins, 3 draws in 11 matches on Sept. 6, 1986. **Div. 2** – 7 away wins, 4 draws in 11 matches on Dec. 26, 1987. **Premier League** – 6 away wins, 5 draws in 11 matches on Dec. 26, 1994.
In the week-end **Premiership** programme on Dec. 7-8-9, 1996 there was not one home win in the ten games (4 aways, 6 draws).

MOST DRAWS IN A SEASON (FOOTBALL LEAGUE)

23 by **Norwich City** (Div. 1, 1978-79) and **Exeter City** (Div. 4, 1986-87). Norwich played 42 matches, Exeter 46.

MOST DRAWS IN ONE DIV. ON ONE DAY

On September 18, 1948 **nine** out of 11 First Division matches were drawn.

MOST DRAWS IN PREMIER DIV. PROGRAMME

In the week-end of December 2, 3, 4, 1995, seven out of the ten matches finished level.

HIGHEST-SCORING DRAWS IN LEAGUE

Leicester City 6, Arsenal 6 (Div. 1 April 21, 1930) **Charlton Athletic 6, Middlesbrough 6** (Div 2 October 22, 1960)
Latest 6-6 draw in first-class football was between Tranmere Rovers and Newcastle United in the Zenith Data Systems Cup 1st. Round on October 1, 1991. The score went from 3-3 at 90 minutes to 6-6 after extra time, and Tranmere won the tie 3-2 on penalties.
Most recent 5-5 draws in top division: Southampton v Coventry (Div. 1, May 4, 1982); Q.P.R. v Newcastle (Div. 1, Sept. 22, 1984).

DRAWS RECORDS

Most consecutive drawn matches in Football League: 8 by **Torquay United** (Div. 3), Oct. 25 – Dec. 13, 1969.
Longest sequence of draws by the same score: six 1-1 results by **Q.P.R.** in season 1957-8.

IDENTICAL RECORDS

There is only **one instance** of two clubs in one division finishing a season with identical records. In 1907-8, **Blackburn Rovers** and **Woolwich Arsenal** were bracketed equal 14th. in the First Division with these figures: P38, W12, D12, L14, Goals 51-63, Pts. 36.

The total of **1195 goals** scored in the Premier League in season 1993-4 was **repeated** in 1994-5.

CHAMPIONS OF ALL DIVISIONS

Wolves and **Burnley** are the only clubs to have won the Championships of the old **Divisions 1, 2, 3 and 4**. Wolves were also **Champions** of the **Third Division North**.

UPS & DOWNS RECORD

Northampton Town went from **Fourth Division** to **First** and back again in nine seasons (1961-9). **Carlisle United** did the same from 1974-87.

NIGHTMARE STARTS

Most goals conceded by a goalkeeper on League debut: 13 by **Steve Milton** when Halifax Town lost 13-0 at Stockport (Div. 3 North) on January 6, 1934.

Post-war: 11 by Lincoln City (11-1) against Crewe's new goalkeeper **Dennis Murray** (Div. 3 North) on September 29, 1951.

RELEGATION ODD SPOTS

In season 1937-8, **Manchester City** were the highest-scoring team in the First Division with 80 goals (3 more than Champions Arsenal), but they finished in 21st place and were relegated – a year after winning the Championship. They scored more goals than they conceded (77).

Twelve years earlier, in 1925-6, City went down to Division 2 despite totalling 89 goals – still the most scored in any division by a relegated team. Man. City also scored 31 F.A. Cup goals that season, but lost the Final 1-0 to Bolton.

Cardiff City were relegated from Div. 1 in season 1928-9, despite conceding fewest goals in the division (59). They also scored fewest (43).

RELEGATION TREBLES

Two Football League clubs have been relegated three seasons in succession. **Bristol City** fell from First Division to Fourth in 1980-1-2, and **Wolves** did the same in 1984-5-6.

OLDEST CLUBS

Oldest Association Football Club is **Sheffield F.C.** (formed in 1855). The minute book for 1857 is still in existence.

The oldest Football League clubs are: **Notts County**, 1862; **Nottingham Forest**, 1865; and **Sheffield Wednesday**, 1866.

FOUR DIVISIONS

In **May, 1957**, the Football League decided to re-group the two sections of the Third Division into Third and Fourth Divisions in **season 1958-9**.

The Football League was reduced to three divisions on the formation of the F.A. Premier League in **1992**.

THREE UP – THREE DOWN

The Football League Annual General Meeting of June 1973 agreed to adopt the promotion and relegation system of three up and three down.

The **new system** came into effect in **season 1973-4** and applied only to the first three divisions; four were still relegated from the Third and four promoted from the Fourth.

It was the first change in the promotion and relegation system for the top two divisions in 81 years.

MOST LEAGUE APPEARANCES

Players with more than 700 Football League appearances (as at end of season 1996-7):-

1005 **Peter Shilton** 1966-97 (286 Leicester, 110 Stoke, 202 Nott'm. Forest, 188 Southampton, 175 Derby, 34 Plymouth, 1 Bolton, 9 Leyton Orient).

824 **Terry Paine** 1956-77 (713 Southampton, 111 Hereford).

797 **Tommy Hutchison** 1968-91 (165 Blackpool, 314 Coventry, 46 Man. City, 92 Burnley, 180 Swansea). In addition, 68 Scottish League apps. for Alloa 1965-68, giving career League app. total of 865.

782 **Robbie James** 1973-94 (484 Swansea, 48 Stoke, 87 Q.P.R., 23 Leicester, 89 Bradford C., 51 Cardiff).

777 **Alan Oakes** 1959-84 (565 Man. City, 211 Chester, 1 Port Vale).

770 **John Trollope** 1960-80 (all for Swindon, record total for one club).

764 **Jimmy Dickinson** 1946-65 (all for Portsmouth).

761 **Roy Sproson** 1950-72 (all for Port Vale).

758 **Billy Bonds** 1964-88 (95 Charlton, 663 West Ham).

758 **Ray Clemence** 1966-88 (48 Scunthorpe, 470 Liverpool, 240 Tottenham).

757 **Pat Jennings** 1963-86 (48 Watford, 472 Tottenham, 237 Arsenal).

757 **Frank Worthington** 1966-88 (171 Huddersfield, 210 Leicester, 84 Bolton, 75 Birmingham, 32 Leeds, 19 Sunderland, 34 Southampton, 31 Brighton, 59 Tranmere, 23 Preston, 19 Stockport).

749 **Ernie Moss** 1968-88 (469 Chesterfield, 35 Peterborough, 57 Mansfield, 74 Port Vale, 11 Lincoln, 44 Doncaster, 26 Stockport, 23 Scarborough, 10 Rochdale).

746 **Les Chapman** 1966-88 (263 Oldham, 133 Huddersfield, 70 Stockport, 139 Bradford C., 88 Rochdale, 53 Preston).

743 **Alan Ball** 1963-84 (146 Blackpool, 208 Everton, 177 Arsenal, 195 Southampton, 17 Bristol Rovers).

743 **John Hollins** 1963-84 (465 Chelsea, 151 QPR, 127 Arsenal).

743 **Phil Parkes** 1968-91 (52 Walsall, 344 Q.P.R., 344 West Ham, 3 Ipswich).

732 **Mick Mills** 1966-88 (591 Ipswich, 103 Southampton, 38 Stoke).

731 **Asa Hartford** 1967-90 (213 W.B.A., 260 Man. City, 3 Nott'm. F., 81 Everton, 28 Norwich, 81 Bolton, 45 Stockport, 4 Oldham, 16 Shrewsbury).

731 **Ian Callaghan** 1959-81 (640 Liverpool, 76 Swansea, 15 Crewe).

725 **Steve Perryman** 1969-90 (655 Tottenham, 17 Oxford Utd., 53 Brentford).

722 **Martin Peters** 1961-81 (302 West Ham, 189 Tottenham, 207 Norwich, 24 Sheffield United).

718 **Mike Channon** 1966-86 (511 Southampton, 72 Man. City, 4 Newcastle, 9 Bristol Rov., 88 Norwich, 34 Portsmouth).

718 **Phil Neal** 1968-89 (186 Northampton, 455 Liverpool, 77 Bolton).

716 **Ron Harris** 1961-83 (655 Chelsea, 61 Brentford).

716 **Mike Summerbee** 1959-79 (218 Swindon, 357 Man. City, 51 Burnley, 3 Blackpool, 87 Stockport).

705 **John Wile** 1968-86 (205 Peterborough, 500 W.B.A.).

● **Stanley Matthews** made 701 League apps. 1932-65 (322 Stoke, 379 Blackpool), incl. 3 for Stoke at start of 1939-40 before season abandoned (war).

LONGEST LEAGUE SEQUENCE

Harold Bell, centre-half of Tranmere Rovers, was ever-present for the first nine post-war seasons (1946-55), achieving a League record of 401 consecutive matches. Counting F.A. Cup games, his run of successive appearances totalled 459.

The longest League sequence since Bell's was 394 appearances by goal-keeper **Dave Beasant** for Wimbledon, Newcastle and Chelsea. His nine-year run began on August 29, 1981 and was ended by a broken finger sustained in Chelsea's League Cup-tie against Portsmouth on October 31, 1990. Beasant's 394 consecutive League games comprised 304 for Wimbledon (1981-8), 20 for Newcastle (1988-9) and 70 for Chelsea (1989-90).

Phil Neal made 366 consecutive First Division appearances for Liverpool between December 1974 and September 1983, a remarkable sequence for an outfield player in top-division football.

EVER-PRESENT DEFENCE

The **entire defence** of Huddersfield Town played in all 42 Second Division matches in season 1952-3, namely, Bill Wheeler (goal), Ron Staniforth and Laurie Kelly (full-backs), Bill McGarry, Don McEvoy and Len Quested (half-backs). In addition, Vic Metcalfe played in all 42 League matches at outside-left.

FIRST SUBSTITUTE USED IN LEAGUE

Keith Peacock (Charlton), away to Bolton (Div. 2) on August 21, 1965.

FROM PROMOTION TO CHAMPIONS

Clubs who have become Champions of England a year after winning promotion: **Liverpool** 1905, 1906; **Everton** 1931, 1932; **Tottenham** 1950, 1951; **Ipswich** 1961, 1962; **Nott'm. Forest** 1977, 1978.

THREE-NATION CHAMPION

Trevor Steven earned eight Championship medals, in three countries: two with Everton (1985, 1987); five with Rangers (1990, 1991, 1993, 1994, 1995) and one with Marseille in 1992.

LEEDS NO-WAY AWAY

Leeds United, in 1992-3, provided the first instance of a club failing to win an away League match in the season following Championship success.

PIONEERS IN 1888 and 1992

Three clubs among the twelve who formed the Football League in 1888 were also founder members of the F.A. Premier League: **Aston Villa, Blackburn Rovers** and **Everton.**

CHAMPIONS (MODERN) WITH TWO CLUBS – PLAYERS

Francis Lee (Man. C. 1968, Derby 1975); **Ray Kennedy** (Arsenal 1971, Liverpool 1979, 1980, 1982); **Archie Gemmill** (Derby 1972, 1975, Nott'm. F. 1978); **John McGovern** (Derby 1972, Nott'm. F. 1978) **Larry Lloyd** (Liverpool 1973, Nott'm. F. 1978); **Peter Withe** (Nott'm. F. 1978, Aston Villa 1981); **John Lukic** (Arsenal 1989, Leeds 1992); **Kevin Richardson** (Everton 1985, Arsenal 1989); **Eric Cantona** (Leeds 1992, Man. United 1993, 1994, 1996, 1997); **David Batty** (Leeds 1992, Blackburn 1995), **Bobby Mimms** (Everton 1987, Blackburn 1995).

CLUB CLOSURES

Four clubs have left the Football League in mid-season: **Leeds City** (expelled Oct. 1919); **Wigan Borough** (Oct. 1931, debts of £20,000); **Accrington Stanley** (March 1962, debts £62,000); **Aldershot** (March 1992, debts £1.2m.). **Maidstone United**, with debts of £650,000, closed August 1992, on the eve of the season.

FOUR-DIVISION MEN

In season 1986-7, **Eric Nixon**, Manchester City goalkeeper, became the first player to appear in **all four divisions** of the Football League **in one season**. He served two clubs in Div. 1: Man. City (5 League games) and Southampton (4); in Div. 2 Bradford City (3); in Div. 3 Carlisle (16); and in Div. 4 for Wolves (16). Total appearances: 44.

Harvey McCreadie, a teenage forward, played in four divisions over two seasons inside a calendar year – from Accrington (Div. 3) to Luton (Div. 1) in January 1960, to Div. 2 with Luton later that season and to Wrexham (Div. 4) in November.

FATHERS & SONS

When player-manager **Ian Bowyer** (39) and **Gary Bowyer** (18) appeared together in the **Hereford United** side at Scunthorpe (Div.4, April 21, 1990), they provided the first instance of father and son playing in the same team in a Football League match for 39 years. Ian Bowyer played as substitute, and Gary scored Hereford's injury-time equaliser in a 3-3 draw.

Alec and **David Herd** were the previous father-and-son duo in League football – for **Stockport County**, 2-0 winners at Hartlepool (Div.3 North) on May 5, 1951.

When **Preston N.E.** won 2-1 at Bury in Div. 3 on January 13, 1990, the opposing goalkeepers were brothers: **Alan Kelly** (21) for Preston and **Gary** (23) for Bury. Their father, **Alan Kelly Senior**, (who kept goal for Preston in the 1964 F.A. Cup Final and won 47 Rep. of Ireland caps) flew from America to watch the sons he taught to keep goal line up on opposite sides.

FATHER & SON ON OPPOSITE SIDES

It happened for the first time in F.A. Cup history (1st. Qual. Round on Sept. 14, 1996) when 21-year-old **Nick Scaife** (Bishop Auckland) faced his father **Bobby** (41), who played for Pickering. Both were in midfield. Home side Bishops won 3-1.

THREE BROTHERS IN DIV. 1 SIDE

Southampton provided the first instance for 65 years of three brothers appearing together in a First Division side on October 22, 1988, when **Danny Wallace** (24) and his 19-year-old twin brothers **Rodney** and **Ray**, played against Sheffield Wednesday. In all, they made 25 appearances together for Southampton until September 1989.

A previous instance in Div. 1 was provided by the Middlesbrough trio, **William**, **John** and **George Carr** with 24 League appearances together from January 1920 to October 1923.

The **Tonner** brothers, **Sam**, **James** and **Jack**, played together in 13 Second Division matches for Clapton Orient in season 1919-20.

SHORTEST MATCH

The 0-0 score in the **Bradford City v. Lincoln City Third Division fixture** on May 11, 1985, abandoned through fire after 40 minutes, was subsequently confirmed as a result. It is the shortest officially completed League match on record, and only the third instance in Football League history of the score of an unfinished match being allowed to stand.

The other occasions: **Middlesbrough 4, Oldham 1** (Div. 1, April 3, 1915), abandoned after 55 minutes when Oldham defender Billy Cook refused to leave the field after being sent off; **Barrow 7, Gillingham 0** (Div. 4, Oct. 9, 1961), abandoned after 75 minutes because of bad light, the match having started late because of Gillingham's delayed arrival.

The last 60 seconds of **Birmingham v Stoke** (Div. 3, 1-1, on Feb. 29, 1992) were played behind locked doors. The ground had been cleared after a pitch invasion.

The First Division fixture, **Sheff. Wednesday v. Aston Villa** (Nov. 26, 1898), was abandoned through bad light after 79½ mins. with Wednesday leading 3-1. The Football League ruled that the match should be completed, and the remaining 10½ minutes were played **four months later** (Mar. 13, 1899), when Wednesday added another goal to make the result 4-1.

A crucial **Manchester derby** (Div.1) was abandoned after 85 minutes, and the result stood, on April 27, 1974, when a pitch invasion at Old Trafford followed the only goal, scored for City by Denis Law, which relegated Manchester United – Law's former club.

F.A. CUP RECORDS

CHIEF WINNERS

Nine Times: Manchester United.
Eight Times: Tottenham Hotspur.
Seven Times: Aston Villa.
Three Times in Succession: The Wanderers (1876-7-8) and Blackburn Rovers (1884-5-6).
Trophy Handed Back: The F.A. Cup became the Wanderers' absolute property in 1878, but they handed it back to the Association on condition that it was not to be won outright by any club.
In Successive Years by Professional Clubs: Blackburn Rovers (in 1890 and 1891); Newcastle United (in 1951 and 1952); Tottenham Hotspur (in 1961 and 1962) and Tottenham again (in 1981 and 1982).
Record Final-tie score: Bury 6, Derby County 0 (1903).
Most F.A. Cup wins at Wembley: Manchester United 8, Arsenal 6, Tottenham Hotspur 6, Newcastle United 5, Liverpool 5.

F.A. CUP: SECOND DIVISION WINNERS

Notts County (1894), Wolves (1908), Barnsley (1912), West Bromwich Albion (1931), Sunderland (1973), Southampton (1976), West Ham United (1980). When Tottenham won the Cup in 1901 they were a Southern League club.

THIRD DIVISION SEMI-FINALISTS

Millwall (1937), Port Vale (1954), York City (1955), Norwich City (1959), Crystal Palace (1976), Plymouth Argyle (1984).

Chesterfield, from the modern Second Division (the old Third), reached the semi-final in 1997.

FOURTH DIVISION QUARTER-FINALISTS

Oxford United (1964), Colchester United (1971), Bradford City (1976), Cambridge United (1990).

F.A. CUP – FOUR TROPHIES

The latest F.A. Cup, first presented at Wembley in 1992, is a replica of the one it replaced and which had been in existence since 1911. The old F.A. Cup is now a museum piece at Lancaster Gate, the F.A. explaining: "It was falling apart and was not going to last much longer."

The new trophy is the fourth F.A. Cup. These were its predecessors:

1895 First F.A. Cup stolen from shop in Birmingham while held by Aston Villa. Never seen again.

1910 Second F.A. Cup presented to Lord Kinnaird on completing 21 years as F.A. president.

1992 Third F.A. Cup "gracefully retired" after 80 years' service (1911-91).

FINALISTS RELEGATED

Four clubs have reached the F.A. Cup Final in a season of relegation, and all lost at Wembley: Man. City 1926, Leicester 1969, Brighton 1983, Middlesbrough 1997.

GIANT-KILLING IN F.A. CUP

(* Home team; R = Replay; Season 1997 = 1996-7)

1997	*Millwall	0	Woking	1R		
1997	*Brighton	1	Sudbury T.	1R		
(Sudbury won on pens.)						
1997	*Blackpool	0	Hednesford	2		
1997	*Cambridge.	0	Woking	1		
1997	*Leyton O.	1	Stevenage	2		
1997	*Hednesford	1	York	0		
1997	*Chesterf'ld	1	Nott'm. F.	0		
1996	*Hitchin	2	Bristol R.	1		
1996	*Woking	2	Barnet	1R		
1996	*Bury	2	Blyth S.	2		
1996	*Gravesend	2	Colchester	0		
1995	*Kingstonian	2	Brighton	1		
1995	*Enfield	1	Cardiff	0		
1995	*Marlow	2	Oxford	0		
1995	*Woking	1	Barnet	0R		
1995	*Hitchin	4	Hereford	2R		
1995	*Torquay	0	Enfield	1R		
1995	*Altrincham	1	Wigan	0		
1995	*Wrexham	2	Ipswich	1		
1995	*Scarboro'	1	Port Vale	0		
1994	*Colchester	3	Sutton	4		
1994	*Yeovil	1	Fulham	0		
1994	*Torquay	0	Sutton	1		
1994	*Halifax	1	W.B.A.	1		
1994	*Birmingham	1	Kid'minster	2		
1994	*Stockport	2	Q.P.R.	1		
1994	*Liverpool	0	Bristol C.	1R		
1994	*Arsenal	1	Bolton	3R		
1994	*Leeds	2	Oxford	3R		
1994	*Luton	2	Newcastle	0R		
1994	*Kid'minster	1	Preston	0		
1994	*Cardiff	1	Man. C.	0		
1993	*Hereford	1	Yeovil	2R		
1993	*Torquay	2	Yeovil	5		
1993	*Altrincham	2	Chester	0R		
1993	*Cardiff	2	Bath	3		
1993	*Ch'field	2	Macc'field	2R		
(Macclesfield won on pens).						
1993	*Marine	4	Halifax	1		
1993	*Stafford	2	Lincoln	1		
1993	*Hartlepool	1	Crystal P.	0		
1993	*Liverpool	0	Bolton	2R		
1992	*Fulham	0	Hayes	2		
1992	*Crawley	4	N'thampton	2		
1992	*Telford	2	Stoke	1R		
1992	*Aldershot	0	Enfield	1		
1992	*Halifax	1	Witton A.	2R		
1992	*Maidstone	1	Kettering	2		
1992	*Walsall	0	Yeovil	1R		
1992	*Farnboro'	4	Torquay	3		
1992	*Wrexham	2	Arsenal	1		
1991	*Scarboro'	0	Leek	2		
1991	*N 'hampton	0	Barnet	1R		
1991	*Hayes	1	Cardiff	0R		
1991	*Chorley	0	Bury	1		
1991	*Shrewsbury	1	Wimbledon	0		
1991	*W.B.A.	2	Woking	4		
1990	*Aylesbury	1	Southend	0		
1990	*Scarboro'	0	Whitley Bay	1		
1990	*Welling	1	Gillingham	0R		
1990	*Whitley Bay	2	Preston	0		
1990	*N'hampton	1	Coventry	0		
1990	*Cambridge	1	Millwall	0R		
1989	*Sutton	2	Coventry	1		
1989	*Halifax	2	Kettering	3R		
1989	*Kettering	2	Bristol R.	1		
1989	*Bognor	2	Exeter	1		
1989	*Leyton O.	0	Enfield	1R		
1989	*Altrincham	3	Lincoln	2		
1989	*Wrexham	2	Runcorn	3R		
1988	*Sutton	3	Aldershot	0		

1988 *Peterboro' ... 1 — Sutton 3
1988 *Carlisle ...... 2 — Macc'field 4
1988 *Macc'field ... 1 — Rotherham 0
1988 *Chester .... 0 — Runcorn 1
1988 *Cambridge .. 0 — Yeovil 1
1987 *Caernarfon .. 1 — Stockport 0
1987 Chorley .... 3 — Wolves ..... 0 R
  (at Bolton)
1987 *Telford .... 3 — Burnley 0
1987 *York C. .... 1 — Caernarfon 2 R
1987 *Aldershot .... 3 — Oxford U 0
1987 *Wigan .... 1 — Norwich C 0
1987 *Charlton ...... 1 — Walsall 2
1986 *Stockport ..... 0 — Telford 1
1986 *Wycombe ..... 2 — Colchester 0
1986 *Dagenham . 2 — Cambridge U 1
1986 *Blackpool ..... 0 — Altrincham 0
1986 *B'ham .... 1 — Altrincham 2
1986 *Peterboro' .... 1 — Leeds 0
1985 *Telford .... 2 — Lincoln 1
1985 *Preston .... 1 — Telford 4
1985 *Telford .... 2 — Bradford C. .. 1
1985 *Blackpool ..... 3 — Darlington . 0 R
1985 *Blackpool ..... 0 — Nott'm. F. .. 0 R
1985 *Wimbledon . 1 — Nott'm. F. .. 0 R
1985 *Orient .... 2 — W.B.A. 1
1985 *Dagenham .. 1 — Peterboro' 0
1985 *Swindon ...... 1 — Dagenham 2 R
1985 *York .... 1 — Arsenal 0
1984 *Halifax .... 2 — Whitby 3
1984 *B'mouth ...... 2 — Man. Utd 0
1984 *Telford .... 3 — Stockport 0
1984 *Telford .... 3 — N'hampton 2 R
1984 Telford .... 4 — *Rochdale 1
1983 *Cardiff .... 2 — Weymouth 2
1981 *Exeter .... 3 — Leicester .. 1 R
1981 *Exeter .... 4 — Newcastle .. 0 R
1980 *Halifax .... 1 — Man. C 0
1980 *Harlow .... 1 — Leicester .. 0 R
1980 *Chelsea ...... 0 — Wigan 1

1979 *Newport ...... 2 — West Ham 1
1978 *Wrexham ..... 4 — Newcastle . 1 R
1978 *Stoke .... 2 — Blyth S 3
1976 *Leeds U ...... 0 — Crystal P. 1
1975 *Brighton ...... 0 — Leatherhead . 1
1975 *Burnley .... 0 — Wimbledon .. 1
1972 *Hereford ...... 2 — Newcastle . 1 R
1971 *Colchester . 3 — Leeds U 2
1969 *Mansfield .... 3 — West Ham 0
1967 *Swindon ...... 3 — West Ham . 0 R
1967 *Man. U .... 1 — Norwich C 2
1966 *Ipswich T .... 0 — Southport . 3 R
1965 *Peterboro' .... 2 — Arsenal 1
1964 *Newcastle ... 1 — Bedford T 2
1964 *Aldershot .... 2 — Aston V .... 1 R
1961 *Coventry ..... 1 — Kings Lynn ... 2
1961 *Chelsea ...... 2 — Crewe A 2
1960 *Man. C .... 1 — South'ton 5
1959 *Norwich C .. 3 — Man. U 0
1959 *Worcester .... 2 — Liverpool 0
1959 *Tooting .... 3 — Bournem'th .. 1
1959 *Tooting .... 2 — N'mpton 1
1958 *Newcastle ... 1 — Scunthorpe .. 3
1957 *Wolves .... 0 — Bournem'th .. 1
1957 *B'mouth ...... 1 — Tottenham 0
1957 *Derby .... 1 — N. Brighton .. 3
1956 *Derby C ...... 1 — Boston U 6
1955 *York C .... 2 — Tottenham 0
1955 *Blackpool ... 0 — York C 2
1954 *Arsenal .... 1 — Norwich C 2
1954 *Port Vale ..... 2 — Blackpool 0
1952 *Everton .... 1 — Leyton O 3
1949 *Yeovil T ...... 2 — Sunderland .. 1
1948 *Colchester ... 1 — Hud'field 0
1948 *Arsenal .... 0 — Bradford 1
1938 *Chelmsford . 4 — South'ton 1
1933 *Walsall .... 2 — Arsenal 0
1922 *Everton .... 0 — Crystal P. 6

YEOVIL TOP GIANT-KILLERS

Yeovil's first round victory against Fulham in season 1993-4 gave them a total of 17 F.A. Cup wins against League opponents. They hold another non-League record by reaching Round 3 eleven times.

This is Yeovil's triumphant Cup record against League clubs: 1924-5 Bournemouth 3-2; 1934-5 Crystal P. 3-0, Exeter 4-1; 1938-9 Brighton 2-1; 1948-9 Bury 3-1, Sunderland 2-1; 1958-9 Southend 1-0; 1960-1 Walsall 1-0; 1963-4 Southend 1-0, Crystal P. 3-1; 1970-1 Bournemouth 1-0; 1972-3 Brentford 2-1; 1987-8 Cambridge 1-0; 1991-2 Walsall 1-0; 1992-3 Torquay 5-2, Hereford 2-1; 1993-4 Fulham 1-0.

NON-LEAGUE BEST IN F.A. CUP

Since League football began in 1888, three non-League clubs have reached the F.A. Cup Final. **Sheffield Wed.** (Football Alliance) were runners-up in 1890, as were **Southampton** (Southern League) in 1900 and 1902. **Tottenham** won the Cup as a Southern League team in 1901.

Otherwise, the **furthest progress** by non-League clubs has been to the **5th. Round** on 5 occasions: Colchester 1948, Yeovil 1949, Blyth Spartans 1978, Telford 1985 and Kidderminster 1994.

Greatest number of non-League sides to reach the **3rd. Round** is 6 in 1978: Blyth, Enfield, Scarborough, Tilbury, Wealdstone and Wigan.

Most to reach **Round 4**: 3 in 1957 (Rhyl, New Brighton, Peterborough) and 1975 (Leatherhead, Stafford and Wimbledon).

TOP-DIVISION SCALPS

Victories in F.A. Cup by non-League clubs over top-division teams this century include:- 1900-1 (Final, replay); **Tottenham** 3, Sheffield Utd. 1 (Spurs then in Southern League); 1919-20 **Cardiff City** 2, Oldham Athletic 0, and Sheffield Wed. 0, **Darlington** 2; 1923-4 **Corinthians** 1, Blackburn Rovers 0; 1947-8 **Colchester Utd.** 1, Huddersfield Town 0; 1948-9 **Yeovil Town** 2, Sunderland 1; 1971-2 **Hereford Utd.** 2, Newcastle 1; 1974-5 Burnley 0, **Wimbledon** 1; 1985-6 Birmingham City 1, **Altrincham** 2; 1988-9 **Sutton United** 2, Coventry City 1.

MOST WEMBLEY FINALS

Six players have appeared in five F.A. Cup Finals at Wembley, replays excluded:-
- Joe Hulme (Arsenal: 1927, lost; 1930 won; 1932 lost; 1936 won; Huddersfield Town: 1938 lost).
- Johnny Giles (Man. United: 1963 won; Leeds Utd: 1965 lost; 1970 drew at Wembley, lost replay at Old Trafford; 1972 won; 1973 lost).
- Pat Rice (all for Arsenal: 1971 won; 1972 lost; 1978 lost; 1979 won; 1980 lost).
- Frank Stapleton (Arsenal: 1978 lost; 1979 won; 1980 lost; Man. United: 1983 won; 1985 won).
- Ray Clemence (Liverpool: 1971 lost; 1974 won; 1977 lost; Tottenham: 1982 won; 1987 lost).
- Mark Hughes (Man. United: 1985 won; 1990 won; 1994 won; 1995 lost; Chelsea: 1997 won).

Stapleton, Clemence and Hughes also played in a replay, making six actual F.A. Cup Final appearances for each of them.

Glenn Hoddle made six F.A. Cup Final appearances at Wembley: 5 for Tottenham (incl. 2 replays), in 1981, 1982 and 1987, and 1 for Chelsea in 1994.

F.A. CUP SEMI-FINALS AT WEMBLEY

1991 Tottenham 3, Arsenal 1; **1993** Sheff. Wed. 2, Sheff. Utd. 1; Arsenal 1, Tottenham 0; **1994** Chelsea 2, Luton 0; Man. Utd. 1, Oldham 1.

FIRST F.A. CUP ENTRANTS (1871-2)

Barnes, Civil Service, Crystal Palace, Clapham Rovers, Donnington School (Spalding), Hampstead Heathens, Harrow Chequers, Hitchin, Maidenhead, Marlow, Queen's Park (Glasgow), Reigate Priory, Royal Engineers, Upton Park and Wanderers. Total 15. Three scratched.

Record F.A. Cup entry .... **674 in 1921**

CUP 'FIRSTS'

Out of Country: Cardiff City, by defeating Arsenal 1-0 in the 1927 Final at Wembley, became the first and only club to take the F.A. Cup out of England.
All-English Winning XI: First club to win the F.A. Cup with all-English XI was West Bromwich Albion, in 1888 and again in 1931. Others since: Bolton (1958),

Man. City (1969), West Ham (1964 and 1975). **Non-English Winning XI:** Liverpool in 1986 (Mark Lawrenson, born Preston, a Rep. of Ireland player). **Won both Cups: Old Carthusians** won the F.A. Cup in 1881 and the F.A. Amateur Cup in 1894 and 1897. **Wimbledon** won Amateur Cup in 1963, F.A. Cup in 1988.

MOST GAMES NEEDED TO WIN F.A. CUP

Barnsley played a record 12 matches (20 hours' football) to win the F.A. Cup in season 1911-12. All six replays (one in Rd. 1, three in Rd. 4 and one in each of semi-final and Final) were brought about by goalless draws.

Arsenal played 11 F.A. Cup games when winning the trophy in 1979. Five of them were in the 3rd. Rd. against Sheffield Wednesday.

LONGEST F.A. CUP TIES

6 matches (11 hours): **Alvechurch v. Oxford City** (4th. qual. round, 1971-2). Alvechurch won 1-0.

5 matches (9 hours, 22 mins – record for competition proper): **Stoke City v. Bury** (3rd. round, 1954-5). Stoke won 3-2.

5 matches: Chelsea v Burnley (4th. round, 1955-6). Chelsea won 2-0.

5 matches: Hull v. Darlington (2nd. round, 1960-1). Hull won 3-0.

5 matches: Arsenal v. Sheff. Wed. (3rd. round, 1978-9). Arsenal won 2-0.

Other marathons (qualifying comp., all 5 matches, 9 hours): **Barrow v. Gillingham** (last qual. round, 1924-5) – winners Barrow; **Leyton v Ilford** (3rd. qual. round, 1924-5) – winners Leyton; **Falmouth Town v. Bideford** (3rd. qual. round, 1973-4) – winners Bideford.

F.A. Cup marathons ended in season 1991-2, when the penalty shoot-out was introduced to decide ties still level after one replay and extra time.

LONGEST ROUND

The longest round in F.A. Cup history was the **third round** in **season 1962-3**. It took 66 days to complete, lasting from January 5 to March 11, and included 261 postponements because of bad weather.

RE-STAGED F.A. CUP TIES

Sixth round, March 9, 1974: Newcastle 4, Nott'm. Forest 3. Match declared void by F.A. and ordered to be replayed following a pitch invasion after Newcastle had a player sent off. Forest claimed the hold-up caused the game to change its pattern. The tie went to two further matches at Goodison Park (0-0, then 1-0 to Newcastle).

Third round, January 5, 1985: Burton Albion 1, Leicester 6 (at Derby). Burton goalkeeper Paul Evans was hit on the head by a missile thrown from the crowd, and continued in a daze. The F.A. ordered the tie to be played again, behind closed doors at Coventry (Leicester won 1- 0).

First round replay, November 25, 1992: Peterborough 9 (Tony Philliskirk 5), Kingstonian 1. Match expunged from records because, at 3-0 after 57 mins, Kingstonian were reduced to ten men when goalkeeper Adrian Blake was concussed by a 50 pence coin thrown from the crowd. The tie was re-staged on the same ground behind closed doors (Peterborough won 1-0).

WAR-TIME MARATHON

Match of 203 minutes: Stockport County's second-leg tie with Doncaster Rovers in the Third Division North Cup, March 30, 1946, lasted 203 minutes and a replay was still necessary.

F.A. CUP FINAL HAT-TRICKS

There have been only three in the history of the competition: **Billy Townley** (Blackburn Rovers, 1890), **Jimmy Logan** (Notts Co., 1894) and **Stan Mortensen** (Blackpool, 1953).

FIVE WINNING MEDALS

The Hon. A.F. Kinnaird (The Wanderers and Old Etonians), **C.H.R. Wollaston** (The Wanderers) and **James Forrest** (Blackburn Rovers) each earned five F.A. Cup winners' medals. Kinnaird, later president of the F.A., played in nine of the first 12 F.A. Cup Finals, and was on the winning side three times for The Wanderers, in 1873 (captain), 1877, 1878 (captain) and twice as captain of Old Etonians (1879, 1882).

MOST WINNERS' MEDALS THIS CENTURY

4 – Mark Hughes (3 for Man. United, 1 for Chelsea).
3 – 17 players: Dick Pym (3 clean sheets in Finals), **Bob Haworth**, **Jimmy Seddon**, **Harry Nuttall**, **Billy Butler** (all Bolton); **David Jack** (2 Bolton, 1 Arsenal); **Bob Cowell**, **Jack Milburn**, **Bobby Mitchell** (all Newcastle); **Dave Mackay** (Tottenham); **Frank Stapleton** (1 Arsenal, 2 Man. Utd.); **Bryan Robson** (3 times winning captain), **Arthur Albiston**, **Gary Pallister** (all Man. Utd.); **Bruce Grobbelaar**, **Steve Nicol**, **Ian Rush** (all Liverpool).

MOST F.A. CUP APPEARANCES

88 by **Ian Callaghan** (79 for Liverpool, 7 for Swansea, 2 for Crewe); 86 by **Stanley Matthews** (37 for Stoke, 49 for Blackpool); 86 by **Peter Shilton** for six clubs (Leicester, Stoke, Nott'm. Forest, Southampton, Derby and Plymouth); 84 by **Bobby Charlton** (80 for Man. United, 4 for Preston N.E.).

THREE-CLUB FINALISTS

Two players have appeared in the F.A. Final for three clubs: **Harold Halse** for Man. United (1909), Aston Villa (1913) and Chelsea (1915); **Ernie Taylor** for Newcastle (1951), Blackpool (1953) and Man. United (1958).

CUP MAN WITH TWO CLUBS IN SAME SEASON

Stan Crowther played for both Aston V. and Manchester Utd. in the 1957-8 F.A. Cup. United signed him directly after the Munich air crash and, in the circumstances, he was given special dispensation to play for them also in the Cup, including the Final.

CAPTAIN'S CUP DOUBLE

Martin Buchan is the only player to have captained Scottish and English F.A. Cup-winning teams – Aberdeen in 1970 and Manchester United in 1977.

MEDALS BEFORE AND AFTER

Two players appeared in F.A. Cup Final teams before and after the war: **Raich Carter** was twice a winner (Sunderland 1937, Derby 1946) and **Willie Fagan** twice on the losing side (Preston 1937, Liverpool 1950).

STARS WHO MISSED OUT

Great players who never won an F.A. Cup winner's medal include: **Tommy Lawton, Tom Finney, Johnny Haynes, Gordon Banks, George Best, Terry Butcher** and **Peter Shilton**.

CUP WINNERS AT NO COST

Not one member of **Bolton Wanderers'** 1958 F.A. Cup-winning team cost the club a transfer fee. Five were Internationals.

ALL-INTERNATIONAL CUP WINNERS

In **Man. United's** 1985 Cup-winning team v. Everton, all 11 players were full Internationals, as was the substitute who played.

NO-CAP CUP WINNERS

Sunderland, in 1973, were the last F.A. Cup-winning team not to include an International player, although some were capped later.

HIGH SCORING SEMI-FINALS

The **record team score** in F.A. Cup semi-finals is 6: 1891-2 WBA 6, Nott'm. Forest 2; 1907-8 Newcastle 6, Fulham 0; 1933-4 Man. City 6, Aston Villa 1.

Most goals in semi-finals (aggregate): 17 in 1892 (4 matches) and 1899 (5 matches). In modern times: 15 in 1958 (3 matches, including Man. United 5, Fulham 3 – highest-scoring semi-final since last war); 16 in 1989-90 (Crystal Palace 4, Liverpool 3; Man. United v Oldham 3-3, 2-1. **All 16 goals** in those three matches were scored by **different players**.

Last hat-trick in an F.A. Cup semi-final was scored by **Alex Dawson** for Man. United in 5-3 replay win against Fulham at Highbury in 1958.

FOUR SPECIAL AWAYS

For the only time in F.A. Cup history, **all four quarter-finals** in season 1986-7 were won by the away team.

F.A. CUP – DRAWS RECORD

In season 1985-6, **seven** of the eight F.A. Cup 5th. Round ties went to replays – a record for that stage of the competition.

LUCK OF THE DRAW

In the F.A. Cup on Jan. 11, 1947, eight of **London's** ten Football League clubs involved in the 3rd. Round were drawn at home (including Chelsea v Arsenal). Only Crystal Palace played outside the capital (at Newcastle).

Contrast: In the 3rd. Round in Jan. 1992, Charlton were the only London club drawn at home (against Barnet), but the venue of the Farnborough v West Ham tie was reversed on police instruction. So Upton Park staged Cup-ties on successive days, with West Ham at home on the Saturday and Charlton (who shared the ground) on Sunday.

Arsenal were drawn away in every round on the way to reaching the F.A. Cup Finals of 1971 and 1972. **Man. United** won the Cup in 1990 without playing once at home.

F.A. CUP: ALL FIRST DIVISION VICTIMS

Only instance of an F.A. Cup-winning club meeting **First Division** opponents in every round was provided by Man. United in 1947-8. They beat Aston Villa, Liverpool, Charlton, Preston, then Derby County in the semi-final and Blackpool in the Final.

HOME ADVANTAGE

For the first time in F.A. Cup history, all eight ties in the 1992-3 5th. Round were won (no replays) by the **clubs drawn at home**. Only other instance of eight home wins at the "last 16" stage of the F.A. Cup was in 1889-90, in what was then the 2nd. Round.

SIXTH ROUND ELITE

For the first time in F.A. Cup 6th. Round history, dating from 1926, when the format of the competition changed, **all eight quarter-finalists** in 1995-6 were from the top division.

F.A. CUP SEMI-FINAL – DOUBLE DERBIES

There have been only two instances of both F.A. Cup semi-finals in the same year being local derbies: **1950** Liverpool beat Everton 1-0 (Maine Road), Arsenal beat Chelsea 1-0 after 2-2 draw (both at Tottenham); **1993** Arsenal beat Tottenham 1-0 (Wembley), Sheff. Wed. beat Sheff. United 2-1 (Wembley).

CUP FINAL HYMN

"**Abide With Me**" was introduced into the F.A. Cup Final community singing in 1927, and has been sung ever since with the exception of 1959. So many complaints followed its omission that it was restored the following year.

LONGEST UNBEATEN RUN IN F.A. CUP

Blackburn Rovers: 24 matches (21 wins, 2 draws, 1 walkover, from Dec. 1883-Nov. 1886), including F.A. Cup hat-trick.

TOP CLUB DISTINCTION

Since the Football League began in 1888, there has never been an F.A. Cup Final in which **neither club** represented the top division.

SPURS OUT – AND IN

Tottenham Hotspur were banned, pre-season, from the 1994-5 F.A. Cup competition because of financial irregularities, but were readmitted on appeal and reached the semi-finals.

F.A. CUP FINAL GUESTS OF HONOUR

1923	King George V, The Duke of Devonshire	1929	Prince of Wales
1924	Duke of York	1930	King George V
1925	Duke of York	1931	Duke of Gloucester
1926	King George V	1932	King George V and Queen Mary
1927	King George V		
1928	King George V and Queen Mary, Duke and Duchess of York	1933	Duke of York
		1934	King George V
		1935	Prince of Wales

1936	Sir Charles Clegg, President of the FA	1968	Princess Alexandra
		1969	Princess Anne
1937	King George VI and Queen Elizabeth	1970	Princess Margaret
		1970rep	Sir Dr Andrew Stephen
1938	King George VI	1971	Duke and Duchess of Kent
1939	King George VI	1972	Queen Elizabeth II and Duke of Edinburgh, Duke and Duchess of Kent
1946	King George VI, Queen Elizabeth, Princess Elizabeth		
		1973	Duke of Kent
1947	Duke and Duchess of Gloucester	1974	Princess Anne, Duke of Kent
		1975	Duke and Duchess of Kent
1948	King George VI	1976	Queen Elizabeth II and Duke of Edinburgh
1949	Princess Elizabeth, Duke of Gloucester		
		1977	Duke and Duchess of Kent
1950	King George VI	1978	Princess Alexandra
1951	King George VI, Queen Elizabeth, Duke of Gloucester, Prince William, Princess Mary	1979	Prince of Wales
		1980	Duke and Duchess of Kent
		1981	Queen Mother
		1981rep	Prince Michael of Kent
1952	Sir Winston Churchill	1982	Princess Anne
1953	Queen Elizabeth II	1982rep	Duke of Kent
1954	Queen Mother, Princess Margaret	1983	Duke of Kent
		1983rep	Princess Michael of Kent
1955	Princess Mary, Duke of Edinburgh	1984	Duke and Duchess of Kent
		1985	Duke of Kent
1956	Queen Elizabeth II	1986	Duchess of Kent
1957	Queen Elizabeth II and Duke of Edinburgh	1987	Duchess of Kent
		1988	Princess of Wales
1958	Queen Elizabeth II and Duke of Edinburgh	1989	Duke and Duchess of Kent
		1990	Duke and Duchess of Kent
1959	Queen Elizabeth II and Duke of Edinburgh	1990rep	Duke and Duchess of Kent
		1991	Prince and Princess of Wales, Duke and Duchess of Kent
1960	Duke of Gloucester		
1961	Duchess of Kent		
1962	Queen Elizabeth II and Duke of Edinburgh	1992	Duke and Duchess of Kent
		1993	Duke and Duchess of Kent
1963	Queen Elizabeth II and Duke of Edinburgh	1993rep	Duchess of Kent
		1994	Duchess of Kent
1964	Earl of Harewood	1995	Prince of Wales and Duke of Kent
1965	Queen Elizabeth II and Duke of Edinburgh		
		1996	Duke and Duchess of Kent
1966	Princess Margaret	1997	Duke and Duchess of Kent
1967	Duke and Duchess of Kent		

LEAGUE CUP RECORDS
(See also League Cup and Goalscoring Sections)

Highest scores: West Ham 10-0 v Bury (2nd. Rd., 2nd. Leg 1983-4; agg. 12-1); Liverpool 10-0 v Fulham (2nd. Rd., 1st. Leg 1986-7; agg. 13-2).

Most League Cup goals (career): 49 Geoff Hurst (43 West Ham, 6 Stoke, 1960-75); 48 Ian Rush (Liverpool); 44 John Aldridge (Newport, Oxford, Liverpool, Tranmere 1979 to date).

Highest scorer (season): 12 Clive Allen (Tottenham 1986-7 in 9 apps).

Most goals in match: 6 Frank Bunn (Oldham v Scarborough, 3rd. Rd., 1989-90).

Fewest goals conceded by winners: 3 by Leeds (1967-8), Tottenham (1970-1), Aston Villa (1995-6).

Most winner's medals: 5 Ian Rush (Liverpool).

Most appearances in Final: 6 Kenny Dalglish (Liverpool 1978-87), Ian Rush (Liverpool 1981-95).

Alan Hardaker Man of the Match Award was introduced in the 1990 Final, in recognition of the League's late secretary who proposed the competition in 1960.

League Cup sponsors: Milk Cup 1981-6, Littlewoods Cup 1987-90, Rumbelows Cup 1991-2, Coca-Cola Cup since 1993. In Jan. 1997 Coca-Cola agreed a new 3-year League Cup deal worth £6m., running to the end of season 1999-2000.

Norwich unique: In 1985, Norwich City became the still only club to win a major domestic cup and be relegated in the same season. They won the League's Milk Cup and went down from the old First Division.

Liverpool's League Cup records: First club to win competition 5 times. **Ian Rush** first player to collect 5 winners' medals in League Cup: 1981-82-83-84-95.
   Rush also first to play in 8 winning teams in Cup Finals **at Wembley**, all with Liverpool (F.A. Cup 1986-89-92; League Cup 1981-82-83-84-95).

DISCIPLINE

SENDINGS-OFF

A total of 341 players with Premier League and Football League clubs were sent off in first-team competitions last season. The record is 376 in 1994-5.

Dismissals comprised 300 in League fixtures (42 Premiership, 253 in Nationwide League, 5 in play-offs), 20 in F.A. Cup, 17 in Coca-Cola League Cup, 4 in Auto Windscreens Shield.

As an experiment the Coca-Cola Cup had a self-contained disciplinary system (red and yellow cards) last season, and it will continue in 1997-8.

Clubs with the worst red-card records in all senior competitions in 1996-7 were Norwich (10), Blackpool (9), Portsmouth (8) and Colchester (8).

Among Premiership clubs (all competitions), Arsenal, Coventry and Southampton had most red cards (6).

Two clubs did not have a player sent off in first-team football last season: W.B.A. and Scunthorpe.

Season-by-season dismissals from the Eighties: **1981-2**, 157 (132 League); **1982-3**, 242 (211 League); **1983-4**, 173 (150 League); **1984-5**, 183 (163 League); **1985-6**, 207 (185 League); **1986-7**, 219 (193 League); **1987-8**, 217 (197 League, incl. 2 in play-offs); **1988-9**, 192 (173 League, incl. 1 in play-offs); **1989-90**, 183 (162 in League, incl. 1 in play-offs); **1990-1**, 238 (204 League, incl. 2 in play-offs); **1991-2**, 278 (245 League, incl. 1 in play-offs); **1992-3**, 277 (229 in League, incl. 3 in play-offs); **1993-4**, 288 (239 in League, incl. 6 in play-offs); **1994-5**, 376 (309 in League, incl. 5 in play-offs); **1995-6**, 320 (279 in League, incl. 1 in play-offs); **1996-7**, 341 (300 League, incl. 5 in play-offs).

November 20, 1982 was the **worst day** for dismissals **in football history** with 15 players sent off (3 League, 12 in the F.A. Cup first round). That was also the blackest day for disciplinary action in the F.A. Cup (previous worst – eight on January 9, 1915).

Most players ordered off in **League football on one day**: 13 on Dec. 14, 1985 (also 4 in Scottish League); 13 on Aug. 19, 1995; 13 on Sept. 9, 1995.

Most players sent off in one **Football League programme**: 15 in week-end of Sat., Dec. 22 (11) and Sun., Dec. 23 (4), 1990.

● In the entire first season of post-war League football (1946-7) only 12 players were sent off, followed by 14 in 1949-50, and the total League dismissals for the first nine seasons after the war was 104.

Worst pre-war total was 28 in each of seasons 1921-2 and 1922-3.

ENGLAND SENDINGS-OFF

Ray Wilkins became only the fourth player England have had sent off in their International history (1872 to date) when he was dismissed for a second bookable offence – throwing ball at referee – in the World Cup Finals match against Morocco in Monterrey on June 6, 1986:-

June 5, 1968 **Alan Mullery**   v. Yugoslavia (Florence, Eur. Champ.)
June 6, 1973 **Alan Ball**   v. Poland (Chorzow, World Cup qual.)
June 15, 1977 **Trevor Cherry**   v. Argentina (Buenos Aires, friendly)
June 6, 1986 **Ray Wilkins**   v. Morocco (Monterrey, World Cup Finals)

Other countries: Most recent sendings-off of players representing the other Home Countries: **N. Ireland – Iain Dowie** v. Norway (Friendly, Belfast, March 1996); **Scotland – John Spencer** v. Japan (Kirin Cup, Hiroshima, May 1995); **Wales – Vinnie Jones** v. Georgia (European Champ., Cardiff, June 1995); **Rep. of Ireland – Jason McAteer** v. Macedonia (World Cup, Skopje, April 1997).

England dismissals at other levels:-

U-23 (4): Stan Anderson (v Bulgaria, Sofia, May 19, 1957); **Alan Ball** (v Austria, Vienna, June 2, 1965); **Kevin Keegan** (v E. Germany, Magdeburg, June 1, 1972); **Steve Perryman** (v Portugal, Lisbon, Nov. 19, 1974).

U-21 (10): Sammy Lee (v Hungary, Keszthely, June 5, 1981); **Mark Hateley** (v Scotland, Hampden Park, April 19, 1982); **Paul Elliott** (v Denmark, Maine Road, Manchester, March 26, 1986); **Tony Cottee** (v W. Germany, Ludenscheid, September 8, 1987); **Julian Dicks** (v Mexico, Toulon, France, June 12, 1988); **Jason Dodd** (v Mexico, Toulon, France, May 29, 1991; 3 Mexico players also sent off in that match); **Matthew Jackson** (v France, Toulon, France, May 28, 1992); **Robbie Fowler** (v Austria, Kafkenberg, October 11, 1994); **Alan Thompson** (v Portugal, Oporto, September 2, 1995); **Terry Cooke** (v Portugal, Toulon, May 30, 1996).

England 'B' (1): Neil Webb (v Algeria, Algiers, December 11, 1990).

FIVE OFF IN ONE MATCH

For the first time since League football began in 1888, **five** players were sent-off (two Chesterfield, three Plymouth) in Div. 2 at Saltergate on **Feb. 22, 1997**. Four were dismissed (two from each side) in a goalmouth brawl in the last minute.

There have been six instances of **four** Football League club players being sent off in one match:

Jan. 8, 1955 Crewe v. Bradford (Div. 3 North), two players from each side.

Dec. 13, 1986 Sheff. United (1 player) v. Portsmouth (3) in Div. 2.

Aug. 18, 1987 Port Vale v. Northampton (Littlewoods Cup 1st. Round, 1st. Leg), two players from each side.

Dec. 12, 1987 Brentford v. Mansfield (Div. 3), two players from each side.

Sept. 6, 1992 First instance in British first-class football of **four players from one side** being sent off in one match. Hereford United's seven survivors, away to Northampton (Div. 3), held out for a 1-1 draw.

Mar. 1, 1977 Norwich v Huddersfield (Div. 1), two players from each side.

Four Stranraer players were sent off away to Airdrie (Scottish Div. 1) on Dec. 3, 1994, and that Scottish record was equalled when **four Hearts men** were ordered off away to Rangers (Prem. Div.) on **Sept. 14, 1996**.

Modern instances of **three players from one side** being sent off:

Dec. 13, 1986 Portsmouth (away to Sheff. United, Div. 2); **Aug. 23, 1989** Falkirk (home to Hearts, Scottish Skol Cup 3rd. Round); **Apr. 20, 1992** Newcastle (away to Derby, Div. 2); **May 2, 1992** Bristol City (away to Watford, Div. 2); **Nov. 23, 1996**

Wycombe W. (home to Preston, Div. 2); **Feb. 8, 1997** Darlington (away to Scarborough, Div. 3).

Aug. 24, 1994: Three Sheff. United players, and one from Udinese, were sent off in the Anglo-Italian Cup at Bramall Lane on Aug. 24, 1994. In addition, United manager Dave Bassett was ordered from the bench.

Most dismissals one team, one match: Five players of America Tres Rios in first ten minutes after disputed goal by opponents Itaperuna in Brazilian cup match in Rio de Janeiro on Nov. 23, 1991. Tie then abandoned and awarded to Itaperuna.

Eight dismissals in one match: Four on each side in S. American Super Cup quarter-final (Gremio, Brazil v Penarol, Uruguay) in Oct. 1993.

Five dismissals in one season – Dave Caldwell (twice with Chesterfield, 3 times with Torquay) in 1987-88.

First instance of **four dismissals in Scottish match**: three **Rangers** players (all English – Terry Hurlock, Mark Walters, Mark Hateley) and **Celtic's** Peter Grant in Scottish Cup quarter-final at Parkhead on Mar. 17, 1991 (Celtic won 2-0).

Four players (3 Hamilton, 1 Airdrie) were sent off in Scottish Div. 1 match on Oct. 30, 1993.

Four players (3 Ayr, 1 Stranraer) were sent off in Scottish Div. 1 match on Aug. 27, 1994.

In Scottish Cup first round replays on Dec. 16, 1996, there were two instances of **three players of one side sent off**: Albion Rovers (away to Forfar) and Huntly (away to Clyde).

FASTEST SENDINGS-OFF

World record – 10 secs: Giuseppe Lorenzo (Bologna) for striking opponent in Italian League match v Parma, December 9, 1990.

Domestic – 19 secs: Mark Smith (Crewe goalkeeper at Darlington, Div. 3, Mar. 12, 1994). **In Div. 1 – 85 secs: Liam O'Brien** (Man. Utd. at Southampton, Jan. 3, 1987). **Premier League – 72 secs: Tim Flowers** (Blackburn goalkeeper v Leeds, Feb. 1, 1995).

In World Cup – 55 secs: Jose Batista (Uruguay v. Scotland at Neza, Mexico, June 13, 1986).

In European competition – 90 secs: Sergei Dirkach (Dynamo Moscow v Ghent UEFA Cup 3rd round, 2nd leg, December 11, 1991).

Fastest F.A. Cup dismissal – 52 secs: Ian Culverhouse (Swindon defender, deliberate hand-ball on goal-line, away to Everton, 3rd. Round, Sunday Jan. 5, 1997).

MOST SENDINGS-OFF IN CAREER

21 – Willie Johnston (Rangers 7, WBA 6, Vancouver Whitecaps 4, Hearts 3, Scotland 1).

WEMBLEY SENDINGS-OFF

Manchester United's **Kevin Moran** is the only player to be sent off in the F.A. Cup Final (v. Everton, 1985).

Arsenal's **Lee Dixon** became the seventh player ordered off in major soccer at Wembley when dismissed in the F.A. Cup semi-final against Tottenham (April 1993), and **Andrei Kanchelskis** (Man. U.) was sent off in the 1994 League Cup Final v Aston Villa. The others, besides Moran, Dixon and Kanchelskis:

Aug. 1948 Boris Stankovic	(Yugoslavia) v. Sweden, Olympic Games.
July 1966 Antonio Rattin	(Argentina captain) v. England, World Cup.
Aug. 1974 Billy Bremner	(Leeds) and **Kevin Keegan** (Liverpool) in F.A. Charity Shield.
Mar. 1977 Gilbert Dresch	(Luxembourg) v. England, World Cup.
June 1995 Tetsuji Hashiratani	(Japan) v. England (Umbro Cup).

In addition, four players have been sent off in **Play-off Finals** at Wembley: **Peter Swan** (Port Vale v W.B.A., 1993); two Stockport players, **Mike Wallace** and **Chris Beaumont**, against Burnley, 1994; and Brentford's **Brian Statham** against Crewe, 1997.

WEMBLEY'S SUSPENDED CAPTAINS

Suspension has prevented four **club captains** playing at Wembley in modern finals, in successive years.

Three were in F.A. Cup Finals – Glenn Roeder (Q.P.R., 1982), **Steve Foster** (Brighton, 1983) and **Wilf Rostron** (Watford, 1984) – and Sunderland's **Shaun Elliott** was barred from the 1985 Milk Cup Final.

Roeder was banned from Q.P.R.'s 1982 Cup Final replay against Tottenham, and Foster was ruled out of the first match in Brighton's 1983 Final against Manchester United.

DECISIONS REVOKED

Sendings-off cancelled by F.A. on "second evidence": **Season 1994-5** Kevin Scott (Tottenham v QPR); Alvin Martin (West Ham v Sheff. Wed.); **season 1995-6** Vinnie Jones (Wimbledon v Liverpool); Henning Berg (Blackburn v Liverpool); **season 1996-7** Paul Stewart (Sunderland v Arsenal); Chris Perkins (Chesterfield v Millwall).

BOOKINGS RECORDS

Most players of one Football League club booked in one match is **TEN** – members of the Mansfield Town team away to Crystal Palace in F.A. Cup third round, January 1963.

Fastest bookings – 3 seconds after kick-off, **Vinnie Jones** (Chelsea, home to Sheff. Utd., F.A. Cup fifth round, February 15, 1992); 5 seconds after kick-off: **Vinnie Jones** (Sheff. Utd., away to Man. City, Div. 1, January 19, 1991). He was sent-off (54 mins) for second bookable offence.

FIGHTING TEAM-MATES

Charlton's **Mick Flanagan** and **Derek Hales** were sent off for fighting each other five minutes from end of F.A. Cup 3rd Round tie at home to Southern League Maidstone on Jan. 9, 1979.

On Sept. 28, 1994 the Scottish F.A. suspended Hearts players **Graeme Hogg** and **Craig Levein** for ten matches for fighting each other in a pre-season "friendly" v Raith.

PLAYERS JAILED

Ten professional footballers found guilty of conspiracy to fraud by "fixing" matches for betting purposes were given prison sentences at Nottingham Assizes on Jan. 26, 1965.

Jimmy Gauld (Mansfield Town), described as the central figure, was given four years. Among the others sentenced, Tony Kay (Sheff. Wed., Everton & England), Peter Swan (Sheff. Wed. & England) and David "Bronco" Layne (Sheff. Wed.) were suspended from football for life by the F.A.

LONG SUSPENSIONS

The longest suspension in modern times for a player in British football was imposed on Man. United's French international captain **Eric Cantona**, following his attack on a spectator as he left the pitch after being sent off at Crystal Palace (Prem. League) on Jan. 25, 1995. He was banned from football for 8 months.

The club immediately suspended him to the end of the season and fined him 2 weeks' wages (est. £20,000). Then, on a disrepute charge, the F.A. fined him £10,000 and extended the ban to September 30 (which FIFA confirmed as world wide).

A subsequent 2-weeks' jail sentence on Cantona for assault was altered, on appeal, to 120 hours' community service, which took the form of coaching schoolboys in the Manchester area.

Mark Dennis, the Q.P.R. defender, was sent off for the 11th time in his career away to Tottenham (Div. 1) on November 14, 1987. (Two of those dismissals were for after-match tunnel offences; in addition, Dennis had then been cautioned 64 times in ten seasons and answered two disrepute charges concerning newspaper articles).

On December 10, the F.A. imposed on him a 53-day suspension, which was amended on appeal (January 25) to an 8-match ban. This was the longest suspension of a Football League player since **Kevin Keegan** (Liverpool) and **Billy Bremner** (Leeds) were each banned for 5 weeks (10 matches) after being sent off in the F.A. Charity Shield at Wembley in August 1974.

On December 6, 1988 Dennis was sent off for **12th. time** in career (Q.P.R. v. Fulham reserves) and fined £1,000.

Steve Walsh (Leicester) has been sent off 12 times in his 15-season career (4 times with Wigan, 8 with Leicester; 11 times in League, once in F.A. Cup; 11 times away, once at home). His latest dismissal was away to West Ham on Oct. 19, 1996.

Before the disciplinary points system was introduced in season 1972-73, offenders were suspended for a specific number of weeks. Other lengthy suspensions imposed by the F.A. for on-field offences:

November 1969: Derek Dougan (Wolves) 8 weeks; **John Fitzpatrick** (Man. Utd.) 8 weeks.

January 1970: Ronnie Rees (Nott'm Forest) 6 weeks; **George Best** (Man. Utd.) 6 weeks.

December 1971: Kevin Lewis (Man. United) 5 months; **Denis Hollywood** and **Brian O'Neil** (both Southampton) 9 weeks.

October 1987: Steve Walsh (Leicester) 9 matches – original ban of 6 games (following the sixth sending-off of his career) increased to 9 when he reached 21 disciplinary points.

April 1988: Chris Kamara (Swindon) suspended to end of season (6 matches).

October 1988: Paul Davis (Arsenal) suspended for 9 matches, and fined a record £3,000, for breaking jaw of Glen Cockerill (Southampton).

January 1992: Frank Sinclair (Chelsea) suspended for 9 matches (fined £600) after being found guilty of assault on referee while playing for W.B.A. on loan.

January 1993: Alan Gough, Fulham goalkeeper, suspended for 42 days by F.A. for assaulting referee in Autoglass Trophy match at Gillingham on December 8.

November 1994: Andy Townsend (Aston Villa) suspended for 6 matches (3 for 21 discip. points, 3 for sending-off).

Seven-month ban: Frank Barson, 37-year-old Watford centre-half, sent off at home to Fulham (Div. 3 South) on September 29, 1928, was suspended by the F.A. for the remainder of the season.

Twelve-month ban: Oldham Athletic full-back **Billy Cook** was given a 12-month suspension for refusing to leave the field when sent off at Middlesbrough (Div. 1), on April 3, 1915. The referee abandoned the match with 35 minutes still to play, and the score (4-1 to Middlesbrough) was ordered to stand.

Long Scottish ban: Billy McLafferty, Stenhousemuir striker, was banned (April 14) for 8½ months, to Jan. 1, 1993, and fined £250 for failing to appear at a disciplinary hearing after being sent off against Arbroath on Feb. 1.

Twelve-match ban: On May 12, 1994 Scottish F.A. suspended then Rangers forward **Duncan Ferguson** for 12 matches for violent conduct v Raith on Apr. 16. On Oct. 11, 1995, Ferguson (then with Everton) sent to jail for 3 months for the assault (served 44 days); Feb. 1, 1996 Scottish judge quashed 7 months that remained of SFA ban on Ferguson.

FINES ETC. – MODERN

For space reasons, this section has been condensed. Fuller details appeared seasonally in previous Annuals.

1988 (July) **Chelsea** fined record £75,000 by F.A. following serious crowd trouble at play-off v Middlesbrough in May.

1988 (November) League fine **Tottenham** £15,000 for failing to fulfil opening-day fixture v Coventry (ground not ready after close-season improvements).

1989 (February) **Brian Clough**, Nott'm. F. manager, fined £5,000 by F.A. (and banned from touchline for rest of season) for striking spectators at League Cup quarter-final v Q.P.R.

1989 (March) **Wimbledon** fined £10,000 by F.A. for making unauthorised loans to players.

1989 (June) League fine **Bradford City** £10,000 for poaching manager Terry Yorath from Swansea. **1989** (November) **Paul McGrath** (Aston Villa) fined £8,500 by F.A. (record for disrepute charge against player) following newspaper criticism of former club, Man. United. F.A. fine **Norwich** £50,000, **Arsenal** £20,000 following player-brawl at Highbury.

1989 (December) **West Ham** and **Wimbledon** each fined £20,000 after player-brawl at League Cup-tie.

1990 (February) **Swindon Town** fined £7,500 by F.A., their former manager **Lou Macari** £1,000 and censured, their chairman **Brian Hillier** suspended from football for 3 years for breach of rules re betting on matches (Newcastle v Swindon, F.A. Cup 4th. Round, Jan. 1988).

1990 (June) **Swindon Town** (promoted to Div.1 via play-offs) demoted to Div. 3, then, on appeal, to Div. 2, by League after pleading guilty to 36 charges of irregular payments to players over four-year period.

1990 (September) **Chesterfield** fined £12,500 by League for failing to fulfil League Cup-tie when hit by injuries.

1990 (November) F.A. deduct 2 League points from **Arsenal**, 1 from **Man. United** and fine both clubs £50,000, following mass player-brawl at Old Trafford.

1991 (January) League fine **Chelsea** record £105,000 for making illegal payments to three players.

1991 (April) League fine **Tottenham** £20,000 (£15,000 of it suspended) for late arrival at Chelsea.

1991 (November) League fine **Tottenham** £17,500 for late payment of transfer instalment to Chelsea for Gordon Durie.

1992 (January) **Birmingham** fined £10,000 by League for fielding ineligible player.

1992 (February) F.A. fine **Michael Thomas** (Liverpool) £3,000 for press criticism of his former manager George Graham (Arsenal).

1992 (April) F. A. fine **Birmingham** £50,000 (suspended to end of season 1992-3) after pitch invasion v Stoke.

1992 (August) F.A. fine **Southampton** £20,000 (£15,000 suspended) for previous season's disciplinary record (5 sent off, 80 cautions, 11 suspensions). F.A. fine **Kevin Keegan** (Newcastle manager) £1,000 on disrepute charge (assistant **Terry McDermott** fined £250) for comments to referee at Derby, April 20. F.A. warn **Kenny Dalglish** (Blackburn manager) on disrepute charge for comments to referee v Wolves, April 14.

1992 (October) *F.A. ban **Gordon Durie** (Tottenham) 3 matches for "feigning injury" v Coventry, Aug. 18 (*ban quashed by F.A. Appeal Board, Dec. 16).

1992 (November) F.A give **Joe Kinnear** (Wimbledon manager) 5-match touchline ban and £750 fine (suspended) for comments to referee at Blackburn, Sept. 19. F.A. fine **Vinnie Jones** (Wimbledon) record individual sum of £20,000 on disrepute charge for narrating "Soccer's hard men" video; Jones also given 6-month playing ban (suspended for 3 years). **Barnet** fined £50,000 by F. League after investigation into club's financial affairs.

1993 (January) Sequel to League match at Tottenham, Dec. 12: F.A. fine Arsenal manager **George Graham** £500 for remarks to referee, suspend **Ian Wright** for 3 matches for throwing punch at opponent.

1993 (March) F.A. fine **Martin Allen** (West Ham) £1,000 (4-match ban) as season's first player to reach 41 discip. points (12 bookings). F.A. fine **Eric Cantona** (Man. U.) £1,000 for spitting at spectators at Leeds, Feb. 8.

1993 (April) F.A. fine **Vinnie Jones** (Wimbledon) £1,000 (4-match ban) for reaching 41 discip. points (his 4th suspension of season). F.A. fine **Man. City** £50,000 (suspended) following F.A. Cup 6th Round pitch invasion v Tottenham, March 7. **Graeme Souness** (Liverpool manager) fined £500 by F.A. and warned for "insulting behaviour" to referee at Crystal Palace, March 23.

1993 (May) League fine **Barnet** £25,000 for irregular payment to player, and warn that further indiscretion could cost them League status.

1993 (August) F.A. fine **Ian Wright** (Arsenal) £5,000 for 'improper gesture' to linesman at F.A. Cup Final replay v Sheff. Wed.. F.A. punish clubs for poor disap. records, season 1992-3: **Southampton** fined £25,000 (suspended), £10,000 of prev. year's fine activated; **Wimbledon** £25,000 (suspended); **Sheff. Utd.** £20,000 (suspended).

1993 (October) F.A. fine **Jim Smith** (Portsmouth manager) £750 for 'insulting comments to referee'; UEFA fine **Cardiff** £1,000 for coin-throwing incident v Standard Liege (CWC).

1993 (November) F.A. fine **Tottenham** £25,000 for 'poaching' manager Ossie Ardiles from WBA. F. League fine **Watford** £10,000 for illegal approach when signing manager Glenn Roeder from Gillingham. UEFA fine **Aberdeen** £4,500 and **Man. U.** £2,260 for offences at European matches. F.A. fine **Bristol C.** £40,000 (£30,000 suspended for 2 years) for improper claims to Football Trust over ground improvements. F.A. fine **Aston Villa** and **Notts Co.** £30,000 each for breach of rules when signing players from Australia.

1994 (January) FIFA fine **Welsh F.A.** £7,055 over incident at Wales-Romania World Cup match in which fan killed by rocket-flare.

1994 (February) F. League fine **Birmingham** £55,000 for 'poaching' manager Barry Fry from Southend.

1994 (March) F.A. fine **Sunderland** £5,000 for 'poaching' Mick Buxton (manager) from Huddersfield. Welsh F.A. fine **Cardiff** £25,000, **Swansea** £30,000 (suspended to season's end) for crowd trouble in match at Cardiff, Dec. 22. **Alex Ferguson** (Man. U. manager) fined £250 by F.A. for remarks to referee at 'A' team match.

1994 (April) F.A. Premier League fine **Everton** record £75,000 (plus £50,000 compensation) for 'poaching' manager Mike Walker from Norwich.

1994 (June) In heaviest punishment ever handed out by F.A., **Tottenham** fined £600,000, deducted 12 Premiership points at start of season 1994-5 and banned from F.A. Cup for same season for 'financial irregularities' involving loans to players during previous administration at club (see Dec. 1994 re appeal). F.A. give **Millwall** 3 sentences (first 2 suspended for 2 years) after crowd trouble at play-off v Derby: fined £100,000; ordered to play 2 matches behind closed doors; 3 League points deducted if further disturbances, home or away, before Dec. 31.

1994 (July) F.A. Appeals Board reduce **Tottenham's** 12-point deduction to 6 points, increase fine from £600,000 to £1.5m., confirm F.A. Cup ban.

1994 (September) F.A. fine **Ian Wright** (Arsenal) £750 for making "gestures' to fans at Q.P.R., April 27.

1994 (October) Football League fine **Preston** £2,500 for late arrival at Darlington (Aug. 13). UEFA fine **Aston Villa** £12,500 for pitch invasion, home to Inter Milan (UEFA Cup, Sept. 29).

1994 (November) UEFA fine **Aston Villa** £9,367 for pitch invasion after UEFA home leg v Trabzonspor (Nov. 1). F.A. fine **Des Walker** (Sheff. W.) £1,200, plus 3-match ban, for head-butting opponent v Ipswich (Nov. 16). F.A. fine **John Fashanu** (Aston Vila) (£6,000) on misconduct charge (newspaper criticism of Eric Cantona (Man. U.).

1994 (December – see June, July) Tribunal annuls 6-point penalty imposed on **Tottenham** and re-instates them in F.A. Cup.

1994 (December) F.A. suspend **Paul Merson** (Arsenal) 2 months from senior football while under treatment for drug abuse.

1995 (January) F.A. fines: **Ian Wright** (Arsenal) £1,000 (4-match ban) for reaching 41 discip. points; **Terry Hurlock** (Fulham) £350, with total 6-week ban for 51 discip. points; **Alan Ball** (Southampton manager) £500 for comments to linesman at Q.P.R. (Dec. 28); **Joe Jordan** (Bristol C. manager) £250 for remarks to match official; **Martin Edwards** (Man. U. Chairman) £100 for remarks to referee at Arsenal (Nov. 26).

1995 (March) League fine **Sunderland** £2,500 for fielding ineligible player (Dominic Matteo, loan transfer from Liverpool registered after transfer deadline). F.A. fines (for 41 discip. points): **Steve Bruce** (Man. U.) £750 and 2-match ban; **Mike Milligan** (Norwich) £500 and 2-match ban; **Francis Benali** (Southampton) £350 and 3-match ban.

1995 (April) F.A. fines: **Robbie Fowler** (Liverpool) £1,000 for hitching shorts to spectators at Leicester, Dec. 26; **Tim Sherwood** (Blackburn) £1,000 and 1-match ban (41 discip. points); **Ken Monkou** (Southampton) £350 and 1-match ban (41 discip. points); **Joe Kinnear** (Wimbledon manager) £1,500 and 6-month touchline ban to Oct. 31 on misconduct charges (verbal abuse of referees); **Vinnie Jones** (Wimbledon) £1,750 on misconduct charge (swearing at Newcastle manager Kevin Keegan after match); **Terry Hurlock** (Fulham) £400 and 4-match suspension (totalling 15-game ban in 1994-5) as first player to reach 61 discip. points in a season.

1995 (May) F.A. fines: **Gary Neville** (Man. U.) and **Carlton Palmer** (Sheff. W.) each £1,000 (41 discip. points); **Roy Keane** (Man. U.) £5,000 on disrepute charge after being sent off in F.A. Cup s-final v Crystal P.

1995 (August) F.A. give suspended fines to 5 clubs for previous season's poor disciplinary records: QPR (£25,000), Wimbledon (£25,000), Burnley (£10,000), Chester (£10,000), Fulham (£10,000).

1995 (September) UEFA suspend **Vinnie Jones** (Wales) for 5 matches (sent off v Georgia, June); UEFA fine **Rangers** £2,500 for supporters' misconduct in Cyprus (E. Cup, August).

1995 (October) F.A. suspend **Julian Dicks** (West Ham) 3 matches on disrepute charge (alleged stamping on Chelsea's John Spencer, Sept. 11).

1995 (November) UEFA fine **Chelsea** £17,000 for misconduct by "unofficial" supporters away to Real Zaragoza (CWC Sf, April 6); F.A. fine **Robert Fleck** (Norwich) £1,000 for abuse of official at Sheff. Utd., Sept. 9); Blackburn fine **Graeme Le Saux** and **David Batty** for brawling away to Spartak Moscow (E. Champions' League, Nov. 22); **UEFA suspend** Le Saux and Batty each for 2 European club matches.

1995 (December) F.A. fine **Bournemouth** £5,000 (suspended) following crowd trouble v Crewe (Sept. 16).

1996 (January) **Tottenham** and **Wimbledon** each given 1-year Euro ban (active for 5 years) by UEFA for fielding weak team in last summer's Inter Toto Cup; on appeal, UEFA quash ban, impose fines instead – **Tottenham** £90,000, **Wimbledon** £60,000 (Premier League's 20 clubs each to pay £9,000 to cover fines/costs. F.A. fine **Man. United** £20,000 for illegal approach to 17-year-old David Brown (Oldham). F.A. fine **Bryan Robson** (Mid'bro' player-manager) £750 and Boro' players **Neil Cox** and **Nigel Pearson** each £500 for abusive remarks to referee at Blackburn, Dec. 16.

1996 (February) Leyton Orient sack **Roger Stanislaus** after F.A. ban him for 12 months – first British-based player to test positive for taking performance-enhancing drug, cocaine-related). F.A. fine **Vinnie Jones** £2,000 (his 5th. large fine in 3 years) for newspaper attack on Chelsea's Ruud Gullit and foreign players generally; F.A. fine **Gary Megson** (Norwich manager) £1,000 on disrepute charge (incident at Derby, Jan. 1).

1996 (March) F.A. fine **Keith Curle** (Man. City) £500 for remarks made to referee (v Everton, Feb. 10).

1996 (April) F.A. fine **Mark Hughes** (Chelsea) £1,000, plus 2-match ban, for reaching 45 discip. points (his third suspension of season); F.A. fine **Mark Ford** (Leeds) £75, with 1-match ban (45 discip. points); **Faustino Asprilla** (Newcastle) fined £10,000 by F.A. and banned from first match 1996-7, on misconduct charges for elbowing/head-butting Keith Curle (Man. City) at Maine Road, Feb. 24 (Curle cleared).

1996 (August) F.A. fine **Neil Ruddock** (Liverpool) £2,000 for exceeding 45 discip. points last season. F.A. fine **Q.P.R.** £25,000 (plus £50,000 suspended) **Wimbledon** £10,000 for prev. season's discip. record and gave suspended fines to 9 clubs: **Mid'bro'** and **Man. C.** each £25,000; **Portsmouth, Luton, Millwall, Gillingham, Burnley, Hartlepool** each £25,000; **Doncaster** £6,000.

1996 (September) **Sunderland** fined £1,000 for fielding suspended Alex Rae in pre-season reserve match.

1996 (October) F.A. fine **Gary Poole** (Birmingham) £1,000, plus 4-match suspensions, for assault on referee at Man. City, Sept. 1; F.A. fine **Bryan Robson** (Mid'bro' manager) £1,500 for remarks to referee at Nott'm. F., Aug. 24; F.A. fine **Graeme Souness** (So'ton manager) £750 for remarks to referee at Leicester, Aug. 21; F.A. fine **Gordon Strachan** (Coventry asst-manager) £2,000 for refusing to leave field when sent off in reserve game; F.A. fine Coventry manager **Ron Atkinson** £750 for remarks to referee at same match.

1996 (November) F.A. fine **Mark Bosnich** (A. Villa goalkeeper) £1,000 for making "Hitler salute" gesture to crowd at Tottenham, Oct. 12; F.A. fine **Liam Daish** (Coventry) £500 for clash with female steward at Chelsea, Aug. 24.

1996 (December) F.A. dock **Brighton** 2 points after pitch invasions v Lincoln, Oct. 1.

1997 (January) Premier League dock **Mid'bro'** 3 points (plus £50,000 fine) for refusing to play at Blackburn, Dec. 21, through injuries; F.A. fine **Gary Megson** (Blackpool manager) £500 for remarks to referee at Millwall, Oct. 30.

1997 (February) F.A. fine **Denis Smith** (Oxford manager) £250 for remarks to match officials v Wolves, Dec. 26; F.A. fine **Neil Lennon** (Leicester) £500 for obscene gestures to Newcastle fans, Oct. 26.

1997 (March) F.A. fine **Norwich** and **Crystal P.** £40,000 each (£30,000 of it suspended until June 1998) after player-brawl at Norwich, Dec. 14; UEFA fine **Man. Utd.** £2,600 after flare thrown on pitch at home to Porto (E. Cup q. final/1); UEFA fine **Robbie Fowler** (Liverpool) £900 for wearing politically motivated under-shirt at CWC q. final/2 v Brann.

1997 (April) F.A. fine **Bolton** £40,000 (£30,000 susp.) and **Wolves** £30,000 (£22,500 susp.) after player-brawl at Bolton, Jan. 18; F.A. fine **Stevenage Borough** (Conf.) £25,000 (susp. 2 years) for seeking £30,000 "bung" from Torquay.

1997 (May) F.A. fine **Billy McKinlay** (Blackburn) £750, **Robbie Mustoe** (Mid'bro') £500 for reaching 45 discip. points in season.

1997 (June) F.A. fine **Plymouth** £30,000 (£22,500 susp.) and **Chesterfield** £20,000 (£15,000 susp.) for player-brawl at Chesterfield, Feb. 22.

1997 (July) F.A. fine **Ian Wright** (Arsenal) £15,000 for remarks made to referee v Blackburn (April 19) and gestures to crowd at Coventry (April 21). He is severely warned as to his future conduct.

MANAGERS

INTERNATIONAL RECORDS
(As at start of season 1997-98)

	P	W	D	L	F	A
Glenn Hoddle	11	9	0	2	18	4
(England – appointed June 1996)						
Bryan Hamilton	28	8	8	12	33	36
(N. Ireland – appointed Feb. 1994)						
Craig Brown	35	18	6	11	42	26
(Scotland – appointed Sept. 1993)						
Bobby Gould	13	4	3	6	18	20
(Wales – appointed Aug. 1995)						
Mick McCarthy	15	4	4	7	24	18
(Rep. of Ireland – appointed Feb. 1996)						

ENGLAND'S MANAGERS

1946-62:	**Walter Winterbottom** (P139, W78, D33, L28).
1963-74:	**Sir Alf Ramsey** (P113, W69, D27, L17).
1974:	**Caretaker – Joe Mercer** (P7, W3, D3, L1).
1974-77:	**Don Revie** (P29, W14, D8, L7).
1977-82:	**Ron Greenwood** (P55, W33, D12, L10).
1982-90:	**Bobby Robson** (P95, W47, D30, L18).
1990-93:	**Graham Taylor** (P38, W18, D13, L7).
1994-96:	**Terry Venables**, coach (P23, W11, D11, L1).
1996-97:	**Glenn Hoddle**, coach (P11, W9, L2).

INTERNATIONAL MANAGER CHANGES

England: Walter Winterbottom 1946-62 (initially coach); **Alf Ramsey** (Feb. 1963-May 1974); **Joe Mercer** (caretaker May 1974); **Don Revie** (July 1974-July 1977); **Ron Greenwood** (Aug. 1977-July 1982); **Bobby Robson** (July 1982-July 1990); **Graham Taylor** (July 1990-Nov. 1993); **Terry Venables**, coach (Jan. 1994-June 1996); **Glenn Hoddle**, coach (from June 1996).

N. Ireland (modern): Billy Bingham (1967-Aug. 1971); **Terry Neill** (Aug. 1971-Mar. 1975); **Dave Clements** (Player-Manager Mar. 1975-1976); **Danny Blanchflower** (June 1976-Nov. 1979); **Billy Bingham** (Feb. 1980-Nov. 1993); **Bryan Hamilton** (since Feb. 1994).

Scotland (modern): Bobby Brown (Feb. 1967-July 1971); **Tommy Docherty** (Sept. 1971- Dec. 1972); **Willie Ormond** (Jan. 1973-May 1977); **Ally MacLeod** (May 1977-Sept.1978); **Jock Stein** (Oct. 1978-Sept. 1985); **Alex Ferguson** (caretaker Oct. 1985-June 1986); **Andy Roxburgh**, coach (July 1986-Sept. 1993); **Craig Brown** (since Sept. 1993).

Wales (modern): Mike Smith (July 1974-Dec. 1979); **Mike England** (Mar. 1980-Feb. 1988); **David Williams** (caretaker Mar. 1988); **Terry Yorath** (Apr. 1988-Nov. 1993); **John Toshack** (Mar. 1994, one match); **Mike Smith** (Mar. 1994-June 1995); **Bobby Gould** (since Aug. 1995).

Rep. of Ireland (modern): Liam Tuohy (Sept. 1971-Nov. 1972); **Johnny Giles** (Oct. 1973-Apr. 1980, initially player-manager); **Eoin Hand** (June 1980-Nov. 1985); **Jack Charlton** (Feb. 1986-Dec. 1995); **Mick McCarthy** (since Feb. 1996).

VENABLES' 11-WIN START

Terry Venables took his record as Australia's national coach to 11 wins out of 11 (goals 39-4) when they beat New Zealand 2-0 in Sydney on July 6. The Socceroos are within two matches of qualifying for the 1998 World Cup Finals. They meet the country who finish fourth in the Asia Zone in a home-and-away play-off in November.

This is Venables' 100 per cent record: Jan. 18 Australia 1, New Zealand 0; Jan. 22 Australia 2, South Korea 1; Jan. 25 Australia 1, Norway 0; Mar. 12 Macedonia 0, Australia 1; apr. 2 Hungary 1, Australia 3; **World Cup**: June 11 Australia 13, Solomon Islands 0; June 13 Australia 5, Tahiti 0; June 17 Solomon Islands 2, Australia 6; June 19 Tahiti 0, Australia 2; June 28 New Zealand 0, Australia 3; July 6 Australia 2, New Zealand 0.

LONGEST-SERVING LEAGUE MANAGERS – ONE CLUB

Fred Everiss, secretary-manager of W.B.A. for 46 years (1902-48); since last war, **Sir Matt Busby**, in charge of Man. United for 26 seasons (Oct 1945-June 1971); **Jimmy Seed** at Charlton for 23 years (1933-56).

SHORT-TERM MANAGERS

		Departed
3 Days	Bill Lambton (Scunthorpe United)	April 1959
7 Days	Tim Ward (Exeter City)	March 1953
7 Days	Kevin Cullis (Swansea City)	February 1996
13 Days	Johnny Cochrane (Reading)	April 1939
16 Days	Jimmy McIlroy (Bolton Wanderers)	November 1970
20 Days	Paul Went (Leyton Orient)	October 1981
28 Days	Tommy Docherty (Q.P.R.)	December 1968
32 Days	Steve Coppell (Man. City)	November 1996
41 Days	Steve Wicks (Lincoln City)	October 1995
44 Days	Brian Clough (Leeds United)	September 1974
44 Days	Jock Stein (Leeds United)	October 1978
48 Days	John Toshack (Wales)	March 1994
49 Days	Brian Little (Wolves)	October 1986
61 Days	Bill McGarry (Wolves)	November 1985
63 Days	Dave Booth (Peterborough United)	January 1991

● In May 1984, Crystal Palace named **Dave Bassett** as manager, but he changed his mind four days later, without signing the contract, and returned to Wimbledon.

EARLY-SEASON MANAGER SACKINGS

1996 Sammy Chung (Doncaster) on morning of season's opening League match; **1996** Alan Ball (Man. City) 12 days; **1994** Kenny Hibbitt (Walsall) and Kenny Swain (Wigan) 20 days; **1993** Peter Reid (Man. C.) 12 days; **1991** Don Mackay (Blackburn) 14 days; **1989** Mick Jones (Peterborough) 12 days; **1980** Bill McGarry (Newcastle) 13 days; **1979** Dennis Butler (Port Vale) 12 days; **1977** George Petchey (Leyton O.) 13 days; **1977** Willie Bell (Birmingham) 16 days; **1971** Len Richley (Darlington) 12 days.

FEWEST MANAGERS

West Ham United have had only eight managers in their history: Syd King, Charlie Paynter, Ted Fenton, Ron Greenwood, John Lyall, Lou Macari, Billy Bonds and Harry Redknapp.

RECORD START FOR MANAGER

Arsenal were unbeaten in 17 League matches from the start of season 1947-8 under new manager Tom Whittaker.

MANAGER DOUBLES

Four managers have won the League Championship with different clubs: **Tom Watson**, secy-manager with Sunderland (1892-3-5) and Liverpool (1901); **Herbert Chapman** with Huddersfield Town (1923-4, 1924-5) and Arsenal (1930-1, 1932-3); **Brian Clough** with Derby County (1971-2) and Nottingham Forest (1977-8); **Kenny Dalglish** with Liverpool (1985-6, 1987-8, 1989-90) and Blackburn (1994-5).

Only manager to win the F.A. Cup with different clubs: **Billy Walker** (Sheff. Wed. 1935, Nott'm. Forest 1959).

Kenny Dalglish (Liverpool) is the only man to achieve the Championship/F.A. Cup double as both player and manager.

FIRST CHAIRMAN-MANAGER

On December 20, 1988, after two years on the board, Dundee United manager **Jim McLean** was elected chairman, too. Scotland's longest-serving manager (appointed by United on November 24, 1971) resigned at end of season 1992-3 (remained chairman).

FIRST DIV (Old)/PREM. LGE. PLAYER–MANAGERS

Les Allen (Q.P.R. 1968-9); **Johnny Giles** (W.B.A. 1976-7); **Howard Kendall** (Everton 1981-2); **Kenny Dalglish** (Liverpool, 1985-90); **Trevor Francis** (Q.P.R., 1988-9); **Terry Butcher** (Coventry, 1990-1), **Peter Reid** (Man. City, 1990-93), **Trevor Francis** (Sheff. Wed., 1991-4), **Glenn Hoddle** (Chelsea, 1993-5), **Bryan Robson** (Middlesbrough, 1994-7), **Ray Wilkins** (Q.P.R., 1994-6), **Ruud Gullit** (Chelsea, since August 1996).

FIRST FOREIGN MANAGER TO WIN F.A. CUP

Ruud Gullit, Chelsea 1997.

MANAGERS OF POST-WAR CHAMPIONS

1947 George Kay (Liverpool); **1948** Tom Whittaker (Arsenal); **1949** Bob Jackson (Portsmouth); **1950** Bob Jackson (Portsmouth); **1951** Arthur Rowe (Tottenham); **1952** Matt Busby (Man. United); **1953** Tom Whittaker (Arsenal).

1954 Stan Cullis (Wolves); **1955** Ted Drake (Chelsea); **1956** Matt Busby (Man. United); **1957** Matt Busby (Man. United); **1958** Stan Cullis (Wolves); **1959** Stan Cullis (Wolves); **1960** Harry Potts (Burnley).

1961 *Bill Nicholson (Tottenham); **1962** Alf Ramsey (Ipswich); **1963** Harry Catterick (Everton); **1964** Bill Shankly (Liverpool); **1965** Matt Busby (Man. United); **1966** Bill Shankly (Liverpool); **1967** Matt Busby (Man United).

1968 Joe Mercer (Man. City); **1969** Don Revie (Leeds); **1970** Harry Catterick (Everton); **1971** *Bertie Mee (Arsenal); **1972** Brian Clough (Derby); **1973** Bill Shankly (Liverpool); **1974** Don Revie (Leeds).

1975 Dave Mackay (Derby); **1976** Bob Paisley (Liverpool); **1977** Bob Paisley (Liverpool); **1978** Brian Clough (Nott'm. Forest); **1979** Bob Paisley (Liverpool); **1980** Bob Paisley (Liverpool); **1981** Ron Saunders (Aston Villa).

1982 Bob Paisley (Liverpool); **1983** Bob Paisley (Liverpool); **1984** Joe Fagan (Liverpool); **1985** Howard Kendall (Everton); **1986** *Kenny Dalglish (Liverpool – player/manager); **1987** Howard Kendall (Everton).

1988 Kenny Dalglish (Liverpool – player/manager); **1989** George Graham (Arsenal); **1990** Kenny Dalglish (Liverpool); **1991** George Graham (Arsenal); **1992**

Howard Wilkinson (Leeds); **1993** Alex Ferguson (Man. United); **1994** *Alex Ferguson (Man. United); **1995** Kenny Dalglish (Blackburn); **1996** *Alex Ferguson (Man. United); **1997** Alex Ferguson (Man. United).

(* Double winners)

ALEX FERGUSON TOP ANGLO MANAGER

With 19 major prizes **Alex Ferguson** has the most successful managerial record with Scottish and English clubs combined. At **Aberdeen** (1978-86) he won ten top prizes: 3 Scottish Championships, 4 Scottish Cups, 1 Scottish League Cup, 1 Cup-Winners' Cup, 1 European Super Cup.

With **Manchester United** he has won 9 major trophies in the last 8 seasons: 1990 F.A. Cup, 1991 Cup-Winners' Cup, 1992 League Cup, 1993 League Championship, 1994 League Championship and F.A. Cup, 1996 Championship and F.A. Cup; 1997 Championship.

MOST SUCCESSFUL ENGLISH-CLUB MANAGER

Bob Paisley, with 20 trophies for Liverpool (1974-83): 6 League Championships, 3 European Cups, 3 League Cups, 1 UEFA Cup, 1 European Super Cup, 6 Charity Shields (1 shared).

RELEGATION 'DOUBLES'

Managers associated with two clubs relegated in same season: **John Bond** in 1985-6 (Swansea and Birmingham); **Ron Saunders** in 1985-6 (W.B.A. and Birmingham); **Bob Stokoe** in 1986-7 (Carlisle and Sunderland); **Billy McNeill** in 1986-7 (Man. City and Aston Villa); **Dave Bassett** in 1987-8 (Watford and Sheff. Utd.).

WEMBLEY STADIUM

Wembley was successful over Manchester (Dec. 1996) in their bid to become England's new national sports stadium. Rebuilding is due to start after the 1999 F.A. Cup Final, with completion aimed at the Final in 2002.

Only the famous Twin Towers (re-sited) will remain. Construction of the 80,000 all-seat stadium will cost an estimated £180m., of which £100m. will come from the National Lottery and the balance from private sector sponsors.

Plans for the new "stadium of dreams" include a retractable roof, and rail station with direct link to the Channel Tunnel.

Over the past decade, more than £80m. was spent on transforming the stadium that opened in 1923 into an arena to match its "Venue of Legends" slogan.

Improvements included the conversion to all-seating (capacity 80,000) in season 1989-90, construction of the Olympic Gallery (capacity 4,000) that encircles the stadium, installation of modern box office and walkways linking Wembley Park station to the ground.

Wembley's charisma was rewarded in May 1992 with the allocation of a fifth European Cup Final.

ORIGINAL CONTRACT

The **Empire Stadium** was built at a cost of **£750,000**. Its construction included 25,000 tons of concrete, 2,000 tons of steel and 104 turnstiles. The original contract (May 1921) between the F.A. and the British Empire Exhibition was for the Cup Final to be played there for 21 years.

INVASION DAY

Memorable scenes were witnessed at the **first F.A. Cup Final at Wembley, April 28, 1923**, between **Bolton Wanderers** and **West Ham United**. An accurate return of the attendance could not be made owing to thousands breaking in, but there were probably more than 150,000 spectators present. The match was delayed for 40 minutes owing to the crowd invading the playing pitch. Official attendance was 126,047.

Gate receipts totalled £27,776. The two clubs and the Football Association each received £6,365 and the F.A. refunded £2,797 to ticket-holders who were unable to get to their seats. Admission has since been by ticket only.

ENGLAND THERE UNTIL 2002

Under an agreement signed in 1983, the Football Association are contracted to playing **England's home matches***, the F.A. Cup Final and Charity Shield at Wembley Stadium until 2002.

* Exceptions were v Sweden (Umbro Cup) at Elland Road, Leeds, on June 8, 1995 – first England home game played away from Wembley since Poland at Goodison Park on Jan. 5, 1966 – and the match v S. Africa at Old Trafford on May 24, 1997.

England previously played elsewhere on their own soil on May 12, 1973, when they met N. Ireland on Everton's ground. Officially, that was a home fixture for Ireland, but the venue was switched from Belfast for security reasons.

MODERN CAPACITY

Capacity of the now all-seated **Wembley Stadium** is 80,000. The last 100,000 attendance was for the 1985 F.A. Cup Final between Man. United and Everton.

WEMBLEY'S FIRST UNDER LIGHTS

November 30, 1955 (England 4, Spain 1), when the floodlights were switched on after 73 minutes (afternoon match played in damp, foggy conditions).
First Wembley International played throughout under lights: England 8, N. Ireland 3 on evening of November 20, 1963 (att: 55,000).

WEMBLEY HAT-TRICKS

Three players have scored hat-tricks in major finals at Wembley: **Stan Mortensen** for Blackpool v Bolton (F.A. Cup Final, 1953), **Geoff Hurst** for England v West Germany (World Cup Final, 1966) and **David Speedie** for Chelsea v Man. City (Full Members Cup, 1985).

ENGLAND'S WEMBLEY DEFEATS

England have lost 15 matches to foreign opponents at Wembley:

Nov.	1953	3-6 v Hungary	Oct.	1982	1-2 v W. Germany
Oct.	1959	2-3 v Sweden	Sept.	1983	0-1 v Denmark
Oct.	1965	2-3 v Austria	June	1984	0-2 v Russia
Apr.	1972	1-3 v W. Germany	May	1990	1-2 v Uruguay
Nov.	1973	0-1 v Italy	Sept.	1991	0-1 v Germany
Feb.	1977	0-2 v Holland	June	1995	1-3 v Brazil
Mar.	1981	1-2 v Spain	Feb.	1997	0-1 v Italy
May	1981	0-1 v Brazil			

A sixteenth defeat came in **Euro 96**. After drawing the semi-final with Germany 1-1, England went out 6-5 on penalties.

FASTEST GOALS AT WEMBLEY

In first-class matches: **38 seconds** by **Bryan Robson** in England's 2-1 win against Yugoslavia on December 13, 1989; **44 seconds** by **Bryan Robson** for England in 4-0 win v N. Ireland on February 23, 1982; **42 seconds** by **Roberto di Matteo** for Chelsea in the 1997 F.A. Cup Final v Middlesbrough.

Fastest goal in **any** match at Wembley: **20 seconds** by **Maurice Cox** for Cambridge University against Oxford on December 5, 1979.

FOUR WEMBLEY HEADERS

When **Wimbledon** beat Sutton United 4-2 in the F.A. Amateur Cup Final at Wembley on May 4, 1963, Irish centre-forward **Eddie Reynolds** headed all four goals.

ENGLAND POSTPONEMENT

Fog at Wembley on November 21, 1979 caused England's European Championship match against Bulgaria to be postponed 24 hours.

WEMBLEY ONE-SEASON DOUBLES

In 1989, **Nottingham Forest** became the first club to win two Wembley Finals in the same season (Littlewoods Cup and Simod Cup).

In 1993, **Arsenal** made history there as the first club to win the League (Coca-Cola) Cup and the F.A. Cup in the same season. They beat Sheffield Wednesday 2-1 in both finals.

SUDDEN DEATH DECIDERS

First Wembley Final decided on sudden death (first goal scored in overtime): April 23, 1995 – **Birmingham** beat Carlisle (1-0, Paul Tait 103 mins.) to win Auto Windscreens Shield.

First instance of a "golden goal" deciding a major International tournament was at Wembley on June 30, 1996, when **Germany** beat the Czech Republic 2-1 in the European Championship Final with Oliver Bierhoff's goal in the 95th. minute.

DOWN WEMBLEY'S MEMORY LANE

April 1923	Wembley's first Cup Final (Bolton 2, West Ham 0). The new stadium's capacity is officially 126,000 but more than 200,000 get in.
April 1938	Preston's George Mutch sends a penalty in off the underside of the crossbar in the last seconds of extra time – the only goal of the Cup Final against Huddersfield.
May 1953	"The Matthews Final," plus a hat-trick by Stan Mortensen in Blackpool's 4-3 win against Bolton.
May 1961	Tottenham (2-0 v Leicester) do more than win the Cup – they complete the first Double this century.
April 1961	England's record victory over Scotland (9-3), their tally topped by a hat-trick from Jimmy Greaves.
July 1966	Alf Ramsey's England win the World Cup, dramatically beating West Germany 4-2 in extra time. The Queen presents football's greatest prize to Bobby Moore, and there's a knighthood for Alf.
May 1968	Matt Busby's dream comes true: Manchester United 4, Benfica 1 in the European Cup Final.
May 1973	Second Division Sunderland shock Leeds in the Cup Final. Has Wembley seen a greater save than Jim Montgomery's that keeps out a "certain" goal by Peter Lorimer?

June 1977	Scotland beat England 2-1 in the Home Championship and their fans go wild, invading the field, pulling down the goalposts and tearing up the pitch.
May 1996	Manchester United beat Liverpool for a record ninth F.A. Cup triumph and become the first English club to do the Double twice.
June 1996	England are just short of reaching the European Championship Final – beaten 6-5 on penalties by Germany.
June 1996	Germany are Kings of Europe for the third time, beating the Czech Republic by the first sudden death goal to decide a major tournament.

SHADOWS OVER SOCCER

DAYS OF TRAGEDY – CLUBS

Season 1988-9 brought the worst disaster in the history of British sport, with the death of *95 Liverpool supporters (200 injured) at the **F.A. Cup semi-final** against Nott'm. Forest at **Hillsborough, Sheffield**, on Saturday, April 15. The tragedy built up in the minutes preceding kick-off, when thousands surged into the ground at the Leppings Lane end. Many were crushed in the tunnel between entrance and terracing, but most of the victims were trapped inside the perimeter fencing behind the goal. The match was abandoned without score after six minutes' play. The dead included seven women and girls, two teenage sisters and two teenage brothers. The youngest victim was a boy of ten, the oldest 67-year-old Gerard Baron, whose brother Kevin played for Liverpool in the 1950 Cup Final. (*Total became 96 in March 1993, when Tony Bland died after being in a coma for nearly four years).

The two worst disasters in one season in British soccer history occurred at the end of 1984-5. On May 11, the last Saturday of the League season, 56 people (two of them visiting supporters) were burned to death – and more than 200 taken to hospital – when fire destroyed the main stand at the **Bradford City-Lincoln City** match at Valley Parade.

The wooden, 77-year-old stand was full for City's last fixture before which, amid scenes of celebration, the club had been presented with the Third Division Championship trophy. The fire broke out just before half-time and, within five minutes, the entire stand was engulfed.

Eighteen days later, on May 29, at the European Cup Final between **Liverpool** and **Juventus** at the Heysel Stadium, Brussels, 39 spectators (31 of them Italian) were crushed or trampled to death and 437 injured. The disaster occurred an hour before the scheduled kick-off when Liverpool supporters charged a Juventus section of the crowd at one end of the stadium, and under pressure, a retaining wall collapsed.

The sequel was a 5-year ban by UEFA on English clubs generally in European competition, with a 6-year ban on Liverpool.

On May 26, 1985 ten people were trampled to death and 29 seriously injured in a crowd panic on the way into the **Olympic Stadium, Mexico City** for the Mexican Cup Final between local clubs National University and America.

More than 100 people died and 300 were injured in a football disaster at Nepal's national stadium in Katmandu in March 1988. There was a stampede when a violent hailstorm broke over the capital. Spectators rushed for cover, but the stadium exits were locked, and hundreds were trapped in the crush.

In South Africa, on January 13, 1991 40 black fans were trampled to death (50 injured) as they tried to escape from fighting that broke out at a match in the gold-mining town of Orkney, 80 miles from Johannesburg. The friendly, between top teams **Kaiser Chiefs** and **Orlando Pirates**, attracted a packed crowd of 20,000. Violence erupted after the referee allowed Kaiser Chiefs a disputed second-half goal to lead 1-0.

Disaster struck at the French Cup semi-final (May 5, 1992), with the death of 15 spectators and 1,300 injured when a temporary metal stand collapsed in the Corsican town of Bastia. The tie between Second Division **Bastia** and French Champions **Marseille** was cancelled.

A total of 318 died and 500 were seriously injured when the crowd rioted over a disallowed goal at the National Stadium in Lima, Peru, on May 24, 1964. **Peru** and **Argentina** were competing to play in the Olympic Games in Tokyo.

That remained sport's heaviest death toll until October 20, 1982, when (it was revealed only in July 1989) 340 Soviet fans were killed in Moscow's Lenin Stadium at the UEFA Cup second round first leg match between **Moscow Spartak** and **Haarlem (Holland)**. They were crushed on an open stairway when a last-minute Spartak goal sent departing spectators surging back into the ground.

Among other crowd disasters abroad: **June 1968** – 74 died in **Argentina**. Panic broke out at the end of a goalless match between River Plate and Boca Juniors at Nunez, Buenos Aires, when Boca supporters threw lighted newspaper torches onto fans in the tiers above.

February 1974 – 49 killed in **Egypt** in crush of fans clamouring to see Zamalek play Dukla Prague.

September 1971 – 44 died in **Turkey**, when fighting among spectators over a disallowed goal (Kayseri v Siwas) led to a platform collapsing.

The then worst disaster in the history of British football, in terms of loss of life, occurred at Glasgow Rangers' ground at **Ibrox Park**, January 2, 1971.

Sixty-six people were trampled to death (100 injured) as they tumbled down Stairway 13 just before the end of the **Rangers v. Celtic** New Year's match. That disaster led to the 1975 Safety of Sports Grounds legislation.

The Ibrox tragedy eclipsed even the Bolton disaster in which 33 were killed and about 500 injured when a wall and crowd barriers collapsed near a corner-flag at the **Bolton v. Stoke** F.A. Cup sixth round tie on March 9, 1946. The match was completed after half an hour's stoppage.

In a previous crowd disaster at **Ibrox** on April 5, 1902 part of the terracing collapsed during the Scotland v. England International and 25 people were killed. The match, held up for 20 minutes, ended 1-1, but was never counted as an official International.

Eight leading players and three officials of **Manchester United** and eight newspaper representatives were among the 23 who perished in the air crash at Munich on February 6, 1958, during take-off following a European Cup-tie in Belgrade. The players were Roger Byrne, Geoffrey Bent, Eddie Colman, Duncan Edwards, Mark Jones, David Pegg, Tommy Taylor and Liam Whelan, and the officials were Walter Crickmer (secretary), Tom Curry (trainer) and Herbert Whalley (coach). The newspaper representatives were Alf Clarke, Don Davies, George Follows, Tom Jackson, Archie Ledbrooke, Henry Rose, Eric Thompson and Frank Swift (former England goalkeeper of Manchester City).

On May 14, 1949, the entire team of Italian Champions, **Torino**, 8 of them Internationals, were killed when the aircraft taking them home from a match against Benfica in Lisbon crashed at Superga, near Turin. The total death toll of 28 included all the club's reserve players, the manager, trainer and coach.

On February 8, 1981, 24 spectators died and more than 100 were injured at a match **in Greece**. They were trampled as thousands of the 40,000 crowd tried to rush out of the stadium at Piraeus after Olympiakos beat AEK Athens 6-0.

On November 17, 1982, 24 people (12 of them children) were killed and 250 injured when fans stampeded at the end of a match at the Pascual Guerrero stadium in **Cali, Colombia.** Drunken spectators hurled fire crackers and broken bottles from the higher stands on to people below and started a rush to the exits.

On December 9, 1987, the 18-strong team squad of **Alianza Lima,** one of Peru's top clubs, were wiped out, together with 8 officials and several youth players, when a military aircraft taking them home from Puccalpa, crashed into the sea off Ventillana, ten miles from Lima. The only survivor among 43 on board was a member of the crew.

On April 28, 1993, 18 members of **Zambia's International** squad and 5 ZFA officials died when the aircraft carrying them to a World Cup qualifying tie against Senegal crashed into the Atlantic soon after take-off from Libreville, Gabon.

On October 16, 1996, 81 fans were crushed to death and 147 seriously injured in the "Guatemala Disaster" at the World Cup qualifier against Costa Rica at the Mateo Flores stadium. The tragedy happened an hour before kick-off, allegedly caused by ticket forgery and overcrowding – 60,000 were reported in the 45,000-capacity ground – and safety problems related to perimeter fencing.

On July 9, 1996, 8 people died, 39 injured in riot after derby match between Libya's two top clubs in Tripoli. Al-Ahli had beaten Al-Ittihad 1-0 by a controversial goal.

On April 6, 1997, 5 spectators were crushed to death at **Nigeria's national stadium** in Lagos after the 2-1 World Cup qualifying victory over Guinea. Only two of five gates were reported open as the 40,000 crowd tried to leave the ground.

DAYS OF TRAGEDY – PERSONAL

Sam Wynne, Bury right-back, collapsed five minutes before half-time in the First Division match away to Sheffield United on April 30, 1927, and died in the dressing-room.

In the Rangers v. Celtic Scottish match on September 5, 1931, **John Thomson**, the 23-year-old Celtic and Scottish International goalkeeper, sustained a fractured skull when diving at an opponent's feet just before half-time and died the same evening.

Sim Raleigh (Gillingham), injured in a clash of heads at home to Brighton (Div. 3 South) on December 1, 1934, continued to play but collapsed in second half and died in hospital the same night.

James Thorpe, 23-year-old Sunderland goalkeeper, was injured during the First Division match at home to Chelsea on February 1, 1936 and died in a diabetic coma three days later.

Derek Dooley, Sheffield Wednesday centre-forward and top scorer in 1951-52 in the Football League with 46 goals in 30 matches, broke a leg in the League match at Preston on February 14, 1953, and, after complications set in, had to lose the limb by amputation.

John White (27), Tottenham Hotspur's Scottish International forward, was killed by lightning on a golf course at Enfield, North London in July, 1964.

Two players were killed by lightning during the Army Cup Final replay at Aldershot in April, 1948.

Tommy Allden (23), Highgate United centre-half was struck by lightning during Highgate's Amateur Cup quarter-final with Enfield Town on February 25, 1967. He died the following day. Four other players were also struck but recovered.

Roy Harper died while refereeing the York City–Halifax Town (Div. 4) match on May 5, 1969.

Jim Finn collapsed and died from a heart attack while refereeing Exeter v Stockport (Div. 4) on September 16, 1972.

Scotland manager **Jock Stein**, 62, collapsed and died minutes after the Wales-Scotland World Cup qualifying match (1-1) at Cardiff on September 10, 1985.

David Longhurst, 25-year-old York City forward, died after being carried off two minutes before half-time in the Fourth Division fixture at home to Lincoln City on September 8, 1990. The match was abandoned (0-0) and the inquest revealed that Longhurst suffered from a rare heart condition.

GREAT SERVICE

"For services to Association Football", **Stanley Matthews** (Stoke City, Blackpool and England), already a C.B.E., became the first professional footballer to receive a knighthood. This was bestowed in 1965, his last season.

Before he retired and five days after his 50th birthday, he played for Stoke to set a record as the oldest First Division footballer (v. Fulham, February 6, 1965).

Over a brilliant span of 33 years, he played in 886 first-class matches, including 54 full Internationals (plus 31 in war time), 701 League games (including 3 at start of season 1939-40, which was abandoned on the outbreak of war) and 86 F.A. Cup-ties, and scored 95 goals. He was never booked in his career.

Sir Stanley celebrated his 82nd birthday last season (February 1, 1997). After spending a number of years in Toronto, he made his home back in the Potteries in 1989, having previously returned to his hometown, Hanley, Stoke-on-Trent in October, 1987 to unveil a life-size bronze statue of himself.

The inscription reads: "Sir Stanley Matthews, CBE. Born Hanley, 1 February 1915. His name is symbolic of the beauty of the game, his fame timeless and international, his sportsmanship and modesty universally acclaimed. A magical player, of the people, for the people."

On his home-coming in 1989, Sir Stanley was made President of Stoke City, the club he joined as a boy of 15 and served as a player for 20 years between 1931 and 1965.

In July 1992 FIFA honoured him with their "Gold merit award" for outstanding services to the game.

Former England goalkeeper **Peter Shilton**, still playing last season at 47, has made more first-class appearances (1,387) than any other footballer in British history. He played his 1,000th. League game in Leyton Orient's 2-0 home win against Brighton on Dec. 22, 1996 and in all played 9 times for Orient last season. He retired from International football after the 1990 World Cup in Italy with 125 caps, then a world record.

Shilton's career spans 32 seasons, 20 of them on the International stage. He made his League debut for Leicester City in May 1966, two months before England won the World Cup.

His 1,387 first-class appearances comprise a record 1,005 in the Football League, 125 Internationals, 102 League Cup, 86 F.A. Cup, 13 for England U-23s, 4 for the Football League and 52 other matches (European Cup, UEFA Cup, World Club Championship, Charity Shield, European Super Cup, Full Members' Cup, Play-offs, Screen Super Cup, Anglo-Italian Cup, Texaco Cup, Simod Cup, Zenith Data Systems Cup and Autoglass Trophy).

Shilton has appeared more times at Wembley (57) than any other player: 52 for England, 2 League Cup Finals, 1 F.A. Cup Final, 1 Charity Shield match, and 1 for the Football League. He passed a century of League appearances with each of his first five clubs: Leicester (286), Stoke (110), Nott'm. Forest (202), Southampton (188) and Derby (175) and subsequently played for Plymouth, Bolton and Leyton Orient.

His club honours, all gained with Nott'm. Forest: League Championship 1978, League Cup 1979, European Cup 1979 and 1980, PFA Player of the Year 1978.

Two other British footballers, also goalkeepers, have made more than 1,000 first-class appearances:

Ray Clemence, formerly with Tottenham, Liverpool and England, retired through injury in season 1987-8 after a career total of 1,119 matches starting in 1965-6. Clemence played 50 times for his first club, Scunthorpe; 665 for Liverpool; 337 for Tottenham; his 67 representative games included 61 England caps.

A third great British goalkeeper, **Pat Jennings**, ended his career (1963-86) with a total of 1,098 first-class matches for Watford, Tottenham, Arsenal and N. Ireland. They were made up of 757 in the Football League, 119 full Internationals, 84 F.A. Cup appearances, 72 League/Milk Cup, 55 European club matches, 2 Charity Shield, 3 Other Internationals, 1 Under-23 cap,

2 Texaco Cup, 2 Anglo-Italian Cup and 1 Super Cup. Jennings played his 119th. and final International on his 41st birthday, June 12, 1986, against Brazil in Guadalajara in the Mexico World Cup.

KNIGHTS OF SOCCER

In the Queen's Birthday Honours on June 11, 1994, **Bobby Charlton**, England's record goalscorer and a Manchester United legend, became the fourth former professional footballer to receive a knighthood for services to the game. The others were **Stanley Matthews** (1965), **Alf Ramsey** (1967) and **Matt Busby** (1968).

PENALTIES

It is now **106 years** since the **penalty-kick** was introduced to the game, following a proposal to the Irish F.A. in 1890 by William McCrum, son of the High Sheriff for Co. Omagh, and approved by the International Football Board on June 2, 1891.

First penalty scored in a first-class match was by John Heath, for Wolves v Accrington Stanley (5-0 in Div. 1, September 14, 1891).

The greatest influence of the penalty has come since the 1970s, with the introduction of the shoot-out to settle deadlocked ties in various competitions.

Man. United were the first club to win a competitive match in British football via a shoot-out (4-3 v Hull, Watney Cup semi-final, August 1970).

In season 1991-2, penalty shoot-outs were introduced to decide **F.A. Cup ties** still level after one replay and extra time.

Wembley saw its first penalty contest 23 years ago in the Charity Shield. So, since 1974, many major matches across the world have been settled thus, including:-

1974 F.A. Charity Shield (Wembley): Liverpool beat Leeds 6-5 (after 1-1).
1976 Eur. Champ. Final (Belgrade): Czech. beat W. Germany 5-3 (after 2-2).
1980 Cup-Winners' Cup Final (Brussels): Valencia beat Arsenal 5-4 (0-0).
1982 World Cup s-final (Seville): West Germany beat France 5-4 (after 3-3).
1984 European Cup Final (Rome): Liverpool beat AS Roma 4-2 (after 1-1).
1984 UEFA Cup Final: Tottenham (home) beat Anderlecht 4-3 (2-2 agg.).
1984 Eur. Champ. s-final (Lyon, France): Spain beat Denmark 5-4 (after 1-1).
1986 European Cup Final (Seville): Steaua Bucharest beat Barcelona 2-0 (0-0). Barcelona missed all four penalties taken.
1986 World Cup q-finals (in Mexico): France beat Brazil 4-3 (after 1-1); West Germany beat Mexico 4-1 (after 0-0); Belgium beat Spain 5-4 (after 1-1).
1987 Freight Rover Trophy Final (Wembley): Mansfield Town beat Bristol City 5-4 (after 1-1).
1987 Scottish League (Skol) Cup Final (Hampden Park): Rangers beat Aberdeen 5-3 (after 3-3).
1988 European Cup Final (Stuttgart): PSV Eindhoven beat Benfica 6-5 (after 0-0).
1988 UEFA Cup Final: Bayer Leverkusen (home) beat Espanol 3-2 (3-3 agg.).
1990 Scottish F.A. Cup Final (Hampden Park): Aberdeen beat Celtic 9-8 (0-0).
1990 World Cup (in Italy): 2nd. Round: Rep. of Ireland beat Rumania 5-4 (after 0-0); q-final: Argentina beat Yugoslavia 3-2 (after 0-0); s-finals: Argentina beat Italy 4-3 (after 1-1); West Germany beat England 4-3 (1-1).

1991 European Cup Final (Bari): Red Star Belgrade beat Marseille 5-3 (after 0-0).

1991 Barclays League Play-off (4th. Div. Final – Wembley): Torquay beat Blackpool 5-4 (after 2-2).

1992 F.A. Cup s-final replay (Villa Park): Liverpool beat Portsmouth 3-1 (after 0-0).

1992 Barclays League Play-off (4th. Div. Final – Wembley): Blackpool beat Scunthorpe 4-3 (after 1-1).

1992 Eur. Champ. s-final (Gothenburg): Denmark beat Holland 5-4 (after 2-2).

1992 African Nations Cup Final (Dakar): Ivory Coast beat Ghana 11-10 (after 0-0).

1993 Barclays League Play-off: (3rd Div. Final – Wembley): York beat Crewe 5-3 (after 1-1).

1993 F.A. Charity Shield (Wembley): Man. Utd. beat Arsenal 5-4 (after 1-1).

1994 League (Coca-Cola) Cup s-final: Aston Villa beat Tranmere 5-4 (after 4-4, 1-3a, 3-1h).

1994 Autoglass Trophy Final (Wembley): Swansea beat Huddersfield 3-1 (after 1-1).

1994 World Cup (in U.S.A.): **2nd. Round**: Bulgaria beat Mexico 3-1 (after 1-1); q-final: Sweden beat Rumania 5-4 (after 2-2); **Final**: Brazil beat Italy 3-2 (after 0-0).

1994 Scottish League (Coca-Cola) Cup Final (Ibrox Park): Raith beat Celtic 6-5 (after 2-2).

1995 Cup-Winners' Cup s-final: Arsenal beat Sampdoria away 3-2 (5-5 agg.).

1995 Copa America Final (Montevideo): Uruguay beat Brazil 5-3 (after 1-1).

1996 European Cup Final (Rome): Juventus beat Ajax 4-2 (after 1-1).

1996 European U-21 Champ. Final (Barcelona): Italy beat Spain 4-2 (after 1-1).

1996 Eur. Champ. q-finals: England beat Spain (Wembley) 4-2 after 0-0; France beat Holland (Anfield) 5-4 after 0-0; **E. Champ. s-finals**: Germany beat England (Wembley) 6-5 after 1-1; Czech Republic beat France (Old Trafford) 6-5 after 0-0.

1997 Auto Windscreens Shield Final (Wembley): Carlisle beat Colchester 4-3 (after 0-0).

1997 UEFA Cup Final: FC Schalke beat Inter Milan 4-1 (after 1-1 agg.).

Footnote: Highest-recorded score in a penalty shoot-out in Britain was **Aldershot's 11-10** victory at home to **Fulham** after their 1-1 draw in the Freight Rover Trophy Southern quarter-final on February 10, 1987. Seven spot-kicks were missed or saved in a record 28-penalty shoot-out at senior level.

Longest-recorded penalty shoot-out was in South America in 1988 – **Argentinos Juniors** beat **Racing Club** 20-19.

Highest-scoring shoot-out in **Int. football** was when North Korea beat Hong Kong 11-10 (after 3-3 draw) in an Asian Cup match in 1975.

F.A. CUP SHOOT-OUTS

In **six seasons** since the introduction of this method to settle F.A. Cup ties (from Round 1) that are level after two matches, a total of **23 ties** have been decided by such means (5 in 1991-2, 6 in 1992-3, 4 in 1993-4, 4 in 1994-5, 4 in 1995-6).

But the **first** penalty contest in the F.A. Cup took place **23 years** ago. In days of the play-off for third place, the 1972 match was delayed until the eve of the following season when losing semi-finalists **Birmingham** and **Stoke** met at St. Andrew's on Aug. 5. The score was 0-0 and Birmingham won 4-3 on penalties.

MISSED CUP FINAL PENALTIES

John Aldridge (Liverpool) became the first player to miss a penalty in the F.A. Cup Final at Wembley – and the second in the competition's history (previously

Charlie Wallace, of Aston Villa, in the 1913 Final against Sunderland at Crystal Palace) – when Wimbledon's Dave Beasant saved his shot in May 1988. Seven previous penalties had been scored in this Final at Wembley.

Tottenham's **Gary Lineker** saw his penalty saved by Nott'm. Forest goalkeeper Mark Crossley in the 1991 F.A. Cup Final.

Another crucial penalty miss at Wembley was by Arsenal's **Nigel Winterburn**, Luton's Andy Dibble saving his spot-kick in the 1988 Littlewoods Cup Final, when a goal would have put Arsenal 3-1 ahead. Instead, they lost 3-2.

Winterburn was the third player to fail with a League Cup Final penalty at Wembley, following **Ray Graydon** (Aston Villa) against Norwich in 1975 and **Clive Walker** (Sunderland), who shot wide in the 1985 Milk Cup Final, also against Norwich, who won 1-0. Graydon had his penalty saved by Kevin Keelan, but scored from the rebound and won the cup for Villa (1-0).

Derby's Martin Taylor saved a penalty from **Eligio Nicolini** in the Anglo-Italian Cup Final at Wembley on March 27, 1993, but Cremonese won 3-1.

LEAGUE PENALTIES RECORD

Most penalties in Football League match: Five – 4 to Crystal Palace (3 missed), 1 to Brighton (scored) in Div. 2 match at Selhurst Park on March 27 (Easter Monday), 1989. Palace won 2-1. Three of the penalties were awarded in a 5-minute spell. The match also produced 6 bookings and a sending-off.

Man. City provided the previous instance of a team missing 3 penalties in a match – against Newcastle (Div. 1) in January, 1912.

SPOT-KICK HAT-TRICKS

Danish International **Jan Molby**'s first hat-trick in English football, for Liverpool in their 3-1 win at home to Coventry (Littlewoods Cup, 4th round replay, Nov. 26, 1986) comprised three goals from the penalty spot.

It was the first such hat-trick in a major match for two years – since **Andy Blair** scored three penalties for Sheff. Wed. against Luton (Milk Cup 4th. round, Nov. 20 1984).

Portsmouth's **Kevin Dillon** scored a penalty hat-trick in the Full Members Cup (2nd rd.) at home to Millwall (3-2) on Nov. 4, 1986.

Alan Slough scored an away-match hat-trick of penalties for Peterborough, beaten 4-3 at Chester (Div. 3, Apr. 29, 1978).

MOST PENALTY GOALS (LEAGUE) IN SEASON

Thirteen by **Francis Lee** for Man. City (Div. 1) in 1971-2. His goal total for the season was 33. In season 1988-9, **Graham Roberts** scored 12 League penalties for Second Division Champions Chelsea.

PENALTY-SAVE SEQUENCES

Ipswich goalkeeper **Paul Cooper** saved eight of the ten penalties he faced in 1979-80. **Roy Brown** (Notts Co.) saved six in a row in season 1972-3.

Andy Lomas, goalkeeper for Chesham United (Diadora League) claimed a record eight **consecutive** penalty saves – three at the end of season 1991-2 and five in 1992-3.

Mark Bosnich (Aston Villa) saved five in two consecutive matches in 1993-4: three in Coca-Cola Cup semi-final penalty shoot-out v Tranmere (Feb. 26), then two in Premiership at Tottenham (Mar. 2).

MISSED PENALTIES SEQUENCE

Against Wolves in Div. 2 on Sept. 28, 1991, **Southend United** missed their seventh successive penalty (five of them the previous season).

SCOTTISH RECORDS

(See also under 'Goals')

RANGERS' MANY RECORDS

Rangers' record-breaking feats include:-
League Champions: 47 times (once joint holders) – world record.
Winning every match in Scottish League (1898-9 season).
Major hat-tricks: Rangers have completed the domestic treble (League Championship, League Cup and Scottish F.A. Cup) a record five times (1948-9, 1963-4, 1975-6, 1977-8, 1992-3).
League & Cup double: 14 times.
Nine successive Championships (1989-97), equalling Celtic's record.

CELTIC'S GRAND SLAM

Celtic's record in 1966-7 was the most successful by a British club in one season. They won the **Scottish League**, the **Scottish Cup**, the **Scottish League Cup**, the **Glasgow Cup** and became the first British club to win the **European Cup**.

Celtic have twice achieved the Scottish treble (League Championship, League Cup and F.A. Cup), in 1966-7 and 1968-9.

They have won the Scottish Cup most times (30), and have completed the League and Cup double 11 times.

Celtic won nine consecutive Scottish League titles (1966-74) under Jock Stein.

SCOTTISH CUP HAT-TRICKS

Aberdeen's feat of winning the Scottish F.A. Cup in 1982-3-4 made them only the third club to achieve that particular hat-trick.

Queen's Park did it twice (1874-5-6 and 1880-1-2), and **Rangers** have won the Scottish Cup three years in succession on three occasions: 1934-5-6, 1948-9-50 and 1962-3-4.

SCOTTISH CUP FINAL DISMISSALS

Three players have been sent off in the Scottish F.A. Cup Final: **Jock Buchanan** (Rangers v. Kilmarnock, 1929), **Roy Aitken** (Celtic v. Aberdeen, 1984) and **Walter Kidd** (Hearts captain v. Aberdeen, 1986).

CELTIC'S RECORD 62

Celtic hold the Scottish League record run of success with 62 matches undefeated, from November 13, 1915 to April 21, 1917, when Kilmarnock won 2-0 at Parkhead.

Greenock Morton in 1963-4 were undefeated in home League matches, obtained a record 67 points out of 72 and scored 135 goals, clinching promotion as early as February 29.

Queen's Park did not have a goal scored against them during the first seven seasons of their existence (1867-74, before the Scottish League was formed).

WORST HOME SEQUENCE

After winning promotion to Div. 1 in 1992, **Cowdenbeath** went a record 40 consecutive home League matches without a win. They ended the sequence when beating Arbroath 1-0 on April 2, 1994.

ALLY'S RECORDS

Ally McCoist became the first player to complete 200 goals in the Premier Division when he scored Rangers' winner (2-1) at Falkirk on December 12, 1992. His first was against Celtic in September 1983, and he reached 100 against Dundee on Boxing Day 1987.

When McCoist scored twice at home to Hibernian (4-3) on December 7, 1996, he became Scotland's record post-war League marksman, beating Gordon Wallace's 264, and his total stood at 268 at the end of the season.

McCoist holds a Scottish League Cup record, too, with a ninth winner's medal in 1996-97, all with the Ibrox club.

STURROCK'S RECORD

Paul Sturrock set an individual scoring record for the Scottish Premier Division with 5 goals in Dundee United's 7-0 win at home to Morton on November 17, 1984.

DOUBLE SCOTTISH FINAL

Rangers v. Celtic drew **129,643** and **120,073** people to the Scottish Cup Final and replay at Hampden Park, Glasgow, in 1963. Receipts for the two matches totalled £50,500.

CHAMPIONS NINE TIMES

Alan Morton won **nine** Scottish Championship medals with Rangers in 1921-23-24-25-27-28-29-30-31. **Ally McCoist** has played in the Rangers side that has won the last nine League titles (1989-97).

SCOTTISH CUP – NO DECISION

The **Scottish F.A.** withheld their Cup and medals in 1908-9 after Rangers and Celtic played two drawn games at Hampden Park. Spectators rioted.

GREAT SCOTS

In February 1988, the Scottish F.A. launched a national **Hall of Fame**, initially comprising the first 11 Scots to make 50 International appearances, to be joined by all future players to reach that number of caps. Each member receives a gold medal, invitation for life at all Scotland's home matches, and has his portrait hung at Scottish F.A. headquarters in Glasgow. Latest to qualify was **Gary McAllister** last season.

NOTABLE SCOTTISH 'FIRSTS'

● The father of League football was a Scot, **William McGregor**, a draper in Birmingham. The 12-club Football League kicked off in September 1888, and McGregor was its first president.

● **Hibernian** were the first British club to play in the European Cup. They reached the semi-final when it began in 1955-6.

● **Celtic** were Britain's first winners of the European Cup, in 1967.

● Scotland's First Division became the **Premier Division** in season 1975-6.

● Football's **first International** was staged at the West of Scotland cricket ground, Partick, on November 30, 1872: Scotland 0, England 0.

● Scotland introduced its **League Cup** in 1945-6, the first season after the war. It was another 15 years before the Football League Cup was launched.

● The Scottish F.A. Cup has been **sponsored** for the last eight seasons, and Tennents' contract continues in 1997-8.

- Scotland pioneered the use in British football of **two substitutes** per team in League and Cup matches.
- The world's **record football score** belongs to Scotland and has stood for 111 years: Arbroath 36, Bon Accord 0 (Scottish Cup first round) on September 12, 1885.
- The Scottish F.A. introduced the **penalty shoot-out** to their Cup Final in 1990.
- On Jan. 22, 1994 all six matches in the **Scottish Premier Division** ended as draws.

SCOTTISH CUP SHOCK RESULTS

1885-86 (1) Arbroath 36, Bon Accord 0
1921-22 (F) Morton 1, Rangers 0
1937-38 (F) East Fife 4, Kilmarnock 2 (replay, after 1-1)
1960-61 (F) Dunfermline 2, Celtic 0 (replay, after 0-0)
1966-67 (1) Berwick Rangers1, Rangers 0
1979-80 (3) Hamilton 2, Keith 3
1984-85 (1) Stirling Albion 20, Selkirk 0
1984-85 (3) Inverness Thistle 3, Kilmarnock 0
1986-87 (3) Rangers 0, Hamilton 1
1994-95 (4) Stenhousemuir 2, Aberdeen 0

Scottish League (Coca-Cola) Cup Final shock
1994-95   Raith 2, Celtic 2 (Raith won 6-5 on pens.)

SCOTTISH FINES (Modern)

1989 (June) fine **Hearts** £93,000, following TV infringement at UEFA Cup q-final.
1990 (May) S.F.A. fine Rangers manager **Graeme Souness** record £5,000 for breaking touchline ban v Hearts on Feb. 17, and extend Souness trackside ban to May 1992. **1991** (February) S.F.A. fine **Rangers** £10,000 and order them to forfeit £13,000 sponsorship money for failing to carry out sponsors' agreement at Cup-tie v Dunfermline in January.
1991 (June) S.F.A. fine **Dundee Utd.** £12,000 for incidents involving referee at Scottish Cup Final defeat by Motherwell.
1992 (October) UEFA fine **Hibernian** £5,730 for crowd trouble at UEFA Cup match v Anderlecht.
1993 (March) UEFA fine **Rangers** £8,000 (later halved) for crowd misconduct away to Bruges in European Cup.
1993 (May) **Rangers** fined £5,000 by League under rule covering "tapping" of players with other clubs.
1993 (August) S.F.A. fine **Airdrie** £10,000, **Dundee** £5,000 for poor disciplinary records, season 1992-3.
1993 (November) UEFA fine **Aberdeen** £4,500 for fan misconduct v Torino (CWC).
1994 (January) S.F.A. fine **Rangers** coach **John McGregor** £3,000 and ban him from touchline until year 2000 for using foul and abusive language to referee at reserve match.
1994 (August) Scottish League fine **Celtic** record £100,000 for poaching manager Tommy Burns from Kilmarnock.
1994 (August) S.F.A. fines for prev. season's disciplinary records: **Dundee** £10,000; **Cowdenbeath**, **East Fife**, **Stranraer** each £1,000.
1994 (November) S.F.A fine **Celtic** manager **Tommy Burns** £2,000 and assistant **Billy Stark** each £2,000 for breach of contract when leaving Kilmarnock.
1995 (March) S.F.A. fine **Celtic** manager **Tommy Burns** £1,000 and ban him from touchline for rest of season (verbal abuse of referee).
1995 (August) S.F.A. fine five clubs for poor disciplinary records in 1994-5:

Dundee Utd. (£5,000), **Falkirk** (£5,000), **Cowdenbeath, East Fife** and **Stranraer** (each £2,000).

1996 (August) Scottish League fine **Ayr** £12,000 for fielding suspended players in Coca-Cola Cup.

1996 (October) S.F.A. fine **Tommy Burns** (Celtic manager) £3,000 for "aggressive altitude" to referee in match v Kilmarnock, April 10.

1996 (November) UEFA fine **Celtic** £42,000 and **Alan Stubbs** £28,000 for using unlicensed agents in summer transfer from Bolton; UEFA ban **Paul Gascoigne** from 4 Champions' League games (sent off away to Ajax, Oct. 17); UEFA fine **Rangers** £2,500 for players' poor discipline v Ajax, Oct. 17.

1996 (December) Scottish League fine **Falkirk** £25,000 for fielding ineligible player and order match v St. Mirren to be replayed.

1997 (January) S.F.A. fine Celtic manager **Tommy Burns** £2,000 for verbal abuse of match officials v Rangers, Nov. 14.

1997 (February) Scottish League fine **Raith** £10,000 for fielding 3 Scandinavian trialists in match (rule permits maximum of 2).

MISCELLANEOUS

NATIONAL ASSOCIATIONS FORMED

F. A. on Oct. 26	1863	F.A. of Wales	1876
Scottish S.F.A.	1873	Irish F.A.	1904

Federation of International Football Associations (FIFA) **1904**

NATIONAL COMPETITIONS LAUNCHED

F. A. Cup	1871	Welsh Cup	1877
Scottish Cup	1873	Irish Cup	1880

Football League **1888**
F.A. Premier League **1992**
Scottish League **1890**
Football League Cup **1960**
Scottish League Cup **1945**
World (Jules Rimet) Cup, at Montevideo **1930**
International Championship **1883-4**
Youth International (16-18 age-groups) **1946-7**
Olympic Games Tournament, at Shepherd's Bush **1908**

INNOVATIONS

Size of Ball: Fixed in **1872.**

Shinguards: Introduced and registered by Sam Weller Widdowson (Nottingham Forest & England) in **1874.**

Referee's Whistle: First used on Nottingham Forest's ground in **1878.**

Professionalism: Legalised in England in the summer of **1885** as a result of agitation by Lancashire clubs.

Goal-nets: Invented and patented in **1890** by Mr. Brodie of Liverpool. They were first used in the North v. South match in January, **1891.**

Referees and Linesmen: Replaced umpires and referees in January, **1891.**

Penalty-kick: Introduced at Irish F.A.'s request in the season **1891-2.** The penalty law ordering the goalkeeper to remain on the goal-line came into force in

September, **1905,** and the order to stand on his goal-line until the ball is kicked arrived in **1929-30.**

White ball: First came into official use in **1951.**

Floodlighting: First F.A. Cup-tie (replay), Kidderminster Harriers v. Brierley Hill Alliance, **1955.**

Electrified pitch to beat frost tried by Everton at Goodison Park in **1958.**

First Soccer Closed-circuit TV: At Coventry City ground in October 1965 (10,000 fans saw their team win at Cardiff, 120 miles away).

Substitutes (one per team) were first allowed in Football League matches at the start of season **1965-6.** Three substitutes (one a goalkeeper) allowed, two of which could be used, in Premier League matches, **1992-93.** The Football League introduced three substitutes for **1993-94.**

Three points for a win: This was introduced by the Football League in **1981-2.**

Offside law amended, player 'level' no longer offside, and 'professional foul' made sending-off offence, **1990.**

Penalty shoot-outs introduced to decide F.A. Cup ties level after one replay and extra time, **1991-2.**

New back-pass rule – goalkeeper must not handle ball kicked to him by team-mate, **1992.**

1994: 3 points for win introduced in World Cup Finals group matches in USA. Also by Scottish League at start of season 1994-5.

CUP AND LEAGUE DOUBLES

League Championship and F.A. Cup: Preston North End, 1889; Aston Villa, 1897; Tottenham Hotspur, 1961; Arsenal, 1971; Liverpool 1986; Man. United 1994, 1996.

F.A. Cup and Promotion: West Bromwich Albion, 1931.

F.A. Cup and Football League Cup: Arsenal, 1993

League Championship and Football League Cup: Nottingham Forest, 1978; Liverpool, 1982; Liverpool, 1983; Liverpool, 1984.

Scottish League Championship and Cup Double: Rangers, (14): 1928-30-34-35-49-50-53-63-64-76-78-92-93-96. Celtic, (11): 1907-8-14-54-67-69-71-72-74-77-88. Aberdeen, (1): 1984.

Scottish Treble (Championship, Cup, League Cup): Rangers 5 times (1949-64-76-78-93); Celtic twice (1967-69).

DERBY DAYS: COMPLETE LEAGUE RESULTS

Arsenal v Tottenham: Played 120 (all in top div.); Arsenal 48 wins, Tottenham 44, Drawn 28.

Aston Villa v Birmingham: Played 96; Villa 39, Birmingham 32, Drawn 25.

Everton v Liverpool: Played 156 (all in top div.); Liverpool 56, Everton 52, Drawn 48.

Ipswich v Norwich: Played 62; Ipswich 32, Norwich 21, Drawn 9.

Man. City v Man. United: Played 124; United 48, City 32, Drawn 44.

Middlesbrough v Newcastle: Played 90; Newcastle 35, Middlesbrough 31, Drawn 24.

Newcastle v Sunderland: Played 118; Newcastle 43, Sunderland 39, Drawn 36 (incl. 1990 play-offs – Sunderland win and draw).

Nott'm. Forest v Notts Co.: Played 86; Forest 35, County 28, Drawn 23.

Sheff. United v Sheff. Wed.: Played 98; United 37, Wednesday 31, Drawn 30.

Port Vale v Stoke City: Played 38; Stoke 15, Port Vale 12, Drawn 11.

Bristol City v Bristol Rovers: Played 80; City 31, Rovers 23, Drawn 26.

Celtic v Rangers: Played 244; Rangers 97, Celtic 74, Drawn 73.

Dundee v Dundee United: Played 98; United 50, Dundee 29, Drawn 19.

Hearts v Hibernian: Played 210; Hearts 87, Hibernian 61, Drawn 62.

YOUNGEST AND OLDEST

Youngest Caps   **Age**

Norman Whiteside (N. Ireland v. Yugoslavia, June 17, 1982)   17 years, 42 days
Ryan Giggs (Wales v. Germany, October 16, 1991)   17 years, 332 days
James Prinsep (England v. Scotland, April 5, 1879)   17 years 252 days
Denis Law (Scotland v. Wales, October 18, 1958)   18 years, 235 days
Jimmy Holmes (Rep. of Ireland v. Austria, May 30, 1971)   17 years 200 days

England's Youngest cap this century: Duncan Edwards (v. Scotland, April 2, 1955), 18 years 183 days.
Youngest England scorer: Tommy Lawton (19 years, 6 days) – penalty against Wales, Ninian Park, Cardiff, October 22, 1938.
Youngest England captain: Bobby Moore (v Czech., away, May 29, 1963), 22 years, 1 month, 17 days.
Youngest player to appear in World Cup Finals: Norman Whiteside (N. Ireland v. Yugoslavia in Spain – June 17, 1982, age 17 years and 42 days (record previously held by Pele – 17 years and 237 days when playing for Brazil in 1958 World Cup in Sweden).
Youngest First Division player: Derek Forster (Sunderland goalkeeper v. Leicester, August 22, 1964) aged 15 years, 185 days.
Youngest First Division scorer: At 16 years and 57 days, schoolboy Jason Dozzell (substitute after 30 minutes for Ipswich Town at home to Coventry City on February 4, 1984). Ipswich won 3-1 and Dozzell scored their third goal.
Youngest F.A. Premier League player: Neil Finn (West Ham goalkeeper at Man. City, January 1, 1996) 17 years, 3 days.
Youngest F.A. Premier League scorer: Andy Turner (Tottenham v Everton, September 5, 1992), 17 years, 166 days.
Youngest First Division hat-trick scorer: Alan Shearer, aged 17 years, 240 days, in Southampton's 4-2 home win v. Arsenal (April 9, 1988) on his full debut. Previously, Jimmy Greaves (17 years, 309 days) with 4 goals for Chelsea at home to Portsmouth (7-4), Christmas Day, 1957.
Youngest to complete 100 Football League goals: Jimmy Greaves (20 years, 261 days) when he did so for Chelsea v. Man. City, November 19, 1960.
Youngest Football League scorer: Ronnie Dix (for Bristol Rovers v Norwich, Div. 3 South, March 3, 1928) aged 15 years, 180 days.
Youngest players in Football League: Albert Geldard (Bradford v. Millwall, Div. 2, September 16, 1929) aged 15 years, 158 days; Ken Roberts (Wrexham v. Bradford, Div. 3 North, September 1, 1951) also 15 years, 158 days.
Youngest player in Scottish League: Goalkeeper Ronnie Simpson (Queens Park) aged 15 in 1946.
Youngest player in F.A. Cup: Andy Awford, Worcester City's England Schoolboy defender, aged 15 years, 88 days when he substituted in second half away to Borehamwood (3rd. qual-round) on October 10, 1987.
Youngest player in F.A. Cup proper: Scott Endersby (15 years, 279 days) when he kept goal for Kettering Town v. Tilbury in first round on November 26, 1977.
Youngest Wembley Cup Final captain: Barry Venison (Sunderland v. Norwich City, Milk Cup Final, March 24, 1985 – replacing suspended captain Shaun Elliott), aged 20 years, 7 months, 8 days.
Youngest F.A. Cup-winning captain: Bobby Moore (West Ham, 1964, v Preston), aged 23 years, 20 days.
Youngest F.A. Cup Final captain: David Nish was 21 years and 7 months old when he captained Leicester C. against Man. City at Wembley on April 26, 1969.
Youngest F.A. Cup Final player: James Prinsep (Clapham Rovers v Old Etonians, 1879) aged 17 years, 245 days.
Youngest F.A. Cup Final player this century: Paul Allen (West Ham v. Arsenal, 1980) aged 17 years, 256 days.
Youngest F.A. Cup Final scorer: Norman Whiteside (Man. United v. Brighton in 1983 replay at Wembley), aged 18 years, 19 days.

Youngest F.A. Cup Final managers: Stan Cullis, Wolves (33) v Leicester, 1949; Steve Coppell, Crystal Palace (34) v Man. United, 1990; Ruud Gullit, Chelsea (34) v Mid'bro', 1997.

Youngest player in Football League Cup: Kevin Davies (Chesterfield sub at West Ham, 2nd Round, 2nd Leg on September 22, 1993) aged 16 years, 180 days.

Youngest Wembley scorer: Norman Whiteside (Man. United v. Liverpool, Milk Cup Final, March 26, 1983) aged 17 years, 324 days.

Youngest Wembley Cup Final goalkeeper: Chris Woods (18 years, 125 days) for Nott'm Forest v. Liverpool, League Cup Final on March 18, 1978.

Youngest Wembley F.A. Cup Final goalkeeper: Peter Shilton (19 years, 7 months) for Leicester City v. Man. City, April 26, 1969.

Youngest senior International at Wembley: Blendi Nollbani (Albania's World Cup goalkeeper v. England, April 26, 1989), aged 17 years, 19 days.

Youngest scorer in full International: Mohamed Kallon (Sierra Leone v Congo, African Nations Cup, April 22, 1995), aged 15 years, 6 months, 16 days.

Youngest player sent off in World Cup Final series: Rigobert Song (Cameroon v Brazil, in USA, June 1994) aged 17 years, 358 days.

Youngest F.A. Cup Final referee: Kevin Howley, of Middlesbrough, aged 35 when in charge of Wolves v. Blackburn, 1960.

Youngest player in England U-23 team: Duncan Edwards (v. Italy, Bologna, January 20, 1954), aged 17 years, 3 months.

Youngest player in England U-21 team: Lee Sharpe (v. Greece, away, February 7, 1989), aged 17 years, 8 months.

Youngest player in Scotland U-21 team: Christian Dailly (v Rumania, Hampden Park, Sept. 11, 1990), aged 16 years, 11 months.

Youngest player in senior football: Cameron Campbell Buchanan, Scottish-born outside right, aged 14 years, 57 days when he played for Wolves v. W.B.A. in War-time League match, September 26, 1942.

Youngest player in peace-time senior match: Eamon Collins (Blackpool v. Kilmarnock, Anglo-Scottish Cup quarter-final 1st. leg, September 9, 1980) aged 14 years, 323 days.

Oldest player to appear in Football League: New Brighton manager Neil McBain (51 years, 120 days) as emergency goalkeeper away to Hartlepool United (Div. 3 North, March 15, 1947).

Other oldest post-war League players: Sir Stanley Matthews (Stoke, 1965, 50 years, 5 days); Peter Shilton (Leyton Orient 1997, 47 years, 126 days); Alf Wood (Coventry, 1958, 43 years, 199 days); Tommy Hutchison (Swansea, 1991, 43 years, 172 days).

Oldest Football League debut: Andrew Cunningham, for Newcastle United at Leicester (Div. 1) on February 2, 1929, aged 38 years, 2 days.

Oldest player to appear in First Division: Sir Stanley Matthews (Stoke City v. Fulham, February 6, 1965), aged 50 years, 5 days.

Oldest player in Premier League: Goalkeeper John Burridge (half-time substitute for Man. City v Newcastle, 0-0, April 29, 1995), aged 43 years, 4 months, 26 days.

Oldest F.A. Cup Final player: Walter (Billy) Hampson (Newcastle Utd. v. Aston Villa on April 26, 1924), aged 41 years, 8 months.

Oldest F.A. Cup-winning team: Arsenal 1950 (average age 31 years, 2 months). Eight of the players were over 30, with the three oldest centre-half Leslie Compton 37, and skipper Joe Mercer and goalkeeper George Swindin, both 35.

Oldest player capped by England: Stanley Matthews (v. Denmark, Copenhagen, May 15, 1957), aged 42 years and 104 days.

Oldest England scorer: Stanley Matthews (v N. Ireland, Belfast, October 6, 1956), aged 41 years, 248 days.

Oldest British International player: Billy Meredith (Wales v. England at Highbury, March 15, 1920), aged 45 years, 8 months.

Oldest "new cap": Arsenal centre-half Leslie Compton, at 38 years, 2 months when he made his England debut in 4-2 win against Wales at Sunderland on

November 15, 1950. **For Scotland:** Goalkeeper Ronnie Simpson (Celtic) at 36 v England at Wembley, April 15, 1967.

Longest Football League career: This spanned 32 years and 10 months, by Stanley Matthews (Stoke, Blackpool, Stoke) from March 19, 1932 until February 6, 1965.

Smallest F.A. Cup-winning captain: 5ft. 4in. – Bobby Kerr (Sunderland v. Leeds, 1973).

SHIRT NUMBERING

Numbering players in Football League matches was made compulsory in 1939. Players wore numbered shirts (1-22) in the F.A. Cup Final as an experiment in 1933 (Everton v. Man. City).

Squad numbers for players were introduced by the F.A. Premier League at the start of the season 1993-4. They were optional in the Football League.

Names on shirts: For first time, players wore names as well as numbers on shirts in League Cup and F.A. Cup Finals, 1993.

SUBSTITUTES

In **1965**, the Football League, by 39 votes to 10, agreed that **one substitute** be allowed for an injured player at any time during a League match.

Two substitutes per team were approved for the League (Littlewoods) Cup and F.A. Cup in season 1986-7 and two were permitted in the Football League for the first time in 1987-8.

Three substitutes (one a goalkeeper), two of which could be used, introduced by the Premier League for season 1992-3. The Football League followed suit for 1993-4.

Three substitutes (one a goalkeeper) were allowed at the World Cup Finals for the first time at US '94.

Three substitutes (any position) introduced by Premier League and Football League in 1995-6.

When Leigh Roose, the Welsh goalkeeper, was injured against England at Wrexham, March 16, 1908, David Davies (Bolton Wanderers) was allowed to take his place as substitute. Thus Wales used 12 players. England won 7-1.

The **first recorded use of a substitute was in 1889** (Wales v. Scotland at Wrexham on April 15) when Sam Gillam arrived late – although he was a Wrexham player – and Alf Pugh (Rhostellyn) was allowed to keep goal until he turned up. The match ended 0-0.

First substitute to score in F.A. Cup Final: Eddie Kelly (Arsenal v. Liverpool, 1971).

END OF WAGE LIMIT

Freedom from the maximum wage system – in force since the formation of the Football League in 1888 – was secured by the Professional Footballers' Association in 1961. About this time Italian clubs renewed overtures for the transfer of British stars and Fulham's **Johnny Haynes** became the first British player to earn a wage of £100 a week.

GREATEST SHOCKS

Excluding such tragedies as the Munich air crash (Feb. 1958), the Bradford fire disaster (May 1985), Heysel (May 1985) and Hillsborough (April 1989), here in date order are, arguably, the greatest shocks in football history:

(1)	Jan. 1933	F.A. Cup 3rd. Round: Walsall 2, Arsenal 0.
(2)	Jan. 1949	F.A. Cup 4th. Round: Yeovil 2, Sunderland 1.
(3)	June 1950	World Cup Finals: U.S.A. 1, England 0 (Belo Horizonte, Brazil).

(4)	Nov. 1953	England 3, Hungary 6 (Wembley).
(5)	Sept. 1962	Cup-Winners' Cup 1st. Round, 1st. Leg: Bangor 2, Napoli 0.
(6)	Mar. 1966	World Cup stolen in London (found a week later).
(7)	June 1966	World Cup Finals: N. Korea 1, Italy 0 (Middlesbrough).
(8)	Jan. 1967	Scottish Cup 1st. Round: Berwick Rangers 1, Glasgow Rangers 0.
(9)	Mar. 1969	League Cup Final: Swindon Town 3, Arsenal 1.
(10)	Feb. 1971	F.A. Cup 5th. Round: Colchester United 3, Leeds 2.
(11)	Jan. 1972	F.A. Cup 3rd. Round: Hereford United 2, Newcastle 1.
(12)	July 1974	Bill Shankly retires as Liverpool manager.
(13)	May 1973	F.A. Cup Final: Sunderland 1, Leeds 0.
(14)	May 1976	F.A. Cup Final: Southampton 1, Man. Utd. 0.
(15)	July 1977	England manager Don Revie defects to coach United Arab Emirates.
(16)	June 1982	World Cup Finals: Algeria 2, West Germany 1 (Gijon, Spain).
(17)	Jan. 1984	F.A. Cup 3rd. Round: Bournemouth 2, Manchester United (holders) 0.
(18)	May 1988	F.A. Cup Final: Wimbledon 1, Liverpool 0 .
(19)	June 1990	World Cup Finals: Cameroon 1, Argentina (World Champions) 0 (Milan).
(20)	Sept. 1990	European Championship (Qual. Round): Faroe Islands 1, Austria 0.
(21)	Feb. 1991	Kenny Dalglish resigns as Liverpool manager.
(22)	Jan. 1992	F.A. Cup 3rd. Round: Wrexham 2, Arsenal 1.
(23)	June 1992	European Championship Final: Denmark 2, Germany (World Champions) 0.
(24)	June 1993	U.S. Cup '93: U.S.A. 2, England 0 (Foxboro, Boston).
(25)	July 1994	World Cup Finals: Bulgaria 2, Germany 1 (New York).

OTHER INTERNATIONAL SHOCKS

(Read in conjunction with Greatest Shocks above)

1982	Spain 0, N. Ireland 1 (World Cup Finals in Spain).
1990	Scotland 0, Costa Rica 1 (World Cup Finals in Italy).
1990	Sweden 1, Costa Rica 2 (World Cup Finals in Italy).
1993	Argentina 0, Colombia 5 (World Cup qual. round).
1993	France 2, Israel 3 (World Cup qual. round).
1993	San Marino score fastest goal in Int. records: 8.3 secs. v England (World Cup qual. round).
1994	Moldova 3, Wales 0; Georgia 5, Wales 0 (both Euro. Champ. qual. round).
1995	Belarus 1, Holland 0 (European Champ. qual. round).

GREAT RECOVERIES

On December 21, 1957, Charlton Athletic were losing 5-1 against Huddersfield Town (Div. 2) at The Valley with only 28 minutes left. From the 15th minute, they were reduced to ten men by injury, but they won 7-6, with left-winger Johnny Summers scoring five goals. Huddersfield remain the only team to score six times in a League match and lose.

Among other notable comebacks: on November 12, 1904 (Div. 1), Sheffield Wednesday were losing 0-5 at home to Everton, but drew 5-5. At Anfield on December 4, 1909 (Div.1), Liverpool trailed 2-5 to Newcastle at half-time, then won 6-5. On Boxing Day, 1927, in Div. 3 South, Northampton Town won 6-5 at home to Luton Town after being 1-5 down at half-time. On September 22, 1984 (Div. 1), Q.P.R. drew 5-5 at home to Newcastle after trailing 0-4 at half-time. On

April 12, 1993 (Div. 1) Swindon were 1-4 down at Birmingham with 30 minutes left, but won 6-4.

Other astonishing turnabouts in Div.1 include: Grimsby (3-5 down) won 6-5 at W.B.A. on Apr. 30, 1932; and Derby beat Man. Utd. 5-4 (from 1-4) on Sept. 5, 1936.

With 5 minutes to play, Ipswich were losing 3-0 at Barnsley (Div. 1, March 9, 1996), but drew 3-3.

On Sunday, Jan. 19, 1997 (Div. 1), Q.P.R. were 0-4 down away to Port Vale at half-time and still trailing 1-4 with 5 minutes left. They drew 4-4.

MATCHES OFF

Worst day for postponements: Feb. 9, 1963, when 57 League fixtures in England and Scotland were frozen off. Only 7 Football League matches took place, and the entire Scottish programme was wiped out

Worst other weather-hit days:

Jan. 12, 1963 and Feb. 2, 1963 – on both those Saturdays, only 4 out of 44 Football League matches were played.

Jan. 1, 1979 – 43 out of 46 Football League fixtures postponed.

Jan. 17, 1987 – 37 of 45 scheduled Football League fixtures postponed; only 2 Scottish matches survived.

Feb. 8-9, 1991 – only 4 of the week-end's 44 Barclays League matches survived the freeze-up (4 of the postponements were on Friday night). In addition, 11 Scottish League matches were off.

Jan. 27, 1996 – 44 Cup and League matches in England and Scotland were frozen off. The ten fixtures played comprised 3 F.A. Cup (4th. Round), 1 in Div. 1, 5 in Scottish Cup (3rd. Round), 1 in Scottish Div. 2.

Fewest matches left on one day by postponements was during the Second World War – Feb. 3, 1940 when, because of snow, ice and fog only one out of 56 regional league fixtures took place. It resulted Plymouth Argyle 10, Bristol City 3.

The Scottish Cup second round tie between Inverness Thistle and Falkirk in season 1978-9 was **postponed 29 times** because of snow and ice. First put off on Jan. 6, it was eventually played on Feb. 22. Falkirk won 4-0.

Pools Panel's busiest days: Jan. 17, 1987 and Feb. 9, 1991 – on both dates they gave their verdict on 48 postponed coupon matches.

FEWEST 'GAMES OFF'

Season 1947-8 was the best since the war for Football League fixtures being played to schedule. Only **six** were postponed.

LONGEST SEASON

The latest that League football has been played in a season was **June 7, 1947**. The season was extended because of mass postponements caused by bad weather in mid-winter.

The latest the F.A. Cup competition has ever been completed was in season 1981-2, when Tottenham beat Q.P.R. 1-0 in a Final replay at Wembley on May 27.

Worst winter hold-up was in season 1962-3. The Big Freeze began on Boxing Day and lasted until March, with nearly 500 first-class matches postponed. The F.A. Cup 3rd. Round was the longest on record – it began with only three out of 32 ties playable on January 5 and ended 66 days and 261 postponements later on March 11. The Lincoln-Coventry tie was put off 15 times. The Pools Panel was launched that winter, on January 26, 1963.

Hottest day for a Football League programme is believed to have been Saturday, September 1, 1906, when temperatures across the country were over 90°.

LEAGUE SECRETARIES

In February 1989, the Football League confirmed the appointment of **David Dent**, 52, as secretary in succession to Graham Kelly, who became chief executive of the F.A.

Mr. Dent, previously assistant and formerly with Coventry City, is only the **sixth secretary** of the League in its 107-year history, following: **Harry Lockett** (1888-1902), **Tom Charnley** (1902-33), **Fred Howarth** (1933-57), **Alan Hardaker** (1957-79) and **Graham Kelly** (1979-88).

F.A. Premier League (1992-97): Chief executive – Rick Parry (succeeded 1997 by Peter Leaver); Secretary – Mike Foster.

FOOTBALL ASSOCIATION SECRETARIES

Ebenezer Morley (1863-66), **Robert Willis** (1866-68), **R.G. Graham** (1868-70), **Charles Adcock** (1870-95, paid from 1887), 1895-1934 **Sir Frederick Wall**, 1934-62 **Sir Stanley Rous**, 1962-73 **Denis Follows**, 1973-89 **Ted Croker** (latterly chief executive), 1989 to date **Graham Kelly** (chief executive).

FOOTBALL'S SPONSORS

Football League: Canon 1983-6; Today Newspaper 1986-7; Barclays 1987-93; Endsleigh Insurance 1993-6; Nationwide 1996-9.

League Cup: Milk Cup 1982-6; Littlewoods 1987-90; Rumbelows 1991-2; Coca-Cola Cup 1993 to date.

Premier League: Carling 1993-2001.

F.A. Cup: Littlewoods 1994-8.

SOCCER HEADQUARTERS

Football Association: 16 Lancaster Gate, London W2 3LW. Chief Executive – Graham Kelly. **F.A. Premier League**: 16 Lancaster Gate, London W2 3LW. Chief Executive – Peter Leaver. **Football League**: Lytham St. Annes, Lancashire FY8 1JG. Secretary – David Dent. **Professional Footballers' Association**: 2 Oxford Court, Bishopsgate, Manchester M2 3WQ. Chief Executive: Gordon Taylor. **Football Trust**: Walkden House, 10 Melton Street, London NW1 2EB. Chief Executive: Peter Lee. **Scottish Football Association**: 6 Park Gardens, Glasgow G3 7YF. Chief Executive – James Farry. **Scottish Football League**: 188 West Regent Street, Glasgow G2 4RY. Secretary – Peter Donald. **Irish Football Association**: 20 Windsor Avenue, Belfast BT9 6EG. Secretary – David Bowen. **Irish Football League**: 87 University Street, Belfast BT7 1HP. Secretary – Mervyn Brown. **League of Ireland**: 80 Merrion Square, Dublin 2. Secretary – Eamonn Morris. **Republic of Ireland F.A.**: 80 Merrion Square, Dublin 2. **Welsh Football Association**: 3 Westgate Street, Cardiff, S. Glamorgan CF1 1JF. **FIFA**: FIFA House, Hitzigweg 11, CH-8032 Zurich, Switzerland. Secretary – Sepp Blatter. **UEFA**: Chemin de la Redoute 54, Case Postale 303, CH-1260, Nyon, Geneva, Switzerland. Secretary – Gerhard Aigner.

WORLD'S LARGEST STADIA
(Source: *FIFA NEWS*)

Capacity 165,000: Maracana, Rio de Janeiro, Brazil; **150,000** Rungnado Stadium, Pyongyang, Korea DPR; **125,000** Magalhaes Pinto Stadium, Belo Horizonte, Brazil; **120,000** Morumbi Stadium, Sao Paulo, Brazil; Stadium of Light, Lisbon, Portugal; Krirangan Stadium, Salt Lake, Calcutta; Senayan Stadium, Jakarta, Indonesia; **119,000** Castelao Stadium, Fortaleza, Brazil; **115,000** Arrudao Stadium, Recife, Brazil; Azteca Stadium, Mexico City; Nou Camp,

Barcelona, Spain; **114,000** Bernabeu Stadium, Madrid; **100,000** Nasser Stadium, Cairo, Egypt; Azadi Stadium, Tehran, Iran; Red Star Stadium, Belgrade, Yugoslavia; Central Stadium, Kiev, USSR.

NEW HOMES OF SOCCER

Newly-constructed League grounds in Britain since the war: 1946 Hull City (Boothferry Park); 1950 Port Vale (Vale Park); 1955 Southend United (Roots Hall); 1988 Scunthorpe United (Glanford Park); 1988 St. Johnstone (McDiarmid Park); 1990 Walsall (Bescot Stadium); 1990 Wycombe (Adams Park); 1992 Chester City (Deva Stadium, Bumpers Lane); 1993 Millwall (New Den); 1994 Clyde (Broadwood Stadium); 1994 Huddersfield Town (Alfred McAlpine Stadium, Kirklees); 1994 Northampton Town (Sixfields Stadium); 1995 Middlesbrough (Riverside Stadium); 1997 Bolton Wand. (Reebok Stadium, Horwich); 1997 Derby County (Pride Park); Stoke City (Britannia Stadium); Sunderland (Monkwearmouth).

GROUND-SHARING

Crystal Palace and **Charlton Athletic** (Selhurst Park, 1985-91); **Bristol Rovers** and **Bath City** (Twerton Park, Bath, 1986-96); **Partick Thistle** and **Clyde** (Firhill Park, Glasgow, 1986-91; in seasons 1990-1, 1991-2 **Chester** shared **Macclesfield Town's** ground (Moss Rose). **Crystal Palace** and **Wimbledon** now share Selhurst Park, starting season 1991-2, when **Charlton** rented Upton Park from **West Ham**. **Clyde** moved to Douglas Park, **Hamilton Academical's** home, in 1991-2. **Stirling Albion** shared **Stenhousemuir's** ground, Ochilview Park, in 1992-3. In 1993-4, **Clyde** shared **Partick's** home until moving to their new ground. In 1994-5, **Celtic** shared Hampden Park with **Queen's Park** (while Celtic Park redeveloped); **Hamilton** shared **Partick's** ground. **Airdrie** shared **Clyde's** Broadwood Stadium. **Bristol Rovers** left Bath City's ground at the start of season 1996-7, sharing Bristol Rugby Club's Memorial Ground. **Dumbarton** and **Clydebank** shared Boghead Park in 1996-7.

ARTIFICIAL TURF

Q.P.R. were the first British club to install an artificial pitch, in 1981. They were followed by **Luton Town** in 1985, and **Oldham Athletic** and **Preston in 1986.** Q.P.R. reverted to grass in 1988, as did Luton and promoted Oldham in season 1991-2 (when artificial pitches were banned in Div. 1). **Preston** were the last Football League club playing "on plastic" in 1993-4, and their Deepdale ground was restored to grass for the start of 1994-5.

Stirling Albion were the **first Scottish club** to play on plastic, in season 1987-8.

ALL-SEATER DEADLINE

Following the **Taylor Report**, Premier League and First Division grounds in England were required to be all-seated by August 1994. But the deadline was extended (May 1994) for five clubs planning to move to new stadiums: Derby, Grimsby, Middlesbrough, Portsmouth and Sunderland.

F.A. SOCCER SCHOOL

The Football Association's **national soccer school**, at Lilleshall, aimed at providing the backbone of England's World Cup challenge in the 1990s, was opened by the Duke of Kent (President) on September 4, 1984. It was sponsored by GM Motors, and the first intake comprised 25 boys aged fourteen.

To date the School of Excellence has produced England Internationals Nick Barmby, Andy Cole, Sol Campbell and Ian Walker. It will close in 1999 and be replaced by academies at leading clubs.

DOUBLE RUNNERS-UP

There have been eight instances of clubs finishing **runner-up in both the League Championship and F.A. Cup in the same season**: 1928 Huddersfield Town; 1932 Arsenal; 1939 Wolves; 1962 Burnley; 1965 and 1970 Leeds United; 1986 Everton; 1995 Manchester United.

CORNER-KICK RECORDS

Not a single corner-kick was recorded when **Newcastle United** drew 0-0 at home to **Portsmouth** (Div.1) on December 5, 1931.

The record for **most corners** in a match for one side is believed to be **Sheffield United's 28** to West Ham's 1 in Div.2 at Bramall Lane on October 14, 1989. For all their pressure, Sheff. United lost 2-0.

Nott'm. Forest led Southampton 22-2 on corners (Premier League, Nov. 28, 1992) but lost the match 1-2.

Tommy Higginson (Brentford) once passed back to his own goalkeeper from a corner kick.

'PROFESSIONAL FOUL' DIRECTIVE

After the 1990 World Cup Finals, F.I.F.A. dealt with the **"professional foul"**, incorporating this directive into the Laws of the Game: "If, in the opinion of the referee, a player who is moving towards his opponents' goal, with an obvious opportunity to score, is intentionally impeded by an opponent through unlawful means – thus denying the attacking player's team the aforesaid goalscoring opportunity – the offender should be sent from the field of play."

SACKED AT HALF-TIME

Leyton Orient sacked **Terry Howard** on his 397th appearance for the club – at half-time in a Second Division home defeat against Blackpool (Feb. 7, 1995) for "an unacceptable performance". He was fined two weeks' wages, given a free transfer and moved to Wycombe Wanderers.

MOST GAMES BY 'KEEPER FOR ONE CLUB

At the end of 1996-7, **Alan Knight** had made 642 League appearances for Portsmouth, over 20 seasons, a record for a goalkeeper at one club. The previous holder was Peter Bonetti with 600 League games for Chelsea (20 seasons, 1960-79).

COLOURFUL REFS

With the launch of the F.A. Premier League in 1992-3, referees wore **green, purple** or **yellow shirts**. Traditional all-black kit was still used when there was a clash with team colours.

PLAYED TWO GAMES ON SAME DAY

Jack Kelsey played full-length matches for both club and country on Wednesday, November 26, 1958. In the afternoon he kept goal for Wales in a 2-2 draw against England at Villa Park, and he then drove to Highbury to help Arsenal win 3-1 in a prestigious floodlit friendly against Juventus.

On the same day, winger **Danny Clapton** played for England (against Wales and Kelsey) and then in part of Arsenal's match against Juventus.

On November 11, 1987, **Mark Hughes** played for Wales against Czechoslovakia (European Championship) in Prague, then flew to Munich and went on as substitute that night in a winning Bayern Munich team, to whom he was on loan from Barcelona.

On February 16, 1993 goalkeeper **Scott Howie** played in Scotland's 3-0 U-21 win v Malta at Tannadice Park, Dundee (k.o. 1.30pm) and the same evening played in Clyde's 2-1 home win v Queen of South (Div. 2).

GOING PUBLIC

Manchester United became the fourth British club (after Tottenham, Hibernian and Millwall) to "go public" with a Stock Exchange share issue in June 1991. Clubs who have since unfolded flotation plans include Chelsea, Preston, Celtic, Leeds, Newcastle, Sunderland, Aston Villa, Birmingham, West Ham, W.B.A. and Sheffield United.

FIRST 'MATCH OF THE DAY'

BBC TV (recorded highlights): Liverpool 3, Arsenal 2 on August 22, 1964.
First complete match to be televised: Arsenal 3, Everton 2 on August 29, 1936.
First League match televised in colour: Liverpool 2, West Ham 0 on November 15, 1969.

OLYMPIC SOCCER WINNERS

1908 Great Britain (in London); **1912** Great Britain (Stockholm); **1920** Belgium (Antwerp); **1924** Uruguay (Paris); **1928** Uruguay (Amsterdam); **1932** No soccer in Los Angeles Olympics.
1936 Italy (Berlin); **1948** Sweden (London); **1952** Hungary (Helsinki); **1956** USSR (Melbourne); **1960** Yugoslavia (Rome); **1964** Hungary (Tokyo).
1968 Hungary (Mexico); **1972** Poland (Munich); **1976** E. Germany (Montreal); **1980** Czechoslovakia (Moscow); **1984** France (Los Angeles); **1988** USSR (Seoul); **1992** Spain (Barcelona); **1996** Nigeria (Atlanta).
Highest scorer in Final tournament: Ferenc Bene (Hungary) 12 goals, 1964.
Record crowd for Olympic Soccer Final: 108,800 (France v. Brazil, Los Angeles 1984).

MOST AMATEUR CUP WINS

Bishop Auckland set the F.A. Amateur Cup record with 10 wins, and in 1957 became the only club to carry off the trophy in three successive seasons. Five wins: Clapton and Crook Town. The competition was discontinued after the Final on April 20, 1974. (Bishop's Stortford 4, Ilford 1, at Wembley).

POOLS – RECORD WINS

Twenty-three winners crashed the £2m. barrier after Littlewoods raised the Treble Chance top prize to that limit at the start of season 1991-2 but, hit by the National Lottery, there were none in 1995-6 or 1996-7.

The Pools began in 1923. Launched with a capital of £100, Littlewoods distributed 4,000 coupons outside Manchester United's ground. Only 35 were returned, stakes totalled £4-7s.-6d. and the first pay-out was £2-12s.

The Treble Chance was introduced in 1946. Prize-money "firsts": £100,000 — 1950; £200,000 — 1957; £500,000 – 1972; £1m. – 1986; £1.5m. – 1990; £2m. – 1991.

Top Winners (all Littlewoods; * = Summer Pools)

Date	Name & Area	£
19/11/94	Syndicate from Worsley, Manchester	2,924,622
22/10/94	Syndicate from Wigan	2,615,854
14/1/95	Andy Paliunovas, Gloucester	2,326,792
27/8/94	Dave Yeomans, Worcester	2,293,110

23/7/94	Maurice Remington, Leicester	*2,281,399
1/10/94	Syndicate from Leeds	2,275,052
7/1/95	Co. Durham Man	2,273,430
6/8/94	David Caldwell, Cheam, Surrey	*2,267,636
16/7/94	Rohan Mitchell, Royal Navy	*2,261,401
24/9/94	Somerset Man	2,257,953
12/2/94	Barry Mallett, Dovercourt, Essex	2,255,387
13/6/92	Justin Daniels, Bournemouth	*2,246,113
11/4/92	South London Man	2,137,917
2/5/92	Suffolk Man	2,110,436
11/12/93	Judith and Terry Smith, Portland	2,077,683
27/11/93	Mary Brown, Liverpool	2,075,151
26/10/91	Rodica Woodcock, South-east London	2,072,220
24/6/95	Audrey Grieve, Scotland	*2,069,767
6/3/93	Terry Saxon (syndicate), Newport, Gwent	2,055,559
8/5/93	Bill Forbes (syndicate), Birmingham	2,029,668
1/2/92	Joyce Beynon, Llantrisant, Mid-Glamorgan	2,027,493
31/10/92	Charlie Hill, Blackpool	2,008,137
15/2/92	Pat Unwin, Stoke-on-Trent	2,000,000

- Jim Wright, from Teignmouth, Devon, set a Fixed Odds record with a payment of £654,375 (Ladbrokes, May 1993). He placed a £1,000 each-way pre-season treble on the champions of the three Football League divisions – Newcastle (8-1), Stoke (6-1), Cardiff (9-1).

- An anonymous Bournemouth punter won £292,000 for a £10 stake with a 13-match Fixed Odds accumulator on Jan. 25-27, 1997 (Ladbrokes). The first 12 selections won on the Saturday, and Raith completed his "lucky 13" with a 4-1 Scottish Cup replay win away to Airdrie two nights later.

POOLS PANEL

The **Pools Panel** was introduced in January 1963 during the **Big Freeze winter**. Originally, 30 coupon matches had to be postponed for the panel to operate; in later seasons the figure was ten and, starting in 1988-9, they gave their verdict when only one coupon fixture was off. The panel assembles at a hotel (originally in London and since 1984 in Manchester) every weekend from the beginning of October to the end of April.

Their busiest day was Jan. 27, 1996, when, because of postponements, they were required to adjudicate on 54 matches (incl. 11 in the Conference).

THE FOOTBALL TRUST

The **Football Trust** founded in 1975 – an initiative of Pools companies Littlewoods, Vernons and Zetters – has been providing support for the game at every level throughout the UK for 22 years, from kit and equipment for school teams to pitches and dressing rooms for local clubs and safety and improvement work throughout the game. Its present priority is to help League clubs fulfil the Taylor Report recommendations that followed the Hillsborough tragedy.

Grants exceeding £140m. have been made to major ground redevelopment projects across Britain, towards the construction of 150 new/refurbished stands in Premier League, Football League and Scottish League and the opening of seven new grounds.

The F.A. Premier League will contribute £20m. to the Football Trust from 1997-2001 during which, via the Trust and the Sports Council Lottery Fund, grants of £55m. will be made for essential work at football grounds throughout England.

RECORD TESTIMONIALS

Two nights after Man. United completed the Double in May, 1994, 42,079 packed Old Trafford for **Mark Hughes'** testimonial (1-3 Celtic). The estimated proceeds of £500,000 equalled the British testimonial record of **Ally McCoist's** match (Rangers 1, Newcastle 2) on August 3, 1993.

The match for **Bryan Robson**, Man. United and England captain, against Celtic at Old Trafford on Tuesday, November 20, 1990 was watched by a crowd of 41,658, and receipts of £300,000 were a then record for a testimonial.

Kenny Dalglish's testimonial (Liverpool v Real Sociedad) at Anfield on August 14, 1990 attracted 30,461 spectators, with receipts estimated at £150,000.

On December 4, 1990, **Willie Miller's** testimonial (Aberdeen v World XI) packed Pittodrie to its 22,500 capacity, and raised an estimated £150,000.

The match for 82-year-old **Sir Matt Busby**, between Man. United and a Rep. of Ireland XI at Old Trafford on Sunday, August 11, 1991 was watched by 35,410 (estimated benefit £250,000).

Ian Rush's testimonial brought an estimated £250,000 from a 25,856 crowd at Anfield on December 6, 1994 (Liverpool 6, Celtic 0).

Three lucrative testimonials were staged in May 1996. Arsenal's **Paul Merson** earned a reported £400,000 (a percentage to charity) from his match against an Int. Man's XI at Highbury (May 9, att: 31,626); the Republic of Ireland's new manager **Mick McCarthy** received an estimated £300,000 from a 40,000 who saw Celtic beaten 3-0 at Lansdowne Road, Dublin on May 26; and **Stuart Pearce** benefited by some £200,000 from a turn-out of 23,815 when Nott'm. Forest beat Newcastle 6-5 at the City Ground on May 8.

Testimonial sums reported in season 1996-7 included: **Bryan Gunn**, Norwich goalkeeper, £250,000 for 21,000 sell-out v Man. United, Nov. 4; **Brian McClair**, Man. United, £380,000 v Celtic, April 14.

WHAT IT USED TO COST . . .

Minimum admission to League football was one shilling in 1939. After the war, it was increased to 1s. 3d. in 1946; 1s. 6d. in 1951; 1s. 9d. in 1952; 2s. in 1955; 2s. 6d. in 1960; 4s. in 1965; 5s. in 1968; 6s. in 1970; and 8s. (40p) in 1972. After that, the fixed minimum charge was dropped.

ENGLAND TOP EURO-PRIZE WINNERS

There have been **118 European club competitions** since the Champions' Cup was launched in season 1955-6; 42 for the European Cup, 39 for the Fairs/UEFA Cup and 37 for the Cup-Winners' Cup.

Despite the five-year enforced absence that followed the Heysel disaster in 1985, **English clubs** still head the European prize list, Arsenal's success in the 1994 Cup-Winners' Cup taking the total to 24 triumphs: 8 in the Champions' Cup, 7 in the Cup-Winners' Cup and 9 in the Fairs/UEFA Cup.

Italy are second with 23 Euro prizes, followed by Spain (22) and West Germany/Germany (15). The 118 winners have come from 16 countries.

England's 24 prizes are shared among 13 clubs: Liverpool 6 (4 EC, 2 UEFA); Tottenham 3 (1 CWC, 2 UEFA); Leeds 2 (2 UEFA); Man. United 2 (1 EC, 1 CWC); Nott'm. Forest 2 (2 EC); Arsenal 2 (1 UEFA, 1 CWC); Aston Villa 1 (EC); Chelsea 1 (CWC); Everton 1 (CWC); Ipswich 1 (UEFA); Man. City 1 (CWC); Newcastle 1 (UEFA); West Ham 1 (CWC).

Scotland's three successes have been achieved by Celtic (EC); Rangers and Aberdeen (both CWC).

EUROPEAN TRIUMPHS, COUNTRY BY COUNTRY

	European Cup	Cup-Winners' Cup	UEFA Cup	Total
England	8	7	9	24
Italy	9	6	8	23
Spain	7	7	8	22
West Germany/Germany	5	4	6	15
Holland	6	1	3	10
Belgium	–	3	1	4
Portugal	3	1	–	4
Scotland	1	2	–	3
USSR	–	3	–	3
France	1	1	–	2
Sweden	–	–	2	2
Yugoslavia	1	–	1	2
Czechoslovakia	–	1	–	1
East Germany	–	1	–	1
Hungary	–	–	1	1
Romania	1	–	–	1
Total:	**42**	**37**	**39**	**118**

BRITAIN'S 27 TROPHIES IN EUROPE

Arsenal's success in the 1993-4 Cup-Winners' Cup took the number of British club triumphs in European to 27 (nine in each competition):

European Cup (9)	Cup-Winners' Cup (9)	Fairs/UEFA Cup (9)
1967 Celtic	1963 Tottenham	1968 Leeds Utd.
1968 Man. United	1965 West Ham Utd.	1969 Newcastle Utd.
1977 Liverpool	1970 Man. City	1970 Arsenal
1978 Liverpool	1971 Chelsea	1971 Leeds Utd.
1979 Nott'm Forest	1972 Rangers	1972 Tottenham
1980 Nott'm Forest	1983 Aberdeen	1973 Liverpool
1981 Aston Villa	1985 Everton	1976 Liverpool
1982 Aston Villa	1991 Man. United	1981 Ipswich Town
1984 Liverpool	1994 Arsenal	1984 Tottenham

EUROPEAN CLUB COMPETITIONS – SCORING RECORDS

European Cup – Record aggregate: 18-0 by Benfica v Dudelange (Lux) (8-0a, 10-0h), prelim. round, 1965-6.
   Record single-match score: 12-0 by Feyenoord v KR Reykjavik (Ice), 1st. round, 1st. leg, 1969-70 (aggregate was 16-0).
Cup-Winners' Cup – Record aggregate: 21-0 by Chelsea v Jeunesse Hautcharage (Lux) (8-0a, 13-0h), 1st. round, 1971-2.
   Record single-match score: 16-1 by Sporting Lisbon v Apoel Nicosia, 2nd. round, 1st. leg, 1963-4 (aggregate was 18-1).
UEFA Cup (prev. Fairs Cup) – Record aggregate: 21-0 by Feyenoord v US Ramelange (Lux) (9-0h, 12-0a), 1st. round, 1972-3.
   Record single-match score: 14-0 by Ajax Amsterdam v Red Boys (Lux) 1st. round, 2nd leg, 1984-5 (aggregate also 14-0).
Record British score in Europe: 13-0 by Chelsea at home to Jeunesse Hautcharage (Lux) in Cup-Winners'Cup 1st. round, 2nd. leg, 1971-2. Chelsea's overall 21-0 in that tie is highest aggregate by British club in Europe.
Individual scoring records for European tie (over two legs): **8 goals** by **Jose Altafini** for the AC Milan v US Luxembourg (European Cup, prelim. round,

1962-3, agg. 14-0) and by **Peter Osgood** for Chelsea v Jeunesse Hautcharage (Cup-Winners' Cup, 1st. round 1971-2, agg. 21-0). Altafini and Osgood each scored 5 goals at home, 3 away.

Individual single-match scoring record in European competition: **6 goals** by Lothar Emmerich when Borussia Dortmund beat Floriana (Malta) 8-0 in Cup-Winners' Cup 1st. round, 2nd. leg, 1965-6.

Most goals in single European campaign: 15 by **Jurgen Klinsmann** for Bayern Munich (UEFA Cup 1995-6).

Most goals (career total) **by British player in European competition:** 31 by Peter Lorimer (Leeds, in 9 campaigns).

EUROPEAN FOOTBALL – BIG RECOVERIES

In the 42-year history of European competition, only four clubs have survived a **4-goal** deficit after the first leg:

1961-2 (Cup-Winners' Cup 1st. Rd.): Leixoes (Portugal) beat Chaux de Fonds 7-6 on agg. (lost 2-6a, won 5-0h).

1962-3 (Fairs Cup 2nd. Rd.): Valencia (Spain) beat **Dunfermline** 1-0 in play-off in Lisbon after 6-6 agg. (Valencia won 4-0h, lost 2-6a).

1984-5 (UEFA Cup 2nd. Rd.): Partizan Belgrade beat **Q.P.R.** on away goals (lost 2-6 away, at Highbury, won 4-0 home).

1985-6 (UEFA Cup 3rd. Rd.): Real Madrid beat Borussia Moenchengladbach on away goals (lost 1-5a, won 4-0h) and went on to win competition.

In the **European Cup**, there are eight instances of clubs reaching the next round after **arrears of three goals** in the first leg:

1958-9 (Prel. Rd.) Schalke beat KB Copenhagen (0-3, 5-2, 3-1).

1965-6 (Q-final) Partizan Belgrade beat Sparta Prague (1-4, 5-0).

1970-1 (S-final) Panathinaikos beat Red Star Belgrade on away goal (1-4, 3-0).

1975-6 (2nd. Rd.) Real Madrid beat **Derby County** (1-4, 5-1).

1985-6 (S-final) Barcelona beat IFK Gothenburg on pens. (0-3, 3-0).

1988-9 (1st. Rd.) Werder Bremen beat Dynamo Berlin (0-3, 5-0).

1988-9 (2nd. Rd.) Galatasaray (Turkey) beat Neuchatel Xamax (Switz.) (0-3, 5-0).

1992-3 (1st. Rd.) **Leeds** beat VfB Stuttgart 2-1 in play-off in Barcelona. Over two legs, VfB won on away goal (3-0h, 1-4 away) but UEFA ordered third match because they broke "foreigners" rule in team selection.

In the **Cup-Winners' Cup**, six clubs have survived a **3-goal** deficit:

1963-4 (Q-final) Sporting Lisbon beat **Man. United** (1-4, 5-0).

1963-4 (S-final) MTK Budapest beat **Celtic** (0-3, 4-0).

1978-9 (2nd. Rd.) Barcelona beat Anderlecht on pens. (0-3, 3-0).

1980-1 (1st. Rd.) Carl Zeiss Jena beat AS Roma (0-3, 4-0).

1984-5 (Q-final) Rapid Vienna beat Dynamo Dresden (0-3, 5-0).

1989-90 (1st. Rd.) Grasshoppers (Switz.) beat Slovan Bratislava (0-3, 4-0).

In the **Fairs Cup/UEFA Cup**, there have been more than 20 occasions when clubs have survived a deficit of **3 goals**, the most notable example being the 1988 UEFA Cup Final, which Bayer Leverkusen won 3-2 on pens., having lost the first leg 0-3 away to Espanol and won the return 3-0 to level the aggregate.

Apart from Leeds, two other British clubs have won a European tie from a 3-goal, first leg deficit: **Kilmarnock** 0-3, 5-1 v Eintracht Frankfurt (Fairs Cup 1st. Round, 1964-5); **Hibernian** 1-4, 5-0 v Napoli (Fairs Cup 2nd. Round, 1967-8).

Three English clubs have gone out of the **UEFA Cup** after leading 3-0 from the first leg: 1975-6 (2nd. Rd.) **Ipswich** lost 3-4 on agg. to Bruges; 1976-7 (Q-final) **Q.P.R.** lost on pens. to AEK Athens after 3-3 agg; 1977-8 (3rd. Rd.) Ipswich lost on pens. to Barcelona after 3-3 agg.

HEAVIEST ENGLISH-CLUB DEFEATS IN EUROPE
(Single-leg scores)

European Cup: Ajax 5, Liverpool 1 (2nd. Rd.), Dec. 1966; Real Madrid 5, Derby 1 (2nd. Rd.), Nov. 1975.

Cup-Winners' Cup: Sporting Lisbon 5, Man. Utd. 0 (Q-final), Mar. 1964.
Fairs/UEFA Cup: Bayern Munich 6, Coventry 1 (2nd. Rd.), Oct. 1970.

SHOCK ENGLISH-CLUB DEFEATS

1968-69 (E. Cup, 1st. Rd.): Man. City beaten by Fenerbahce, 1-2 agg.
1971-72 (CWC, 2nd. Rd.): Chelsea beaten by Atvidaberg on away goals.
1993-94 (E. Cup, 2nd. Rd.): Man. United beaten by Galatasaray on away goals.
1994-95 (UEFA Cup, 1st. Rd.): Blackburn beaten by Trelleborgs, 2-3 agg.

P.F.A. FAIR PLAY TROPHY
(Bobby Moore Fair Play Trophy from 1993)

1988	Liverpool	1993	Norwich
1989	Liverpool	1994	Crewe
1990	Liverpool	1995	Crewe
1991	Nott'm. Forest	1996	Crewe
1992	Portsmouth	1997	Crewe

RECORD MEDALS SALE

"The **Billy Wright Collection**" – caps, medals and other memorabilia from his illustrious career – fetched over £100,000 at Christies' ninth annual football sale in Glasgow on Nov. 21, 1996.

At the sale in Oct. 1993, trophies, caps and medals earned by **Ray Kennedy**, 42-year-old former England, Arsenal and Liverpool player, fetched a then record total of £88,407. Kennedy, who suffers from Parkinson's Disease, received £73,000 after commission.

The P.F.A. paid £31,080 for a total of 60 lots – including a record £16,000 for his 1977 European Cup winner's medal – to be exhibited at their Manchester museum. An anonymous English collector paid £17,000 for the medal and plaque commemorating Kennedy's part in the Arsenal Double in 1971.

Previous record for one player's medals, shirts etc. collection: £30,000 (**Bill Foulkes**, Man. Utd. in 1992). The sale of **Dixie Dean**'s medals etc. in 1991 realised £28,000.

VARSITY MATCH

Oxford and **Cambridge** drew 0-0 in the 113th Varsity soccer match at Fulham on March 29 last. Cambridge have won 45, Oxford 42, with 26 draws. The fixture began in 1874.

LONGEST UNBEATEN CUP RUN

Liverpool established the longest unbeaten Cup sequence by a Football League club: 25 successive rounds in the League/Milk Cup between semi-final defeat by Nottingham Forest (1-2 agg.) in 1980 and defeat at Tottenham (0-1) in the third round on October 31, 1984. During this period Liverpool won the tournament in four successive seasons, a feat no other Football League club has achieved in any competition.

HIGH HALF-TIME SCORES

Tottenham 10, Crewe 1 (F.A. Cup 4th. Rd. replay, Feb. 3, 1960; result 13-2); Tranmere 8, Oldham 1 (Div. 3N., Dec. 26, 1935; result 13-4); Chester 8, York 0 (Div. 3N., Feb. 1, 1936; result 12-0; believed to be record half-time scores in League football).

• On March 4, 1933 Coventry beat Q.P.R. (Div. 3 South) 7-0, having led by that score at half-time.

• Only instance of club failing to win League match after leading 5-0 at half-time: Sheff. Wed. 5, Everton 5 (Div. 1, Nov. 12, 1904; Wednesday scored 5 in first half, Everton 5 in second).

TOP SECOND-HALF TEAM

Most goals scored by a team in one half of a League match is eleven. Stockport led Halifax 2-0 at half-time in Div. 3 North on Jan. 6, 1934 and won 13-0.

FIVE NOT ENOUGH

Last team to score 5 in League match and lose: Reading, beaten 7-5 at Doncaster (Div. 3, Sept. 25, 1982).

LONG SERVICE WITH ONE CLUB

Bob Paisley was associated with Liverpool for 57 years from 1939, when he joined them from Bishop Auckland, until he died in February 1996. He served them as player, trainer, coach, assistant-manager, manager, director and vice-president.

Ronnie Moran, who joined Liverpool in 1952, is still with the club as coach.

Ernie Gregory served West Ham for 52 years as goalkeeper and coach. He joined them as boy of 14 from school in 1935, retired in May 1987.

Ted Sagar, Everton goalkeeper, 23 years at Goodison Park (1929-52, but only 16 League seasons because of War).

Roy Sproson, defender, played 21 League seasons for his only club, Port Vale (1950-71).

Pat Bonner, goalkeeper, 19 seasons with Celtic (1978-97).

Danny McGrain, defender, 17 years with Celtic (1970-87).

LONGEST CURRENT MEMBERSHIPS OF TOP DIVISION

Arsenal (since 1919), **Everton** (1954), **Liverpool** (1962), **Coventry** (1967).

TIGHT AT HOME

Fewest home goals conceded in League season (modern times): 4 by **Liverpool** (Div. 1, 1978-9); 4 by **Man. United** (Premier League, 1994-5) – both in 21 matches.

TRIBUNAL-FEE RECORDS

Top tribunal fee: £2.5m for **Chris Bart-Williams** (Sheff. Wed. to Nott'm. Forest, June 1995).

Biggest discrepancy: **Andy Walker**, striker, Bolton to Celtic, June 1994: Bolton asked £2.2m, Celtic offered £250,000. Tribunal decided £550,000.

LONGEST THROW-IN?

That by Notts County's **Andy Legg** was measured (season 1994-5) at 41 metres (45 yards) and claimed as the longest throw by any footballer in the world.

BALL JUGGLING: WORLD RECORD CLAIM

Sam Ik (South Korea) juggled a ball non-stop for 18 hours, 11 minutes, 4 seconds in March 1995.

SUBS' SCORING RECORD

Barnet's 5-4 home win v Torquay (Div. 3, Dec. 28, 1993) provided the first instance of **all four substitutes** scoring in a major League match in England.

FOOTBALL'S OLDEST ANNUAL

Now in its 111th edition, this publication began as the 16-page *Athletic News Football Supplement & Club Directory* in 1887. From the long-established *Athletic News*, it became the *Sunday Chronicle Annual* in 1946, the *Empire News* in 1956, the *News of the World & Empire News* in 1961 and, since 1965, the *News of the World Annual*.

FOOTBALL LEAGUE COCA-COLA CUP FIRST ROUND

Macclesfield v Hull
Rochdale v Stoke
Chester v Carlisle
Lincoln v Burnley
Port Vale v York
Wigan v Chesterfield
Oldham v Grimsby
Tranmere v Hartlepool
Wrexham v Sheffield Utd
Crewe v Bury
Doncaster v Nott'm Forest
Scarborough v Scunthorpe
Rotherham v Preston
Darlington v Notts Co
Blackpool v Manchester C
Huddersfield v Bradford
Mansfield v Stockport
Oxford v Plymouth

Charlton v Ipswich
Norwich v Barnet
Reading v Swansea
Brentford v Shrewsbury
Walsall v Exeter
Wycombe v Fulham
Cardiff v Southend
Colchester v Luton
Gillingham v Birmingham
Northampton v Milwall
Peterborough v Portsmouth
Cambridge v WBA
Bristol C v Bristol R
Swindon v Watford
Bournemouth v Torquay
Brighton v L Orient
QPR v Wolves.

To be played weeks commencing Aug 11 & 25.

SCOTTISH LEAGUE COCA-COLA CUP 1997-98

1st Round – Sat., Aug. 2
Berwick v Brechin
Arbroath v Queen of the South
Inverness Cal. Th. v Stenhousemuir
Forfar v Albion
Ross County v Montrose
Cowdenbeath v Alloa
Dumbarton v Queens Park
East Stirling v Stranraer

2nd Round – Sat., Aug. 9
Dundee v E. Stirling or Stranraer
Hibernian v Cowdenbeath or Alloa
Livingston v Hearts
St. Mirren v Clydebank

Hamilton Acad. v Rangers
Raith v Forfar or Albion
Arbroath or Queen of South v Dundee Utd.
St. Johnstone v Clyde
Berwick or Brechin v Celtic
Partick Thistle v Stirling Albion
Dumbarton or Queens Park v Aberdeen
Dunfermline v Ayr
Ross County or Montrose v Falkirk
Motherwell v Inverness Cal.Th. or Stenhousemuir
Greenock Morton v Airdrie

LEAGUE CHAMPIONS' RECORDS

Season	Champions	P	W	D	L	F	A	Pts
1888-89	Preston North End	22	18	4	0	74	15	40
1889-90	Preston North End	22	15	3	4	71	30	33
1890-91	Everton	22	14	1	7	63	29	29
1891-92	Sunderland	26	21	0	5	93	36	42
1892-93	Sunderland	30	22	4	4	100	36	48
1893-94	Aston Villa	30	19	6	5	84	42	44
1894-95	Sunderland	30	21	5	4	80	37	47
1895-96	Aston Villa	30	20	5	5	78	45	45
1896-97	Aston Villa	30	21	5	4	73	38	47
1897-98	Sheffield United	30	17	8	5	56	31	42
1898-99	Aston Villa	34	19	7	8	76	40	45
1899-1900	Aston Villa	34	22	6	6	77	35	50
1900-01	Liverpool	34	19	7	8	59	35	45
1901-02	Sunderland	34	19	6	9	50	35	44
1902-03	Sheffield Wednesday	34	19	4	11	54	36	42
1903-04	Sheffield Wednesday	34	20	7	7	48	28	47
1904-05	Newcastle United	34	23	2	9	72	33	48
1905-06	Liverpool	38	23	5	10	79	46	51
1906-07	Newcastle United	38	22	7	9	74	46	51
1907-08	Manchester United	38	23	6	9	81	48	52
1908-09	Newcastle United	38	24	5	9	65	41	53
1909-10	Aston Villa	38	23	7	8	84	42	53
1910-11	Manchester United	38	22	8	8	72	40	52
1911-12	Blackburn Rovers	38	20	9	9	60	43	49
1912-13	Sunderland	38	25	4	9	86	43	54
1913-14	Blackburn Rovers	38	20	11	7	78	42	51
1914-15	Everton	38	19	8	11	76	47	46
1919-20	West Bromwich Albion	42	28	4	10	104	47	60
1920-21	Burnley	42	23	13	6	79	36	59
1921-22	Liverpool	42	22	13	7	63	36	57
1922-23	Liverpool	42	26	8	8	70	31	60
1923-24	Huddersfield Town	42	23	11	8	60	33	57
1924-25	Huddersfield Town	42	21	16	5	69	28	58
1925-26	Huddersfield Town	42	23	11	8	92	60	57
1926-27	Newcastle United	42	25	6	11	96	58	56
1927-28	Everton	42	20	13	9	102	66	53
1928-29	Sheffield Wednesday	42	21	10	11	86	62	52
1929-30	Sheffield Wednesday	42	26	8	8	105	57	60
1930-31	Arsenal	42	28	10	4	127	59	66
1931-32	Everton	42	26	4	12	116	64	56
1932-33	Arsenal	42	25	8	9	118	61	58
1933-34	Arsenal	42	25	9	8	75	47	59
1934-35	Arsenal	42	23	12	7	115	46	58
1935-36	Sunderland	42	25	6	11	109	74	56
1936-37	Manchester City	42	22	13	7	107	61	57
1937-38	Arsenal	42	21	10	11	77	44	52
1938-39	Everton	42	27	5	10	88	52	59
1946-47	Liverpool	42	25	7	10	84	52	57

Season	Champions	P	W	D	L	F	A	Pts
1947-48	Arsenal	42	23	13	6	81	32	59
1948-49	Portsmouth	42	25	8	9	84	42	58
1949-50	Portsmouth	42	22	9	11	74	38	53
1950-51	Tottenham Hotspur	42	25	10	7	82	44	60
1951-52	Manchester United	42	23	11	8	95	52	57
1952-53	Arsenal	42	21	12	9	97	64	54
1953-54	Wolverhampton Wanderers	42	25	7	10	96	56	57
1954-55	Chelsea	42	20	12	10	81	57	52
1955-56	Manchester United	42	25	10	7	83	51	60
1956-57	Manchester United	42	28	8	6	103	54	64
1957-58	Wolverhampton Wanderers	42	28	8	6	103	47	64
1958-59	Wolverhampton Wanderers	42	28	5	9	110	49	61
1959-60	Burnley	42	24	7	11	85	61	55
1960-61	Tottenham Hotspur	42	31	4	7	115	55	66
1961-62	Ipswich Town	42	24	8	10	93	67	56
1962-63	Everton	42	25	11	6	84	42	61
1963-64	Liverpool	42	26	5	11	92	45	57
1964-65	Manchester United	42	26	9	7	89	39	61
1965-66	Liverpool	42	26	9	7	79	34	61
1966-67	Manchester United	42	24	12	6	84	45	60
1967-68	Manchester City	42	26	6	10	86	43	58
1968-69	Leeds United	42	27	13	2	66	26	67
1969-70	Everton	42	29	8	5	72	34	66
1970-71	Arsenal	42	29	7	6	71	29	65
1971-72	Derby County	42	24	10	8	69	33	58
1972-73	Liverpool	42	25	10	7	72	42	60
1973-74	Leeds United	42	24	14	4	66	31	62
1974-75	Derby County	42	21	11	10	67	49	53
1975-76	Liverpool	42	23	14	5	66	31	60
1976-77	Liverpool	42	23	11	8	62	33	57
1977-78	Nottingham Forest	42	25	14	3	69	24	64
1978-79	Liverpool	42	30	8	4	85	16	68
1979-80	Liverpool	42	25	10	7	81	30	60
1980-81	Aston Villa	42	26	8	8	72	40	60
1981-82	Liverpool	42	26	9	7	80	32	87
1982-83	Liverpool	42	24	10	8	87	37	82
1983-84	Liverpool	42	22	14	6	73	32	80
1984-85	Everton	42	28	6	8	88	43	90
1985-86	Liverpool	42	26	10	6	89	37	88
1986-87	Everton	42	26	8	8	76	31	86
1987-88	Liverpool	40	26	12	2	87	24	90
1988-89	Arsenal	38	22	10	6	73	36	76
1989-90	Liverpool	38	23	10	5	78	37	79
1990-91	Arsenal	38	24	13	1	74	18	83
1991-92	Leeds United	42	22	16	4	74	37	82
1992-93	Manchester United	42	24	12	6	67	31	84
1993-94	Manchester United	42	27	11	4	80	38	92
1994-95	Blackburn Rovers	42	27	8	7	80	39	89
1995-96	Manchester United	38	25	7	6	73	35	82
1996-97	Manchester United	38	21	12	5	76	44	75

OLYMPIC SOCCER FINALS

Year	Venue	Participants	Winners	Runners-up	Score	Attendance	Tournament Top Scorer
1908	London	6	Great Britain	Denmark	2-0	8,000	11 – Sophus Nielsen (Denmark)
1912	Stockholm	13	Great Britain	Denmark	4-2	14,000	10 – Gottfried Fuchs (Germany)
1920	Antwerp	14	Belgium	Czechoslovakia	2-0		7 – Herbert Karlsson (Sweden)
	(Final abandoned 39 mins – Czechs disqualified after walking off in protest when player sent off)						
1924	Paris	23	Uruguay	Switzerland	3-0	41,000	8 – Pedro Petrovic (Uruguay)
1928	Amsterdam	17	Uruguay	Argentina	2-1		9 – Domingo Tarasconi (Argentina)
				(Replay after 1-1)			
1932	Los Angeles – No soccer tournament						
1936	Berlin	16	Italy	Austria	2-1	100,000	7 – Annibale Frossi (Italy)
1948	London	18	Sweden	Yugoslavia	3-1		7 – Gunnar Nordahl (Sweden)
1952	Helsinki	25	Hungary	Yugoslavia	2-0	60,000	7 – Rajko Mitic & Branko Zebec (both Yugoslavia)
1956	Melbourne	11	USSR	Yugoslavia	1-0	100,000	4 – Dimitar Milanov (Bulgaria)
1960	Rome	16	Yugoslavia	Denmark	3-1		7 – Milan Galic & Borivoje Kostic (both Yugoslavia)
1964	Tokyo	14	Hungary	Czechoslovakia	2-1	80,000	12 – Ferenc Bene (Hungary)
1968	Mexico	16	Hungary	Bulgaria	4-1		7 – Kunishige Kamamoto (Japan)
1972	Munich	16	Poland	Hungary	2-1		9 – Kazimierz Deyna (Poland)
1976	Montreal	13	E. Germany	Poland	3-1	71,619	6 – Andrzej Szarmach (Poland)
1980	Moscow	16	Czechoslovakia	E. Germany	1-0	80,000	5 – Sergey Andreev (USSR)
1984	Los Angeles	16	France	Brazil	2-0	108,800	5 – Damel Xuereb (France); Bovivoje Cvetkovic & Stjepan Deveric (both Yugoslavia)
1988	Seoul	16	USSR	Brazil	2-1	74,000	7 – Farias Romario (Brazil)
1992	Barcelona	16	Spain	Poland	3-2	95,000	7 – Andrzej Juskowiak (Poland)
1996	Athens (Georgia, USA)	16	Nigeria	Argentina	3-2	86,117	6 – Bebeto (Brazil) Crespo (Argentina)

TRANSFER TRAIL
By Albert Sewell

For space reasons, it is no longer possible to include every million-pound transfer involving British clubs since the first such deal: **Trevor Francis** from Birmingham to Nott'm. Forest (£1,180,000) in Feb. 1979.

Alan Shearer became the world's first £15m. player when he moved from Blackburn to Newcastle in July 1996. Key:

★ = British record fee at that time
A = Record all-British deal
B = Record for goalkeeper
C = Record for defender
D = Record deal between English and Scottish clubs
E = Record fee paid by Scottish club
F = Record fee to Scottish club
G = Record all-Scottish deal

H = Record paid for winger
J = Record received for winger
K = Record for teenager
L = Most expensive foreign import
M = Record English-club signing
N = Record British striker

(• Fees as at time of transfer, i.e. not including any subsequent increases)

	Player	From	To	Date	£
AMN★	Alan Shearer	Blackburn	Newcastle	7/96	15,000,000
	Juninho	Mid'bro'	Atl. Madrid	7/97	12,000,000
★	Stan Collymore	Nottm. F.	Liverpool	6/95	8,500,000
J	Andrei Kanchelskis	Everton	Fiorentina	1/97	8,000,000
L★	Dennis Bergkamp	Inter Milan	Arsenal	6/95	7,500,000
★	Andy Cole	Newcastle	Man. Utd.	1/95	7,000,000
	Fabrizio Ravanelli	Juventus	Mid'bro'	7/96	7,000,000
	Stan Collymore	Liverpool	Aston Villa	5/97	7,000,000
H	Marc Overmars	Ajax Amsterdam	Arsenal	6/97	7,000,000
	Faustino Asprilla	Parma	Newcastle	2/96	6,700,000
★	David Platt	Bari	Juventus	6/92	6,500,000
★	Paul Ince	Man. Utd.	Inter Milan	6/95	6,000,000
	Les Ferdinand	Q.P.R.	Newcastle	6/95	6,000,000
	Nick Barmby	Mid'bro'	Everton	10/96	5,750,000
★	David Platt	Aston Villa	Bari	7/91	5,500,000
★	Paul Gascoigne	Tottenham	Lazio	6/92	5,500,000
	Nick Barmby	Tottenham	Mid'bro'	8/95	5,250,000
	David Platt	Juventus	Sampdoria	7/93	5,200,000
F	Trevor Steven	Rangers	Marseille	8/91	5,000,000
	Chris Sutton	Norwich	Blackburn	7/94	5,000,000
	Andrei Kanchelskis	Man. Utd.	Everton	8/95	5,000,000
	Paul Merson	Arsenal	Mid'bro'	7/97	5,000,000
	Roberto Di Matteo	Lazio	Chelsea	7/96	4,900,000
	David Platt	Sampdoria	Arsenal	7/95	4,750,000
	Juninho	Sao Paulo	Mid'bro'	10/95	4,750,000
	Chris Armstrong	Crystal P.	Tottenham	6/95	4,500,000
	Lee Sharpe	Man. Utd.	Leeds	8/96	4,500,000
	Gianfranco Zola	Parma	Chelsea	11/96	4,500,000
C	Slaven Bilic	West Ham	Everton	5/97	4,500,000
E	Paul Gascoigne	Lazio	Rangers	7/95	4,300,000
	Jason McAteer	Bolton	Liverpool	9/95	4,500,000
	Tomas Brolin	Parma	Leeds	11/95	4,300,000
	Ruel Fox	Newcastle	Tottenham	10/95	4,200,000
★	Chris Waddle	Tottenham	Marseille	7/89	4,250,000
G	Duncan Ferguson	Dundee U.	Rangers	7/93	4,000,000
D	Duncan Ferguson	Rangers	Everton	12/94	4,000,000
	Warren Barton	Wimbledon	Newcastle	6/95	4,000,000
	David Batty	Blackburn	Newcastle	2/96	4,000,000
	Emerson	FC Porto	Mid'bro'	5/96	4,000,000
	Jorg Albertz	Hamburg	Rangers	7/96	4,000,000

311

	Player	From	To	Date	Fee
	Sasa Curcic	Bolton	Aston Villa	8/96	4,000,000
	Lorenzo Amoruso	Fiorentina	Rangers	5/97	3,950,000
	Roy Keane	Nott'm. F.	Man. Utd.	7/93	3,750,000
	Phil Babb	Coventry	Liverpool	9/94	3,600,000
	John Scales	Wimbledon	Liverpool	9/94	3,500,000
	Savo Milosevic	P'zan. Belgrade	Aston Villa	6/95	3,500,000
	Alan Stubbs	Bolton	Celtic	5/96	3,500,000
	Gary Speed	Leeds	Everton	6/96	3,500,000
	Karel Poborsky	Slavia Prague	Man. Utd.	7/96	3,500,000
	Patrick Vieira	AC Milan	Arsenal	8/96	3,500,000
	Sebastian Rozental	Univ. Cath (Chile)	Rangers	1/97	3,500,000
	Ramon Vega	Cagliari	Tottenham	1/97	3,500,000
	Oyvind Leonhardsen	Wimbledon	Liverpool	6/97	3,500,000
	Marco Negri	Perugia	Rangers	6/97	3,500,000
	Teddy Sheringham	Tottenham	Man. Utd.	6/97	3,500,000
	Tony Yeboah	Eint. F'furt	Leeds	1/95	3,400,000
★	Alan Shearer	Southampton	Blackburn	7/92	3,300,000
	John Hartson	Arsenal	West Ham	2/97	3,300,000
	Mark Draper	Leicester	Aston Villa	7/95	3,250,000
	Patrik Berger	Bor. Dortmund	Liverpool	7/96	3,250,000
★	Ian Rush	Liverpool	Juventus	6/87	3,200,000
	Gheorghe Popescu	Tottenham	Barcelona	5/95	3,200,000
	Garry Flitcroft	Man. City	Blackburn	3/96	3,200,000
	Daniel Amokachi	Bruges	Everton	8/94	3,000,000
	Gary McAllister	Leeds	Coventry	7/96	3,000,000
	Benito Carbone	Inter Milan	Sheff. W.	10/96	3,000,000
	Pierre van Hooijdonk	Celtic	Nott'm. F.	3/97	3,000,000
	Emmanuel Petit	Monaco	Arsenal	6/97	3,000,000
	Sergio Porrino	Juventus	Rangers	6/97	3,000,000
	Stephan Henchoz	Hamburg	Blackburn	6/97	3,000,000
	Dean Saunders	Derby	Liverpool	7/91	2,900,000
	Gheorghe Popescu	PSV Eindhov'n	Tottenham	9/94	2,900,000
	Ian Rush	Juventus	Liverpool	8/88	2,800,000
	Chris Coleman	Crystal P.	Blackburn	12/95	2,800,000
	Gary Lineker	Everton	Barcelona	6/86	2,750,000
	Andy Sinton	Q.P.R.	Sheff. W.	8/93	2,750,000
	David Batty	Leeds	Blackburn	10/93	2,750,000
	Mike Sheron	Stoke	Q.P.R.	7/97	2,750,000
	Brian Deane	Sheff. Utd.	Leeds	7/93	2,700,000
	Des Walker	Sampdoria	Sheff. W.	7/93	2,700,000
	Paul Warhust	Sheff. W.	Blackburn	9/93	2,700,000
	Darren Peacock	Q.P.R.	Newcastle	3/94	2,700,000
	Basile Boli	Marseille	Rangers	6/94	2,700,000
	Andy Booth	Huddersfield	Sheff. Wed.	7/96	2,700,000
	Gianluca Festa	Inter Milan	Mid'bro'	1/97	2,700,000
	Philippe Albert	Anderlecht	Newcastle	8/94	2,650,000
	Carlton Palmer	Sheff. W.	Leeds	6/94	2,600,000
	Ilie Dumitrescu	Steaua Buch.	Tottenham	7/94	2,600,000
K	Lee Bowyer	Charlton	Leeds	7/96	2,600,000
	Jonas Bjorklund	Vicenza	Rangers	7/96	2,600,000
	John Scales	Liverpool	Tottenham	12/96	2,600,000
	Keith Curle	Wimbledon	Man. City	8/91	2,500,000
	Ian Wright	Crystal P.	Arsenal	9/91	2,500,000
	Terry Phelan	Wimbledon	Man. City	8/92	2,500,000
	Craig Short	Notts Co.	Derby	9/92	2,500,000
	Kevin Gallacher	Coventry	Blackburn	3/93	2,500,000
	Neil Ruddock	Tottenham	Liverpool	7/93	2,500,000
	Bryan Roy	Foggia	Nott'm. F.	6/94	2,500,000
	John Hartson	Luton	Arsenal	1/95	2,500,000
	Gareth Southgate	Crystal P.	Aston Villa	6/95	2,500,000
	David Ginola	Paris St. Germain	Newcastle	7/95	2,500,000

Player	From	To	Date	Fee
Stefan Schwarz	Arsenal	Fiorentina	7/95	2,500,000
Oleg Salenko	Valencia	Rangers	7/95	2,500,000
Kevin Campbell	Arsenal	Nott'm. F.	6/95	2,500,000
Chris Bart-Williams	Sheff. W.	Nott'm. F.	6/95	2,500,000
Darko Kovacevic	Sheff. W.	R. Sociedad	6/96	2,500,000
Franck Lebouef	Strasbourg	Chelsea	6/96	2,500,000
John Spencer	Chelsea	Q.P.R.	11/96	2,500,000
Steffen Iversen	Rosenborg	Tottenham	11/96	2,500,000
Gary Breen	Birmingham	Coventry	1/97	2,500,000
Per Pedersen	Odense	Blackburn	2/97	2,500,000
Jon Daal Tomasson	Herenveen (Holl.)	Newcastle	4/97	2,500,000
Lee Clark	Newcastle	Sunderland	6/97	2,500,000
Martin Dahlin	Roma	Blackburn	7/97	2,500,000
Trevor Steven	Marseille	Rangers	7/92	2,400,000
Craig Short	Derby	Everton	7/95	2,400,000
Florin Raducioiu	Espanol	West Ham	7/96	2,400,000
★ Mark Hughes	Man. Utd.	Barcelona	5/86	2,300,000
Gary Pallister	Mid'bro'	Man. Utd.	8/89	2,300,000
Paul Stewart	Tottenham	Liverpool	7/92	2,300,000
Dean Saunders	Liverpool	Aston Villa	9/91	2,300,000
Paul Furlong	Watford	Chelsea	5/94	2,300,000
Andreas Thom	B. Leverkusen	Celtic	7/95	2,300,000
Dan Petrescu	Sheff. W.	Chelsea	10/95	2,300,000
Paul Kitson	Newcastle	West Ham	2/97	2,300,000
Tommy Johnson	Aston Villa	Celtic	3/97	2,300,000
Michael Johansen	FC Copenhagen	Bolton	6/96	2,280,000
Per Frandsen	FC Copenhagen	Bolton	6/96	2,280,000
Nigel Clough	Nott'm. Forest	Liverpool	6/93	2,275,000
Ruel Fox	Norwich	Newcastle	2/94	2,250,000
Paul Kitson	Derby	Newcastle	9/94	2,250,000
B Nigel Martyn	Crystal P.	Leeds	7/96	2,250,000
Celestine Babayaro	Anderlecht	Chelsea	4/97	2,250,000
Ed de Goey	Feyenoord	Chelsea	6/97	2,250,000
Tony Cottee	West Ham	Everton	7/88	2,200,000
Mark Wright	Derby	Liverpool	7/91	2,200,000
Gordon Durie	Chelsea	Tottenham	8/91	2,200,000
Stan Collymore	Southend	Nott'm. F.	6/93	2,200,000
Brian Laudrup	Fiorentina	Rangers	6/94	2,200,000
Vinny Samways	Tottenham	Everton	8/94	2,200,000
Robbie Elliott	Newcastle	Bolton	7/97	2,200,000
Teddy Sheringham	Nott'm. F.	Tottenham	8/92	2,100,000
Robert Fleck	Norwich	Chelsea	8/92	2,100,000
Andy Townsend	Chelsea	Aston Villa	7/93	2,100,000
Paul Gascoigne	Newcastle	Tottenham	7/88	2,000,000
Alexei Mikhailichenko	Sampdoria	Rangers	6/91	2,000,000
Teddy Sheringham	Millwall	Nott'm. F.	7/91	2,000,000
Paul Parker	Q.P.R.	Man. Utd.	8/91	2,000,000
David Rocastle	Arsenal	Leeds	7/92	2,000,000
Martin Keown	Everton	Arsenal	2/93	2,000,000
Tim Flowers	Southampton	Blackburn	11/93	2,000,000
Jurgen Klinsmann	Monaco	Tottenham	7/94	2,000,000
Dion Dublin	Man. Utd.	Coventry	9/94	2,000,000
Tommy Johnson	Derby	Aston Villa	1/95	2,000,000
Glenn Helder	Vit. Arnhem	Arsenal	2/95	2,000,000
Darko Kovacevic	R.S. Belgrade	Sheff. W.	10/95	2,000,000
Dejan Stefanovic	R.S. Belgrade	Sheff. W.	10/95	2,000,000
Noel Whelan	Leeds	Coventry	12/95	2,000,000
Eoin Jess	Aberdeen	Coventry	2/96	2,000,000
Ben Thatcher	Millwall	Wimbledon	7/96	2,000,000
Gilles Grimandi	Monaco	Arsenal	6/97	2,000,000
Jimmy Hasselbaink	Boavista	Leeds	6/97	2,000,000

| David Ginola | Newcastle | Tottenham | 7/97 | 2,000,000 |
| Alan Rogers | Tranmere | Nott'm. F. | 7/97 | 2,000,000 |

Biggest under-£2m. transfers since last season's Annual went to press:

July 1996: **Paul Gerrard**, Oldham to Everton £1.5m.

Aug. 1996: **Niall Quinn**, Sunderland to Man. C. £1.3m; **Reggie Genaux**, Standard Liege to Coventy £1m; **Paul Dickov**, Arsenal to Man. C. £1m.

Oct. 1996: **Ulrich van Gobbel**, Galatasaray, Turk. to Southampton £1.3m; **Eyal Berkovic**, Maccabi Haifa to Southampton £1m; **Neil Shipperley**, Southampton to Crystal P. £1m.

Nov. 1996: **Jamie Pollock**, Mid'bro' to Bolton £1.5m; **Darren Huckerby**, Newcastle to Covertry £1m.

Dec. 1996: **Vladimir Kinder**, Slovan Brat. to Mid'bro' £1m.

Jan. 1997: **Matt Elliott**, Oxford to Leicester £1.6m; **Kevin Horlock**, Swindon to Man. C. £1.5m; **Florin Raducioiu**, West Ham to Espanol £1.4m; **Robert Molenaar**, Valendam (Holl.) to Leeds £1m.

Feb. 1997: **Mark Schwarzer**, Bradford C. to Mid'bro' £1.5m; **John Ebbrell**, Everton to Sheff. Utd. £1m.

Mar. 1997: **Steve Lomas**, Man. C. to West Ham £1.6m; **Des Hamilton**, Bradford C. to Newcastle £1.5m; **Mark Bowen**, West Ham to Shimizh-S-Ruse (Jap.) £1m.

May 1997: **Staale Stensaas**, Rosenborg (Nov.) to Rangers £1.75m; **Neil Cox**, Mid'bro' to Bolton £1.5m; **Matthew Upson**, Luton to Arsenal £1m; **Kevin Kilbane**, Preston to WBA £1m.

June 1997: **Patrick Blondeau**, Monaco to Sheff. Wed. £1.8m; **Eyal Berkovic**, Southampton to West Ham £1.75m; **Lois Boa Morte**, Sp. Lisbon to Arsenal £1.75m; **Bernard Lambourde**, Bordeaux to Chelsea £1.5m; **Gjorji Hristov**, Partizan Belgrade to Barnsley £1.5m; **Andrew Impey**, QPR to West Ham £1.2m.

July 1997: **Iwan Roberts**, Wolves to Norwich £1m; **Darren Jackson**, Hibernian to Celtic £1.25m; **John Oster**, Grimsby to Everton £1.5m.

Record stages: Prior to Trevor Francis becoming the subject of the first £1m. transfer, this is how the record was broken, stage by stage from the time of the first £1,000 deal in 1905:

Player	From	To	Date	£
Alf Common	Sunderland	Mid'bro'	2/1905	1,000
Syd Puddefoot	West Ham	Falkirk	2/22	5,000
Warney Cresswell	S. Shields	Sunderland	3/22	5,500
Bob Kelly	Burnley	Sunderland	12/25	6,500
David Jack	Bolton	Arsenal	10/28	10,890
Bryn Jones	Wolves	Arsenal	8/38	14,500
Billy Steel	Morton	Derby	9/47	15,000
Tommy Lawton	Chelsea	Notts Co.	11/47	20,000
Len Shackleton	Newcastle	Sunderland	2/48	20,500
Johnny Morris	Man. Utd.	Derby	2/49	24,000
Eddie Quigley	Sheff. W.	Preston	12/49	26,500
Trevor Ford	Aston Villa	Sunderland	10/50	30,000
Jackie Sewell	Notts Co.	Sheff. W.	3/51	34,500
Eddie Firmani	Charlton	Sampdoria	7/55	35,000
John Charles	Leeds	Juventus	4/57	65,000
Denis Law	Man. City	Torino	6/61	100,000
Denis Law	Torino	Man. Utd.	7/62	115,000
Allan Clarke	Fulham	Leicester	6/68	150,000
Allan Clarke	Leicester	Leeds	6/69	165,000
Martin Peters	West Ham	Tottenham	3/70	200,000
Alan Ball	Everton	Arsenal	12/71	220,000
David Nish	Leicester	Derby	8/72	250,000
Bob Latchford	Birmingham	Everton	2/74	350,000
Graeme Souness	Mid'bro'	Liverpool	1/78	352,000
Kevin Keegan	Liverpool	Hamburg	6/77	500,000
David Mills	Mid'bro'	W.B.A.	1/79	516,000

• **World's first £1m. transfer:** Guiseppe Savoldi, Bologna to Napoli, July 1975.

TOP FOREIGN SIGNINGS

Player	From	To	Date	£
*Ronaldo	Barcelona	Inter Milan	6/97	18,000,000
Gianluigi Lentini	Torino	AC Milan	7/92	13,000,000
Gianluca Vialli	Sampdoria	Juventus	6/92	12,500,000
Ronaldo	PSV Eindhoven	Barcelona	7/96	12,500,000
Christian Vieri	Juventus	Athletico Madrid	7/97	12,000,000
Enrico Chiesa	Sampdoria	Parma	7/96	11,000,000
Jean-Pierre Papin	Marseille	AC Milan	6/92	10,000,000
Alen Boksic	Marseille	Lazio	10/93	8,400,000
Dennis Bergkamp	Ajax	Inter Milan	6/93	8,000,000
Roberto Baggio	Juventus	AC Milan	7/95	8,000,000
Roberto Baggio	Fiorentina	Juventus	5/90	7,700,000
Gianluca Pagliuca	Sampdoria	Inter Milan	8/94	7,500,000
Daniel Fonseca	Cagliari	Napoli	6/92	7,000,000
Igor Shalimov	Foggia	Inter Milan	5/92	6,500,000
David Platt	Bari	Juventus	6/92	6,500,000
Ruud Gullit	PSV Eindh'n	AC Milan	6/87	6,000,000
Luca Marchegiani	Torino	Lazio	7/93	6,000,000
Thomas Hassler	Juventus	Roma	7/91	5,800,000
K.-H. Riedle	Wer. Bremen	Lazio	4/90	5,500,000
Vitor Baia	Porto	Barcelona	7/96	5,500,000
Claudio Caniggia	Atalanta	Roma	5/92	5,500,000
K.-H. Riedle	Lazio	B. Dortmund	7/93	5,500,000
Thomas Hassler	Cologne	Juventus	4/90	5,400,000
Dragan Stojkovic	Red Star	Marseille	7/90	5,250,000
Diego Maradona	Barcelona	Napoli	6/84	5,000,000
Thomas Doll	Hamburg	Lazio	6/91	5,000,000
Christian Karembeu	Nantes	Sampdoria	7/95	5,000,000
Romario	Flamenco	Valencia	7/96	5,000,000
Diego Maradona	Boca Juniors	Barcelona	6/82	4,800,000
Lajos Detari	Eint. F'furt	Olympiakos	7/88	4,700,000
Hristo Stoichkov	Barcelona	Parma	7/95	4,600,000
Diego Maradona	Napoli	Seville	9/92	4,500,000
George Weah	Paris SG	AC Milan	5/95	4,500,000
Clarence Seedorf	Ajax	Sampdoria	7/95	4,500,000
Roberto Carlos	Palmeiras	Inter Milan	7/95	4,500,000
Paulo Futre	At. Madrid	Benfica	1/93	4,200,000

* Transfer awaited confirmation by FIFA at time of going to press.

WORLD RECORD GOALKEEPER FEE
£7.5m for **Gianluca Pagliuca** (Sampdoria to Inter Milan, Aug. 1994).

RECORD FEE BETWEEN NON-LEAGUE CLUBS

£85,000 for **Carl Alford**, 24-year-old striker from Kettering (GMVC) to neighbours Rushden & Diamonds (Beazer Homes League), March 1996.

DECEMBER D-DAY

In all five Premiership seasons, the **bottom** club on December 31 was relegated in the final table: 1993 Nott'm. Forest; 1994 Swindon; 1995 Ipswich; 1996 Bolton; 1997 Nott'm. Forest.

KEITH NOW A DON

Keith Burkinshaw, 61, who managed Tottenham from 1976-84 and later WBA, is back in senior football as general manager of **Aberdeen**.

SOCCER DIARY 1996-97

July 1996

2 Andy Booth, Huddersfield striker, to **Sheff. W.** (£2.75m). **Huddersfield** pay club record £1.2m for **Bristol R.** forward **Marcus Stewart.** London-based media group **Caspian** in £20m takeover of **Leeds Utd. 3 Southampton** replace manager **Dave Merrington** with **Graeme Souness** (3-year contract). **Leeds** sign 19-year-old **Lee Bowyer** from **Charlton** – free of £2.6m is **record for teenager. 4 Mid'bro'** sign Juventus striker **Fabrizio Ravanelli** for club record £7m. **West Ham** sign **Florin Raducioiu** from Espanol for £2.4m (club record). **5 Blackpool** appoint **Gary Megson** manager. **Chelsea** pay club record £4.9m for **Roberto di Matteo** from Lazio. **Man. Utd.** Sign striker **Ole Gunnar Solskjaer** from Molde (Nor.), £1.5m. **Rangers** sign **Joachim Bjorklund** from Vicenza (It.), £2.6m. **8 Nott'm. F.** sign striker **Dean Saunders** from Galatasaray (Turk.), £1.5m. **9 Barcelona** buy Brazil striker **Ronaldo** from PSV Eindhoven, £12.5m. **11 Keith Wiseman, Southampton** vice-chairman, succeeds **Sir Bert Millichip** as FA chairman. **12 A. Villa** sign full-back **Fernando Nelson** from Sp. Lisbon, £1.75m. **19 Man. Utd.** buy **Karel Poborsky** from Slavia Prague, £3.5m. **22 Richard Hall, Southampton** def. to West Ham, £1.4m. **24 Coventry** pay Leeds £3m for Scotland captain **Gary McAllister. Man. Utd.** sign **Jordi Cruyff**, son of Johan, from Barcelona, £800,000. **25 New record goalkeeper fee** (£2.25m) for **Nigel Martyn**, Crystal P. to Leeds. **27 Rangers** sign **Jorg Albertz** from Hamburg, £4m. **29** England striker **Alan Shearer** becomes world's **first £15m player** (Blackburn to Newcastle). **31 Paul Gerrard,** Oldham to **Everton,** £1.5m.

August 1996

3 Nigeria first African country to win **Olympic soccer** title (3-2 v Argentina in Georgia, USA). **4** Entrepreneur **Chris Wright** completes £10m takeover of QPR. **11 Charity Shield** (Wembley): **Man. Utd.** 4, Newcastle 0. **Leeds** pay **Man. Utd.** £4.5m for **Lee Sharpe. 12 Arsenal** sack manager **Bruce Rioch. Terry Venables,** ex-England manager, takes control of **Portsmouth. 14** Aston V. pay club record £4m for **Bolton's Sasa Curcic.** Managerless **Arsenal** buy **Patrick Vieira** from AC Milan, £3.5m. **15 Liverpool** sign **Patrik Berger** from Borx. Dortmund, £3.25m. **Sunderland** pay club record £1.3m for **Niall Quinn** (Man. C.) from Arsenal. **Ray Clemence** quits **Barnet** as manager to become **England** goalkeeper coach. **17** Start of League season: In Champions **Man. Utd's** 3-0 win at Wimbledon, **David Beckham** scores last minute goal from 55 yards. Tottenham captain **Gary Mabbutt** breaks left leg at Blackburn (out for season). **21 Kenny Dalglish** resigns as Blackburn's dir. of football. **26** Ten days into season, **Alan Ball** quits as **Man. C.** manager. **28** Manager **Andy King** leaves **Mansfield.**

September 1996

1 World Cup: **England** start **Glenn Hoddle's** reign with 3-0 win in Moldova; Austria 0; **Scotland** 0; **Wales** 6 San Marino 0; **N. Ireland** 0, Ukraine 1; Liechtenstein 0, **Rep. of Ireland** 5. **4 Ray Wilkins** leaves as QPR player-manager, signs on month's loan for **Hibs. 9 Leeds** sack **Howard Wilkinson** as manager after 8 years. **10 George Graham** returns to football management with **Leeds** after 19-month exile; **David O'Leary** (also ex-Arsenal) joins him as No. 2. **13 Stewart Houston** leaves as Arsenal caretaker to manage QPR. **16** Arsenal name Frenchman **Arsene Wenger** (from Grampus 8, Japan) as new manager from Oct. 1. **Rotherham** part company with joint managers **Archie Gemmill, John McGiven** and appoint **Danny Bergara. Steve Archibald** sacked as E. Fife manager, replaced by **Jimmy Bone. 24 York** knock Everton out of Coca-Cola Cup (3-2, 4-3 agg.). **30** Departing managers: **Alan Smith** (Wycombe), **Alex Miller** (Hibernian).

October 1996

1 Mansfield appoint **Steve Parkin** (30) youngest manager in League. **5** World Cup: Latvia 0, **Scotland** 2; **Wales** 1, Holland 3; **N. Ireland** 1, Armenia 1. **Paul Barnes** scores all 5 in Burnley's 5-2 win v Stockport (Div. 2). **7 Steve Coppell** (Crystal P. tech. dir.) becomes **Man. City's** 8th. manager in ten years; **Cardiff** manager **Phil Neal** joins him as No. 2. **8 Man. Utd.** announce profit of £16.7m. **9** World Cup: **England** 2, Poland 1; **Rep. of Ireland** 0, Macedonia 0; Estonia v **Scotland** (Tallinn) – no match; **Estonia** refuse to turn up after change of kick-off, Scotland kick off against invisible opponents, then "match abandoned" (3 seconds). **14 Sheff. Wed.** make record signing: **Benito Carbone** (Inter Milan) £3m. **15 Southampton** pay their record £1.3m for Dutch def. **Ulrich van Gobbel** from Galatasaray, Turk. **16 Paul Gascoigne** sent off as Rangers lose 4-1 away to Ajax (Champions' League). **20 Premier League: Newcastle** 3 points clear after 5-0 home win v **Man. Utd. 22 Coca-Cola Cup** (3rd. Rd.): Blackburn 0, Stockport 1. Multi-millionaire **Matthew Harding, Chelsea** vice-chairman, among 5 killed in helicopter crash in Cheshire on way home from Coca-Cola Cup defeat at Bolton. **Wycombe** appoint **John Gregory** (A. Villa coach) manager. **25** Manager **Ray Harford** quits **Blackburn** (bottom Prem. League); **Tony Parkes** caretaker for rest of season. **26 Man. Utd.** (5th) 5 points behind leaders Arsenal after 3-6 defeat at Southampton. **28 Leyton Orient** sack manager **Pat Holland**. **30 Everton** pay their record fee (£5.75m) for **Nick Barmby** (Mid'bro').

November 1996

1 Grimsby sack manager Brian Laws. **4 Gordon Strachan** becomes Coventry player-manager (**Ron Atkinson** to dir. of football). **Leyton Orient** appoint **Tommy Taylor** manager (from **Cambridge Utd.**). Hartlepool manager Keith Houchen replaced by **Mick Tait**. **6 Alex Ferguson** completes 10 years as **Man. Utd.** manager. Death of **Tommy Lawton**, 77. **7 Liverpool** fine **Stan Collymore** £20,000 for refusing to play in reserves. **8 Steve Coppell** quits after 32 days as **Man. C.** manager. **Chelsea** sign Gianfranco Zola from Parma (£4.5m). **9** World Cup: Georgia 0, **England** 2; Holland 7, **Wales** 1 (their worst World Cup defeat); Germany 1, **N. Ireland** 1. **10** World Cup: **Scotland** 1, Sweden 0; **Rep. of Ireland** 0, Iceland 0. **Darlington** sack manager **Jim Platt**, appoint **David Hodgson** for second time. **11 Russell Osman** new manager of **Cardiff**. **13 Roy McFarland** becomes manager of **Cambridge Utd. 19 Australia** appoint Terry Venables national coach. **21 John Spencer**, Chelsea to QPR (£2.5m, Rangers' record). **22 Darren Huckerby**, Newcastle to Coventry (£1m). **24 Scottish Coca-Cola Cup Final:** Rangers 4, Hearts 3. **26 Duane Darby** scores 6 in Hull's 8-4 replay win v Whitby (FA Cup 1). **28 Tottenham** pay £2.5m (Norwegian record) for **Steffen Iversen** from Rosenborg.

December 1996

2 Rick Parry (chief exec.) to leave **Premier League** at season's end to join Liverpool (chief exec.). **3 Crewe** extend manager **Dario Gradi's** contract by 10 years to 2007. **Kilmarnock** sack manager **Alex Totten**. **7 Ally McCoist** becomes **record post-war Scottish League scorer** with 265th. goal in Rangers' 4-3 win v Hibs. **8 Tottenham** beat Leeds to capture **John Scales** from Liverpool (£2.6m). **9 Premier League** clubs agree record £36m, 4-year sponsorship extension with Carling (1997-2001). FA dock **Brighton** 2 points for pitch invasion v Lincoln, Oct. 1. **11 Brighton** replace manager **Jimmy Case** with **Steve Gritt** (ex-Charlton). **14 Robbie Fowler** scores 4 in Liverpool's 5-1 win v Mid'bro', taking his club total to 102 goals in 4½ seasons and 165 games. **15 Cesare Maldini**, 64, named **Italy's** new coach, replacing Arrigo Sacchi. **16 Blackburn** name Swede **Sven Goran Eriksson** (Sampdoria) manager, w/effect June (see Feb. 24). **19 Frank Clark** resigns as Nott'm. F. manager; player **Stuart Pearce** caretaker. **20 Mid'bro'** call off next day's fixture at Blackburn, claiming 23 players injured/ill (will face Premier League inquiry). **21 Falkirk** replace manager **Eamonn Bannon** with **Alex Totten** (ex-Kilmarnock). **22** (Sun) **Peter Shilton** (47) first player to reach **1000 League apps** (in Leyton Orient's 2-0 home win v Brighton). **23 Notts County** sack management team **Colin Murphy, Steve Thompson. Bobby Williamson** new **Kilmarnock** manager. **29 Man. C.** appoint **Frank Clark** manager. **30** New **Hibs** manager is **Jim Duffy**, from Dundee.

January 1997

1 New Year Honours: MBE for Arsenal 'keeper **David Seaman** and Celtic's **Paul McStay; OBE** for **Glen Kirton**, tournament dir. of Euro 96. **Deep freeze** hits New Year's Day soccer – 30 English, 10 Scottish games off. Prem. leaders **Liverpool** lose 1-0 at Chelsea. **3** Worst weather-affected **FA Cup 3rd. Rd.** since 1979 – 13 ties frozen off. **6** FA appoint **Howard Wilkinson** (ex-Leeds manager) first technical director in English football (4-year contract). **Tottenham** pay **Cagliari** £3.5m for Swiss defender **Ramon Vega. 8** Newcastle rocked – manager **Kevin Keegan** resigns ("I feel I have taken this club as far as I can"). **Grimsby** confirm **Kenny Swain** as manager after 2 months as caretaker. **9** Leeds pay Dutch club **Volendam** £1m for centre-back **Robert Molenaar. 11** Mid'bro' buy defender **Gianluca Festa** from Inter Milan (£2.7m). **Aston V.** give manager **Brian Little** 5-year renewal of contract. **14** Newcastle appoint **Kenny Dalglish** Manager (3½-year contract). Premier League **dock** bottom club **Mid'bro' 3** points and fine them £50,000 for calling off match at Blackburn on Dec. 21. **16** New **Notts County** manager is **Sam Allardyce. Leicester** buy Oxford def. **Matt Elliott** for £1.6m (record both clubs). **20** FIFA vote **Ronaldo** (Barcelona & Brazil) World Player of Year. **21** WBA sack manager **Alan Buckley. 25** FA Cup (4): Everton 3, Bradford C. 3. **26** (Sun) **FA Cup** (4): **Chelsea** (2 down at half-time) beat Liverpool 4-2. **FA** appoint **Don Howe** technical co-ordinator coaching. **29** Man. Utd. (2-1 v Wimbledon) go top of Premier League (for rest of season). **Andrei Kanchelskis, Everton** to Fiorentina (£8m., Everton record). **30** Coventry pay club record £2.5m for **Gary Breen** (Birmingham).

February 1997

3 Plymouth sack manager **Neil Warnock**, replace him with **Mick Jones. 4** FA Cup (4R): Wimbledon knock out **holders Man. Utd.** 1-0; (4) Bolton 2, Chesterfield 3 (Kevin Davies hat-trick). **6** WBA appoint **Ray Harford** manager. West Ham sign striker **Paul Kitson** from Newcastle (£2.3m). **10** Millwall (in administration, debts £10m) sack manager **Jimmy Nicholl**, chief exec. **Graham Hortop**, & trade and list 12 players. They appoint **John Docherty** manager (second time). **Billy Bingham** resigns as **Blackpool** dir. of football. **11** World Cup: Estonia 0, Scotland 0 (Monaco). Oldham manager **Graeme Sharp** resigns. **12** England 0, Italy 1 (England's **first home defeat** in W. Cup). **Terry Venables**, chairman, buys 51% control of **Portsmouth** for £1. **14** West Ham pay club record £3.3m for Arsenal striker **John Hartson. 15** FA Cup (5): **Chesterfield** (1-0 v Nott'm. F.) reach q-finals for first time. **21** Mark Schwarzer, Bradford C. goalkeeper, to **Mid'bro'** (£1.5m). **Per Pederssen** (Odense, Den,) to Blackburn, £2.5m. Oldham appoint **Neil Warnock** manager. **22** Four players (2 each side) sent off after brawl in Chesterfield v Plymouth match (Div. 2). **24** Nott'm. F. taken over (£19.1m) by consortium of property magnates Nigel Wray and Irving Scholar (ex-Tottenham) and Phil Soar (chief exec.). **Brian Laws** replaces **Mick Buxton** as **Scunthorpe** manager. **26** Blackburn snubbed by Sven Goran Eriksson (see Dec. 16), appoint Inter Milan's **Roy Hodgson** manager (w/effect July). **27** Premier League appoint **Peter Leaver** chief. exec. **Dave Bassett** quits as Crystal P. manager, joins Nott'm. F. as general manager; Palace make **Steve Coppell** caretaker.

March 1997

4 Winchester Crown Court: After 34-day trial, jury fail to reach verdict in **"match-fixing"** trial of Bruce Grobbelaar (ex-Liverpool), former Wimbledon players John Fashanu and Hans Segers and Malaysian businessman Heng Suan Lim. Retrial ordered for June. **10** Nott'm. F. pay club record £3m for Celtic's Dutch striker **Pierre van Hooijdonk. 24** Manager **Joe Jordan** leaves Bristol C., replaced by **John Ward. 26** FA Appeal Board turns down Mid'bro's appeal against 3-point deduction (see Jan. 14). **27** Manager **Joe Royle** leaves Everton ("mutual consent"); captain Dave Watson caretaker for rest of season. **Transfer deadline** day: £9m. spent – top deal £1.6m (Steve Lomas, Man. C. to West Ham). **28 Tommy Johnson**, Aston V. to Celtic (£2.3m). **29** Easter Sat. (No Premier League programme). World Cup: **Scotland** 2, Estonia 0; **Wales** 1, Belgium 2; **N. Ireland** 0, Portugal 0. Friendly: **England** 2, Mexico 0.

April 1997

1 Bolton valued at £22m in takeover by Mosaic Investments; **Newcastle** valued at £194m on Stock Market debut. **2** World Cup: **Scotland** 2, Austria 0; Macedonia 3, **Rep. of Ireland** 2; Ukraine 2, **N. Ireland** 1. **5 Bolton**, 17 points clear with 5 games left, clinch promotion to Prem. League with 2-1 win v QPR. **6 Coca-Cola Cup Final** (Wembley): Leicester 1, Mid'bro' 1. **8 Fulham** and **Wigan** promoted to Div. 2. **9 Eur. Cup** s-final (1) Bor. Dortmund 1, **Man. Utd.** 0. **10 Cup-Winners' Cup** s-final (1): Paris SG 3, **Liverpool** 0. **13 FA Cup** s-finals: Wimbledon 0, Chelsea 3; Mid'bro' 3, Chesterfield 3. **Alan Shearer** voted PFA Player of Year for second time. **16 Coca-Cola Cup Final** rep. (Hillsborough): Leicester 1, Mid'bro' 0, aet. **19** Manager **Lou Macari** to quit **Stoke** at season's end. **21 Chelsea** sign **Celestine Babayaro** from **Anderlecht**, £2.25m. **Rotherham** (relegated) sack manager Danny Bergara. **22 FA Cup** s-final rep: Chesterfield 0, Mid'bro' 3. **23 Eur. Cup** s-final (2): **Man. Utd.** 0, Bor. Dortmund 1 (agg. 0-2). **24 Cup-Winners' Cup** s-final (2): **Liverpool** 2, Paris SG 0 (agg. 2-3). **26 Barnsley** (2-0 v Bradford C.) promoted to top div. for first time; **Bury** (0-0 at Watford) promoted for second year running. **Elton John** returns to **Watford** as chairman. **28 Stockport** (1-0 at Chesterfield) promoted to Div. 1 (their highest level since 1938). **30** World Cup: **England** 2, Georgia 0; Sweden 2, **Scotland** 1; Romania 1, **Rep. of Ireland** 0; Armenia 1, **N. Ireland** 0.

May 1997

2 Celtic sack manager **Tommy Burns**. **Millwall** manager **John Docherty** resigns. **3 Nott'm F.** relegated from Premier League after 1-1 v Wimbledon; **Brighton** (1-1 at Hereford) avoid demotion – **Hereford** finish bottom. **Macclesfield** beat Kettering 4-1 to clinch League place as Conf. champions. **5 Chelsea** fan **Tony Banks** appointed New Labour's **Minister for Sport. 6** Liverpool's 2-1 defeat at Wimbledon makes **Man. Utd.** Premier League champions for **fourth time in 5 seasons. Shrewsbury** sack manager **Fred Davies**. **7 Brian Laudrup's** goal (1-0 v Dundee Utd.) gives **Rangers** a **record-equalling** ninth successive Scottish Championship. **8** Football League chairmen reject proposal to regionalise and extend Div. 3. **Dave Bassett** becomes manager of **Nott'm F.** (from gen. manager). **Billy Bonds** appointed **Millwall** manager. **9** Joint managers **Jimmy Quinn** and **Mick Gooding** leave **Reading**. **11** (Sun): Four crucial results on last day of Premier League season: Villa 1, Southampton 0 (but **Saints** safe); Leeds 1, Mid'bro' 1 (**Boro' down**); Tottenham 1, Coventry 2 (**Coventry safe**); Wimbledon 1, Sunderland 0 (**Sunderland down**, a year after promotion). **Boro'** relegated because of 3 points docked. **12 Watford** re-appoint **Graham Taylor** manager (from gen. manager). **13 Aston Villa's** record signing: Stan Collymore from Liverpool, £7m. **14** New British **record fee for defender**: £4.5m for **Slaven Bilic** (West Ham to Everton). **15** Sir **Stanley Matthews**, first Footballer of Year in 1948, presents 50th award to Gianfranco **Zola** (Chelsea). **16 FA Cup Final**: Chelsea 2, Mid'bro' 0 (**Roberto di Matteo** scores in 42 secs., fastest Cup Final goal at Wembley). **18** Eric **Cantona** (31), Man. Utd. captain, retires as player. **21** World Cup: **Rep. of Ireland** 5, Liechtenstein 0 (David Connolly hat-trick). Departing managers: Grimsby sack **Kenny Swain**; Chris **Nicholl** (**Walsall**) resigns. **Shrewsbury** appoint **Jake King** (former captain) manager, from Telford. **23** Jimmy **Hill**, 68, resigns after 10 years as Fulham chairman. Grimsby appoint **Alan Buckley** manager (second time). **24** Friendly: **England** 2, S. Africa 1 (Old Trafford). **Kilmarnock** win **Scottish Cup** (1-0 v Falkirk). **Northampton** win Div. 3 play-off final (1-0 v Swansea). **Southampton's** management team resign: Graeme **Souness** and dir. of football **Lawrie McMenemy**. **25 Crewe** win Div. 2 play-off final (1-0 v Brentford). **Rotherham** appoint their ex-player **Ronnie Moore**

manager. **26 Crystal Palace** win Div. 1 play-off final (1-0 v Sheff. Utd.). **27** Friendly: **Scotland** 0, **Wales** 1. **29 European Cup Final** (Munich): Bor. Dortmund 3, Juventus 1. **Fulham** taken over: **Mohamed Al Fayed**, owner of Harrods, buys club for £30m. **Rangers** pay club record £3,950,000 for **Lorenzo Amoruso** from Fiorentina. **31** World Cup: Poland 0, **England** 2.

June 1997

1 Friendly: Malta 2, **Scotland** 3. **2 West Ham** in double signing: **Eyal Berkovic** from Southampton (£1.75m), Andy Impey (QPR, £1.2m). **Scott Booth** leaves **Aberdeen** for Bor. Dortmund, free (out of contract). **Sunderland** pay their record £2.5m for Lee Clark (Newcastle). New **World Cup record score**: Iran beat the Maldives 17-0 in Asia qual. zone. **3** Oyvind Leonhardsen, Wimbledon to Liverpool, £3.5m. **4** Winchester Crown Court: **Match-fixing retrial** begins (see March 4). **Arsenal** manager **Arsene Wenger** returns to his former club **Monaco** to sign two more Frenchmen (£5m): **Gilles Grimandi** and **Emmanuel Petit**. **Tournoi de France: England** 2, Italy 0. **8** World Cup: Belarus 0, **Scotland** 1. Tournoi de France: France 0, **England** 1. **Rep. of Ireland** extend manager **Mick McCarthy's** contract to 2000. **10 Tournoi de France** (won by England): Brazil 1, **England** 0. **Rangers** sign **Sergio Porrini** (Juventus def.), £3m. **11 Wimbledon** takeover: Norwegians Kjell Inge Roekke and Bjorn Rune Gjelstan to buy club for £30m; previous owner **Sam Hammam** stays £2.5m. Prem. newcomers **Barnsley** pay their record £1.5m for striker **Georgi Hristov** (Partizan Belgrade). **12 Graeme Souness** (ex-So'ton) becomes coach to **Torino** (Serie B). **Leeds** sign **Jimmy Hasselbaink** (Boavista), £2m. **14** OBE for Rangers manager **Walter Smith** in Queen's Birthday Honours, MBE for 81-year-old **Ken Aston**, former Int. referee. **Arsenal** to sign Lois Boa Vista (Sp. Lisbon forward), £1.75m. **17 Arsenal** sign Dutch Int. winger **Marc Overmars** from Ajax (£7m). **Chelsea** buy Bernard **Lambourde** (Bordeaux) £1.5m. **18 Rangers** sign striker **Marco Negri** from Perugia (It.) £3.5m. **20** Brazil striker **Ronaldo** becomes **world's costliest player** in £18m move from Barcelona to Inter Milan. **Don Howe** steps down as FA technical co-ordinator, returns to **Arsenal** as head youth coach. **Jimmy Nicholl** appointed Raith manager (second time). **21 Celtic** appoint **Jock Brown**, BBC Scottish TV commentator, general manager. **23 Southampton** name **Dave Jones** as manager (**Stockport** receive £200,000 compensation). **24 David Lloyd**, Britain's Davis Cup tennis captain, buys **Hull City** for £2.4m. **John Toshack** appointed coach of Besiktas, Turk. **Patrick Blondeau**, Monaco to **Sheff. Wed.** (£1.8m). **26** Everton appoint **Howard Kendall** manager (third time); **Sheff. Utd.** seek £1m. compensation. **Walsall's** new manager is former Danish Int. **Jan Sorensen. 27** Teddy Sheringham, **Tottenham** to **Man. Utd.** £3.5m. **Burnley** manager **Adrian Heath** becomes Howard Kendall's No. 2 at **Everton. 30 Reading** appoint **Terry Bullivant** manager, from Barnet, who replace him with Lincoln's assistant **John Still**.

QUOTE-UNQUOTE

PAULINE COPE, goalkeeper, after Millwall Lionesses beat Wembley Ladies in the Women's F.A. Cup Final at Upton Park in May: "To hang my knickers on the same peg as Trevor Brooking is my biggest dream come true."

STUART PEARCE: "The best present I've ever had was the 25ft. flag-pole bearing the cross of St. George that my wife Liz gave me one Christmas. It stands proudly on our lawn."

Arsenal's **IAN WRIGHT**, after being fined £15,000 by the F.A. (July 10) on his latest misconduct charges: "You will see a new me this season. I know what I must do and I will do it."

FINAL WHISTLE –
OBITUARIES 1996-97

June

ALLENBY CHILTON, 78, was the dominant centre-half in Man. United's first great post-war team, earning a Cup-winner's medal in 1948 and Championship honours in 1952. He played 352 League and 36 FA Cup matches for the club and was capped twice by England. He left Old Trafford in March 1955 to become player-manager of Grimsby, and during 4 seasons there took them to the Third Div. North title in 1956. He managed Wigan (1960-61) and Hartlepool (1962-63), then became a publican.

BOB DENNISON, 84, managed Northampton (1949-54), Mid'bro' (1954-63) and Hereford (1963-67) and from 1967 served Coventry as chief scout and assistant-manager until retiring in 1978. He played pre-war for Newcastle, Nott'm. Forest and Fulham, and his football career spanned 6 decades.

July

VIC LAMBDEN, 70, was one of the most prolific marksmen in Bristol Rovers history, scoring 117 goals in 269 League games after joining them in Oct. 1945. Top scorer for 4 seasons, he was ever-present in the side that won Div. 3 South in 1952-53.

FRANTISEK PLANIKA, 92, captained the Czech team that finished World Cup runners-up to Italy in Rome in 1934, also played in 1938 tournament. He was capped 73 times and rated Europe's best goalkeeper in the 1930s. He won 9 Czech Championships and their domestic cup 6 times.

BILLY REES, 72, Welsh Int. inside-forward (4 caps), played in Cardiff's Third Div. South Championship team of 1946-47. He moved to Tottenham (£14,000) in June 1949 and to Leyton Orient (£14,500) in 1950.

JOHN (JOCK) WALLACE, 60, former Rangers and Leicester manager, died after a long battle with Parkinson's Disease. He kept goal for Workington, Berwick Rangers, Airdrie, WBA and, second time round with Berwick, player-managed the side that created the biggest shock in Scottish Cup history, beating Rangers 1-0 in Jan. 1967. From coaching at Ibrox, he succeeded Willie Waddell as Rangers manager in 1972 and ended Celtic's domination, twice taking Gers to the Scottish treble, in 1976 and 1978. A believer in Commando-style training, he managed Leicester (1978-82), left briefly for Motherwell, returned in charge of Rangers (1983-86) and after coaching in Seville (1986-87) managed Colchester from Jan.-Dec. 1989. Facing ill health, he spent his last years on the Costa del Sol.

August

TOMMY GODWIN, 69, Rep. of Ireland and Bournemouth goalkeeper, died at his home at Bournemouth. Capped 13 times, he played for the Rep. when they recorded their first victory on English soil (2-0 at Goodison Park, Sept. 1949).

JIMMY GORDON, 80, was a wing-half with Newcastle and Mid'bro', playing 380 games for the North-east clubs (1935-54). He later coached under Brian Clough at Derby and Nott'm. Forest, helping both clubs to win the Championship and Forest to lift the European Cup twice.

September

JIMMY DUNCANSON, 76, who joined Rangers as a forward in 1939, starred in the immediate post-war period, winning Championship medals in 1947-49-50, a hat-trick of Scottish Cup honours (1948-49-50) and League Cup-winner's medals in 1947-49. He was capped by Scotland against N. Ireland in Nov. 1946. He left Ibrox for St. Mirren in 1950 and ended his career with Stranraer.

BILL HICKS, 84, former sports editor of the *News Chronicle* and *Daily Mail*. He was a stickler for facts, especially football, and with the *Chronicle* insisted that every fixture involving League clubs was mentioned, however small the print or fee.

GEORGE HUNT, 86, was Tottenham's record scorer pre-war with 138 goals in

198 matches. He joined Spurs from Chesterfield in 1930 and left them for Arsenal in Oct. 1937, but stayed only 5 months at Highbury, moving to Bolton in March 1938. After the war, aged 36, he joined Sheff. Wed. (Nov. 1946), returning in May 1948 to Bolton, where he served on the training staff for 20 years.

ARTHUR JONES, 50, Macclesfield's chairman, was found dead from gunshot wounds at his office. He joined the club in 1991 and became chairman 2 years later. During his office, they won the Conference in 1995, and the FA Trophy at Wembley in 1996. He had the Moss Rose ground brought up to standard in preparation for League status which, denied Macclesfield in 1995, was achieved 8 months after their chairman's death.

TONY PULLEIN, 62, editor of the old *Football Monthly* magazine for ten years and a contributor to many club programmes. He was once on Bournemouth's books and a former secretary of the Nat. Fed. of Supporters' Clubs.

October

ALF BENTLEY, 64, was groomed in goalkeeping with Kent League side Snowdown Colliery, and joined Coventry in Oct. 1955. But he was reserve to Reg Matthews and, after 29 League apps., moved to Gillingham for 4 seasons.

MATTHEW HARDING, 42, multi-millionaire vice-chairman of Chelsea, was among 5 who died when their helicopter crashed in woods near Middlewich, Cheshire, on the way home from a Coca-Cola Cup defeat at Bolton. A Chelsea fan from boyhood, he made his money in re-insurance brokerage and became Britain's 89th. richest man with a personal fortune put at £170m. The est. £25m. he poured into the club contributed vastly to Chelsea's modern revival and the spectacular redevelopment of Stamford Bridge. The fans loved him because, for all his wealth, he was "one of them."

EDDIE LYONS, 76, former Brentford trainer, physio and assistant-manager. He served the club for 30 years from 1955.

November

TOMMY LAWTON, 77, who died (Nov. 6) in Nottingham from pneumonia after a long illness, was as complete and powerful a centre-forward as English football has ever seen. Bolton-born, he began his career – interrupted by the war and spanning 21 years, 1935-56 – with Burnley, moving to Everton (£6,500) in Jan. 1937. More than anything else, his 34 goals in 38 games, took the Championship to Goodison Park in 1938-39. After Army service, he returned briefly to Everton before an £11,500 transfer to Chelsea in Nov. 1945. Two years later he became football's first £20,000 player with a surprise move out of the top division to Notts County, where gates rapidly lifted from 9,000 to 35,000 as he led them to the Third Div. South title in 1950. In March 1952, he returned to London with Second Div. Brentford (£12,000) and briefly player-managed them. In Sept. 1953, aged 34, he was recalled to the top company in a £10,000 transfer to Champions Arsenal, who had started the season badly. After 3 years at Highbury, he became player-manager of non-league Kettering, taking them to the Southern League title, and he returned to Meadow Lane as manager. But his one season back in charge of Notts County (1957-58) ended in relegation. He later ran a village pub near Nottingham, returned to Kettering (manager and director), then went back to County in a coaching, scouting role. From 1984 he wrote a column for the *Nottingham Evening Post*. In his career, Tommy Lawton scored 231 goals in 390 League apps, plus 22 in 23 full Internationals for England (1938-48). Despite his robust approach, he was never booked. He shot powerfully with both feet and was supreme in the air as, with dark hair slicked back, he met his wingers' crosses with bullet headers. He played in an era when the top wage never exceeded £12 a week, plus bonuses of £2 for a win, £1 for a draw.

ALF SMIRKE, 79, a pre-war player with Sheff. Wed., was Southend's left winger from 1946-48. He completed his career with Gateshead.

December

LES BLIZZARD, 73, originally a wing-half with QPR, then Bournemouth, he made a name in the Southern League Yeovil side that reached the FA Cup 5th. Round in 1949. He followed Alec Stock to Leyton Orient, for whom he played 221

League games, mostly at centre-half, from 1950-57.

SYD CANN, 85, was Man. City's right-back in the 1933 Cup Final, having joined them from his native Torquay in 1930. He moved to Charlton in June 1935, but the war virtually ended his playing career. He managed Southampton from 1949-51, subsequently coached Isthmian League Wycombe (Amateur Cup Final 1957), then Norwich (1961-62) and completed 45 years in the game as Sutton United's coach (1962-73).

JOHN CRAVEN, 49, a midfield player who totalled 360 League apps. for 4 clubs: Blackpool 1965-71, Crystal P. 1971-73, Coventry 1973-77, Plymouth 1977-78. He quit English football for Canada, playing for Vancouver Whitecaps and Calgary Boomers before settling in California, where he had just started a PE teaching career when he died.

ANDY McLAREN, 74, began a nomadic career with Preston in 1939 but, because of the war, waited until Christmas Day 1946 to make his First Div. debut. He shone in a right-wing partnership with Tom Finney and was capped 4 times by Scotland, continuing his career via Sheff. United, Barrow, Bradford Park Avenue, Southport and Rochdale.

BOBBY ROBINSON, 46, died at his Forfar home. Capped 4 times by Scotland (1974-75) when with Dundee, he also played for Falkirk, Dundee Utd., Hearts and Raith. He was in the Dundee team that beat Celtic in the 1974 League Cup Final.

HARRY THREADGOLD, 72, kept goal in nearly 500 games over 12 years for Chester, Sunderland and Southend, for whom he made 319 League apps. (1953-63).

January 1997

GUILLERMO CANEDO, 76, FIFA senior vice-president, died in his native Mexico after a long illness. He organised the 1970 and 1986 World Cups in Mexico, and his grasp of television potential led to football's biggest event being projected to massive trans-world audiences.

DON DORMAN, 74, was a legendary talent-spotter for Birmingham City, scouting for them for more than 25 years. Among the stars he discovered was 16-year-old Trevor Francis, who was to become Britain's first £1m. player. As an inside-forward, Dorman began with Birmingham (1946-51) and later played for Coventry (1951-54) and Walsall (1954-57).

ERIC GARBUTT, 76, kept goal for Newcastle in 52 League games (1946-49) before a broken leg against Mid'bro' ended his career. In his most memorable match, he was virtually a spectator, watching Len Shackleton score 6 in Newcastle's 13-0 win against Newport in Oct. 1946.

ROY SPROSON, 66, was Port Vale's "Mr Loyalty," serving them for 28 years (1949-77) as wing-half, full-back, scout, coach and manager. Stoke-born, he made 761 League apps. for his only club, helping them reach the FA Cup semi-final and win Div. 3 North in 1954. He managed the club from 1974-77.

SID TICKRIDGE, 73, played 100 post-war games at full-back for Tottenham, then moved to Chelsea (£10,000) in March 1951. After 4 years at Stamford Bridge, he joined Brentford, where injury ended his playing career in Jan. 1957. He later served Millwall as assistant-manager, then returned to Spurs to work part-time with their youth and reserve teams for 17 years while employed in the accounts section of a national newspaper.

GEORGE YOUNG, 74, legendary captain of Rangers and Scotland, he led out his country 48 times in 53 Int. apps. (1948-57), including successive Wembley wins against England in 1949 and 1951. A 6ft. 2in., 15st. centre-half he helped Rangers win 6 League Championships, 4 Scottish Cups and 2 League Cups. Despite his physique, he was fairness personified. England's Tom Finney, whom he encountered in a number of Ints., remembered him as: "A giant octopus. You would beat him and think you were past him but then, with perfect timing, out would come that right leg and reclaim the ball."

February

WILF CHITTY, 84, who played on Chelsea's left wing in the 1930s, died at Caterham. He began with Woking, served Chelsea from 1930-38, then moved to Plymouth Argyle. He played for Reading during the war and ended his League career there in 1946-47. He later scouted for Fulham and, until 1995, for West Ham.

COLIN LIDDELL, 71, outside-left for Queens Park, Morton, Hearts and Rangers (1942-56). Played for Morton in 1948 Scottish Cup Final v Rangers and fetched the then Scottish record fee of £10,000 when sold to Hearts the following season.

BILL McCULLOUGH, 64, served Barrow for 26 years, including 15 as chairman and the last 7 as president.

STAN PEARSON, whose career with Man. United as one of the game's outstanding inside-forwards spanned 1935-54, died at Alderley Edge, Cheshire, aged 78. He played in a dazzling forward line in company with Delaney, Morris, Rowley and Mitten, he was creator and marksman, scoring 180 goals in 342 League and Cup apps. Salford-born, he went to Old Trafford as a 16-year-old and played in the United side that won promotion to the First Division in 1938. When the war ended – he served in the Army in India and Burma – Pearson was 26, and resumed his career in the great side created by Matt Busby. United were runners-up in 4 of the first 5 post-war seasons, and Pearson scored in the classic 1948 FA Cup Final triumph against Blackpool. With 22 goals, he top-scored for the Championship-winning team of 1951-52, and was capped 8 times for England (1948-52). He left United in Feb. 1954 a £4,500 transfer to Second Div. Bury, where he spent 3 seasons before completing his career as player, then manager of Chester in Div. 3 North (1959-61). Then he ran a newsagents shop and post office at Prestbury until the Eighties, remaining a devoted United follower.

REG RYAN, 71, a stocky inside-forward, played for both Irish Int. teams – 16 times for the Republic (1950-56) and once for N. Ireland. Dublin-born, he spent his 15-season League career with WBA (1946-55), played in their Cup-winning team of 1954), Derby (1955-58) and Coventry (1958-61).

BILL WHEATLEY, 86, president and former chairman of Brentford, died in a car crash. He helped the club fight off the takeover bid by QPR in the 1960s.

March

FRANK BRENNAN, 72, was a member of Newcastle United's FA Cup-winning teams of 1951 and 1952 and widely regarded as the most commanding centre-half in the club's history. Born just outside Glasgow, he began his career in wartime with Airdrieonians in 1941 and transferred to Newcastle (£7,000) in May 1946. A craggy 6ft. 3in., superb in the air, he helped them win promotion to the First Div. in 1948 and was capped 7 times by Scotland. A contractual dispute led to his missing Newcastle's third Cup Final in 5 seasons in 1955 and a year later he joined non-League North Shields, taking them to the 1969 Amateur Cup Final. He managed Darlington in 1971-72 and after giving up football ran a sports shop in Newcastle before retiring to Whitley Bay.

LEN MILLARD, 78, was captain and left-back in WBA's F.A. Cup-winning team in 1954. They were his only club (1937-58), and his 600-plus apps. included 436 in the Football League.

BOBBY PARKER, 73, who began as a right-back with Partick Thistle, was with Heart of Midlothian for 46 years (1947-93) as player, captain, trainer, coach, scout, manager, director and chairman. He played in Hearts Championship-winning team of 1959-60, and helped bring on a young star-to-be named Dave Mackay.

JIMMY ROGERS, 67, was a bold-running, right-wing sharp-shooter for Bristol City, with 102 goals in 270 League apps. in two spells (1950-56, 1958-62), between which he was with Coventry. He played in the Bristol side that won Div. 3 South in 1954-55.

BOB WOOD, 84, from Wearside, was appointed a League referee in 1946. In 25 years with the whistle, he sent off only 2 players and booked 6.

April

DENIS COMPTON, 78, played cavalier cricket for Middlesex and England and scintillating football for Arsenal, and his death, 5 days after a third hip operation, was of added poignance on St. George's Day (April 23), for English sport has known no greater patriot. No more popular entertainer either. He was a natural at both games, and while his batting was sheer genius, he was a crowd-pleaser on the football field too – a dashing, dribbling, hard-shooting left-winger. He joined then mighty Arsenal from amateur club Nunhead in Sept. 1932, signed pro' in May 1935 and made his First Div. debut, with a goal, at home to Derby in Sept. 1936. On return from Army service in India, he played with big brother Leslie (also the Middlesex wicket-keeper) in Arsenal's Championship-winning team of 1947-48 and, with right knee heavily bandaged, in the 1950 FA Cup Final triumph against Liverpool. The war took 6 years from a scintillating career, which was also disrupted by knee operations, so that his peace-time League apps. (1936-50) were restricted to 54 (15 goals) compared with 174 wartime games (74 goals) for the club. He played in 14 war Ints. for England. He reflected on his sporting life: "I was jolly lucky, doing something I enjoyed well enough to earn a living." With his picture on the advertising hoardings (£1,000 a year from Brylcreem), he set a trend that earns today's sports stars millions. In 1958 he was awarded the CBE for his services to cricket. His services to both games as a sporting idol were beyond measure, and Westminster Abbey could not accommodate all who wished to attend the memorial service of Denis Charles Scott Compton on July 1.

EDDIE QUIGLEY, whose £26,500 transfer from Sheff. Wed. to Preston in Dec. 1949 made him football's then most expensive player, died at Blackpool, aged 75. Bury-born, he spent his entire career in the North, as a goalscorer for Bury (1941-47), Sheff. Wed. (1947-49), Preston (1949-51), Blackburn (1951-56) and finally back to Bury. He learned the management ropes in 6 years with non-League Mossley and then, as Bury's youth manager, discovered Colin Todd among many others. Between managing Stockport in 1966 and 1976-77, he was in charge at Blackburn from 1967-70 and then general manager there.

PETER TAYLOR, LORD TAYLOR OF GOSFORTH, 66, Lord Chief Justice from 1992-96 and lifelong Newcastle supporter, was responsible for the official report into the Hillsborough Disaster in 1989. It changed the face of our football, with recommendations that brought safer conditions for supporters and all-seat stadiums.

May

TREVOR PORTEOUS, 63, who was Stockport County personified, died from a heart attack while playing bowls. Over 41 years – he joined the club from Hull in June 1956 – he served them as player and player-manager (364 apps. 1956-65), physio, secretary, groundsman, youth development officer and supporters' club secretary.

DR DAVID TARGETT was Aston Villa's medical officer for 25 years and became a director of the club in 1983.

JACKIE WHARTON, 76, began as an outside-right with Plymouth and served 4 clubs in the immediate post-war period: Preston, Man. City, Blackburn and Newport. He spent most of his career with Blackburn, making 129 League apps. in 5 years (1948-53). His son Terry was also a right-winger (Wolves and Bolton).

July

GEORGE ANTONIO, 82, former Stoke, Derby, Doncaster and Mansfield wing-half (1935-50), died at Shrewsbury. He coached in Shropshire and continued playing minor football until well into his fifties.

IVOR ALLCHURCH, 67, one of Wales' all-time greats, died at his home in Swansea. He was known as the "Golden Boy", and in his 20-year career (1948-68) scored 251 goals in 694 League apps. for Swansea (two spells), Newcastle and Cardiff. An inside forward with superb ball control, he was capped 68 times (1951-66), including Wales' only appearance in the World Cup finals in Sweden in 1958, and his 23 goals were at the time a record for his country. He was awarded the MBE in 1966.

(Sources: National and provincial newspapers, Association of Football Statisticians and FIFA News)

MILESTONES OF SOCCER

1848 First code of rules compiled at Cambridge Univ.
1855 Sheffield F.C., world's oldest football club, formed
1862 Notts County (oldest League club) formed
1863 Football Association founded – their first rules of game agreed
1871 F.A. Cup introduced
1872 First official International: Scotland 0, England 0. Corner-kick introduced
1873 Scottish F.A. formed; Scottish Cup introduced
1874 Shinguards introduced. Oxford v Cambridge, first match
1875 Crossbar introduced (replacing tape)
1876 F.A. of Wales formed
1877 Welsh Cup introduced
1878 Referee's whistle first used
1880 Irish F.A. founded; Irish Cup introduced
1883 Two-handed throw-in introduced
1885 Record first-class score (Arbroath 36, Bon Accord 0 – Scottish Cup).
Professionalism legalised
1886 International Board formed
1887 Record F.A. Cup score (Preston N.E. 26, Hyde 0)
1888 Football League founded by Wm. McGregor. First matches on Sept. 8
1889 Preston win Cup and League (first club to complete Double)
1890 Scottish League and Irish League formed
1891 Goal-nets introduced. Penalty-kick introduced
1892 Inter-League games began. Football League Second Division formed
1893 F.A. Amateur Cup launched
1894 Southern League formed
1895 F.A. Cup stolen from Birmingham shop window – never recovered
1897 First Players' Union formed. Aston Villa win Cup and League
1898 Promotion and relegation introduced
1901 Maximum wage rule in force (£4 a week). Tottenham Hotspur first professional club to take F.A. Cup South. First 100,000 attendance (110,802) at
F.A. Cup Final
1902 Ibrox Park disaster (25 killed). Welsh League formed
1904 F.I.F.A. founded (7 member countries)
1905 First £1,000 transfer (Alf Common, Sunderland to Middlesbrough)
1907 Players' Union revived
1908 Transfer fee limit (£350) fixed in January and withdrawn in April.
1911 New F.A. Cup trophy – in use to 1991. Transfer deadline introduced
1914 King George V first reigning monarch to attend F.A. Cup Final
1916 Entertainment Tax introduced
1919 League extended to 44 clubs
1920 Third Division (South) formed
1921 Third Division (North) formed
1922 Scottish League (Div. II) introduced
1923 Beginning of football pools. First Wembley Cup Final
1924 First International at Wembley (England 1, Scotland 1). Rule change allows
goals to be scored direct from corner-kicks
1925 New offside law
1926 Huddersfield Town complete first League Championship hat-trick
1927 First League match broadcast (radio): Arsenal v Sheff. Utd. (Jan 22). First
radio broadcast of Cup Final (winners Cardiff C.). Charles Clegg,
president of F.A., becomes first knight of football
1928 First £10,000 transfer – David Jack (Bolton to Arsenal). W.R. ('Dixie') Dean
(Everton) creates League record – 60 goals in season. Britain withdraws
from F.I.F.A.
1930 Uruguay first winners of World Cup
1931 West Bromwich Albion win Cup and promotion
1933 Players numbered for first time in Cup Final (1-22)
1934 Sir Frederick Wall retires as F.A. secretary; successor Stanley Rous. Death

	of Herbert Chapman (Arsenal manager)
1935	Arsenal equal Huddersfield Town's Championship hat-trick record. Official two-referee trials
1936	Joe Payne's 10-goal League record (Luton 12, Bristol Rovers 0)
1937	British record attendance: 149,547 at Scotland v England match
1938	First live TV transmission of F.A. Cup Final. F.A.'s 75th anniversary. Football League 50th Jubilee. New pitch marking – arc on edge of penalty-area. Laws of Game re-drafted by Stanley Rous. Arsenal pay record £14,500 fee for Bryn Jones (Wolverhampton Wanderers)
1939	Compulsory numbering of players in Football League. First six-figure attendance for League match (Rangers v Celtic, 118,567). All normal competitions suspended for duration of Second World War
1944	Death of Sir Frederick Wall (84), F.A. secretary 1896-1934
1945	Scottish League Cup introduced
1946	British associations rejoin F.I.F.A.. Bolton disaster (33 killed) during F.A. Cup tie with Stoke City. Walter Winterbottom appointed England's first director of coaching
1947	Great Britain beat Rest of Europe 6-1 at Hampden Park, Glasgow. First £20,000 transfer – Tommy Lawton, Chelsea to Notts Co.
1949	Stanley Rous, secretary F.A., knighted. England's first home defeat outside British Champ. (0-2 v Eire)
1950	Football League extended from 88 to 92 clubs. World record crowd (203,500) at World Cup Final, Brazil v Uruguay, in Rio. Scotland's first home defeat by foreign team (0-1 v Austria)
1951	White ball comes into official use
1952	Newcastle first club to win F.A. Cup at Wembley in successive seasons
1953	England's first Wembley defeat by foreign opponents (3-6 v Hungary)
1954	Hungary beat England 7-1 in Budapest
1955	First F.A. Cup match under floodlights (prelim. round replay, Sept. 14): Kidderminster Harriers v Brierley Hill Alliance
1956	First F.A. Cup ties under floodlights in competition proper (Jan. 7). First League match by floodlight (Feb. 22, Portsmouth v Newcastle). Real Madrid win the first European Cup
1957	Last full Football League programme on Christmas Day. Entertainment Tax withdrawn
1958	Manchester United air crash at Munich (Feb. 6). League re-structured into four divisions
1959	Football League establish fixtures copyright; pools must pay for use
1960	Record transfer fee: £55,000 for Denis Law (Huddersfield to Man. C.). Wolves win Cup, miss Double and Championship hat-trick by one goal. For fifth time in ten years F.A. Cup Final team reduced to ten men by injury. F.A. recognise Sunday football. Football League Cup launched
1961	Tottenham complete the first Championship-F.A. Cup double this century. Maximum wage (£20 a week) abolished in High Court challenge by George Eastham. First British £100-a-week wage paid (by Fulham to Johnny Haynes). First £100,000 British transfer – Denis Law, Man. C. to Torino. Sir Stanley Rous elected president of F.I.F.A.
1962	Man. United raise record British transfer fee to £115,000 for Denis Law
1963	F.A. Centenary. Football League's 75th anniversary. Season extended to end of May due to severe winter. First pools panel. English "retain and transfer" system ruled illegal in High Court test case
1964	Rangers' second great hat-trick – Scottish Cup, League Cup and League. Football League and Scottish League guaranteed £500,000 a year in new fixtures copyright agreement with Pools. First televised 'Match of the Day' (BBC2): Liverpool 3, Arsenal 2 (August 22)
1965	Bribes scandal – ten players jailed (and banned for life by F.A.) for match-fixing 1960-63. Stanley Matthews knighted in farewell season. Arthur Rowley (Shrewsbury Town) retires with record of 434 League goals. Substitutes allowed for injured players in Football League matches (one per team)

1966 England win World Cup (Wembley)

1967 Alf Ramsey, England manager, knighted; O.B.E. for captain Bobby Moore. Celtic become first British team to win European Cup. First substitutes allowed in F.A. Cup Final (Tottenham v Chelsea) but not used. Football League permit loan transfers (two per club)

1968 First F.A. Cup Final televised live in colour (BBC2 – W.B.A. v Everton). Manchester United first English club to win European Cup

1971 Arsenal win League Championship and F.A. Cup

1973 Football League introduce 3-up, 3-down promotion/relegation between Divisions 1, 2 and 3 and 4-up, 4-down between Divisions 3 and 4

1974 First F.A. Cup ties played on Sunday (Jan. 6). League football played on Sunday for first time (Jan. 20). Last F.A. Amateur Cup Final. Joao Havelange (Brazil) succeeds Sir Stanley Rous as F.I.F.A. president

1975 Scottish Premier Division introduced

1976 Football League introduce goal difference (replacing goal average)

1977 Liverpool achieve the double of League Championship and European Cup. Don Revie defects to Saudi Arabia when England manager – successor Ron Greenwood

1978 Freedom of contract for players accepted by Football League. P.F.A. lifts ban on foreign players in English football. Football League introduce Transfer Tribunal. Viv Anderson (Nottingham Forest) first black player to win a full England cap. Willie Johnston (Scotland) sent home from World Cup Finals in Argentina after failing dope test

1979 First all-British £500,000 transfer – David Mills, M'bro' to W.B.A. First British million pound transfer (Trevor Francis – B'ham to Nott'm. F.). Andy Gray moves from Aston Villa to Wolves for a record £1,469,000 fee

1981 Tottenham win 100th F.A. Cup Final. Liverpool first British side to win European Cup three times. Three points for a win introduced by Football League. Q.P.R. install Football League's first artificial pitch. Sept. 29, death of Bill Shankly, manager-legend of Liverpool 1959-74. Record British transfer – Bryan Robson (W.B.A. to Man. Utd.), £1,500,000

1982 Aston Villa become sixth consecutive English winners of European Cup. Tottenham retain F.A. Cup – first club to do so since Spurs 1961 and 1962. Football League Cup becomes the (sponsored) Milk Cup

1983 Liverpool complete the League Championship-Milk Cup double for second year running. Manager Bob Paisley retires. Aberdeen first club to do Cup-Winners' Cup and domestic double. Football League clubs vote to keep own match receipts. Football League sponsored by Canon, Japanese camera and business equipment manufacturers – 3-year agreement starting 1983-4. Football League agree 2-year contract for live TV coverage of ten matches per season (5 Friday night, BBC, 5 Sunday afternoon, ITV)

1984 One F.A. Cup tie in rounds 3, 4, 5 and 6 shown live on TV (Friday or Sunday). Aberdeen take Scottish Cup for third successive season, win Scottish Championship, too. Tottenham win UEFA Cup on penalty shoot-out. Liverpool win European Cup on penalty shoot-out to complete unique treble with Milk Cup and League title (as well as Championship hat-trick). N. Ireland win the final British Championship. France win European Championship – their first honour. F.A. National Soccer School opens at Lilleshall. Britain's biggest score this century: Stirling Alb. 20, Selkirk 0 (Scottish Cup)

1985 Bradford City fire disaster – 56 killed. First £1m. receipts from match in Britain (F.A. Cup Final). Kevin Moran (Man. United) first player to be sent off in F.A. Cup Final. Celtic win 100th Scottish F.A. Cup Final. European Cup Final horror (Liverpool v Juventus, riot in Brussels) 39 die. UEFA ban all English clubs indefinitely from European competitions. No TV coverage at start of League season – first time since 1963 (resumption delayed until January 1986). Sept: first ground-sharing in League history – Charlton move from The Valley to Selhurst Park (C. Palace)

1986 Liverpool complete League and Cup double in player-manager Kenny Dalglish's first season in charge. Swindon (4th Div. Champions) set

League points record (102). League approve reduction of First Division to 20 clubs by 1988. Everton chairman Philip Carter elected president of Football League. July 18, death of Sir Stanley Rous (91). 100th edition of *News of the World* Football Annual. League Cup sponsored for next three years by Littlewoods (£2m.). Football League voting majority (for rule changes) reduced from ¾ to ⅔. Wales move HQ from Wrexham to Cardiff after 110 years. Two substitutes in F.A. Cup and League (Littlewoods) Cup. Two-season League/TV deal (£6.2m.):- BBC and ITV each show seven live League matches per season, League Cup semi-finals and Final. Football League sponsored by *Today* newspaper. Luton Town first club to ban all visiting supporters; as sequel are themselves banned from League Cup. Oldham and Preston install artificial pitches, making four in F. League (following Q.P.R. and Luton).

1987 May: League introduce play-off matches to decide final promotion/relegation places in all divisions. Re-election abolished – bottom club in Div. 4 replaced by winners of GM Vauxhall Conference. Two substitutes approved for Football League 1987-88. Red and yellow disciplinary cards (scrapped 1981) re-introduced by League and F.A.. Football League sponsored by Barclays. First Div. reduced to 21 clubs

1988 Football League Centenary. First Division reduced to 20 clubs

1989 Soccer gets £74m. TV deal: £44m. over 4 years, ITV; £30m. over 5 years, BBC/BSB. But it costs Philip Carter the League Presidency. Ted Croker retires as F.A. chief executive; successor Graham Kelly, from Football League. Hillsborough disaster: 95 die at F.A. Cup semi-final (Liverpool v Nott'm. F.). Arsenal win closest-ever Championship with last kick. Peter Shilton sets England record with 109 caps.

1990 Nott'm. Forest win last Littlewoods Cup Final. Both F.A. Cup semi-finals played on Sunday and televised live. Play-off finals move to Wembley; Swindon win place in Div. 1, then relegated back to Div. 2 (breach of financial regulations) – Sunderland promoted instead. Pools betting tax cut from 42½ to 40%. England reach World Cup semi-final in Italy and win F.I.F.A. Fair Play Award. Peter Shilton retires as England goalkeeper with 125 caps (world record). Graham Taylor (Aston Villa) succeeds Bobby Robson as England manager. Int. Board amend offside law (player 'level' no longer offside). F.I.F.A. make "pro foul" a sending-off offence. English clubs back in Europe (Man. U. and Aston V.) after 5-year exile

1991 First F.A. Cup semi-final at Wembley (Tottenham 3, Arsenal 1). Bert Millichip (F.A. chairman) and Philip Carter (Everton chairman) knighted. End of artificial pitches in Div. 1 (Luton, Oldham). Scottish League reverts to 12-12-14 format (as in 1987-8). Penalty shoot-out introduced to decide F.A. Cup ties level after one replay

1992 Introduction of fourth F.A. Cup (previous trophy withdrawn). F.A. launch Premier League (22 clubs). Football League reduced to three divisions (71 clubs). Record TV-sport deal: BSkyB/BBC to pay £304m. for 5-year coverage of Premier League. ITV do £40m., 4-year deal with F. League. Channel 4 show Italian football live (Sundays). F.I.F.A. approve new back-pass rule (goalkeeper must not handle ball kicked to him by team-mate). New League of Wales formed. Record all-British transfer, £3.3m.: Alan Shearer (So'ton to Blackburn). Charlton return to The Valley after 7-year absence

1993 Barclays end 6-year sponsorship of F. League. For first time both F.A. Cup semi-finals at Wembley (Sat., Sun.). Arsenal first club to complete League Cup/F.A. Cup double. Rangers pull off Scotland's domestic treble for fifth time. F.A. in record British sports sponsorship deal (£12m. over 4 years) with brewers Bass for F.A. Carling Premiership, from Aug. Brian Clough retires after 18 years as Nott'm. F. manager; as does Jim McLean (21 years manager of Dundee U.). Football League agree 3-year, £3m. sponsorship with Endsleigh Insurance. Premier League introduce squad numbers with players' names on shirts. Record British transfer: Duncan Ferguson, Dundee U. to Rangers (£4m.). Record English-club signing: Roy Keane,

Nott'm. F. to Man. U. (£3.75m.). Graham Taylor resigns as England manager after World Cup exit (Nov.). Death in Feb. of Bobby Moore (51), England World-Cup winning captain 1966.

1994 Death of Sir Matt Busby (Jan.). Terry Venables appointed England coach (Jan.). Man. United complete the Double. Last artificial pitch in English football goes – Preston revert to grass, summer 1994. Bobby Charlton knighted. Scottish League format changes to four divisions of ten clubs. Record British transfer: Chris Sutton, Norwich to Blackburn (£5m.). Sept: FA announce first sponsorship of F.A. Cup – Littlewoods Pools (4-year, £14m. deal, plus £6m. for Charity Shield). Death of Billy Wright, 70 (Sept).

1995 New record British transfer: Andy Cole, Newcastle to Man. U. (£7m.). First England match abandoned through crowd trouble (v Rep. of Ireland, Dublin). Blackburn Champions for first time since 1914. Premiership reduced to 20 clubs. British transfer record broken again (June): Stan Collymore, Nott'm. F. to Liverpool (£8½m.). Starting season 1995-96, teams allowed to use 3 substitutes per match, not necessarily including a goalkeeper. Dec: European Court of Justice upholds Bosman ruling, barring transfer fees for players out of contract and removing limit on number of foreign players clubs can field.

1996 Death in Feb. of Bob Paisley (77), ex-Liverpool, most successful manager in English Football. F.A. appoint Chelsea manager Glenn Hoddle to succeed Terry Venables as England coach after Euro 96. Man. United first English club to achieve Double twice (and in 3 seasons). Football League completes £125m., 5-year TV deal with BSkyB starting 1996-97. England stage European Championship, reach semi-finals, lose on pens to tournament winners Germany. Keith Wiseman succeeds Sir Bert Millichip as F.A. Chairman. Linesmen become known as "referees' assistants". Coca-Cola Cup experiment with own disciplinary system (red, yellow cards). Alan Shearer football's first £15m. player (Blackburn to Newcastle). Nigeria first African contry to win Olympic soccer. Nation-wide Building Society sponsor Football League in initial 3-year deal worth £5.25m. Peter Shilton first player to make 1000 League apps.

1997 Howard Wilkinson appointed English football's first technical director. England's first home defeat in World Cup (0-1 v Italy). Ruud Gullit (Chelsea) first foreign coach to win F.A. Cup. Rangers equal Celtic's record of 9 successive League titles. Man. United win Premier League for fourth time in 5 seasons. New record World Cup score: Iran 17, Maldives 0 (qual. round). Season 1997-98 starts Premiership's record £36m., 4-year sponsorship extension with brewers Bass (Carling).

McSTAY BOWS OUT

A recurring ankle injury forced 32-year-old **Paul McStay** to retire from football in May. He played 16 seasons for Celtic, his only club, and was capped 76 times by Scotland.

EASTER BLANK

For the first time since League football began in 1888-89, there was no top-division football last Easter. The "blank" was arranged to assist International preparation – though England had only a friendly fixture, other countries faced World Cup qualifying matches.

COVENTRY'S JINX GROUND

Coventry City have **never** won a League fixture **away to Aston Villa** – and they have been trying since 1936. The clubs' 23 meetings at Villa Park have produced 13 wins for Villa and ten draws (goals 36-12).

ENGLISH LEAGUE ROLL CALL
APPEARANCES & SCORERS 1996-97
(Figures in brackets = appearances as substitute)

F.A. CARLING PREMIERSHIP

ARSENAL

Ground: Arsenal Stadium, Highbury, London N5 1BU.
Telephone: 0171-704-4000. **Clubcall:** 0891 202020. **Club Nickname:** Gunners.
First-choice Colours: Red shirts; white shorts; white/red stockings.

Adams, T 21	Helder, G .... –(2)	Parlour, R .... 17(13)
Anelka, N .... –(4)	Hillier, D .... –(2)	Platt, D .... 27(1)
Bergkamp, D ...... 28(1)	Hughes, S .... 9(5)	Rose, M 1
Bould, S 33	Keown, M 33	Seaman, D 22
Clarke, A .... –(1)	Linighan, A .... 10(1)	Selley, I .... –(1)
Dickov, P .... 1(6)	Lukic, J 15	Shaw, P .... 1(7)
Dixon, L .... 31(1)	McGowan, G 1	Vieira, P .... 30(1)
Garde, R .... 7(4)	Marshall, S .... 6(2)	Winterburn, N 38
Harper, L 1	Merson, P 32	Wright, I .... 30(5)
Hartson, J .... 14(5)	Morrow, S .... 5(9)	

League Goals (62): Wright 23, Bergkamp 12, Merson 6, Platt 4, Adams 3, Hartson 3, Dixon 2, Parlour 2, Shaw 2, Vieira 2, Hughes 1, Keown 1, Linighan 1.
Coca-Cola Cup Goals (8): Wright 5, Bergkamp 1, Merson 1, Platt 1. **FA Cup Goals (3):** Bergkamp 1, Hughes 1, Hartson 1 **UEFA Cup Goals (4):** Merson 2, Wright 2.
'Player of Year': Martin Keown. **Sponsors:** JVC.
Average Home League Attendance 1996-97: 37,537. **Capacity for 1997-98:** 38,500 (all-seated).
Record Attendance: 73,295 v Sunderland (Div. 1) 9 March 1935.

ASTON VILLA

Ground: Villa Park, Trinity Road, Birmingham B6 6HE.
Telephone: 0121-327-2299. **Clubcall:** 0891 121148. **Club Nickname:** Villans.
First-choice Colours: Claret and blue shirts; white shorts; claret and blue stockings.

Bosnich, M 20	Johnson, T .... 10(9)	Staunton, S 30
Curcic, S .... 17(5)	Milosevic, S .... 29(1)	Taylor, I .... 29(5)
Draper, M .... 28(1)	Murray, S 1	Tiler, C .... 9(2)
Ehiogu, U 38	Nelson, F .... 33(1)	Townsend, A 34
Farrelly, G .... 1(2)	Oakes, M .... 18(2)	Wright, A 38
Hughes, D .... 4(3)	Scimeca, R .... 11(6)	Yorke, D 37
Joachim, J .... 3(12)	Southgate, G 28	

League Goals (47): Yorke 17, Milosevic 9, Johnson 4, Ehiogu 3, Joachim 3, Staunton 2, Taylor 2, Townsend 2, Southgate 1, Tiler 1, Wright 1, Opponents 2.
Coca-Cola Cup Goals (2): Taylor 1, Yorke 1. **F.A. Cup Goals (4):** Yorke 2, Curcic 1, Ehiogu 1. **UEFA Cup Goals (1):** Johnson 1.
'Player of Year': Dwight Yorke. **Sponsors:** AST Computer.
Average Home League Attendance 1996-97: 36,027. **Capacity for 1997-98:** 39,339 (all-seated).
Record Attendance: 76,588 v Derby County (F.A. Cup 6) 2 March 1946.

BLACKBURN ROVERS

Ground: Ewood Park, Blackburn, Lancashire BB2 4JF.
Telephone: 01254-698888. **Clubcall:** 0891 121179. **Club Nickname:** Rovers

First-choice Colours: Blue and white shirts; white shorts; blue and white stockings.

Beattie, J 1	Flowers, T 36	Marker, N .... 5(2)
Berg, H 36	Gallacher, K 34	Pearce, I .... 7(5)
Bohinen, L .... 17(6)	Given, S 2	Pedersen, P .... 6(5)
Coleman, C 8	Gudmundsson, N ... –(2)	Ripley, S .... 5(8)
Croft, G .... 4(1)	Hendry, C 35	Sherwood, T 37
Donis, G .... 11(11)	Kenna, J 37	Sutton, C .... 24(1)
Duff, D 1	Le Saux, G 26	Warhurst, P .... 5(6)
Fenton, G .... 5(8)	McKinlay, W .... 23(2)	Wilcox, J .... 26(2)
Flitcroft, G .... 27(1)		

League Goals (42): Sutton 11, Gallacher 10, Flitcroft 3, Sherwood 3, Berg 2, Bohinen 2, Donis 2, Warhurst 2, Wilcox 2, Fenton 1, Hendry 1, Le Saux 1, McKinlay 1, Pedersen 1.
Coca-Cola Cup Goals (4): Flitcroft 1, Gallacher 1, Sherwood 1, Sutton 1.
F.A. Cup Goals (2): Bohinen 1, Sherwood 1.
'Player of Year': Tim Sherwood. **Sponsors**: CIS ASICS.
Average Home League Attendance 1996-97: 24,947. **Capacity for 1997-98**: 31,367 (all-seated).
Record Attendance: 61,783 v Bolton Wanderers (F.A. Cup 6) 2 March 1929.

CHELSEA

Ground: Stamford Bridge, Fulham Road, London SW6 1HS.
Telephone: 0171-385-5545. **Clubcall**: 0891 121159. **Club Nickname**: Blues.
First-choice Colours: Blue shirts; blue shorts; white stockings.

Burley, C .... 26(5)	Hitchcock, K .... 10(2)	Newton, E .... 13(2)
Clarke, S 31	Hughes, M .... 32(3)	Nicholls, M .... 3(5)
Clement, N 1	Hughes, P .... 8(4)	Parker, P .... 1(3)
Colgan, N 1	Johnsen, E .... 14(4)	Petrescu, D 34
Di Matteo, R .... 33(1)	Kharine, D 5	Phelan, T .... 1(1)
Duberry, M .... 13(2)	Lebouef, F 26	Sherin, J .... –(1)
Forrest, C .... 2(1)	Lee, D 1	Sinclair, F .... 17(2)
Granville, D .... 3(2)	Minto, S .... 24(1)	Vialli, G .... 23(5)
Gullit, R .... 6(6)	Morris, J .... 6(5)	Wise, D .... 27(4)
Grodas, F .... 20(1)	Myers, A .... 15(3)	Zola, G .... 22(1)

League Goals (58): Vialli 9, M Hughes 8, Zola 8, Di Matteo 7, Lebouef 6, Minto 4, Petrescu 3, Wise 3, Burley 2, P Hughes 2, Duberry 1, Gullit 1, Lee 1, Myers 1, Sinclair 1, Opponent 1.
Coca-Cola Cup Goals (6): Spencer 2, M Hughes 1, Minto 1, Morris 1, Petrescu 1. **F.A. Cup Goals (19)**: M Hughes 5, Wise 5, Zola 4, Di Matteo 2, Lebouef 1, Newton 1, Petrescu 1.
'Player of Year': Gianfranco Zola. **Sponsors**: Autoglass.
Average Home League Attendance 1996-97: 27,617. **Capacity for 1997-98**: 31,500 (increasing to 35,000) (all-seated).
Record Attendance: 82,905 v Arsenal (Div. 1) 12 October 1935.

COVENTRY CITY

Ground: Highfield Road, King Richard Street, Coventry CV2 4FW.
Telephone: 01203-234000. **Clubcall**: 0891 121166. **Club Nickname**: Sky Blues.
First-choice Colours: Sky blue and navy shirts; navy shorts; navy stockings.

Boland, W .... –(1)	Genaux, R .... 3(1)	O'Neill, M 1
Borrows, B .... 16(7)	Hall, M .... 10(2)	Richardson, K ...... 25(3)
Breen, G .... 8(1)	Huckerby, D .... 21(4)	Salako, J 23
Burrows, D .... 17(1)	Isaias, M .... –(1)	Shaw, R 35
Daish, L 20	Jess, E .... 19(8)	Strachan, G .... 3(6)
Dublin, D .... 33(1)	McAllister, G 38	Telfer, P .... 31(3)
Ducros, A .... 1(4)	Ndlovu, P .... 10(10)	Whelan, N .... 34(1)
Evtusho, K 3	Ogrizovic, S 38	Williams, P .... 29(3)

League Goals (38): Dublin 13, McAllister 6, Whelan 6, Huckerby 5, Williams 2. Daish 1, Ndlovu 1, Salako 1, Opponents 3.
Coca-Cola Cup Goals (4): Telfer 2, Daish 1, McAllister 1. **F.A. Cup Goals (7)**: Huckerby 2, Jess 2, Whelan 2, Opponent 1.
'Player of Year': To be announced. **Sponsors**: To be advised.
Average Home League Attendance 1996-97: 19,625. **Capacity for 1997-98**: 23,662 (all-seated).
Record Attendance: 51,455 v Wolves (Div. 2) 29 April 1967.

DERBY COUNTY
Ground: Pride Park Stadium, Derby DE24 8XL.
Telephone: 01332-667503. **Clubcall**: 0891 121187. **Club Nickname**: Rams.
First-choice Colours: White shirts; black shorts; white stockings.

Asanovic, A 34	Parker, P 4	Sturridge, D .... 29(1)
Carbon, M .... 6(5)	Poom, M 4	Taylor, M 3
Carsley, L .... 15(9)	Powell, C 35	Trollope, P .... 13(1)
Dailly, C .... 31(5)	Powell, D .... 27(6)	Van der Laan, R .. 15(3)
Flynn, S .... 10(7)	Rahmberg, M .... −(1)	Wanchope, P .... 2(3)
Gabbiadini, M .... 5(9)	Rowett, G .... 35(1)	Ward, A .... 25(6)
Hoult, R .... 31(1)	Simpson, P .... −(22)	Willems, R .... 7(9)
Laursen, J .... 35(4)	Solis, M .... −(2)	Yates, D .... 8(2)
McGrath, P 23	Stimac, I 21	

League Goals (45): Sturridge 11, Ward 8, Asanovic 6, Dailly 3, Rowett 2, Simpson 2, Van der Laan 2, Willems 2, Flynn 1, Laursen 1, D Powell 1, Stimac 1, Trollope 1, Wanchope 1, Opponents 1.
Coca-Cola Cup Goals (2): Simpson 1, Sturridge 1. **F.A. Cup Goals (8)**: Van der Laan 3, Sturridge 2, Willems 2, Ward 1.
'Player of Year': Chris Powell. **Sponsors**: Puma.
Average Home League Attendance 1996-97: 17,888. **Capacity for 1997-98**: 30,000 (all-seated).
Record Attendance: 41,826 v Tottenham Hotspur (Div. 1) 20 September 1969.

EVERTON
Ground: Goodison Park, Liverpool L4 4EL.
Telephone: 0151-330-2200. **Clubcall**: 0891 121199. **Club Nickname**: Toffees.
First-choice Colours: Blue shirts; white shorts; blue stockings.

Allen, G .... −(1)	Grant, T .... 11(7)	Rideout, P 5
Ball, M .... 2(3)	Hills, S .... −(2)	Short, C .... 19(4)
Barmby, N .... 22(3)	Hinchcliffe, A 18	Southall, N 34
Barrett, E 36	Hottiger, M .... 4(4)	Speed, G 37
Branch, M .... 13(12)	Kanchelskis, A 20	Stuart, G .... 29(6)
Dunne R .... 6(1)	Limpar, A 1	Thomsen, C .... 15(1)
Ebbrell, J 2	Parkinson, J 28	Unsworth, D .... 32(2)
Ferguson, D .... 31(2)	Phelan, T 15	Watson, D 29
Gerrard, P .... 4(1)		

League Goals (44): Ferguson 10, Speed 9, Stuart 5, Unsworth 5, Barmby 4, Kanchelskis 4, Branch 3, Short 2, Hinchcliffe 1, Watson 1.
Coca-Cola Cup Goals (3): Kanchelskis 1, Rideout 1, Speed 1. **F.A. Cup Goals (5)**: Kanchelskis 2, Barmby 1, Ferguson 1, Speed 1.
'Player of Year': Gary Speed. **Sponsors**:
Average Home League Attendance 1996-97: 36,186. **Capacity for 1997-98**: 40,177 (all-seated).
Record Attendance: 78,299 v Liverpool (Div. 1) 18 September 1948.

LEEDS UNITED
Ground: Elland Road, Leeds, West Yorkshire LS11 0ES.
Telephone: 0113-226-6000. **Clubcall**: 0891 121180. **Club Nickname**: United.
First-choice Colours: White shirts; white shorts; white stockings.

Beeney, M .... 1(1)	Halle, G 20	Molenaar, R 12
Beesley, P 11	Harte, I .... 10(4)	Palmer, C .... 26(2)
Blunt, J .... –(1)	Hateley, M .... 5(1)	Radebe, L .... 28(4)
Bowyer, L 32	Jackson, M .... 11(6)	Rush, I .... 34(2)
Boyle, P .... –(1)	Jobson, R 10	Sharpe, L 26
Couzens, A .... 7(3)	Kelly, G .... 34(2)	Shepherd, P 1
Deane, B .... 27(1)	Kewell, H .... –(1)	Tinkler, M .... 1(2)
Dorigo, T .... 15(3)	Laurent, P .... 2(2)	Wallace, R .... 17(5)
Ford, M 15	Lilley, D .... 4(2)	Wetherall, D .... 25(4)
Gray, A .... 1(6)	Martyn, N 37	Yeboah, A .... 6(1)

League Goals (28): Deane 5, Sharpe 5, Bowyer 4, Rush 3, Wallace 3, Harte 2, Couzens 1, Ford 1, Kelly 1, Molenaar 1, Opponents 2.
Coca-Cola Cup Goals (5): Wallace 3, Harte 1, Sharpe 1. **F.A. Cup Goals (6):** Bowyer 2, Wallace 2, Deane 1, Opponent 1.
'Player of Year': Nigel Martyn. **Sponsors:** Packard Bell.
Average Home League Attendance 1996-97: 32,109. **Capacity for 1997-98:** 40,000 (all-seated).
Record Attendance: 57,892 v Sunderland (F.A. Cup 5) 15 March 1967.

LEICESTER CITY

Ground: City Stadium, Filbert Street, Leicester LE2 7FL.
Telephone: 0116 2915000. **Clubcall:** 0891 121185. **Club Nickname:** Foxes.
First-choice Colours: Blue shirts; white shorts; blue stockings.

Campbell, S .... 4(6)	Kaamark, P .... 9(1)	Prior, S .... 33(1)
Claridge, S .... 29(3)	Keller, K 31	Robins, M .... 5(3)
Elliott, M 16	Lawrence, J .... 2(13)	Rolling, F 1
Grayson, S 36	Lennon, N 35	Taylor, S .... 20(5)
Guppy, S .... 12(1)	Lewis, N .... 4(2)	Walsh, S 22
Heskey, E 35	Marshall, I .... 19(9)	Watts, J .... 22(4)
Hill, C .... 6(1)	Parker, G .... 22(9)	Whitlow, M .... 14(3)
Izzet, M .... 34(1)	Poole, K .... –	Wilson, S .... –(2)

League Goals (46): Claridge 11, Heskey 10, Marshall 8, Elliott 5, Izzet 3, Parker 2, Walsh 2, Lennon 1, Robins 1, Watts 1, Wilson 1, Opponent 1.
Coca-Cola Cup Goals (12): Claridge 2, Grayson 2, Heskey 2, Lawrence 2, Izzet 1, Lennon 1, Parker 1, Robins 1. **F.A. Cup Goals (6):** Marshall 2, Claridge 1, Parker 1, Walsh 1, Opponent 1.
'Player of Year': Simon Grayson. **Sponsors:** Walkers Crisps.
Average Home League Attendance 1996-97: 20,183. **Capacity for 1997-98:** 21,500 (all-seated).
Record Attendance: 47,298 v Tottenham Hotspur (F.A. Cup 5) 18 February 1928.

LIVERPOOL

Ground: Anfield Road, Liverpool L4 0TH.
Telephone: 0151-263-2361. **Clubcall:** 0891 121184. **Club Nickname:** Reds.
First-choice Colours: Red shirts; red shorts; red stockings.

Babb, P .... 21(1)	James, D 38	Owen, M .... 1(1)
Barnes, J .... 34(1)	Jones, L .... –(2)	Redknapp, J .... 18(5)
Berger, P .... 13(10)	Jones, R 2	Ruddock, N .... 15(2)
Bjornebye, S 38	Kennedy, M .... –(5)	Scales, J 3
Carragher, J .... 1(1)	Kvarme, B 15	Thomas, M .... 29(2)
Collymore, S .... 25(5)	McAteer, J .... 36(1)	Thompson, D .... –(2)
Fowler, R 32	McManaman, S 37	Wright, M 33
Harkness, S .... 5(2)	Matteo, D .... 22(4)	

League Goals (62): Fowler 18, Collymore 12, McManaman 7, Berger 6, Barnes 4, Thomas 3, Bjornebye 2, Redknapp 2, Babb 1, Carragher 1, McAteer 1, Owen 1, Ruddock 1, Opponents 3.
Coca-Cola Cup Goals (10): Fowler 5, McManaman 2, Berger 1, Redknapp 1, Wright 1. **F.A. Cup Goals (3):** Collymore 2, Fowler 1. **Cup-Winners' Cup Goals**

(18): Fowler 7, Barnes 3, Berger 2, Bjornebye 2, Collymore 2, McManaman 1, Wright 1.
'Player of Year': To be announced. **Sponsors**: Carlsberg/Reebok.
Average Home League Attendance 1996-97: 39,552. **Capacity for 1997-98**: 35,000 all-seated (rising to 45,000 in February on completion of new stand).
Record Attendance: 61,905 v Wolves (F.A. Cup 4) 2 February 1952.

MANCHESTER UNITED
Ground: Sir Matt Busby Way, Old Trafford, Manchester M16 0RA.
Telephone: 0161-872-1661. **Clubcall**: 0891 121161. **Club Nickname**: Red Devils. **First-choice Colours**: Red shirts; white shorts; black stockings.

Beckham, D .... 33(3)	van der Gouw, R 2	O'Kane, J 1
Butt, N .... 24(2)	Irwin, D .... 29(2)	Pallister, G 27
Cantona, E 36	Johnsen, R .... 26(5)	Poborsky, K .... 15(7)
Casper, C .... −(2)	Keane, R 21	Schmeichel, P 36
Clegg, M .... 3(1)	McClair, B .... 4(15)	Scholes, P .... 16(8)
Cole, A .... 10(10)	May, D .... 28(1)	Solskjaer, O .... 25(8)
Cruyff, J .... 11(5)	Neville, G .... 30(1)	Thornley, B .... 1(1)
Giggs, R .... 25(1)	Neville, P .... 15(3)	

League Goals (76): Solskjaer 18, Cantona 11, Beckham 8, Cole 6, Butt 5, Cruyff 3, Giggs 3, May 3, Pallister 3, Poborsky 3, Scholes 3, Keane 2, Irwin 1, Neville G 1, Opponents 6.
Coca-Cola Cup Goals (2): Poborsky 1, Scholes 1. **F.A. Cup Goals (3)**: Scholes 2, Beckham 1. **European Cup Goals (10)**: Cantona 3, Beckham 2, Giggs 2, Cole 1, May 1, Solskjaer 1. **Charity Shield Goals (4)**: Cantona 1, Butt 1, Beckham 1, Keane 1.
'Player of Year': To be announced. **Sponsors**: Sharp Electronics.
Average Home League Attendance 1996-97: 55,081. **Capacity for 1997-98**: 56,387 (all-seated).
Record Attendance: 76,962 Wolves v Grimsby Town (F.A. Cup Semi-final) 25 March 1939. **Club record**: 70,504 v Aston Villa (Div. 1) 27 December 1920.
Note: 83,260 saw Man. United v Arsenal (Div. 1) 17 January 1948 (at Maine Road).

MIDDLESBROUGH
Ground: Cellnet Riverside Stadium, Middlesbrough, Cleveland TS3 6RS.
Telephone: 01642-877700. **Boro Livewire**: 0891 424200. **Club Nickname**: Boro'.
First-choice Colours: Red shirts; white shorts; red stockings.

Barmby, N 10	Hendrie, J .... −(1)	Ravanelli, F 33
Beck, M .... 22(3)	Hignett, C .... 19(3)	Roberts, B .... 9(1)
Blackmore, C ...... 14(2)	Juninho .... 34(1)	Robson, B 1
Branco .... 1(1)	Kinder, V .... 4(2)	Schwarzer, M 7
Campbell, A .... −(3)	Liddle, C 5	Stamp, P .... 16(8)
Cox, N .... 29(2)	Miller, A 10	Summerbell, M ..... −(2)
Emerson 32	Moore, A .... 10(7)	Vickers, S .... 26(3)
Festa, G 13	Morris, C .... 3(1)	Walsh, G 12
Fjortoft, J .... 2(4)	Mustoe, R 32	Whelan, P 9
Fleming, C 29	Pearson, N .... 17(1)	Whyte, D .... 20(1)
Freestone, C .... −(3)		

League Goals (51): Ravanelli 16, Juninho 13, Beck 5, Emerson 4, Hignett 4, Blackmore 2, Mustoe 2, Barmby 1, Festa 1, Kinder 1, Stamp 1, Opponent 1.
Coca-Cola Cup Goals (23): Ravanelli 8, Beck 4, Branco 2, Emerson 2, Fleming 1, Hignett 1, Juninho 1, Stamp 1, Vickers 1, Whyte 1. **F.A. Cup Goals (18)**: Ravanelli 6, Beck 2, Hignett 2, Juninho 2, Cox 1, Emerson 1, Festa 1, Fjortoft 1, Stamp 1, Opponent 1.
'Player of Year': Juninho. **Sponsors**: Cellnet.
Average Home League Attendance 1996-97: 29,871. **Capacity for 1997-98**: 30,500 (all-seated).
Record Attendance – Riverside Stadium: 30,215 v Tottenham (Prem. league)

19 October 1996. Previous ground (Ayresome Park): 53,596 v Newcastle United (Div. 1) 27 December 1949.

NEWCASTLE UNITED

Ground: St. James' Park, Newcastle-upon-Tyne, Tyne and Wear NE1 4ST.
Telephone: 0191-201-8400. **Clubcall**: 0891 121190. **Club Nickname**: Magpies.
First-choice Colours: Black and white shirts; black and white shorts; black stockings.

Albert, P .... 27(5)	Crawford, J .... –(2)	Kitson, P .... –(2)
Asprilla, F .... 17(7)	Elliott, R 29	Lee, R .... 32(1)
Barton, W .... 14(4)	Ferdinand, L .... 30(1)	Peacock, D 35
Batty, D 32	Gillespie, K .... 23(9)	Shearer, A 31
Beardsley, P .... 22(3)	Ginola, D .... 20(4)	Srnicek, P 22
Beresford, J .... 18(1)	Hislop, S 16	Watson, S .... 33(3)
Clark, L .... 9(16)	Howey, S .... 8(1)	

League Goals (73): Shearer 25, Ferdinand 16, Elliott (R) 7, Lee 5, Beardsley 5, Asprilla 4, Clark 2, Albert 2, Watson 1, Gillespie 1, Ginola 1, Howey 1, Peacock 1, Batty 1, Barton 1.
Coca-Cola Cup Goals (2): Beardsley 1, Shearer 1. **F.A. Cup Goals (4)**: Clark 1, Ferdinand 1, Lee 1, Shearer 1. **UEFA Cup Goals (14)**: Asprilla 5, Ferdinand 4, Beardsley 2, Albert 1, Ginola 1, Shearer 1.
'Player of Year': No official award. **Sponsors**: Newcastle Breweries.
Average Home League Attendance 1996-97: 36,466. **Capacity for 1997-98**: 36,610 (all-seated).
Record Attendance: 68,386 v Chelsea (Div. 1) 3 September 1930.

NOTTINGHAM FOREST

Ground: City Ground, Nottingham NG2 5FJ.
Telephone: 01159 526000. **Clubcall**: 0891 121174. **Club Nickname**: Reds.
First-choice Colours: Red shirts; white shorts; red stockings.

Allen, C 16	Guinan, S .... –(1)	O'Neil, B .... 3(1)
Bart-Williams, C 16	Haaland, A .... 33(2)	Pearce, S 33
Blatherwick, S 7	Henesy, D .... 1(1)	Phillips, D .... 23(11)
Campbell, S .... 15(1)	Hooijdonk, P 8	Roy, B .... 10(12)
Chettle, S .... 31(1)	Howe, S .... –(1)	Saunders, D 33
Clough, N .... 10(3)	Jerkan, N 14	Silenzi, A .... 1(1)
Cooper, C 36	Lee, J .... 8(8)	Warner, V .... 2(1)
Crossley, M 33	Lyttle, D .... 30(2)	Woan, I .... 29(3)
Fettis, A 4	McGregor, P .... 2(5)	Wright, T 1
Gemmill, S .... 19(6)		

League Goals (31): Campbell 6, Haaland 6, Pearce 5, Roy 3, Saunders 3, Cooper 2, Bart-Williams 1, Clough 1, van Hooijdonk 1, Lyttle 1, Woan 1.
Coca-Cola Cup Goals (3): Cooper 1, Roy 1, Lee 1. **F.A. Cup Goals (5)**: Saunders 2, Woan 1, Allen 1.
'Player of Year': Colin Cooper. **Sponsors**:
Average Home League Attendance 1996-97: 23,233. **Capacity for 1997-98**: 30,602 (all-seated).
Record Attendance: 49,945 v Manchester United (Div. 1) 28 October 1967.

SHEFFIELD WEDNESDAY

Ground: Hillsborough, Sheffield, South Yorkshire S6 1SW.
Telephone: 0114 221 2121. **Clubcall**: 0891 121186. **Club Nickname**: Owls.
First-choice Colours: Blue and white shirts; black shorts; black stockings.

Atherton, P 37	Briscoe, L .... 5(1)	Donaldson, O .... 2(3)
Blinker, R ...... 915(18)	Carbone, B .... 24(1)	Hirst, D .... 20(5)
Booth, A .... 32(3)	Clarke, M .... –(1)	Humphreys, R .... 14(15)
Bright, M .... –(1)	Collins, W .... 8(4)	Hyde, G .... 15(4)

Newsome, J 10	Pembridge, M ...... 33(1)	Trustfull, O .... 9(10)
Nicol, S .... 19(4)	Pressman, K 38	Walker, D 36
Nolan, S 38	Sheridan, J .... –(2)	Whittingham, G .... 29(4)
Oakes, S .... 7(12)	Stefanovic, D .... 27(2)	Williams, M .... –(1)

League Goals (50): Booth 10, Hirst 6, Pembridge 6, Carbone 5, Humphreys 3, Trustfull 3, Whittingham 3, Atherton 2, Donaldson 2, Hyde 2, Stefanovic 2, Blinker 1, Collins 1, Newsome 1, Nolan 1, Oakes 1, Walker 1.
Coca-Cola Cup Goals (1): Whittingham 1. **F.A. Cup Goals (10)**: Booth 3, Humphreys 2, Hyde 1, Pembridge 1, Whittingham 1, Opponents 2.
'Player of Year': Mark Pembridge. **Sponsors**: Sanderson Electronics.
Average Home League Attendance 1996-97: 25,693. **Capacity for 1997-98**: 39,859 (all-seated).
Record Attendance: 72,841 v Manchester City (F.A. Cup 5) 17 February 1934.

SOUTHAMPTON
Ground: The Dell, Milton Road, Southampton, Hampshire SO15 2XH.
Telephone: 01703-220505. **Clubcall**: 0891 121178. **Club Nickname**: Saints.
First-choice Colours: Red and white striped shirts; black shorts; red and white stockings.

Basham, S .... 1(5)	Le Tissier, M .... 25(6)	Robinson, M .... 3(4)
Beasant, D .... 13(1)	Lundekvam, C ...... 28(1)	Shipperley, N .... 9(1)
Benali, F .... 14(4)	Maddison, N ...... 14(4)	Slater, R .... 22(8)
Berkovic, E .... 26(2)	Magilton, J .... 31(6)	Taylor, M 18
Charlton, S .... 24(3)	Monkou, K .... 8(5)	Van Gobbel U. ...... 24(1)
Dia .... –(1)	Moss, N 3	Venison, B 2
Dodd, J 23	Neilson, A .... 24(5)	Warren, C .... –(1)
Dryden, R .... 28(1)	Oakley, M .... 23(5)	Watkinson, R .... –(2)
Evans, M .... 8(4)	Ostenstad, E ...... 29(1)	Watson, N .... 7(1)
Heaney, N .... 4(4)	Potter, G .... 2(6)	Woods, C 4
Hughes, D .... 1(5)		

League Goals (50): Le Tissier 13, Ostenstad 10, Berkovic 4, Magilton 4, Evans 4, Oakley 3, Slater 2, Watson 2, Dodd 1, Dryden 1, Heaney 1, Maddison 1, Van Gobbel 1, Shipperley 1, Opponents 2.
Coca-Cola Cup Goals (18): Dryden 3, Le Tissier 3, Ostenstad 3, Watson 3, Berkovic 2, Magilton 2, Charlton 1, Van Gobbel 1. **F.A. Cup Goals (1)**: Ostenstad 1.
'Player of Year': Egil Ostenstad. **Sponsors**: Sandersons.
Average Home League Attendance 1996-97: 15,100. **Capacity for 1997-98**: 15,250 (all-seated).
Record Attendance: 31,044 v Manchester United (Div. 1) 8 October 1969.

SUNDERLAND
Ground: Stadium Park, Sunderland, Tyne & Wear SR5 1BT.
Telephone: 0191-551-5000. **Clubcall**: 0891 121140. **Club Nickname**:
First-choice Colours: Red and white striped shirts; black shorts; black with red turnover stockings.

Agnew, S .... 11(4)	Howey, L .... 9(3)	Quinn, N .... 8(4)
Aiston, S .... –(2)	Johnston, A .... 4(2)	Rae, A .... 13(10)
Ball, K 32	Kelly, D .... 23(1)	Russell, C .... 10(19)
Bracewell, P 38	Kubicki, D .... 28(1)	Scott, M 15
Bridges, M .... 10(15)	Melville, A 30	Smith, M .... 6(5)
Coton, T 10	Mullin, J .... 9(1)	Stewart, P .... 20(4)
Eriksson, J 1	Ord, R 33	Waddle, C 7
Gray, M .... 31(3)	Perez, L .... 28(1)	Williams, D .... 10(1)
Hall, G 32		

League Goals (35): Russell 4, Stewart 4, Ball 3, Bridges 3, Gray 3, Agnew 2, Melville 2, Ord 2, Quinn 2, Rae 2, Williams 2, Johnston 1, Mullin 1, Scott 1, Waddle 1, Opponents 2.

337

Coca-Cola Cup Goals (4): Ball 1, Quinn 1, Rae 1, Scott 1. **F.A. Cup Goals (1)**: Gray 1.
'Player of Year': Lionel Perez. **Sponsors**: Vaux Breweries.
Average Home League Attendance 1996-97: 20,973. **Capacity for 1997-98**: 42,000 (all seated).
Record Attendance: 75,118 v Derby County (F.A. Cup 6) 8 March 1933.

TOTTENHAM HOTSPUR
Ground: White Hart Lane, 748 High Road, Tottenham, London N17 0AP.
Telephone: 0181-365-5000. **Spurs Line**: 0891 335555. **Club Nickname**: Spurs.
First-choice Colours: White shirts; navy shorts; white stockings.

Allen, R .... 9(3)	Dozzell, J .... 10(7)	Nielsen, A .... 28(1)
Anderton, D .... 14(2)	Edinburgh, J ...... 21(3)	Rosenthal, R ...... 4(16)
Armstrong, C 12	Fenn, N .... −(4)	Scales, J .... 10(2)
Austin, D .... 13(2)	Fox, R .... 19(6)	Sheringham, T 29
Baardsen, E .... 1(1)	Howells, D 32	Sinton, A .... 32(1)
Calderwood, C ..... 33(1)	Iversen, S 16	Vega, R 8
Campbell, S 38	McVeigh, P .... 2(1)	Walker, I 37
Carr, S .... 24(2)	Mabbutt, G 1	Wilson, C .... 23(3)
Clapham, J .... −(1)	Nethercott, S .... 2(7)	

League Goals (44): Sheringham 7, Iversen 6, Nielsen 6, Sinton 6, Armstrong 5, Anderton 3, Allen 2, Dozzell 2, Howells 2, Fox 1, McVeigh 1, Rosenthal 1, Vega 1, Wilson 1.
Coca-Cola Cup Goals (7): Allen 2, Anderton 2, Armstrong 1, Campbell 1, Sheringham 1. **F.A. Cup Goals**: None.
'Player of Year': Sol Campbell. **Sponsors**: Hewlett Packard.
Average Home League Attendance 1996-97: 31,067. **Capacity for 1997-88**: 33,208 (subject to ground redevelopment).
Record Attendance: 75,038 v Sunderland (F.A. Cup 6) 5 March 1938.

WEST HAM UNITED
Ground: Boleyn Ground, Green Street, Upton Park, London E13 9AZ.
Telephone: 0181-548-2748. **Clubcall**: 0891 121165. **Club Nickname**: Hammers. **First-choice Colours**: Claret and blue shirts; white shorts; claret stockings.

Bilic, S 35	Hall, R 7	Newell, M .... 6(1)
Bishop, I .... 26(3)	Hartson, J 11	Omoyinmi, M .... −(1)
Bowen, M .... 15(2)	Hughes, M .... 31(2)	Porfirio, H .... 15(8)
Boylan, L .... −(1)	Jones, S .... 5(3)	Potts, S .... 17(3)
Breacker, T .... 22(4)	Kitson, P 14	Raducioiu, F .... 6(5)
Cottee, T .... 2(1)	Lampard, F .... 3(10)	Rieper, M .... 26(2)
Dicks, J 31	Lazaridis, S .... 13(9)	Rowland, K .... 11(4)
Dowie, I .... 18(5)	Lomas, S 7	Sealey, L .... 1(1)
Dumitrescu, I .... 3(4)	Mautone, S 1	Slater, R .... 2(1)
Ferdinand, R .... 11(4)	Miklosko, L 36	Williamson, D ...... 13(2)
Futre, P .... 4(5)	Moncur, J .... 26(1)	

League Goals (39): Kitson 8, Dicks 6, Hartson 5, Hughes 3, Ferdinand 2, Porfirio 2, Radicioiu 2, Moncur 2, Bilic 2, Bishop 1, Bowen 1, Lazaridis 1, Rieper 1, Rowland 1, Opponents 2.
Coca-Cola Cup Goals (8): Dicks 2, Dowie 2, Bilic 1, Cottee 1, Porfirio 1, Raducioiu 1. **F.A. Cup Goals (1)**: Porfirio 1.
'Player of Year': Julian Dicks. **Sponsors**: To be announced.
Average Home League Attendance 1996-97: 23,342. **Capacity for 1997-98**: 26,012 (all-seated).
Record Attendance: 43,322 v Tottenham Hotspur (Div. 1) 17 October 1970.

WIMBLEDON

Ground: Selhurst Park, London SE25 6PY.
Telephone: 0181-771-2233. **Clubcall:** 0891 121175. **Club Nickname:** Crazy Gang. **First-choice Colours:** Navy blue shirts; navy blue shorts; navy blue stockings.

Ardley, N .... 33(1)	Euell, J .... 4(3)	Jupp, D 6
Blackwell, D .... 22(5)	Fear, P .... 9(9)	Kimble, A .... 28(3)
Castledine, S .... 4(2)	Gayle, M .... 34(2)	Leonhardsen, O 27
Clarke, A .... 4(7)	Goodman, J .... 6(7)	McAllister, B .... 19(4)
Cort, C .... –(1)	Harford, M .... 3(10)	Perry, C 37
Cunningham, K 36	Heald, P 2	Reeves, A .... –(2)
Earle, R 32	Holdsworth, D .... 10(15)	Sullivan, N 36
Ekoku, E .... 28(2)	Jones, V 29	Thatcher, B 9

League Goals (49): Ekoku 11, Gayle 8, Earle 7, Holdsworth 5, Leonhardsen 5, Jones 3, Ardley 2, Euell 2, Castledine 1, Clarke 1, Goodman 1, Harford 1, Perry 1, Opponent 1.
Coca-Cola Cup Goals (9): Gayle 3, Holdsworth 2, Castledine 1, Ekoku 1, Fear 1, Leonhardsen 1. **F.A. Cup Goals (9):** Earle 2, Gayle 2, Holdsworth 2, Perry 1.
'Player of Year': Chris Perry. **Sponsors:** Elonex.
Average Home League Attendance 1996-97: 15,156. **Capacity for 1997-98:** 26,409 (all-seated).
Record Attendance: 30,115 v Manchester United (Premier Division), Selhurst Park, 9 May 1993; 45,701 v Leeds United (F.A. Cup 4R), switched from Plough Lane to Selhurst Park, 10 Feb. 1975.

NATIONWIDE LEAGUE – FIRST DIVISION

BARNSLEY

Ground: Oakwell, Barnsley, South Yorkshire S71 1ET.
Telephone: 01226-211211. **Clubcall:** 0891 121152. **Club Nickname:** Reds.
First-choice Colours: Red shirts; white shorts; red & white stockings.

Appleby, M 35	Hurst, G .... –(2)	Sheridan, D .... 39(2)
Bosancic, J .... 17(8)	Jones, S .... 12(6)	Shirtliff, P .... 12(1)
Bochenski, S .... –(1)	Liddell, A .... 25(13)	Ten Heuvel, L .... –(2)
Bullock, M .... 7(21)	Marcelle, C .... 26(14)	Thompson, N 24
Davis, S 24	Moses, A .... 25(3)	Van der Velden, C .. 1(1)
De Zeeuw, A 43	Redfearn, N 43	Watson, D 46
Eaden, N 46	Regis, D .... –(4)	Wilkinson, P 45
Hendrie, J 36		

League Goals (76): Redfearn 17, Hendrie 15, Wilkinson 9, Liddell 9, Marcelle 8, Thompson 5, Eaden 3, Davis 3, de Zeeuw 2, Moses 2, Sheridan 2, Bosancic 1.
Coca-Cola Cup Goals (4): Wilkinson 2, Redfearn 1, Regis 1. **F.A. Cup Goals (4)** Bullock 1, Hendrie 1, Marcelle 1, Redfearn 1.
'Player of Year': Neil Redfearn. **Sponsors:** ORA Electronics (UK).
Average Home League Attendance 1996-97: 11,356. **Capacity for 1997-98:** 18,510 (all-seated).
Record Attendance: 40,255 v Stoke City (F.A. Cup 5) 15 February 1936.

BIRMINGHAM CITY

Ground: St. Andrew's, Birmingham B9 4NH.
Telephone: 0121-772-0101. **Clubcall:** 0891 121188. **Club Nickname:** Blues.
First-choice Colours: Blue shirts; white shorts; blue stockings.

Ablett, G .... 39(3)	Bowen, J .... 19(5)	Castle, S .... 4(4)
Barnett, D 6	Breen, G .... 20(2)	Cook, T .... 1(3)
Bass, J .... 12(2)	Brown, K 11	Devlin, P .... 32(6)
Bennett, I 40	Bruce,S .... 30(2)	Donowa, L .... –(4)

Edwards, C .... 1(2)	Holland, C .... 28(4)	Newell, M .... 11(4)
Finnan, S 3	Horne, B 33	O'Connor, M 24
Forster, N .... 4(3)	Hughes, B .... 10(1)	Otto, R .... 1(3)
Frain, J 1	Hunt, J .... 6(8)	Poole, K .... 9(1)
Francis, K .... 4(15)	Jackson, M 10	Robinson, S .... 6(4)
Furlong, P .... 37(6)	Johnson, M .... 28(7)	Sutton, S 6
Gabbiadini, M .... –(2)	Legg, A .... 22(9)	Tait, P .... 18(8)
Grainger, M .... 21(2)	Limpar, A .... 3(1)	Wassell, D 6

League Goals (52): Devlin 16, Furlong 10, Legg 4, O'Connor 4, Bowen 3, Forster 3, Grainger 3, Hunt 2, Ablett 1, Breen 1, Francis 1, Newell 1, Opponents 3.
Coca-Cola Cup Goals (4): Newell 2, Devlin 1, Furlong 1. **F.A. Cup Goals (6):** Devlin 2, Francis 2, Furlong 1, Bruce 1.
'Player of Year': Paul Devlin. **Sponsors:** Auto Windscreen.
Average Home League Attendance 1996-97: 17,751. **Capacity for 1997-98:** 25,812 (all-seated).
Record Attendance: 66,844 v Everton (F.A. Cup 5) 11 February 1939.

BOLTON WANDERERS

Ground: Reebok Stadium, Horwich, Lancashire.
Telephone: 01204-389200. **Clubcall:** 0891 121164. **Club Nickname:** Trotters.
First-choice Colours: White shirts; blue shorts; blue stockings.

Bergsson, G .... 30(3)	Lee, D .... 12(12)	Sheridan, J .... 12(8)
Blake, N 42	McAnespie, S .... 11(2)	Small, B .... 10(1)
Branagan, K 36	McGinlay, J 43	Taggart, G 43
Burnett, W .... –(1)	Paatelainen, M ...... 3(7)	Taylor, S .... 2(9)
Fairclough, C 46	Phillips, J 36	Thompson, A 35
Frandsen P .... 40(1)	Pollock, J .... 18(2)	Todd, A .... 6(9)
Green, S .... 7(7)	Sellars, S .... 40(2)	Ward, G .... 10(1)
Johansen, M .... 24(9)		

League Goals (100): McGinlay 24, Blake 19, Thompson 11, Fairclough 8, Sellars 8, Frandsen 5, Johansen 5, Pollock 4, Bergsson 3, Taggart 3, Lee 2, Paatelainen 2, Sheridan 2, Green 1, Taylor 1, Opponents 2.
Coca-Cola Cup Goals (11): McGinlay 5, Blake 3, Frandsen 1, Taggart 1, Taylor 1.
F.A. Cup Goals (9): Blake 2, Green 2, Pollock 2, McGinlay 1, Taylor 1, Thompson 1.
'Player of Year': Chris Fairclough. **Sponsors:** Reebok.
Average Home League Attendance 1996-97: 15,826. **Capacity for 1997-98:** 25,000 (all-seated).
Record Attendance: 69,912 v Manchester City (F.A. Cup 5) 18 February 1933.

BRADFORD CITY

Ground: The Pulse Stadium, Valley Parade, Bradford, West Yorkshire BD8 7DY.
Telephone: 01274-773355. **Clubcall:** 0930 191196. **Club Nickname:** Bantams.
First-choice Colours: Claret and amber shirts; black shorts; black stockings.

Blake, R .... 3(2)	Midgley, C .... –(1)	Roberts, B 2
Brightwell, D 2	Mitchell, D 6	Sansam, C .... –(1)
Cowans, G .... 23(1)	Mohan, N 44	Sas, M 31
Davison, A 10	Moore, I 6	Schwarzer, M 13
Dreyer, J .... 27(1)	Murray, S .... 13(4)	Shutt, C .... 10(12)
Duxbury, L 33	Newell, M 7	Smithard, M .... –(1)
Edhino 15	Nixon, E 12	Stallard, M .... 13(9)
Gould, J 9	O'Brien, A .... 18(4)	Steiner, R .... 14(1)
Hamilton, D .... 24(8)	Oliveira, R 2	Sundgot, O .... 11(9)
Huxford, R .... 1(1)	Ormondroyd, I .... –(1)	Vanhala, C .... –(1)
Jacobs, W .... 37(2)	Pehrsson, M 1	Waddle, C 25
Kiwomya, A .... 20(7)	Pepper, C 11	Watson, G 3
Kulcsar, G 9	Pinto, S .... 7(11)	Wilder, C .... 4(3)
Liburd, R .... 33(3)	Regtop, E .... 5(3)	Wright, T .... 2(9)

340

League Goals (47): Sundgot 6, Edhino 5, Pepper 5, Waddle 5, Steiner 4, Duxbury 3, Jacobs 3, Sas 3, Shutt 3, O'Brien 2, Dreyer 1, Kiwomya 1, Liburd 1, Murray 1, Regtop 1, Stallard 1, Watson 1, Wright 1.
Coca-Cola Cup Goals (1): Stallard 1. **F.A. Cup Goals (5)**: Dreyer 3, Steiner 1, Waddle 1.
'Player of Year': Wayne Jacobs. **Sponsors**: JCT 600.
Average Home League Attendance 1996-97: 12,925 **Capacity for 1997-98**: 18,011 (seats 10,511, standing 7,500).
Record Attendance: 39,146 v Burnley (F.A. Cup 4) 11 March 1911.

CHARLTON ATHLETIC

Ground: The Valley, Floyd Road, Charlton, London SE7 8BL.
Telephone: 0181-333-4000. **Clubcall**: 0891 121146. **Club Nickname**: Addicks.
First-choice Colours: Red shirts; white shorts; red stockings.

Allen, B .... 10(5)	Leaburn, C .... 40(4)	Poole, G .... 14(2)
Balmer, S .... 28(4)	Lee, J .... 7(1)	Robinson, J .... 41(1)
Barness, A 45	Lisbie, K .... 4(25)	Robson, M .... 8(7)
Bright, M .... 4(2)	Mortimer, P .... 10(1)	Rufus, R .... 33(1)
Brown, S .... 22(5)	Newton, S .... 39(4)	Salmon, M 28
Chapple, P .... 25(3)	Nicholls, K .... 34(4)	Scott, K 9
Jones, K .... 14(5)	O'Connell, B .... 3(5)	Stuart, J 10
Jones, S 2	Otto, R .... 5(2)	Sturgess, P .... 1(2)
Kinsella, M 37	Petterson, A 21	Whyte, D .... 18(3)

League Goals (52): Leaburn 8, Whyte 7, Kinsella 6, Allen 4, Lee 3, Newton 3, Robinson 3, Robson 3, Balmer 2, Barness 2, Bright 2, Chapple 2, O'Connell 2, Lisbie 1, Mortimer 1, Nicholls 1, Poole 1, Stuart 1.
Coca-Cola Cup Goals (8): Allen 2, Robinson 2, Whyte 2, Leaburn 1, Newton 1.
F.A. Cup Goals (2): Kinsella 1, Robson 1.
'Player of Year': Andy Petterson. **Sponsors**: Greenwich Council.
Average Home League Attendance 1996-97: 11,082. **Capacity for 1997-98**: 16,000 (all-seated).
Record Attendance: 75,031 v Aston Villa (F.A. Cup 5) 12 February 1938.

CRYSTAL PALACE

Ground: Selhurst Park, London SE25 6PU.
Telephone: 0181-768-6000. **Clubcall**: 0891 400333. **Club Nickname**: Eagles.
First-choice Colours: Red and blue shirts; white shorts; white stockings.

Andersen, L .... 7(7)	Harris, J .... –(2)	Pitcher, D 3
Boxall, D .... 4(2)	Hopkin, D .... 38(3)	Quinn, R .... 17(4)
Cyrus, A 1	Houghton, R .... 18(3)	Roberts, A 45
Davies, G .... 5(1)	Linighan, A 19	Rodger, S .... 9(2)
Day, C 24	McKenzie, L .... 4(17)	Scully, A .... –(1)
Dyer, B .... 39(4)	Mimms, B 1	Shipperley, N ..... 29(3)
Edworthy, M .... 42(3)	Muscat, K .... 42(2)	Trollope, P .... –(9)
Freedman, D ...... 33(11)	Nash, C 21	Tuttle, D 39
Gordon, D .... 26(4)	Ndah, G .... 5(21)	Veart, C .... 35(5)

Play-offs – Appearances: Davies 1, Dyer 3, Edworthy 3, Freedman –(2), Gordon 3, Hopkin 3, Houghton 1, Linighan 3, Muscat 2, Nash 3, Roberts 3, Rodger 3, Shipperley 3, Tuttle 2, Veart –(1).
League Goals (78): Dyer 17, Hopkin 13, Shipperley 12, Freedman 11, Veart 6, Gordon 3, Ndah 3, Linighan 2, McKenzie 2, Muscat 2, Roberts 2, Tuttle 2, Anderson 1, Houghton 1, Quinn 1. **Play-off Goals (5)**: Freedman 2, Hopkin 2, Shipperley 1.
Coca-Cola Cup Goals (8): Hopkin 2, Veart 2, Edworthy 1, Freedman 1, Muscat 1, Quinn 1. **F.A. Cup Goals (2)**: Dyer 1, Veart 1.
'Player of Year': David Hopkin. **Sponsors**: TDK.
Average Home League Attendance 1996-97: 16,085. **Capacity for 1997-98**: 26,309 (all-seated).

GRIMSBY TOWN

Ground: Blundell Park, Cleethorpes, South Humberside DN35 7PY.
Telephone: 01472-697111. **Clubcall**: 0891 555855. **Club Nickname**: Mariners.
First-choice Colours: Black and white shirts; black shorts; white stockings.

Appleton, M 10	Lester, J .... 16(6)	Rodger, G .... 27(1)
Black, K .... 19(5)	Lever, M .... 20(1)	Shakespeare, C .... 23(3)
Childs, G .... 19(8)	Livingstone, S .... 23(9)	Smith, R .... 12(2)
Fickling, A .... 20(7)	Love, A 3	Southall, L .... 23(11)
Forrester, J .... 4(9)	McDermott, J 29	Trollope, P .... 6(1)
Gallimore, A .... 36(6)	Mendonca, C 45	Walker, J .... –(1)
Handyside, P .... 8(1)	Miller, A 3	Webb, N .... 3(1)
Jobling, K .... 24(4)	Neil, J .... –(1)	Widdrington, T .... 41(1)
Laws, B 3	Oster, J .... 21(3)	Woods, N .... 21(3)
Lee, J .... 2(5)	Pearcey, J 40	Wrack, D .... 5(7)

League Goals (60): Mendonca 18, Livingstone 6, Lester 5, Southall 4, Widdrington 4, Appleton 3, Oster 3, Fickling 2, Lee 2, Rodger 2, Shakespeare 2, Childs 1, Forrester 1, Gallimore 1, Handyside 1, McDermott 1, Trollope 1, Woods 1, Wrack 1, Opponent 1.
Coca-Cola Cup Goals (1): Mendonca 1. **F.A. Cup Goals (1)**: Oster 1.
'Player of Year': Graham Rodger. **Sponsors**: Europe's Food Town Consortium.
Average Home League Attendance 1996-97: 5,859. **Capacity for 1997-98**: 8,870 (all-seated).
Record Attendance: 31,651 v Wolves (F.A. Cup 5) 20 February 1937.

HUDDERSFIELD TOWN

Ground: Alfred McAlpine Stadium, Leeds Road, Huddersfield, West Yorkshire HD1 6PX.
Telephone: 01484-420335. **Clubcall**: 0891 121635. **Club Nickname**: Terriers.
First-choice Colours: Blue and white shirts; white shorts; white stockings.

Baldry, S .... 2(6)	Dyson, J .... 18(5)	Makel, L 19
Beresford, D 6	Edmondson, D 10	Morrison, A .... 9(1)
Browning, M 13	Edwards, R .... 24(9)	Norman, T 4
Bullock, D .... 26(1)	Facey, D .... 1(2)	Payton, A 38
Burnett, W .... 33(2)	Francis, S 19	Reid, P .... 20(2)
Collins, Sam .... 3(1)	Glover, L 11	Rowe, R .... 1(6)
Collins, Simon ...... 10(6)	Gray, K .... 36(3)	Ryan, R .... 2(3)
Cowan, T 42	Heary, T .... 2(3)	Sinnott, L .... 29(1)
Crosby, G .... 19(5)	Illingworth, J .... 2(1)	Stewart, M .... 19(1)
Dalton, P .... 17(12)	Jenkins, D 33	Tisdale, P .... 1(1)
Davies, S 3	Kaye, P .... –(1)	Williams, M 2
Dunn, I .... 1(4)	Lawson, I .... 8(10)	

League Goals (48): Payton 17, Stewart 7, Dalton 4, Cowan 3, Edwards 3, Lawson 3, Makel 3, Crosby 2, Beresford 1, Bullock 1, Gray 1, Morrison 1, Opponents 2.
Coca-Cola Cup Goals (9): Stewart 4, Payton 2, Collins 1, Cowan 1, Edwards 1.
F.A. Cup Goals (2): Crosby 1, Edwards 1.
'Player of Year': Tom Cowan. **Sponsors**: Panasonic.
Average Home League Attendance 1996-97: 12,175. **Capacity for 1997-98**: 19,600 (all-seated).
Record Attendance (Leeds Road): 67,037 v Arsenal (F.A. Cup 6) 27 February 1932. **New Ground**: 18,775 v Birmingham (Div. 2) 6 May 1995.

IPSWICH TOWN

Ground: Portman Road, Ipswich, Suffolk IP1 2DA.
Telephone: 01473-219211. **Clubcall**: 0839 664488. **Club Nickname**: Super Blues. **First-choice Colours**: Blue shirts; white shorts; blue stockings.

Creaney, G 6	Mathie, A .... 11(1)	Swailes, C 23
Cundy, J 13	Milton, S .... 8(15)	Tanner, A .... 10(6)
Dyer, K .... 2(11)	Mowbray, T 8	Taricco, M 41
Forrest, C 6	Naylor, R .... 19(8)	Thomsen, C .... 10(1)
Gregory, N .... 10(7)	Niven, S 2	Uhlenbeek, G ... 34(4)
Gudmundsson, N ... 2(6)	Petta, B .... 1(5)	Vaughan, T .... 27(5)
Howe, S .... 2(1)	Scowcroft, J .... 40(1)	Wark, J 2
Jean, E .... –(1)	Sedgley, S 39	Williams, D 43
Marshall, I 2	Sonner, M .... 22(7)	Wright, R 40
Mason, P .... 41(2)	Stockwell, M .... 42(1)	

Play-offs – Appearances: Dyer 1(1), Gregory 1(1), Gudmundsson 1(1), Mason 1, Scowcroft 2, Sedgley 2, Stockwell 2, Swailes 2, Taricco 2, Uhlenbeek 2, Vaughan 2, Williams 2, Wright 2.
League Goals (68): Mason 12, Scowcroft 9, Sedgley 7, Stockwell 7, Gregory 6, Mathie 4, Naylor 4, Tanner 4, Taricco 3, Cundy 2, Gudmundsson 2, Sonner 2, Vaughan 2, Creaney 1, Swailes 1, Williams 1, Opponent 1. **Play-off Goals (3):** Gudmundsson 1, Scowcroft 1, Stockwell 1.
Coca-Cola Cup Goals(15): Mathie 5, Mason 3, Marshall 1, Milton 1, Naylor 1, Scowcroft 1, Sedgley 1, Sonner 1, Stockwell 1. **F.A. Cup Goals:** None.
'Player of Year': Mauricio Taricco. **Sponsors:** Greene King.
Average Home League Attendance 1996-97: 11,953. **Capacity for 1997-98:** 22,600 (all-seated).
Record Attendance: 38,010 v Leeds United (F.A. Cup 6) 8 March 1975.

MANCHESTER CITY

Ground: Maine Road, Moss Side, Manchester M14 7WN.
Telephone: 0161-224-5000. **Clubcall:** 0891 121191. **Club Nickname:** Citizens.
First-choice Colours: Light blue shirts; white shorts; navy stockings.

Atkinson, D .... 7(1)	Foster, J 3	Lomas, S 35
Beagrie, P .... –(1)	Frontzeck, M ...... 8(3)	Margetson, M 17
Beesley, P 6	Greenacre, C .... –(4)	McGoldrick, E 33
Brannan, G 11	Heaney, N .... 10(5)	Phillips, M .... 1(3)
Brightwell, I .... 36(1)	Hiley, S .... 2(1)	Rodger, S 8
Brown, M .... 7(4)	Horlock, K 18	Rosler, U .... 43(1)
Clough, N .... 18(5)	Immel, E 4	Summerbee, N .... 43(1)
Creaney, N .... 1(4)	Ingram, R .... 13(5)	Symons, K 44
Crooks, L .... 8(7)	Kavelashvili, M .... 6(18)	Wassall, D .... 14(1)
Dibble, A .... 12(1)	Kernaghan, A .... 9(1)	Whitley, J .... 12(11)
Dickov, P .... 25(4)	Kinkladze, G 39	Wright, T 13

League Goals (59): Rosler 15, Kinkladze 12, Dickov 5, Horlock 4, Summerbee 4, Lomas 3, Atkinson 2, Brightwell 2, Clough 2, Kavelashvili, Brannan 1, Creaney 1, Heaney 1, Rodger 1, Whitley 1, Opponents 3.
Coca-Cola Cup Goals (1): Rosler 1. **F.A. Cup Goals (4):** Summerbee 2, Heaney 1, Rosler 1.
'Player of Year': Georgi Kinkladze. **Sponsors:** Brother.
Average Home League Attendance 1996-97: 26,753. **Capacity for 1997-98:** 33,000 (all-seated).
Record Attendance: 84,569 v Stoke City (F.A. Cup 6) 3 March 1934.

NORWICH CITY

Ground: Carrow Road, Norwich, Norfolk NR1 1JE.
Telephone: 01603-760760. **Clubcall:** 0891 121144. **Club Nickname:** Canaries.
First-choice Colours: Yellow shirts; yellow shorts; yellow stockings.

Adams, N 45	Carey, S .... 8(6)	Gunn, B 39
Akinbiyi, A .... 3(9)	Crook, I .... 33(4)	Jackson, M 19
Bellamy, C .... –(3)	Eadie, D 42	Johnson, A .... 24(3)
Bradshaw, D .... 11(6)	Fleck, R .... 33(3)	Marshall, A 7
Broughton, D .... 3(5)	Forbes, A .... 3(7)	Milligan, M 37

Mills, D .... 27(5)	Polston, J .... 27(4)	Scott, Kevin 9
Moore, N 2	Rocastle, D 11	Simpson, K .... 1(2)
Newman, R 44	Rush, M .... –(2)	Sutch, D .... 43(1)
O'Neill, K .... 23(3)	Scott, Keith .... 5(8)	Wright, J .... 3(1)
Ottosson, U .... 4(3)		

League Goals (63): Eadie 17, Adams 13, O'Neill 6, Johnson 5, Fleck 4, Scott (Keith) 3, Sutch 3, Crook 2, Jackson 2, Polston 2, Broughton 1, Milligan 1, Newman 1, Ottosson 1, Opponents 2.
Coca-Cola Cup Goals (3): Adams 2, Johnson 1. **F.A. Cup Goals (2)**: Polston 1, Adams 1.
'Player of Year': Darren Eadie. **Sponsors**: Colman's.
Average Home League Attendance 1996-97: 14,720. **Capacity for 1997-98**: 21,994 (all-seated).
Record Attendance: 43,984 v Leicester City (F.A. Cup 6) 30 March 1963.

OLDHAM ATHLETIC

Ground: Boundary Park, Oldham, Lancashire OL1 2PA.
Telephone: 0161-624-4972. **Clubcall**: 0891 121142. **Club Nickname**: Latics.
First-choice Colours: Red and blue shirts; white shorts; red and blue stockings.

Allott, M .... –(5)	Hallworth, J 4	Ormondroyd, I ...... 26(4)
Banger, N .... 16(6)	Henry, N .... 21(1)	Pemberton, M .... –(3)
Barlow, S .... 25(11)	Hodgson, D .... 11(1)	Redmond, S 24
Beresford, D ...... 24(11)	Holt, A .... 1(1)	Reid, P 9
Duxbury, L .... 11(1)	Hughes, A .... 7(1)	Richardson, Lee .. 26(5)
Fleming, C .... 44(6)	Kelly G 42	Richardson, Lloyd .. –(1)
Foran, M .... –(1)	McCarthy, S .... 18(4)	Rickers, P .... 46(1)
Gannon, J 1	McNivern, D .... 2(7)	Ritchie, A .... 4(6)
Garnett, S .... 22(1)	McNivern, S .... 11(9)	Rush, A .... 6(2)
Graham, R .... 15(1)	Morrow, J .... 1(1)	Serrant, C .... 34(6)
Halle, G .... 18(2)	Orlygsson, T .... 23(8)	Snodin, I .... 13(1)

League Goals (51): Barlow 12, Ormondroyd 8, Banger 5, McCarthy 4, Richardson 4, Rickers 4, Halle 3, Redmond 2, Rush 2, Reid 1, Allott 1, Duxbury 1, Garnott 1, Graham 1, Henry 1, Orlygsson 1.
Coca-Cola Cup Goals (4): McCarthy 2, Banger 1, Richardson 1. **F.A. Cup Goals**: None.
'Player of Year': Gary Kelly. **Sponsors**: J.D. Sports.
Average Home League Attendance 1996-97: 7,045. **Capacity for 1997-98**: 13,700 (all-seated).
Record Attendance: 47,671 v Sheffield Wednesday (F.A. Cup 4) 25 January 1930.

OXFORD UNITED

Ground: Manor Ground, London Road, Headington, Oxford OX3 7RS.
Telephone: 01865-761503. **Clubline**: 0891 440055. **Club Nickname**: U's.
First-choice Colours: Yellow shirts; navy shorts; navy stockings.

Aldridge, M .... 18(12)	Gray, M .... 41(2)	Purse, D .... 25(7)
Angel, M .... 15(9)	Jackson, E 3	Robinson, L .... 36(2)
Beauchamp, J ...... 35(9)	Jemson, N 44	Rush, D .... 4(10)
Elliott, M 26	Marsh, S .... 6(2)	Smith, D 45
Ford, M 42	Massey, S .... 15(14)	Weatherstone, S .... –(1)
Ford, R .... 29(4)	Moody, P .... 20(19)	Whitehead, P 43
Gabbiadini, M 5	Murphy, M .... 5(24)	Whyte, C 10
Gilchrist, P 38	Phillips, M .... –(1)	Wilsterman, B 1

League Goals (64): Jemson 18, Aldridge 8, Beauchamp 7, Elliott 4, Ford 4, Moody 4, Massey 3, Murphy 3, Angel 2, Gilchrist 2, Gray 2, Gabbiadini 1, Marsh* 1, Purse 1, Rush 1, Opponents 3.
Coca-Cola Cup Goals (11): Jemson 5, Moody 2, Aldridge 1, Elliott 1, Ford (M.) 1, Ford (R.) 1. **F.A. Cup Goals**: None.

'Player of Year': Paul Whitehead. **Sponsors**: Unipart.
Average Home League Attendance 1996-97: 7,609. **Capacity for 1997-98**: 9,524 (seats 2,803, standing 6,721).
Record Attendance: 22,730 v Preston N.E. (F.A. Cup 6) 29 February 1964.

PORTSMOUTH

Ground: Fratton Park, Frogmore Road, Portsmouth, Hampshire PO4 8RA.
Telephone: 01705-731204. **Clubcall**: 0891 121182. **Club Nickname**: Pompey.
First-choice Colours: Blue shirts; white shorts; red stockings.

Allen, M .... 3(1)	Flahavan, A 24	Rees, J .... 1(2)
Awford, A .... 37(2)	Hall, P .... 36(6)	Russell, L .... 18(2)
Bradbury, L .... 38(3)	Hillier, D 21	Simpson, F .... 40(1)
Burton, D .... 12(9)	Igoe, S .... 22(18)	Svensson, M .... 17(2)
Butters, G 7	Knight, A 22	Thomson, A .... 22(6)
Carter, J .... 23(4)	McLoughlin, A ..... 33(3)	Turner, A .... 22(1)
Cook, A .... 6(2)	Perrett, R .... 31(1)	Waterman, D .... 1(3)
Dobson, A 4	Pethick, R .... 27(8)	Whitbread, A 24
Durnin, J .... 16(19)		

League Goals (59): Bradbury 15, Hall 13, Svensson 6, McLoughlin 5, Simpson 4, Durnin 3, Hillier 2, Igoe 2, Russell 2, Turner 2, Burton 1, Carter 1, Perrett 1, Rees 1, Thomson 1.
Coca-Cola Cup Goals (3): Burton 2, Carter 1. **F.A. Cup Goals (9)**: Bradbury 2, Hall 2, Burton 1, Hillier 1, McLouglin 1, Svensson 1, Thomson 1.
'Player of Year': Lee Bradbury. **Sponsors**: KJC Mobile Phones.
Average Home League Attendance 1996-97: 8,857. **Capacity for 1997-98**: 19,400 (all-seated after work completed in November).
Record Attendance: 51,385 v Derby County (F.A. Cup 6) 26 February 1949.

PORT VALE

Ground: Vale Park, Hamil Road, Burslem, Stoke-on-Trent, Staffs ST6 1AW.
Telephone: 01782-814134. **Clubcall**: 0891 121636. **Club Nickname**: Valiants.
First-choice Colours: White shirts; black shorts; black stockings.

Aspin, N 32	Hill, A .... 36(2)	Musselwhite, P 33
Bogie, I .... 28(3)	Holwyn, J .... 5(2)	Naylor, T .... 40(13)
Corden, W .... 5(6)	Huesden, A 13	Porter, A 44
Foyle, M .... 9(27)	Janson, J .... 10(1)	Stokes, D .... 8(2)
Glover, D .... 40(2)	Koordes, R .... 7(6)	Talbot, S .... 25(7)
Griffiths, G .... 24(2)	McCarthy, J 45	Tankard, A 37
Guppy, S 34	Mills, L .... 22(11)	Walker, R .... 9(9)

League Goals (58): Naylor 17, Mills 13, Guppy 6, McCarthy 4, Talbot 4, Foyle 3, Porter 3, Glover 2, Bogie 1, Hill 1, Janson 1, Tankard 1, Opponents 2.
Coca-Cola Cup Goals (9): Naylor 3, McCarthy 2, Mills 2, Bogie 1, Foyle 1. **F.A. Cup Goals**: None.
'Player of Year': Lee Mills. **Sponsors**: Tunstall Assurance Friendly Society.
Average Home League Attendance 1996-97: 7,385. **Capacity for 1997-98**: 23,079 (seats 17,769, standing 5,310).
Record Attendance: 50,000 v Aston Villa (F.A. Cup 5) 20 February 1960.

QUEENS PARK RANGERS

Ground: Rangers Stadium, South Africa Road, Shepherds Bush, London W12 7PA.
Telephone: 0181-743-0262. **Clubcall**: 0891 121162. **Club Nickname**: R's.
First-choice Colours: Blue and white hoops; white shorts; white stockings.

Barker, S 38	Charles, L .... 6(7)	Hateley, M .... 8(5)
Brazier, M .... 22(5)	Dichio, D .... 31(5)	Impey, A .... 26(6)
Brevett, R 44	Gallen, K 2	Jackson, M 7
Challis, T 2	Graham, M .... 16(12)	Maddix, D .... 18(7)

Mahoney-Johnson, M .	–(2)	Perry, M	2	Slade, S	11(6)
McDermott, A	6	Plummer, C	4(1)	Sommer, J	33
McDonald, A	38(1)	Quashie, N	9(4)	Spencer, J	25
Morrow, S	5	Ready, K	28(1)	Wilkins, R	4
Murray, P	26(6)	Roberts, T	13	Yates, S	16
Peacock, G	27	Sinclair, T	39		

League Goals (64): Spencer 17, Dichio 7, Murray 5, Peacock 5, Barker 4, Slade 4, Gallen 3, Sinclair 3, Brazier 2, Impey 2, McDermott 2, McDonald 2, Charles 1, Hateley 1, Morrow 1, Perry 1, Yates 1, Opponents 3.
Coca-Cola Cup Goals (3): Brazier 1, Dichio 1, Impey 1. **F.A. Cup Goals (7):** Hateley 2, Peacock 2, McDonald 1, Sinclair 1, Spencer 1.
'Player of Year': John Spencer. **Sponsors:** Ericsson.
Average Home League Attendance 1996-97: 12,554. **Capacity for 1997-98:** 19,148 (all-seated).
Record Attendance: 35,353 v Leeds United (Div. 1) 27 April 1974.

READING
Ground: Elm Park, Norfolk Road, Reading, Berkshire RG3 2EF.
Telephone: 01189-507878. **Clubcall:** 0891 121000. **Club Nickname:** Royals.
First-choice Colours: White and blue hoops; white shorts; white stockings.

Bernal, A	41	Hammond, N	1	Morley, T	36(1)
Bibbo, S	5	Holsgrove, P	12	Nogan, L	21(10)
Blatherwick, S	6(1)	Hopkins, J	17(1)	Parkinson, P	15(10)
Bodin, P	38	Hunter, B	26(1)	Quinn, J	10(13)
Booty, M	14	Lambert, J	20(10)	Roach, N	2(1)
Brown, K	5	Lovell, S	16(8)	Smith, B	–(1)
Caskey, D	26(9)	Mautone, S	15	Swales, S	3
Gilkes, M	27(5)	McPherson, K	39	Wdowczyk, D	8
Glasgow, B	2(2)	Meaker, M	15(10)	Williams, M	21(8)
Gooding, M	40(3)	Mihaylov, B	8	Wright, T	17

League Goals (58): Morley 22, Nogan 6, Lambert 5, Lovell 5, Quinn 4, Williams 3, Hunter 2, Holsgrove 2, McPherson 2, Bodin 1, Blatherwick 1, Gilkes 1, Meaker 1, Roach 1, Opponents 2.
Coca-Cola Cup Goals (1): Parkinson 1. **F.A. Cup Goals (3):** Caskey 1, Lambert 1, Morley 1.
'Player of Year': Trevor Morley. **Sponsors:** Auto Trader.
Average Home League Attendance 1996-97: 9,160. **Capacity for 1997-98:** 15,000 (seats 2,242, standing 12,758).
Record Attendance: 33,042 v Brentford (F.A. Cup 5) 17 February 1927.

SHEFFIELD UNITED
Ground: Bramall Lane, Sheffield, South Yorkshire S2 4SU.
Telephone: 0114-221-5757. **Clubcall:** 0891 888650. **Club Nickname:** Blades.
First-choice Colours: Red and white shirts; black shorts; black stockings.

Anthony, G	–(2)	Hutchison, D	38(3)	Spackman, N	19(4)
Beard, M	9(7)	Katchuoro, P	28(12)	Starbuck, P	1(1)
Bettney, C	–(1)	Kelly, A	39	Taylor, G	26(8)
Ebbrell, J	1	Nilsen, R	32(1)	Tiler, C	6
Fjortoft, J	15(2)	Parker, P	7(3)	Tracey, S	7
Hartfield, C	1(1)	Patterson, M	34(1)	Vonk, M	17
Hawes, S	–(2)	Sandford, L	25(5)	Walker, A	20(17)
Henry, N	9	Scott, A	4(4)	Ward, M	34
Hodgson, D	12(1)	Short, C	22(2)	White, D	31(6)
Hodgson, N	9	Simpson, P	2(4)	Whitehouse, D	30
Holdsworth, D	37				

Play-offs – Appearances: Fjortoft 3, Henry 2, Holdsworth 3, Hutchison 2(1), Katchuoro 3, Kelly 2, Nilsen 2(1), Sandford 1(1), Short 1(1), Spackman 1, Taylor –(2), Tiler 3, Tracey 1, Walker –(2), Ward 3, White 3, Whitehouse 3.

League Goals (75): Katchouro 12, Walker 12, Fjortoft 11, Taylor 11, White 6, Whithouse 6, Ward 4, Hutchison 3, Sandford 2, Vonk 2, Holdsworth 1, Patterson 1, Scott 1, Tiler 1, Opponents 2. **Play-off Goals (3)**: Fjortoft 1, Katchouro 1, Walker 1. **F.A. Cup Goals**: None.
Coca-Cola Cup Goals (8): Vonk 2, Walker 2, Katchouro 1, Taylor 1, Ward 1, White 1. **F.A. Cup Goals**: None.
'Player of Year': Peter Katchouro. **Sponsors**: Wards.
Average Home League Attendance 1996-97: 16,638. **Capacity for 1997-98**: 30,370 (all-seated).
Record Attendance: 68,287 v Leeds United (F.A. Cup 5) 15 February 1936.

SOUTHEND UNITED

Ground: Roots Hall, Victoria Avenue, Southend-on-Sea, Essex SS2 6NQ.
Telephone: 01702-304050. **Clubcall**: 0839 664444. **Club Nickname**: Shrimpers.
First-choice Colours: Blue/yellow shirts; blue shorts; blue stockings.

Boere, J .... 27(9)	Harris, A .... 43(1)	Roget, L 25
Byrne, P .... 23(9)	Jones, M .... −(1)	Royce, S 43
Clarke, A 7	Lapper, M .... 23(5)	Sansome, P 3
Codner, R .... 3(1)	Marsh, M 35	Selley, I .... 3(1)
Dublin, K 46	McNally, M .... 32(2)	Stimson, M .... 7(2)
Dursun, P .... −(1)	Nielsen, F .... 17(7)	Thomson, A .... 14(3)
Gridelet, P .... 37(7)	Patterson, M 4	Tilson, S .... 27(1)
Hails, J .... 32(5)	Poric, A 7	Williams, P .... 24(9)
Hanlon, R .... 1(1)	Rammell, A .... 26(10)	

League Goals (42): Boere 9, Rammell 9, Williams 6, Marsh 5, Thomson 5, Nielsen 3, Byrne 3, Gridelet 1, Lapper 1, Tilson 1, Opponent 1.
Coca-Cola Cup Goals (2): Nielsen 1, Rammell 1. **F.A. Cup Goals**: None.
'Player of Year': Keith Dublin. **Sponsors**: Telewest Communications.
Average Home League Attendance 1996-97: 5,175. **Capacity for 1997-98**: 12,306 (all-seated).
Record Attendance: 31,033 v Liverpool (F.A. Cup 3) 10 January 1979.

STOKE CITY

Ground: Britannia Stadium, Sideway, Stoke-on-Trent, Staffs.
Telephone: 01782-413511. **Clubcall**: 0891 121040. **Club Nickname**: Potters.
First-choice Colours: Red and white shirts; white shorts; red and white stockings.

Beeston, C .... 17(1)	Griffin, A .... 29(5)	Prudhoe, M 13
Carruthers, M .... −(1)	Kavanagh, G .... 32(6)	Rodger, S 5
Cranson, I 6	Keen, K .... 5(11)	Sigurdsson, L 45
Crowe, D .... −(1)	Macari, M .... 15(15)	Sheron, M 41
Da Costa, A .... 1(1)	MacKenzie, N .... 5(17)	Stein, M 11
Devlin, M .... 13(8)	McMahon, G .... 31(4)	Stokoe, G .... −(2)
Dreyer, J 12	McNally, M 3	Sturridge, S 5
Flynn, S 5	Muggleton, C 33	Wallace, R 45
Forsyth, R 40	Nyamah, K .... −(7)	Whittle, J .... 35(2)
Gayle, J .... 8(4)	Pickering, A .... 39(1)	Worthington, N 12

League Goals (51): Sheron 19, Forsyth 8, Kavanagh 4, Stein 4, Macari 3, McMahon 3, Wallace 2, Dreyer 1, Gayle 1, Griffin 1, Keen 1, MacKenzie 1, Opponents 3.
Coca-Cola Cup Goals (6): Sheron 5, Worthington 1. **F.A. Cup Goals**: None.
'Player of Year': Mike Sheron. **Sponsors**: Britannia.
Average Home League Attendance 1996-97: 12,698. **Capacity for 1997-98**: 28,000 (all-seated).
Record Attendance: 51,380 v Arsenal (Div. 1) 29 March 1937.

SWINDON TOWN

Ground: County Ground, County Road, Swindon, Wiltshire SN1 2ED.
Telephone: 01793-430430. **Clubcall**: 0891 121640. **Club Nickname**: Robins.

First-choice Colours: Red shirts; red shorts; red stockings.

Allen, P .... 5(3)	Drysdale, J .... 13(1)	O'Sullivan, W .... 16(9)
Allison, W .... 39(2)	Elkins, G .... 19(4)	Pattimore, M .... –(1)
Anthony, G 3	Finney, S .... 8(12)	Robinson, M 43
Broomes, M 12	Gooden, T .... 7(6)	Seagraves, M .... 27(1)
Bullock, D .... 12(1)	Holcroft, P .... 2(1)	Smith, A .... 13(5)
Collins, L .... 3(1)	Horlock, K 28	Talia, F 15
Coughlan, G 3	Kerslake, D 8	Taylor, S 2
Cowe, S .... 28(10)	King, P 5	Thorne, P .... 24(8)
Culverhouse, I 31	Leitch, S 36	Walters, M .... 24(3)
Darras, F .... 30(5)	McMahon, S .... 2(1)	Watson, K .... 17(9)
Digby, F 31	Mildenhall, S .... –(1)	

League Goals (52): Allison 11, Thorne 8, Horlock 8, Walters 7, Cowe 6, Finney 2, Allen 1, Broomes 1, Bullock 1, Elkins 1, Gooden 1, Leitch 1, O'Sullivan 1, Robinson 1, Smith 1, Watson 1.
Coca-Cola Cup Goals (7): Allison 2, Thorne 2, Leitch 1, Walters 1, Opponent 1.
F.A. Cup Goals: None.
'Player of Year': Fraser Digby. **Sponsors**:To be confirmed.
Average Home League Attendance 1996-97: 9,917. **Capacity for 1997-98**: 15,728 (all-seated).
Record Attendance: 32,000 v Arsenal (F.A. Cup 3) 15 January 1972.

TRANMERE ROVERS

Ground: Prenton Park, Prenton Road West, Birkenhead, Merseyside L42 9PN.
Telephone: 0151-608-4194. **Clubcall**: 0891 121646. **Club Nickname**: Rovers.
First-choice Colours: White shirts; blue shorts; white stockings.

Aldridge, J .... 32(11)	Jones, G .... 13(17)	Nixon, E 25
Bonetti, I .... 9(4)	Jones, L 8	O'Brien, L 41
Branch, G .... 22(13)	Mahon, A .... 14(11)	Rogers, D .... 28(3)
Brannan, G .... 31(3)	McGreal, J 24	Stevens, G 31
Challinor, D .... 4(1)	Moore, I .... 14(7)	Teale, S 33
Cook, P .... 30(6)	Morgan, A .... –(1)	Thomas, A .... 28(2)
Coyne, D 21	Morrissey, J .... 21(10)	Thorn, A 19
Higgins, D .... 21(1)	Nevin, P .... 10(11)	Woods, W 1
Irons, K .... 34(7)		

League Goals (63): Aldridge 18, Brannan 6, Jones (G.) 6, Branch 5, Jones (L.) 5, Irons 5, Moore 3, Cook 3, Higgins 2, Mahon 2, Nevin 2, Bonetti 1, Morrissey 1, O'Brien 1, Thorn 1, Opponents 2.
Coca-Cola Cup Goals (5): Aldridge 2, Bonetti 1, Branch 1, Morrissey 1. **F.A. Cup Goals**: None.
'Player of Year': David Higgins. **Sponsors**: Wirral Borough Council.
Average Home League Attendance 1996-97: 8,170. **Capacity for 1997-98**: 16,700 (all-seated).
Record Attendance: 24,424 v Stoke City (F.A. Cup 4) 5 February 1972.

WEST BROMWICH ALBION

Ground: The Hawthorns, Halfords Lane, West Bromwich, West Midlands B71 4LF. **Offices**: Tom Silk Building, Halfords lane, West Bromwich, West Midlands, B71 4BR.
Telephone: 0121-525-8888. **Clubcall**: 0891 121193. **Club Nickname**: Baggies, Throstles.
First-choice Colours: Navy blue and white stripes; white shorts; navy blue and white stockings.

Agnew, P 2191	Crichton, P 30	Gilbert, D .... 11(7)
Ashcroft, L .... 2(3)	Coldicott, S .... 13(6)	Groves, P .... 27(2)
Bennett, D .... –(1)	Cunnington, S .... –(3)	Hamilton, I 39
Burgess, D 33	Darby, J .... 13(4)	Holmes, P .... 37(1)
Butler, P .... 12(5)	Donovan, K .... 17(15)	Hunt, A .... 42(3)

Joseph, R .... –(2)	Nicholson, S .... 16(2)	Smith, D .... 21(3)
Mardon, P .... 11(2)	Peschisolido, P .... 30(7)	Sneekes, R .... 42(3)
McDermott, A 6	Potter, G .... 2(4)	Spink, N 4
Miller, A 12	Raven, P 33	Taylor, R .... 16(16)
Murphy, S .... 16(1)	Rodosthenous, M ... –(1)	

League Goals (68): Hunt 15, Peschisolido 15, Taylor 10, Sneekes 8, Hamilton 5, Groves 4, Coldicott 3, Murphy 2, Smith 2, Burgess 1, Gilbert 1, Holmes 1, Raven 1.
Coca-Cola Cup Goals (4): Donovan 1, Groves 1, Hamilton 1, Hunt 1. **F.A. Cup Goals**: None.
'Player of Year': Ian Hamilton. **Sponsors**: West Bromwich Building Society.
Average Home League Attendance 1996-97: 15,151. **Capacity for 1997-98**: 25,296 (all-seated).
Record Attendance: 64,815 v Arsenal (F.A. Cup 6) 6 March 1937.

WOLVERHAMPTON WANDERERS

Ground: Molineux, Waterloo Road, Wolverhampton, West Midlands WV1 4QR.
Telephone: 01902-655000. **Clubcall**: 0891 121103. **Club Nickname**: Wolves.
First-choice Colours: Gold shirts; black shorts; gold stockings.

Atkins, M .... 44(1)	Froggatt, S 27	Romano, S .... 1(3)
Bull, S 43	Gilkes, M 5	Smith, J .... 36(2)
Corica, S .... 33(3)	Goodman, D .... 19(8)	Stowell, M 46
Crowe, G .... 5(1)	Law, B .... 4(3)	Thomas, G .... 15(6)
Curle, K 20	Leadbeatter, R ...... –(1)	Thompson, A ...... 26(6)
Dennison, R .... 9(5)	Osborn, S .... 33(2)	Van der Laan, R 7
Dowe, I .... 5(3)	Pearce, D 4	Venus, M .... 36(4)
Emblen, N .... 27(1)	Richards, D .... 19(2)	Williams, A 6
Ferguson, D .... 10(6)	Roberts, I .... 24(9)	Wright, J .... –(2)
Foley, D .... –(5)	Robinson, C .... 1(1)	Young, E 1

Play-offs – Appearances: Atkins 2, Bull 2, Curle 2, Ferguson 2, Foley –(2), Goodman 1, Osborn 2, Roberts 2, Smith 2, Stowell 2, Thomas 2, Thompson 1, Williams 2.
League Goals (68): Bull 23, Roberts 12, Goodman 6, Osborn 5, Atkins 4, Ferguson 3, Thomas 3, Corica 2, Curle 2, Froggatt 2, Thompson 2, Dennison 1, Foley 1, Gilkes 1, Richards 1. **Play-off Goals (3)**: Atkins 1, Smith 1, Williams 1.
Coca-Cola Cup Goals (1): Osborn 1. **F.A. Cup Goals (1)**: Ferguson 1.
'Player of Year': Steve Bull. **Sponsors**: Goodyear.
Average Home League Attendance 1996-97: 24,763. **Capacity for 1997-98**: 28,500 (all-seated).
Record Attendance: 61,315 v Liverpool (F.A. Cup 5) 11 February 1939.

SECOND DIVISION

BLACKPOOL

Ground: Bloomfield Road, Blackpool, Lancashire FY1 6JJ.
Telephone: 01253-404331. **Clubcall**: 0891 121648. **Club Nickname**: Seasiders.
First-choice Colours: Tangerine shirts; tangerine shorts; tangerine stockings.

Banks, S 46	Clarkson, P 17	Onwere, U .... 5(4)
Barlow, A .... 43(3)	Darton, S .... 8(7)	Ormerod, B .... –(4)
Bonner, M .... 25(4)	Dixon, D .... 3(8)	Philpott, L .... 20(6)
Brabin, G .... 30(2)	Ellis, T .... 41(4)	Preece, A .... 35(6)
Bradshaw, D .... 4(6)	Linighan, D 42	Quinn, J .... 37(1)
Brightwell, I .... 1(1)	Lydiate, J .... 18(2)	Russell, K .... –(1)
Bryan, M 34	Malkin, C .... 8(7)	Thorpe, L .... 2(7)
Butler, T .... 41(1)	Mellon, M 43	Woods, B 3
Carden, P .... –(1)		

League Goals (60): Ellis 15, Quinn 13, Preece 10, Clarkson 5, Mellon 4, Malkin 3, Philpott 3, Brabin 2, Barlow 1, Bonner 1, Bryan 1, Darton 1, Linighan 1.
Coca-Cola Cup Goals (7): Ellis 3, Quinn 3, Philpott 1. **F.A. Cup Goals (1):** Quinn 1. **Auto Windscreens Shield Goals (5):** Ellis 2, Butler 1, Mellon 1, Preece 1.
'Player of Year': Steve Banks. **Sponsors:** Telewest Communication.
Average Home League Attendance 1996-97: 4,987. **Capacity for 1997-98:** 11,047 (seats 3,036, standing 8,011).
Record Attendance: 38,098 v Wolves (Div. 1) 17 September 1955.

A.F.C. BOURNEMOUTH

Ground: Dean Court, Bournemouth, Dorset BH7 7AF.
Telephone: 01202-395381. **Clubcall:** 0891 121163. **Club Nickname:** Cherries.
First-choice Colours: Red, black and white shirts; white shorts; white stockings.

Bailey, J 40	Fletcher, S .... 33(2)	O'Brien, R 1
Beardsmore, R 37	Glass, J 35	O'Neill, J .... 7(11)
Brissett, J .... 16(9)	Gordon, D .... 14(2)	Omoyinmi, M .... 5(2)
Christie, I .... 3(1)	Hayter, J .... –(2)	Rawlinson, M ...... 22(3)
Coll, O 16	Holland, M 45	Robinson, S .... 34(6)
Cotterell, L .... 2(7)	Howe, E .... 7(6)	Town, D .... 16(10)
Cox, I 44	Marshall, A 11	Vincent, J .... 28(1)
Dean, M .... 10(2)	Morris, M .... –(1)	Watson, M .... 6(9)
Ferdinand, R 10	Murray, R .... 20(12)	Young, N 44

League Goals (43): Cox 8, Fletcher 7, Holland 7, Robinson 7, Brissett 4, Rawlinson 2, Town 2, Watson 2, Bailey 1, Gordon 1, Murray 1, O'Neill 1.
Coca-Cola Cup Goals (1): Fletcher 1. **F.A. Cup Goals:** None. **Auto Windscreens Shield Goals:** None.
'Player of Year': Ian Cox. **Sponsors:** Patrick/Sewards.
Average Home League Attendance 1996-97: 4,580. **Capacity for 1997-98:** 10,440 (seats 3,080, standing 7,360).
Record Attendance: 28,779 v Manchester United (F.A. Cup 6) 2 March 1957.

BRENTFORD

Ground: Griffin Park, Braemar Road, Brentford, Middlesex TW8 0NT.
Telephone: 0181-847-2511. **Clubcall:** 0891 121108. **Club Nickname:** Bees.
First-choice Colours: Red and white shirts; black shorts; black stockings.

Abrahams, P ...... –(5)	Dennis, K .... 9(3)	MacPherson, M ..... 2(1)
Anderson, I 45	Fernandes, T 2	McGhee, D 44
Asaba, C 44	Forster, N 25	Omigie, J .... 7(5)
Ashby, B 40	Goddard, R .... –(1)	Rapley, K .... 1(1)
Bates, J 39	Harvey, L .... 2(9)	Slade, S 4
Bent, M .... 29(5)	Hurdle, G .... 28(1)	Smith, P 46
Canham, S 13	Hutchings, C ..... 23(4)	Statham, B .... 11(7)
Dearden, K 44	Janney, M .... 1(1)	Taylor, R 42

Play-offs – Appearances: Anderson 3, Asaba 2, Ashby –(1), Bates 3, Bent 3, Canham –(2), Dearden 3, Dennis 1, Hurdle 3, Hutchings 3, McGhee 3, Smith 3, Statham 3, Taylor 3.
League Goals (56): Asaba 24, Forster 10, Taylor 8, Bent 3, Bates 2, Hutchings 2, Ashby 1, Anderson 1, Canham 1, Janney 1, Omigie 1, McGhee 1, Smith 1.
Play-off Goals (4): Taylor 2, Bent 1, Smith 1.
Coca-Cola Cup Goals (2): Forster 1, Taylor 1. **F.A. Cup Goals (5):** Taylor 2, Forster 1, McGhee 1, Smith 1. **Auto Windscreens Shield Goals (4):** Asaba 1, Forster 1, Omigie 1, Taylor 1.
'Player of Year': Barry Ashby. **Sponsors:** Ericsson.
Average Home League Attendance 1996-97: 5,920. **Capacity for 1997-98:** 12,763 (seats 8,921, standing 3,842).
Record Attendance: 39,626 v Preston N.E. (F.A. Cup 6) 5 March 1938.

BRISTOL CITY

Ground: Ashton Gate, Bristol BS3 2EJ.
Telephone: 0117-963-0630. **Clubcall**: 0891 121176. **Club Nickname**: Robins.
First-choice Colours: Red shirts; white shorts; red and white stockings.

Agostino, P .... 33(10)	Goater, S .... 39(3)	Partridge, S .... –(6)
Allen, P .... 12(1)	Goodridge, G .... 19(9)	Paterson, S .... 15(4)
Barnard, D 44	Hewlett, M .... 34(2)	Plummer, D .... –(1)
Bent, J .... 17(4)	Kuhl, M .... 23(9)	Seal, D .... –(11)
Blackmore, C 5	McLeary, A .... 1(2)	Shail, M .... 10(1)
Brennan, J .... 7(1)	Naylor, S 35	Taylor, S 29
Carey, L .... 40(2)	Nugent, K .... 20(17)	Tinnion, B .... 29(3)
Cundy, J 6	Owers, G 46	Welch, K 11
Edwards, N 31		

Play-offs – Appearances: Agostino –(1), Allen 2, Barnard 2, Bent –(1), Carey –(2), Edwards 2, Goater 2, Goodridge –(1), Hewlett 2, Kuhl 1, Nugent 2, Owers 2, Paterson 1, Shail 2, Taylor 1, Tinnion 1(1), Welch 2.
League Goals (69): Goater 23, Barnard 11, Agostino 9, Goodridge 6, Nugent 6, Owers 4, Bent 3, Hewlett 2, Taylor 1, Tinnion 1, Opponents 3. **Play-off Goals (2)**: Barnard 1, Owers 1.
Coca-Cola Cup Goals (5): Agostino 1, Barnard 1, Goater 1, Owers 1, Partridge 1. **F.A. Cup Goals (11)**: Agastino 5, Hewlett 2, Kuhl 2, Goodridge 1, Nugent 1.
Auto Windscreens Shield Goals (2): Goater 1, Owers 1.
'Player of Year': Darren Barnard. **Sponsors**: Sanderson Computer Recruitment.
Average Home League Attendance 1996-97: 10,794. **Capacity for 1997-98**: 21,497 (all-seated).
Record Attendance: 43,335 v Preston N.E. (F.A. Cup 5) 16 February 1935.

BRISTOL ROVERS

Ground: The Beeches, Broomhill Road, Brislington, Bristol BS7 0AQ.
Telephone: 0117-977-2000. **Clubcall**: 0891 664422. **Club Nickname**: Pirates.
First-choice Colours: Blue shirts; white shorts; blue stockings.

Alsop, J .... 10(6)	Gayle, B 7	Morgan, S 1
Archer, L .... 18(3)	Gurney, A .... 21(3)	Parmenter, S .... 10(4)
Beadle, P .... 36(6)	Harris, J 6	Power, G 16
Bennett, F .... 6(5)	Hayfield, M .... 12(5)	Pritchard, D 26
Browning, M .... 24(2)	Higgs, S 2	Ramasut, T .... 5(6)
Clapham, J .... 4(1)	Holloway, I .... 29(2)	Skinner, J .... 29(5)
Clark, B .... 26(1)	Lockwood, M .... 36(3)	Tillson, A 38
Collett, A 44	Low, J .... –(3)	White, T .... 18(3)
Cureton, J .... 32(6)	Martin, L 25	Zabek, L .... –(1)
French, J .... 3(1)	Miller, P .... 22(3)	

League Goals (47): Beadle 12, Cureton 11, Alsop 3, Archer 2, Browning 2, Gurney 2, Harris 2, Miller 2, Parmenter 2, Skinner 2, Tillson 2, Bennett 1, Clark 1, Holloway 1, Lockwood 1, Opponent 1.
Coca-Cola Cup Goals (2): Gurney 1, Archer 1. **F.A. Cup Goals (1)**: Parmenter 1.
Auto Windscreens Shield Goals (1): Harris 1.
'Player of Year': Andy Collett. **Sponsors**: Bradshaws Snack Box.
Average Home League Attendance 1996-97: 5,629. **Capacity for 1997-98**: 8,205 (seats 1,601, standing 6,604).
Record Attendance (at previous ground, Eastville): 38,472 v Preston N.E. (F.A. Cup 4) 30 January 1960.

BURNLEY

Ground: Turf Moor, Brunshaw Road, Burnley, Lancashire BB10 4BX.
Telephone: 01282-700000. **Clubcall**: 0891 121153. **Club Nickname**: Clarets.
First-choice Colours: Claret and blue shirts; claret and white shorts; white stockings.

Barnes, P 39(1)	Hodgson, D 1	Robinson, L 3(6)
Beresford, M 40	Hoyland, J 24(10)	Russell, W 6(9)
Brass, C 38(8)	Huxford, R 2(11)	Smith, P 30(8)
Cooke, A 19(17)	Little, G 5(7)	Swan, P 15(7)
Eyres, D 36(1)	Matthew, D 29(3)	Thompson, S 14(8)
Gleghorn, N 32(1)	Nogan, K 30(1)	Vinnicombe, C 6(5)
Guinan, S –(6)	Overson, V 6(6)	Weller, P 21(13)
Harrison, G 32(3)	Parkinson, G 43	Winstanley, M 34(1)
Heath, A –(2)		

League Goals (71): Barnes 23, Cook 11, Nogan 11, Matthew 5, Eyres 4, Gleghorn 4, Smith 4, Swan 2, Weller 2, Hoyland 1, Parkinson 1, Thompson 1.
Coca-Cola Cup Goals (7): Eyres 3, Nogan 2, Cooke 1, Matthew 1. **F.A. Cup Goals (4):** Barnes 1, Eyres 1, Gleghorn 1, Matthew 1. **Auto Windscreens Shield Goals (2):** Eyres 1, Nogan 1.
'Player of Year': Chris Brass. **Sponsors:** Endsleigh Insurance Services.
Average Home League Attendance 1996-97: 10,122. **Capacity for 1997-98:** 22,546 (all-seated).
Record Attendance: 54,775 v Huddersfield Town (F.A. Cup 4) 23 February 1924.

BURY

Ground: Gigg Lane, Bury, Lancashire BL9 9HR.
Telephone: 0161-764-4881. **Clubcall:** 0930 190003. **Club Nickname:** Shakers.
First-choice Colours: White shirts; blue shorts; blue stockings.

Armstrong, G 16(16)	Jepson, R 24	Randall, A 14(7)
Battersby, A 9(2)	Johnrose, L 44(2)	Reid, S 6(1)
Bimson, S 1(1)	Johnson, D 33(9)	Rigby, A 1(15)
Butler, P 40	Kiely, D 46	Scott, A 2(6)
Carter, M 28(12)	Lucketti, C 38	Stant, P 3(6)
Daws, N 46	Matthews, R 22(7)	West, D 46
Hughes, I 14(9)	O'Kane, J 11(12)	Woodward, A 17(4)
Jackson, M 29	Pugh, D 16(2)	

League Goals (62): Carter 11, Jepson 9, Johnson 8, Matthews 5, Johnrose 4, Jackson 3, O'Kane 3, West 3, Armstrong 2, Battersby 2, Butler 2, Daws 2, Pugh 2, Randall 2, Stant 1, Opponents 3.
Coca-Cola Cup Goals (3): Carter 1, Jackson 1, Pugh 1. **F.A. Cup Goals:** None.
Auto Windscreens Shield Goals (10): Carter 2, Jepson 2, Johnson 2, Butler 1, Daws 1, Lucketti 1, Pugh 1.
'Player of Year': Chris Lucketti. **Sponsors:** Birthdays.
Average Home League Attendance 1996-97: 4,319 **Capacity for 1997-98:** 11,869 (seats 9,369, standing 2,500).
Record Attendance: 35,000 v Bolton Wanderers (F.A. Cup 3) 9 January 1960.

CHESTERFIELD

Ground: Recreation Ground, Saltergate, Chesterfield, Derbyshire S40 4SX.
Telephone: 01246-209765. **Clubcall:** 0891 555818. **Club Nickname:** Spireites.
First-choice Colours: Blue shirts; white shorts; blue stockings.

Allison, N –(2)	Hanson, D 3	Mason, A 1(1)
Beaumont, C 29(4)	Hewitt, J 36(1)	Mercer, W 35
Bowater, J –(1)	Holland, P 24(1)	Mitchell, A 1(1)
Carr, D 12	Howard, J 26(9)	Morgan, P 2
Curtis, T 40	Jules, M 41(1)	Morris, A 19(8)
Davies, K 28(6)	Law, N 4(3)	Patterson, G 7(2)
Dunn, I 10(1)	Leaning, A 9	Perkins, C 26(4)
Dyche, S 36	Lomas, J –(2)	Rogers, L 14(3)
Ebdon, M 11(1)	Lormor, A 25(11)	Scott, A 4(1)
Gaughan, S 14(4)	Lund, G 7(3)	Williams, M 42

League Goals (42): Howard 9, Lormor 8, Morris 4, Curtis 3, Davies 3, Holland 3, Scott 3, Williams 3, Beaumont 1, Ebdon 1, Hanson 1, Hewitt 1, Law 1, Opponent 1.

Coca-Cola Cup Goals (2): Gaughan 1, Lormor 1. **F.A. Cup Goals (13)**: Davies 4, Howard 2, Beaumont 1, Curtis 1, Dyche 1, Hewitt 1, Lormor 1, Morris 1, Williams 1. **Auto Windscreens Shield Goals**: None.
'Player of Year': Sean Dyche. **Sponsors**: North Derbyshire Health.
Average Home League Attendance 1996-97: 4,638. **Capacity for 1997-98**: 8,880 (seats 3,408, standing 5,472).
Record Attendance: 30,698 v Newcastle United (Div. 2) 7 April 1939.

CREWE ALEXANDRA
Ground: Gresty Road, Crewe, Cheshire CW2 6EB.
Telephone: 01270-213014. **Clubcall**: 0891 664564. **Club Nickname**: Railwaymen.
First-choice Colours: Red shirts; red shorts; white stockings.

Adebola, D .... 27(4)	Johnson, S .... 8(3)	Rivers, M .... 23(3)
Anthrobus, S 10	Kearton, J 30	Savage, R 41
Bankole, A 3	Launders, B .... 6(3)	Smith, P .... –(1)
Barr, B .... 29(5)	Lightfoot, C .... 16(9)	Smith, S .... 34(4)
Billing, P .... 9(6)	Little, C .... 3(12)	Taylor, M 6
Charnock, P .... 24(7)	Macauley, S .... 40(2)	Tierney, F .... 18(13)
Ellison, L 3	Mautone, S 3	Unsworth, L .... 28(1)
Garvey, S .... 10(7)	Moralee, J 7	Westwood, A .... 43(1)
Gayle, M 4	Murphy, D .... 44(1)	Whalley, G 37

Play-offs – Appearances: Adebola 3, Charnock 3, Garvey –(2), Johnson –(3), Kearton 3, Lightfoot –(2), Little 3, Macauley 3, Murphy 3, Rivers 3, Smith 3, Tierney –(1), Unsworth 3, Westwood 3, Whalley 3.
League Goals (56): Adebola 16, Murphy 10, Rivers 6, Barr 4, Smith 4, Tierney 3, Whalley 3, Ellison 2, Macauley 2, Westwood 2, Charnock 1, Johnson 1, Lightfoot 1, Savage 1. **Play-off Goals (5)**: Little 2, Smith 2, Rivers 1.
Coca-Cola Cup Goals (1): Adebola 1. **F.A. Cup Goals (10)**: Murphy 3, Adebola 1, Garvey 1, Lightfoot 1, Macauley 1, Smith 1, Westwood 1, Opponent 1. **Auto Windscreens Shield Goals (3)**: Murphy 2, Tierney 1.
'Player of Year': Danny Murphy. **Sponsors**: Boldon James.
Average Home League Attendance 1996-97: 3,978. **Capacity for 1997-98**: 6,000 (seats 5,000, standing 1,000).
Record Attendance: 20,000 v Tottenham Hotspur (F.A. Cup 4) 30 January 1960

GILLINGHAM
Ground: Priestfield Stadium, Redfern Avenue, Gillingham, Kent ME7 4DD.
Telephone: 01634-851854. **Clubcall**: 0891 332211. **Club Nickname**: Gills.
First-choice Colours: Blue shirts; blue shorts; white stockings.

Akinbiyi, A 19	Galloway, J .... 6(3)	O'Connor, M .... 18(4)
Armstrong, C 10	Gould, I 3	Onuora, I .... 37(3)
Bailey, D .... 16(14)	Green, R .... 28(1)	Pennock, A 26
Bryant, M .... 38(1)	Harris, M .... 19(2)	Piper, L .... 4(15)
Butler, S .... 29(8)	Hessenthaler, A 38	Puttnam, D .... 5(9)
Butters, G 30	Humphrey, J 9	Ratcliffe, S 43
Carpenter, R 1	Manuel, S .... 3(8)	Smith, N 42
Chapman, I .... 20(3)	Marshall, A 5	Stannard, J 38
Ford, J .... 2(2)	Morris, M 6	Thomas, G .... 4(6)
Fortune-West, L 7		

League Goals (60): Onwora 21, Butler 9, Akinbiyi 7, Ratcliffe 6, Bailey 2, Fortune-West 2, Green 2, Hessenthaler 2, Pennock 2, Chapman 1, Galloway 1, Harris 1, Piper 1, Puttnam 1, Smith 1, Opponent 1.
Coca-Cola Cup Goals (8): Ratcliffe 2, Butler 1, Fortune-West 1, Onuora 1, Puttnam 1, Smith 1, Torpey 1. **F.A. Cup Goals (3)**: Butler 1, Hessenthaler 1, Onuora 1. **Auto Windscreens Shield Goals (1)**: Piper 1.
'Player of Year': Andy Hessenthaler. **Sponsors**: Invicta Radio.
Average Home League Attendance 1996-97: 6,033. **Capacity for 1997-98**: 11,110 (seats 3,610, standing 7,500).

Record Attendance: 23,002 v Q.P.R. (F.A. Cup 3) 10 January 1948.

LUTON TOWN

Ground: Kenilworth Stadium, 1 Maple Road, Luton, Bedfordshire LU4 8AW.
Telephone: 01582-411622; 01582-416976 (ticket office). **Clubcall**: 0891
121123. **Club Nickname**: Hatters.
First-choice Colours: White shirts; blue shorts; white and blue stockings.

Alexander, G .... 44(1)	Hughes, C 36	Oldfield, D .... 31(7)
Davis, S .... 43(1)	James, J 44	Patterson, D .... 8(2)
Douglas, S .... 2(7)	Johnson, M 44	Showler, P .... 21(2)
Evers, S 1	Kiwomya, A 5	Skelton, A .... 2(1)
Feuer, I 46	Linton, D .... 3(4)	Thomas, M 42
Fotiadis, A .... 9(8)	McGowan, G 2	Thorpe, T .... 39(2)
Grant, K .... 8(17)	McLaren, P .... 13(11)	Upson, M .... −(1)
Guentchev, B ..... 15(12)	Marshall, D .... 9(15)	Waddock, G .... 38(1)
Harvey, R .... 1(1)		

Play-offs – Appearances: Alexander 2, Davis 2, Feuer 2, Fotiadis 1(1), Grant
−(1), James 1, Johnson 1, McLaren 2, Marshall −(2), Oldfield 2, Patterson 2,
Showler 1, Thomas 2, Thorpe 2, Waddock 2.
League Goals (71): Thorpe 28, Davis 8, Oldfield 6, Showler 6, Marshall 4,
Hughes 4, Fotiadis 3, Thomas 3, Alexander 2, Grant 2, Waddock 2, Guentchev 1,
James 1, Kiwomya 1. **Play-off Goals (3)**: Oldfield 3.
Coca-Cola Cup Goals (9): Oldfield 2, Grant 2, Thorpe 2, James 1, Hughes 1,
Opponent 1. **F.A. Cup Goals (6)**: Marshall 3, Hughes 1, Johnson 1, Thorpe 1.
Auto Windscreens Shield Goals (2): Davis 1, Grant 1.
'Player of Year': Tony Thorpe. **Sponsors**: Universal Salvage Auctions.
Average Home League Attendance 1996-97: 6,294. **Capacity for 1997-98**:
9,970 (all-seated).
Record Attendance: 30,069 v Blackpool (F.A. Cup 6) 4 March 1959.

MILLWALL

Ground: The New Den, Zampa Road, London SE16 3LN.
Telephone: 0171-232-1222. **Clubcall**: 0891 400300. **Club Nickname**: Lions.
First-choice Colours: Blue shirts; white shorts; blue stockings.

Berry, G .... 13(1)	Harle, M .... 12(9)	Robertson, G .... −(1)
Bircham, M 6	Hartley, P .... 35(9)	Roche, S .... 4(3)
Bowry, B .... 26(2)	Hockton, D .... −(2)	Rogan, A .... 26(2)
Bright, M 3	Huckerby, D 6	Sadler, R .... 7(3)
Cadette, R 7	Iga, A .... −(1)	Savage, D .... 32(3)
Canoville, D .... −(2)	Lavin, G .... 7(2)	Sinclair, D .... 6(2)
Carter, T 46	McLeary, A 15	Stevens, K 6
Crawford, S .... 40(2)	McRobert, L .... 3(1)	Van Blerk, J .... 2(2)
Dair, J .... 21(3)	Malkin, C .... 7(2)	Webber, D .... 28(1)
Dolby, T .... 15(6)	Neill, L .... 35(4)	Wilkins, R 3
Doyle, M .... 19(9)	Newman, R .... 39(2)	Witter, T 33
Fitzgerald, S 7		

League Goals (50): Crawford 11, Rogan 8, Hartley 4, Neill 4, Huckerby 3,
Newman 3, Savage 3, Dolby 2, Malkin 2, Webber 2, Bowry 1, Bright 1, Cadette 1,
Dair 1, Doyle 1, Harle 1, Opponents 2.
Coca-Cola Cup Goals (1): Malkin 1. **F.A. Cup Goals (2)**: Malkin 1, Savage 1.
Auto Windscreens Shield Goals (6): Crawford 3, Dair 2, Savage 1.
'Player of Year': Lucas Neill. **Sponsors**: ':Lve TV'.
Average Home League Attendance 1996-97: 7,756. **Capacity for 1997-98**:
20,146 (all-seated).
Record Attendance At New Den: 20,093 v Arsenal (F.A. Cup 3) 10 January
1994. At previous ground, The Den: 48,672 v Derby County (F.A. Cup 5) 20
February 1937.

NOTTS COUNTY

Ground: Meadow Lane, Nottingham NG2 3HJ.
Telephone: 0115-952-9000. **Clubcall**: 0891 888684. **Club Nickname**: Magpies.
First-choice Colours: Black and white shirts; black shorts; black stockings.

Agana, T .... 17(5)	Hogg, G 35	Regis, D .... 7(3)
Arkins, V .... 13(2)	Hunt, J .... 5(3)	Richardson, I .... 15(4)
Baraclough, I ..... 36(3)	Jones, G .... 21(5)	Ridgeway, I .... 4(3)
Battersby, A .... 6(11)	Kennedy, P .... 20(1)	Robinson, P .... 33(4)
Cunnington, S ...... 6(2)	Ludlam, C 1	Rogers, P .... –(1)
Derry, S .... 37(2)	Martindale, G .... 16(12)	Simpson, M 2
Diuk, W .... –(1)	Mendez, G .... 2(1)	Strodder, G 28
Dudley, C .... 6(4)	Mitchell, P 1	Walker, R .... 12(3)
Farrell, S .... 10(4)	Murphy, S 16	Ward, D 38
Finnan, S .... 18(5)	Nogan, L 6	White, D .... 7(2)
Galloway, M .... 4(1)	Pollitt, N 8	Wilder, C 37
Gallagher, T 1	Redmile, M 23	Wilkes, T 3
Hendon, I 12		

League Goals (33): Martindale 6, Agana 3, Jones 3, Baraclough 2, Derry 2, Dudley 2, Redmile 2, Regis 2, Robinson 2, Strodder 2, Arkins 1, Battersby 1, Farrell 1, Richardson 1, Opponents 3.
Coca-Cola Cup Goals (1): Jones 1. **F.A. Cup Goals (5)**: Agana 1, Arkins 1, Jones 1, Kennedy 1, Robinson 1. **Auto Windscreens Shield Goals (2)**: Hunt 1, Martindale 1.
'Player of Year': N/A. **Sponsors**: SAPA.
Average Home League Attendance 1996-97: 4,239. **Capacity for 1997-98**: 20,300 (all-seated).
Record Attendance: 47,310 v York City (F.A. Cup 6) 12 March 1955.

PETERBOROUGH UNITED

Ground: London Road, Peterborough, Cambridge PE2 8AL.
Telephone: 01733-63947. **Clubcall**: 0891 121654. **Club Nickname**: Posh.
First-choice Colours: Blue shirts; white shorts; blue and white stockings.

Basham, M .... 4(1)	Edwards, A 25	Neal, A 4
Billington, D .... 2(3)	Etherington, M 1	O'Connor, M 18
Bodley, M 31	Farrell, S .... 4(3)	Otto, R 15
Boothroyd, A ..... 24(2)	Foran, M .... 2(2)	Payne, D 36
Bullimore, W .... 2(3)	Griemink, B 27	Ramage, C 7
Carruthers, M .... 13(1)	Griffiths, C .... 2(10)	Regis, D .... 4(3)
Carter, A .... 3(5)	Heald, S .... 34(2)	Rowe, E .... 10(12)
Charlery, K .... 36(1)	Houghton, S .... 26(5)	Sheffield, J 16
Clark, S .... 30(4)	Huxford, R 7	Spearing, T .... 11(2)
Cleaver, C .... 6(7)	Le Bihan, N 2	Tyler, M 3
De Souza, M 8	Linton, D 8	Welsh, S 6
Donowa, L .... 16(6)	McKeever, M .... 2(1)	Williams, M 6
Drury, A 5	Morrison, D .... 4(7)	Willis, R .... 34(6)
Ebdon, M .... 12(8)		

League Goals (55): Houghton 8, Willis 6, Charlery 5, Carruthers 4, Otto 4, Clark 3, Farrell 3, O'Connor 3, Rowe 3, De Souza 2, Heald 2, Morrison 2, Payne 2, Boothroyd 1, Cleaver 1, Donowa 1, Drury 1, Ebdon 1, Griffiths 1, Regis 1, Opponent 1.
Coca-Cola Cup Goals (3): Charlery 1, Farrell 1, Griffiths 1. **F.A. Cup Goals (11)**: Charlery 6, Carruthers 2, Grazioli 1, Griffiths 1, Houghton 1. **Auto Windscreens Shield Goals (6)**: Donowa 2, Otto 2, Charlery 1, Heald 1.
'Player of Year': Derek Payne. **Sponsors**: Thomas Cook Group.
Average Home League Attendance 1996-97: 5,297. **Capacity for 1997-98**: 15,500 (seats 11,000, standing 4,500).
Record Attendance: 30,096 v Swansea (F.A. Cup 5) 20 February 1965.

PLYMOUTH ARGYLE

Ground: Home Park, Plymouth, Devon PL2 3DQ.
Telephone: 01752-562561. **Clubcall**: 0839 442270. **Club Nickname**: Pilgrims.
First-choice Colours: Green and white shirts; black shorts; green stockings.

Barlow, M .... 38(2)	Grobbelaar, B 36	Patterson, M .... 11(1)
Billy, C .... 44(1)	Heathcote, M .... 41(1)	Perkins, S .... 1(3)
Blackwell, K 4	Illman. N .... 12(13)	Phillips, L .... –(2)
Clayton, G .... –(1)	James, A 34	Rowbotham, J ...... 12(3)
Collins, S .... 11(1)	Leadbitter, C .... 17(2)	Saunders, M ...... 22(3)
Corazzin, C .... 22(8)	Littlejohn, A .... 33(4)	Simpson, M .... 10(2)
Curran, C .... 20(2)	Logan, R .... 19(9)	Williams, P 46
Dungey, J 6	Mauge, R .... 29(6)	Wotton, P .... 5(4)
Evans, M 33		

League Goals (47): Evans 11, Littlejohn 6, Corazzin 5, Illman 4, Logan 4, Billy 3, Mauge 3, Saunders 3, Williams 3, Barlow 1, Collins 1, Heathcote 1, James 1, Wotton 1.
Coca-Cola Cup Goals: None. **F.A. Cup Goals (9)**: Evans 3, Littlejohn 2, Mauge 2, Billy 1, Corazzin 1. **Auto Windscreens Shield Goals (3)**: Wotton 2, Illman 1.
'Player of Year': Chris Billy. **Sponsors**: Rotolok.
Average Home League Attendance 1996-97: 6,495. **Capacity for 1997-98**: 19,800 (seats 6,620, standing 13,180).
Record Attendance: 43,596 v Aston Villa (Div. 2) 10 October 1936.

PRESTON NORTH END

Ground: Deepdale, Lowthorpe Road, Preston, Lancashire PR1 6RU.
Telephone: 01772-902020. **Clubcall**: 0891 660220. **Club Nickname**: Lilywhites.
First-choice Colours: White and navy shirts; navy shorts; white and navy stockings.

Ashcroft, L .... 26(1)	Holt, M .... 8(10)	O'Hanlon, K 13
Atkinson, G .... 12(5)	Jackson, M 7	Patterson, D 2
Barrick, D .... 30(6)	Kay, J 7	Rankine, M .... 19(4)
Beckford, D .... –(2)	Kidd, R .... 33(2)	Reeves, D .... 33(1)
Bennett, G .... 10(6)	Kilbane, K .... 32(16)	Saville, A 12
Brown, M .... 5(1)	Lucas, D 2	Sparrow, P 6
Bryson, I .... 32(8)	McDonald, N ...... 11(10)	Squires, J .... 6(2)
Cartwright, L 14	McKenna, P .... 4(1)	Stallard, M 4
Davey, S .... 30(7)	Mimms, B 27	Teale, S 5
Gage, K 16	Moilanen, T 4	Wilcox, R 36
Gregan, S 20	Moyes, D 26	Wilkinson, S .... 8(2)
Gregory, J 1	Nogan, K 5	

League Goals (49): Reeves 11, Ashcroft 8, Davey 6, Moyes 4, Bennett 3, Bryson 3, Holt 3, Wilkinson 3, Kilbane 2, Cartwright 1, Gregan 1, McKenna 1, Saville 1, Stallard 1, Opponent 1.
Coca-Cola Cup Goals (8): Wilkinson 4, Atkinson 1, Davey 1, Holt 1, McDonald 1.
F.A. Cup Goals (6): Ashcroft 3, Reeves 3. **Auto Windscreens Shield Goals (2)**: Atkinson 1, Bennett 1.
'Player of Year': David Moyes. **Sponsors**: Baxi.
Average Home League Attendance 1996-97: 9,405. **Capacity for 1997-98**: 15,295 (seats 9,131, standing 6,164).
Record Attendance: 42,684 v Arsenal (Div. 1) 23 April 1938.

ROTHERHAM UNITED

Ground: Millmoor, Rotherham, South Yorkshire S60 1HR.
Telephone: 01709-512434. **Clubcall**: 0891 664442. **Club Nickname**: Merry Millers. **First-choice Colours**: Red and white shirts; white shorts; red and white stockings.

Bain, K .... 10(2)	Barnes, P 2	Berry, T .... 19(11)

Blades, P	9(1)	Garner, D	30	McGlashan, J	28(3)
Bowman, R	13	Gayle, B	19(1)	McKenzie, R	6(5)
Bowyer, G	10(1)	Glover, L	16(6)	Monington, M	28
Breckin, I	42	Goodwin, S	7(1)	Pell, R	2
Cherry, S	20	Hayward, A	32(2)	Pilkington, K	17
Clarke, A	1(1)	Hurst, P	25(5)	Richardson, N	10(4)
Crawford, J	11	James, M	–(3)	Roscoe, A	39(4)
Dillon, P	11(2)	Jean, E	7(11)	Sandeman, B	20(1)
Dobbin, J	17(2)	Landon, R	7(1)	Slawson, S	2(3)
Druce, M	16(4)	McDougald, J	14(4)	Smith, S	9(2)
Farrelly, S	7		

League Goals (39): Jean 6, Berry 4, Druce 4, Hayward 4, Breckin 3, Goodwin 3, Bowyer 2, Garner 2, McDougald 2, Sandeman 2, Blades 1, Dillon 1, Glover 1, Richardson 1, Opponents 3.
Coca-Cola Cup Goals: None. **F.A. Cup Goals (1)**: McGlashan 1. **Auto Windscreens Shield Goals**: None.
'Player of Year': Andy Roscoe. **Sponsors**: Parkgate Retail World.
Average Home League Attendance 1996-97: 2,844. **Capacity for 1997-98**: 11,533 (seats 4,486, standing 7,047).
Record Attendance: 25,000 v Sheff. Wed. (Div. 2) 26 January 1952; 25,000 v Sheff. Wed. (Div. 2) 13 December 1952.

SHREWSBURY TOWN
Ground: Gay Meadow, Shrewsbury, Shropshire SY2 6AB.
Telephone: 01743-360111. **Clubcall**: 0891 888611. **Club Nickname**: Shrews/Blues.
First-choice Colours: Blue shirts; blue shorts; blue stockings.

Anthrobus, S	33	Edwards, P	23	Stevens, I	41
Bennett, F	2(2)	Evans, P	42	Tate, C	–(1)
Bent, J	6	Gall, B	23	Taylor, L	13(3)
Berkley, A	20(4)	Nielson, T	19(3)	Taylor, M	33(4)
Blamey, N	6	Nwadike, E	1(1)	Walton, D	23(1)
Briscoe, A	–(1)	Reed, I	–(3)	Ward, N	5(9)
Brown, M	17(2)	Rowbotham, D	11(3)	Whiston, P	26(1)
Cope, J	3(1)	Scott, R	20(7)	Wrack, D	3(1)
Currie, D	25(12)	Seabury, K	34(4)	Wray, S	1
Dempsey, M	37(3)	Spink, D	39(2)		

League Goals (49): Stevens 17, Anthrobus 6, Evans 6, Spink 4, Bennett 3, Currie 2, Brown 1, Nielson 1, Rowbotham 1, Scott 1, M Taylor 1, Walton 1, Ward 1, Whiston 1, Opponents 1.
Coca-Cola Cup Goals (1): Scott 1. **F.A. Cup Goals (1)**: Stevens 1. **Auto Windscreens Shield Goals (6)**: Evans 3, Anthrobus 1, Berkley 1, Stevens 1.
'Player of Year': Dean Spink. **Sponsors**: Ternhill Communications.
Average Home League Attendance 1996-97: 3,178. **Capacity for 1997-98**: 8,500 (seats 3,000, standing 5,500).
Record Attendance: 18,917 v Walsall (Div. 3) 26 April 1961.

STOCKPORT COUNTY
Ground: Edgeley Park, Hardcastle Road, Edgeley, Stockport SK3 9DD.
Telephone: 0161-286-8888. **Clubcall**: 0891 121638. **Club Nickname**: County.
First-choice Colours: Blue shirts; white shorts; blue stockings.

Angell, B	30(4)	Connelly, S	45	Jeffers, J	25(9)
Armstrong, A	38(1)	Cooper, K	11(1)	Jones, P	46
Bennett, T	43	Cowans, G	6(1)	Landon, R	–(2)
Bound, M	4	Dinning, T	12(8)	Marsden, C	34(1)
Cavaco, L	19(8)	Durkan, K	36(5)	Mike, A	–(1)
Charanga, M	–(3)	Flynn, M	46	Mutch, A	15(18)
Charlery, K	8(2)	Gannon, J	38(2)	Nash, M	–(3)

Searle, D .... 7(3)   Todd, L .... 39(2)   Ware, P .... 4(4)

League Goals (59): Angell 15, Armstrong 9, Cavaco 5, Gannon 4, Mutch 4, Bennett 3, Cooper 3, Durkan 3, Jeffers 3, Dinning 2, Flynn 2, Evans 1, Marsden 1, Opponents 4.
Coca-Cola Cup Goals (20): Mutch 4, Angell 3, Armstrong 3, Bennett 2, Cavaco 2, Connelly 1, Flynn 1, Gannon 1, Ware 1, Opponents 2. **F.A. Cup Goals (6):** Durkan 3, Angell 1, Armstrong 1, Flynn 1. **Auto Windscreens Shield Goals (5):** Angell 1, Cavaco 1, Dinning 1, Marsden 1, Opponent 1.
'Player of Year': Paul Jones. **Sponsors:** Robinson's Best Bitter.
Average Home League Attendance 1996-97: 6,424. **Capacity for 1997-98:** 12,100 (seats 9,350, standing 2,750).
Record Attendance: 27,833 v Liverpool (F.A. Cup 5) 11 February 1950.

WALSALL

Ground: Bescot Stadium, Bescot Crescent, Walsall, West Midlands WS1 4SA.
Telephone: 01922-22791. **Clubcall:** 0891 555800. **Club Nickname:** Saddlers.
First-choice Colours: Red shirts; black shorts; white stockings.

Beckford, D .... 3(5)	Keister, J .... 30(6)	Roper, I .... 5(6)
Blake, M .... 35(3)	Lightbourne, K 45	Ryder, S .... –(1)
Bradley, D .... 21(5)	Marsh, C .... 28(2)	Thomas, W .... 14(6)
Butler, M .... 20(3)	Mountfield, D 42	Viveash, A 46
Daniel, R .... 8(2)	Ntamark, C .... 36(2)	Walker, J 36
Donowa, L 6	Platt, C .... –(1)	Watson, A .... 22(14)
Evans, D .... 27(1)	Ricketts, M .... 2(9)	Wilson, K .... 36(1)
Hodge, J .... 32(5)	Rogers, D .... 1(1)	Wood, T 10
Keates, D .... 1(1)		

League Goals (54): Lightbourne 20, Viveash 9, Wilson 7, Watson 5, Blake 4, Hodge 4, Butler 1, Donowa 1, Keister 1, Ntamark 1, Ricketts 1.
Coca-Cola Cup Goals (1): Lightbourne 1. **F.A. Cup Goals (7):** Lightbourne 4, Wilson 2, Viveash 1. **Auto Windscreens Shield Goals:** None.
'Player of Year': Adrian Viveash. **Sponsors:** Banks Brewery.
Average Home League Attendance 1996-97: 3,892. **Capacity for 1997-98:** 9,000 (seats 6,700, standing 2,300).
Record Attendance (at Bescot Stadium): 10,628 England v Switz 'B' Int., May 20, 1991. **Club:** 8,619 Walsall v Leeds (F.A. Cup 3) 7 January 1995. **At previous ground,** Fellows Park): 25,433 v Newcastle United (Div. 2) 29 August 1961.

WATFORD

Ground: Vicarage Road, Watford, Hertfordshire WD1 8ER.
Telephone: 01923-496000. **Clubcall:** – **Club Nickname:** Hornets.
First-choice Colours: Yellow shirts; red shorts; red stockings.

Andrews, W .... 16(9)	Lowndes, N .... –(3)	Porter, G 6
Armstrong, C 14	Ludden, D .... 18(2)	Ramage, C .... 9(1)
Bazeley, D .... 38(3)	Millen, K 42	Robinson, P .... 8(4)
Chamberlain, A 3	Miller, K 42	Scott, K 6
Connolly, D .... 12(1)	Mooney, T .... 33(3)	Slater, S .... 11(3)
Easton, C 16	Noel-Williams, G .. 9(16)	Talboys, S .... 2(1)
Flash, R .... –(1)	Page, R .... 34(1)	Ward, D 7
Gibbs, N .... 42(2)	Palmer, S 40	White, D .... 19(3)
Johson, C 1	Penrice, G .... 21(10)	Williams, N 9
Johnson, R .... 35(2)	Phillips, K .... 13(2)	

League Goals (45): Mooney 13, Andrews 4, Phillips 4, Bazeley 3, Ramage 3, White 3, Connolly 2, Johnson 2, Millen 2, Noel-Williams 2, Scott 2, Easton 1, Gibbs 1, Palmer 1, Penrice 1, Slater 1.
Coca-Cola Cup Goals (2): Andrews 1, Porter 1. **F.A. Cup Goals (9):** Connolly 3, Bazeley 3, Noel-Williams 1, White 1.
Auto Windscreens Shield Goals (4): Andrews 1, Bazeley 1, Connolly 1, Page 1.
'Player of Year': Kevin Miller. **Sponsors:** CTX Computer Products.

Average Home League Attendance 1996-97: 8,894. **Capacity for 1997-98**: 22,100 (all-seated).
Record Attendance: 34,099 v Manchester United (F.A. Cup 4) 3 February 1969.

WREXHAM

Ground: Racecourse Ground, Mold Road, Wrexham, Clwyd LL11 2AH.
Telephone: 01978-262129. **Clubcall**: 0891 121642. **Club Nickname**: Robins.
First-choice Colours: Red shirts; white shorts; white stockings.

Bennett, G 15	Hughes, B .... 20(3)	Phillips, W 26
Brace, D 26	Humes, T 34	Ridler, D .... 7(4)
Brammer, D .... 18(2)	Jones, B .... 14(8)	Roberts, P .... −(1)
Carey, B 38	Jones, L .... 2(3)	Russell, K .... 37(4)
Cartwright, M 3	Jones, P 6	Skinner, C .... 22(5)
Chalk, M .... 33(10)	McGregor, M .... 37(1)	Solomon, J 2
Connolly, K .... 27(3)	Marriott, A 43	Ward, P 23
Cross, J .... 11(7)	Morris, S .... 10(7)	Watkin, S .... 24(2)
Hardy, P 13	Owen, G .... 12(10)	Williams, S .... 3(1)

League Goals (54): Connolly 14, Watkin 7, Bennett 5, Phillips 5, Humes 4, Morris 4, Skinner 4, Hughes 3, Cross 2, Brace 1, Brammer 1, Chalk 1, McGregor 1, Owen 1, Ward 1.
Coca-Cola Cup Goals (1): Skinner 1. **F.A. Cup Goals (17)**: Hughes 6, Russell 3, Watkin 3, Morris 2, Connolly 1, Humes 1, Ward 1. **Auto Windscreens Shield Goals**: None.
'Player of Year': Andy Marriott. **Sponsors**: Wrexham Lager.
Average Home League Attendance 1996-97: 4,245. **Capacity for 1997-98**: 9,500 (seats 5,000, standing 4,500).
Record Attendance: 34,445 v Manchester United (F.A. Cup 4) 26 January 1957.

WYCOMBE WANDERERS

Ground: Adams Park, Hillbottom Road, High Wycombe, Bucks. HP1 4HJ.
Telephone: 01494-472100. **Clubcall**: 0891 446855. **Club Nickname**: Chairboys.
First-choice Colours: Blue shirts; navy blue shorts; navy blue stockings.

Bell, M 46	Farrell, M .... 17(10)	Parkin, B 24
Brown, S .... 28(6)	Forsyth, M .... 22(1)	Patterson, G .... 6(3)
Carroll, D .... 42(1)	Harkin, M .... −(4)	Read, P .... 7(6)
Cheesewright, J 18	Kavanagh, J 27	Scott, K 9
Cornforth, J .... 8(2)	Lawrence, M .... 12(1)	Simpson, M .... 16(4)
Cousins, J .... 36(1)	McCarthy, P .... 36(3)	Skiverton, T .... 2(4)
Crossley, M .... 7(2)	McGavin, S .... 33(2)	Stallard, M 12
Davis, N 13	Mahoney-Johnson,	Taylor, M 4
De Souza, M .... 29(4)	M .... 2(2)	Wilkins, R 1
Evans, T .... 38(4)	Markman, D .... −(2)	Williams, J .... 11(8)

League Goals (51): Carroll 9, McGavin 9, Brown 6, De Souza 5, Read 4, Stallard 4, Scott 3, Bell 2, Evans 2, Forsyth 2, Mahoney-Johnson 2, Lawrence 1, Simpson 1, Williams 1.
Coca-Cola Cup Goals (4): Williams 2, McCarthy 1, Evans 1. **F.A. Cup Goals (8)**: Williams 4, De Souza 2, Carroll 1, McGavin 1. **Auto Windscreens Shield Goals (1)**: McGavin 1.
'Player of Year': Micky Bell. **Sponsors**: Verco Office Furniture.
Average Home League Attendance 1996-97: 5,232. **Capacity for 1997-98**: 10,000 (seats 7,306, standing 2,694).
Record Attendance (Adams Park) 9,007 v West Ham (F.A. Cup 3) January 7, 1995.

YORK CITY

Ground: Bootham Crescent, York, North Yorkshire YO3 7AQ.
Telephone: 01904-624447. **Clubcall**: 0891 664545. **Club Nickname**: Minstermen. **First-choice Colours**: Red shirts; navy shorts; red stockings.

Atkin, P	6(4)	Harrison, T	–(1)	Reed, M		2
Atkinson, P	13(1)	Himsworth, G	32(1)	Rowe, R		9(1)
Barras, A	46	Jordan, S	7(8)	Rush, D		1(1)
Bull, G	33(7)	McMillan, A	46	Sharples, J		28
Bushell, S	26(5)	Murty, G	25(2)	Stephenson, P	33(2)
Campbell, N	5(6)	Naylor, G	–(1)	Tinkler, M		9
Clarke, T	17	Pepper, N	26(3)	Tolson, N		39(1)
Cresswell, R	9(8)	Pouton, A	18(4)	Tutill, S		13(2)
Gilbert, D	9	Prudhoe, M	2	Warrington, A	27
Greening, J	–(5)	Randall, A	13(3)	Williams, D	–(1)
Hall, W	12(1)					

League Goals (47): Pepper 12, Tolson 12, Bushell 3, Rowe 3, Bull 2, Himsworth 2, Murty 2, Randall 2, Barras 1, Campbell 1, Gilbert 1, Jordan 1, Pouton 1, Sharples 1, Stephenson 1, Tinkler 1, Opponent 1.
Coca-Cola Cup Goals (7): Tolson 3, Bull 1, Bushell 1, Murty 1, Pepper 1. **F.A. Cup Goals (6):** Tolson 2, Barras 1, Himsworth 1, Pepper 1. Opponent 1. **Auto Windscreens Shield Goals (1):** Himsworth 1.
'Player of Year': Tony Barras. **Sponsors:** Portakabin.
Average Home League Attendance 1996-97: 3,361. **Capacity for 1997-98:** 9,534 (seats 3,669, standing 5,865).
Record Attendance: 28,123 v Huddersfield Town (F.A. Cup 6) 5 March 1938.

THIRD DIVISION

BARNET

Ground: Underhill Stadium, Westcombe Drive, Barnet, Herts. EN5 2BE.
Telephone: 0181-441-6932. **Clubcall:** 0891 121544. **Club Nickname:** Bees.
First-choice Colours: Black and amber shirts; black shorts; black and amber stockings.

Adams, K	1(2)	Goodhind, W	1(3)	Primus, L		46
Brady, M	1(7)	Hardyman, P	13(2)	Rattray, K		9
Brazil, G	15(4)	Harrison, L	21	Samuels, D		13(4)
Campbell, J	36(7)	Hodges, L	28(2)	Simpson, P		29(4)
Constantinou, G	1	Howarth, L	37(1)	Stockley, S		21
Codner, R	20(4)	McDonald, D	10(7)	Taylor, M		25
Devine, S	30(1)	Mills, D	–(2)	Thompson, N		1
Dunwell, R	1	Ndah, J	12(2)	Tomlinson, M	19(12)
Ford, J	13	Pardew, A	23(3)	Wilson, P.		37
Gale, S	40(3)	Patterson, G	3			

League Goals (46): Devine 11, Wilson 5, Hodges 5, Campbell 4 Ndah 4, Primus 3, Brazil 2, Gale 2, Hardyman 2, Simpson 2, Codner 1, Ford 1, Howarth 1, Samuels 1, Tomlinson 1, Opponent 1.
Coca-Cola Cup Goals (7): Simpson 2, Campbell 1, Codner 1, Devine 1, Tomlinson 1, Wilson 1. **F.A. Cup Goals (8):** Devine 4, Hodges 2, Campbell 1, Simpson 1. **Auto Windscreens Shield Goals (1):** Samuels 1.
'Player of Year': Linvoy Primus. **Sponsors:** To be confirmed.
Average Home League Attendance 1996-97: 2,145. **Capacity for 1997-98:** 4,057 (seats 1,902, standing 2,155).
Record Attendance: 11,026 v Wycombe W. (F.A. Amateur Cup 4) 1954.

BRIGHTON & HOVE ALBION

Administration office: Hanover House, 118 Queens Road, Brighton, BN1 3XG.
Telephone: 01273-778855. **Club Line:** 0891 440066. **Club Nickname:** Seagulls.
First-choice Colours: Blue and white stripes; blue shorts; white stockings.

Adekola, D	1	Baird, I	34(1)	Hobson, G		35(2)
Allan, D	31	Fox, M	–(2)	Humphrey, J		11
Andrews, P	1(6)	Fox, S	5(7)	Johnson, R		21(8)

Martin, D 1	Morris, M .... 11(1)	Reinelt, R .... 7(5)
Maskell, C 37	Mundee, D .... 27(2)	Rust, N 25
Mayo, K .... 22(2)	Neal, A 8	Smith, P .... 26(4)
McDonald, P .... 40(5)	Ormerod, M 21	Storer, S .... 37(5)
McGarrigle, K ..... 9(4)	Parris, G .... 17(1)	Tuck, S 27
Minton, J .... 22(3)	Peake, J .... 27(3)	Warren, C 3

League Goals (53): Maskell 14, Baird 13, Storer 6, McDonald 4, Mundee 4, Minto 3, Reinelt 3, Andrews 1, Hobson 1, Morris 1, Parris 1, Peake 1, Smith 1.
Coca-Cola Cup Goals: None. **F.A. Cup Goals (1)**: Maskell 1. **Auto Windscreens Shield Goals (3)**: Maskell 1, McDonald 1, Virgo 1.
'Player of Year': Stuart Storer. **Sponsors**: Sandtex.
Average Home League Attendance 1996-97: 5,845.
Record Attendance (Goldstone Ground): 36,747 v Fulham (Div. 2) 27 December 1958.

CAMBRIDGE UNITED
Ground: Abbey Stadium, Newmarket Road, Cambridge CB5 8LN.
Telephone: 01223-566500. **Clubcall**: 0891 555885. **Club Nickname**: U's.
First-choice Colours: Black and amber shirts; black shorts; black and amber stockings.

Ashbee, I .... 16(2)	Hayes, A .... 19(6)	Preece, D .... 19(6)
Barnwell, J .... 36(5)	Hyde, M 38	Raynor, P 44
Barrett, S 45	Joseph, Marc .... 5(3)	Richards, T .... 13(9)
Beall, M .... 33(3)	Joseph, Matthew ... 44	Taylor, J .... 19(2)
Benjamin, T .... 1(6)	Kyd, M .... 22(6)	Thompson, D .... 18(7)
Brazil G. 1	Marshall, S 1	Turner, R .... 2(5)
Craddock, J 41	McGleish, S 10	Vowden, C .... 5(1)
Foster, C 7	Miguel, S .... –(1)	Wanless, P .... 26(3)
Granville, D 37	Pack, L .... –(1)	Wilde, A .... –(1)
Hay, D .... –(4)	Palmer, L .... –(1)	Wilson, P 7

League Goals (53): Hyde 7, Kyd 7, McGleish 7, Barnwell 6, Raynor 4, Richards 4, Taylor 4, Wanless 3, Beall 2, Thompson 2, Ashbee 1, Benjamin 1, Brazil 1, Craddock 1, Turner 1, Opponents 2.
Coca-Cola Cup Goals (1): Thompson 1. **F.A. Cup Goals (3)**: Barnwell 1, Beall 1, Kyd 1. **Auto Windscreens Shield Goals**: None.
'Player of Year': Matthew Joseph. **Sponsors**: Premier Holidays Travel.
Average Home League Attendance 1996-97: 3,362. **Capacity for 1997-98**: 9,667 (seats 3,241, standing 6,426).
Record Attendance: 14,000 v Chelsea (Friendly) 1 May 1970.

CARDIFF CITY
Ground: Ninian Park, Sloper Road, Cardiff, South Glamorgan CF1 8SX.
Telephone: 01222-398636. **Clubcall**: 0891 121171. **Club Nickname**: Bluebirds.
First-choice Colours: Blue shirts; white shorts; blue stockings.

Baddeley, L .... 4(5)	Gardner, J .... 19(9)	Phillips, L .... 2(1)
Bennett, M .... 5(9)	Haworth, S .... 20(4)	Philliskirk, T .... 27(6)
Burton, D 5	Jarman, L .... 27(4)	Rodgerson, I .... 15(6)
Coldicott, S 6	Lloyd, K .... 27(4)	Rollo, J .... 3(7)
Dale, C .... 28(5)	McStay, P 1	Scott, A .... 1(1)
Davies, G 6	Michael, J .... –(1)	Stoker, G 17
Eckhardt, J .... 34(1)	Middleton, C .... 40(1)	Ware, P 5
Elliott, A 36	Mountain, P 5	White, S .... 32(6)
Flack, S 1	O'Halloran, K 8	Williams, S 5
Fleming, H .... 9(1)	Partridge, S .... 14(1)	Young, S 32
Fowler, J .... 37(1)	Perry, J 35	

Play-off – Appearances: Dale 2, Eckhardt 2, Fowler 2, Haworth 2, Jarman 2, Lloyd 2, Middleton 2, Perry 2, Philliskirk –(1), Rollo –(2), Stoker 2, White –(2), Williams 2, Young 2.

League Goals (56): White 13, Dale 9, Haworth 9, Eckhardt 5, Fowler 4, Middleton 4, Stoker 3, Burton 2, Davies 2, Bennett 1, Gardner 1, Lloyd 1, Philliskirk 1, Young 1. **Play-off Goals(2):** Fowler 1, Haworth 1.
Coca-Cola Cup Goals (1): Dale 1. **F.A. Cup Goals (2):** Middleton 1, White 1.
Auto Windscreens Shield Goals (3): Dale 2, Eckhardt 1.
'Player of Year': Jeff Eckhardt. **Sponsors:** South Wales Echo.
Average Home League Attendance 1996-97: 3,030. **Capacity for 1997-98:** 14,129 (seats 11,800, standing 2,329).
Record Attendance: 61,566 Wales v England 14 October 1961. **Club record:** 57,800 v Arsenal (Div. 1) 22 April 1953.

CARLISLE UNITED

Ground: Brunton Park, Warwick Road, Carlisle, Cumbria CA1 1LL.
Telephone: 01228-26237. **Clubcall:** 0891 230011. **Club Nickname:** Cumbrians.
First-choice Colours: Blue shirts; white shorts; white stockings.

Archdeacon, O 46	Freestone, C .... 3(2)	Prokas, R .... 10(3)
Aspinall, W .... 39(1)	Hayward, S 43	Reeves, D 8
Bass, J .... 3(2)	Heath, S .... –(1)	Robinson, J .... 6(1)
Caig, A 46	Hopper, T .... 13(7)	Shirtliff, P 5
Conway, P .... 22(3)	Jansen, M .... 4(15)	Smart, A .... 25(3)
Currie, D .... 5(10)	Kerr, D .... –(1)	Thorpe, J .... 2(3)
Delap, R .... 25(7)	McAlindon, G .... 3(9)	Thomas, R .... 23(12)
Dobie, S .... –(2)	Peacock, L .... 37(7)	Varty, W .... 31(1)
Edmondson, D 19	Pounewatchy, S 42	Walling, D 46

League Goals (67): Smart 11, Conway 9, Peacock 9, Hayward 8, Archdeacon 7, Aspinall 5, Delap 4, Reeves 3, Freestone 2, McAlindon 2, Walling 2, Dobie 1, Hopper 1, Jansen 1, Pouneworthy 1, Prokas 1.
Coca-Cola Cup Goals (6): Thomas 2, Archdeacon 1, Hayward 1, Aspinall 1, Reeves 1. **F.A. Cup Goals (8):** Archdeacon 2, Peacock 1, Conway 1, Edmondson 1, McAlindon 1, Opponents 2. **Auto Windscreens Shield Goals (12):** Archdeacon 4, Conway 3, Walling 2, Pounewatchy 1, McAlindon 1, Thomas 1.
'Player of Year': Owen Archdeacon. **Sponsors:** Eddie Stobart Limited.
Average Home League Attendance 1996-97: 5,440. **Capacity for 1997-98:** 16,651 (seats 7,987, standing 8,664).
Record Attendance: 27,500 v Birmingham (F.A. Cup 3) 5 January 1957; 27,500 v Middlesbrough (F.A. Cup 5) 7 January 1970.

CHESTER CITY

Ground: Deva Stadium, Bumpers Lane, Chester CH1 4LT.
Telephone: 01244-371376/371809. **Clubcall:** 0891 121633. **Club Nickname:** Blues.
First-choice Colours: Blue and white shirts; blue shorts; blue stockings.

Alsford, J 43	Jackson, P 32	Reid, S 27
Aiston, S 14	Jenkins, I 39	Richardson, N 9
Brown, G .... –(1)	Jones, J .... 3(14)	Rimmer, S .... 22(4)
Brown, W 2	Knowles, C 2	Rodgers, D .... 4(1)
Cutler, N 5	McDonald, R 22	Shelton, G .... 18(4)
Davidson, R 40	Milner, A .... 38(8)	Sinclair, R 37
Fisher, N .... 19(11)	Murphy, J .... 4(7)	Tallon, G 1
Flitcroft, D .... 30(2)	Noteman, K .... 30(5)	Whelan, S .... 18(7)
Helliwell, I .... 8(1)	Priest, C .... 30(2)	Woods, M .... 9(12)

Play-offs – Appearances: Aiston 2, Alsford 2, Davidson 2, Flitcroft 2, Jenkins 2, Jones –(1), McDonald 2, Milner 2, Priest 2, Reid 2, Rimmer –(1), Sinclair 2, Whelan 1, Woods 1(1).
League Goals (55): Milner 12, Noteman 9, Flitcroft 6, McDonald 6, Rimmer 4, Davidson 2, Alsford 2, Priest 2, Shelton 2, Fisher 1, Helliwell 1, Jackson 1, Jones 1, Murphy 1, Reid 1, Whelan 1, Woods 1, Opponents 2. **Play-off Goals:** None.
Coca-Cola Cup Goals (1): Noteman 1. **F.A. Cup Goals (4):** Milner 2, Rimmer 2.
Auto Windscreens Shield Goals (1): McDonald 1.

'Player of Year': Ronnie Sinclair. **Sponsors**: Saunders Honda.
Average Home League Attendance 1996-97: 2,262. **Capacity for 1997-98**: 5,734 (seats 3,094, standing 2,640).
Record Attendance (Deva Stadium): 5,368 v Preston (Div. 3) April 2, 1994.
Previous ground, Sealand Road: 20,500 v Chelsea (F.A. Cup 3) 16 January 1952.

COLCHESTER UNITED

Ground: Layer Road, Colchester, Essex CO2 7JJ.
Telephone: 01206-508800. **Clubcall**: 0891 737300. **Club Nickname**: U's.
First-choice Colours: Blue and white shirts; blue shorts; white stockings.

Abrahams, P .... 27(2)	Forbes, S 1	McCarthy, T .... 34(1)
Adcock, T .... 26(10)	Fry, C .... 31(11)	Pitcher, G .... –(1)
Barnes, O 11	Gibbs, P .... 18(2)	Reinelt, R .... 8(13)
Betts, S 10	Greene, D 44	Sale, M 10
Buckle, P 24	Gregory, D .... 32(6)	Stamps, S .... 7(1)
Caldwell, G 6	Haydon, N .... –(1)	Taylor, J 8
Cawley, P 28	Kelly, A .... 2(1)	Vaughan, J 5
Duguid, K .... 10(10)	Kinsella, M 7	Whitton, S .... 36(3)
Dunne, J .... 23(12)	Lock, A .... 1(5)	Wilkins, R 40
Emberson, C 35	Locke, A .... 22(10)	

League Goals (62): Adcock 11, Abrahams 7, Whitton 6, Fry 5, Taylor 5, Locke 4, Reinelt 4, Duguid 3, Sale 3, Kinsella 2, Wilkins 2, Betts 1, Cawley 1, Forbes 1, Greene 1, Gregory 1, Haydon 1, Lock 1, Opponents 3.
Coca-Cola Cup Goals (5): Reinelt 2, Adcock 1, Dunne 1, Fry 1. **F.A. Cup Goals (1)**: Wilkins 1. **Auto Windscreens Shield Goals (9)**: Buckle 3, Abrahams 2, Adcock 2, Fry 1, Greene 1.
'Player of Year': Chris Fry. **Sponsors**: Home – Guardian Direct; Away – Ashbys.
Average Home League Attendance 1996-97: 3,251. **Capacity for 1997-98**: 7,650 (seats 1,960, standing 5,690).
Record Attendance: 19,072 v Reading (F.A. Cup 1) 27 November 1948.

DARLINGTON

Ground: Feethams, Darlington, County Durham DL1 5JB.
Telephone: 01325-465097. **Clubcall**: 0891 101555. **Club Nickname**: Quakers.
First-choice Colours: White shirts; white shorts; black and white stockings.

Atkinson, B .... 25(5)	Faulkner, D .... 2(2)	Moilanen, T 16
Atkinson, J .... 2(3)	Gregan, S 16	Naylor, G .... 27(9)
Barbara, D .... 1(5)	Hope, R 20	Newell, P 20
Barnard, M .... 35(2)	Hunt, D .... –(1)	Oliver, M .... 34(5)
Blake, R .... 29(2)	Innes, C .... 1(14)	Painter, R .... 2(4)
Brumwell, P .... 31(7)	Kelly, R .... 13(9)	Reed, A 14
Brydon, L .... 18(7)	Key, D .... –(3)	Roberts, D .... 42(2)
Byrne, W .... 1(1)	Laws, B 10	Robinson, P .... –(3)
Carss, A .... 20(9)	Lowe, K .... 5(2)	Shaw, S .... 35(4)
Crosby, A 43	Lucas, D 7	Shutt, C 3
Devos, J .... 7(1)	McClelland, J 1	Twynham, G .... 21(8)

League Goals (64): Roberts 16, Blake 10, Naylor 10, Oliver 8, B Atkinson 4, Shaw 3, Twynham 3, Kelly 2, Shutt 2, Barbara 1, Brumwell 1, Crosby 1, Opponents 2.
Coca-Cola Cup Goals (4): Roberts 2, Blake 1, Painter 1. **F.A. Cup Goals (4)**: Brumwell 1, Crosby 1, Naylor 1, Shaw 1. **Auto Windscreens Shield Goals (1)**: Barbara 1.
'Player of Year': Andy Crosby. **Sponsors**: Chaddington Property and Darlington Building Society.
Average Home League Attendance 1996-97: 2,651. **Capacity for 1997-98**: 4,875 (seats 656, standing 4,219).
Record Attendance: 21,023 v Bolton Wanderers (League Cup 3) 14 November 1960.

DONCASTER ROVERS

Ground: Belle Vue, Doncaster, South Yorkshire DN4 5HT.
Telephone: 01302-539441. **Clubcall**: 0891 664428. **Club Nickname**: Rovers.
First-choice Colours: Red shirts; red shorts; red and white stockings.

Anderson, L 6	Fahy, A .... –(5)	Omandjianian, D .... –(1)
Beirne, M 1	Gore, I .... 35(1)	Pemberton, M 9
Birch, P .... 26(1)	Gray, A 1	Piearce, S .... 8(11)
Bullimore, W 4	Ireland, S 27	Robertson, P .... 3(1)
Clark, I .... 8(12)	Larmour D .... 3(17)	Ryan, T .... 22(6)
Coady, L 1	Lester, J .... 5(6)	Schofield, J 42
Colcombe, S .... 9(3)	McDonald, M 33	Smith, M .... 12(6)
Cramb, C .... 40(1)	Marquis, P 3	Utley, D .... 19(4)
Cunningham, D 11	Messer, G .... –(1)	Walker, S 1
Dixon, K .... 13(3)	Mike, A 5	Warren, L .... 21(4)
Doling, S .... 3(2)	Moore, D 41	Weaver, S 2
Donnelly, M .... –(2)	Murphy, J .... 30(1)	Wheeler, A 1
Esdaille, D .... 16(2)	O'Connor, G 18	Williams, D 27

League Goals (52): Cramb, 18, Schofield 7, Moore 5, Dixon 3, Birch 2, Clark 2,
Ireland 2, McDonald 2, Smith 2, Colcombe 1, Esdaille 1, Gore 1, Lester 1, Mike 1,
Pemberton 1, Piearce 1, Utley 1, Opponent 1.
Coca-Cola Cup Goals (1): Cramb 1. **F.A. Cup Goals (1)**: Cramb 1. **Auto
Windscreens Shield Goals (1)**: Cramb 1.
'Player of Year': Darren Moore. **Sponsors**:
Average Home League Attendance 1996-97: 2,087. **Capacity for 1997-98**:
8,608 (seats 1,259, standing 7,349).
Record Attendance: 37,149 v Hull City (Div. 3N) 2 October 1948.

EXETER CITY

Ground: St. James' Park, Wells Street, Exeter, Devon EX4 6PX.
Telephone: 01392-254073. **Clubcall**: 0891 446868. **Club Nickname**: Grecians.
First-choice Colours: Red and white shirts; black shorts; red stockings.

Baddeley, L .... 8(3)	Fox, P 5	Myers, C .... 31(2)
Bailey, D .... 32(3)	Gayle, B 10	Pears, R .... 6(2)
Bayes, A 41	Ghazghazi, S .... 1(5)	Rees, J 7
Birch, P .... 1(1)	Hare, M .... 16(9)	Rice, G .... 9(5)
Blake, N 46	Hodges, L .... 16(1)	Richardson, J ...... 43(1)
Braithwaite, L .... 26(12)	Hughes, D .... 33(3)	Richardson, N 14
Chamberlain, M .. 22(4)	McConnell, B ..... 20(14)	Rowbotham, D 25
Crowe, G 10	McKeown, G 3	Sharpe, J .... 19(2)
Dailly, M .... 8(9)	Medlin, N .... 7(4)	Steele, T .... 14(14)
Flack, S .... 20(7)	Minett, J 13	

League Goals (48): Rowbotham 10, Blake 6, Braithwaite 5, Crowe 5, Flack 4,
Chamberlain 3, Steele 3, Bailey 2, Myers 2, Hare 1, Hughes 1, Medlin 1, Pears 1,
J Richardson 1, Sharpe 1, Opponents 2.
Coca-Cola Cup Goals: None. **F.A. Cup Goals (3)**: Flack 1, Rowbotham 1,
Sharpe 1. **Auto Windscreens Shield Goals (1)**: Rowbotham 1.
'Player of Year': Darren Rowbotham. **Sponsors**: Concept Incorporated.
Average Home League Attendance 1996-97: 3,014. **Capacity for 1997-98**:
10,570 (seats 1,664, standing 8,906).
Record Attendance: 20,984 v Sunderland (F.A. Cup 6) 4 March 1931.

FULHAM

Ground: Craven Cottage, Stevenage Road, London SW6 6HH.
Telephone: 0171-736-6561. **Club Line**: 0891 440044. **Club Nickname**: Cottag-
ers. **First-choice Colours**: White shirts; black shorts; white stockings.

Adams, M .... 2(1)	Blake, M .... 40(1)	Carpenter, R 34
Angus, T .... 28(4)	Brooker, P 26	Cockerill; G .... 27(5)

Conroy, M .... 40(3)	Lange, T 18	Scott, R .... 36(7)
Cullip, D .... 23(6)	Lawrence, M .... 13(2)	Soloman, J .... 1(3)
Cusack, N .... 44(1)	McAree, R .... 5(4)	Stewart, S .... 2(1)
Davis, S .... –(1)	Mison, M .... 1(3)	Thomas, M .... 6(19)
Freeman, D .... 38(7)	Morgan, S 44	Walton, M 28
Hartfield, C .... 1(1)	Parker, P 3	Warren, C .... 8(1)
Herrera, M 26		

League Goals (72): Conroy 21, Freeman 9, Scott 9, Morgan 8, Blake 7, Carpenter 5, Watson 3, Brooker 2, Cusack 2, Angus 1, Cockerill 1, Cullip 1, McAree 1, Warren 1, Opponent 1.
Coca-Cola Cup Goals (6): Brooker 2, Conroy 2, Morgan 1, Watson 1. **F.A. Cup Goals:** None. **Auto Windscreens Shield Goals (2):** Cusack 1, Scott 1.
'Player of Year': Mike Conroy. **Sponsors:** GMB.
Average Home League Attendance 1996-97: 6,673. **Capacity for 1997-98:** 14,969 (seats 5,119, standing 9,850).
Record Attendance: 49,335 v Millwall (Div. 2) 8 October 1938.

HARTLEPOOL UNITED
Ground: Victoria Park, Clarence Road, Hartlepool, Cleveland TS24 8BZ.
Telephone: 01429-222077. **Clubcall:** – **Club Nickname:** Pools.
First-choice Colours: White and blue shirts; blue shorts; blue stockings.

Allon, J .... 27(2)	Halliday, S .... 28(3)	McAuley, S 38
Baker, P 6	Hislop, K .... 22(3)	McDonald, C 9
Baron, M 16	Homer, C .... –(1)	McGuckin, I .... 21(1)
Beech, C 42	Horace, A .... –(1)	Mike, A 7
Bradley, R 12	Houchen, K .... 3(3)	O'Connor, P 30
Brown, S 6	Howard, S .... 26(6)	Pears, S 16
Clegg, D .... 24(9)	Ingram, D .... 34(3)	Proctor, M 6
Cooper, M 33	Irvine, S .... 2(2)	Sunderland, J .... 6(7)
Cullen, J .... 5(1)	Knowles, D 7	Tait, M .... 16(3)
Davies, G .... 30(2)	Lee, G .... 23(1)	Walton, P .... 2(2)
Elliot, A .... 2(2)	Lucas, R 7	Winstanley, C .... –(1)

League Goals (53): Allon 10, Beech 9, Cooper 3, Halliday 3, Howard 6, Baker 2, Clegg 1, Bradley 1, Brown 1, Davies 1, Ingram 1, Irvine 1, Mike 1, McAuley 1, Sunderland 1.
Coca-Cola Cup Goals (4): Allon 2, Beech 1, Davies 1. **F.A. Cup Goals:** None.
Auto Windscreens Shield Goals: None.
'Player of Year': Chris Beech. **Sponsors:** Camerons.
Average Home League Attendance 1996-97: 2,085. **Capacity for 1997-98:** 7,229 (seats 3,966, standing 3,263).
Record Attendance: 17,426 v Manchester United (F.A. Cup 3) 5 January 1957.

HEREFORD UNITED
Ground: Edgar Street, Hereford HR4 9JU.
Telephone: 01432-276666. **Clubcall:** 0891 121645. **Club Nickname:** Bulls.
First-choice Colours: Black shirts; white shorts; black stockings.

Agana, P .... 3(2)	Foster, I .... 4(15)	Pitman, J .... 4(4)
Bartlett, N .... –(3)	Hargreaves, C ...... 42(2)	Preedy, P .... 2(7)
Beeston, C 9	Hibbard, M .... 5(2)	Sandeman, B 7
Brough, J 32	Jordan, R 1	Smith, D 7
Cook, G .... 17(3)	Kottila, M .... 11(2)	Stoker, G .... 20(2)
Cross, N 5	Law, N 14	Sutton, W 4
Debont, A 27	McGorry, B 7	Townsend, Q .... 6(1)
Downing, K 16	Mahon, G .... 10(1)	Turner, G 6
Ellison, A .... –(1)	Matthewson, T 35	Warner, R .... 16(5)
Fishlock, M .... 29(1)	Norton, D 45	Williams, J .... 8(3)
Forsyth, M 12	O'Toole, G 1	Wood, T 19
Foster, A .... 42(1)		

League Goals (50): A Foster 16, Smith 9, Hargreaves 3, Stoker 3, Williams 3, Agana 2, Beeston 2, Matthewson 2, Preedy 2, Brough 1, Cross 1, Fishlock 1, Hibbard 1, Kottila 1, Mahon 1, McGorry 1, Norton 1.
Coca-Cola Cup Goals (4): Smith 2, A. Foster 1, Norton 1. **F.A. Cup Goals**: None. **Auto Windscreens Shield Goals**: None.
'Player of Year': Dean Smith. **Sponsors**: Sun Valley Poultry.
Average Home League Attendance 1996-97: 2,931. **Capacity for 1997-98**: 8,843 (seats 2,761, standing 6,082).
Record Attendance: 18,114 v Sheffield Wednesday (F.A. Cup 3) 4 January 1958.

HULL CITY

Ground: Boothferry Park, Boothferry Road, Hull, North Humberside HU4 6EU.
Telephone: 01482-351119. **Clubcall**: – Club Nickname: Tigers.
First-choice Colours: Amber shirts; black shorts; amber and black stockings.

Allison, N 11	Fewings, P .... 3(9)	Peacock, R .... 34(6)
Brien, T .... 28(3)	Gilbert, K .... 15(4)	Quigley, M .... 23(6)
Brown, A .... 7(19)	Gordon, G .... 19(1)	Rioch, G .... 38(1)
Carroll, R 23	Greaves, M .... 23(7)	Sansam, C .... 2(1)
Darby, D .... 40(1)	Joyce, W 45	Sharman, S .... 2(2)
Davison, A 9	Lowthorpe, A ...... 13(1)	Trevitt, S .... 21(1)
Dewhurst, R ...... 20(2)	Mann, N .... 24(8)	Turner, R 5
Dickinson, A .... –(1)	Marks, J .... 7(3)	Wharton, P .... –(1)
Doncel, A .... 22(4)	Mason, A .... 4(2)	Wilson, S .... 14(1)
Ellington, L .... –(2)	Maxfield, S .... 10(7)	Wright, I 41
Elliott, S 3		

League Goals (44): Darby 13, Joyce 5, Gordon 4, Peacock 4, Mason 3, Mann 2, Greaves 2, Doncel 2, Turner 2, Brien 1, Brown 1, Gilbert 1, Longthorpe 1, Quigley 1, Rioch 1, Trevitt 1.
Coca-Cola Cup Goals (4): Rioch 2, Quigley 1, Gordon 1. **F.A. Cup Goals (9)**: Darby 6, Peacock 1, Mann 1, Joyce 1. **Auto Windscreens Shield Goals (3)**: Darby 1, Joyce 1, Wright 1.
'Player of Year': Duane Darby. **Sponsors**: University of Hull.
Average Home League Attendance 1996-97: 3,412. **Capacity for 1997-98**: 12,996 (seats 5,495, standing 7,501).
Record Attendance: 55,019 v Manchester United (F.A. Cup 6) 26 February 1949.

LEYTON ORIENT

Ground: Leyton Stadium, Brisbane Road, Leyton, London E10 5NE.
Telephone: 0181-539-2233. **Clubcall**: 0891 121150. **Club Nickname**: O's.
First-choice Colours: Red and white shirts; black shorts; red stockings.

Ansah, A .... –(2)	Heidenstrom, B ...... 3(1)	Morrison, D 8
Arnott, A .... 28(3)	Hendon, I 28	Naylor, D 44
Atkin, P 5	Hodges, L 3	Riches, S .... 2(3)
Ayorinde, S .... 6(6)	Howes, S .... 3(2)	Sealey, L 12
Baker, J .... 15(5)	Hyde, P 13	Shearer, L .... 7(1)
Caldwell, P 3	Inglethorpe, A .... 10(6)	Shilton, P 9
Castle, S 4	Joseph, R 15	Timmons, C 6
Channing, J 40	Kelly, A .... 6(3)	Warren, M .... 25(2)
Chapman, D .... 31(9)	Ling, M .... 39(5)	Weaver, L 9
Clapham, J 6	McCarthy, A .... 3(1)	West, C .... 22(1)
Fortune-West, L .... 1(4)	McGleish, S 28	Whyte, C 1
Garland, P .... 13(8)	Martin, A .... 16(1)	Wilkins, R 3
Griffiths, C 13	Martin, D 8	Winston, S .... 3(8)
Hanson, D .... 15(10)		

League Goals (50): Inglethorpe 8, McGleish 7, Channing 5, Griffiths 5, Arnott 3, Hanson 3, Naylor 3, West 3, Ayorinde 2, Chapman 2, Ling 2, Timmons 2, Castle 1, Hendon 1, Kelly 1, Warren 1, Winston 1.
Coca-Cola Cup Goals (1): Kelly. **F.A. Cup Goals (3)**: Channing 1, West 1, Winston 1. **Auto Windscreens Shield Goals (1)**: Ling 1.

'**Player of Year**': Mark Warren. **Sponsors**: Acclaim Entertainments.
Average Home League Attendance 1996-97: 4,315. **Capacity for 1997-98**:
12,573 (seats 7,145, standing 5,428).
Record Attendance: 34,345 v West Ham United (F.A. Cup 4) 25 January 1964.

LINCOLN CITY

Ground: Sincil Bank, Lincoln LN5 8LD.
Telephone: 01522-880011. **Clubcall**: 0891 664666. **Club Nickname**: Imps.
First-choice Colours: Red and white shirts; white shorts; white stockings.

Ainsworth, G 46	Cort, C .... 5(1)	Richardson, B 36
Alcide, C .... 38(4)	Dennis, J .... 23(5)	Robertson, J .... 15(1)
Austin, K 44	Fleming, T 37	Stant, P 22
Barnett, J .... 33(2)	Foron, M .... 1(1)	Sterling, W .... 15(6)
Bimson, S .... 13(2)	Holmes, S .... 27(1)	Stones, C .... –(2)
Bos, G .... 18(5)	Hone, M .... 26(3)	Taylor, J 5
Brown, G 34	Martin, J .... 29(5)	Vaughan, J 10
Brown, S .... 9(6)	Minett, J .... 2(2)	Whitney, J 18

League Goals (70): Ainsworth 22, Stant 16, Alcide 8, Holmes 4, Martin 4,
Whitney 3, Brown S 2, Dennis 2, Taylor 2, Bos 1, Brown G 1, Cort 1, Robertson 1,
Opponents 3.
Coca-Cola Cup Goals (13): Bos 3, Ainsworth 2, Alcide 2, Holmes 2, Fleming 1,
Hone 1, Martin 1, Whitney 1. **F.A. Cup Goals (1)**: Bos 1. **Auto Windscreens
Shield Goals**: None.
'**Player of Year**': Gareth Ainsworth. **Sponsors**: Lincolnshire Echo.
Average Home League Attendance 1996-97: 3,163. **Capacity for 1997-98**:
10,918 (seats 9,251, standing 1,667).
Record Attendance: 23,196 v Derby County (League Cup 4) 15 November 1967.

MANSFIELD TOWN

Ground: Field Mill, Quarry Lane, Mansfield, Notts. NG18 5DA.
Telephone: 01623-23567. **Clubcall**: 0891 121311. **Club Nickname**: Stags.
First-choice Colours: Amber and blue shirts; amber and blue shorts; blue
stockings.

Bowling, I 46	Harper, S .... 37(6)	Sale, M .... 12(6)
Christie, I 8	Hassell, R .... –(1)	Sedgemore, B ...... 37(3)
Clarke, D .... 17(14)	Helliwell, I .... 4(3)	Sherlock, P .... 14(10)
Clifford, M .... 3(4)	Holbrook, L .... –(1)	Walker, J .... 32(4)
Cresswell, I 5	Hurst, I .... 5(1)	Watkiss, S .... 30(6)
Doolan, J 41	Ireland, S .... 5(1)	Weaver, N .... –(1)
Eustace, S .... 42(1)	Kerr, D 9	Williams, L .... 7(10)
Ford, T .... 25(3)	Kilcline, B .... 30(2)	Williams, R .... –(5)
Hackett, W .... 35(3)	Martindale, G 5	Wood, S .... 23(13)
Hadley, S .... 31(3)	Robinson, I .... 3(8)	Young, C .... –(2)

League Goals (47): Doolan 6, Sale 5, Eustace 4, Hadley 4, Sedgemore 4,
Kilcline 3, Walker 3, Wood 3, Clarke 2, Ford 2, Harper 2, Martindale 2, Cresswell
1, Hackett 1, Helliwell 1, Watkiss 1, Opponents 3.
Coca-Cola Cup Goals: None. **F.A. Cup Goals (4)**: Doolan 1, Eustace 1, Ford 1,
Wood 1. **Auto Windscreens Shield Goals**: None.
'**Player of Year**': Ian Bowling. **Sponsors**: Mansfield Brewery.
Average Home League Attendance 1996-97: 2,282. **Capacity for 1997-98**:
6,722 (seats 2,695, standing 4,027).
Record Attendance: 24,567 v Nottingham Forest (F.A. Cup 3) 10 January 1953.

NORTHAMPTON TOWN

Ground: Sixfields Stadium, Upton Way, Northampton NN5 5QA.
Telephone: 01604-757773. **Clubcall**: 0839 664477. **Club Nickname**: Cobblers.
First-choice Colours: Claret shirts; white shorts; claret stockings.

Burns, C 6	Lee, C .... 12(17)	Sampson, I 43
Clarkson, I 45	Lyne, N 1	Smart, A 1
Colkin, L .... 1(5)	Maddison, L 34	Stant, P .... 4(1)
Cooper, M .... 37(4)	Martin, D .... 10(2)	Thompson, G .... –(1)
Frain, J 13	O'Shea, D .... 29(6)	Turley, B 1
Gayle, J .... 9(4)	Parrish, S .... 37(2)	Warburton, R 35
Gibb, A .... 6(12)	Peer, D .... 7(14)	Warner, M .... 1(8)
Grayson, N .... 32(8)	Rennie, D .... 42(1)	White, J .... 15(17)
Hunter, R .... 26(10)	Rush, M 14	Woodman, A 45
Kirby, R .... –(1)		

Play-offs – Appearances: Clarkson 3, Cooper 1, Frain 3, Gayle 3, Gibb –(1), Grayson 3, Hunter 3, Lee 1(2), Parrish 3, Peer –(3), Rennie 3, Sampson 3, Warburton 3, White 1(1), Woodman 3.
League Goals (67): Grayson 12, Cooper 10, Parrish 8, Lee 7, Hunter 6, Sampson 5, Warburton 4, Rennie 3, Rush 3, Stant 2, White 2, Gayle 1, Gibb 1, Peer 1, Opponents 2. **Play-off Goals (5)**: Frain 1, Gayle 1, Parrish 1, Sampson 1, Warburton 1.
Coca-Cola Cup Goals (3): Lee 2, Opponent 1. **F.A. Cup Goals**: None. **Auto Windscreens Shield Goals (3)**: Martin 2, Gayle 1.
'Player of Year': Ian Clarkson. **Sponsors**: Elite Business Systems.
Average Home League Attendance 1996-97: 4,822. **Capacity for 1997-98**: 7,653 (all-seated).
Record Attendance (Sixfields Stadium): 7,478 v Arsenal (Friendly), 13 August 1996. Previous (County Ground): 24,523 v Fulham (Div. 1) 23 April 1966.

ROCHDALE

Ground: Spotland, Sandy Lane, Rochdale, Lancashire OL11 5DS.
Telephone: 01706-44648. **Clubcall**: 0891 555858. **Club Nickname**: Dale.
First-choice Colours: Blue shirts; white shorts; blue stockings.

Bailey, M .... 13(2)	Formby, K .... 12(4)	Painter, P .... 21(6)
Bayliss, D .... 22(2)	Gouck, A .... 22(6)	Robson, G .... –(3)
Brown, M 5	Gray, I 46	Russell, A .... 35(4)
Cecere, M .... 2(2)	Hill, K 43	Stuart, M .... 28(3)
Deary, J .... 37(1)	Johnson, A 46	Taylor, J .... –(1)
Dowell, W .... 6(1)	Lancaster, D .... 1(5)	Thackeray, A 17
Farrell, A .... 37(3)	Leonard, M 39	Thompson, D .... 9(19)
Fensome, A .... 38(2)	Martin, D .... –(1)	Whitehall, S .... 27(8)

League Goals (58): Russell 9, Whitehall 9, Painter 7, Stuart 7, Deary 5, Johnson 4, Leonard 4, Gouck 3, Hill 3, Farrell 2, Cecere 1, Formby 1, Thomson 1, Opponents 2.
Coca-Cola Cup Goals (2): Deary 1, Whitehall 1. **F.A. Cup Goals (3)**: Deary 1, Johnson 1, Thackeray 1. **Auto Windscreens Shield Goals**: None.
'Player of Year': Alan Johnson. **Sponsors**: Carcraft.
Average Home League Attendance 1996-97: 1,827. **Capacity for 1997-98**: 9,032 (seats 4,638, standing 4,394).
Record Attendance: 24,231 v Notts County (F.A. Cup 2) 10 December 1949.

SCARBOROUGH

Ground: McCain Stadium, Seamer Road, Scarborough, North Yorkshire YO12 4HF.
Telephone: 01723-375094. **Clubcall**: None. **Club Nickname**: Boro.
First-choice Colours: White shirts; white shorts; white stockings.

Bennett, G 46	Daws, A .... 4(2)	Lucas, R .... 19(9)
Bennett, T .... 4(1)	Hanby, R .... 1(3)	McElhatton, M .... 26(2)
Bochenski, S .... 5(14)	Hicks, S .... 36(2)	Martin, K 3
Brodie, S .... 23(1)	Ironside, I 39	Midgley, C 6
Brooke, A .... 28(6)	Kay, J 34	Mitchell, J .... 23(20)
Currie, D 16	Knowles, D .... 12(5)	Moilanen, T 4

368

Mowbray, D .... 2(1) Russell, M .... 1(4) Wells, M .... 22(8)
Rigby, A 5   Sunderland, J .... –(2)   Williams, A 1
Ritchie, A .... 26(5) Sutherland, J .... 17(4) Williams, G 45
Rockett, J 40   Thompstone, I ...... 12(7) Worrall, B .... 6(9)

League Goals (65): Bennett 10, Williams 10, Ritchie 9, Mitchell 8, Currie 6, Brodie 5, Rockett 5, Brooke 2, Midgley 2, Thompstone 2, Bochenski 1, Hicks 1, McElhatton 1, Rigby 1, Wells 1, Worrall 1.
Coca-Cola Cup Goals (6): Bennett 2, Ritchie 2, Daws 1, Williams 1. **F.A. Cup Goals (2):** Kay 1, Ritchie 1. **Auto Windscreens Shield Goals:** None.
'Player of Year': Jason Rockett. **Sponsors:** ERREA.
Average Home League Attendance 1996-97: 2,455. **Capacity for 1997-98:** 6,000 (seats 3,496, standing 2,504).
Record Attendance: 9,000 v Luton Town (F.A. Cup 3) 8 January 1938.

SCUNTHORPE UNITED
Ground: Glanford Park, Doncaster Road, Scunthorpe, South Humberside DN15 8TD.
Telephone: 01724-848077. **Clubcall:** 0891 121652. **Club Nickname:** Iron.
First-choice Colours: Sky blue and claret shirts; blue shorts; blue stockings.

Baker, D 21   Francis, J .... 1(6) McFarlane, A .... 7(11)
Borland, J .... –(12) Gavin, M .... 10(4)   Moss, D 4
Bradley, R 22   Hope, C 46   Paterson, J .... 10(18)
Calvo-Garcia, A ... 8(18) Housham, S .... 30(5)   Samways, M 25
Clarke, T 15   Jackson, K .... –(17)   Sertori, M .... 42(1)
Clarkson, P 28   Jones, G .... 9(2)   Turnbull, L .... 11(13)
D'Auria, D 39   Knill, A 30   Walker, J .... 8(1)
Dunn, I 3   Laws, B .... 2(5)   Walsh, M .... 32(7)
Eyre, J .... 41(1) Lucas, D 6   Wilson, P A 37
Forrester, J 10   McAuley, S 9   Wilson, P D .... –(2)

League Goals (59): Clarkson 13, Baker 9, Eyre 8, Forrester 6, Jones 5, Hope 5, McFarlane 3, Housham 3, Bradley 1, Garcia 1, Jackson 1, P A Wilson 1, Opponents 3.
Coca-Cola Cup Goals (2): Clarkson 1, Moss 1. **F.A. Cup Goals (8):** Baker 5, Clarkson 2, D'Auria 1. **Auto Windscreens Shield Goals (2):** Hope 2.
'Player of Year': John Eyre. **Sponsors:** Pleasure Island.
Average Home League Attendance 1996-97: 2,607. **Capacity for 1997-98:** 9,183 (seats 6,410, standing 2,773).
Record Attendance Glanford Park: 8,775 v Rotherham (Div. 4) 1 May 1989. At previous ground (Old Show Ground): 23,935 v Portsmouth (F.A. Cup 4) 30 January 1954.

SWANSEA CITY
Ground: Vetch Field, Swansea, West Glamorgan SA1 3SU.
Telephone: 01792-474114. **Clubcall:** 0891 121639. **Club Nickname:** Swans.
First-choice Colours: White shirts; white shorts; white stockings.

Ampadu, K .... 25(4) Garnett, S 6   Molby, J .... 26(2)
Appleby, R .... 8(3) Heggs, C .... 5(9)   Moreira, J 10
Brayson, P 11   Hills, J 11   O'Leary, K .... 9(3)
Brown, L .... 13(8) Jenkins, S .... 21(2)   Penney, D 44
Casey, R .... 3(6) Jones, L 1   Phillips, G .... –(1)
Chapple, S .... 10(7) Jones, S 46   Price, J .... 1(1)
Clode, M .... 16(2) King, R 2   Thomas, D .... 31(5)
Coates, J .... 38(2) Lacey, D .... 9(2)   Torpey, S .... 37(2)
Edwards, C 36   McDonald, C .... 3(7)   Walker, K 31
Freestone, R 45   McGibbon, P 1   Willer, T 7

Play-offs – Appearances: Ampadu 3, Appleby 1, Brown –(1), Coates 3, Edwards 3, Freestone 3, Heggs 2(1), S. Jones 2, Molby 1, Moreira 3, Penney 3, Thomas 3, Torpey 3, Walker 3.

League Goals (62): Penney 13, Torpey 9, Thomas 9, Molby 6, Brayson 5, Ampadu 4, Brown 3, Coates 3, Heggs 2, Jenkins 2, Appleby 1, Clode 1, S. Jones 1, O'Leary 1, Walker 1, Opponent 1. **Play-off Goals**: Heggs 1, Thomas 1, Torpey 1.
Coca-Cola Cup Goals: None. **F.A. Cup Goals (1)**: Torpey 1. **Auto Windscreens Shield Goals (1)**: Thomas 1.
'Player of Year': Steve Jones. **Sponsors**: South Wales Evening Post.
Average Home League Attendance 1996-97: 3,850. **Capacity for 1997-98**: 11,477 (seats 3,635, standing 7,842).
Record Attendance: 32,796 v Arsenal (F.A. Cup 4) 17 February 1968.

TORQUAY UNITED

Ground: Plainmoor, Torquay, Devon TQ1 3PS.
Telephone: 01803-328666. **Clubcall**: 0891 664565. **Club Nickname**: Gulls.
First-choice Colours: Yellow and navy shirts; navy shorts; yellow and navy stockings.

Adcock, P .... –(1)	Hawthorne, M ...... 25(9)	Newland, R 11
Baker, P .... 10(1)	Hinshelwood, D ...... 7(1)	Oatway, A .... 39(2)
Barrow, L .... 45(1)	Hockley, W .... –(2)	Preston, M .... –(2)
Bedeau, A .... 3(4)	Hodges, K .... –(1)	Stamps, S .... 30(1)
Chandler, D 4	Howell, J .... 2(2)	Thirlby, A .... 1(11)
Crane, S .... –(3)	Jack, R .... 30(3)	Thomas, W .... 1(10)
Gittens, J 33	Laight, E .... 6(4)	Tucker, L .... –(1)
Gregg, M 1	McCall, S .... 23(1)	Watson, A 46
Gregory, A 5	McFarlane, A 19	Wilmot, R 34
Hancox, R .... 6(5)	Mitchell, P .... 22(2)	Winter, S .... 36(1)
Hapgood, L .... –(1)	Ndah, J .... 9(2)	Wright, M .... 7(2)
Hathaway, I .... 21(14)	Nelson, G .... 30(4)	

League Goals (46): Jack 10, Nelson 8, Winter 6, Baker 4, Gittens 3, McFarlane 3, Stamps 3, Hawthorne 2, Bedeau 1, Hathaway 1, Laight 1, McCall 1, Ndah 1, Oatway 1, Watson 1.
Coca-Cola Cup Goals (3): Baker 3. **F.A. Cup Goals**: None. **Auto Windscreens Shield Goals (1)**: Watson 1.
'Player of Year': Alex Watson. **Sponsors**:
Average Home League Attendance 1996-97: 2,288 **Capacity for 1997-98**: 6,000 (seats 2,300, standing 3,700).
Record Attendance: 21,908 v Huddersfield Town (F.A. Cup 4) 29 January 1955.

WIGAN ATHLETIC

Ground: Springfield Park, Wigan, Lancashire WN6 7BA.
Telephone: 01942-244433. **Clubcall**: 0891 121655. **Club Nickname**: Latics.
First-choice Colours: Blue and white shirts; blue and green shorts; blue and white stockings.

Biggins, W .... 20(13)	Jones, G .... 39(1)	Pender, J .... 27(2)
ishop, C .... 20(1)	Kilford, I .... 24(11)	Rogers, P .... 18(2)
Butler, J .... 20(4)	Kirby, R .... 5(1)	Saville, A .... 17(3)
Butler, L 46	Lancashire, G ...... 15(9)	Seba, J .... –(1)
Carragher, M .... 12(6)	Lowe, D .... 31(11)	Sharp, K .... 30(5)
Diaz, I .... 26(13)	McGibbon, P 10	Ward, M 5
Greenall, C 46	Martinez, R .... 38(5)	Whittaker, S .... 2(1)
Johnson, G 37	Morgan, S .... 18(5)	

League Goals (84): Jones 31, Lancashire 9, Kilford 8, Diaz 6, Lowe 6, Martinez 4, Saville 4, Biggins 3, Rogers 3, Johnson 3, Greenall 2, Sharp 2, McGibbon 1, Morgan 1, Opponent 1.
Coca-Cola Cup Goals (6): Lancashire 4, Jones 1, Greenall 1. **F.A. Cup Goals**: None. **Auto Windscreens Shield Goals (2)**: Jones 1, Martinez 1.
'Player of Year': Graeme Jones. **Sponsors**: JJB Sports.
Average Home League Attendance 1996-97: 3,899. **Capacity for 1997-98**: 7,466 (seats 1,128, standing 6,338).
Record Attendance: 27,500 v Hereford United (F.A. Cup 2) 12 December 1953.

SCOTTISH LEAGUE ROLL CALL
APPEARANCES & SCORERS 1996-97
(Figures in brackets = appearances as substitute)

PREMIER DIVISION

ABERDEEN

Ground: Pittodrie Stadium, Aberdeen. **Capacity:** 21,634 (all-seated).
Telephone: 01224-650400. **Colours:** Red and white. **Nickname:** Dons.

Anderson, R 14	Ingolfsson, M .... 1(5)	Stillie, D 8
Bernard, P .... 13(1)	Irvine, B .... 24(1)	Tzvetanov, T. 27
Booth, S .... 8(11)	Kiriakov, I .... 26(1)	Walker, J 19
Buchan, M .... 9(5)	Kombouare, A 30	Watt, M 9
Craig, M .... 2(3)	Kpedekpo, M .... –(5)	Windass, D 29
Dodds, W 31	McKimmie, S 14	Woodthorpe, C .... 14(5)
Glass, S .... 20(4)	Miller, J .... 26(4)	Wyness, D .... 1(6)
Grant, B 2	Rowson, D .... 30(4)	Young, D .... 22(4)
Inglis, J 15	Shearer, D .... 2(19)	

League Goals (45): Dodds 15, Windass 10, Miller 4, Shearer 4, Kombouare 3, Rowson 2, Craig 1, Glass 1, Irvine 1, Kiriakov 1, Young 1, Opponents 2.
Coca-Cola Cup Goals (10): Windass 5, Dodds 4, Glass 1. **Scottish League Cup Goals (2):** Booth 1, Dodds 1. **UEFA Cup Goals (11):** Dodds 4, Glass 2, Irvine 1, Rowson 1, Shearer 1, Windass 1, Young 1.

CELTIC

Ground: Celtic Park, Glasgow. **Capacity:** 50,600.
Telephone: 0141-556-2611. **Colours:** Green and white. **Nickname:** Bhoys.

Annoni, E 3	Hay, C .... 4(10)	McLaughlin, B ...... 8(12)
Anthony, M .... –(2)	Hughes, J .... 5(1)	McNamara, J 30
Boyd, T 31	Johnson, T .... 3(1)	McStay, P .... 14(1)
Cadete, J .... 30(1)	Kelly, P 1	O'Donnell, P 19
Di Canio, P .... 25(1)	Kerr, J .... 25(1)	O'Neil, B .... 15(1)
Donnelly, S .... 20(9)	Mackay, M .... 18(2)	Stubbs, A 20
Elliot, B .... –(1)	Marshall, G 11	Thom, A .... 18(5)
Grant, P .... 21(2)	McBride, J .... –(2)	Van Hooijdonk, P . 19(2)
Gray, S .... 7(4)	McKinlay, T .... 24(3)	Weighorst, M .... 11(6)
Hannah, D .... 14(4)		

League Goals (78): Cadete 25, Van Hooijdonk 14, Di Canio 12, Thom 7, Donnelly 4, Hay 4, O'Donnell 2, O'Neil 2, Wieghorst 2, Johnson 1, Mackay 1, McLaughlin 1, McNamara 1, McStay 1, Opponent 1.
Coca-Cola Cup Goals (8): Cadete 5, Thom 2, Van Hooijdonk 1. **Scottish Cup Goals (11):** Di Canio 3, Cadete 2, Mackay 2, O'Donnell 2, Johnson 1, Van Hooijdonk 1. **UEFA Cup Goals (1):** Cadete.

DUNDEE UNITED

Ground: Tannadice Park, Dundee. **Capacity:** 12,608 (all-seated).
Telephone: 01382-833166. **Colours:** Tangerine and black. **Nickname:** Dark Blues.

Benneker, A .... 6(1)	Dolan, J .... 11(2)	Key, L 4
Black, P .... –(1)	Duffy, C .... 6(7)	McInally, J .... 12(4)
Bowman, D .... 26(2)	Easton, C .... 1(1)	McKimmie, S 6
Coyle, O .... 6(4)	Hannah, D .... 9(3)	McKinnon, R .... 17(9)
Dijkstra, S 22	Johnson, I .... 2(5)	McLaren, A .... 29(5)

McQuilken, J .... 6(3) Perry, M .... 33(2) Thompson, S .... –(1)
McSwegan, G .... 15(16) Pressley, S .... 36 Walker, P .... 2(1)
Malpas, M .... 26 Robertson, A .... 1(3) Winters, R .... 27(9)
Maxwell, A .... 10 Shannon, R .... 7(2) Wirmola, J .... 1(2)
Olofsson, K .... 22(3) Sinclair, D .... 3(3) Zetterlund, L 25
Pedersen, E 25

League Goals (76): Olofsson 12, Winters 8, McSwegan 7, McKinnon 6, McLaren 3, Hannah 2, Pressley 2, Duffy 1, Malpas 1, McInally 1, Zetterlund 1, Opponents 2.
Coca-Cola Cup Goals (4): Coyle 2, McSwegan 1, Winters 1. **Scottish Cup Goals (8):** Winters 3, McLaren 2, McSwegan 1, Olofsson 1, Opponent 1.

DUNFERMLINE ATHLETIC

Ground: East End Park, Dunfermline. **Capacity:** 15,925.
Telephone: 01383-724295. **Colours:** Black and white. **Nickname:** Pars.

Bingham, D .... 5(12) Ireland, C .... 7(2) Robertson, C 31
Britton, G .... 27(6) Lemajic, Z .... 8 Sharp, R .... 14(1)
Clark, J .... 8 McCulloch, M .... 4(5) Shaw, G .... –(3)
Curran, H .... 18(2) Millar, M .... 19(4) Smith, A .... 30(5)
Den Bieman, I ..... 21(7) Miller, C .... 19(3) Tod, A 35
Fleming, D .... 23(3) Moore, A .... 13(13) Welsh, S 20
Fraser, J .... 2 Petrie, S .... 24(4) Westwater, I .... 28(1)
French, H .... 34(1) Rice, B .... 4(4) Young, S 2

League Goals (52): Britton 13, Smith 10, Millar 6, Tod 4, French 3, Moore 3, Petrie 3, Curran 2, Fleming 2, Bingham 1, Clark 1, Den Bieman 1, Ireland 1, Young 1, Opponent 1.
Coca-Cola Cup Goals (8): Bingham 2, Britton 2, French 2, Moore 2. **Scottish Cup Goals (5):** Smith 2, Curran 1, French 1, Petrie 1.

HEART OF MIDLOTHIAN

Ground: Tynecastle Park, Edinburgh. **Capacity:** 18,000 (all-seated).
Telephone: 0131-200-7200. **Colours:** Maroon and white. **Nickname:** Jam Tarts.

Beckford, D .... 6(2) Holmes, D .... 1 Naysmith, G 10
Bruno, P .... 11(2) Horn, R .... 1 Paille, S .... 12(7)
Burns, J .... –(2) Locke, G .... 11 Pointon, N .... 24(1)
Callaghan, S .... 4 Mackay, G .... 20(7) Ritchie, P .... 27(1)
Cameron, C .... 36 McCann, N .... 25(5) Robertson, J .... 25(2)
Colquhoun, J .... 4(7) McKenzie, R .... 3 Rousset, G 33
Frail, S .... 4(5) McManus, A .... 10(5) Salvatori, S .... 12(2)
Fulton, S .... 25(4) McPherson, D .... 26 Thomas, K .... 4(9)
Goss, J .... 7(3) Murie, D .... 6(1) Thorn, K 1
Hamilton, J .... 12(6) Murray, A .... 2(2) Weir, D 34

League Goals (46): Robertson 14, Cameron 8, Weir 6, Hamilton 5, McCann 3, Ritchie 3, Paille 2, Fulton 1, Mackay 1, McPherson 1.
Coca-Cola Cup Goals (11): Robertson 2, Beckford 2, Cameron 2, Fulton 1, McCann 1, Paille 1, Weir 1.
Scottish Cup Goals (6): Robertson 2, Cameron 1, Hamilton 1, Pointon 1, Weir 1.
European Cup-Winners' Cup Goals (1): McPherson 1.

HIBERNIAN

Ground: Easter Road, Edinburgh. **Capacity:** 16,115 (all-seated).
Telephone: 0131-661-2159. **Colours:** Green and white. **Nickname:** Hibees.

Cameron, I .... 9(8) Dow, A .... 17(5) Hunter, G .... 16(1)
Charnley, J .... 9 Elliot, D .... 5(2) Jackson, C .... 15(4)
Dennis, S .... 4 Grant, B .... 9(3) Jackson, D 30
Dods, D .... 17(3) Harper, K .... 23(3) Lavety, B .... 6(4)
Donald, G .... 8(3) Hughes, J .... 4 Leighton, J 35

Love, G .... 6(1)
McAllister, K ...... 10(9)
McGinlay, P 29
McLaughlin, J 9
McQuilken, J 9
Millen, A .... 16(3)
Miller, G .... 3(3)

Miller, W 31
Power, L 6
Reid, C 1
Renwick, M .... 6(3)
Riippa, J 1
Riley, P .... –(1)
Schmugge, T 1

Shannon, R 5
Tosh, P 6
Weir, M .... 1(7)
Welsh, B 17
Wilkins, N .... 15(1)
Wright, K .... 17(9)

League Goals (38): Jackson 11, McGinlay 6, Harper 5, Wright 4, Dow 2, Charnley 1, Dennis 1, Donald 1, McAllister 1, Power 1, Tosh 1, Weir 1, Opponents 3.
Play-Off Goals (5): Johnson 2, Tosh 1, Wright 1, Opponents 1. **Coca-Cola Cup Goals (4)**: Dow 1, Lavety 1, McGinlay 1, Wright 1. **Scottish Cup Goals (3)**: Jackson 1, McGinlay 1, Miller 1.

KILMARNOCK

Ground: Rugby Park, Kilmarnock. **Capacity**: 18,128 (all-seated).
Telephone: 01563-525184. **Colours**: White and blue. **Nickname**: Killie.

Anderson, D .... 16(1)
Bagen, D .... 16(1)
Brown, T .... 7(17)
Burke, A .... 14(4)
Findlay, W .... 15(4)
Hamilton, S 6
Henry, J .... 18(4)
Holt, G .... 10(2)
Kerr, A .... 2(2)

Kerr, D 27
Lauchlan, J .... 7(2)
Lekovic, D 30
MacPherson, A 33
McGowne, K .... 30(1)
McIntyre, J .... 29(2)
McKee, C .... 14(11)
Meldrum, C 6

Mitchell, A .... 23(7)
Montgomerie, S .. 20(2)
Prytz, R .... 1(2)
Reilly, M .... 31(2)
Roberts, M .... 2(9)
Tallon, G 4
Whitworth, N 6
Wright, P .... 29(2)

League Goals (41): Wright 15, McIntyre 6, Burke 3, Henry 2, McKee 2, Mitchell 2, Reilly 2, Roberts 2, Brown 1, Findlay 1, Holt 1, Lauchlan 1, Montgomerie 1, Opponents 2.
Coca-Cola Cup Goals: None. **Scottish Cup Goals (10)**: Henry 3, Wright 3, McIntyre 2, Brown 1, McGowne 1.

MOTHERWELL

Ground: Fir Park, Motherwell. **Capacity**: 13,742 (all-seated).
Telephone: 01698-333333. **Colours**: Claret and amber. **Nickname**: 'Well

Arnott, D .... 11(4)
Burns, A .... 16(14)
Christie, K .... 3(1)
Coyle, O 15
Coyne, T .... 24(3)
Davies, W .... 20(5)
Denham, G .... 5(4)
Dolan, J 18
Essandoh, R .... –(1)

Falconer, W 21
Hendry, J .... 5(1)
Howie, S 30
Lehtonen, J .... 4(2)
Martin, B 34
May, E 34
McCart, C .... 16(3)
McCulloch, L .... 1(14)
McMillan, S .... 13(3)

McSkimming, S 23
Philliben, J .... 11(6)
Roddie, A .... 8(4)
Ross, I .... 21(9)
Valakari, S 11
Van der Gaag, M 26
Weir, M 5
Wishart, F .... 15(3)
Woods, S 6

League Goals (44): Coyne 11, Coyle 7, Van Der Gaag 6, McSkimming 4, Arnott 3, Falconer 2, May 2, Ross 2, Weir 2, Burns 1, Davies 1, Philliben 1, Opponents 2.
Coca-Cola Cup Goals: None. **Scottish Cup Goals (6)**: Coyle 3, Davies 1, McSkimming 1, Van Der Gaag 1.

RAITH ROVERS

Ground: Stark's Park, Kirkcaldy. **Capacity**: 10,271.
Telephone: 01592-263514. **Colours**: Navy blue and white. **Nickname**: Rovers.

Andersen, V .... 18(1)
Andersen, S 7
Bergersen, K 6
Bonar, P .... 9(7)

Browne, P 4
Craig, D 28
Dargo, C .... 1(4)
Dennis, S 16

Duffield, P .... 23(10)
Geddes, A 3
Hallum, C 6
Harvey, P .... 10(8)

Kirk, S .... 19(7)	McGill, D .... 3(6)	Skonhoff, O 1
Kirkwood, D .... 13(4)	McInally, J 4	Stein, J .... –(2)
Krivokapic, M 6	Millar, J .... 25(2)	Taylor, A .... 13(4)
Lennon, D 35	Millen, A 13	Thomson, S.Y. 27
Lorimer, D .... 1(2)	Mitchell, G 20	Thomson, S.M. .... 18(4)
Makela, J 8	Rougier, A .... 27(3)	Twaddle, K .... 23(5)
McCulloch, G .... 3(3)	Scott, C 6	

League Goals (29): Duffield 5, Lennon 5, Twaddle 4, Andersen 3, Craig 2, Taylor 2, Thomson 2, Bergersen 1, Bonar 1, Kirk 1, Kirkwood 1, Makela 1, Rougier 1.
Coca-Cola Cup Goals (2): Rougier 2. **Scottish Cup Goals (6):** Andersen 2, Craig 1, Kirk 1, Kirkwood 1, Rougier 1.

RANGERS

Ground: Ibrox Stadium, Glasgow. **Capacity:** 50,411 (all-seated).
Telephone: 0141-427-8500. **Colours:** Royal blue. **Nickname:** Gers.

Albertz, J .... 31(1)	Gascoigne, P .... 23(3)	Moore, C 23
Andersen, E .... 6(11)	Goram, A 25	Petric, G .... 23(3)
Bjorklund, J 28	Gough, R 27	Robertson, D .... 21(1)
Boyack, S .... –(1)	Hateley, M 4	Rozental, S .... –(1)
Cleland, A 32	Laudrup, B 33	Shields, G 6
Dibble, A 7	McCall, S 7	Snelders, T 4
Durie, G .... 14(2)	McCoist, A .... 13(12)	Steven, T .... 5(3)
Durrant, I .... 4(4)	McInnes, D .... 10(11)	Van Vossen, P .... 6(8)
Ferguson, B 1	McLaren, A .... 17(1)	Wilson, S 1
Ferguson, I .... 17(6)	Miller, C .... 7(6)	Wright, S 1
Fitzgerald, D .... –(1)		

League Goals (85): Laudrup 16, Gascoigne 13, Albertz 10, McCoist 10, Andersen 9, Durie 5, Gough 5, Van Vossen 5, Robertson 4, Petric 2, Ferguson 1, Hateley 1, McInnes 1, Miller 1, Moore 1, Steven 1.
Coca-Cola Cup Goals (20): Van Vossen 4, Albertz 3, Gascoigne 3, McCoist 3, Andersen 2, Laudrup 2, McInnes 2, Durie 1. **Scottish Cup Goals (5):** Andersen 1, McCoist 1, Robertson 1, Rozental 1, Steven 1. **European Cup Goals (15):** McCoist 6, Laudrup 2, Durrant 1, Gascoigne 1, Gough 1, McInnes 1, Miller 1, Petric 1, Van Vossen 1.

FIRST DIVISION

AIRDRIEONIANS

Ground: Broadwood Stadium, Cumbernauld. **Capacity:** 8,029 (all-seated).
Telephone: 01236-762067. **Colours:** White and red. **Nickname:** Diamonds.

Black, K .... 26(2)	Jack, P 30	Martin, J 27
Boyle, A .... 19(7)	Johnston, F .... 15(6)	Rhodes, A 9
Connelly, G .... 1(3)	Lawrence, A .... 10(17)	Sandison, J 36
Connolly, P .... 24(11)	Mackay, G 8	Smith, A .... 21(7)
Cooper, S .... 18(5)	McIntyre, T .... 5(2)	Stewart, A 31
Davies, J 31	McPhee, B .... 24(4)	Sweeney, S 26
Eadie, K .... 9(6)	Martin, A .... –(1)	Wilson, M .... 21(8)
Hetherston, P 5		

League Goals (56): Connolly 8, Cooper 8, McPhee 8, Eadie 7, Davies 6, Black 4, Lawrence 3, Stewart 3, Smith 2, Jack 1, Johnston 1, Mackay 1, Sandison 1, Sweeney 1, Wilson 1, Opponent 1.
Play-Off Goals (2): Connolly 1, Black 1. **Coca-Cola Cup Goals (3):** Cooper 1, Eadie 1, Hetherston 1. **Scottish Cup Goals (1):** Sandison 1. **League Challenge Cup Goals:** None.

CLYDEBANK

Ground: Boghead Park, Dumbarton. **Capacity:** 5,007.
Telephone: 0141-955-9048. **Colours:** White and red. **Nickname:** Bankies.

Adamson, C 1	Grady, J 36	Melvin, W .... 1(2)
Agnew, P .... 25(3)	Hardie, D .... –(1)	Miller, S .... 11(13)
Barnes, D 7	Irons, D 35	Murdoch, S .... 13(2)
Bowman, G 22	Lovering, P .... 25(1)	Nicholls, J .... 32(1)
Brannigan, K 35	Macfarlane, I 16	Robertson, J ...... 6(20)
Brown, J .... 12(1)	McKelvie, D .... –(1)	Robertson, S 2
Connaghan, D .... 1(1)	McKinstrey, J .... 2(3)	Sutherland, C 9
Connell, G .... 26(3)	McMahon, S .... 12(9)	Teale, G .... 32(1)
Currie, T .... 24(4)	Matthews, G 10	Templeton, R 1

League Goals (31): Grady 8, Teale 6, Agnew 5, McMahon 3, Brown 2, Connell 2, Nicholls 2, Brannigan 1, Miller 1, Opponent 1.
Coca-Cola Cup Goals: None. **Scottish Cup Goals:** None. **League Challenge Cup Goals:** None.

DUNDEE

Ground: Dens Park Stadium, Dundee. **Capacity:** 14,481.
Telephone: 01382-826104. **Colours:** Navy blue, white. **Nickname:** Dark Blues.

Adamczuk, D 30	Farningham, R .... 3(5)	Raeside, R 34
Anderson, I .... 28(7)	Ferguson, I .... 5(8)	Robertson, H 15
Annand, E 5	Hamilton, J 12	Shaw, G .... 18(3)
Bain, K 12	McGlynn, G 11	Skonnord, O .... 1(3)
Bayne, G .... –(2)	McKeown, S .... 17(3)	Smith, B 36
Cargill, A .... –(4)	McQueen, T .... 15(1)	Thomson, W 25
Charnley, J 15	Magee, K .... 10(15)	Tosh, P .... 19(4)
Crole, L 1	O'Driscoll, J .... 18(3)	Tully, C .... 16(5)
Duffy, J 2	Power, J .... 9(1)	Ward, M 1
Elliott, J .... 1(3)	Rae, G .... 11(6)	Winnie, D 26

League Goals (47): O'Driscoll 10, Anderson 5, Shaw 5, Power 4, Raeside 4, Tosh 4, Charnley 3, Annand 2, Rae 2, Adamczuk 1, Ferguson 1, Hamilton 1, McKeown 1, Robertson 1, Winnie 1, Opponents 2.
Coca-Cola Cup Goals (7): Hamilton 5, Raeside 1, Tosh 1. **Scottish Cup Goals (5):** Anderson 2, Power 2, O'Driscoll 1. **League Challenge Cup Goals (6):** Tosh 2, Farmingham 1, Hamilton 1, Magee 1, Shaw 1.

EAST FIFE

Ground: Bayview Park, Methil. **Capacity:** 5,433.
Telephone: 01333-426323. **Colours:** Black and gold. **Nickname:** Fifers.

Allan, G .... 30(2)	Dwarika, A .... 12(6)	McStay, J 9
Andrew, R .... 27(4)	Dyer, M .... 9(2)	Mair, I .... –(1)
Archibald, S 5	Fennell, K 1	Moffat, B .... 7(1)
Baillie, L .... 5(5)	Gartshore, P .... 15(8)	Nicoll, G .... 1(4)
Beaton, D 5	Gibb, R 30	Ritchie, I 13
Bogie, G .... 5(3)	Hamilton, L 30	Robertson, D .... 5(2)
Cameron, R .... 13(2)	Hope, D .... 5(5)	Ronald, P 8
Carmichael, D ...... –(1)	Hutcheon, S .... 18(6)	Rushford, C 1
Christie, K 9	Johnston, G 16	Scott, R 15
Cusick, J .... 25(5)	Kinnell, A .... –(1)	Stiggsson, O 3
Demmin, C .... 1(5)	Lewis, G .... 6(10)	Sweeney, C .... –(1)
Dixon, A .... 26(2)	Macfarlane, C .... 9(2)	Winiarski, S .... 6(9)
Donaghy, M 23	McPherson, G ...... 1(3)	Yates, D 2

League Goals (28): Dyer 4, Ronald 4, Scott 3, Allan 2, Hutcheon 2, Macfarlane 2, Andrew 1, Baillie 1, Beaton 1, Cameron 1, Christie 1, Cusick 1, Donaghy 1, Moffat 1, Winiarski 1, Opponents 2.
Coca-Cola Cup Goals (1): Dwarika 1. **Scottish Cup Goals (3):** Christie 2, Baillie 1. **League Challenge Cup Goals (2):** Archibald 1, Scott 1.

FALKIRK

Ground: Brockville Park, Falkirk. **Capacity:** 9,706.
Telephone: 01324-624121. **Colours:** Navy blue. **Nickname:** Bairns.

Berry, N 9	Hagen, D .... 31(3)	McKenzie, S .... 26(2)
Corrigan, M .... 8(9)	Hamilton, B ...... 18(1)	Mathers, P 16
Crabbe, S .... 10(2)	Huttenen, T 2	Mitchell, G ...... 17(3)
Craig, A .... 10(3)	James, K .... 17(1)	Nelson, C 20
Crawford, G .... –(2)	Kaijasilta, P .... –(1)	Oliver, N .... 14(1)
De Massis, S ...... –(1)	Kelly, T .... –(1)	Olson, P .... –(1)
Elliot, D .... 8(9)	Kidd, W 1	Seaton, A .... 26(3)
Fellner, G .... 4(3)	Lawrie, A .... 7(5)	Tortolano, J ..... 11(1)
Ferguson, D ...... 13(1)	McAllister, K ...... 14(1)	Waddle, C 4
Foster, W .... 10(4)	McGowan, J 29	Ward, K .... 9(1)
Graham, A .... 5(2)	McGraw, M .... 20(9)	Whiteside, G ...... –(1)
Gray, A .... 13(5)	McGrillen, P ..... 24(7)	

League Goals (42): McGraw 8, McGrillen 7, Fellner 4, Ferguson 3, James 3, McAllister 3, Craig 2, McGowan 2, Elliot 1, Foster 1, Gray 1, Hagen 1, Hamilton 1, McKenzie 1, Mitchell 1, Oliver 1, Waddle 1, Ward 1.
Coca-Cola Cup Goals (2): Craig 2. **Scottish Cup Goals (9):** Craig 2, Hagen 2, James 2, McAllister 1, McGraw 1, McGrillen 1. **League Challenge Cup Goals (2):** Hagen 1, McGraw 1.

GREENOCK MORTON

Ground: Cappielow Park, Greenock. **Capacity:** 14,267.
Telephone: 01475-723571. **Colours:** Royal blue and white. **Nickname:** Ton.

Aitken, S .... 10(3)	Hunter, J 3	Mahood, A 27
Anderson, J 31	Inglis, N 4	Mason, B .... 2(2)
Blaikie, A .... 4(1)	Johnstone, D .... 11(2)	Matheson, R .... 8(13)
Blair, P .... 11(5)	Lilley, D 25	Rajamaki, M ..... 23(10)
Collins, P 35	Lindberg, J 24	Reid, B 26
Cormack, P 25	McArthur, N ...... 24(3)	Slavin, B 1
Flannery, P .... 6(14)	McCahill, S 22	Willoughby, J .... –(1)
Hawke, W .... 25(7)	McPherson, C .... 17(12)	Wylie, D 32

League Goals (42): Lilley 15, Hawke 7, Anderson 4, Rajamaki 4, Flannery 3, Mahood 3, Lindberg 2, Blair 1, Cormack 1, McPherson 1, Reid 1.
Coca-Cola Cup Goals (4): Lilley 2, Anderson 1, Cormack 1. **Scottish Cup Goals (11):** Hawke 3, Lilley 2, Mahood 2, Blair 1, Cormack 1, Mason 1, Rajamaki 1.
League Challenge Cup Goals (8): Lilley 3, Flannery 2, Anderson 1, Matheson 1, Rajamaki 1.

PARTICK THISTLE

Ground: Firhill Stadium, Glasgow. **Capacity:** 20,906.
Telephone: 0141-945-4811. **Colours:** Red and yellow. **Nickname:** Jags.

Adams, C .... 26(4)	Henderson, N ...... 12(4)	Milne, C .... 22(3)
Apiliga, R 1	Hillcoat, J 26	Moss, D 31
Archibald, A .... 2(2)	Hringsson, H ...... 1(2)	Ritchie, J .... –(1)
Ayton, S 3	Lyons, A .... 29(6)	Slavin, J .... 17(1)
Cairns, M 10	MacDonald, W ..... 10(5)	Smith, T .... –(1)
Dinnie, A .... 13(1)	McCall, I 1	Stirling, J 34
Docherty, S ...... 8(14)	McKenzie, J ...... –(1)	Te Jero, J .... –(1)
Evans, G 29	McWilliams, J ...... 19(4)	Turner, T .... 7(4)
Farrell, D 31	Maskrey, S .... 29(2)	Watson, G 35

League Goals (49): Moss 11, Evans 9, Adams 8, Stirling 7, Lyons 3, Farrell 2, Henderson 2, Maskrey 2, McWilliams 2, Dinnie 1, Docherty 1, Macdonald 1.
Coca-Cola Cup Goals (4): Evans 3, Stirling 1. **Scottish Cup Goals:** None.
League Challenge Cup Goals (6): Stirling 2, Evans 1, Henderson 1, Maskrey 1, McWilliams 1.

ST. JOHNSTONE

Ground: McDiarmid Park, Perth. **Capacity:** 10,673 (all-seated).
Telephone: 01738-626961. **Colours:** Royal blue and white. **Nickname:** Saints.

Bowman, G	4	Griffin, D	26(3)	O'Halloran, K	4(1)
Brown, G	–(1)	Jenkinson, L	22(3)	O'Neil, J	25(4)
Colquhoun, J	6	King, C	2(2)	Preston, A	23(9)
Dasovic, N	14	McAnespie, K	1(8)	Robertson, S	2
Davidson, C	18(2)	McCluskey, S	7(3)	Scott, P	24(5)
Donaldson, E	3(1)	McGowne, K	2	Sekerlioglu, A	22(2)
Farquhar, G	3(2)	McQuillan, J	32	Tosh, S	22(5)
Ferguson, I	3(5)	Main, A	34	Weir, J	32
Fymr, J	3(1)	O'Boyle, G	23(2)	Whiteford, A	8(3)
Grant, R	31(2)				

League Goals (74): Grant 19, O'Boyle 12, Scott 12, Jenkinson 6, Sekerlioglu 6, O'Neil 3, Tosh 3, Weir 3, Davidson 2, Ferguson 2, McAnespie 2, Colquhoun 1, Griffin 1, McCluskey 1, Preston 1.
Coca-Cola Cup Goals (6): Grant 2, O'Boyle 2, Scott 1, Tosh 1. **Scottish Cup Goals:** None. **League Challenge Cup Goals (15):** Grant 5, Farquhar 2, O'Boyle 2, O'Neil 1, Preston 1, Sekerlioglu 1, Scott 1, Whiteford 1, Opponent 1.

ST. MIRREN

Ground: St. Mirren Park, Paisley. **Capacity:** 15,410.
Telephone: 0141-889-2558. **Colours:** Black and white. **Nickname:** Saints.

Archdeacon, P	1(5)	Gillies, R	29	Mendes, J	32(4)
Baker, M	31	Hetherston, B	20(2)	Munro, S	25(1)
Combe, A	36	Iwelumo, C	2(12)	Murray, H	–(1)
Dick, J	24(1)	McGarry, S	5(6)	Smith, B	20(5)
Fallon, W	–(2)	McGuire, J	–(3)	Taylor, S	11(1)
Fenwick, P	27	McLaren, J	–(1)	Turner, T	17
Foster, W	8	McLaughlin, B	27(1)	Watson, S	26
Galloway, G	1(1)	McWhirter, N	26(1)	Yardley, M	28(2)

League Goals (48): Yardley 15, Fenwick 6, Gillies 6, Watson 4, Dick 3, Hetherston 3, Mendes 3, Foster 2, Turner 2, McGarry 1, Munro 1, Taylor 1, Opponent 1.
Coca-Cola Cup Goals (5): Gillies 1, Hetherston 1, Iwelumo 1, Taylor 1, Yardley 1.
League Challenge Cup Goals (1): Hetherston 1.

STIRLING ALBION

Ground: Forthbank Stadium, Stirling. **Capacity:** 3,808.
Telephone: 01786-450399. **Colours:** Red and white. **Nickname:** Albion.

Bennett, J	26(7)	McCormick, S	29(2)	Mortimer, P	–(1)
Bone, A	34	McGeown, M	36	Paterson, A	34
Carberry, G	10(1)	McGrotty, G	–(12)	Paterson, G	33
Deas, P	32	McLaren, S	8(15)	Taggart, C	22(3)
Forrest, E	1	McLeod, J	5(1)	Tait, T	22(4)
Gibson, J	28(8)	McQuilter, R	31	Watson, P	–(1)
Hjartarsson, G	20(1)	Mitchell, C	13(1)	Wood, D	5(8
Jack, S	7(8)				

League Goals (54): Bone 9, McCormick 8, Tait 6, Bennett 5, Hjartarsson 5, McLaren 4, Paterson G 4, McQuilter 2, Paterson A 2, Taggart 2, Deas 1, Gibson 1, Wood 1, Opponents 3.
Coca-Cola Cup Goals (1): Gibson 1. **Scottish Cup Goals:** None. **League Challenge Cup Goals (4):** Bone 3, Gibson 1.

SECOND DIVISION

AYR UNITED

Ground: Somerset Park, Ayr. **Capacity:** 12,178.
Telephone: 01292-263435. **Colours:** White, black, red. **Nickname:** Honest Men.

Bell, R .... 5(1)	Henderson, D .... 19(10)	Mercer, J .... 1(12)
Biggart, K .... –(3)	Hood, G .... 20(1)	Scott, R .... 17(1)
Castilla, D 1	Horace, A .... 21(1)	Smith, C .... –(1)
Clarke, J .... –(1)	Humphries, M 22	Smith, H 35
Connor, R 18	Jamieson, W 26	Smith, P .... 27(6)
Coyle, R .... 29(1)	Kerrigan, S .... 22(5)	Smith, T .... 19(2)
Dalziel, G .... –(1)	Kinnaird, P .... 13(14)	Traynor, J .... 30(4)
English, I 17	Law, M .... 10(6)	Ward, M 1
George, D .... 17(3)	McStay, J .... 6(4)	Watson, P .... 20(6)

League Goals (61): Kerrigan 14, Smith PM 9, English 7, Scott 6, Horace 5, Smith TW 4, Jamieson 3, George 2, Kinnaird 2, Mercer 2, Traynor 2, Biggart 1, Connor 1, Henderson 1, Hood 1, Opponent 1.
Coca-Cola Cup Goals (7): English 2, Kerrigan 2, Connor 1, Henderson 1, Hood 1. **Scottish Cup Goals:** None. **League Challenge Cup Goals:** None.

BERWICK RANGERS

Ground: Shielfield Park, Berwick-upon-Tweed. **Capacity:** 4,131.
Telephone: 01289-307424. **Colours:** Black and gold. **Nickname:** Borderers.

Burgess, M 9	Irvine, N .... 24(1)	Reid, A .... 28(3)
Clegg, N .... 11(3)	Laidler, M 15	Robinson, D .... 14(2)
Coates, S 3	Lamont, W 3	Smith, I .... –(1)
Collier, D 16	Little, G .... 6(7)	Smith, S 3
Craig, K .... 18(8)	Ludlow, L .... 3(3)	Stewart, A .... 24(2)
Finlayson, D 19	McGlynn, D .... 7(5)	Walton, K .... 31(4)
Forrester, P .... 24(6)	McParland, J .... 8(1)	Ward, B .... 1(1)
Fraser, G 33	Manson, C .... 8(3)	Watkins, D .... 7(4)
Garrity, J .... 1(1)	Miller, G .... 2(5)	Wilson, M 4
Graham, T .... 27(3)	Neil, M .... 21(1)	Young, N 8
Grant, D .... 28(4)	Paxton, G .... –(3)	

League Goals (32): Forrester 6, Neil 4, Robinson 4, Clegg 3, Craig 2, Little 2, Manson 2, McGlynn 2, Walton 2, Grant 1, McParland 1, Miller 1, Reid 1.
Coca-Cola Cup Goals: None. **Scottish Cup Goals (4):** McParland 2, Neil 1, Walton 1. **League Challenge Cup Goals:** None.

BRECHIN CITY

Ground: Glebe Park, Brechin. **Capacity:** 3,960.
Telephone: 01356-622856. **Colours:** Red and white. **Nickname:** City.

Allan, R 12	Conway, F 35	Kerrigan, S .... 25(4)
Baillie, R .... 7(1)	Dailly, M 3	McKellar, J .... 19(12)
Black, R .... 1(2)	Farnan, C 35	McNeill, W .... 1(9)
Brand, R .... 20(8)	Ferguson, S .... 17(3)	Ross, A .... –(2)
Brown, R 34	Feroz, C .... 16(15)	Scott, W 30
Buick, G .... 18(2)	Garden, S .... 24(1)	Smith, G .... 8(1)
Cairney, H 31	Heddle, I .... 11(5)	Sorbie, S .... 22(6)
Christie, J .... 27(2)		

League Goals (36): Kerrigan 7, Brand 6, Feroz 4, McKellar 4, Sorbie 4, Brown 3, Christie 2, Conway 2, Ferguson 2, Buick 1, Farnan 1.
Coca-Cola Cup Goals (3): Feroz 2, Kerrigan 1. **Scottish Cup Goals (6):** Brand 2, Sorbie 2, Brown 1, Kerrigan 1. **League Challenge Cup Goals:** None.

CLYDE

Ground: Broadwood Stadium, Cumbernauld. **Capacity:** 8,029 (all-seated).
Telephone: 01236-451511. **Colours:** White and black. **Nickname:** Bully Wee.

Annand, E 29	Gibson, L ...... –(2)	McLean, M 29
Balfour, R 7	Gillies, K ...... 24(2)	McPhee, G ...... –(1)
Brown, J ...... 25(1)	Harrison, T ...... 3(5)	Mathieson, M ...... 19(8)
Brownlie, P ...... 30(3)	Knox, K 36	O'Neill, Martin ...... 21(8)
Campbell, P ...... 16(8)	McCheyne, G ...... 4(4)	O'Neill, Michael .. 12(11)
Carrigan, B ...... 5(8)	McConnell, I ...... 8(2)	Parks, G ...... –(2)
Coleman, S ...... –(1)	McEwan, J ...... 31(3)	Prunty, J ...... 15(2)
Ferguson, G ...... 20(1)	McInulty, S ...... 28(3)	Robertson, G 1
Gibson, A ...... 33(2)	McLay, J ...... –(1)	

League Goals (42): Annand 21, Brownlie 5, Mathieson 4, O'Neill 4, Gibson 2, Knox 2, McCheyne 2, Carrigan 1, Prunty 1.
Coca-Cola Cup Goals (2): Annand 1, Brown 1, **Scottish Cup Goals (9):** Annand 2, Gibson 2, Brownlie 1, Mathieson 1, McEwan 1, McInulty 1, O'Neil 1. **League Challenge Cup Goals (3):** Mathieson 2, Knox 1.

DUMBARTON

Ground: Boghead Park, Dumbarton. **Capacity:** 5,007.
Telephone: 01389-762569 **Colours:** White and black. **Nickname:** Sons.

Barnes, D 11	MacFarlane, I 9	Mellis, A 1
Bruce, J 9	McCabe, G 4	Melvin, M 23
Dallas, S ...... 15(1)	McCuaig, R ...... –(1)	Mooney, M ...... 18(4)
Davidson, W ...... 12(4)	McGall, J ...... –(6)	Parks, G 4
Dennison, P 2	McGarvey, M ...... 7(5)	Reid, D ...... –(1)
Glancy, M ...... 24(8)	McGivern, S ...... 1(1)	Reilly, R ...... 2(6)
Goldie, J ...... 1(3)	McKenzie, G ...... 4(1)	Scott, J ...... –(1)
Gow, S ...... 21(3)	McKinnon, C 34	Sharp, L 35
Granger, A ...... 2(4)	Marsland, J ...... 30(1)	Ward, R ...... 26(9)
Hringsson, H 3	Meechan, J 36	Wilson, W 21
King, T 27	Meechan, K 14	

League Goals (44): Ward 7, Glancy 6, Meechan 6, Sharp 5, McKinnon 4, Wilson 4, Hringsson 3, Dallas 2, King 2, Granger 1, McGivern 1, Mooney 1, Reilly 1, Opponent 1.
Coca-Cola Cup Goals (1): Dallas 1. **Scottish Cup Goals:** None. **League Challenge Cup Goals:** None.

HAMILTON ACADEMICAL

Ground: Cliftonhill Stadium, Coatbridge. **Capacity:** 1,238.
Telephone: 01698-286103. **Colours:** Red and white. **Nickname:** Accies.

Baptie, C ...... 11(4)	Lorimer, D ...... –(3)	McQuade, J ...... –(4)
Clark, G ...... 15(17)	McBride, J ...... 2(1)	Paris, S 2
Cunnington, E 8	McCormick, S ...... 16(3)	Quitongo, J ...... 31(3)
Davidson, W ...... 5(7)	McCulloch, S ...... 19(5)	Renicks, S 33
Ferguson, A 27	McEntegart, S ...... 24(2)	Ritchie, P 36
Fotheringham, K .. 6(8)	McFarlane, D ..... 10(10)	Scott, C 5
Geraghty, M ...... –(1)	McGill, D 8	Sherry, J 24
Hillcoat, C 36	McIntosh, M 33	Thomson, A ...... 32(3)
Hillcoat, J 2	McKenzie, P ...... 11(7)	

League Goals (75): Ritchie 31, McCormick 7, McIntosh 7, McFarlane 6, Sherry 6, McGill 4, Quitongo 3, Clark 2, Fotheringham 2, McEntegart 2, Thomson 2, Davidson 1, Hillcoat 1, McCulloch 1.
Coca-Cola Cup Goals (1): Sherry 1. **Scottish Cup Goals (6):** Ritchie 3, Clark 2, McEntegart 1. **League Challenge Cup Goals (3):** Quitongo 3.

LIVINGSTON

Ground: Almondvale Stadium, Livingston. **Capacity:** 6,100 (all-seated).
Telephone: 01506-417000. **Colours:** Gold and black. **Nickname:** Livi Lions.

Alleyne, D .... 14(9)	Duthie, M .... 32(1)	Sinclair, C .... 4(7)
Bailey, L .... 13(10)	Forrest, G 5	Smart, C .... 10(7)
Callaghan, T 32	Graham, T 15	Tierney, P 22
Callaghan, W .... 7(14)	Harvey, G .... 27(2)	Watson, G .... 20(2)
Campbell, S 30	Laidlaw, S .... 4(9)	Williamson, S 32
Davidson, G .... 20(1)	McLeod, G 19	Young, J .... 21(13)
Douglas, R 36	McMartin, G .... 33(1)	

League Goals (56): Harvey 15, Bailey 8, Duthie 7, McLeod 5, Young 5, Callaghan 3, Campbell 3, McMartin 3, Laidlaw 2, Alleyne 1, Forrest 1, Graham 1, Tierney 1, Williamson 1.
Coca-Cola Cup Goals (2): Callaghan 1, Young 1. **Scottish Cup Goals (1):** Bailey 1. **League Challenge Cup Goals (1):** Young.

QUEEN OF THE SOUTH

Ground: Palmerston Park, Dumfries. **Capacity:** 6,412.
Telephone: 01387-254853. **Colours:** Royal blue. **Nickname:** Doonhammers.

Aitken, A 14	Hughes, J .... 2(2)	McFarlane, A 6
Alexander, R .... 5(6)	Irvine, C .... –(1)	McKeown, B 26
Brown, J 15	Kennedy, D .... 20(1)	McKeown, D .... 27(2)
Bryce, T .... 34(1)	Laing, D .... 5(4)	Mallan, S .... 28(6)
Brydson, E .... –(4)	Lancaster, I .... 3(3)	Mathieson, D 36
Cleeland, M .... –(1)	Lee, P .... –(1)	Nesovic, A .... 26(4)
Cochrane, G .... 7(2)	Leslie, S .... 17(3)	Rowe, J .... 25(1)
Doig, C .... 2(2)	Lilley, D .... 20(2)	Thomson, J 16
Flannigan, C .... 26(2)	Maclean, J .... 2(5)	Townsley, D .... 29(2)
Herriot, S .... –(3)	McAllister, J .... 4(2)	Wilson, S 1

League Goals (55): Mallan 13, Bryce 12, Flannigan 11, Nesovic 5, Rowe 5, Alexander 2, Townsley 2, Leslie 1, Lilley 1, McFarlane 1, McKeown 1, Thomson 1.
Coca-Cola Cup Goals: None. **Scottish Cup Goals (4):** Nesovic 2, Leslie 1, Mallan 1. **League Challenge Cup Goals (4):** Flannigan 2, Mallan 1, Nesovic 1.

STENHOUSEMUIR

Ground: Ochilview Park, Stenhousemuir. **Capacity:** 2,710.
Telephone: 01324-562992. **Colours:** Maroon, sky blue and white. **Nickname:** Warriors.

Alexander, N 12	Haddow, L .... 27(1)	McGeachie, G ...... 20(5)
Armstrong, G 34	Henderson, J .... 35(1)	McKee, K 13
Banks, A .... 16(2)	Hume, A .... 5(18)	Roseburgh, D .... 8(14)
Brown, S 3	Hunter, P .... 29(1)	Sprott, A .... 23(8)
Campbell, M .... 7(5)	Hutchison, G .... 29(1)	Stewart, I .... 2(2)
Christie, M .... 7(1)	Innes, C .... 23(1)	Thomson, J .... 12(1)
Ellison, S 24	Little, I 35	Whiteford, S .... –(1)
Fisher, J 31	Logan, P .... 1(4)	

League Goals (49): Little 14, Haddow 10, Hunter 7, Henderson 4, Hutchison 4, Hume 3, Fisher 2, Roseburgh 2, Innes 1, Sprott 1, Stewart 1.
Coca-Cola Cup Goals (1): Sprott 1. **Scottish Cup Goals (1):** Hume 1. **League Challenge Cup Goals:** None.

STRANRAER

Ground: Stair Park, Stranraer. **Capacity:** 6,100.
Telephone: 01776-703271. **Colours:** Royal blue and white. **Nickname:** Blues.

Black, T 26	Crawford, D .... 14(6)	Duffy, B 27
Campbell, M 1	Docherty, R .... 25(6)	Duffy, J .... –(1)

Duncan, G .... 9(6)	Jack, A .... –(1)	McMillan, J .... 9(17)
Friels, G .... 1(5)	Lansdowne, A 30	McStay, R .... –(1)
Gallacher, I .... 14(4)	McAulay, I .... 25(1)	Matthews, G 9
Gallagher, A 13	McCaffrey, J 25	Millar, G 20
Hay, G 9	McCrindle, S .... –(3)	Robertson, J ..... 20(11)
Higgins, G .... 17(4)	McIntyre, P 28	Sloan, T .... 26(5)
Howard, N .... 2(1)	McLaren, J .... –(1)	Young, G .... 24(6)
Hughes, J .... 22(5)		

League Goals (29): McIntyre 7, Young 5, Docherty 3, Sloan 3, Crawford 2, Higgins 2, McCaffrey 2, Black 1, Lansdowne 1, McAuley 1, McMillan 1, Opponent 1.
Coca-Cola Cup Goals (3): Docherty 1, Sloan 1, Young 1. **Scottish Cup Goals (1):** Young 1. **League Challenge Cup Goals (9):** Sloan 3, Docherty 1, McAuley 1, McCaffrey 1, McIntyre 1, McMillan 1, Opponents 1.

THIRD DIVISION

ALBION ROVERS

Ground: Cliftonhill Stadium, Coatbridge. **Capacity:** 1,238.
Telephone: 01236-606334. **Colours:** Yellow and black. **Nickname:** Wee Rovers.

Angus, I 8	Kennedy, A 1	Mitchell, C .... 11(2)
Boal, B .... 8(6)	Leonard, M .... 1(2)	Moore, V 27
Brown, M 6	MacFarlane, C ..... 10(2)	Pickering, M 13
Byrne, D 29	McGowan, N .... 16(1)	Reilly, R .... 4(10)
Clark, M .... 14(3)	McGuire, D .... 8(8)	Robertson, S 1
Cody, S .... 8(1)	McInally, A .... 13(3)	Ross, S 24
Davidson, A 1	McInnes, E 1	Russell, P .... –(1)
Dickson, J .... 17(4)	McInnes, I .... 9(3)	Shepherd, A 5
Duncan, C 10	McKenna, A .... –(1)	Tannock, R 4
Gallagher, J .... 7(1)	McKenzie, D ..... 17(15)	Walker, T .... 20(4)
Gardner, R 16	McKilligan, N ..... 28(2)	Watters, W .... 23(1)
Harty, I .... 4(5)	Martin, P 25	Webster, D .... 2(1)
Kelly, G .... 4(1)	Mitchell, A 1	

League Goals (50): Watters 11, McKenzie 7, Walker 6, Gardner 5, Moore 5, Dickson 4, McGuire 3, Clark 2, Boal 1, Cody 1, Kelly 1, Martin 1, McKilligan 1, Shepherd 1, Opponent 1.
Coca-Cola Cup Goals (7): McGuire 3, McKenzie 2, MacFarlane 1, McInally 1.
Scottish Cup Goals: None. **League Challenge Cup Goals (1):** McKenzie 1.

ALLOA ATHLETIC

Ground: Recreation Park, Alloa. **Capacity:** 4,111.
Telephone: 01259-722695. **Colours:** Gold and black. **Nickname:** Wasps.

Balfour, R 15	Lamont, W 1	Monaghan, M 19
Cadden, S .... –(1)	Little, T .... 10(10)	Nelson, M .... 21(3)
Cameron, J 1	Mackay, S .... 10(3)	Pew, D .... 20(1)
Cowan, M 30	McAnenay, M ..... 10(15)	Piggot, J .... 5(9)
Dick, A .... –(1)	McAneny, P ..... 30(2)	Simpson, P .... 8(3)
Dwyer, P .... 14(1)	McAvoy, N 4	Tennant, S 2
Gilmour, J .... 14(16)	McCormack, J 25	Valentine, C 35
Irvine, W 33	McCulloch, K ..... 11(4)	Wilson, M .... 14(2)
Johnston, N .... –(2)	Mathieson, M 3	Wilson, S 22
Kane, K .... 27(1)	Moffat, B .... 12(3)	Wylie, R .... –(2)

League Goals (50): Irvine 12, Dwyer 11, Cowan 3, McAneny 3, Moffat 3, Pew 3, Piggot 3, Simpson 3, Gilmour 2, McCormack 2, Kane 1, Mackay 1, McAnenay 1, Nelson 1, Wilson 1.

Coca-Cola Cup Goals (4): Dwyer 1, Irvine 1, McAneny 1, McAvoy 1. **Scottish Cup Goals (4):** Dwyer 1, Irvine 1, McAnenay 1, McKay 1. **League Challenge Cup Goals (3):** Irvine 3.

ARBROATH
Ground: Gayfield Park, Arbroath. **Capacity:** 6,488.
Telephone: 01241-872157. **Colours:** Maroon, white. **Nickname:** Red Lichties.

Arthur, G	9	Longmuir, K	2(3)	Pew, D	13
Balfour, G	10	Mackie, B	3	Phinn, J	2
Bilsland, B	6	McAulay, J	36	Reynolds, C	9
Clark, P	3(1)	McCarron, J	19(5)	Roberts, P	7(7)
Crawford, J	26	McCormick, S	2(2)	Scott, S	11(16)
Dunn, G	–(1)	McVicar, D	20(1)	Tennant, S	2
Florence, S	20(7)	McWalter, M	23(1)	Valentine, S	1
Gallagher, J	24(1)	Moonlight, P	1(1)	Ward, J	14(1)
Gardner, R	10	Morrison, P	8(2)	Waters, M	7
Grant, B	15(2)	Murray, I	–(1)	Watters, W	10
Hinchcliffe, C	27	Orr, J	6(1)	Welsh, B	1(7)
Hope, D	10	Peters, S	17	Wylie, R	21
Kerr, J	1				

League Goals (31): Grant 5, McAuley 4, Watters 4, McCarron 3, McWalter 3, McVicar 2, Pew 2, Scott 2, Gallagher 1, Hope 1, McCormick 1, Reynolds 1, Wylie 1, Opponent 1.
Coca-Cola Cup Goals: None. **Scottish Cup Goals (5):** McCormick 2, McCarron 1, Grant 1, Wylie 1. **League Challenge Cup Goals (2):** Peters 1, Welsh 1.

COWDENBEATH
Ground: Central Park, Cowdenbeath. **Capacity:** 5,258.
Telephone: 01383-610166. **Colours:** Royal blue and white. **Nickname:** Cowden.

Ballie, R	15(2)	Lockhart, D	–(1)	Nolan, T	6
Bowmaker, K	15(5)	McKinnon, M	–(2)	Petrie, E	15(2)
Brough, G	5(7)	McMahon, B	13	Ritchie, A	24(7)
Conn, S	28	Malloy, B	3(5)	Russell, N	30
Coulston, D	12(14)	Manson, S	1(1)	Scott, M	14(3)
Fairley, S	–(1)	Meldrum, G	33	Sinclair, C	30
Godfrey, A	4	Millar, G	2(1)	Stewart, W	22(8)
Hamilton, A	12(5)	Millar, P	2	Winter, C	31(1)
Huston, A	–(1)	Moffat, J	2	Wood, G	23
Humphreys, M	22(3)	Munro, K	32		

League Goals (38): Wood 6, Coulston 5, Stewart 5, Sinclair 4, McMahon 3, Winter 3, Bowmaker 2, Conn 2, Nolan 2, Petrie 2, Scott 2, Malloy 1, Ritchie 1.
Coca-Cola Cup Goals (1): Sinclair 1. **Scottish Cup Goals (1):** Scott 1. **League Challenge Cup Goals:** None.

EAST STIRLINGSHIRE
Ground: Firs Park, Falkirk. **Capacity:** 1,880.
Telephone: 01324-623583. **Colours:** White and black. **Nickname:** The Shire.

Abercromby, M	15(4)	Hunter, M	14(9)	McStay, R	1
Campbell, C	22	Inglis, G	25(3)	Muirhead, D	12(11)
Cochrane, M	7(10)	Jack, A	–(1)	Murray, N	3(3)
Conway, V	2(1)	Kerr, R	3	Neill, A	36
Devine, W	1	Lamont, W	3	Nisbet, I	1
Farquhar, A	2(4)	McBride, M	31	Patterson, P	7(7)
Hamilton, G	20(1)	McDougall, G	22	Ramsay, S	20(5)
Hringsson, H	1	McKenzie, C	1	Ronald, P	21(3)
Hughes, J	1	McNamee, P	1(2)	Ross, B	13(1)

Russell, G 30	Stirling, D .... 19(4)	Wilson, E 10
Scott, M .... −(8)	Watt, D 25	Wilson, S 1
Sneddon, S .... 26(1)		

League Goals (36): Inglis 9, McBride 5, Watt 5, Neill 3, Snedden 3, Muirhead 2, Ramsay 2, Abercromby 1, Hringsson 1, Hunter 1, McKenzie 1, Ronald 1, Opponents 2.
Coca-Cola Cup Goals (1): Ramsay 1. **Scottish Cup Goals (4):** Stirling 2, Abercromby 1, Inglis 1. **League Challenge Cup Goals (1):** Ramsay 1.

FORFAR ATHLETIC

Ground: Station Park, Forfar. **Capacity:** 8,732.
Telephone: 01307-463576. **Colours:** Sky blue and navy. **Nickname:** Sky Blues.

Allison, J .... 34(1)	Gray, A 1	McPhee, I .... 6(3)
Arthur, G 6	Hamilton, J .... 31(1)	Mann, R .... 31(1)
Bowes, M .... 30(2)	Hannigan, P .... 24(10)	Morgan, A 36
Cargill, A .... 15(1)	Higgins, G .... 8(1)	Nairn, J .... −(1)
Craig, D 33	Honeyman, B .... 29(6)	Orr, J .... −(2)
Donegan, S .... 24(1)	Inglis, G 1	Roberts, P .... 7(11)
Farquharson, S .... −(1)	Lee, I .... 31(2)	Robertson, D 6
Glennie, S .... 18(2)	Loney, J .... 23(9)	Sexton, S .... 2(1)

League Goals (74): Honeyman 17, Morgan 16, Hannigan 7, Mann 7, Roberts 6, Loney 4, Cargill 3, Higgins 3, Lee 3, Allison 2, Craig 2, Bowes 1, Glennie 1, McPhee 1, Opponents 2.
Coca-Cola Cup Goals (2): Higgins 1, Inglis 1. **Scottish Cup Goals (4):** Allison 1, Honeyman 1, Lee 1, Morgan 1. **League Challenge Cup Goals:** None.

INVERNESS CALEDONIAN THISTLE

Ground: Caledonian Stadium, Inverness. **Capacity:** 5,280.
Telephone: 01463-222880. **Colours:** Royal blue and red. **Nickname:** Caley.

Addicoat, W .... 6(8)	Hercher, A .... 10(3)	Sinclair, N .... −(3)
Bennett, G .... 3(6)	MacArthur, I 34	Stewart, I .... 34(2)
Calder, J 35	McLean, S .... 17(3)	Teasdale, M 36
Cherry, P 31	MacMillan, D 1	Thomson, B .... 21(2)
Christie, C .... 30(3)	Noble, M 34	Tokely, R .... 13(11)
De-Barros, M ...... 4(18)	Ross, D .... 26(5)	Wilson, B .... 27(2)
Hastings, R 34		

League Goals (70): Stewart 27, Thomson 10, McLean 8, Wilson 5, Hercher 4, Ross 4, Christie 3, Noble 2, Teasdale 2, Tokely 2, Addicoat 1, Cherry 1, De-Barros 1.
Coca-Cola Cup Goals: None. **Scottish Cup Goals (2):** McLean 1, Stewart 1.
League Challenge Cup Goals (3): Cherry 1, Stewart 1, Thomson 1.

MONTROSE

Ground: Links Park Stadium, Montrose. **Capacity:** 4,338.
Telephone: 01674-673200. **Colours:** Royal blue and white. **Nickname:** Gable Endies.

Bird, J .... 24(3)	Ingram, N .... 20(9)	Slythe, M .... −(1)
Butter, J 12	Larter, D 24	Smith, S .... 9(4)
Cassie, S .... −(1)	MacDonald, I .... 24(2)	Stephen, L .... 3(10)
Cooper, C .... 19(2)	McGlashan, C 30	Taylor, S .... 26(5)
Craib, M 26	Mailer, C .... 31(1)	Thomson, N .... 7(3)
Dorward, R 2	Masson, C 8	Tindal, K 31
Fisher, D .... 20(2)	Masson, P 14	Tosh, J .... 2(4)
Glass, S .... 11(5)	Purves, S .... 13(4)	Winiarski, S 10
Haro, M 30		

League Goals (46): McGlashan 11, Taylor 9, Ingram 4, Tindal 4, Smith 3, Bird 2, Haro 2, Masson C 2, Masson P 2, Cooper 1, Craib 1, Fisher 1, MacDonald 1, Mailer 1, Winiarski 1, Opponent 1.
Coca-Cola Cup Goals: None. **Scottish Cup Goals:** None. **League Challenge Cup Goals (9):** McGlashan 4, Glass 1, Ingram 1, P. Masson 1, Smith 1, Taylor 1.

QUEEN'S PARK

Ground: Hampden Park, Glasgow. **Capacity:** 9,222 (all-seated – only North Stand and North Stand Gantry will be used).
Telephone: 0141-632-1275. **Colours:** White and black. **Nickname:** Spiders.

Arbuckle, D 31	Ferry, D .... 21(11)	Maxwell, I 33
Bruce, G 31	Fitzpatrick, I .... 14(2)	Orr, G .... 9(1)
Callan, D .... 1(1)	Fraser, R .... 7(1)	Reilly, R .... −(1)
Cameron, C .... −(3)	Graham, D 29	Smith, D .... −(9)
Caven, R .... 27(2)	Hardie, M .... 14(9)	Smith, J .... 7(1)
Edgar, S 16	Kennedy, K .... 19(9)	Smith, M .... 12(6)
Elder, G 24	King, D .... 9(3)	Starr, S 5
Falconer, M ...... 8(14)	McGoldrick, K 31	Wilson, D .... 18(6)
Ferguson, P 9	McLauchlan, M .... 21(8)	

League Goals (46): Ferry 7, Kennedy 6, Maxwell 5, McGoldrick 5, McLauchlan 5, Hardie 4, Edgar 3, Graham 3, Caven 2, Falconer 2, Orr 2, Arbuckle 1, Fitzpatrick 1.
Coca-Cola Cup Goals (3): Falconer 1, Maxwell 1, McGoldrick 1. **Scottish Cup Goals (3):** Caven 1, Falconer 1, Opponent 1. **League Challenge Cup Goals (1):** Falconer 1.

ROSS COUNTY

Ground: Victoria Park, Dingwall. **Capacity:** 5,320.
Telephone: 01349-862253. **Colours:** Navy blue and white. **Nickname:** County

Adams, D .... 31(3)	Fotheringham, K .... 4(3)	Macleod, A.D. ...... 16(8)
Bellshaw, J .... 27(3)	Furphy, W .... 16(3)	Matheson, D 2
Bradshaw, P .... 1(2)	Gilbert, K 13	McBain, R .... 26(1)
Broddle, J .... 27(2)	Golabek, S .... 9(7)	Milne, C .... −(2)
Clark, J 1	Grant, B .... 1(4)	Morgan, K 7
Connelly, G .... 13(5)	Hart, R .... −(4)	Ross, A 22
Cooper, N 4	Herd, W .... 28(2)	Somerville, C ...... 7(1)
Cormack, D 4	Hewitt, J .... 2(5)	Watt, W 1
Farrell, G .... 22(1)	Hutchison, S 25	Williamson, R .... 16(3)
Ferguson, S .... 13(3)	Mackay, D 24	Wood, G .... 6(1)
Ferries, K .... 27(9)	Macleod, A.J. 1	

League Goals (58): Adams 22, Ross 9, Macleod 6, McBain 4, Ferguson 3, Golabek 3, Farrell 2, Ferries 2, Clarke 1, Connelly 1, Gilbert 1, Hart 1, Herd 1, Hewitt 1, Wood 1.
Coca-Cola Cup Goals (1): Adams 1. **Scottish Cup Goals (3):** Ross 3. **League Challenge Cup Goals:** None.

QUOTE-UNQUOTE

PROF. TOM CANNON, chief executive of the Management Charter Institute in the City of London, on Alex Ferguson: "He is the best exponent of psychological warfare since Montgomery in the Second World War. He doesn't have a persecution complex, but it's very convenient for him to pretend he has. Even when he is at his angriest, it is purposeful anger. He provokes his opponents, then appears to apologise, which only provokes them even more."

GRAHAM RIX, Ruud Gullit's right-hand man, assessing Chelsea's up-and-coming trainees: "I wish I was 16 again."

PLAYING STAFFS 1997-98

(As notified at time of going to press)

F.A. CARLING PREMIERSHIP

ARSENAL

Name	Height ft. in.	Previous Club	Birthplace	Birthdate
Goalkeepers				
Bartram, Vince	6. 2	Bournemouth	Birmingham	7.08.68
Lukic, John	6. 4	Leeds	Chesterfield	11.12.60
Manninger, Alex	—	Casino Graz	Salzburg	
Seaman, David	6. 4	Q.P.R.	Rotherham	19.09.63
Defenders				
Adams, Tony	6. 3	—	Romford	10.10.66
Bould, Steve	6. 4	Stoke	Stoke	16.11.62
Crowe, Jason	5. 7	—	Kent	30.09.78
Dixon, Lee	5. 8	Stoke	Manchester	17.03.64
Grimandi, Gilles	5. 9	AS Monaco	Gap, Fra	11.11.70
Hughes, Richard	—	Atalanta, It	—	
Keown, Martin	6. 1	Everton	Oxford	24.07.66
Linighan, Andy	6. 4	Norwich	Hartlepool	18.06.62
McGowan, Gavin	5. 8	—	Blackheath	16.01.76
Marshall, Scott	6. 1	—	Edinburgh	1.05.73
Petit, Emmanuel	6. 0	AS Monaco	Dieppe, Fra	22.09.70
Taylor, Ross	5. 10	—	Southend	14.01.77
Upson, Matthew	6. 0	Luton	Hartismere	18.04.79
Winterburn, Nigel	5. 8	Wimbledon	Nuneaton	11.12.63
Midfield				
Black, Michael	5. 8	—	Chigwell	6.10.76
Garde, Remi	5. 9	Strasbourg	L'Arbresle, Fra	3.04.66
Gislason, Valur	5. 10	Fram	Reykjavik, Ice	8.09.77
Helder, Glenn	5. 11	Vitesse Arnhem	Leiden, Hol.	28.10.68
Hughes, Stephen	6. 0	—	Wokingham	18.09.76
Mendez, Alberto	5. 8	Feucht	Nurenberg, Ger	24.10.74
Parlour, Ray	5. 10	—	Romford	7.03.73
Pereira, Luis Boa Morte	5. 10	Sporting Lisbon	Lisbon, Port	4.08.77
Platt, David	5. 10	Sampdoria, Ita.	Chadderton	10.06.66
Overmars, Marc	5. 8	Ajax, Amsterdam	Emst, Holland	29.03.73
Selley, Ian	5. 9	—	Chertsey	14.06.74
Shaw, Paul	5. 11	—	Burnham	4.09.73
Vieira, Patrick	6. 3	AC Milan	Dakar, Senegal	23.06.76
Forwards				
Anelka, Nicolas	6. 1	Paris St Germain	Versailles	14.03.79
Bergkamp, Dennis	6. 0	Inter Milan, Ita.	Amsterdam, Hol.	10.05.69
Kiwomya, Chris	5. 9	Ipswich	Huddersfield	2.12.69
Rankin, Isaiah	5. 10	—	Edmonton	22.05.78
Wright, Ian	5. 9	Crystal Palace	Woolwich	3.11.63

ASTON VILLA

Name	Height ft. in.	Previous Club	Birthplace	Birthdate
Goalkeepers				
Bosnich, Mark	6. 1	Sydney Croatia, Aust.	Fairfield, Aust.	13.01.72
Oakes, Michael	6. 2	—	Northwich	30.10.73

Name	Height ft. in.	Previous Club	Birthplace	Birthdate
Rachel, Adam	5. 11	–	Birmingham	10.12.76
Defenders				
Charles, Gary	5. 9	Derby	London	13.04.70
Collins, Lee	6. 1	–	Birmingham	10.09.77
Ehiogu, Ugo	6. 2	W.B.A.	London	3.11.72
Grayson, Simon	6. 0	Leicester City	Ripon	16.12.69
Hines, Leslie	5. 7	–	Iserlohn, Ger.	7.01.77
Hughes, David	6. 4	–	Wrexham	1.02.78
Murray, Scott	5. 10	Fraserburgh	Aberdeen	26.05.74
Nelson, Fernando	5. 11	Sporting Lisbon, Por.	Lisbon, Por.	5.11.71
Petty, Ben	6. 0	–	Solihull	22.03.77
Scimeca, Riccardo	6. 1	–	Leamington Spa	13.06.75
Southgate, Gareth	6. 0	Crystal Palace	Watford	3.09.70
Staunton, Steve	6. 0	Liverpool	Drogheda	19.01.69
Wright, Alan	5. 4	Blackburn	Ashton-u-Lyme	28.09.71
Midfield				
Draper, Mark	5. 10	Leicester City	Longeaton	11.11.70
Jaszcun, Tommy	5. 10	–	Kettering	16.09.77
Kirby, Alan	5. 7	–	Waterford	8.09.77
Lescott, Aaron	5. 8	–	Birmingham	2.12.78
Taylor, Ian	6. 1	Sheff. Wed.	Birmingham	4.06.68
Townsend, Andy	5. 11	Chelsea	Maidstone	23.07.63
Forwards				
Byfield, Darren	5. 11	–	Birmingham	29.09.76
Collymore, Stan	6. 3	Liverpool	Stone, Staffs	22.01.71
Davis, Neil	5. 8	Redditch Utd.	Bloxwich	15.08.73
Hendrie, Lee	5. 9	–	Birmingham	18.05.77
Joachim, Julian	5. 7	Leicester City	Boston	12.09.74
Lee, Alan	6. 2	–	Galway	21.08.78
Middleton, Darren	6. 0	–	Lichfield	28.12.78
Milosevic, Savo	6. 0	Partizan Bel., Yug.	Bijelina, Serbia	2.09.73
Walker, Richard	6. 0	–	Birmingham	8.11.77
Yorke, Dwight	5. 11	St. Clair's, Tobago	Tobago	3.11.71

BARNSLEY

Name	Height ft. in.	Previous Club	Birthplace	Birthdate
Goalkeepers				
Bullock, Tony	6. 1	Leek Town	Warrington	18.02.72
Lees, Lars	6. 5	Bayer Leverkusen		
Watson, David	5. 9	–	Barnsley	10.11.73
Defenders				
Appleby, Matt	5. 10	Darlington	Middlesbrough	16.04.72
Davis, Steven	6. 0	Burnley	Birmingham	26.07.65
De Zeeuw, Arjan	6. 1	Telstar, Hol.	Castricum, Hol.	16.04.70
Eden, Nicholas	5. 8	–	Sheffield	12.12.72
Hulson, Shane	5. 9	–	Barnsley	17.12.78
Hume, Mark	6. 1	–	Barnsley	21.05.78
Jones, Dean	6. 0	–	Barnsley	12.10.77
Jones, Scott	5. 7	–	Sheffield	1.05.75
Krizan, Ales	–	Maribor, Slov	–	–
Morgan, Christopher	5. 11	–	Barnsley	13.02.78
Moses, Adrian	5. 8	–	Doncaster	4.05.75
Perry, Jonathan	6. 0	–	Hamilton, N.Z.	22.11.76
Sheridan, Darren	5. 4	Winsford Town	Manchester	8.12.67
Shirtliff, Peter	6. 0	Wolves	Sheffield	6.04.61
Thompson, Neil	5. 10	Ipswich	Beverley	2.10.63
Midfield				
Bosancic, Jovo	5. 11	Campanaior	Novi Sad	7.08.70

Bullock, Martin	5. 4	Eastwood Town	Derby	5.03.75
Gregory, Andrew	5. 7	–	Barnsley	8.10.76
McClare, Sean	5. 7	–	Rotherham	12.01.78
Redfearn, Neil	5. 8	Oldham	Bradford	20.06.65
Shenton, Daniel	5.11	–	Sheffield	29.09.78
Tinkler, Eric		Cagliari, It	South Africa	
Forwards				
Bagshaw, Paul	5. 7	–	Sheffield	29.05.79
Beckett, Duane	5. 8	–	Sheffield	31.01.78
Beckett, Luke	5. 8	–	Sheffield	25.11.76
Hendrie, John	5. 7	Middlesbrough	Lennoxtown	24.10.63
Hristov, Georgi		Partizan Belgrade	Macedonia	
Liddell, Andy	5. 6	–	Leeds	28.06.73
Marcelle, Clinton	5. 4	Felguiras	Port of Spain	9.11.68
Prendergast, Rory	5. 8	–	Pontefract	6.04.78
Regis, David	6. 0	Southend	Paddington	3.03.64
Rose, Karl	5. 4	–	Barnsley	12.10.78
Ten Heuvel, Laurens	5.10	Den Bosch, Hol.	Duivendrecht, Hol.	6.06.76
Wilkinson, Paul	6. 1	Middlesbrough	Louth	30.10.64

BLACKBURN ROVERS

Name	Height ft. in.	Previous Club	Birthplace	Birthdate
Goalkeepers				
Filan, John	5.11	Coventry	Sydney, Aust	8.02.70
Flowers, Tim	6. 2	Southampton	Kenilworth	3.02.67
Defenders				
Berg, Henning	6. 0	Lillestrom, Nor.	Eidsvoll, Nor.	1.09.68
Coleman, Chris	6. 2	Crystal Palace	Swansea	10.06.70
Croft, Gary	5. 8	Grimsby	Stafford	17.02.74
Henchoz, Stephan	6. 1	Hamburg	Switzerland	
Hendry, Colin	6. 1	Man. City	Keith	7.12.65
Kenna, Jeff	5.11	Southampton	Dublin	27.08.70
Le Saux, Graeme	5.10	Chelsea	Jersey	17.10.68
Marker, Nicky	6. 0	Plymouth	Exeter	3.05.65
Valery, Patrick	5.11	Bastia	France	
Midfield				
Bohinen, Lars	5.11	Nott'm. Forest	Vadso, Nor.	8.09.66
Donis, Georgios	6. 0	Panathinaikos, Gre.	Greece	29.10.69
Fenton, Graham	5.10	Aston Villa	Wallsend	22.05.74
Flitcroft, Garry	6. 0	Man. City	Bolton	6.11.72
Gallacher, Kevin	5. 8	Coventry	Clydebank	23.11.66
Holmes, Matthew	5. 7	West Ham	Luton	1.08.69
McKinlay, Billy	5. 8	Dundee Utd.	Glasgow	22.04.69
Pearce, Ian	6. 3	Chelsea	Bury St. Edmunds	7.05.74
Ripley, Stuart	6. 0	Middlesbrough	Middlesbrough	20.11.67
Sherwood, Tim	6. 1	Norwich	St. Albans	6.02.69
Forwards				
Andersson, Anders	–	Malmo, Swe	–	
Dahlin, Martin	–	Roma	Sweden	
Pedersen, Per	6. 0	Odense	Denmark	
Sutton, Chris	6. 3	Norwich	Nottingham	10.03.73
Wilcox, Jason	6. 0	–	Bolton	15.07.71

BOLTON WANDERERS

Name	Height ft. in.	Previous Club	Birthplace	Birthdate
Goalkeepers				
Branagan, Keith	6. 0	Millwall	Fulham	10.07.66

Name	Height ft. in.	Previous Club	Birthplace	Birthdate
Glennon, Matthew	6. 2	–	Stockport	8.10.78
Ward, Gavin	6. 2	Bradford City	Sutton Coldfield	30.06.70
Defenders				
Aliofrer, Hasney	6. 0	–	Manchester	17.07.78
Bergsson, Gudni	6. 1	Tottenham	Iceland	21.07.65
Coleman, Simon	6. 0	Sheff. Wed.	Worksop	13.06.68
Cox, Neil	6. 0	Middlesbrough	Scunthorpe	8.10.71
Doherty, Martin	6. 2	–	Manchester	17.10.78
Elliott, Robbie	5. 10	Newcastle	Newcastle	25.12.73
Fairclough, Chris	5. 11	Leeds	Nottingham	12.04.64
McAnespie, Steve	5. 9	Raith	Kilmarnock	1.02.72
Phillips, Jimmy	6. 0	Middlesbrough	Bolton	8.02.66
Small, Bryan	5. 9	Aston Villa	Birmingham	15.11.71
Spooner, Nicholas	5. 10	–	Manchester	5.06.71
Strong, Greg	6. 2	Wigan	Bolton	5.09.75
Taggart, Gerry	6. 1	Barnsley	Belfast	18.10.70
Todd, Andrew	5. 10	Middlesbrough	Derby	21.09.74
Midfield				
Frandsen, Per	6. 1	FC Copenhagen	Copenhagen, Den.	6.08.70
Johansen, Michael	5. 6	FC Copenhagen	Golstrup, Den.	22.07.72
Pollock, Jamie	5. 11	Osasuna	Stockton	16.02.74
Sellars, Scott	5. 8	Newcastle	Sheffield	27.11.65
Sheridan, John	5. 9	Sheffield Wed	Stretford	7.10.64
Thompson, Alan	6. 0	Newcastle	Newcastle	22.12.73
Whitehead, Stuart	5. 11	Bromsgrove	Bromsgrove	17.07.76
Forwards				
Blake, Nathan	5. 11	Sheff. Utd.	Cardiff	27.01.72
Gunnlaugsson, Arnar	6. 0	IA Akranes, Ice	Iceland	
McGinlay, John	5. 9	Millwall	Inverness	8.04.64
Paatelainen, Mixu	6. 0	Aberdeen	Helsinki, Fin.	3.02.67
Potter, Lee	6. 0	–	Bolton	3.09.78
Taylor, Scott	5. 10	Millwall	Chertsey	5.05.76

CHELSEA

Name	Height ft. in.	Previous Club	Birthplace	Birthdate
Goalkeepers				
Colgan, Nick	6. 1	Drogheda	Drogheda	19.10.73
De Goey, Ed	–	Feyenoord	–	–
Grodas, Frode	6. 2	Lillestrom, Nor	Norway	24.10.64
Hitchcock, Kevin	6. 1	Mansfield	Custom House	5.10.62
Kharine, Dmitri	6. 3	CSKA Moscow, Rus.	Moscow, Rus.	16.08.68
Defenders				
Babayaro, Celestine	6. 0	Anderlecht	Kadun	29.08.78
Clarke, Steve	5. 9	St. Mirren	Saltcoats	29.08.63
Clement, Neil	5. 10	–	Reading	3.10.78
Duberry, Michael	6. 2	–	Enfield	14.10.75
Granville, Danny	5. 10	Cambridge	Islington	10.01.75
Gullit, Ruud	6. 1	Sampdoria, Ita.	Surinam	1.09.62
Lebouef, Frank	5.10	Strasbourg	Paris	22.01.68
Lambourde, Bernard	–	Bordeaux, Fra	France	–
Lee, David	6. 3	–	Kingswood	26.11.69
Petrescu, Dan	5. 9	Sheff. Wed.	Bucharest, Rom.	22.12.67
Sinclair, Frank	5. 8	–	Lambeth	3.12.71
Midfield				
Burley, Craig	6. 1	–	Ayr	24.09.71
Di Matteo, Roberto	5. 10	Lazio, Ita.	Berne, Swi.	29.05.70
Hughes, Paul	5. 11	–	London	19.04.76
Morris, Jody	5. 4	–	London	28.12.78

Myers, Andy	5.8	–	Hounslow	3.11.73
Newton, Eddie	5.9	–	Hammersmith	13.12.71
Poyet, Gustavo		Real Zaragoza	Uruguay	
Rocastle, David	5.9	Man. City	Lewisham	2.05.67 Hull
Wise, Dennis	5.6	Wimbledon	Kensington	15.12.66
Forwards				
Flo, Tor Andre	6.2	Brann Bergen	Norway	–
Hughes, Mark	5.10	Man. Utd.	Wrexham	1.11.63
Nicholls, Mark	5.10	–	Middlesex	30.05.77
Stein, Mark	5.7	Stoke	Capetown, S.A.	28.01.66
Vialli, Gianluca	5.11	Juventus, Ita.	Cremona, Ita.	9.07.64
Zola, Gianfranco	5.6	Parma	Sardinia	5.07.66

COVENTRY CITY

Name	Height ft. in.	Previous Club	Birthplace	Birthdate
Goalkeepers				
Hedman, Magnus	–	IFK Stockholm.	Sweden	–
Ogrizovic, Steve	6.5	Shrewsbury	Mansfield	12.09.57
Defenders	Nilsson			
Andrews, John	6.1	–	Cork	29.09.78
Borrows, Brian	5.10	Bolton	Liverpool	20.12.60
Breen, Gary	6.1	Birmingham	London	12.12.73
Burrows, David	5.10	Everton	Dudley	25.10.68
Daish, Liam	6.2	Birmingham	Portsmouth	23.09.68
Goodwin, Scott	5.9	–	Hull	13.09.78
Hall, Marcus	6.1	–	Coventry	24.03.76
Prenderville, Barry	6.1	–	Dublin	16.10.76
Shaw, Richard	5.9	Crystal Palace	Brentford	11.09.68
Williams, Paul	6.0	Derby	Burton	26.03.71
Willis, Adam	6.1	–	Nuneaton	21.09.76
Midfield				
Barnett, Christopher	5.11	–	Derby	20.12.78
Boland, Willie	5.9	–	Ennis	6.08.75
Devaney, Martin	5.10	–	Cheltenham	1.06.80
Eustace, John	5.11	–	Solihull	3.11.79
McAllister, Gary	6.1	Leeds Utd	Motherwell	25.12.64
Quinn, Barry	6.0	–	Dublin	9.05.79
Richardson, Kevin	5.7	Aston Villa	Newcastle	4.12.62
Shilton, Sam	5.11	– (Son of Peter)	Nottingham	21.07.78
Soltvedt, Trond Egil	6.1	Rosenborg	Voss, Norway	15.02.67
Strachan, Gordon	5.6	Leeds	Edinburgh	9.02.57
Telfer, Paul	5.9	Luton	Edinburgh	21.10.71
Forwards				
Blake, Aslam	6.0	–	Birmingham	9.10.79
Dublin, Dion	6.1	Man. Utd.	Leicester	22.04.69
Ducros, Andrew	5.6	–	Evesham	16.09.77
Faulconbridge, Craig	6.1	–	Nuneaton	20.04.78
Haworth, Simon	6.3	Cardiff	Cardiff	30.03.77
Johansen, Martin	–	FC Copenhagen	Denmark	–
Huckerby, Darren	5.11	Newcastle	Nottingham	23.04.76
Lightbourne, Kyle	6.2	Walsall	Bermuda	29.09.68
O'Neill, Michael	5.11	Hibernian	Portadown	5.07.69
Salako, John	5.11	Crystal Palace	Nigeria	11.02.69
Whelan, Noel	6.2	Leeds	Leeds	30.12.74

Nilsson R.
Moldovan, Viorel
Boateng George
Romania
Feyenoord
£3.5m

389

CRYSTAL PALACE

Name	Height ft. in.	Previous Club	Birthplace	Birthdate
Goalkeepers				
Miller, Kevin	6. 1	Watford	Falmouth	15.03.69
Nash, Carlo	6. 5	Clitheroe	–	13.09.73
Ormshaw, Gareth	6. 0		Durban	8.07.79
Defenders				
Boxall, Danny	5. 8		Croydon	24.08.77
Burton, Sagi	6. 2		Birmingham	25.11.77
Davies, Gareth	6. 1	Hereford	Hereford	11.12.73
Edworthy, Marc	5. 8	Plymouth	Barnstaple	24.12.72
Gordon, Dean	6. 0	–	Thornton Heath	10.02.73
Hibburt, James	6. 0		Ashford	30.10.79
Linighan, Andy	6. 4	Arsenal	Hartlepool	18.06.62
Mullins, Hayden	6. 0	–	Reading	27.03.79
Muscat, Kevin	6. 0	–	Crawley	7.08.73
Quinn, Robert	5. 11		Sidcup	8.11.76
Tuttle, David	6. 2	Sheff. Utd.	Reading	6.02.72
Midfield				
Carlisle, Wayne	6. 0		Lisburn	9.09.79
Ginty, Rory	5. 9	–	Galway	23.01.77
Graham, Gareth	5. 7	–	Belfast	6.12.78
Hopkin, David	5. 9	Chelsea	Glasgow	21.08.70
Kennedy, Richard	5. 10	–	Waterford	28.08.78
Pitcher, Darren	5. 9	Charlton	Mile End	12.10.69
Roberts, Andy	5. 10	Millwall	Dartford	20.03.74
Rodger, Simon	5. 9	Bognor Regis	Shoreham	3.10.71
Savage, Robbie	5. 10	Crewe	Wrexham	18.10.74
Scully, Tony	5. 7	–	Dublin	12.06.76
Thomson, Steve	5. 8	–	Glasgow	23.01.78
Veart, Carl	5. 10	Sheff. Utd.	Whyalla, Aust.	21.05.70
Warhurst, Paul	6. 0	Blackburn	Stockport	26.09.69
Forwards				
Dyer, Bruce	5. 11	Watford	Ilford	13.04.75
Folan, Anthony	5. 10	–	Lewisham	18.09.78
Freedman, Dougie	5. 9	Barnet	Glasgow	21.01.74
Harris, Jason	6. 1	–	Sutton	24.11.76
McKenzie, Leon	5. 10	–	Croydon	17.05.78
Martin, Andrew	6. 0	–	Cardiff	28.02.80
Morrison, Clinton	6. 1	–	Tooting	14.05.79
Ndah, George	6. 1	–	Camberwell	23.12.74
Shipperley, Neil	6. 1	Southampton	Chatham	30.10.74
Stevens, David	5. 10	–	Ashford	29.04.79
Wordsworth, Dean	6. 2	Bromley	London	2.07.72

DERBY COUNTY

Name	Height ft. in.	Previous Club	Birthplace	Birthdate
Goalkeepers				
Hoult, Russell	6. 4	Leicester City	Leicester	22.11.72
Poom, Mart	6. 5	Tallscflora Tallin	Estonia	3.02.72
Defenders				
Carbon, Matt	6. 3	Lincoln City	Nottingham	8.06.75
Carsley, Lee	5. 9	–	Birmingham	28.02.74
Dailly, Christian	5. 10	Dundee Utd.	Dundee	23.10.73
Laursen, Jacob	5. 11	Silkeborg, Den.	Vejle, Den.	6.10.71
Rowett, Gary	6. 1	Everton	Bromsgrove	6.03.74
Stimac, Igor	6. 2	Hadjuk Split, Cro.	Methoric	24.01.70

390

Yates, Dean	6.2	Notts County	Leicester	26.10.67
Midfield				
Asanovic, Aljosa	5.10	Hadjuk Split, Cro.	Split, Cro.	14.12.65
Eranio, Stefano	5.10	AC Milan	Genoa	
Flynn, Sean	5.7	Coventry	Birmingham	13.03.68
Powell, Chris	5.10	Southend	Lambeth	8.09.69
Powell, Darryl	6.1	Portsmouth	Lambeth	15.01.71
Solis, Mauricio	5.8	Herediano	Costa Rica	
Trollope, Paul	5.9	Torquay	Swindon	3.06.72
Van der Laan, Robin	5.11	Port Vale	Schiedam, Hol.	5.09.68
Forwards				
Gabbiadini, Marco	5.10	Crystal Palace	Nottingham	20.01.68
Hunt, Jonathan	5.10	Birmingham City	London	2.11.71
Simpson, Paul	5.6	Oxford Utd.	Carlisle	26.07.66
Sturridge, Dean	5.7	–	Birmingham	27.07.73
Wanchope, Paulo	6.4	Herediano	Costa Rica	
Ward, Ashley	6.0	Norwich	Manchester	24.11.70
Willems, Ron	6.0	Grasshoppers, Swi.	Epa, Hol.	20.09.66

EVERTON

Name	Height ft. in.	Previous Club	Birthplace	Birthdate
Goalkeepers				
Gerrard, Paul	6.2	Oldham	Heywood, Lancs.	22.01.73
Southall, Neville	6.1	Bury	Llandudno	16.09.58
Defenders				
Allen, Graham	6.0	–	Bolton	8.04.77
Ball, Michael	–	–	Liverpool	2.10.79
Barrett, Earl	5.11	Aston Villa	Rochdale	28.04.67
Bilic, Slaven	6.2	West Ham	Croatia	11.09.68
Dunne, Richard	6.0	Home Farm	Dublin	21.09.79
Hinchcliffe, Andy	5.10	Man. City	Manchester	5.02.69
O'Connor, Jon	5.10	–	Darlington	19.10.76
Phelan, Terry	5.9	Chelsea	Manchester	16.03.67
Short, Craig	6.2	Derby	Bridlington	26.06.68
Unsworth, David	5.11	–	Preston	16.10.73
Watson, Dave	6.0	Norwich	Liverpool	20.11.61
Midfield				
Farrelly, Gareth	6.0	Aston Villa	Dublin	28.08.75
Grant, Tony	5.7	–	Liverpool	14.11.74
Hills, John	5.10	Blackpool	Blackpool	21.04.78
Parkinson, Joe	5.11	Bournemouth	Eccles	11.06.71
Speed, Gary	5.9	Leeds	Hawarden	8.09.69
Stuart, Graham	5.8	Chelsea	Tooting	24.10.70
Thomsen, Claus	6.0	Ipswich	Aarhus, Den	31.05.70
Forwards				
Barmby, Nick	5.6	Middlesbrough	Hull	11.02.74
Branch, Michael	5.10	–	Liverpool	18.10.78
Ferguson, Duncan	6.2	Rangers	Stirling	27.12.71
Oster, John	5.7	Grimsby	Boston	8.12.78

LEEDS UNITED

Name	Height ft. in.	Previous Club	Birthplace	Birthdate
Goalkeepers				
Beeney, Mark	6.4	Brighton	Pembury	30.12.67
Bridges, Simon	–	–	–	14.10.78
Martyn, Nigel	6.2	Crystal Palace	St Austell	11.08.66

Defenders

Name	ft. in.	Previous Club	Birthplace	Birthdate
Butler, John	–	–	–	28.10.79
Dorigo, Tony	5. 10	Chelsea	Melbourne, Aust.	31.12.65
Halle, Gunnar	5. 11	Oldham	Larvik, Nor.	11.08.65
Harte, Ian	5. 7	–	Drogheda	31.08.77
Jobson, Richard	6. 2	Oldham	Hull	9.05.63
Kelly, Gary	5. 9	Home Farm	Drogheda	9.07.74
Maybury, Alan	–	–	Dublin	8.08.78
Molenaar, Robert	6. 1	Volendam	Holland	27.02.69
Radebe, Lucas	6. 2	Kaizer Chiefs, S.A.	South Africa	12.04.69
Robertson, David	6. 0	Rangers	Aberdeen	17.10.68
Shepherd, Paul	6. 0	–	Leeds	17.11.77
Wetherall, David	6. 3	Sheff. Wed.	Sheffield	14.03.71

Midfield

Name	ft. in.	Previous Club	Birthplace	Birthdate
Blunt, Jason	5. 8	–	Penzance	16.08.77
Bowyer, Lee	5. 9	Charlton	London	3.01.77
Brolin, Tomas	5. 8	Parma	Huoiksvall, Swe.	29.11.66
Foster, Martin	–	–	–	29.10.77
Haaland, Alf-Inge	5. 10	Nott'm F.	Stavanger, Nor.	23.11.72
Jackson, Mark	5. 8	–	–	20.10.77
Kewell, Harry	–	–	Australia	22.09.78
McPhail, Stephen	–	–	–	9.12.79
Palmer, Carlton	6. 2	Sheff. Wed.	Oldbury	5.12.65
Ribeiro, Bruno	–	Vit. Setubal	Portugal	22.10.75

Forwards

Name	ft. in.	Previous Club	Birthplace	Birthdate
Boyle, Wesley	–	–	Portadown	30.03.70
Deane, Brian	6. 3	Sheff. Utd.	Leeds	7.02.68
Gray, Andy	5. 10	–	Harrogate	15.11.77
Hasselbaink, Jimmy	6. 2	Boavista	–	27.03.72
Laurent, Pierre	5. 10	Bastia	France	13.12.70
Lilley, Derek	5. 11	Morton	Scotland	9.02.72
Matthews, Lee	–	–	Middlesbrough	6.01.79
Rush, Ian	6. 0	Liverpool	Flint	20.10.61
Sharpe, Lee	6. 0	Man. Utd.	Halesowen	27.05.71
Wallace, Rod	5. 7	Southampton	Lewisham	2.10.69
Wright, Andy	–	–	Leeds	21.10.78
Yeboah, Tony	6. 0	Eint. Frankfurt, Ger.	Kumasi, Ghana	6.06.66

LEICESTER CITY

Name	Height ft. in.	Previous Club	Birthplace	Birthdate
Goalkeepers				
Keller, Kasey	6. 2	Millwall	Washington (USA)	29.11.69
Wilson, Stevie	6. 0	–	Leicester	28.11.78
Defenders				
Branston, Guy	6. 1	–	Leicester	9.01.79
Elliott, Matt	6. 3	Oxford Utd.	Roehampton	1.11.68
Emerson, Paul	6. 1	–	Newtonards	29.08.79
Fox, Martin	5. 8	–	Sutton-in-Ashfield	21.04.79
Kaamark, Pontus	5. 10	Gothenburg, Swe.	Vasteras, Swe.	5.04.69
Prior, Spencer	6. 3	Norwich City	Rochford	22.04.71
Ullathorne, Robert	5. 8	Osasuna (Spain)	Wakefield	11.10.71
Walsh, Steve	6. 3	Wigan	Fulwood	3.11.64
Watts, Julian	6. 3	Sheff. Wed.	Sheffield	17.03.71
Wenlock, Stephen	5. 8	–	Peterborough	11.03.78
Whitlow, Mike	6. 0	Leeds	Northwich	13.01.68
Midfield				
Campbell, Stuart	5. 8	–	Corby	9.12.77
Izzet, Mustapha	5. 6	Chelsea	Hackney	31.10.74

Name	Height ft. in.	Previous Club	Birthplace	Birthdate
Lennon, Neil	5. 10	Crewe	Lurgan	25.06.71
McMahon, Sam	5. 10	–	Newark	10.02.76
Oakes, Stefan	5. 11	–	Leicester	6.09.78
Mitchell, Ross	5. 11	–	Halifax	24.08.78
Parker, Garry	6. 0	Aston Villa	Oxford	7.09.65
Taylor, Scott	5. 9	Reading	Portsmouth	28.11.70
Forwards				
Arcos-Diaz, Miguel	5. 6	–	Loughborough	1.09.78
Claridge, Steve	6. 0	Birmingham	Portsmouth	10.04.66
Guppy, Steve	5. 11	Port Vale	Winchester	29.03.69
Heskey, Emile	6. 2	–	Leicester	11.01.78
Jaffa, Graeme	5. 6	–	Falkirk	8.05.79
Marshall, Ian	6. 2	Ipswich Town	Liverpool	20.03.66
Neil, Gary	6. 0	–	Glasgow	16.08.78
Robins, Mark	5. 8	Norwich	Ashton-u-Lyme	22.12.69
Skeldon, Kevin	5. 11	–	Edinburgh	27.04.78
Wilson, Stuart	5. 6	–	Leicester	16.09.77

LIVERPOOL

Name	Height ft. in.	Previous Club	Birthplace	Birthdate
Goalkeepers				
James, David	6. 5	Watford	Welwyn	1.08.70
Naylor, Roy	–	–	Liverpool	18.09.78
Nielsen, Jorgen	6. 0	Hvidovre	Nykabing	6.05.71
Warner, Tony	6. 4	–	Liverpool	11.05.74
Defenders				
Babb, Phil	6. 0	Coventry	Lambeth	30.11.70
Bjornebye, Stig	5. 10	Rosenborg, Nor.	Norway	11.12.69
Brazier, Phil	–	–	Liverpool	3.09.77
Harkness, Steve	5. 10	Carlisle	Carlisle	27.08.71
Jones, Rob	5. 8	Crewe	Wrexham	5.11.71
Kvarme, Bjorn	5. 11	Rosenborg, Nor.	Trondheim	17.6.72
Matteo, Dominic	6. 1	–	Dumfries	24.04.74
Roberts, Gareth	–	–	Wrexham	6.02.78
Ruddock, Neil	6. 2	Tottenham	Battersea	9.05.68
Wright, Mark	6. 2	Derby	Dorchester, Oxon	1.08.63
Midfield				
Barnes, John	5. 11	Watford	Kingston, Jam.	7.11.63
Berger, Patrik	6. 1	Bor. Dortmund	Prague	10.11.73
Carragher, James	6. 1	–	Liverpool	28.01.78
Cassidy, Jamie	5. 9	–	Liverpool	21.11.77
Culshaw, Thomas	5. 10	–	Liverpool	10.10.78
Dalglish, Paul	5. 10	Celtic	Glasgow	18.02.77
Friars, Sean	–	–	Derry	15.05.79
Kennedy, Mark	5. 11	Millwall	Dublin	15.05.76
Leonhardsen, Oyvind	5. 11	Wimbledon	Kristiansund, Nor.	17.08.70
McAteer, Jason	5. 11	Bolton	Birkenhead	18.06.71
McManaman, Steve	6. 0	–	Liverpool	11.02.72
Maxwell, Leyton	–	–	St Asaph	3.10.79
Murphy, Danny	5. 9	Crewe	Chester	18.03.77
Redknapp, Jamie	6. 0	Bournemouth	Barton-on-Sea	25.06.73
Rizzo, Nicky	5. 10	Sydney Olympic	Sydney, Aus.	9.06.79
Thomas, Michael	5. 9	Arsenal	Lambeth	24.08.67
Thompson, David	5. 7	–	Liverpool	12.09.77
Turkington, Eddie	–	–	Merseyside	15.05.78
Williams, Danny	–	–	Wrexham	12.07.79
Forwards				
Byrne, Niall	–	–	Dublin	3.09.79

393

Name	Height ft. in.	Previous Club	Birthplace	Birthdate
Fowler, Robbie	5. 11	–	Liverpool	9.04.75
Newby, John	–	–	Warrington	28.11.78
Owen, Michael	5. 8	–	Chester	14.12.79

MANCHESTER UNITED

Name	Height ft. in.	Previous Club	Birthplace	Birthdate
Goalkeepers				
Schmeichel, Peter	6. 4	Brondby, Den.	Gladsaxe, Den.	18.11.63
Van der Gouw, Raimond	6. 3	Vitesse Arnhem, Hol.	Oldenzaal, Hol.	24.03.63
Defenders				
Casper, Chris	6. 0	–	Burnley	28.04.75
Clegg, Michael	5. 8	–	Tameside	3.07.77
Curtis, John	5. 9	–	Nuneaton	3.09.78
Irwin, Denis	5. 8	Oldham	Cork	31.10.65
Johnsen, Ronny	6. 2	Besiktas, Tur.	Oslo, Nor.	10.06.69
McGibbon, Patrick	6. 1	Portadown	Lurgan	6.09.73
May, David	6. 0	Blackburn	Oldham	24.06.70
Neville, Gary	5. 10	–	Bury	18.02.75
Neville, Phil	5. 10	–	Bury	21.01.77
O'Kane, John	5. 10	–	Nottingham	15.11.74
Pallister, Gary	6. 4	Middlesbrough	Ramsgate	30.06.65
Midfield				
Beckham, David	6. 0	–	Leytonstone	2.05.75
Butt, Nicky	5. 10	–	Manchester	21.01.75
Davies, Simon	6. 0	–	Winsford	23.04.74
Keane, Roy	5. 10	Nott'm. Forest	Cork	10.08.71
McClair, Brian	5. 10	Celtic	Airdrie	8.12.63
Poborsky, Karel	5. 9	Slavia Prague	Czech Rep.	30.03.72
Forwards				
Cole, Andy	5. 11	Newcastle	Nottingham	15.10.71
Cooke, Terry	5. 7	–	Marston Green	5.08.76
Cruyff, Jordi	6. 1	Barcelona	Amsterdam	9.02.74
Giggs, Ryan	5. 11	–	Cardiff	29.11.73
Nevland, Erik	5. 11	Viking Stavanger	Stavanger, Nor	10.11.77
Scholes, Paul	5. 6	–	Salford	16.11.74
Sheringham, Teddy	6. 0	Tottenham	Highams Park	2.04.66
Solskjaer, Ole Gunnar	5. 9	Molde, Nor.	Norway	–
Thornley, Ben	5. 9	–	Bury	21.04.75
Tomlinson, Graeme	5. 9	Bradford City	Keighley	10.12.75

NEWCASTLE UNITED

Name	Height ft. in.	Previous Club	Birthplace	Birthdate
Goalkeepers				
Given, Shay	6. 0	Blackburn	Lifford	20.04.76
Harper, Stephen	6. 0	–	Easington	14.03.75
Hislop, Shaka	6. 6	Reading	London	22.02.69
Srnicek, Pavel	6. 2	Banik Ostrava, Cze.	Ostrava, Cze.	10.03.68
Defenders				
Albert, Philippe	6. 3	Anderlecht, Bel.	Bouillon, Bel.	10.08.67
Barton, Warren	5. 11	Wimbledon	Stoke Newington	19.03.69
Beresford, John	5. 5	Portsmouth	Sheffield	4.09.66
Elliot, Stuart	5. 8	–	Hendon	27.08.77
Hamilton, Des	5. 10	Bradford C.	Bradford	15.08.76
Howey, Steve	6. 1	–	Sunderland	26.10.71
Hughes, Aaron	6. 0	–	–	8.11.79

Name	ft. in.		Previous Club	Birthplace	Birthdate
Peacock, Darren	6.	2	Q.P.R.	Bristol	3.02.68
Watson, Steve	6.	1	–	North Shields	1.04.74
Midfield					
Batty, David	5.	8	Blackburn	Leeds	2.12.68
Gillespie, Keith	5.	9	Man. Utd.	Larne	18.02.75
Kelly, Patrick	5.	10	Celtic	–	26.04.78
Ketsbaia, Temur	5.	11	AEK Athens	Georgia	18.03.68
Lee, Robert	5.	11	Charlton	West Ham	1.02.66
Forwards					
Asprilla, Faustino	5.	9	Parma, Ita.	Tulua, Col.	10.11.69
Beardsley, Peter	5.	8	Everton	Newcastle	18.01.61
Brayson, Paul	5.	4	–	Newcastle	16.09.77
Ferdinand, Les	5.	11	Q.P.R.	Acton	8.12.66
Gudjansson, Bjarni	5.	8	Akranes	Iceland	26.02.79
Shearer, Alan	5.	11	Blackburn	Newcastle	13.08.76
Tomasson, Jon	6.	0	SC Heerenveen	Denmark	29.08.76

SHEFFIELD WEDNESDAY

Name	Height ft. in.		Previous Club	Birthplace	Birthdate
Goalkeepers					
Clarke, Matthew	6.	3	Rotherham	Sheffield	3.11.73
Pressman, Kevin	6.	2	–	Fareham	6.11.67
Defenders					
Atherton, Peter	5.	10	Coventry	Orrell	6. 04.70
Billington, David	6.	0	Peterborough	Oxford	15.10.80
Blondeau, Patrick	6.	0	AS Monaco	France	–
Newsome, Jon	6.	2	Norwich	Sheffield	6.09.70
Nicol, Steve	5.	10	Notts County	Irvine	11.12.61
Nolan, Ian	5.	11	Tranmere	Liverpool	9.07.70
Walker, Des	5.	11	Sampdoria, Ita.	Hackney	26.11.65
Weaver, Simon	5.	10	–	Doncaster	20.12.77
Midfield					
Collins, Wayne	5.	11	Crewe	Manchester	4.03.69
Hercock, David	5.	10	Cambridge	Peterborough	17.04.77
Hyde, Graham	5.	8	–	Doncaster	10.11.70
Jones, Ryan	6.	3	–	Sheffield	23.07.73
Kotylo, Krystof	5.	10	–	Sheffield	28.09.77
Oakes, Scott	5.	11	Luton	Leicester	5.08.72
Pembridge, Mark	5.	7	Derby	Merthyr Tydfil	29.11.70
Poric, Adem	5.	11	St. George, Budapest	London	22.04.73
Stefanovic, Dejan	6.	2	R.S. Belgrade, Yug.	Belgrade, Yug.	28.10.74
Trustfull, Orlando	6.	1	Feyernood	Amsterdam	4.08.70
Forwards					
Batty, Mark	5.	10	–	Nottingham	30.01.79
Blinker, Regi	5.	9	Feyenoord	Rotterdam	2.06.69
Booth, Andy	6.	1	Huddersfield	Huddersfield	17.03.73
Briscoe, Lee	5.	11	–	Pontefract	30.09.75
Carbone, Benito	5.	6	Inter Milan	Begnara	14.08.71
Donaldson, O'Neill	5.	11	Doncaster	Birmingham	24.11.69
Hirst, David	6.	0	Barnsley	Barnsley	7.12.67
Humphreys, Richie	5.	10	–	Sheffield	30.11.77
McKeever, Mark	5.	10	Peterborough	Derry	16.11.78
Platts, Mark	5.	11	–	Sheffield	23.05.79
Smith, Gavin	5.	10	–	Sheffield	24.09.77
Whittingham, Guy	5.	10	Aston Villa	Evesham	10.11.64

395

SOUTHAMPTON

Name	Height ft. in.	Previous Club	Birthplace	Birthdate
Goalkeepers				
Beasant, Dave	6. 4	Chelsea	Willesden	20.03.59
Flahavan, Daryl	5. 10	–	Southampton	9.09.77
Moss, Neil	6. 2	Bournemouth	New Milton	10.05.75
Taylor, Maik	6. 3	Barnet	Germany	4.09.71
Defenders				
Blamey, Nathan	5. 10	–	Plymouth	10.06.77
Charlton, Simon	5. 7	Huddersfield	Huddersfield	25.10.71
Dodd, Jason	5. 11	Bath City	Bath	2.11.70
Dryden, Richard	5. 11	Bristol City	Stroud	14.06.69
Lundekvam, Claus	6. 3	SK Brann	Norway	22.02.73
Monkou, Ken	6. 3	Chelsea	Surinam	29.11.64
Neilson, Alan	5. 11	Newcastle	Wegberg, Ger.	26.09.72
Piper, David	5. 10	–	Bournemouth	31.10.77
Spedding, Duncan	6. 2	–	Camberley	7.09.77
Van Gobbel, Ulrich	6. 0	Galatasaray	Surinam	16.01.71
Midfield				
Benali, Francis	5. 10	–	Southampton	30.12.68
Hughes, David	5. 10	–	St. Albans	30.12.72
Maddison, Neil	5. 10	–	Darlington	2.10.69
Magilton, Jim	6. 1	Oxford Utd.	Belfast	6.05.69
Oakley, Matthew	5. 10	–	Peterborough	17.08.77
Potter, Graham	6. 1	Stoke	Solihull	20.05.75
Robinson, Matthew	5. 11	–	Exeter	23.12.74
Sheerin, Paul	5. 10	–	Edinburgh	28.08.74
Slater, Robbie	5. 10	West Ham	Ormskirk	26.11.64
Tisdale, Paul	5. 9	–	Malta	14.01.73
Venison, Barry	5. 10	Galatasaray	Consett	16.08.64
Forwards				
Basham, Steve	5. 10	–	Southampton	2.12.77
Bennett, Frankie	5. 7	–	Birmingham	3.01.69
Davies, Kevin	6. 0	Chesterfield	Sheffield	26.03.77
Evans, Michael	6. 1	Plymouth Arg.	Plymouth	1.01.73
Le Tissier, Matthew	6. 1	Vale Recreation	Guernsey	14.10.68
Ostenstad, Egil	5. 11	Stavanger	Haugesund	2.01.72
Warren, Christer	5. 10	–	Poole	10.10.74
Watkinson, Russell	6. 0	Woking	Epsom	3.12.77
Williams, Andrew	5. 10	–	Bristol	8.10.77

TOTTENHAM HOTSPUR

Name	Height ft. in.	Previous Club	Birthplace	Birthdate
Goalkeepers				
Baardsen, Espen	6. 5	San. Fran. All Blacks	San Rafael	7.12.77
Brown, Simon	6. 1	–	Chelmsford	3.12.76
Marriott, Alan	6. 0	–	Bedford	3.09.78
Walker, Ian	6. 1	–	Watford	31.10.71
Defenders				
Arber, Mark	6. 0	–	South Africa	9.10.77
Austin, Dean	6. 0	Southend	Hemel Hempstead	26.04.70
Calderwood, Colin	6. 0	Swindon	Stranraer	20.01.65
Campbell, Sol	6. 1	–	Newham	18.09.74
Carr, Stephen	5. 7	–	Dublin	29.08.76
Darcy, Ross	6. 0	–	Balbriggan	21.03.78
Davies, Darren	5. 10	–	Port Talbot	13.08.78
Edinburgh, Justin	5. 10	Southend	Basildon	18.12.69

Domingues, José — Portugal

Name	Height ft. in.	Previous Club	Birthplace	Birthdate
Mabbutt, Gary	5. 9	Bristol Rovers	Bristol	23.08.61
Maher, Kevin	6. 0	–	Ilford	17.10.76
Nethercott, Stuart	5. 11	–	Chadwell Heath	21.03.73
Scales, John	6. 2	Liverpool	Harrogate	4.07.66
Townley, Leon	6. 0	–	Loughton	16.02.76
Vega, Ramon	6. 3	Cagliari	Zurich	14.06.71
Wilson, Clive	5. 7	Q.P.R.	Manchester	13.11.61
Midfield				
Brady, Garry	5. 8	–	Glasgow	7.09.76
Clapham, Jamie	5. 9	–	Lincoln	7.12.75
Clemence, Stephen	5. 11	–	Liverpool	31.03.78
Dozzell, Jason	6. 1	Ipswich	Ipswich	9.12.67
Gain, Peter	6. 1	–	Hammersmith	11.11.76
Ginola, David	6. 0	Newcastle	Gassin, Fra.	25.01.67
Hill, Danny	5. 9	–	Edmonton	1.10.74
Howells, David	5. 11	–	Guildford	15.12.67
Nielsen, Allan	5. 8	Brondby	Esbjerg	13.03.71
Sinton, Andy	5. 8	Sheff. Wed.	Newcastle	19.03.66
Webb, Simon	5. 11	–	Castle Bar	19.01.78
Forwards				
Allen, Rory	5. 9	–	Beckenham	17.10.77
Anderton, Darren	6. 1	Portsmouth	Southampton	3.03.72
Armstrong, Chris	6. 0	Crystal Palace	Newcastle	19.06.71
Fenn, Neale	5. 10	–	Edmonton	18.01.77
Fox, Ruel	5. 6	Newcastle	Ipswich	14.01.68
Iversen, Steffen	6. 1	Rosenborg	Oslo	10.11.76
McVeigh, Paul	5. 11	–	Belfast	6.12.77
Mahorn, Paul	5. 8	–	Whipps Cross	13.08.73

WEST HAM UNITED

Name	Height ft. in.	Previous Club	Birthplace	Birthdate
Goalkeepers				
Finn, Neil	5. 10	–	London	29.12.78
Miklosko, Ludek	6. 5	Banik Ostrava, Cze.	Ostrava, Cze.	9.12.61
Sealey, Les	6. 1	Leyton Orient	London	29.09.57
Defenders				
Blaney, Steven	6. 0	–	Orsett	24.03.77
Breacker, Tim	5. 11	Luton	Bicester	2.07.65
Coyne, Chris	6. 1	Perth	Brisbane, Aus.	20.12.78
Dicks, Julian	5. 10	Liverpool	Bristol	8.08.68
Ferdinand, Rio	6. 2	–	London	7.11.78
Hall, Richard	6. 2	Southampton	Ipswich	14.03.72
Moore, Jason	5. 8	–	Dover	16.02.79
Philson, Graeme	5. 1	Coleraine	Londonderry	24.03.75
Potts, Steve	5. 7	–	Hartford, U.S.A.	7.05.67
Rieper, Marc	6. 4	Brondby, Den.	Rodoure, Den.	5.06.68
Terrier, David		Metz, Fra.	France	
Midfield				
Berkovic, Eyal	–	Southampton	Israel	2.04.72
Bishop, Ian	5. 9	Man. City	Liverpool	29.05.65
Canham, Scott	5. 8	–	West Ham	5.11.74
Hughes, Michael	5. 7	Strasbourg, Fra.	Belfast	2.08.71
Impey, Andrew	5. 7	QPR	Hammersmith	13.09.77
Lampard, Frank	6. 0	–	London	21.06.78
Lazaridis, Stan	5. 9	West Adelaide, Aust.	Perth, Aust.	16.08.72
Lomas, Steve	6. 0	Man. City	Hanover	18.01.74
Moncur, John	5. 7	Swindon	Stepney	22.09.66
Omoyinmi, Emmanuel	5. 6	–	Nigeria	28.12.77

397

Abba Sannassi Marc Keller CD Karlsruhe

Rowland, Keith	5. 10	Bournemouth	Portadown	1.09.71
Williamson, Daniel	5. 10	–	Newham	5.12.73
Forwards				
Boogers, Marco	6. 1	Sp. Rotterdam, Hol.	Dordrecht, Hol.	12.01.67
Dowie, Iain	6. 1	Crystal Palace	Hatfield	9.01.65
Hartson, John	6. 1	Arsenal	Swansea	5.04.75
Hodges, Lee	5. 5	–	London	2.03.78
Kitson, Paul	5. 10	Newcastle	Murton	9.01.71

GK Forrest Craig
Sinclair Trev

WIMBLEDON QPR

Name	Height ft. in.	Previous Club	Birthplace	Birthdate
Goalkeepers				
Heald, Paul	6. 2	Leyton Orient	Rotherham	20.09.68
Murphy, Brendan	5. 11	Hull	Wexford	19.08.75
Sullivan, Neil	6. 0	Sutton United	Sutton	24.02.70
Defenders				
Blackwell, Dean	6. 1	–	Camden	5.12.69
Cunningham, Kenny	6. 0	Millwall	Dublin	28.06.71
Hawkins, Peter	5. 11	–	Kent	18.09.78
Hodges, Danny	6. 0	–	Greenwich	14.09.76
Jupp, Duncan	6. 0	Fulham	Guildford	25.01.75
Kimble, Alan	5. 8	Cambridge Utd.	Poole	6.08.66
McAllister, Brian	5. 11	–	Glasgow	30.11.70
Pearce, Andy	6. 4	Sheff. Wed.	Bradford	20.04.66
Perry, Chris	5. 8	–	Carshalton	26.04.73
Reeves, Alan	6. 1	Rochdale	Birkenhead	19.11.67
Thatcher, Ben	5. 10	Millwall	Swindon	30.11.75
Midfield				
Ardley, Neal	5. 8	–	Epsom	1.09.72
Castledine, Stewart	5. 11	–	Wandsworth	22.01.73
Earle, Robbie	5. 10	Port Vale	Newcastle-u-Lyme	27.01.65
Fear, Peter	5. 10	–	Sutton	10.09.73
Francis, Damien	5. 11	–	Wandsworth	27.02.79
Gardner, James	5. 10	–	London	22.10.78
Hughes, Ceri	5. 10	Luton	Pontypridd	26.2.71
Jones, Vinnie	6. 0	Chelsea	Watford	5.01.65
Forwards				
Clarke, Andy	5. 8	Barnet	Islington	22.07.67
Cort, Carl	5. 11	–	London	1.11.76
Ekoku, Efan	6. 1	Norwich	Manchester	8.06.67
Euell, Jason	6. 2	–	London	6.02.77
Gayle, Marcus	6. 2	Brentford	Hammersmith	27.09.70
Goodman, Jon	5. 11	Millwall	Walthamstow	2.06.71
Harford, Mick	6. 3	Coventry	Sunderland	12.02.59
Hinds, Leigh	5. 10	–	London	17.08.78
Holdsworth, Dean	5. 11	Brentford	Walthamstow	8.11.68
O'Connor, Richard	5. 10	–	London	30.08.78
Renner, Victor	6. 0	–	London	10.04.79

Hughes Michael
Solbakken Spaal   Lillstrom
MF Kennedy
S Leaburn

NATIONWIDE FOOTBALL LEAGUE

First Division

BIRMINGHAM CITY

Name	Height ft. in.	Previous Club	Birthplace	Birthdate
Goalkeepers				
Bennett, Ian	6. 0	Peterborough	Worksop	10.10.71
Defenders				
Ablett, Gary	6. 0	Everton	Liverpool	19.11.65
Brown, Kenny	5. 8	West Ham	Upminster	11.07.67
Bruce, Steve	6. 0	Man. Utd.	Corbridge	31.12.60
Dukes, Lee	5. 9	–	Walsall	24.10.79
Grainger, Martin	5. 10	Brentford	Enfield	23.08.72
Hinton, Craig	5. 11	–	Wolverhampton	26.11.77
Johnson, Michael	5. 11	Notts County	Nottingham	4.07.73
Wassall, Darren	6. 0	Derby County	Edgbaston	27.06.68
Midfield				
Bowen, Jason	5. 6	Swansea	Methyr Tydfil	24.08.72
Holland, Chris	5. 9	Newcastle Utd.	Whalley	11.09.75
Horne, Barry	5. 10	Everton	St. Asaph	18.05.62
Hughes, Bryan	5. 9	Wrexham	Liverpool	19.06.76
Legg, Andrew	6. 0	Notts County	Neath	28.07.66
O'Connor, Martyn	5. 8	Peterborough	Walsall	10.12.67
Otto, Ricky	5. 10	Southend	London	9.11.67
Robinson, Steve	5. 8	–	Nottingham	17.01.75
Tait, Paul	6. 1	–	Sutton Coldfield	31.07.71
Forwards				
Barnes, Steve	5. 4	Welling United	Wembley	5.01.76
Devlin, Paul	5. 8	Stafford Rangers	Birmingham	14.04.72
Forinton, Howard	–	Yeovil	Boston, Lincs	18.09.75
Forster, Nicky	5. 9	Brentford	Caterham	08.09.73
Francis, Kevin	6. 7	Stockport	Birmingham	6.12.67
Furlong, Paul	6. 0	Chelsea	Wood Green	1.10.68
Hey, Toni	–	Fortuna, Cologne	Birmingham	–
Ndlovu, Peter	5. 8	Coventry	Zimbabwe	25.02.73
Newell, Michael	6. 0	Chelsea	Liverpool	27.01.65

BRADFORD CITY

Name	Height ft. in.	Previous Club	Birthplace	Birthdate
Goalkeepers				
Gould, Jonathan	6. 1	Coventry	Paddington	18.07.68
Defenders				
Dreyer, John	6. 1	Stoke City	Alnwick	11.06.63
Jacobs, Wayne	5. 9	Rotherham	Sheffield	3.02.69
Kulcsar, George	6. 1	Royal Antwerp	Budapest	12.08.67
Liburd, Richard	5. 10	Middlesbrough	Nottingham	26.09.73
Mohan, Nicky	6. 1	Leicester City	Middlesbrough	6.10.70
Moore, Darren	6. 2	Doncaster	Birmingham	22.04.74
O'Brien, Andy	6. 0	–	Harrogate	29.06.79
Sas, Marco	6. 0	FC Breda, Hol.	Vlardingaan	06.02.70

Wilder, Chris	5. 10	Notts County	Stockbridge	23.09.67
Youds, Eddie	6. 1	Ipswich	Liverpool	3.05.70
Midfield				
Jansson, Jan	–	Norrkoping, Swe.	–	–
Kiwomya, Andy	5. 9	Scunthorpe	Huddersfield	1.10.67
Midgeley, Craig	5. 8		Bradford	24.05.67
Murray, Shaun	5. 7	Scarborough	Newcastle	7.02.70
Forwards				
Beagrie, Peter	5. 8	Man. City	Middlesbrough	28.11.65
Blake, Robbie	5. 9	Darlington	Middlesbrough	04.03.76
Edhino	5. 8	Guimaraes, Port.	Brazil	21.02.67
Lawrence, Jamie	6. 0	Leicester	Balham	8.03.70
Pepper, Nigel	5. 11	York City	Rotherham	25.04.68
Steiner, Robert	–	Norrkoping, Swe.	–	–
Sundgot, Ole Bjorn	5. 11	Molde FK	Olsumd	21.03.72
Watson, Gordon	5. 11	Southampton	Sidcup	20.03.71

BURY

Name	Height ft. in.	Previous Club	Birthplace	Birthdate
Goalkeepers				
Bracey, Lee	6. 0	Halifax Town	London	11.09.68
Kiely, Dean	6. 0	York	Salford	10.10.70
Philips, Paul	5. 11	–	Manchester	15.11.78
Defenders				
Butler, Paul	6. 2	Rochdale	Manchester	2.11.72
Lucketti, Chris	6. 0	Halifax Town	Manchester	28.09.71
West, Dean	5. 8	Lincoln City	Wakefield	5.12.72
Woodward, Andrew	6. 0	Crewe	Stockport	23.09.73
Winrow, Brian	5. 11	–	Oldham	19.05.79
Midfield				
Armstrong, Gordon	6. 0	Sunderland	Newcastle	15.07.67
Crossland, Mark	6. 0	Lincoln	Ashton-u-Lyne	14.12.78
Daws, Nicky	5. 11	Altrincham	Manchester	15.03.70
Forrest, Martyn	5. 7	–	Bury	2.01.79
Hughes, Ian	5. 11	–	Bangor, N Wales	2.08.74
Johnrose, Lennie	5. 10	Hartlepool	Preston	29.11.69
Jepson, Ronnie	6. 1	Huddersfield	Audley	12.05.63
Rigby, Tony	5. 10	Barrow	Ormskirk	10.08.72
Forwards				
Battersby, Tony	5. 10	Notts County	Doncaster	30.08.75
Hirst, Matthew	6. 2	Millwall	St. Albans	14.11.77
Johnson, David	5. 6	Man. Utd.	Kingston, Jam.	15.08.76
Matthews, Rob	5. 11	York	Slough	14.10.70
Pugh, David	6. 2	Chester	Liverpool	19.09.64

CHARLTON ATHLETIC

Name	Height ft. in.	Previous Club	Birthplace	Birthdate
Goalkeepers				
Petterson, Andy	6. 1	Luton	Freemantle, Aust.	26.09.69
Salmon, Mike	6. 2	Wrexham	Leyland	14.07.64
Defenders				
Balmer, Stuart	6. 1	Celtic	Falkirk	20.06.69
Barness, Anthony	5. 10	Chelsea	Lewisham	25.03.72
Brown, Steve	6. 1	–	Brighton	13.05.72
Chapple, Phil	6. 2	Cambridge Utd.	Norwich	26.11.66

Name	Height ft. in.	Previous Club	Birthplace	Birthdate
Poole, Gary	6. 0	Birmingham	Stratford	11.09.67
Rufus, Richard	6. 1	–	Lewisham	12.01.75
Midfield				
Jones, Keith	5. 9	Southend	Dulwich	14.10.64
Kinsella, Mark	5. 9	Colchester	Dublin	12.08.72
Newton, Shaun	5. 8	Brighton	Camberwell	20.08.75
Nicholls, Kevin	–	–	Newham	02.01.79
O'Connell, Brendan	5. 9	Barnsley	Waterloo	12.11.66
Robinson, John	5. 10	Brighton	Bulawayo, Zim.	29.08.71
Forwards				
Allen, Bradley	5. 7	Q.P.R.	Harold Wood	13.09.71
Emblen, Paul	–	Tonbridge Angels	–	–
Jones, Steve	6. 0	West Ham	Cambridge	17.03.70
Leaburn, Carl	6. 3	–	Lewisham	30.03.69
Mendonca, Clive	5. 10	Grimsby Town	Tullington	09.09.68

CREWE ALEXANDRA

Name	Height ft. in.	Previous Club	Birthplace	Birthdate
Goalkeepers				
Bankole, Ademole	6. 3	–	Lagos	9.09.69
Cutler, Neil	6. 1	WBA	Birmingham	3.09.76
Gayle, Mark	6. 2	Walsall	Bromsgrove	21.10.69
Kearton, Jason	6. 1	Everton	Ipswich	9.07.69
Defenders				
Johnson, Seth	5. 10	–	Birmingham	12.03.79
Lightfoot, Chris	6. 1	Wigan	Warrington	1.04.70
Macauley, Steve	6. 1	Fleetwood Town	Lytham	4.03.69
Smith, Shaun	5. 10	Halifax Town	Leeds	9.04.71
Unsworth, Lee	5. 11	Ashton United	Eccles	25.02.73
Westwood, Ashley	5. 11	Man. Utd.	Bridgnorth	31.08.76
Midfield				
Charnock, Phil	5. 10	Liverpool	Southport	14.02.75
Launders, Brian	5. 10	Crystal Palace	Dublin	8.01.76
Rivers, Mark	5. 10	–	Crewe	26.11.75
Tierney, Francis	5. 10	–	Liverpool	10.09.75
Whalley, Gareth	5. 9	–	Manchester	19.12.73
Forwards				
Adebola, Dele	6. 3	–	Lagos	23.06.75
Anthrobus, Steve	6. 2	Shrewsbury	Wandsworth	10.11.68
Garvey, Steve	5. 9	–	Manchester	22.11.73
Little, Colin	5. 8	Hyde United	Wythenshawe	4.11.72
Moralee, Jamie	5. 11	Watford	Wandsworth	7.12.71

HUDDERSFIELD TOWN

Name	Height ft. in.	Previous Club	Birthplace	Birthdate
Goalkeepers				
Francis, Steve	6. 1	Reading	Billericay	29.05.64
O'Connor, Derek	5. 11	–	Dublin	9.03.78
Defenders				
Collins, Sam	6. 2	–	Pontefract	5.06.77
Cowan, Tom	5. 8	Sheff. Utd.	Bellshill	28.08.69
Dyson, Jon	6. 1	–	Mirfield	18.12.71
Edmondson, Darren	6. 0	Carlisle Utd.	Cumbria	4.11.71
Gray, Kevin	6. 0	Mansfield	Sheffield	7.01.72
Jenkins, Steve	5. 11	Swansea	Merthyr Tydfil	16.07.72
Morrison, Andy	6. 1	Blackpool	Inverness	30.07.70

Name	ft. in.	Previous Club	Birthplace	Birthdate
Ryan, Robbie	5. 10	–	Dublin	16.05.77
Midfield				
Baldry, Simon	5. 10	–	Huddersfield	12.02.76
Browning, Marcus	6. 0	Bristol Rovers	Bristol	22.04.71
Burnett, Wayne	5. 11	Bolton Wanderers	Lambeth	4.09.71
Dalton, Paul	5. 11	Plymouth	Middlesbrough	25.04.67
Heary, Thomas	5. 9	–	Dublin	14.02.79
Illingworth, Jeremy	5. 10	–	Huddersfield	20.05.77
Makel, Lee	5. 9	Blackburn	Sunderland	11.01.73
Murphy, Stephen	5. 11	–	Dublin	5.04.78
Forwards				
Beresford, David	5. 4	Oldham	Manchester	11.11.76
Edwards, Rob	5. 9	Crewe	Manchester	23.02.70
Facey, Delroy	5. 11	–	Huddersfield	22.04.80
Kaye, Peter	5. 7	–	Huddersfield	04.11.77
Lawson, Ian	5. 11	–	Huddersfield	4.11.77
Payton, Andy	5. 9	Barnsley	Burnley	3.10.67
Stewart, Marcus	5. 10	Bristol Rovers	Bristol	7.11.72

IPSWICH TOWN

Name	Height ft. in.	Previous Club	Birthplace	Birthdate
Goalkeepers				
Forrest, Craig	6. 5	–	Vancouver, Can.	20.09.67
Wright, Richard	6. 2	–	Ipswich	5.11.77
Defenders		Clapham Jamie (LB)		
Brown, Wayne	6. 0	–	Barking	20.08.77
Ellis, Kevin	6. 2	–	Great Yarmouth	12.05.77
Gaughan, Kevin	6. 0	–	Glasgow	6.03.78
Mowbray, Tony	6. 1	Celtic	Saltburn	22.11.63
Swailes, Chris	6. 2	Doncaster	Gateshead	19.10.70
Taricco, Mauricio	5. 8	Argentinos Jun.	Buenos Aires	10.03.73
Venus, Mark	6. 0	Wolves	Hartlepool	6.04.67
Wark, John	5. 11	Middlesbrough	Glasgow	4.08.57
Midfield				
Bell, Leon	5. 8	–	Ipswich	23.09.77
Mason, Paul	5. 9	Aberdeen	Liverpool	3.09.63
Milton, Simon	5. 10	Bury Town	Fulham	23.08.63
Petta, Bobby	5. 9	Feyenoord, Hol.	Rotterdam, Hol.	6.08.74
Sonner, Danny	5. 11	Burnley	Wigan	9.01.72
Stockwell, Mick	5. 9	–	Chelmsford	14.02.65
Tanner, Adam	6. 0	–	Maldon	25.10.73
Uhlenbeek, Gus	5. 10	Tops, SV	Surinam	20.08.70
Williams, Geraint	5. 7	Derby	Treorchy	5.01.62
Forwards				
Gregory, Neil	5. 11	–	Ndola, Zambia	7.10.72
Mathie, Alex	5. 10	Newcastle	Bathgate	20.12.68
Naylor, Richard	6. 1	–	Leeds	28.02.77
Scowcroft, James	6. 1	–	Bury St. Edmunds	15.11.75

MANCHESTER CITY

Name	Height ft. in.	Previous Club	Birthplace	Birthdate
Goalkeepers				
Brown, Michael	5. 9	–	Stanraer	6.11.79
Margetson, Martyn	6. 0	–	Neath	8.09.71
Weaver, Nick	6. 3	Mansfield	Sheffield	2.03.79
Wright, Tommy	6. 1	Nott'm Forest	Belfast	29.08.63

Defenders

Name	Height ft. in.	Previous Club	Birthplace	Birthdate
Beesley, Paul	6. 1	Leeds	Wigan	21.09.65
Brannan, Ged	6. 0	Tranmere	Liverpool	15.01.72
Brightwell, Ian	5. 10	–	Lutterworth	9.04.68
Callaghan, Anthony	5. 7	–	Manchester	11.01.78
Edghill, Richard	5. 9	–	Oldham	23.09.74
Fenton, Anthony	5. 10	–	Preston	23.11.79
Fenton, Nicholas	5. 10	–	Preston	23.11.79
Foster, John	5. 10	–	Manchester	19.09.73
Gallagher, Ben	5. 8	–	Rugby	12.10.78
Hiley, Scott	5. 9	Birmingham	Plymouth	27.09.68
Ingram, Rae	5. 11	–	Manchester	6.12.74
Kernaghan, Alan	6. 2	Middlesbrough	Otley	25.04.67
Rimmer, Stephen	6. 3	–	Liverpool	23.05.79
Symons, Kit	6. 1	Portsmouth	Basingstoke	8.03.71
Vaughan, Tony	6. 0	Ipswich	Manchester	11.10.75
Wiekens, Gerrard	6. 1	Veendam, Hol.	Tolhviswyk	25.02.73

Midfield

Name	Height ft. in.	Previous Club	Birthplace	Birthdate
Brisco, Neil	6. 0	–	Wigan	28.01.78
Brown, Michael	5. 10	–	Hartlepool	25.01.77
Clough, Nigel	5. 10	Liverpool	Sunderland	19.03.66
Crooks, Lee	5. 11	–	Wakefield	14.01.78
Kinkladze, Georgi	5. 8	Dinamo Tbilisi	Tbilisi, Geo.	6.07.73
Horlock, Kevin	6. 0	Swindon	Erith	1.11.72
Mason, Gary	5. 8	–	Edinburgh	15.10.79
McGlinchey, Brian	5. 7	–	Derry	26.10.77
McGoldrick, Eddie	5. 10	Arsenal	London	30.04.65
Morley, Neil	5. 8	–	Warrington	16.11.78
Summerbee, Nick	5. 10	Swindon	Altrincham	26.08.71
Thomas, Scott	5. 9	–	Bury	30.10.74
Whitley, Jeff	5. 9	–	Zambia	28.01.79
Whitley, Jim	5. 9	–	Zambia	14.04.75

Forwards

Name	Height ft. in.	Previous Club	Birthplace	Birthdate
Creaney, Gerry	5. 10	Portsmouth	Coatbridge	13.04.70
Dickov, Paul	5. 5	Arsenal	Glasgow	1.11.72
Greenacre, Chris	5. 11	–	Halifax	23.12.77
Heaney, Neil	5. 9	Southampton	Middlesbrough	3.11.71
Kavelashvili, Mikhail	5. 11	S. Vladikavkaz, Rus.	Georgia	22.07.71
Kelly, Ray	5. 11	Athlone Town	Ballinasloe	29.12.76
Phillips, Martin	5. 9	Exeter City	Exeter	13.03.76
Rosler, Uwe	6. 0	Nurnburg, Ger.	Attenburg, Ger.	15.11.68

MIDDLESBROUGH

Name	Height ft. in.	Previous Club	Birthplace	Birthdate
Goalkeepers				
Roberts, Ben	6. 1	Bradford C.	Bishop Auckland	22.06.75
Schwarzer, Mark	6. 5	Bradford C.	Sydney, Aus	06.10.72
Walsh, Gary	6. 3	Oldham	Wigan	21.03.68
Defenders				
Blackmore, Clayton	5. 8	Man. Utd.	Neath	23.09.64
Festa, Gianluca	6. 0	Inter Milan	Cagliari	15.03.69
Fleming, Curtis	5. 10	St. Patrick's Ath.	Manchester	8.10.68
Gavin, Jason	5. 10	Crumlin Utd.	Dublin	14.03.80
Harrison, Craig	5. 10	–	Gateshead	10.11.77
Kinder, Vladimir	5. 10	Slovan Bratislava	Bratislava	14.03.69
Liddle, Craig	5. 11	Blyth Spartans	Chester-le-Street	21.10.71
Pearson, Nigel	6. 1	Sheff. Wed.	Nottingham	21.08.63
Vickers, Steve	6. 1	Tranmere	Bishop Auckland	13.10.67

Name	Height ft. in.	Previous Club	Birthplace	Birthdate
White, Alan	5. 11	–	Darlington	22.03.76
White, Darren	–	–	Easington	13.01.79
Whyte, Derek	5. 11	Celtic	Glasgow	31.08.68
Midfield				
Cummins, Michael	5. 8	Crumlin Utd.	Dublin	1.06.78
Emerson	6. 0	Porto, Por.	Rio de Janeiro	
Hignett, Craig	5. 9	Crewe	Whiston	12.01.70
Moore, Alan	5. 10	Rivermount	Dublin	25.11.74
Moreira, Fabio	–	Desportivo de Chaves	Brazil	14.03.72
Mustoe, Robbie	5. 10	Oxford Utd.	Oxford	28.08.68
Ormerod, Anthony	–	–	Middlesbrough	31.03.79
Stamp, Phil	5. 10	–	Middlesbrough	12.12.75
Summerbell, Mark	5. 10	–	Durham	30.10.76
Swalwell, Andrew	–	–	Middlesbrough	29.03.79
Forwards				
Beck, Mikkel	6. 2	Fortuna Cologne	Aarhus, Den.	12.05.73
Campbell, Andrew	5. 11	–	Stockton-on-Tees	18.04.79
Connor, Paul	6. 0	–	Bishop Auckland	12.01.79
Freestone, Chris	5. 10	Arnold Town	Nottingham	4.09.71
Merson, Paul	6. 0	Arsenal	Harlesden	20.03.68
O'Brien, Ronnie	–	St. Joseph's, Dublin	–	–
Ravanelli, Fabrizio	6. 1	Juventus, Ita.	Perugia, Ita.	11.12.68

NORWICH CITY

Name	Height ft. in.	Previous Club	Birthplace	Birthdate
Goalkeepers				
Green, Robert	6. 2	–	Chertsey	18.01.80
Gunn, Bryan	6. 2	Aberdeen	Thurso	22.12.63
Marshall, Andy	6. 2	–	Bury	14.04.75
Defenders				
Bradshaw, Carl	5. 10	Sheff. Utd.	Sheffield	2.10.68
Brownrigg, Andrew	6. 0	Hereford	Sheffield	2.06.76
Davis, Kori	6. 0	–	Germany	12.02.79
Fleming, Craig	5. 11	Oldham	Calder	6.10.71
Green, Joe	6. 3	–	Wisbech	2.11.78
Jackson, Matt	6. 0	Everton	Leeds	19.10.71
Kenton, Darren	5. 9	–	Wandsworth	13.09.78
Marshall, Lee	6. 0	Enfield	London	21.01.79
Mills, Danny	5. 11	–	Norwich	18.05.77
Newman, Rob	6. 2	Bristol City	Bradford-on-Avon	13.12.63
Polston, John	5. 11	Tottenham	Walthamstow	10.06.68
Scott, Kevin	6. 4	Tottenham	Easington	11.12.66
Midfield				
Adams, Neil	5. 8	Oldham	Stoke-on-Trent	23.11.65
Bellamy, Craig	5. 8	–	Cardiff	13.07.79
Carey, Shaun	5. 8	–	Kettering	13.05.76
Hilton, Damian	6. 2	–	Norwich	6.09.77
Llewellyn, Chris	5. 11	–	Swansea	29.08.79
Milligan, Mike	5. 8	Oldham	Manchester	20.02.67
Shore, Jamie	5. 9	–	Bristol	01.09.77
Simpson, Karl	5. 11	–	Newmarket	12.10.76
Sutch, Daryl	6. 0	–	Lowestoft	11.09.71
Tipple, Gavin	5. 9	–	Welwyn	2.02.79
Wilson, Che	5. 9	–	Ely	17.01.79
Forwards				
Broughton, Drew	6. 3	–	Hitchin	25.10.78

Name	Height ft. in.	Previous Club	Birthplace	Birthdate
Coote, Adrian	6. 2	–	Gt Yarmouth	03.09.78
Eadie, Darren	5. 8	–	Chippenham	10.06.75
Fleck, Robert	5. 9	Chelsea	Glasgow	11.08.65
Forbes, Adrian	5. 7	–	London	23.01.79
O'Neill, Keith	6. 1	–	Dublin	16.02.76
Roberts, Iwan	6. 2	Wolves	Bangor, N. Wales	26.06.68

NOTTINGHAM FOREST

Name	Height ft. in.	Previous Club	Birthplace	Birthdate
Goalkeepers				
Crossley, Mark	6. 0	–	Barnsley	16.06.69
Fettis, Alan	6. 2	Hull	Belfast	1.02.71
Henry, David	6. 3	Crusaders	Belfast	12.11.77
Pascolo, Marco	–	Cagliari, It	Basle	–
Defenders				
Blatherwick, Steve	6. 1	Notts County	Nottingham	20.09.73
Bonalair, Thierry	–	Neuchatel Xamax	Paris	14.06.66
Chettle, Steve	6. 1	–	Nottingham	27.09.68
Cooper, Colin	5. 9	Millwall	Durham	28.02.67
Follett, Richard	5. 9	–	Leamington Spa	29.08.79
George, Daniel	6. 1	–	Lincoln	22.10.78
Harewood, Marlon	6. 1	–	Hampstead	25.08.79
Jerkan, Nikola	6. 2	Real Oviedo, Spa.	Zagreb, Cro.	8.12.64
Lyttle, Des	5. 8	Swansea	Wolverhampton	26.09.71
Pearce, Stuart	5. 10	Coventry	Shepherds Bush	24.04.62
Rogers, Alan	5. 10	Tranmere	Liverpool	3.01.77
Thom, Stuart	6. 2	–	Dewsbury	27.12.76
Midfield				
Allen, Chris	5. 11	Oxford Utd.	Oxford	18.11.72
Archer, Paul	5. 8	–	Leicester	25.04.78
Armstrong, Craig	5. 11	–	South Shields	23.05.75
Bart-Williams, Chris	5. 11	Sheff. Wed.	Sierra Leone	16.06.74
Burns, John	5. 10	–	Dublin	4.12.77
Cowling, Lee	5. 9	–	Doncaster	22.09.77
Dawson, Andrew	5. 9	–	Northallerton	20.10.78
Finnigan, John	5. 8	–	Wakefield	28.03.76
Fitchett, Scott	5. 8	–	Manchester	20.01.79
Gemmill, Scot	5. 11	–	Paisley	2.01.71
Grim, Robert	5. 11	–	London	10.09.78
Howe, Stephen	5. 7	–	Annitsford	6.11.73
Johnson, Andy	6. 0	Norwich	Bristol	2.05.74
Melton, Stephen	5. 11	–	Lincoln	3.10.78
Phillips, David	5. 11	Norwich	Wegberg, Ger.	29.07.63
Smith, Paul	5. 11	Hastings Town	Hastings	25.01.76
Stone, Steve	5. 8	–	Gateshead	20.08.71
Thomas, Geoff	6. 1	Wolves	Manchester	5.08.64
Todd, Andrew	6. 0	Eastwood	Nottingham	22.02.79
Turner, Barry	5. 9	–	Nottingham	1.12.78
Warner, Vance	6. 0	–	Leeds	3.09.74
Woan, Ian	5. 10	Runcorn	Wirral	14.12.67
Forwards				
Campbell, Kevin	6. 1	Arsenal	Lambeth	4.02.70
Guinan, Stephen	6. 1	–	Birmingham	24.12.75
Hooijdonk, Pierre	6. 4	Celtic	Steenbergen	29.11.69
McGregor, Paul	5. 10	–	Liverpool	17.12.74
Moore, Ian	5. 11	Tranmere	Birkenhead	26.08.76
Saunders, Dean	5. 8	Galatasaray	Swansea	21.06.64

OXFORD UNITED

Name	Height ft. in.	Previous Club	Birthplace	Birthdate
Goalkeepers				
Jackson, Elliott	6. 0	–	Swindon	27.08.77
Whitehead, Phil	6. 2	Barnsley	Halifax	17.12.69
Defenders				
Ford, Mike	6. 0	Cardiff	Bristol	9.02.66
Gilchrist, Phil	6. 0	Hartlepool	Stockton	25.08.73
Marsh, Simon	5. 11	–	Perivale	29.01.77
Purse, Darren	6. 2	Leyton Orient	London	14.02.77
Robinson, Les	5. 8	Doncaster	Shirebrook	1.03.67
Whelan, Phil	6. 4	Middlesbrough	Stockport	7.03.72
Wilsterman, Brian	6. 1	Beerschot	Surinam	19.11.66
Midfield				
Ford, Bobby	5. 9	–	Bristol	22.09.74
Gray, Martin	5. 10	Sunderland	Stockton	17.08.71
Lewis, Mickey	5. 8	Derby	Birmingham	15.02.65
Massey, Stuart	5. 10	Crystal Palace	Crawley	17.11.64
McGregor, Marc	5. 10	–	Southend	30.04.78
Murphy, Matt	5. 10	Corby Town	Northampton	20.08.71
Powell, Paul	5. 9	–	Wallingford	30.06.78
Smith, David	5. 10	Norwich	Liverpool	26.12.70
Forwards				
Aldridge, Martin	5. 11	Northampton	Northampton	6.12.74
Angel, Mark	5. 9	Sunderland	Sunderland	23.08.75
Beauchamp, Joey	5. 10	Swindon	Oxford	13.03.71
Jemson, Nigel	5. 10	Notts County	Hutton	10.08.69
Stevens, Mark	6. 5	–	Swindon	3.12.77
Weatherstone, Simon	5. 9	–	Reading	26.01.80

PORTSMOUTH

Name	Height ft. in.	Previous Club	Birthplace	Birthdate
Goalkeepers				
Flahavan, Aaron	6. 1	–	Southampton	15.12.75
Knight, Alan	6. 1	–	Balham	3.07.61
Defenders				
Awford, Andy	5. 9	–	Worcester	14.07.72
Hinshelwood, Danny	5. 9	Nott'm. Forest	Bromley	12.12.75
Perrett, Russell	6. 2	Lymington	Barton-on-Sea	18.06.73
Pethick, Robbie	5. 10	Weymouth	Tavistock	8.09.70
Rees, Gavin	6. 1	–	Haverford West	1.11.78
Russell, Lee	5. 10	–	Southampton	3.09.69
Thomson, Andrew	6. 3	Swindon	Swindon	28.03.74
Waterman, David	5. 10	–	Guernsey	16.05.77
Whitbread, Adrian	6. 0	West Ham	Epping	22.10.71
Midfield				
Allen, Martin	5. 10	West Ham	Reading	14.08.65
Cook, Andy	5. 9	Swansea City	Romsey	10.08.69
Durnin, John	5. 10	Oxford Utd.	Liverpool	18.08.65
Hillier, David	5. 10	Arsenal	London	18.12.69
Igoe, Samuel	5. 6	–	Spelthorne	30.09.75
Jukes, Nathan	5. 10	–	Worcester	10.04.79
McLoughlin, Alan	5. 8	Southampton	Manchester	20.04.67
Simpson, Fitzroy	5. 8	Man. City	Trowbridge	26.02.70
Thompson, Mark	6. 2	–	Southampton	17.09.77
Turner, Andy	5. 10	Tottenham	Woolwich	23.03.75
Williams, Adam	5. 11	–	Rustington	4.10.78

Forwards

Name	ft.	in.	Previous Club	Birthplace	Birthdate
Bundy, Scott	6.	1	–	Southampton	20.10.77
Bradbury, Lee	6.	0	–	Isle of Wight	3.07.75
Carter, Jimmy	5.	10	Arsenal	London	9.11.65
Hall, Paul	5.	9	Torquay	Manchester	3.07.72
Karimzadeh, Askan	6.	0	–	Tehran	11.09.78
Simpson, Robert	5.	9	Tottenham	Luton	3.03.76
Svensson, Mathias	6.	0	If. Elfsborg	Boras, Sweden	24.09.74

PORT VALE

Name	Height ft.	in.	Previous Club	Birthplace	Birthdate
Goalkeepers					
Boswell, Matthew	6.	2	–	Shrewsbury	19.08.77
Musselwhite, Paul	6.	1	Scunthorpe	Portsmouth	22.12.68
Van Heusden, Arjan	6.	2	Noordwijk, Hol.	Alphen, Hol.	11.12.72
Defenders					
Aspin, Neil	6.	0	Leeds	Gateshead	12.04.65
Glover, Dean	5.	11	Middlesbrough	Birmingham	29.12.63
Griffiths, Gareth	6.	4	Rhyl	Winsford	10.04.70
Hill, Andy	5.	11	Man. City	Maltby	20.01.65
Holwyn, Jermaine	6.	2	Ajax, Hol.	Amsterdam, Hol.	16.04.73
Stokes, Dean	5.	7	Halesowen Town	Birmingham	23.05.70
Tankard, Allen	5.	10	Wigan	Islington	21.05.69
Midfield					
Bogie, Ian	5.	7	Leyton Orient	Newcastle	6.12.67
Corden, Wayne	5.	10	–	Leek	1.11.75
Koordes, Rogier	6.	1	–	Holland	13.06.72
McCarthy, Jon	5.	9	York	Middlesbrough	18.08.70
Porter, Andy	5.	9	–	Holmes Chapel	17.09.68
Talbot, Stewart	5.	10	Moor Green	Birmingham	14.06.73
Forwards					
Foyle, Martin	5.	10	Oxford Utd.	Salisbury	2.05.63
Mills, Lee	6.	1	Derby	Mexborough	10.07.70
Naylor, Tony	5.	6	Crewe	Manchester	29.03.67
O'Reilly, Justin	6.	0	Gresley Rovers	Derby	29.06.73

QUEENS PARK RANGERS

Name	Height ft.	in.	Previous Club	Birthplace	Birthdate
Goalkeepers					
Harper, Lee	6.	1	Arsenal	Dulwich	30.10.71
Hurst, Richard	6.	0	–	Hammersmith	23.12.76
Roberts, Tony	6.	0	–	Bangor, N Wales	4.08.69
Sommer, Jurgen	6.	5	Luton	New York	27.02.69
Defenders					
Bardsley, David	5.	10	Oxford Utd.	Manchester	11.09.64
Brevett, Rufus	5.	8	Doncaster	Derby	24.09.69
Challis, Trevor	5.	8	–	Paddington	23.10.75
Graham, Mark	5.	7	–	Newry	24.10.74
Maddix, Danny	5.	11	Tottenham	Ashford, Kent	11.10.67
Morrow, Stephen	6.	0	Arsenal	Bangor, N.I.	2.07.70
Owen, Karl	5.	11	–	Coventry	12.10.79
Perry, Mark	5.	10	–	Perivale	19.10.78
Plummer, Chris	6.	2	–	Isleworth	12.10.76
Ready, Karl	6.	1	–	Neath	14.08.72
Rose, Matthew	5.	11	Arsenal	Dartford	24.09.75
Yates, Steve	5.	10	Bristol Rovers	Bristol	29.01.70

Midfield

Name	ft. in.	Previous Club	Birthplace	Birthdate
Barker, Simon	5. 9	Blackburn	Bolton	4.11.64
Brazier, Matthew	5. 8	–	Whipps Cross	2.07.76
Murray, Fraser	5. 8	–	Paisley	24.09.79
Murray, Paul	5. 8	Carlisle	Carlisle	31.08.76
Peacock, Gavin	5. 8	Chelsea	Eltham	18.11.67
Quashie, Nigel	6. 0	–	Nunhead	20.07.78

Forwards

Charles, Lee	5. 11	Chertsey	Hillingdon	20.08.71
Gallen, Kevin	5. 11	–	Hammersmith	21.09.75
Graham, Richard	5. 7	–	Newry	05.08.79
Mahoney-Johnson, Michael	5. 10	–	Paddington	6.11.76
Sheron, Mike	5. 9	Stoke	Liverpool	11.01.72
Sinclair, Trevor	5. 10	Blackpool	Dulwich	2.03.73
Slade, Steven	5. 10	Tottenham	Romford	6.10.75
Spencer, John	5. 7	Chelsea	Glasgow	11.09.70

READING

Name	Height ft. in.	Previous Club	Birthplace	Birthdate
Goalkeepers				
Biboo, Salvatore	6. 2	Sheff. Utd.	Basingstoke	24.08.74
Hammond, Nicky	6. 0	Plymouth	Hornchurch	7.09.67
Mautone, Steve	6. 2	West Ham	Myrtleford, Aus.	10.08.70
Defenders				
Bernal, Andy	5. 10	Syd. Olympic, Aust.	Canberra, Aust.	16.05.66
Bodin, Paul	6. 0	Swindon	Cardiff	13.09.64
Booty, Martyn	5. 8	Crewe	Leicester	30.05.71
Hunter, Barry	6. 4	Wrexham	Coleraine	18.11.68
McPherson, Keith	5. 11	Northampton	Greenwich	11.09.63
Swales, Stephen	5. 8	Scarborough	Whitby	26.12.73
Thorp, Michael	6. 0	–	Wallingford	5.12.75
Wdowczyk, Dariusz	5. 11	Celtic	Warsaw	21.09.62
Midfield				
Caskey, Darren	5. 8	Tottenham	Basildon	21.08.74
Freeman, Andrew	5. 10	Crystal Palace	Reading	8.09.77
Glasgow, Byron	5. 6	–	London	18.02.79
Holsgrove, Paul	6. 2	Millwall	Wellington	26.08.69
Parkinson, Phil	6. 0	Bury	Chorley	1.12.67
Smith, Ben	5. 9	Arsenal	Chelmsford	23.11.78
Forwards				
Lambert, James	5. 7	–	Henley	14.09.73
Lovell, Stuart	5. 10	–	Sydney, Aust.	9.01.72
Morley, Trevor	5. 11	West Ham	Nottingham	20.03.61
Nogan, Lee	5. 10	Watford	Cardiff	21.05.69
Williams, Martin	5. 9	Luton	Luton	12.07.73

SHEFFIELD UNITED

Name	Height ft. in.	Previous Club	Birthplace	Birthdate
Goalkeepers				
Heritage, Paul	6. 2	–	Sheffield	17.04.79
Kelly, Alan	6. 3	Preston	Preston	11.08.68
Tracey, Simon	6. 0	Wimbledon	Woolwich	9.12.67
Defenders				
Beard, Mark	5. 11	Millwall	Roehampton	8.10.74
Borbokis, Vassilis	5. 11	AEK Athens	Serres, Gre.	10.02.69

Name	ft. in.	Previous Club	Birthplace	Birthdate
Capper, David	6. 0		Stoke	8.09.78
Dyer, Liam	5. 11		Doncaster	2.05.78
Hocking, Matthew	5. 11		Boston	30.01.78
Holdsworth, David	6. 0	Watford	Walthamstow	8.08.68
James, Owen	5. 11		Derby	1.09.78
Nilsen, Roger	5. 11	Viking Stavanger	Tromso, Nor.	8.08.69
Sandford, Lee	6. 0	Stoke	Basingstoke	22.04.68
Short, Chris	5. 10	Notts County	Munster	9.05.70
Tiler, Carl	6. 2	Aston Villa	Sheffield	11.02.70
Vonk, Michel	6. 3	Man. City	Alkmaar, Hol.	28.10.68
Midfield				
Davies, Kevin	5. 11		Sheffield	15.11.78
Ebbrell, John	5. 10	Everton	Bromborough	1.10.69
Hawes, Steven	5. 8		High Wycombe	17.07.78
Henry, Nick	5. 6	Oldham	Liverpool	21.02.69
Hutchison, Don	6. 2	West Ham	Gateshead	9.05.71
Ludlam, Ryan	6. 0		Carlisle	12.05.79
Patterson, Mark	5. 8	Bolton	Darwen	24.05.65
Quinn, Wayne	5. 10		Truro	19.11.76
Spackman, Nigel	6. 0	Chelsea	Romsey	2.12.60
Ward, Mitch	5. 8		Sheffield	19.06.71
White, David	6. 1	Leeds	Manchester	30.10.67
Whitehouse, Dane	5. 9		Sheffield	14.10.70
Forwards				
Bettney, Chris	5. 10		Chesterfield	27.10.77
Fjortoft, Jan Aage	6. 3	Middlesbrough	Aalesund	10.01.67
Katchouro, Peter	5. 11	D. Minsk, Belarus	Belarus	2.08.72
Scott, Andy	6. 1	Sutton Utd.	Epsom	2.08.72
Taylor, Gareth	6. 2	Crystal Palace	Weston-s-Mare	25.02.73
Tracey, Richard	5. 11		Dewsbury	09.07.77
Walker, Andy	5. 8	Celtic	Glasgow	6.04.65

STOCKPORT COUNTY

Name	Height ft. in.	Previous Club	Birthplace	Birthdate
Goalkeepers				
Edwards, Neil	5. 8	Leeds	Aberdare	5.12.70
Jones, Paul	6. 3	Wolves	Chirk	18.04.67
Defenders				
Bennett, Tom	5. 11	Wolves	Falkirk	12.12.69
Bound, Matthew	6. 2	Southampton	Trowbridge	9.11.72
Connelly, Sean	5. 10	Hallam	Sheffield	26.06.70
Da Costa, Nelson	5. 10	Belonese	Angola	8.12.78
Dinning, Tony	5. 11	Newcastle	Wallsend	12.04.75
Flynn, Mike	6. 0	Preston	Oldham	23.02.69
Gannon, Jim	6. 2	Sheff. Utd.	London	7.09.68
Jones, Lea	6. 0		Southport	25.09.77
Killduff, Danny	6. 1		Stockport	27.12.78
Todd, Lee	5. 5	Hartlepool	Hartlepool	7.03.72
Midfield				
Ansell, Gary	5. 10		Rochford	8.11.78
Cowans, Gordon	5. 7	Bradford C.	Durham	27.10.58
Durkan, Kieron	5. 10	Wrexham	Chester	1.12.73
Marsden, Chris	5. 11	Notts County	Sheffield	3.01.69
Forwards				
Angell, Brett	6. 2	Sunderland	Marlborough	20.08.68
Armstrong, Alun	6. 0	Newcastle	Gateshead	22.02.75
Cardew, Simon	5. 9		Urmston	26.10.78
Cavaco, Luis	5. 9	Estoril, Por.	Portugal	1.03.72

Charana, Manuel	5. 10	Belonense	Portugal	24.10.76
Charley, Ken	6. 0	Peterborough	Stepney	28.11.64
Jeffers, John	5. 10	Port Vale	Liverpool	5.10.68
Landon, Richard	6. 3	Plymouth	Worthing	22.03.70
Lewis, Gary	5. 9	–	Bolton	5.10.78
Mutch, Andy	5. 10	Swindon	Liverpool	28.12.63
Nash, Martin	5. 11	Vancouver	Regina	27.12.75
Shearer, Lee	5. 9	–	London	30.09.78

STOKE CITY

Name	Height ft. in.	Previous Club	Birthplace	Birthdate
Goalkeepers				
Fraser, Stuart	6. 0	–	Cheltenham	01.08.78
Morgan, Philip	6. 2	Ipswich	Stoke	18.12.74
Muggleton, Carl	6. 1	Celtic	Leicester	13.09.68
Defenders				
Birch, Mark	5. 11	–	Stoke	5.01.77
Clarke, Clive	5. 11	–	Dublin	14.01.80
Griffin, Andrew	5. 8	–	Wigan	17.03.79
McNally, Mark	5. 11	Southend	Motherwell	10.03.71
Pickering, Ally	5. 9	Coventry	Manchester	22.06.67
Sigurdsson, Larus	6. 0	Thor FC, Ice.	Akuveyni, Ice.	4.06.73
Whittle, Justin	6. 1	Celtic	Derby	18.03.71
Woods, Stephen	5. 11	–	Davenham	15.12.76
Midfield				
Cairns, Kwesi	5. 5	–	London	5.08.79
Devlin, Mark	5. 10	–	Irvine	18.01.73
Forsyth, Richard	5. 10	Birmingham	Dudley	3.10.70
Heath, Robert	5. 8	–	Stoke	31.04.78
Kavanagh, Graham	5. 10	Middlesbrough	Dublin	02.12.73
Keen, Kevin	5. 7	Wolves	Amersham	25.02.67
MacKenzie, Neil	6. 2	–	Birmingham	15.04.76
O'Connor, James	5. 7	–	Dublin	1.09.79
Schreuder, Dick	–	Waalwijk, Hol.	–	–
Stokoe, Graham	6. 1	–	Chester-le-Street	17.12.75
Wallace, Ray	5. 7	Leeds	Greenwich	2.10.69
Forwards				
Crowe, Dean	5. 5	–	Stockport	6.06.79
Macari, Michael	5. 7	–	Kilwinning	4.02.73
Macari, Paul	5. 8	–	Manchester	23.08.76
McMahon, Gerard	5. 11	Tottenham	Belfast	29.12.73
Nyamah, Kofi	5. 10	Kettering	London	20.06.75
Stewart, Paul	5. 11	Sunderland	Manchester	7.10.64
Sturridge, Simon	5. 5	Birmingham	Birmingham	9.12.69

SUNDERLAND

Name	Height ft. in.	Previous Club	Birthplace	Birthdate
Goalkeepers				
Coton, Tony	6. 2	Man. Utd.	Tamworth	19.05.61
Perez, Lionel	5. 11	Bordeaux	Bagnols Ceze	24.04.67
Preece, David	6. 0	–	Sunderland	28.08.76
Zeotebier, Edwin	–	Volendam, Hol.	–	–
Defenders				
Ball, Kevin	5. 9	Portsmouth	Hastings	12.11.64
Hall, Gareth	5. 8	Chelsea	Croydon	12.03.69
Heckingbottom, Paul	5. 10	Man. Utd.	Sunderland	12.03.69

Name	ft. in.	Previous Club	Birthplace	Birthdate
Heiselberg, Kim	5. 11	Esberg	Tarm, Den.	21.09.77
Holloway, Darren	5. 11	–	Bishop Auckland	3.10.77
Kubicki, Dariusz	5. 10	Aston Villa	Warsaw	6.06.63
Melville, Andy	6. 1	Oxford Utd.	Swansea	29.11.68
Ord, Richard	6. 2	–	Easington	3.03.70
Scott, Martin	5. 9	Bristol City	Sheffield	7.01.68
Midfield				
Agnew, Steve	5. 9	Leicester City	Shipley	9.11.65
Aiston, Sam	5. 10	Newcastle	Newcastle	21.11.76
Bracewell, Paul	5. 8	Newcastle	Heswall	19.07.62
Clark, Lee	5. 7	Newcastle	Wallsend	27.10.72
Eriksson, Jan	6. 0	Helsinborgs	Sundsvall	
Gray, Michael	5. 9	–	Sunderland	3.08.64
Johnston, Allan	5. 9	Rennes	Glasgow	14.12.73
Mawson, David	5. 11	–	Sunderland	4.03.77
Pickering, Stephen	5. 9	–	Sunderland	25.09.76
Rae, Alex	5. 9	Millwall	Glasgow	30.09.69
Smith, Martin	5. 11	–	Sunderland	13.11.74
Forwards				
Bridges, Michael	5. 10	–	Whitley Bay	5.08.78
Byrne, Chris	5. 11	Macclesfield	–	
Howey, Lee	6. 3	–	Sunderland	1.04.69
Kelly, David	5. 11	Wolves	Birmingham	25.11.65
Mullin, John	5. 9	Burnley	Bury	11.08.75
Phillips, Kevin	5. 7	Watford	Hitchin	25.07.73
Quinn, Niall	6. 4	Man. City	Dublin	6.10.66
Russell, Craig	5. 11	–	South Shields	4.02.74

SWINDON TOWN

Name	Height ft. in.	Previous Club	Birthplace	Birthdate
Goalkeepers				
Digby, Fraser	6. 1	Man. Utd.	Sheffield	23.04.67
Mildenhall, Stephen	6. 5	–	Swindon	13.05.78
Talia, Frank	6. 1	Blackburn	Melbourne, Aust.	20.07.72
Defenders				
Culverhouse, Ian	5. 10	Norwich	Bishop's Stortford	22.09.64
Darras, Frederick	–	–	Calais	19.08.66
Drysdale, Jason	5. 10	Newcastle	Bristol	17.11.70
Elkins, Gary	5. 9	Wimbledon	Wallingford	4.05.66
King, Phil	5. 8	Aston Villa	Bristol	28.12.67
McDonald, Alan	6. 2	Q.P.R.	Belfast	12.10.63
O'Sullivan, Wayne	5. 8	–	Cyprus	25.02.74
Robinson, Mark	5. 9	Newcastle	Rochdale	21.11.68
Seagraves, Mark	6. 0	Bolton	Bootle	22.10.66
Midfield				
Bullock, Darren	5. 8	Huddersfield	Worcester	12.02.69
Collins, Lee	5. 8	–	Bellshill	3.02.74
Gooden, Ty	5. 8	Wycombe	Canvey Island	23.10.72
Holcroft, Peter	–	–	Liverpool	3.01.76
Leitch, Scott	5. 9	–	Motherwell	06.10.69
Smith, Alex	5. 8	–	Liverpool	15.02.76
Walters, Mark	5. 9	Liverpool	Birmingham	2.06.64
Watson, Kevin	5. 9	Tottenham	Hackney	3.01.74
Forwards				
Allison, Wayne	6. 1	Bristol City	Huddersfield	16.10.68
Cowe, Steve	5. 7	Aston Villa	Gloucester	29.09.74
Finney, Steve	5. 10	Man. City	Hexham	31.10.73
Thorne, Peter	6. 0	Blackburn	Manchester	21.06.73

411

TRANMERE ROVERS

Name	Height ft. in.	Previous Club	Birthplace	Birthdate
Goalkeepers				
Coyne, Danny	5. 11	–	Prestatyn	27.08.73
Nixon, Eric	6. 4	Man. City	Manchester	4.10.62
Simonson, Steve	6. 4	–	South Shields	3.04.79
Defenders				
Challinor, Dave	6. 1	–	Chester	2.10.75
McGreal, John	5. 11	–	Birkenhead	2.06.72
Stevens, Gary	5. 11	Rangers	Barrow	27.03.63
Teale, Shaun	6. 0	Aston Villa	Southport	10.03.64
Thomas, Tony	5. 11	–	Liverpool	12.07.71
Thorn, Andy	6. 0	Wimbledon	Carshalton	12.11.66
Thompson, Andy	5. 4	Wolves	Cannock	9.11.67
Midfield				
Connelly, Stuart	5. 8	Stella Maris	Dublin	8.12.77
Cook, Paul	5. 11	Coventry	Liverpool	22.02.67
Irons, Kenny	5. 10	–	Liverpool	4.11.70
Mahon, Alan	5. 10	–	Dublin	4.04.78
Morgan, Alan	5. 10	–	Aberystwyth	2.11.73
O'Brien, Liam	6. 1	Newcastle	Dublin	5.09.64
Forwards				
Aldridge, John	5. 11	Real Sociedad, Spa.	Liverpool	18.09.58
Branch, Graham	6. 2	Heswall	Liverpool	12.02.72
Jones, Gary	6. 3	–	Chester	10.05.75
Jones, Lee	5. 8	–	Wrexham	29.05.73
Morrissey, John	5. 8	Wolves	Liverpool	8.03.64
Nevin, Pat	5. 6	Everton	Glasgow	6.09.63

WEST BROMWICH ALBION

Name	Height ft. in.	Previous Club	Birthplace	Birthdate
Goalkeepers				
Crichton, Paul	6. 1	Grimsby	Pontefract	3.10.68
Germaine, Gary	6. 2	–	Birmingham	2.08.76
Miller, Alan	6. 3	Middlesbrough	Epping	29.03.70
Spink, Nigel	6. 2	Aston Villa	Chelmsford	8.08.58
Defenders				
Burgess, Daryl	5. 11	–	Birmingham	20.04.71
Holmes, Paul	5. 10	Everton	Stockbridge	18.02.68
Joseph, Roger	5. 11	Leyton Orient	Paddington	24.12.65
McDermott, Andrew	5. 9	Q.P.R.	Sydney, Aus.	20.03.77
Mardon, Paul	6. 0	Birmingham	Bristol	14.09.69
Murphy, Shaun	6. 1	Notts Co.	Sydney, Aus.	5.11.70
Nicholson, Shane	5. 10	Derby	Newark	3.06.70
Potter, Graham	5. 11	Southampton	Birmingham	20.05.75
Raven, Paul	6. 1	Doncaster	Salisbury	28.07.70
Midfield				
Butler, Peter	5. 9	Notts County	Halifax	27.08.66
Coldicott, Stacy	5. 8	–	Redditch	29.04.74
Donovan, Kevin	5. 8	Huddersfield	Halifax	17.12.71
Gilbert, David	5. 4	Grimsby	Lincoln	22.06.63
Hamilton, Ian	5. 9	Scunthorpe	Stevenage	14.12.67
Kilblane, Kevin	6. 0	Preston N.E.	Preston	1.02.77
Smith, David	5. 8	Birmingham	Stonehouse	29.03.68
Sneekes, Richard	5. 11	Bolton	Amsterdam	30.10.68
Forwards				
Bennett, Dean	5. 10	Aston Villa	Wolverhampton	13.12.77

Name	Height ft. in.	Previous Club	Birthplace	Birthdate
Hunt, Andy	6. 0	Newcastle	Thurrock	9.06.70
Hughes, Lee	–	Kidderminster	Birmingham	22.05.76
Rodosthenous, Mike	5. 11	–	Islington	25.08.76
Taylor, Bob	5. 10	Bristol City	Easington	3.02.67

WOLVERHAMPTON WANDERERS

Name	Height ft. in.	Previous Club	Birthplace	Birthdate
Goalkeepers				
Stowell, Mike	6. 2	Everton	Portsmouth	19.04.65
Defenders				
Atkins, Mark	6. 1	Blackburn	Doncaster	14.08.68
Curle, Keith	6. 0	Man. City	Bristol	14.11.63
Emblen, Neil	6. 2	Millwall	Bromley	19.06.71
Richards, Dean	6. 2	Bradford City	Bradford	9.06.74
Smith, James	5. 6	–	Birmingham	17.09.74
Williams, Adrian	6. 2	Reading	Reading	16.08.71
Midfield				
Corica, Steve	5. 8	Leicester City	Cairns, Aust.	24.03.73
Daley, Tony	5. 8	Aston Villa	Birmingham	18.10.67
Ferguson, Darren	5. 10	Man. Utd.	Glasgow	9.02.72
Froggatt, Steve	5. 10	Aston Villa	Lincoln	9.03.73
Gilkes, Michael	5. 8	Reading	Hackney	20.07.65
Leadbeater, Richard	–	–	–	27.10.77
Osborn, Simon	5. 10	Q.P.R.	New Addington	19.01.72
Robinson, Carl	6. 3	–	Llandrudod	13.10.76
Sedgley, Steve	6. 1	Ipswich	Enfield	26.05.68
Forwards				
Bull, Steve	5. 11	W.B.A.	Tipton	28.03.65
Crowe, Glen	5. 10	–	Dublin	25.12.77
Foley, Dominic	6. 1	St. James Gate	Dublin	7.07.76
Goodman, Don	5. 10	Sunderland	Leeds	9.05.66
Wright, Jermaine	5. 9	Millwall	Greenwich	15.08.75

Second Division

BLACKPOOL

Name	Height ft. in.	Previous Club	Birthplace	Birthdate
Goalkeepers				
Banks, Steven	6. 0	Gillingham	Hillingdon	9.02.72
Heighton, Henry	6. 0	–	Sunderland	27.11.78
Defenders				
Bradshaw, Darren	5. 11	Peterborough	Sheffield	19.03.67
Bryan, Marvin	6. 0	Q.P.R.	Paddington	2.08.75
Butler, Tony	6. 2	Gillingham	Stockport	28.09.72
Couzens, Andy	5. 9	Leeds	Leeds	4.06.75
Cross, Jamie	5. 10	–	Blackpool	29.08.79
Dixon, Ben	6. 1	Lincoln	Lincoln	16.09.74
Linighan, David	6. 2	Ipswich	Hartlepool	9.01.65
Lydiate, Jason	5. 11	Bolton	Manchester	29.10.71
Midfield				
Bonner, Mark	5. 10	–	Ormskirk	7.06.74
Brabin, Gary	5. 11	Bury	Liverpool	9.02.70

Clarkson, Phil	5. 10	Scunthorpe Utd.	Garstang	13.11.68
Haddow, Paul	5. 8	–	Fleetwood	11.10.78
Mellon, Micky	5. 8	W.B.A.	Paisley	18.03.72
Philpott, Lee	5. 9	Leicester	Hackney	21.02.70
Russell, Keith	5. 10	Hednesford	Aldridge	21.01.74
Forwards				
Carden, Paul	5. 8	–	Liverpool	29.03.79
Ellis, Tony	5. 11	Preston	Salford	20.10.64
Malkin, Chris	6. 3	Millwall	Hoylake	4.06.67
Ormerod, Brett	5. 11	Accrington S.	Blackburn	18.10.76
Preece, Andy	6. 1	Crystal Palace	Evesham	27.03.67
Quinn, James	6. 1	Birmingham	Coventry	15.12.74

BOURNEMOUTH

Name	Height ft. in.	Previous Club	Birthplace	Birthdate
Goalkeepers				
Glass, Jimmy	6. 1	Crystal Palace	Epsom	1.08.73
Wells, David	6. 2	–	Portsmouth	29.12.77
Defenders				
Cotterill, Leo	5. 9	Ipswich	Cambridge	2.09.74
Coll, Owen	6. 0	Tottenham	Donegal	9.04.76
Howe, Eddie	5. 9	–	Amersham	29.11.77
Jenkins, Jamie	5. 10	–	Pontypool	1.01.79
Vincent, Jamie	5. 10	Crystal Palace	London	18.06.75
Young, Neil	5. 9	Tottenham	Harlow	31.08.73
Midfield				
Beardsmore, Russell	5. 6	Man. Utd.	Wigan	28.09.68
Brissett, Jason	5. 9	Peterborough	Redbridge	7.09.74
Cox, Ian	6. 0	Crystal Palace	Croydon	25.03.71
Dean, Michael	5. 9	–	Weymouth	9.03.78
Griffin, Anthony	5. 10	–	Bournemouth	22.03.79
Holland, Matthew	5. 9	West Ham	Bury	11.04.74
Murray, Robert	5. 11	–	Hammersmith	31.10.74
Rawlinson, Mark	5. 8	Man. Utd.	Bolton	9.06.75
Forwards				
Bailey, John	5. 8	Enfield	London	6.05.69
Fletcher, Steven	6. 2	Hartlepool	Hartlepool	26.06.72
Hayter, James	5. 10	–	Sandown, I.O.W.	9.04.79
O'Neill, Jon	5. 11	Celtic	Glasgow	3.01.74
Robinson, Stephen	5. 7	Tottenham	Crumlin	10.12.74
Town, David	5. 9	–	Bournemouth	9.12.76

BRENTFORD

Name	Height ft. in.	Previous Club	Birthplace	Birthdate
Goalkeepers				
Dearden, Kevin	5. 11	Tottenham	Luton	8.03.70
Fernandes, Tamar	6. 3	–	Paddington	7.12.74
Defenders				
Ashby, Barry	6. 2	Watford	Brent	21.11.70
Bates, Jamie	6. 1	–	Croydon	24.02.68
Hurdle, Gus	5. 10	Fulham	London	14.10.73
Statham, Brian	5. 11	Tottenham	Zimbabwe	21.05.69
Midfield				
Anderson, Ijah	5. 8	Southend	Hackney	30.12.75
Bent, Marcus	6. 0	–	London	19.05.78
Canham, Scott	5. 10	West Ham Utd.	London	5.11.74

Dennis, Kevin	5. 10	Arsenal	–	14.12.76
Goddard, Richard	6. 3	Arsenal	–	31.03.78
Harvey, Lee	5. 11	Nott'm Forest	Harlow	21.12.66
Hutchings, Carl	6. 0	–		24.09.74
Myall, Stuart	5. 9	Brighton	Eastbourne	12.11.74
Wormull, Simon	5. 10	Tottenham	Crawley	1.12.76
Forwards				
Asaba, Carl	6. 1	Dulwich Hamlet	London	28.01.73
McGhee, David	5. 10	–	Sussex	19.06.76
McPherson, Malcolm	5. 10	West Ham	Glasgow	19.12.74
Omigie, Joe	6. 2	Donna	Hammersmith	13.06.72
Rapley, Kevin	5. 9	–		21.09.77
Taylor, Rob	6. 1	Leyton Orient	Norwich	30.04.71

BRISTOL CITY

Name	Height ft. in.	Previous Club	Birthplace	Birthdate
Goalkeepers				
Naylor, Stuart	6. 4	W.B.A.	Leeds	6.12.62
Phillips, Steven	6. 1	Paulton Rov.	Bath	6.05.78
Welch, Keith	6. 1	Rochdale	Bolton	3.10.68
Defenders				
Barnard, Darren	5. 10	Chelsea	Rintein, Ger.	30.11.71
Bell, Michael	5. 10	Wycombe W.	Newcastle	15.11.71
Brennan, James	5. 9	Sora Lazio, Can.	Toronto, Can.	8.05.77
Dyche, Sean	6. 0	Chesterfield	Kettering	28.06.71
Edwards, Rob	6. 0	Carlisle	Kendal	1.01.73
Hale, Matthew	5. 6	–	Bristol	2.02.79
Hobbs, Darren	6. 2	–	Bristol	18.01.79
Langan, Kevin	6. 0	–	Jersey	7.04.78
Paterson, Scott	5. 11	Liverpool	Aberdeen	13.05.72
Shail, Mark	6. 1	Yeovil	Sandviken, Swe.	15.10.66
Taylor, Shaun	6. 1	Swindon Town	Plymouth	26.02.63
Midfield				
Carey, Louis	5. 10	–	Bristol	22.01.77
Doherty, Thomas	5. 7	–	Bristol	17.03.79
Hewlett, Matthew	6. 1	–	Bristol	25.02.76
Owers, Gary	6. 0	Sunderland	Newcastle	3.10.68
Plummer, Dwayne	5. 10	–	Bristol	12.05.78
Tinnion, Brian	5. 11	Bradford City	Stanley	23.02.68
Tisdale, Paul	5. 9	Southampton	Malta	14.01.73
Vanes, Michael	5. 6	–	Cayman Isl.	16.03.79
Forwards				
Barclay, Dominic	5. 9	–	Bristol	5.09.76
Bent, Junior	5. 5	Huddersfield	Huddersfield	1.03.70
Bokoto, Mommainais	5. 11	Maria Aalter	France	20.10.74
Cramb, Colin	6. 0	Doncaster	Lanark	23.06.74
Goater, Shaun	6. 0	Rotherham	Hamilton, Berm.	25.02.70
Goodridge, Gregory	5. 6	Q.P.R.	Barbados	10.02.75
Seal, David	5. 11	Eendracht, Bel.	Sydney, Aust.	26.1.72

BRISTOL ROVERS

Name	Height ft. in.	Previous Club	Birthplace	Birthdate
Goalkeepers				
Collett, Andy	6. 0	Middlesbrough	Stockton	28.10.73
Higgs, Shane	6. 2	–	Oxford	13.05.77

Defenders

Clark, Billy	6. 0	Bournemouth	Christchurch	19.05.67
Foster, Stephen	6. 1	Woking	Mansfield	3.12.74
Martin, Lee	6. 0	Celtic	Hyde	5.02.68
Perry, Jason	6. 1	Cardiff City	Caerphilly	2.04.70
Power, Graeme	5. 11	Q.P.R.	London	7.03.77
Pritchard, David	5. 7	Telford United	Wolverhampton	27.05.72
Tillson, Andy	6. 2	Q.P.R.	Huntingdon	30.06.66
White, Tom	5. 11	–	Bristol	26.01.76

Midfield

Brown, Justin	5. 11	–	Leeds	9.11.78
French, John	5. 10	–	Bristol	25.09.76
Hayfield, Matthew	5. 10	–	Bristol	8.08.75
Holloway, Ian	5. 8	Q.P.R.	Kingswood	12.03.63
Lockwood, Matthew	5. 9	Q.P.R.	Rochford	17.10.76
Lowe, Joshua	6. 0	–	Bristol	15.02.79
Morgan, Brian	6. 1	–	Bristol	12.07.78
Ramasut, Tom	5. 10	Norwich	Cardiff	30.08.77
Skinner, Justin	6. 0	Fulham	Chiswick	30.01.69
Zabek, Lee	6. 0	–	Bristol	13.10.78

Forwards

Alsop, Julian	6. 4	Halesowen	Nuneaton	28.05.73
Archer, Lee	5. 6	–	Bristol	6.11.72
Beadle, Peter	6. 2	Watford	London	13.05.72
Bennett, Frankie	5. 7	Southampton	Birmingham	13.01.69
Cureton, Jamie	5. 7	Norwich	Bristol	28.08.75
Hayles, Barry	5. 9	Stevenage	London	17.04.72
Miller, Paul	6. 0	Wimbledon	Bisley	31.01.68
Parmenter, Steve	5. 9	Q.P.R.	Chelmsford	22.01.77
Teague, Simon	5. 6	–	Henley	23.02.79

Bennie Gary

BURNLEY

Name	Height ft. in.	Previous Club	Birthplace	Birthdate
Goalkeepers				
Beresford, Marlon	6. 1	Sheff. Wed.	Lincoln	2.09.69
Woods, Chris	6. 2	Sunderland	Boston	14.11.59
Defenders				
Gentile, Marco	–	Maastricht	–	–
Hoyland, Jamie	6. 0	Sheff. Utd.	Sheffield	23.01.66
Overson, Vince	6. 2	Stoke	Kettering	15.05.62
Swan, Peter	6. 3	Plymouth	Leeds	28.09.66
Vinnicombe, Chris	5. 8	Rangers	Exeter	20.10.70
West, Gareth	6. 2	–	Oldham	1.08.78
Winstanley, Mark	6. 1	Bolton	St. Helens	22.01.68
Midfield				
Barnes, Paul	5. 11	Birmingham	Leicester	16.11.67
Ford, Mark	5. 7	Leeds	Pontefract	10.10.75
Gleghorn, Nigel	6. 0	Stoke	Seaham	12.08.62
Harrison, Gerry	5. 9	Huddersfield	Lambeth	15.04.72
Little, Glen	6. 3	Glentoran	Wimbledon	15.10.75
Matthew, Damian	5. 11	Crystal P.	Islington	23.09.70
Weller, Paul	5. 8	–	Brighton	6.03.75
Forwards				
Cooke, Andy	5. 11	Newtown	Stoke	20.01.74
Duerden, Ian	5. 11	–	Burnley	27.03.78
Eastwood, Phil	5. 10	–	Blackburn	6.04.78
Eyres, David	5. 10	Blackpool	Liverpool	26.02.64
Smith, Paul	6. 1	–	Easington	22.01.76
Waddle, Chris	6. 1	Sheff. Wed.	Gateshead	14.12.60

CARLISLE UNITED

Name	Height ft. in.	Previous Club	Birthplace	Birthdate
Goalkeepers				
Caig, Anthony	6. 1	–	Whitehaven	11.04.74
Day, Richard	6. 3	–	Chelmsford	25.01.79
Dixon, George	6. 1	–	Whitehaven	24.10.78
Defenders				
Archdeacon, Owen	5. 9	Barnsley	Greenock	4.03.66
Delap, Rory	6. 0	–	Birmingham	6.07.76
Hopper, Tony	5. 11	–	Carlisle	31.05.76
Pounewatchy, Stephane	6. 0	FC Guegnon	Paris	10.02.68
Taylor, Lee	6. 0	–	Whitehaven	12.09.77
Thorpe, Jeff	5. 11	–	Whitehaven	17.11.72
Varty, William	6. 2	–	Workington	1.10.76
Walling, Dean	6. 0	Guiseley	Leeds	17.04.69
Midfield				
Aspinall, Warren	5. 8	Bournemouth	Wigan	13.09.67
Boertien, Paul	6. 0	–	Halthwistle	20.01.79
Conway, Paul	6. 1	Oldham	London	17.04.70
Hampton, James	5. 10	–	Leeds	7.07.79
Prokas, Richard	5. 10	–	Penrith	22.01.76
Sandwith, Kevin	5. 11	–	Workington	30.04.78
Forwards				
Dobie, Scott	6. 0	–	Workington	10.10.78
Jansen, Matthew	5. 10	–	Carlisle	20.10.77
McAlindon, Gareth	5. 10	Newcastle	Hexham	6.04.77
Peacock, Lee	6. 0	–	Paisley	9.10.76
Smart, Allan	6. 0	Preston N.E.	Perth	8.07.74
Stevens, Ian	5. 11	Shrewsbury	Malta	21.10.66

CHESTERFIELD

Name	Height ft. in.	Previous Club	Birthplace	Birthdate
Goalkeepers				
Leaning, Andy	6. 2	Lincoln City	York	18.05.63
Mercer, Billy	6. 2	Sheff. Utd.	Liverpool	22.05.69
Defenders				
Carr, Darren	6. 3	Crewe	Bristol	4.09.68
Jules, Mark	5. 9	Scarborough	Bradford	5.09.71
Perkins, Chris	5. 11	Mansfield	Nottingham	9.01.74
Rogers, Lee	5. 11	Doncaster	Doncaster	28.10.66
Williams, Mark	6. 0	Shrewsbury	Cheshire	28.09.70
Willis, Roger	6. 1	Peterborough	Sheffield	17.06.67
Midfield				
Beaumont, Chris	5. 11	Stockport Co.	Sheffield	5.12.65
Curtis, Tom	5. 8	Derby	Exeter	1.03.73
Dunn, Iain	5. 10	Huddersfield	–	1.04.70
Ebdon, Marcus	5. 10	Peterborough	Pontypool	17.10.70
Gaughan, Steve	6. 0	Doncaster	Doncaster	14.04.70
Hewitt, Jamie	5. 10	Doncaster	Chesterfield	17.05.68
Holland, Paul	5. 10	Sheff. Utd.	Lincoln	8.07.73
Lomas, James	5. 11	–	–	–
Forwards				
Howard, Jonathan	5. 10	Rotherham	Sheffield	7.10.71
Lormor, Tony	6. 0	Peterborough	Ashington	29.10.70
Morris, Andrew	6. 4	Rotherham	Sheffield	17.11.67
Wilkinson, Steve	5. 10	Preston	Lincoln	1.9.68

FULHAM

Name	Height ft. in.	Previous Club	Birthplace	Birthdate
Goalkeepers				
Arendse, Andre	–	Cape Town Spurs	South Africa	–
Walton, Mark	6. 4	Fakenham Town	Merthyr Tydfil	1.06.69
Defenders				
Aggrey, Jimmy	6. 5	Chelsea	London	26.10.78
Blake, Mark	6. 0	Shrewsbury	Portsmouth	17.12.67
Cullip, Danny	6. 0	Oxford United	Berkshire	17.09.76
Cusack, Nick	6. 0	Oxford United	Rotherham	24.12.65
Herrera, Robbie	5. 6	Q.P.R.	Torquay	12.06.70
Lawrence, Matt	5. 10	Wycombe	Northampton	19.06.74
McGuckin, Ian	6. 2	Hartlepool	Middlesbrough	24.0.4.73
Stewart, Simon	6. 1	Sheff. Wed.	Leeds	1.11.73
Watson, Paul	5. 8	Gillingham	Hastings	14.01.75
Midfield				
Arnott, Andy	6. 1	Leyton Orient	Chatham	18.10.73
Carpenter, Richard	5. 11	Gillingham	Sheppey	30.09.72
Cockerill, Glenn	5. 10	Leyton Orient	Grimsby	25.08.59
Hayward, Steve	5. 11	Carlisle United	Walsall	8.09.71
McAree, Rod	5. 7	Dungannon	Dungannon	10.08.74
Morgan, Simon	5. 10	Leicester City	Birmingham	5.09.66
Smith, Neil	5. 8	Gillingham	London	30.09.71
Thomas, Martin	5. 8	Leyton Orient	Lyndhurst	12.09.73
Forwards				
Brooker, Paul	5. 8	–	London	25.11.76
Conroy, Mike	6. 0	Preston	Glasgow	31.12.65
Freeman, Darren	5. 11	Gillingham	Brighton	22.08.73
Moody, Paul	6. 3	Oxford Utd.	Portsmouth	13.06.67
Newhouse, Aidan	6. 2	Wimbledon	Wallasey	25.05.72
Scott, Rob	6. 1	Sheff. Utd.	Epsom	15.08.73

GILLINGHAM

Name	Height ft. in.	Previous Club	Birthplace	Birthdate
Goalkeepers				
Stannard, Jim	6. 2	Fulham	London	6.10.62
Defenders				
Bryant, Matt	6. 1	Bristol City	Bristol	21.09.70
Butters, Guy	6. 3	Portsmouth	Hillingdon	30.10.69
Chapman, Ian	5. 8	Brighton	Brighton	31.05.70
Green, Richard	6. 1	Swindon	Wolverhampton	22.11.67
Harris, Mark	6. 3	Swansea	Reading	15.07.63
Masters, Neil	6. 0	Wolves	Lisburn	25.05.72
Thomas, Glen	6. 0	Barnet	Hackney	6.10.67
Midfield				
Hessenthaler, Andy	5. 7	Watford	Gravesend	17.06.65
O'Connor, Mark	5. 9	Bournemouth	Rochdale	10.03.63
Pennock, Adrian	6. 0	Bournemouth	Ipswich	27.03.71
Ratcliffe, Simon	6. 0	Brentford	Davyhulme	8.02.67
Smith, Paul	5. 11	Brentford	Lenham	18.09.71
Forwards				
Akinbiyi, Adeola	6. 1	Norwich	Hackney	10.10.74
Bailey, Dennis	5. 10	Q.P.R.	Lambeth	30.11.65
Butler, Steve	6. 1	Cambridge Utd.	Birmingham	27.01.62
Fortune-West, Leo	6. 3	Stevenage Borough	Stratford	9.04.71
Onoura, Ifem	6. 0	Mansfield	Glasgow	28.07.67
Piper, Lenny	5. 8	Wimbledon	London	8.08.77
Puttnam, Dave	5. 11	Lincoln City	Leicester	3.02.67

GRIMSBY TOWN

Name	Height ft. in.	Previous Club	Birthplace	Birthdate
Goalkeepers				
Love, Andrew	6. 2	–	Grimsby	28.03.79
Pearcey, Jason	6. 1	Mansfield	Leamington Spa	23.07.71
Defenders				
Bloomer, Matthew	6. 1	–	Grimsby	–
Chapman, Ben	5. 7	–	Scunthorpe	–
Fickling, Ashley	5.10	Sheff. Utd.	Sheffield	15.11.72
Gallimore, Tony	5.11	Carlisle	Crewe	21.02.72
Handyside, Peter	6. 1	–	Dumfries	31.07.74
Jobling, Kevin	5. 9	Leicester City	Sunderland	1.01.68
Lever, Mark	6. 3	–	Beverley	29.03.70
McDermott, John	5. 7	–	Middlesbrough	3.02.69
Rodger, Graham	6. 2	Luton	Glasgow	1.04.67
Smith, Richard	5.11	Leicester City	Lutterworth	3.10.70
Midfield				
Black, Kingsley	5. 8	Nott'm F.	Luton	22.06.68
Brown, James	5.10	–	–	–
Groves, Paul	5.11	W.B.A.	Derby	28.02.66
Neil, James	5. 8	–	Bury St. Edmunds	28.02.76
Widdrington, Tommy	5.10	Southampton	Newcastle	21.11.71
Wrack, Darren	5. 9	Derby	Cleethorpes	5.05.76
Forwards				
Clarke, Daryl	5.10	–	–	–
Lester, Jack	5.10	–	Sheffield	8.10.75
Livingstone, Steve	6. 1	Chelsea	Middlesbrough	8.09.69
Stephenson, Lee	5.11	–	Grimsby	–

LUTON TOWN

Name	Height ft. in.	Previous Club	Birthplace	Birthdate
Goalkeepers				
Abbey, Nathan	6. 1	–	London	11.07.78
Davis, Kelvin	6. 1	–	Bedford	29.06.76
Feuer, Ian	6. 7	West Ham	Las Vegas	20.05.71
Defenders				
Davis, Steve	6. 2	Burnley	Hexham	30.10.68
James, Julian	5.10	–	Tring	22.03.70
Johnson, Marvin	6. 0	–	Wembley	29.10.68
Patterson, Darren	6. 2	Crystal Palace	Belfast	15.10.69
Thomas, Mitchell	6. 2	West Ham	Luton	2.10.64
Willmott, Chris	6. 1	–	Bedford	30.09.77
Midfield				
Alexander, Graham	5.10	Scunthorpe	Coventry	10.10.71
Evers, Sean	5. 8	–	Hitchin	10.10.77
Kean, Robert	5. 7	–	Luton	3.06.78
McLaren, Paul	6. 0	–	High Wycombe	17.11.76
Showler, Paul	5. 7	Bradford City	Doncaster	10.10.66
Waddock, Gary	5.10	Bristol Rovers	Kingsbury	17.03.62
Forwards				
Douglas, Stuart	5.10	–	London	9.04.78
Fotiadis, Andrew	5.11	–	Hitchin	6.09.77
Grant, Kim	5.10	Charlton	Ghana	25.09.72
Marshall, Dwight	5. 7	Plymouth	Jamaica	3.10.65
Oldfield, David	6. 0	Leicester City	Perth, Aust.	30.05.68
Thorpe, Tony	5. 9	Leicester City	Leicester	10.04.74

MILLWALL

Name	Height ft. in.	Previous Club	Birthplace	Birthdate
Goalkeepers				
Carter, Tim	6. 2	Oxford Utd.	Bristol	5.10.67
Horne, Brian	–	Hartlepool	–	–
Nurse, David	6. 4	Man. City	Kings Lynn	12.10.76
Smith, Phil	–	–	–	–
Defenders				
Aris, Steve	–	–	London	27.07.79
Bircham, Marc	–	–	London	11.05.78
Connor, James	6. 0	–	Middlesbrough	22.08.74
Fitzgerald, Scott	6. 0	Wimbledon	London	13.08.69
Lavin, Gerard	5. 10	Watford	Corby	5.02.74
Newman, Ricky	5. 10	Crystal P.	Guildford	5.08.70
Stevens, Keith	6. 0	–	Merton	21.06.64
Sturges, Paul	5. 11	Charlton	Dartford	4.08.75
Webber, Damian	6. 4	Bognor Regis	Rustington	8.10.68
Witter, Tony	6. 1	Q.P.R.	London	12.08.65
Midfield				
Bowry, Bobby	5. 10	Crystal Palace	Croydon	19.05.71
Canoville, Dean	6. 1	–	Perivale	30.11.78
Dair, Jason	5. 11	Raith	Dunfermline	15.06.74
Doyle, Maurice	5. 8	Q.P.R.	Ellesmere Port	17.10.69
Hartley, Paul	5. 9	Hamilton	Baillieston	19.10.76
McRobert, Lee	5. 9	Sittingbourne	Bromley	4.10.72
Neill, Lucas	6. 1	–	Sydney, Aust.	9.03.78
Robertson, Graham	–	Raith Rovers	Edinburgh	12.11.76
Roche, Stephen	–	–	Dublin	2.10.78
Savage, Dave	6. 2	Longford Town	Dublin	30.07.73
Forwards				
Crawford, Steve	5. 10	Raith	Dunfermline	9.01.74
Hockton, Danny	–	–	–	7.02.79
Markey, Brendan	–	Bohemians	Dublin	19.05.76
Sadlier, Richard	6. 2	–	Dublin	14.01.79

Wilkinson Paul   *Barnsley*

NORTHAMPTON TOWN

Name	Height ft. in.	Previous Club	Birthplace	Birthdate
Goalkeepers				
Turley, Billy	6. 3	Evesham	Wolverhampton	15.07.73
Woodman, Andy	6. 3	Exeter	Denmark Hill	11.08.71
Defenders				
Clarkson, Ian	5. 11	Stoke City	Solihull	4.12.70
Colkin, Lee	5. 11	–	Nuneaton	15.07.74
Frain, John	5. 9	Birmingham City	Birmingham	8.10.68
Rennie, David	6. 0	Coventry City	Edinburgh	29.08.64
Sampson, Ian	6. 2	Sunderland	Wakefield	14.11.68
Warburton, Ray	6. 0	York	Rotherham	7.10.67
Midfield				
Hunter, Roy	5. 10	W.B.A.	Saltburn	29.10.73
Martin, David	6. 1	Leyton Orient	East Ham	25.04.63
Parrish, Sean	5. 10	Doncaster Rovers	Wrexham	14.03.72
Peer, Dean	6. 2	Walsall	Dudley	8.08.69
Warner, Michael	5. 9	Tamworth	Harrogate	17.01.74
Forwards				
Gayle, John	6. 2	Stoke City	Bromsgrove	30.07.64
Gibb, Alistair	5. 9	Norwich	Salisbury	17.02.76
Grayson, Neil	5. 10	Boston Utd.	York	1.11.64

Lee, Christian	6. 1	Doncaster	Aylesbury	8.10.76
White, Jason	6. 0	Scarborough	Meriden	19.10.71
Wilson, Kevin	5. 8	Walsall	Banbury	18.04.61

OLDHAM ATHLETIC

Name	Height ft. in.	Previous Club	Birthplace	Birthdate
Goalkeepers				
Ironside, Ian	6. 2	Scarborough	Sheffield	8.03.64
Kelly, Gary	5. 10	Bury	Preston	3.08.66
Defenders				
Garnett, Sean	6. 2	Swansea	Wallasey	22.11.69
Graham, Richard	6. 3	–	Dewsbury	28.11.74
Hodgson, Doug	6. 1	Sheffield Utd.	Frankston, Aus.	27.02.69
Holt, Andy	6. 1	–	Manchester	21.05.78
McNivern, Scott	5. 9	–	Blackpool	27.05.78
Ramsden, Gavin	5. 11	–	Manchester	4.11.78
Redmond, Steve	6. 0	Man. City	Liverpool	2.11.67
Serrant, Carl	5. 11	–	Bradford	12.09.75
Sinnott, Lee	6. 2	Huddersfield	Walsall	12.07.65
Midfield				
Duxbury, Lee	5. 10	Bradford City	Keighley	7.10.69
Hughes, Andrew	5. 10	–	Stockport	2.01.78
Orlygsson, Toddy	5. 11	Stoke	Odense, Den.	2.08.66
Reed, Paul	5. 10	Huddersfield	Oldbury	6.08.71
Richardson, Lee	5. 11	Aberdeen	Halifax	12.03.69
Richardson, Lloyd	6. 0	–	Dewsbury	7.10.77
Rickers, Paul	5. 8	–	Castleford	9.05.75
Forwards				
Barlow, Stuart	5. 10	Everton	Liverpool	16.07.68
McCarthy, Sean	6. 0	Bradford City	Bridgend	12.09.67
McNiven, David	5. 10	–	Leeds	27.05.78
Ormandroyd, Ian	6. 5	Bradford City	Bradford	22.09.64
Ritchie, Andy	5. 11	Scarborough	Manchester	28.11.60
Rush, Matthew	5. 11	Norwich City	Hackney	6.08.71

PLYMOUTH ARGYLE

Name	Height ft. in.	Previous Club	Birthplace	Birthdate
Goalkeepers				
Blackwell, Kevin	5. 11	Huddersfield	Luton	21.12.58
Dungey, James	5. 10	–	Plymouth	7.02.78
Prudhoe, Mark	6. 0	Stoke	Washington	11.11.63
Defenders				
Billy, Chris	6. 0	Huddersfield	Huddersfield	2.01.73
Curran, Chris	5. 11	Torquay	Birmingham	17.09.71
Heathcote, Mick	6. 2	Cambridge Utd.	Durham	10.09.65
James, Anthony	6. 3	Hereford	Sheffield	27.06.67
Logan, Richard	6. 0	Huddersfield	Barnsley	24.05.69
Patterson, Mark	5. 10	Derby	Leeds	13.09.68
Williams, Paul	5. 6	Huddersfield	Leicester	11.09.69
Midfield				
Barlow, Martin	5. 7	–	Barnstaple	25.06.71
Collins, Simon	6. 0	Huddersfield	Pontefract	16.12.73
Mauge, Ronnie	5. 10	Bury	Islington	10.03.69
Saunders, Mark	5. 9	Tiverton	Reading	23.07.71
Wotton, Paul	5. 10	–	Plymouth	17.08.77

Forwards

Name	ft.	in.	Previous Club	Birthplace	Birthdate
Corazzin, Carlo	5.	9	Cambridge Utd.	Canada	25.12.71
Illman, Neil	5.	7	Eastwood Town	Doncaster	29.04.75
Littlejohn, Adrian	5.	9	Sheff. Utd.	Wolverhampton	26.09.70

PRESTON NORTH END

Name	Height ft. in.		Previous Club	Birthplace	Birthdate
Goalkeepers					
Lucas, David	6.	0	–	Preston	23.11.77
Moilanen, Teuvo	6.	2	FF Jaro, Fin.	Oulu, Fin.	12.12.73
O'Hanlon, Kelham	6.	0	Dundee Utd.	Saltburn	16.05.62
Mimms, Bobby	6.	4	Blackburn	York	12.10.63
Defenders					
Barrick, Dean	5.	7	Cambridge Utd.	Hemsworth	30.09.69
Gage, Kevin	5.	10	Sheff. Utd.	Chiswick	21.04.64
Jackson, Michael	6.	0	Bury	Chester	4.12.73
Kidd, Ryan	6.	0	Port Vale	Radcliffe	6.10.71
Morgan, Paul	6.	0	–	Belfast	23.10.78
Moyes, David	6.	1	Hamilton	Glasgow	25.04.63
Murdock, Colin	6.	3	Man. Utd.	Ballymena	2.07.75
Parkinson, Gary	5.	11	Burnley	Thornaby	10.01.68
Sparrow, Paul	6.	0	Crystal Palace	London	24.03.75
Squires, Jamie	6.	1	–	Preston	15.11.75
Midfield					
Ashcroft, Lee	5.	10	W.B.A.	Preston	7.09.72
Atkinson, Graeme	5.	8	Hull	Hull	11.11.71
Cartwright, Lee	5.	8	–	Rossendale	19.09.72
Darby, Julian	6.	0	W.B.A.	Bolton	3.10.67
Davey, Simon	5.	10	Carlisle	Swansea	1.10.70
Gregan, Sean	6.	2	Darlington	Cleveland	29.03.74
McDonald, Neil	5.	11	Bolton	Wallsend	2.11.65
McKenna, Paul	5.	10	–	Chorley	20.10.77
Rankine, Mark	5.	10	Wolves	Doncaster	30.09.69
Forwards					
Holt, Michael	5.	9	Blackburn	Burnley	28.07.77
Nogan, Kurt	5.	10	Burnley	Cardiff	9.09.70
Reeves, David	6.	0	Carlisle	Birkenhead	19.11.67

SOUTHEND UNITED

Name	Height ft. in.		Previous Club	Birthplace	Birthdate
Goalkeepers					
Henriksen, Tony	6.	3	Randes Freja	Denmark	25.04.73
Royce, Simon	6.	2	Heybridge Swifts	Forest Gate	9.09.71
Defenders					
Dublin, Keith	5.	11	Watford	Brent	29.01.66
Harris, Andrew	5.	10	Liverpool	South Africa	26.02.77
Roget, Leo	6.	1	–	Ilford	1.08.77
Stimpson, Mark	5.	10	Portsmouth	London	27.12.67
Midfield					
Byrne, Paul	5.	11	Celtic	Dublin	30.06.72
Gridelet, Phil	6.	1	Barnsley	Edgware	30.04.67
Hails, Julian	5.	10	Fulham	Lincoln	20.11.67
Houghton, Ray	5.	7	Crystal Palace	Glasgow	9.01.62
Marsh, Mike	5.	8	Galatasaray, Tur.	Liverpool	21.07.69
Nielsen, John	5.	9	Ikast	Denmark	7.04.72

Forwards

Name	Height ft.	in.	Previous Club	Birthplace	Birthdate
Boere, Jeroen	6.	3	Crystal Palace	Arnhem, Hol.	18.11.67
Rammell, Andy	6.	2	Barnsley	Nuneaton	10.02.67
Thomson, Andy	5.	10	Queen of the South	Motherwell	1.04.71
Williams, Paul	5.	7	Torquay	London	16.08.65

WALSALL

Name	Height ft.	in.	Previous Club	Birthplace	Birthdate
Goalkeepers					
Naisbitt, Darren	5.	10	Middlesbrough	–	–
Walker, Jim	5.	11	Notts County	Sutton-in-Ashfield	9.07.73
Defenders					
Evans, Wayne	5.	10	Welshpool	Welshpool	25.08.71
Mountfield, Derek	6.	1	Carlisle	Liverpool	2.11.62
Rogers, Darren	5.	9	Wycombe	Birmingham	9.04.70
Roper, Ian	6.	3	–	Nuneaton	20.06.77
Ryder, Stuart	6.	1	–	Sutton Coldfield	6.11.73
Viveash, Adrian	6.	1	Swindon	Swindon	30.09.69
Midfield					
Keates, Dean	5.	4	–	Walsall	30.06.78
Keister, John	5.	8	–	Manchester	11.11.70
Platt, Clive	6.	3	–	London	27.10.77
Thomas, Wayne	–	–	–	–	–
Forwards					
Hodge, John	5.	6	Swansea	Skelmersdale	1.04.69
Ricketts, Michael	6.	2	–	Birmingham	4.12.78
Watson, Andrew	5.	9	Blackpool	Leeds	1.04.67

WATFORD

Name	Height ft.	in.	Previous Club	Birthplace	Birthdate
Goalkeepers					
Chamberlain, Alec	6.	2	Sunderland	Ely	20.06.64
Day, Chris	6.	2	Crystal Palace	Whipps Cross	28.07.75
Defenders					
Bazeley, Darren	5.	10	–	Northampton	5.10.72
Belgrave, Kevin	5.	10	–	Bedford	20.04.78
Foster, Colin	6.	4	West Ham	Chislehurst	16.07.64
Gibbs, Nigel	5.	7	–	St. Albans	20.11.65
Ludden, Dominic	5.	7	Leyton Orient	Basildon	30.03.74
Millen, Keith	6.	2	Brentford	Croydon	26.09.66
Page, Robert	6.	0	–	Llwynypia	3.09.74
Rooney, Mark	6.	0	–	London	19.05.78
Midfield					
Easton, Clint	5.	10	–	Barking	1.10.77
Flash, Richard	5.	9	–	Birmingham	8.04.76
Johnson, Richard	5.	10	–	Kurri Kurri, Aust.	27.04.74
Palmer, Steve	6.	1	Ipswich	Brighton	31.03.68
Porter, Gary	5.	6	–	Sunderland	6.03.66
Ramage, Craig	5.	9	Derby	Derby	30.03.70
Slater, Stuart	5.	9	–	Sudbury	27.03.69
Talboys, Steve	5.	10	Wimbledon	Bristol	18.09.66
Forwards					
Andrews, Wayne	5.	10	–	London	25.11.77
Lee, Jason	6.	3	Nott'm F.	Newham	9.05.71
Lowndes, Nathan	5.	11	Leeds	Salford	2.06.77
Mooney, Tommy	5.	11	Southend	Middlesbrough	11.08.71

Penrice, Gary	5. 8	Q.P.R.	Bristol	23.03.64
Phillips, Kevin	5. 7	Baldock Town	Hitchin	25.07.73
Simpson, Colin	6. 1	–	Oxford	30.04.76
Thomas, David	5. 10	Swansea City	Caerphilly	26.09.75

WIGAN ATHLETIC

Name	Height ft. in.	Previous Club	Birthplace	Birthdate
Goalkeepers				
Butler, Lee	6. 2	Barnsley	Sheffield	30.05.66
Carroll, Roy	6. 2	Hull City	Northern Ireland	30.09.77
Farnworth, Simon	5. 11	Preston	Chorley	28.10.63
Defenders				
Bishop, Charlie	6. 0	Barnsley	Nottingham	16.02.68
Fitzhenry, Neil	6. 0	–	Wigan	24.09.78
Green, Scott	5. 11	Bolton	Walsall	15.01.70
Greenall, Colin	5. 11	Lincoln City	Billinge	30.12.63
Johnson, Gavin	5. 11	Luton	Stowmarket	10.10.70
Morgan, Steve	5. 9	Coventry City	Oldham	19.09.68
Pender, John	6. 0	Burnley	Luton	19.11.63
Sharp, Kevin	5. 9	Leeds	Ontario, Can.	19.09.74
Midfield				
Diaz, Isidro	5. 7	CF Balaguer, Spa.	Valencia, Spa.	15.05.72
Kilford, Ian	5. 10	Nott'm. Forest	Bristol	6.10.73
Martinez, Roberto	5. 11	CF Balaguer, Spa.	Balaguer, Spa.	13.07.73
Rogers, Paul	6. 0	Notts Co.	Portsmouth	21.03.65
Forwards				
Black, Tony	5. 8	Bamber Bridge	Barrow-in-Furness	15.07.69
Jones, Graeme	6. 0	Doncaster	Gateshead	13.03.70
Lancashire, Graham	5. 10	Preston	Blackpool	19.10.72
Lee, David	5. 7	Bolton	Whitefield	5.11.67
Lowe, David	5. 10	Leicester City	Liverpool	30.08.65
Saville, Andy	6. 0	Preston NE	Hull	12.12.64

WREXHAM

Name	Height ft. in.	Previous Club	Birthplace	Birthdate
Goalkeepers				
Cartwright, Mark	6. 2	York	Chester	13.01.73
Edwards, Leigh	6. 1	–	Wrexham	19.09.78
Marriott, Andy	6. 1	Nott'm. Forest	Sutton-in-Ashfield	11.10.70
Walsh, Dave	6. 1	–	Wrexham	29.04.79
Defenders				
Brace, Deryn	5. 7	Norwich	Haverfordwest	15.03.75
Carey, Brian	6. 3	Leicester City	Cork	31.05.68
Hardy, Phil	5. 7	–	Chester	9.04.73
Humes, Tony	6. 0	Ipswich	Blyth	19.03.66
Jones, Barry	5. 11	Liverpool	Prescot	20.06.70
McGregor, Mark	5. 10	–	Chester	16.02.77
Morris, Rob	5. 10	–	Oswestry	4.09.78
Ridler, Dave	5. 8	–	Liverpool	12.03.76
Shone, Gareth	6. 0	–	Aldershot	5.01.79
Midfield				
Brammer, David	5. 9	–	Bromborough	28.02.75
Chalk, Martyn	5. 6	Stockport	Louth	30.08.69
Cross, Jonathan	5. 10	–	Wallasey	2.03.75
Griffiths, Andy	5. 11	–	Wirral	21.11.78
Owen, Gareth	5. 7	–	Chester	21.10.71

Name	Height ft. in.	Previous Club	Birthplace	Birthdate
Phillips, Wayne	5. 10	–	Bangor, N Wales	15.12.70
Skinner, Craig	5. 9	Plymouth	Bury	21.10.70
Thomas, Steve	5. 10	–	Hartlepool	23.06.79
Ward, Peter	5. 10	Stockport	County Durham	15.10.64
Williams, Scott	6. 0	–	Bangor, N Wales	7.08.74
Forwards				
Bennett, Gary	5. 11	Preston NE	Kirkby	20.09.63
Connolly, Karl	5. 9	–	Prescot	9.02.70
Morris, Steve	5. 10	Liverpool	Liverpool	13.05.76
Roberts, Neil	5. 10	–	Wrexham	7.04.78
Roberts, Paul	5. 11	Porthmadog	Bangor, N Wales	29.07.77
Russell, Kevin	5. 8	Notts County	Portsmouth	6.12.66
Spink, Dean	6. 1	Shrewsbury	Birmingham	22.01.67
Watkin, Steve	5. 10	–	Wrexham	16.06.71

WYCOMBE WANDERERS

Name	Height ft. in.	Previous Club	Birthplace	Birthdate
Goalkeepers				
Parkin, Brian	6. 2	Bristol Rovers	Birkenhead	12.10.65
Taylor, Martin	5. 11	Derby Co	Tamworth	9.12.66
Defenders				
Brown, Steve	6. 0	Northampton	Northamptom	6.07.66
Cousins, Jason	5. 10	Brentford	Hayes	4.10.70
Forsyth, Mike	5. 11	Notts Co	Liverpool	20.03.66
Kavanagh, Jason	5. 9	Derby Co	Birmingham	23.11.71
McCarthy, Paul	6. 0	Brighton	Cork	4.08.71
Patton, Aaron	5. 8	–	–	–
Patton, Alan	5. 11	–	–	–
Ryan, Keith	5. 11	Berkhamsted	Northampton	25.06.70
Midfield				
Carroll, David	6. 0	Ruislip Manor	Paisley	20.09.66
Cornforth, John	6. 1	Birmingham	Whitley Bay	7.10.67
Harkin, Maurice	5. 9	–	–	–
McGavin, Steve	5. 9	Birmingham	North Walsham	24.01.69
Simpson, Michael	5. 9	Notts Co	Nottingham	28.02.74
Wraight, Gary	5. 9	–	–	–
Forwards				
Read, Paul	5. 11	Arsenal	Harrow	25.09.73
Scott, Keith	6. 3	Norwich	Oadby	9.06.67
Stallard, Mark	6. 0	Bradford City	Derby	24.10.74

YORK CITY

Name	Height ft. in.	Previous Club	Birthplace	Birthdate
Goalkeepers				
Warrington, Andy	6. 3	–	Sheffield	10.06.76
Defenders				
Atkinson, Paddy	5. 9	Newcastle	Singapore	22.05.70
Barras, Tony	6. 0	Stockport	Stockton-on-Tees	29.03.71
Hall, Wayne	5. 9	Hatfield Main	Rotherham	25.10.68
McMillan, Andy	5. 10	–	South Africa	22.06.68
Reed, Martin	6. 1	–	Scarborough	10.01.78
Sharples, John	6. 0	Ayr	Bury	26.01.73
Tutill, Steve	5. 11	–	Derwent	1.10.69
Midfield				
Bushell, Steve	5. 9	–	Manchester	28.12.72
Jordan, Scott	5. 9	–	Newcastle	19.07.75

Murty, Graeme	5. 10	–	Middlesbrough	13.11.74
Pouton, Alan	6. 0	Newcastle	Newcastle	1.02.77
Tinkler, Mark	5. 11	Leeds	Bishop Auckland	24.10.74
Forwards				
Bull, Gary	5. 10	Birmingham	Tipton	12.06.66
Campbell, Neil	5. 10	–	Middlesbrough	26.01.77
Cresswell, Richard	5. 11	–	Bridlington	20.09.77
Greening, Jonathan	5. 10	–	Scarborough	2.01.79
Himsworth, Gary	5. 7	Darlington	Appleton	19.12.69
Rowe, Rodney	5. 8	Huddersfield	Huddersfield	30.07.75
Rush, David	5. 11	Oxford	Sunderland	15.05.71
Stephenson, Paul	5. 9	Brentford	Newcastle	2.01.68
Tolson, Neil	6. 1	Bradford City	Wordley	25.10.73

Third Division

BARNET

Name	Height ft. in.	Previous Club	Birthplace	Birthdate
Goalkeepers				
Harrison, Lee	6. 2	Fulham	Billericay	12.09.71
Defenders				
Adams, Keiran	5. 11	–	St. Ives, Cambs	20.10.77
Ford, Jon	6. 2	Gillingham	Birmingham	12.04.68
Hardyman, Paul	5. 8	Wycombe	Portsmouth	11.03.64
Harle, Michael	6. 0	Millwall	Lewisham	3.10.72
Howarth, Lee	6. 2	Mansfield	Bolton	3.01.68
McDonald, David	5. 10	Peterborough	Dublin	2.01.71
Primus, Linvoy	6. 0	Charlton	Stratford	14.09.73
Stockley, Sam	6. 0	Southampton	Tiverton	5.09.77
Midfield				
Campbell, Jamie	6. 2	Luton	Birmingham	21.10.72
Goodhind, Warren	5. 11	–	South Africa	16.08.77
Hodges, Lee	5. 11	Tottenham	Epping	4.09.73
Mills, Danny	5. 11	Charlton	Sidcup	13.02.75
Simpson, Phil	5. 8	Stevenage Borough	London	18.10.69
Wilson, Paul	5. 9	Barking	Forest Gate	26.09.64
Forwards				
Brady, Matthew	5. 10	–	London	27.10.77
Devine, Sean	6. 0	Omonia Nicosia, Cyp.	Lewisham	6.09.72
Samuels, Dean	6. 2	Borehamwood	Hackney	29.03.73

BRIGHTON & HOVE ALBION

Name	Height ft. in.	Previous Club	Birthplace	Birthdate
Goalkeepers				
Ormerod, Mark	6. 0	–	Bournemouth	5.02.76
Rust, Nicholas	6. 0	Arsenal	Cambridge	25.09.74
Defenders				
Allan, Derek	6. 0	Southampton	Irvine	24.12.74
Hobson, Gary	6. 1	Hull	Hull	12.11.72
McNally, Ross	6. 1	–	Dublin	6.09.78
Morris, Mark	6. 2	Bournemouth	Carshalton	26.09.62
Saul, Eric	5. 7	–	Dublin	28.10.78

Smith, Peter	6. 1	Alma Swanley	Stone	12.07.69
Tuck, Stuart	5. 11	–	Brighton	1.10.74
Yorke-Johnson, Ross	6. 0	–	Brighton	2.01.76

Midfield

Armstrong, Paul	5. 10	–	Dublin	5.10.78
Mayo, Kerry	5. 10	–	Cuckfield	21.09.77
Mundee, Denny	5. 10	Brentford	Swindon	10.10.68
Peake, Jason	5. 10	Rochdale	Leicester	29.09.71
Reinelt, Robert	5. 11	Colchester Utd.	Epping	11.03.74
Thompson-Minton, Jeff	5. 6	Tottenham	Hackney	28.12.73

Forwards

Baird, Ian	6. 0	Plymouth Argyle	Rotherham	1.04.64
McDonald, Paul	5. 6	Southampton	Motherwell	20.04.68
Maskell, Craig	5. 8	Southampton	Aldershot	10.04.68
Rowlands, James	5. 8	–	Aberdare	31.05.79
Storer, Stuart	5. 11	Exeter	Rugby	16.01.67
Westcott, John	5. 6	–	Eastbourne	31.05.79

CAMBRIDGE UNITED

Name	Height ft. in.	Previous Club	Birthplace	Birthdate
Goalkeepers				
Barrett, Scott	5. 11	Stoke City	Derby	2.04.63
Marshall, Shaun	6. 0	–	–	30.06.79
Defenders				
Craddock, Jody	6. 0	Christchurch	Redditch	25.07.75
Joseph, Marc	6. 0	–	Leicester	10.11.76
Thompson, David	6. 0	Blackpool	Ashington	20.11.68
Vowden, Colin	6. 0	Cambridge City	Newmarket	13.09.71
Wanless, Paul	6. 1	Lincoln City	Banbury	14.12.73
Midfield				
Ashbeem Ian	–	–	–	–
Beall, Matthew	5. 7	–	Enfield	4.12.77
Hayes, Adrian	6. 2	–	Norwich	22.05.78
Hyde, Micah	5. 9	–	Newham	10.11.74
Joseph, Matthew	5. 7	Arsenal	Bethnal Green	30.09.72
Preece, David	5. 6	Swindon	Bridgnorth	28.05.63
Raynor, Paul	5. 9	Preston	Nottingham	29.04.66
Wilde, Adam	–	–	–	–
Williamson, David	–	–	–	–
Forwards				
Barnwell-Edinboro, Jamie	5. 9	Wigan	Hull	26.12.75
Benjamin, Trevor	–	–	Kettering	8.02.79
Kyd, Michael	5. 8	–	Hackney	21.05.77
Richards, Anthony	6. 2	Sudbury	Newham	17.09.73
Taylor, John	6. 3	Colchester	Norwich	24.08.64

CARDIFF CITY

Name	Height ft. in.	Previous Club	Birthplace	Birthdate
Goalkeepers				
Elliott, Anthony	6. 0	Carlisle	Nuneaton	30.11.69
Hallworth, Jon	6. 1	Oldham	Stockport	26.10.65
Defenders				
Eckhardt, Jeff	6. 0	Stockport	Sheffield	7.09.65
Jarman, Lee	6. 2	–	Cardiff	16.12.77
Lloyd, Kevin	5. 10	Hereford	Llanidloes	26.09.70

| Phillips, Lee | 6. 0 | – | Aberdare | 18.03.79 |
| Young, Scott | 6. 1 | – | Tonypandy | 14.01.76 |

Midfield

Cross, John	5. 9	–	Barking	6.04.76
Fowler, Jason	6. 1	Bristol City	Bristol	20.08.74
Middleton, Craig	5. 9	–	Nuneaton	10.09.70
Partridge, Scott	5. 9	Bristol City	Leicester	13.10.74
Rollo, James	5. 10	–	Wisbech	27.05.76
Stoker, Gareth	5. 9	Hereford	Bishop Auckland	22.02.73

Forwards

Dale, Carl	5. 8	Chester	Colwyn Bay	29.04.66
Nugent, Kevin	6. 1	Bristol City	Edmonton	10.04.64
Philliskirk, Tony	6. 1	Burnley	Sunderland	10.02.65
White, Steve	5. 11	Hereford	Chipping Sodbury	2.01.59

CHESTER CITY

Name	Height ft. in.	Previous Club	Birthplace	Birthdate
Goalkeepers				
Brown, Wayne	6. 0	Weston	Southampton	14.01.77
Sinclair, Ronnie	5. 9	Stoke C.	Stirling	19.11.64
Defenders				
Alsford, Julian	6. 2	Watford	Poole	24.12.72
Davidson, Ross	5. 8	Sheff. Utd.	Chertsey	13.11.73
Jackson, Peter	6. 0	Huddersfield	Bradford	6.04.61
Jenkins, Iain	5. 9	Everton	Prescot	24.11.72
Rogers, Dave	6. 1	Tranmere	Liverpool	25.08.75
Whelan, Spencer	6. 2	Liverpool	Liverpool	17.09.71
Woods, Matthew	6. 1	Everton	Gosport	9.09.76
Midfield				
Brown, Greg	5. 10	–	Manchester	31.07.78
Fisher, Neil	5. 10	Bolton	St. Helens	7.11.70
Flitcroft, David	5. 11	Preston	Bolton	14.01.74
Giles, Martin	5. 10	–	Shrewsbury	1.01.79
Priest, Chris	5. 10	Everton	Leigh	18.10.73
Reid, Shaun	5. 9	Bury	Huyton	13.10.65
Richardson, Nick	6. 1	Bury	Halifax	11.04.67
Shelton, Gary	5. 7	Bristol City	Nottingham	21.03.58
Forwards				
Jones, Jon	5. 11	Aston Villa	Wrexham	27.10.78
McDonald, Rod	5. 10	Falkirk	London	20.03.67
Milner, Andy	6. 0	Rochdale	Kendal	10.02.67
Murphy, John	6. 1	–	Whiston	18.10.76
Noteman, Kevin	5. 10	Doncaster	Preston	15.10.69

COLCHESTER UNITED

Name	Height ft. in.	Previous Club	Birthplace	Birthdate
Goalkeepers				
Caldwell, Garrett	6. 0	–	Princeton	6.11.73
Emberson, Carl	6. 1	Millwall	Epsom	13.07.73
Defenders				
Armitage, Gavin	5. 11	–	London	–
Betts, Simon	5. 7	Scarborough	Middlesbrough	3.03.73
Cawley, Peter	6. 3	Barnet	London	15.09.65
Dunne, Joe	5. 10	Gillingham	Dublin	25.05.73
Greene, David	6. 2	Luton	Luton	26.10.73
Gregory, David	5. 11	Peterborough	Colchester	23.01.70

Name	Height ft. in.	Previous Club	Birthplace	Birthdate
Haydon, Nicky	5. 9	Colchester	Barking	10.08.78
Skelton, Aaron	6. 0	Luton	Welwyn	22.11.74
Stamps, Scott	5. 10	Torquay	Edgbaston	20.03.75
Midfield				
Abrahams, Paul	5. 8	Brentford	Colchester	31.10.73
Buckle, Paul	5. 7	Exeter	Hayfield	16.12.70
Forbes, Stephen	6. 2	Millwall	London	24.12.75
Hathaway, Ian	5. 6	Torquay	Wordsley	22.08.68
Sandford, David	5. 11	Colchester	London	–
Whitton, Steve	6. 0	Ipswich	East Ham	4.12.60
Wilkins, Richard	6. 0	Hereford	Streatham	28.05.65
Forwards				
Adcock, Tony	5. 10	Luton	Bethnal Green	27.02.63
Duguid, Karl	5. 11	–	Hitchin	21.03.78
Lock, Tony	5. 8	–	Harlow	3.09.76
Sale, Mark	6. 5	Macclesfield	Burton-on-Trent	27.02.72

DARLINGTON

Name	Height ft. in.	Previous Club	Birthplace	Birthdate
Goalkeepers				
Papaconstantinou, Lucas	6. 4	Alabama States	Canada	10.05.74
Preece, David	6. 2	Sunderland	Sunderland	28.08.76
Defenders				
Barnard, Mark	6. 0	Rotherham	Sheffield	27.11.75
Brydon, Lee	5. 11	Liverpool	Stockton	15.11.74
Crosby, Andy	6. 2	Doncaster	Rotherham	3.03.73
Devos, Jason	6. 4	Montreal	Vancouver	2.01.74
Hope, Richard	6. 3	Blackburn	Stockton	28.06.78
Shaw, Simon	5. 11	–	Middlesbrough	21.09.73
Midfield				
Atkinson, Brian	5. 9	Sunderland	Darlington	19.01.71
Brumwell, Phil	5. 11	Sunderland	Darlington	8.08.75
Lowe, Kenny	5. 10	Gateshead	Sedgefield	6.11.61
Oliver, Michael	5. 9	Stockport	Cleveland	1.08.75
Tarrant, Neil	6. 0	–	Darlington	24.06.79
Forwards				
Naylor, Glenn	5. 10	York	Howden	11.08.72
Roberts, Darren	6. 0	Chesterfield	Birmingham	12.10.69
Robinson, Paul	5. 10	–	Sunderland	20.11.78
Shutt, Carl	5. 10	Bradford C.	Sheffield	10.10.61

DONCASTER ROVERS

Name	Height ft. in.	Previous Club	Birthplace	Birthdate
Goalkeepers				
Williams, Dean	6. 1	Brentford	Lichfield	5.01.72
Defenders				
Gore, Ian	5. 11	Torquay	Liverpool	10.01.68
Hawthorne, Mark	5. 11	–	Sunderland	21.08.79
Utley, Darren	6. 0	–	Barnsley	28.09.77
Midfield				
Clark, Ian	5. 11	Stockton	Stockton	23.10.74
Cunningham, Harvey	5. 9	Droylsden	Manchester	11.09.68
Esdaille, Darren	5. 8	Hyde	Manchester	4.11.74
Ireland, Simon	5. 11	Mansfield	Halifax	23.11.71
McDonald, Martin	6. 0	Southport	Glasgow	4.12.73

Schofield, Jon	5. 11	Lincoln City	Barnsley	16.05.65
Smith, Mike	5. 11	Runcorn	Liverpool	28.09.73
Warren, Lee	6. 0	Hull	Manchester	28.02.69
Forwards				
Dixon, Kerry	6. 1	Watford	Luton	24.07.61
Pemberton, Martin	5. 11	Oldham	Bradford	1.02.76

EXETER CITY

Name	Height ft. in.	Previous Club	Birthplace	Birthdate
Goalkeepers				
Bayes, Ashley	6. 1	Torquay	Lincoln	19.04.72
Fox, Peter	5. 10	Stoke	Scunthorpe	5.07.57
Defenders				
Baddeley, Lee	6. 1	Cardiff City	Cardiff	12.07.74
Blake, Noel	6. 4	Dundee	Jamaica	31.02.62
Cyrus, Andy	5. 8	Crystal Palace	Lambeth	30.09.76
Gale, Shaun	6. 1	Barnet	Reading	8.10.69
Hare, Matthew	6. 0	–	Barnstaple	26.12.76
Richardson, Jon	6. 1	–	Nottingham	29.08.75
Vittles, James	5. 10	–	Sidmouth	15.10.78
Midfield				
Birch, Paul	5. 6	Doncaster Rov.	West Bromwich	20.11.62
Gardner, Jimmy	5. 10	Cardiff City	Dunfermline	29.09.67
McConnell, Barry	5. 11	–	Exeter	1.01.77
Medlin, Nicky	5. 9	–	Camborne	23.11.76
Minett, Jason	5. 10	Lincoln City	Peterborough	12.08.71
Forwards				
Braithwaite, Leon	6. 0	Bishop's Stortford	Hackney	13.12.72
Flack, Steve	6. 1	Cardiff City	Cambridge	29.05.72
Fry, Chris	5. 8	Colchester Utd.	Cardiff	23.10.69
Ghazghazi, Suryan	5. 7	–	Honiton	24.08.77
Rowbotham, Darren	5. 10	Shrewsbury T.	Cardiff	22.10.68

HARTLEPOOL UNITED

Name	Height ft. in.	Previous Club	Birthplace	Birthdate
Goalkeepers				
O'Connor, Paul	5. 11	–	Easington	17.08.71
Pears, Stephen	6. 0	Liverpool	Brandon	22.01.62
Defenders				
Barron, Michael	5. 11	Middlesbrough	Lumley	22.12.74
Bradley, Russell	6. 2	Scunthorpe	Birmingham	28.03.66
Davies, Glenn	6. 2	Burnley	Brighton	20.07.76
Downey, Glen	6. 1	–	Newcastle	20.09.78
Ingram, Denny	5. 10	–	Sunderland	27.06.76
Knowles, Darren	5. 10	–	Sunderland	20.06.76
Lee, Graeme	5. 6	–	Sheffield	8.10.70
Lucas, Richard	6. 2	–	Middlesbrough	31.05.78
McDonald, Chris	5. 10	–	Chapel Town	22.09.70
Walton, Paul	5. 9	–	Sunderland	2.07.79
Midfield				
Beech, Christopher	5. 10	–	Blackpool	16.09.74
Cooper, Mark	5. 8	Exeter	Wakefield	18.12.68
Cullen, Jon	6. 0	–	Durham	10.01.73
Gallagher, Ian	5. 10	–	Hartlepool	30.05.78
Howard, Steven	6. 1	–	Durham	10.05.76

Name	Height ft. in.		Previous Club	Birthplace	Birthdate
Hutt, Stephen	6.	2	–	Middlesbrough	19.02.79
Miller, Thomas	6.	1	–	Easington	8.01.79
Proctor, Mark	5.	10	–	Middlesbrough	30.01.61
Tait, Mick	5.	11	Gretna	Wallsend	30.09.56
Forwards					
Allon, Joe	5.	11	Port Vale	Gateshead	12.11.66
Baker, Paul	6.	1	–	Newcastle	5.01.63
Halliday, Stephen	5.	10	Charlton	Sunderland	3.05.76
Irvine, Stuart	5.	9	–	Hartlepool	1.03.79

HULL CITY

Name	Height ft. in.		Previous Club	Birthplace	Birthdate
Goalkeepers					
Wilson, Steve	5.	10	–	Hull	24.04.74
Defenders					
Brien, Tony	6.	0	W.B.A.	Dublin	10.02.69
Dewhurst, Robert	6.	3	Blackburn	Keighley	10.09.71
Doncel, Antonio	6.	0	Ferrol (Spain)	Lugo (Spain)	31.01.67
Greaves, Mark	6.	1	Brigg Town	Hull	22.01.75
Lowthorpe, Adam	5.	7	–	Hull	7.08.75
Marks, Jamie	5.	9	Leeds	Belfast	18.03.77
Rioch, Gregor	5.	11	Peterborough	Sutton Coldfield	24.06.75
Sharman, Sam	5.	10	Sheffield Wed.	Hull	7.11.77
Trevitt, Simon	5.	11	Huddersfield	Dewsbury	20.12.67
Wilkinson, Ian	6.	2	–	Hull	19.09.77
Wright, Ian	6.	1	Bristol Rovers	Lichfield	10.03.72
Midfield					
Dickinson, Patrick	5.	10	–	Vancouver	6.05.78
Joyce, Warren	5.	9	Burnley	Oldham	20.01.65
Mann, Neil	5.	10	Grimsby	Nottingham	19.11.72
Maxfield, Scott	5.	8	Doncaster	Thorne	13.07.76
Quigley, Michael	5.	7	Man. City	Manchester	2.10.70
Wharton, Paul	5.	4	Leeds	Newcastle	26.06.77
Forwards					
Brown, Andy	6.	3	Leeds	Edinburgh	11.10.76
Darby, Duane	5.	11	Doncaster	Birmingham	17.10.73
Fewings, Paul	5.	11	–	Hull	18.02.78
Gordon, Gavin	6.	1	–	Manchester	24.06.79
Hateley, Mark	6.	1	Rangers	Liverpool	7.11.61
Peacock, Richard	5.	10	–	Sheffield	29.10.72

Rocastle Drus

LEYTON ORIENT

Name	Height ft. in.		Previous Club	Birthplace	Birthdate
Goalkeepers					
Hyde, Paul	6.	1	Leicester	Hayes	7.04.63
Defenders					
Caldwell, Peter	6.	1	Q.P.R.	Dorchester	5.06.72
Channing, Justin	5.	11	Bristol Rovers	Reading	19.11.68
McCarthy, Alan	5.	11	Q.P.R.	Tooting	11.01.72
Shearer, Lee	5.	10	–	Southend	23.10.77
Smith, Dean	6.	0	Hereford	West Bromwich	19.03.71
Midfield					
Ayorinde, Sam	5.	10	–	Lagos	20.10.74
Baker, Joe	5.	10	Charlton	London	19.04.77
Garland, Peter	5.	10	Charlton	Croydon	20.01.71
Hanson, David	5.	9	–	Huddersfield	19.11.68

Ling, Martin	5. 7	Swindon	West Ham	15.07.66
Martin, David	6. 1	Gillingham	East Ham	25.04.63
Warren, Mark	6. 1	–	Clapton	12.11.74
Forwards				
Arnott, Andy	6. 1	Gillingham	Chatham	18.10.73
Griffiths, Carl	5. 9	Peterborough	Welshpool	16.07.71
Inglethorpe, Alex	5. 11	Watford	Epsom	14.11.71
Morrison, David	5. 11	Peterborough	Waltham Forest	30.11.74

LINCOLN CITY

Name	Height ft. in.	Previous Club	Birthplace	Birthdate
Goalkeepers				
Richardson, Barry	6. 1	Preston	Wallsend	5.08.69
Vaughan, John	5. 10	Preston NE	Isleworth	26.06.64
Defenders				
Austin, Kevin	5. 9	Leyton Orient	Hackney	12.02.73
Bimson, Stuart	5. 11	Bury	Liverpool	29.09.69
Brown, Grant	6. 0	Leicester City	Sunderland	19.11.69
Fleming, Terry	5. 9	Preston	Marston Green	5.01.73
Holmes, Stephen	6. 2	Preston	Middlesbrough	13.01.71
Robertson, John	6. 2	Wigan	Liverpool	8.01.74
Westley, Shane	6. 2	Cambridge Utd.	Canterbury	16.06.65
Whitney, Jonathon	5. 10	Huddersfield	Nantwich	23.12.70
Midfield				
Hone, Mark	6. 1	Southend Utd.	Sidcup	31.03.68
Martin, Jae	5. 11	Birmingham	London	5.02.76
Sterling, Worrell	5. 7	Bristol Rov.	London	8.06.65
Forwards				
Ainsworth, Gareth	5. 9	Preston	Blackburn	10.05.73
Alcide, Colin	6. 2	Emley	Huddersfield	14.04.72
Barnett, Jason	5. 9	Wolves	Shrewsbury	21.04.76
Bos, Gijesbert	6. 0	Ijsselmeervogels	Spackenburg	22.02.73
Brown, Stephen	6. 0	Gillingham	Southend	6.12.73
Stant, Philip	6. 0	Bury	Bolton	13.10.62

MACCLESFIELD TOWN

Name	Height ft. in.	Previous Club	Birthplace	Birthdate
Goalkeepers				
Oakes, Andy	6. 1	Barnton	Northwich	11.01.77
Price, Ryan	6. 5	Birmingham	Coven	13.03.70
Defenders				
Foey, Ceg	6. 1	Whitton Albion	Manchester	12.03.65
Gee, Danny	5. 11	Barnton	Northwich	6.05.74
Howarth, Neil	6. 1	Burnley	Bolton	15.11.71
Payne, Steve	5. 11	Huddersfield	Castleford	1.08.75
Sodje, Efetobore	6. 1	Stevenage Bor.	Greenwich	5.10.72
Tinson, Darren	5. 10	Northwich V.	Connahs Quay	15.11.69
Midfield				
Gardiner, Mark	5. 10	Crewe A.	Cirencester	25.12.66
Hitchen, Steven	5. 9	Blackburn	Salford	28.11.76
Leendis, Andy	5. 8	Oldham	Cheadle	4.07.78
Sorvel, Neil	5. 10	Crewe A.	Whiston	2.03.73
Wood, Steve	5. 8	Ashton Utd	Oldham	23.06.63
Forwards				
Askey, John	6. 0	–	Stoke	4.11.64

Davenport, Peter	5. 10	Southport	Birkenhead	24.03.61
Landon, Richard	6. 1	Stockport Co.	Worthing	22.03.70
Mitchell, Neil	5. 6	Blackpool	Lytham	7.11.74
Ohandjanian, Demis	5. 8	Aston Villa	Stockport	1.05.78
Peel, Nathan	6. 0	Burnley	Clitheroe	17.05.72
Power, Phil	5. 7	Stalybridge C.	Salford	25.07.67

MANSFIELD TOWN

Name	Height ft. in.	Previous Club	Birthplace	Birthdate
Goalkeepers				
Bowling, Ian	6. 4	Bradford City	Sheffield	27.07.65
Defenders				
Eustace, Scott	6. 0	Leicester City	Leicester	13.06.75
Ford, Tony	5. 11	Barrow	Grimsby	14.05.69
Hackett, Warren	6. 0	Doncaster	Newham	16.12.71
Peters, Mark	6. 0	Peterborough	St. Asaph	6.07.72
Watkiss, Stuart	6. 2	Hereford	Wolverhampton	8.05.66
Midfield				
Clark, Darrell	5. 11	–	Mansfield	16.12.77
Doolan, John	6. 1	Everton	Liverpool	7.05.74
Kerr, David	5. 11	Man. City	Dumfries	6.09.74
Walker, John	5. 8	Grimsby	Glasgow	12.12.73
Williams, Lee	5. 7	Tranmere Rovers	Birmingham	3.02.73
Forwards				
Christie, Iyseden	5. 10	Coventry	Coventry	14.11.76
Hadley, Stewart	6. 1	Derby	Derby	30.12.73
Harper, Steve	5. 10	Doncaster	Stoke	3.02.69
Williams, Ryan	5. 5	–	Chesterfield	31.08.78

NOTTS COUNTY

Name	Height ft. in.	Previous Club	Birthplace	Birthdate
Goalkeepers				
Pollitt, Michael	6. 4	Darlington	Bolton	29.02.72
Ward, Darren	5. 11	Mansfield	Worksop	11.05.74
Defenders				
Baraclough, Ian	6. 1	Mansfield	Leicester	4.12.70
Derry, Shaun	5. 11	–	Nottingham	6.12.77
Hendon, Ian	6. 0	Leyton Orient	Ilford	5.12.71
Hogg, Graeme	6. 1	Hearts	Aberdeen	17.06.64
Mitchell, Paul	5. 10	–	Nottingham	8.11.78
Redmile, Matthew	6. 3	–	Nottingham	12.11.76
Strodder, Gary	6. 1	W.B.A.	Mirfield	1.04.65
Midfield				
Cunnington, Shaun	5. 9	W.B.A.	Bourne	4.01.66
Finnan, Steve	5. 9	Birmingham	Chelmsford	20.04.76
Galloway, Michael	5. 11	–	Nottingham	13.10.74
Marshall, Ben	6. 0	–	Kirkby-in-Ashfield	5.09.79
Richardson, Ian	5. 10	Birmingham	Barking	22.10.70
Robinson, Philip	5. 9	Chesterfield	Stafford	6.01.67
Robson, Mark	5. 7	Charlton Ath.	Newham	22.05.69
Forwards				
Dudley, Craig	6. 0	–	Ollerton	12.09.79
Farrell, Sean	6. 1	Peterborough	Watford	28.02.69
Jones, Gary	6. 0	Southend	Huddersfield	6.04.69
Martindale, Gary	5. 11	Peterborough	Liverpool	24.06.71
White, Devon	6. 3	Watford	Nottingham	2.03.64

PETERBOROUGH UNITED

Name	Height ft. in.	Previous Club	Birthplace	Birthdate
Goalkeepers				
Griemink, Bart	6. 3	Birmingham	Montreal	29.03.72
Sheffield, Jon	6. 0	Cambridge Utd.	Bedworth	1.02.69
Tyler, Mark	5. 11	–	Norwich	2.04.77
Defenders				
Bodley, Michael	6. 1	Southend	Hayes	14.09.67
Boothroyd, Adrian	5. 10	Mansfield	Bradford	8.02.71
Drury, Adam	5. 10	–	Cottenham	29.08.78
Edwards, Andrew	6. 2	Birmingham	Epping	17.09.71
Foran, Mark	6. 4	Sheff. Utd.	Aldershot	30.10.73
Heald, Gregory	6. 2	Enfield	London	26.09.71
Neal, Ashley	6. 1	Huddersfield	Northampton	16.12.74
Midfield				
Bullimore, Wayne	5. 9	Mansfield	Bradford	12.09.70
Castle, Steve	5. 10	Birmingham	Barkingside	17.05.66
Houghton, Scott	5. 5	Walsall	Hitchin	22.10.71
Lewis, Neil	5. 8	Leicester	Wolverhampton	28.06.74
Linton, Desmond	6. 1	Luton	Birmingham	5.09.71
Willis, Roger	6. 1	Southend	Sheffield	17.06.67
Forwards				
Carruthers, Martin	5. 11	Stoke	Nottingham	7.08.72
Cleaver, Christopher	5. 9	–	Hitchin	24.03.79
De Souza, Miguel	5. 11	Wycombe	Newham	11.02.70
Grazioli, Giuliano	5. 11	Wembley	London	23.03.75
Inman, Niall	5. 9	–	Wakefield	6.02.78
Quinn, Jimmy	6. 0	Reading	Belfast	18.11.59
Rowe, Ezekul	5. 10	Chelsea	Stoke Newington	30.10.73

ROCHDALE

Name	Height ft. in.	Previous Club	Birthplace	Birthdate
Goalkeepers				
Gray, Ian	6. 2	Oldham	Manchester	25.02.75
Defenders				
Barlow, Andy	5. 10	Blackpool	Oldham	24.11.65
Bayliss, Dave	6. 0	–	Liverpool	8.06.76
Fensome, Andy	5. 7	Preston	Northampton	18.02.69
Hill, Keith	6. 0	Plymouth	Bolton	17.05.69
Johnson, Alan	6. 0	Lincoln	Wigan	19.02.71
Irwin, Nick	5. 10	–	Salford	25.12.78
Midfield				
Bailey, Mark	5. 9	Stoke	Stoke	12.08.76
Bryson, Ian	5. 10	Preston	Kilmarnock	26.11.62
Farrell, Andy	5. 11	Wigan	Colchester	7.10.65
Gouck, Andy	5. 10	Blackpool	Blackpool	8.06.72
Russell, Alex	5. 11	Burscough	Crosby	17.03.73
Forwards				
Carter, Mark	5. 10	Bury	Liverpool	17.12.60
Leonard, Mark	6. 0	Wigan	St. Helens	27.09.62
Painter, Rob	5. 10	Darlington	Wigan	26.01.71
Robson, Glen	6. 1	–	Sunderland	25.09.77
Stuart, Mark	5. 10	Huddersfield	Chiswick	15.12.66

ROTHERHAM UNITED

Name	Height ft. in.	Previous Club	Birthplace	Birthdate
Goalkeepers				
Barnes, Philip	6. 1	–	Sheffield	2.03.79
Pettinger, Paul	–	Leeds	Sheffield	1.10.75
Defenders				
Breckin, Ian	5. 11	–	Rotherham	24.02.75
Clark, Martin	–	Southport	Accrington	12.09.70
Dillon, Paul	5. 9	–	Limerick	22.10.78
Heath, Stephen	–	Carlisle	Hull	15.11.77
Hurst, Paul	5. 4	–	Sheffield	25.09.74
Monington, Mark	6. 1	Burnley	Mansfield	21.10.70
Pell, Robert	6. 0	–	Leeds	5.02.79
Richardson, Neil	6. 0	–	Sunderland	3.03.68
Midfield				
Berry, Trevor	5. 6	Aston Villa	Haslemere	1.08.74
Garner, Darren	5. 9	Dorchester Town	Plymouth	10.12.71
Goodwin, Shaun	5. 8	–	Rotherham	14.06.69
Hudson, Danny	–	–	Mexborough	25.06.79
McKenzie, Robert	5. 9	–	Northumberland	22.03.79
Roscoe, Andy	5. 10	Bolton	Liverpool	4.06.73
Shuttleworth, Barry	5. 8	Bury	Accrington	9.07.77
Forwards				
Druce, Mark	6. 0	Oxford	Oxford	3.03.74
Glover, Lee	5. 11	Port Vale	Kettering	24.04.70
Hayward, Andy	6. 0	Frickley	Barnsley	21.06.70
McDougald, Junior	5. 9	Brighton	Texas	12.01.75

SCARBOROUGH

Name	Height ft. in.	Previous Club	Birthplace	Birthdate
Goalkeepers				
Martin, Kevin	6. 1	–	Bromsgrove	22.06.76
Defenders				
Aitken, Paul	6. 0	York City	Nottingham	3.09.69
Bennett, Gary	6. 0	Sunderland	Manchester	4.12.61
Carr, Graeme	5. 9	–	Chester-le-Street	28.10.78
Kay, John	5. 10	Sunderland	Great Lumley	29.01.64
Lee, Mark	6. 0	–	Consett	31.05.79
Rockett, Jason	6. 1	Rotherham	London	26.09.69
Sutherland, Colin	6. 0	Clydebank	Glasgow	15.03.75
Midfield				
Bazglya, Eammon	5. 7	–	London	25.10.78
Bennett, Troy	6. 0	Barnsley	Barnsley	25.12.75
McElhatton, Michael	6. 1	Bournemouth	Kerry	16.04.75
Russell, Matthew	5. 11	–	Dewsbury	17.01.78
Van der Velden, Carel	6. 0	Barnsley	Arnhem, Hol.	3.08.72
Worrall, Ben	5. 6	Swindon	Swindon	7.12.75
Forwards				
Bochenski, Simon	5. 10	Barnsley	Worksop	6.12.75
Brodie, Steven	5. 8	Sunderland	Sunderland	14.01.73
Mitchell, Jamie	5. 7	Norwich	Glasgow	6.11.76
Robinson, Liam	5. 8	Burnley	Bradford	26.12.65
Tate, Chris	6. 0	Sunderland	York	27.12.77
Williams, Gareth	5. 10	Northampton	Isle of Wight	12.03.67

SCUNTHORPE UNITED

Name	Height ft. in.	Previous Club	Birthplace	Birthdate
Goalkeepers				
Clarke, Tim	6. 4	York	Stourbridge	16.05.65
Defenders				
Hope, Chris	6. 0	Nott'm. Forest	Sheffield	14.11.72
Housham, Steve	5. 10	–	Gainsborough	24.02.76
Laws, Brian	5. 10	Darlington	Wallsend	14.10.61
McAuley, Sean	5. 11	Hartlepool	Sheffield	23.06.72
Sertori, Mark	6. 1	Bury	Manchester	1.09.67
Walsh, Michael	5. 11	–	Rotherham	5.08.77
Wilcox, Russ	6. 0	Preston	Hemsworth	25.03.64
Midfield				
Calvogarcia, Alex	5. 9	Ordizia	Spain	1.01.72
D'Auria, David	5. 9	Scarborough	Swansea	26.03.70
Gavin, Mark	5. 10	Exeter	–	17.10.63
Harsley, Paul	5. 8	Grimsby	Scunthorpe	29.05.78
Marshall, Lee	5. 7	Eastwood Town	Nottingham	1.08.75
Patterson, Jamie	5. 4	Hearts	Dumfries	26.04.73
Shakespeare, Craig	5. 11	Grimsby	Birmingham	26.10.63
Walker, Justin	5. 9	Nott'm F.	Nottingham	6.09.75
Forwards				
Eyre, John	5. 10	Oldham	Hull	9.10.74
Forrester, Jamie	6. 0	Grimsby	Bradford	1.11.74
Stamp, Darren	6. 2	–	Hull	21.09.78

SHREWSBURY TOWN

Name	Height ft. in.	Previous Club	Birthplace	Birthdate
Goalkeepers				
Edwards, Paul	6. 2	Crewe	Liverpool	22.02.65
Gall, Benny	6. 2	Dordrecht	Copenhagen	14.03.71
Defenders				
Blaney, Nathan	5. 10	Southampton	Plymouth	10.06.77
Nwadike, Emeka	6. 1	Wolves	Camberwell	9.08.78
Scott, Richard	5. 9	Birmingham	Dudley	29.09.74
Seabury, Kevin	5. 9	–	Shrewsbury	24.11.73
Taylor, Lee	6. 0	Faweh	Hammersmith	24.02.76
Walton, David	6. 2	Sheff. Utd.	Bedlington	10.04.73
Whiston, Peter	6. 0	Southampton	Widnes	4.01.68
Wilding, Peter	6. 0	Telford	Shrewsbury	28.11.68
Midfield				
Cope, James	5. 11	–	Birmingham	4.10.77
Dempsey, Mark	5. 8	Leyton Orient	Dublin	10.12.72
Evans, Paul	5. 8	–	Oswestry	1.09.74
Reed, Ian	5. 8	–	Lichfield	4.09.75
Taylor, Mark	5. 9	Sheff. Wed.	Walsall	22.02.66
Forwards				
Berkley, Austin	5. 9	Swindon	Gravesend	28.01.73
Briscoe, Tony	6. 0	–	Birmingham	16.08.78
Brown, Michael	5. 9	Preston NE	Birmingham	8.02.68
Corns, Stuart	5. 11	–	Shrewsbury	1.07.79
Currie, Darren	5. 9	West Ham	Hampstead	29.11.74
Ward, Nicholas	5. 10	–	Wrexham	30.11.77
Wray, Shaun	6. 1	–	Dudley	14.03.78

SWANSEA CITY

Name	Height ft. in.	Previous Club	Birthplace	Birthdate
Goalkeepers				
Freestone, Roger	6. 3	Chelsea	Newport, Gwent	19.08.68
Jones, Lee	6. 3	AFC Porth	Pontypridd	9.08.70
Miles, Ben	6. 1	Southall	Middlesex	13.04.76
Defenders				
Clode, Mark	5. 10	Plymouth	Plymouth	24.02.73
Jones, Steve	5. 10	Cheltenham	Bristol	25.12.70
King, Robert	5. 8	Torquay	Merthyr	2.09.77
Moreira, Joao	6. 2	Benfica, Por.	Portugal	30.06.70
O'Leary, Kristian	6. 0	–	Port Talbot	30.08.77
Midfield				
Ampadu, Kwame	5. 10	W.B.A.	Bradford	20.12.70
Chapple, Shaun	5. 11	–	Swansea	14.02.73
Edwards, Christian	6. 2	–	Caerphilly	23.11.75
Grey, Jonathan	5. 11	–	Swansea	2.09.77
Lacy, Damian	5. 9	–	Bridgend	3.08.77
Molby, Jan	6. 2	Liverpool	Denmark	4.07.63
Phillips, Gareth	5. 8	–	Porth	19.07.79
Price, Jason	6. 2	Aberaman	Aberdare	12.04.77
Walker, Keith	6. 0	St. Mirren	Edinburgh	17.04.66
Forwards				
Appleby, Richard	5. 9	Ipswich	Middlesbrough	18.09.75
Brown, Linton	5. 10	Hull	Hull	12.04.68
Casey, Ryan	6. 0	–	Coventry	3.01.79
Coates, Jonathan	5. 8	–	Swansea	27.06.75
Heggs, Carl	6. 1	W.B.A.	Leicester	11.10.70
Jenkins, Lee	5. 9	–	Pontypool	28.06.79
McDonald, Colin	5. 7	Falkirk	Edinburgh	10.04.74
Torpey, Steve	6. 3	Bradford City	Islington	8.12.70

TORQUAY UNITED

Name	Height ft. in.	Previous Club	Birthplace	Birthdate
Goalkeepers				
Gregg, Matthew	6. 1	–	Cheltenham	30.11.78
Defenders				
Barrow, Lee	5. 11	Scarborough	Worksworth	1.05.73
Gittins, John	5. 11	Portsmouth	Birmingham	22.01.64
Robinson, Jamie	6. 1	Carlisle	Liverpool	26.02.72
Thomas, Wayne	5. 11	–	Gloucester	17.05.79
Watson, Alex	6. 2	Bournemouth	Liverpool	5.04.68
Midfield				
Gibbs, Paul	5. 10	Colchester United	Gorleston	26.10.72
McCall, Steve	5. 11	Plymouth	Carlisle	15.10.60
Oatway, Charlie	5. 6	Cardiff	Hammersmith	28.11.73
Preston, Michael	5. 8	–	Plymouth	22.11.77
Forwards				
Bedeau, Anthony	5. 9	–	London	24.03.79
Hockley, Wayne	5. 8	–	Torbay	6.09.78
Jack, Rodney	5. 6	Lambada	St. Vincent	28.09.72
McFarlane, Andrew	6. 3	Scunthorpe	Wolverhampton	30.11.68

Mahé LB
Brattbakk
Harald (s)
Larsson Henrik (s)

SCOTTISH LEAGUE SQUADS 1997-98

PREMIER DIVISION

Blinker.

ABERDEEN: Russell Anderson; Paul Bernard; Baldur Bett; Scott Booth; Robert Brown; Duncan Buchan; Martin Buchan; Michael Craig; William Dodds; Russell Duncan; Ryan Esson; Stephen Glass; Iain Good; John Inglis; Ilian Kiriakov; Antoine Kombouare; Malcolm Kpedekpo; James Leighton; Joseph Miller; Michael Newlands; Brian O'Neill; David Rowson; Duncan Shearer; Derek Stillie; Tzanko Tzvetanov; Joseph Walker; Michael Watt; Karl Williamson; Dean Windass; Colin Woodthorpe; Dennis Wyness; Darren Young; Derek Young. **Manager:** Roy Aitken.

Mahé · Henrik Larsson

CELTIC: Enrico Annoni; Marc Anthony; Patrick Bonner; Paul Borland; Thomas Boyd; Jorge Cadete; John Convery; Gerard Crossley; Craig Culkin; Paolo Di Canio; Simon Donnelly; John Dow; Eamonn Duggan; Barry Elliot; Patrick Fitzpatrick; James Gallagher; Peter Grant; Stuart Gray; David Hannah; Christopher Hay; Thomas Johnson; Patrick Kelly; James Kerr; Gerard Lyttle; Peter MacDonald; Malcolm Mackay; Gordon Marshall; John McBride; Andrew McCondichie; Timothy McGrath; Philip McKeown; Thomas McKinlay; Brian McLaughlin; Jackie McNamara; Paul McStay; Graeme Morrison; Ryan Morrison; Andrew O'Brien; Philip O'Donnell; Brian O'Neill; John Potter; James Smith; Alan Stubbs; Andreas Thom; Brian Vaughan; Morten Wieghort. **Manager:** Wim Jansen.

Binley Craig (MF)

Marc Rieper (CB)

Paul Lambert (Ex Borussia D)

Craig Binley

DUNDEE UNITED: Armand Benneker; Paul Black; David Bowman; Paul Boylan; Craig Brown; Joseph Bryers; Gareth Dailly; Hugh Davidson; Christopher Devine; Sieb Dijkstra; James Dolan; Barry Donachie; Cornelius Duffy; Craig Easton; Steven Fallon; Paul Gallacher; Dale Gray; Ian Johnson; Marino Keith; Grahame Kennedy; Maurice Malpas; Alastair Maxwell; Stephen McConalogue; Kevin McDonald; Stewart McKimmie; Raymond McKinnon; Andrew McLaren; Gary McSwegan; Michael Neil; Kjell Olofsson; James Paterson; Erik Pedersen; Mark Perry; Steven Pressley; David Sinclair; Andrew Stewart; Steven Thompson; Richard Thomson; Paul Walker; Robert Winters; Lars Zetterlund. **Manager:** Tommy McLean.

DUNFERMLINE ATHLETIC: David Bingham; Gerard Britton; Henry Curran; Ivo Den Bieman; Derek Fleming; John Fraser; Hamish French; Craig Ireland; Zoran Lemajic; Gregg Loudon; Craig Martin; Mark McCulloch; Marc Millar; Colin Miller; Allan Moore; Stewart Petrie; Craig Robertson; Raymond Sharp; Gregory Shaw; Greg Shields; Andrew Smith; Andrew Tod; Steven Welsh; Ian Westwater; Scott Young. **Manager:** Robert Paton.

HEART OF MIDLOTHIAN: Mark Bradley; John Burns; Stuart Callaghan; Colin Cameron; Stephen Frail; Stephen Fulton; Jeremy Goss; Alisdair Graham; James Hamilton; Myles Hogarth; Derek Holmes; Robert Horn; Gary Locke; Neil McCann; Roderick McKenzie; Allan McManus; David McPherson; David Murie; Grant Murray; Gary Naysmith; Robbie Neilson; Steven O'Donnell; Kris O'Neil; Neil Pointon; Paul Ritchie; John Robertson; Gilles Rousset; Stefano Salvatori; Scott Severin; Kevin Thomas; David Weir. **Manager:** James Jefferies.

HIBERNIAN: Scott Bannerman; Graeme Bryson; Ian Cameron; John Campbell; Jamie Carter; James Charnley; Mark Dempsie; Shaun Dennis; Darren Dods;

Graeme Donald; Andrew Dow; David Elliot; Andrew Frame; Jason Gardiner; Brian Grant; Kevin Harper; Russel Huggon; John Hughes; Martin Hughes; Gordon Hunter; Christopher Jackson; Darren Jackson; Barry Lavety; John Martin; Stuart McCaffrey; Ian McDonald; Patrick McGinlay; Timothy McLean; James McQuilken; Greg Miller; Kenneth Miller; William Miller; Andrew Newman; Eric Paton; Lee Power; Christopher Reid; Michael Renwick; Paul Riley; Robert Shannon; Paul Tosh; Brian Welsh; Keith Wright. **Manager:** Jim Duffy.

KILMARNOCK: Damiano Agostini; Derek Anderson; David Bagen; Martin Baker; Alexander Burke; John Dillon; Kevin Doig; Anthony Elliott; William Findlay; Martin Graham; Steven Hamilton; Garry Hay; John Henry; Gary Holt; Alan Kerr; Dylan Kerr; James Lauchlan; Dragoje Lekovic; Rodney Lennox; Angus MacPherson; Gary McCutcheon; Kevin McGowne; James McIntyre; Colin McKee; John McLelland; Colin Meldrum; Alistair Mitchell; Samuel Montgomerie; Steven Morrison; Mark Reilly; Mark Roberts; Mark Skilling; Gerrit Tallon; Robert Vincent; Neil Whitworth; Paul Wright. **Manager:** Bobby Williamson.

MOTHERWELL: Douglas Arnott; Alexander Burns; Kevin Christie; Owen Coyle; Thomas Coyne; Stephen Craigan; William Davies; Greig Denham; Mario Dorner; William Falconer; Garry Gow; John Hendry; Scott Howie; Brian Martin; Edward May; David McCallum; Christopher McCart; Lee McCulloch; Stephen McMillan; Shaun McSkimming; John Philliben; Franz Resch; Ian Ross; Simo Valakari; Mitchell Van Der Gaag; Michael Weir; Stephen Woods. **Manager:** Alex McLeish.

RANGERS: Jorg Albertz; Lorenzo Amoruso; Erik Bo Andersen; Joachim Bjorklund; Gary Bollan; Steven Boyack; John Brown; Mark Brown; Steven Carson; Alexander Cleland; Gordon Durie; Ian Durrant; Barry Ferguson; Ian Ferguson; Darren Fitzgerald; Paul Gascoigne; Gennaro Gattuso; James Gibson; Andrew Goram; David Graham; Brian Laudrup; Peter MacDonald; Robert Malcolm; Steven McAdam; Stuart McCall; Alistair McCoist; Brian McGinty; Derek McInnes; Paul McKnight; Alan McLaren; Paul McShane; Charles Miller; Craig Moore; Marco Negri; Barry Nicholson; Antti Niemi; Gordan Petric; Sergio Porrio; Michael Rae; Kevin Robison; Maurice Ross; Sebastian Rozental; Theodorus Snelders; Stale Stensaas; Michael Stone; Jonas Thern; Peter Van Vossen; Tony Vidmar; Kirk Willoughby; Scott Wilson; Stephen Wright; David Young. **Manager:** Walter Smith.

ST. JOHNSTONE: Gary Bowman; Gordon Brown; Nick Dasovic; Callum Davidson; Euan Donaldson; Gary Farquhar; Ian Ferguson; Roderick Grant; Daniel Griffin; Leigh Jenkinson; Charles King; Alan Main; Stuart Malcolm; Kieran McAnespie; Stuart McCluskey; Marc McCulloch; John McQuillan; George O'Boyle; Keith O'Halloran; John O'Neil; Stewart Orr; Allan Preston; Stephen Robertson; Philip Scott; Attila Sekerlieglu; Steven Tosh; James Weir; Andrew Whiteford. **Manager:** Paul Sturrock.

FIRST DIVISION

AIRDRIEONIANS: Kenneth Black; Gordon Connelly; Patrick Connolly; Stephen Cooper; John Davies; Peter Hetherston; Paul Jack; Forbes Johnston; Alan Lawrence; Gary Mackay; John Martin; John McClelland; Gerard McKenna; Brian McPhee; Andrew Rhodes; James Sandison; Anthony Smith; Alexander Stewart; Sean Sweeney; Marvyn Wilson. **Manager:** Alex McDonald.

AYR UNITED: Paul Agnew; Robert Bell; Steven Bonar; John Bradford; Gordon

Burns; David Castilla; Robert Connor; Ronald Coyle; Gordon Dalziel; Isaac English; Duncan George; Darren Henderson; Gregg Hood; Alain Horace; Mark Humphries; William Jamieson; Steven Kerrigan; Richard Newall; John Kenneth Nolan; Neil Scally; Robert Scott; Henry Smith; Thomas Smith; David Stewart; John Traynor; Derek Vennard; Paul Watson. **Manager:** Gordon Dalziel.

DUNDEE: Dariusz Adamczuk; Iain Anderson; Edward Annand; Graham Bayne; Paul Clark; Michael Dickie; John Elliott; Raymond Farningham; James Grady; Brian Irvine; James Langfield; Kevin Magee; Stephen McDermott; Gary McGlynn; James McInally; Steven Milne; Jerry O'Driscoll; Gavin Rae; Robert Raeside; Hugh Robertson; George Shaw; Mark Slater; Barry Smith; William Thomson; Craig Tully; Lee Wilkie. **Manager:** John McCormack.

FALKIRK: Neil Berry; Derek Buchanan; Martyn Corrigan; Scott Crabbe; Albert Craig; Graeme Crawford; James Cunning; Derek Ferguson; Andrew Gray; David Hagen; Brian Hamilton; Christopher Horn; Kevin James; Walter Kidd; Andrew Lawrie; Paul Mathers; Kevin McAllister; Jamie McGowan; Mark McGraw; Paul McGrillen; Scott McKenzie; Craig Nelson; Neil Oliver; Stephen Peters; Andrew Seaton; Joseph Tortolano; Kenneth Ward. **Manager:** Alex Totten.

GREENOCK MORTON: Stephen Aitken; John Anderson; Alan Blaikie; Paul Blair; Derek Collins; Peter Cormack; Ross Fanning; Patrick Flannery; Maurice George; Warren Hawke; James Hunter; Neil Inglis; Douglas Johnstone; Janne Lindberg; Alan Mahood; Barry Mason; Ross Matheson; Scott McArthur; Francis McAulay; Stephen McCahill; Craig McPherson; Marc Powers; Marko Rajamaki; Brian Reid; Bryan Slavin; John Willoughby; David Wylie. **Manager:** Allan McGraw.

HAMILTON ACADEMICAL: Martin Bonnar; David Campbell; Gary Clarke; Edward Cunnington; William Davidson; Allan Ferguson; Michael Geraghty; Christopher Hillcoat; Steven McCormick; Scott McCulloch; Sean McEntegart; David McFarlane; Martin McIntosh; Paul McKenzie; John McQuade; Andrew Neilson; Jose Quitongo; Steven Renicks; Paul Ritchie; James Sherry; Steven Thomson. **Manager:** Alex Clark.

PARTICK THISTLE: Charles Adams; Robert Apiliga; Alan Archibald; Stephen Docherty; Robert Dunn; Gareth Evans; David Farrell; Nicholas Henderson; Andrew Lyons; William MacDonald; Callum Milne; David Moss; Jered Stirling; Gregg Watson. **Manager:** John McVeigh.

RAITH ROVERS: Paul Bonar; Paul Browne; Kevin Byers; David Craig; Lee Dair; Craig Dargo; Peter Duffield; Paul Harvey; Stephen Kirk; Daniel Lennon; Greig McCulloch; Derek McGill; John Millar; Andrew Millen; Graham Mitchell; Anthony Rougier; Colin Scott; Jay Stein; Scott Thomson; Kevin Twaddle; Guido Van De Kamp; David Wilson. **Manager:** Jimmy Nicholl.

ST. MIRREN: Paul Archdeacon; Thomas Brown; Alan Combe; James Dick; Paul Fenwick; Richard Gillies; Brian Hetherston; Christopher Iwelumo; Steven McGarry; James McGuire; Barry McLaughlin; Norman McWhirter; Junior Mendes; David Milne; Hugh Murray; Alan Prentice; Derek Scrimgour; Brian Smith; Stuart Taylor; Thomas Turner; Stephen Watson; Mark Yardley. **Manager:** Tony Fitzpatrick.

STIRLING ALBION: John Bennett; Alexander Bone; Garrett Carberry; James Chalmers; Paul Deas; Edward Forrest; John Gibson; Gretar Hjartarsson; Stephen

McCormick; Mark McGeown; Stuart McLaren; Ronald McQuilter; Paul Mortimer; Andrew Paterson; Gary Paterson; Raymond Stewart; Craig Taggart; Thomas Tait. **Manager:** Kevin Drinkell.

SECOND DIVISION

BRECHIN CITY: Raymond Allan; Richard Baillie; Roddy Black; Ralph Brand; Robert Brown; Garry Buick; Henry Cairney; Harry Cargill; Graeme Christie; Francis Conway; Marcus Dailly; Graham Davidson; Neil Ewen; Craig Farnan; Scott Ferguson; Craig Feroz; Stuart Garden; Ian Heddle; Andrew Hutcheon; Steven Kerrigan; James McKellar; William McNeill; Walter Scott; Greig Smith; Ronnie Smollet; Stuart Sorbie. **Manager:** John Young.

CLYDE: Robert Balfour; James Brown; David Brownlie; Paul Brownlie; Paul Campbell; Brian Carrigan; Andrew Gibson; Thomas King; Keith Knox; Craig McEwan; Stephen McInulty; Mark McLean; Stephen McPeake; Gary McPhee; John McStay; Martin O'Neill; Michael O'Neill; James Prunty; Paul Stewart. **Manager:** Gardner Speirs.

CLYDEBANK: Kenneth Brannigan; James Brown; Denis Connaghan; Graham Connell; Thomas Currie; Paul Lovering; Ian MacFarlane; James McKinstrey; Scott Miller; Scott Murdoch; David Nicholls; Gary Teale. **Player-coach:** Ian McColl.

EAST FIFE: Gilbert Allan; Benjamin Andrew; David Beaton; William Burns; John Cusick; Alan Dixon; Mark Donaghy; Arnold Dwarika; Matthew Dyer; Philip Gartshore; Richard Gibb; Ronald Hildersley; George Johnston; Andrew Kinnell; Colin MacFarlane; Barrie Moffat; Graham Nicoll; Innes Ritchie; Paul Ronald. **Manager:** Jimmy Bone.

FORFAR ATHLETIC: John Allison; Mark Bowes; Andrew Cargill; Sean Christie; Douglas Craig; John Donegan; Stuart Farquharson; Barry Gardiner; Stuart Glennie; Alastair Gray; James Hamilton; Paul Hannigan; Ben Honeyman; Iain Lee; James Loney; Ian Lowe; Robert Mann; Martin McLauchlan; Barry McLean; Ian McPhee; Andrew Morgan; James Nairn; Alan Rattray; Paul Roberts; Dean Robertson. **Manager:** Ian McPhee.

INVERNESS CALEDONIAN THISTLE: Wayne Addicoat; James Calder; Paul Cherry; Charles Christie; Marco De-Barros; Leslie Fridge; Richard Hastings; Alan Hercher; Iain MacArthur; Scott McLean; Michael Noble; David Ross; Iain Stewart; Michael Teasdale; Brian Thomson; Ross Tokely; Barry Wilson. **Manager:** Steven Paterson.

LIVINGSTON: David Alleyne; Lee Bailey; Graeme Davidson; Robert Douglas; Mark Duthie; Gordon Forrest; Thomas Graham; Graham Harvey; Michael Korotkich; Steven Laidlaw; Ian McCaldon; Gordon McLeod; Grant McMartin; Horace Stoute; Peter Tierney; Graham Watson; Stewart Williamson; Jason Young. **Manager:** James Leishman.

QUEEN OF THE SOUTH: Andrew Aitken; Rowan Alexander; Craig Allen; Thomas Bryce; Marc Cleeland; Craig Flannigan; Craig Irving; David Kennedy; Derek Laing; Steven Leslie; David Lilley; Jeffrey MacLean; Stephen Mallan; David Mathieson;

James McAllister; Desmond McKeown; Alexander Nesovic; Steven Pettit; John Rowe; James Thomson; Derek Townsley. **Managers:** Rowan Alexander/Mark Shanks.

STENHOUSEMUIR: Neil Alexander; Graeme Armstrong; Alan Banks; Scott Brown; Gordon Buchanan; Mark Campbell; Martin Christie; Steven Ellison; James Falconer; Stephen Farrell; James Fisher; Richard Fox; Lloyd Haddow; James Henderson; Gary Houston; Andrew Hume; Paul Hunter; Gareth Hutchison; Christopher Innes; Ian Little; Desmond McClung; Kevin McKee; Connell McNelis; Brian Roberts; David Roseburgh; Adrian Sprott; Craig Stewart; Ian Stewart; David Stoddart; Steven Whiteford. **Manager:** Terry Christie.

STRANRAER: Thomas Black; Mark Campbell; Derek Crawford; Robert Docherty; Bernard Duffy; Gavin Friels; Iain Gallacher; Graham Hay; Gary Higgins; James Hughes; Paul Kinnaird; Alan Lansdowne; Gary Matthews; Ian McAulay; John McCaffrey; Scott McCrindle; Paul McIntyre; John McMillan; Israel Money; John Robertson; Gordon Young. **Manager:** I. Campbell Money.

THIRD DIVISION

ALBION ROVERS: Bryan Boal; David Byrne; Martin Clark; Stephen Cody; John Dickson; Cameron Duncan; Robert Gardner; Ian Harty; Gerard Kelly; Mark Leonard; Paul Martin; Neil McGowan; Anthony McInally; Ian McInnes; David McKenzie; Neil McKilligan; Anthony Mitchell; Colin Mitchell; Vincent Moore; Mark Pickering; Stuart Robertson; Stephen Ross; Anthony Shepherd; Thomas Walker; William Watters; David Webster. **Manager:** Vincent Moore.

ALLOA: Stephen Cadden; Mark Cowan; Peter Dwyer; William Irvine; Kevin Kane; Thomas Little; Giacomo Lonzi; Stuart Mackay; Miller Mathieson; Paul McAneny; Neil McAvoy; John McCormack; Keith McCulloch; Michael Monaghan; Mark Nelson; Neil Nicholson; David Pew; Paul Simpson; Craig Valentine; Mark Wilson; Robert Wilson; Stuart Wilson. **Manager:** Thomas Hendrie.

ARBROATH: Gary Balfour; Steven Burns; Jonathan Crawford; Steven Florence; John Gallagher; Brian Grant; Craig Hinchcliffe; Douglas Hope; John McAulay; James McCarron; Stephen McCormick; Mark McWalter; James Phinn; Craig Reynolds; Steven Scott; Michael Waters; Roderick Wylie. **Manager:** David Baikie.

BERWICK RANGERS: Michael Burgess; Neil Clegg; Darren Collier; David Finlayson; Paul Forrester; Graeme Fraser; Thomas Graham; Derek Grant; Neil Irvine; Thomas King; Mark Laidler; Graham Little; Craig Manson; Martin Neil; Alastair Reid; Grant Stewart; Kevin Walton; Barry Ward; Neil Young. **Manager:** Jimmy Thomson.

COWDENBEATH: Robert Baillie; Kevin Bowmaker; Samuel Conn; Douglas Coulston; Ross Godfrey; Alistair Hamilton; Martin Humphreys; Barry McMahon; Graham Meldrum; James Moffat; Kenneth Munro; Thomas Nolan; Edward Petrie; Alan Ritchie; Neil Russell; Martin Scott; Craig Sinclair; William Stewart; Murray Urquhart; Craig Winter. **Manager:** Samuel Conn.

DUMBARTON: Derek Barnes; Craig Brittain; Jamie Bruce; Stephen Dallas;

William Davidson; Martin Glancy; Joseph Goldie; Stephen Gow; Steven Hamill; James Marsland; Martin McGarvey; Graeme McKenzie; Colin McKinnon; James Meechan; Kenneth Meechan; Adrian Mellis; Martin Melvin; Martin Mooney; David Reid; Robert Reilly; John Scott; Lee Sharp; Hugh Ward; William Wilson. **Manager:** Ian Wallace.

EAST STIRLINGSHIRE: Mark Abercromby; Colin Campbell; Matthew Cochrane; Graeme Hamilton; Murray Hunter; Martin McBride; Gordon McDougall; David Muirhead; Alan Neill; Gordon Parks; Paul Patterson; Steven Ramsay; Brian Ross; Gordon Russell; Scott Snedden; David Watt. **Manager:** John Brownlie.

MONTROSE: John Bird; Justin Brown; James Butter; Craig Cooper; Mark Craib; Ross Dorward; Alistair Ferrie; Graeme Ferris; David Fisher; Scott Glass; Mark Haro; Stephen Kydd; David Larter; Graham Lawrie; Innes MacDonald; Craig Mailer; Ronald Massie; Christopher Masson; Paul Masson; Colin McGlashan; Stewart Purves; Mark Robb; Michael Ross; Shaun Smith; Scott Taylor; Neil Thomson; Kevin Tindal; James Tosh; Stefan Winiarski. **Manager:** Tom Campbell.

QUEEN'S PARK: David Arbuckle; Alan Bryson; Ross Caven; Graeme Elder; Marc Falconer; Paul Ferguson; Daniel Ferry; Iain Fitzpatrick; David Graham; Martin Hardie; David King; Kevin McGoldrick; Garry Orr; Colin Smith; James Smith; Mark Smith; Scott Starr; Derek Wilson. **Coach:** Graeme Elder.

ROSS COUNTY: Derek Adams; Johnston Bellshaw; Paul Bradshaw; Julian Broddle; Gordon Connelly; Neale Cooper; David Cormack; Gerard Farrell; Steven Ferguson; Keith Ferries; William Furphy; Kenneth Gilbert; Stuart Golabek; Richard Hart; William Herd; Stephen Hutchison; David Mackay; Andrew MacLeod; Jamie MacPherson; David Matheson; Roy McBain; Kevin Morgan; Alexander Ross; Ross Ruickbie; Robert Williamson; Garry Wood. **Manager:** Neale Cooper.

QUOTE-UNQUOTE

BRIAN LABONE, reflecting on Mike Trebilcock's two goals when Everton beat Sheff. Wed. in the 1996 Final: "Among the graffiti, when we got home to Merseyside with the Cup, was one that said 'Trebilcock loves the Beverley Sisters.' "

TEDDY SHERINGHAM, 31, after this summer's £3.5m. move from Tottenham to Man. United: "It has taken 14 seasons to reach the pinnacle of my career."

BILL SHANKLY: "Never pick your team until the final training session is over."

COLIN HUTCHINSON, Chelsea managing director, after the capture of Ruud Gullit: "One of the reasons he agreed to sign, he says, was that he had always won things playing for teams who wore white socks."

TONY GUBBA (BBC TV) on Ryan Giggs: "It looks like he's got wings on his feet."

TONY ADAMS, Arsenal captain, on a goal conceded: "I thought it was offside. But then I always do."

MATTHEW LE TISSIER, asked by a Southampton player in a 5-a-side practice: "Why do you always have to do the difficult thing?": "Because I find the difficult thing easy."

LEAGUE FIXTURES 1997-98

F.A. Premier League: F.A. Carling Premiership.
Football League: Nationwide Football League.

Saturday, August 9
Premiership
Barnsley v West Ham United
Blackburn Rovers v Derby County
Coventry City v Chelsea
Everton v Crystal Palace
Leeds United v Arsenal
Leicester City v Aston Villa
Newcastle United v Sheffield Wed.
Southampton v Bolton Wand.
Wimbledon v Liverpool

First Division
Birmingham City v Stoke City
Bradford City v Stockport Co.
Bury v Reading
Manchester City v Portsmouth
Middlesbrough v Charlton Athletic
Norwich City v Wolves
Oxford United v Huddersfield T.
Port Vale v Nott'm. Forest
Q.P.R. v Ipswich Town
Swindon Town v Crewe Alexandra
W.B.A. v Tranmere Rovers

Second Division
Blackpool v Luton Town
Bristol Rovers v Plymouth Argyle
Chesterfield v Walsall
Fulham v Wrexham
Gillingham v Preston N.E.
Grimsby Town v Bristol City
Millwall v Brentford
Northampton T. v Bournemouth
Oldham Athletic v York City
Southend United v Carlisle United
Watford v Burnley
Wigan Athletic v Wycombe Wand.

Third Division
Chester City v Lincoln City
Colchester Utd. v Darlington
Exeter City v Hartlepool United
Leyton Orient v Cardiff City
Macclesfield Town v Torquay United
Mansfield Town v Hull City
Notts County v Rochdale
Peterborough Utd. v Scunthorpe Utd.
Rotherham United v Barnet
Scarborough v Cambridge United
Shrewsbury Town v Doncaster Rov.
Swansea City v Brighton & H.A.

Sunday, August 10
Premiership
Tottenham H. v Manchester Utd.

First Division
Sheffield United v Sunderland

Monday, August 11
Premiership
Arsenal v Coventry City

Tuesday, August 12
Premiership
Crystal Palace v Barnsley

Wednesday, August 13
Premiership
Aston Villa v Blackburn Rovers
Derby County v Wimbledon
Liverpool v Leicester City
Manchester Utd. v Southampton
Sheffield Wed. v Leeds United
West Ham United v Tottenham H.

Friday, August 15
First Division
Bradford City v Stoke City
Nott'm. Forest v Norwich City

Saturday, August 16
First Division
Charlton Athletic v Oxford United
Crewe Alexandra v W.B.A.
Huddersfield T. v Birmingham City
Portsmouth v Port Vale
Reading v Swindon Town
Stockport Co. v Bury
Sunderland v Manchester City
Tranmere Rovers v Q.P.R.
Wolves v Sheffield United

Second Division
Bournemouth v Wigan Athletic
Brentford v Chesterfield
Bristol City v Blackpool
Burnley v Gillingham
Carlisle United v Watford
Plymouth Argyle v Grimsby Town
Preston N.E. v Millwall
Walsall v Fulham

Wrexham v Oldham Athletic
Wycombe Wand. v Northampton T.
York City v Bristol Rovers

Third Division
Barnet v Exeter City
Brighton & H.A. v Macclesfield Town
Cambridge United v Rotherham Utd.
Cardiff City v Chester City
Darlington v Swansea City
Doncaster Rov. v Peterborough Utd.
Hartlepool United v Colchester Utd.
Hull City v Notts County
Lincoln City v Shrewsbury Town
Rochdale v Mansfield Town
Scunthorpe Utd. v Leyton Orient
Torquay United v Scarborough

Sunday, August 17
First Division
Ipswich Town v Middlesbrough

Monday, August 18
Second Division
Luton Town v Southend United

Friday, August 22
First Division
Manchester City v Tranmere Rovers

Third Division
Colchester Utd. v Barnet
Scarborough v Brighton & H.A.

Saturday, August 23
Premiership
Blackburn Rovers v Liverpool
Coventry City v Bolton Wand.
Everton v West Ham United
Leeds United v Crystal Palace
Leicester City v Manchester Utd.
Newcastle United v Aston Villa
Southampton v Arsenal
Tottenham H. v Derby County
Wimbledon v Sheffield Wed.

First Division
Birmingham City v Reading
Bradford City v Ipswich Town
Bury v Charlton Athletic
Middlesbrough v Stoke City
Norwich City v Crewe Alexandra
Oxford United v Nott'm. Forest
Port Vale v Sunderland
Q.P.R. v Stockport Co.
Sheffield United v Portsmouth
Swindon Town v Huddersfield T.

Second Division
Blackpool v Wycombe Wand.

Bristol Rovers v Carlisle United
Chesterfield v Preston N.E.
Fulham v Luton Town
Gillingham v Walsall
Grimsby Town v Wrexham
Millwall v York City
Northampton T. v Bristol City
Oldham Athletic v Bournemouth
Southend United v Burnley
Watford v Brentford
Wigan Athletic v Plymouth Argyle

Third Division
Chester City v Cambridge United
Exeter City v Darlington
Leyton Orient v Rochdale
Macclesfield Town v Doncaster Rov.
Mansfield Town v Cardiff City
Notts County v Lincoln City
Peterborough Utd. v Hull City
Rotherham United v Hartlepool Utd.
Shrewsbury Town v Torquay United
Swansea City v Scunthorpe Utd.

Sunday, August 24
Premiership
Barnsley v Chelsea

First Division
W.B.A. v Wolves

Monday, August 25
Premiership
Blackburn Rovers v Sheffield Wed.

Tuesday, August 26
Premiership
Leeds United v Liverpool

Wednesday, August 27
Premiership
Barnsley v Bolton Wand.
Coventry City v West Ham United
Everton v Manchester Utd.
Leicester City v Arsenal
Southampton v Crystal Palace
Tottenham H. v Aston Villa
Wimbledon v Chelsea

Friday, August 29
First Division
Stockport Co. v Birmingham City

Saturday, August 30
Premiership
Arsenal v Tottenham H.
Aston Villa v Leeds United
Chelsea v Southampton
Crystal Palace v Blackburn Rovers

Derby County v Barnsley
Manchester Utd. v Coventry City
Sheffield Wed. v Leicester City
West Ham United v Wimbledon

First Division
Charlton Athletic v Manchester City
Huddersfield T. v Sheffield United
Ipswich Town v W.B.A.
Nott'm. Forest v Q.P.R.
Portsmouth v Oxford United
Reading v Bradford City
Stoke City v Swindon Town
Sunderland v Norwich City
Tranmere Rovers v Middlesbrough
Wolves v Bury

Second Division
Bournemouth v Blackpool
Brentford v Grimsby Town
Bristol City v Wigan Athletic
Burnley v Bristol Rovers
Carlisle United v Northampton T.
Luton Town v Oldham Athletic
Plymouth Argyle v Chesterfield
Preston N.E. v Watford
Walsall v Southend United
Wycombe Wand. v Fulham
York City v Gillingham

Third Division
Barnet v Chester City
Brighton & H.A. v Leyton Orient
Cambridge Utd. v Shrewsbury Town
Cardiff City v Notts County
Darlington v Rotherham United
Doncaster Rov. v Exeter City
Hartlepool Utd. v Macclesfield Town
Hull City v Swansea City
Lincoln City v Scarborough
Rochdale v Peterborough Utd.
Scunthorpe Utd. v Mansfield Town
Torquay United v Colchester Utd.

Sunday, August 31
Premiership
Liverpool v Newcastle United

First Division
Crewe Alexandra v Port Vale

Monday, September 1
Premiership
Bolton Wand. v Everton

Tuesday, September 2
First Division
Charlton Athletic v Sheffield United
Crewe Alexandra v Bury
Huddersfield T. v Bradford City

Ipswich Town v Swindon Town
Portsmouth v Norwich City
Reading v Q.P.R.
Stockport Co. v Middlesbrough
Sunderland v Oxford United
Tranmere Rovers v Birmingham City

Second Division
Bournemouth v Bristol Rovers
Brentford v Gillingham
Bristol City v Fulham
Burnley v Oldham Athletic
Carlisle United v Wigan Athletic
Luton Town v Millwall
Plymouth Argyle v Watford
Preston N.E. v Grimsby Town
Walsall v Northampton T.
Wrexham v Blackpool
Wycombe Wand. v Southend United
York City v Chesterfield

Third Division
Barnet v Swansea City
Cambridge United v Colchester Utd.
Cardiff City v Shrewsbury Town
Darlington v Scarborough
Doncaster Rov. v Leyton Orient
Hartlepool United v Notts County
Hull City v Rotherham United
Lincoln City v Mansfield Town
Rochdale v Macclesfield Town
Scunthorpe Utd. v Chester City
Torquay United v Exeter City

Wednesday, September 3
First Division
Nott'm. Forest v Manchester City
Stoke City v W.B.A.
Wolves v Port Vale

Third Division
Brighton & H.A. v Peterborough Utd.

Friday, September 5
First Division
Bradford City v Sunderland

Saturday, September 6
First Division
Birmingham City v Ipswich Town
Bury v Tranmere Rovers
Manchester City v Crewe Alexandra
Norwich City v Charlton Athletic
Port Vale v Stockport Co.
Q.P.R. v Portsmouth
Sheffield United v Stoke City
Swindon Town v Nott'm. Forest
W.B.A. v Reading

Second Division
Blackpool v Carlisle United

Bristol Rovers v Walsall
Chesterfield v Burnley
Fulham v Plymouth Argyle
Gillingham v Bournemouth
Grimsby Town v York City
Millwall v Bristol City
Northampton T. v Luton Town
Oldham Athletic v Preston N.E.
Southend United v Brentford
Watford v Wycombe Wand.

Third Division
Chester City v Hull City
Colchester Utd. v Brighton & H.A.
Exeter City v Cardiff City
Leyton Orient v Cambridge United
Macclesfield Town v Darlington
Mansfield Town v Doncaster Rov.
Notts County v Scunthorpe Utd.
Peterborough Utd. v Barnet
Rotherham United v Lincoln City
Scarborough v Hartlepool United
Shrewsbury Town v Rochdale
Swansea City v Torquay United

Sunday, September 7
First Division
Oxford United v Wolves

Monday, September 8
Second Division
Wigan Athletic v Wrexham

Tuesday, September 9
First Division
Middlesbrough v Huddersfield T.

Friday, September 12
First Division
Bury v Manchester City

Third Division
Colchester Utd. v Scarborough

Saturday, September 13
Premiership
Arsenal v Bolton Wand.
Barnsley v Aston Villa
Coventry City v Southampton
Crystal Palace v Chelsea
Derby County v Everton
Leicester City v Tottenham H.
Liverpool v Sheffield Wed.
Manchester Utd. v West Ham United
Newcastle United v Wimbledon

First Division
Bradford City v Middlesbrough
Huddersfield T. v Ipswich Town

Norwich City v Port Vale
Portsmouth v Crewe Alexandra
Q.P.R. v W.B.A.
Reading v Oxford United
Sheffield United v Nott'm. Forest
Stoke City v Stockport Co.
Swindon Town v Tranmere Rovers
Wolves v Charlton Athletic

Second Division
Bournemouth v Luton Town
Bristol Rovers v Gillingham
Fulham v Grimsby Town
Millwall v Southend United
Oldham Athletic v Northampton T.
Plymouth Argyle v Brentford
Preston N.E. v Walsall
Watford v Chesterfield
Wigan Athletic v Blackpool
Wrexham v Bristol City
Wycombe Wand. v Carlisle United
York City v Burnley

Third Division
Brighton & H.A. v Darlington
Cambridge United v Barnet
Cardiff City v Rochdale
Chester City v Shrewsbury Town
Hartlepool United v Torquay United
Hull City v Lincoln City
Leyton Orient v Exeter City
Macclesfield Town v Swansea City
Notts County v Mansfield Town
Rotherham Utd. v Peterborough Utd.
Scunthorpe Utd. v Doncaster Rov.

Sunday, September 14
Premiership
Blackburn Rovers v Leeds United

First Division
Birmingham City v Sunderland

Friday, September 19
Second Division
Brentford v Wycombe Wand.

Saturday, September 20
Premiership
Aston Villa v Derby County
Bolton Wand. v Manchester Utd.
Everton v Barnsley
Leeds United v Leicester City
Sheffield Wed. v Coventry City
Southampton v Liverpool
Tottenham H. v Blackburn Rovers
West Ham United v Newcastle United
Wimbledon v Crystal Palace

First Division
Crewe Alexandra v Q.P.R.

Ipswich Town v Stoke City
Manchester City v Norwich City
Middlesbrough v Birmingham City
Nott'm. Forest v Portsmouth
Oxford United v Sheffield United
Port Vale v Bury
Stockport Co. v Huddersfield T.
Sunderland v Wolves
Tranmere Rovers v Reading
W.B.A. v Swindon Town

Second Division
Blackpool v Oldham Athletic
Bristol City v Bournemouth
Burnley v Preston N.E.
Carlisle United v Plymouth Argyle
Chesterfield v Bristol Rovers
Gillingham v Watford
Grimsby Town v Millwall
Northampton T. v Wigan Athletic
Southend United v Fulham
Walsall v York City

Third Division
Barnet v Scunthorpe Utd.
Doncaster Rov. v Cambridge United
Exeter City v Rotherham United
Lincoln City v Cardiff City
Mansfield Town v Chester City
Peterborough Utd. v Leyton Orient
Rochdale v Hull City
Scarborough v Macclesfield Town
Shrewsbury Town v Notts County
Swansea City v Colchester Utd.
Torquay United v Brighton & H.A.

Sunday, September 21
Premiership
Chelsea v Arsenal

First Division
Charlton Athletic v Bradford City

Third Division
Darlington v Hartlepool United

Monday, September 22
Premiership
Liverpool v Aston Villa

Tuesday, September 23
Premiership
Bolton Wand. v Tottenham H.
Wimbledon v Barnsley

Wednesday, September 24
Premiership
Arsenal v West Ham United
Coventry City v Crystal Palace
Leicester City v Blackburn Rovers

Manchester Utd. v Chelsea
Newcastle United v Everton
Sheffield Wed. v Derby County
Southampton v Leeds United

Friday, September 26
First Division
Norwich City v Ipswich Town

Saturday, September 27
Premiership
Aston Villa v Sheffield Wed.
Barnsley v Leicester City
Chelsea v Newcastle United
Crystal Palace v Bolton Wand.
Derby County v Southampton
Everton v Arsenal
Leeds United v Manchester Utd.
Tottenham H. v Wimbledon
West Ham United v Liverpool

First Division
Bury v W.B.A.
Charlton Athletic v Stockport Co.
Crewe Alexandra v Tranmere Rovers
Manchester City v Swindon Town
Nott'm. Forest v Stoke City
Oxford United v Bradford City
Port Vale v Q.P.R.
Portsmouth v Reading
Sheffield United v Birmingham City
Wolves v Huddersfield T.

Second Division
Bournemouth v Grimsby Town
Blackpool v Southend United
Brentford v Burnley
Bristol City v Luton Town
Carlisle United v Gillingham
Northampton T. v Millwall
Oldham Athletic v Bristol Rovers
Plymouth Argyle v Walsall
Watford v York City
Wigan Athletic v Fulham
Wrexham v Chesterfield
Wycombe Wand. v Preston N.E.

Third Division
Barnet v Lincoln City
Brighton & H.A. v Rochdale
Cambridge United v Cardiff City
Colchester Utd. v Exeter City
Darlington v Mansfield Town
Hartlepool United v Shrewsbury Town
Macclesfield T. v Peterborough Utd.
Rotherham United v Chester City
Scarborough v Notts County
Scunthorpe Utd. v Hull City
Swansea City v Leyton Orient
Torquay United v Doncaster Rov.

Sunday, September 28
Premiership
Blackburn Rovers v Coventry City

First Division
Sunderland v Middlesbrough

Tuesday, September 30
Second Division
Wrexham v Millwall

Friday, October 3
First Division
Huddersfield T. v Nott'm. Forest

Saturday, October 4
Premiership
Arsenal v Barnsley
Bolton Wand. v Aston Villa
Coventry City v Leeds United
Manchester Utd. v Crystal Palace
Newcastle United v Tottenham H.
Sheffield Wed. v Everton
Southampton v West Ham United
Wimbledon v Blackburn Rovers

First Division
Birmingham City v Crewe Alexandra
Bradford City v Wolves
Ipswich Town v Manchester City
Q.P.R. v Charlton Athletic
Reading v Sunderland
Stockport Co. v Portsmouth
Stoke City v Bury
Swindon Town v Port Vale
Tranmere Rovers v Norwich City
W.B.A. v Oxford United

Second Division
Bristol Rovers v Wrexham
Burnley v Wycombe Wand.
Chesterfield v Bournemouth
Fulham v Oldham Athletic
Gillingham v Bristol City
Grimsby Town v Wigan Athletic
Luton Town v Watford
Millwall v Blackpool
Preston N.E. v Brentford
Southend United v Northampton T.
Walsall v Carlisle United
York City v Plymouth Argyle

Third Division
Cardiff City v Barnet
Chester City v Hartlepool United
Doncaster Rov. v Brighton & H.A.
Exeter City v Scarborough
Hull City v Torquay United
Leyton Orient v Macclesfield Town
Lincoln City v Cambridge United

Mansfield Town v Colchester Utd.
Notts County v Darlington
Peterborough Utd. v Swansea City
Rochdale v Scunthorpe Utd.
Shrewsbury T. v Rotherham United

Sunday, October 5
Premiership
Liverpool v Chelsea

First Division
Middlesbrough v Sheffield United

Monday, October 6
Premiership
Leicester City v Derby County

Saturday, October 11
First Division
Bradford City v Sheffield United
Huddersfield T. v Charlton Athletic
Ipswich Town v Sunderland
Middlesbrough v Nott'm. Forest
Q.P.R. v Norwich City
Reading v Crewe Alexandra
Stockport Co. v Oxford United
Swindon Town v Bury
Tranmere Rovers v Portsmouth
W.B.A. v Manchester City

Second Division
Bristol Rovers v Watford
Burnley v Carlisle United
Chesterfield v Wigan Athletic
Fulham v Blackpool
Gillingham v Wycombe Wand.
Grimsby Town v Northampton T.
Luton Town v Plymouth Argyle
Millwall v Oldham Athletic
Preston N.E. v Bournemouth
Southend United v Bristol City
Walsall v Wrexham
York City v Brentford

Third Division
Cardiff City v Scunthorpe Utd.
Chester City v Brighton & H.A.
Doncaster Rov. v Hartlepool United
Exeter City v Swansea City
Hull City v Scarborough
Leyton Orient v Rotherham United
Lincoln City v Torquay United
Mansfield Town v Cambridge United
Notts County v Macclesfield Town
Peterborough Utd. v Colchester Utd.
Rochdale v Darlington
Shrewsbury Town v Barnet

449

Sunday, October 12

First Division
Birmingham City v Wolves
Stoke City v Port Vale

Friday, October 17

Second Division
Bristol City v York City
Carlisle United v Preston N.E.

Saturday, October 18

Premiership
Aston Villa v Wimbledon
Blackburn Rovers v Southampton
Chelsea v Leicester City
Crystal Palace v Arsenal
Derby County v Manchester Utd.
Everton v Liverpool
Leeds United v Newcastle United
West Ham United v Bolton Wand.

First Division
Bury v Birmingham City
Crewe Alexandra v Middlesbrough
Manchester City v Reading
Norwich City v Stockport Co.
Nott'm. Forest v Tranmere Rovers
Oxford United v Ipswich Town
Port Vale v Bradford City
Portsmouth v W.B.A.
Sheffield United v Q.P.R.
Sunderland v Huddersfield T.
Wolves v Swindon Town

Second Division
Bournemouth v Fulham
Blackpool v Grimsby Town
Brentford v Walsall
Northampton T. v Gillingham
Oldham Athletic v Chesterfield
Plymouth Argyle v Southend United
Watford v Millwall
Wigan Athletic v Luton Town
Wrexham v Burnley
Wycombe Wand. v Bristol Rovers

Third Division
Barnet v Hull City
Brighton & H.A. v Exeter City
Cambridge United v Rochdale
Colchester Utd. v Shrewsbury Town
Darlington v Doncaster Rov.
Hartlepool United v Leyton Orient
Macclesfield Town v Mansfield Town
Rotherham United v Cardiff City
Scarborough v Peterborough Utd.
Scunthorpe Utd. v Lincoln City
Swansea City v Notts County
Torquay United v Chester City

Sunday, October 19

Premiership
Tottenham H. v Sheffield Wed.

First Division
Charlton Athletic v Stoke City

Monday, October 20

Premiership
Barnsley v Coventry City

Tuesday, October 21

First Division
Bury v Q.P.R.
Crewe Alexandra v Ipswich Town
Oxford United v Middlesbrough
Port Vale v Huddersfield T.
Portsmouth v Bradford City
Sheffield United v Stockport Co.
Sunderland v Swindon Town

Second Division
Bournemouth v Millwall
Blackpool v Chesterfield
Brentford v Bristol Rovers
Bristol City v Preston N.E.
Carlisle United v Luton Town
Northampton T. v York City
Oldham Athletic v Grimsby Town
Plymouth Argyle v Burnley
Watford v Fulham
Wigan Athletic v Gillingham
Wrexham v Southend United
Wycombe Wand. v Walsall

Third Division
Barnet v Rochdale
Cambridge United v Hull City
Colchester Utd. v Doncaster Rov.
Darlington v Cardiff City
Hartlepool Utd. v Peterborough Utd.
Macclesfield Town v Exeter City
Rotherham United v Notts County
Scarborough v Chester City
Scunthorpe Utd. v Shrewsbury Town
Swansea City v Mansfield Town
Torquay United v Leyton Orient

Wednesday, October 22

First Division
Charlton Athletic v Birmingham City
Manchester City v Stoke City
Norwich City v Reading
Nott'm. Forest v W.B.A.
Wolves v Tranmere Rovers

Third Division
Brighton & H.A. v Lincoln City

Friday, October 24
First Division
Reading v Nott'm. Forest

Third Division
Doncaster Rov. v Swansea City

Saturday, October 25
Premiership
Coventry City v Everton
Liverpool v Derby County
Manchester Utd. v Barnsley
Newcastle United v Blackburn Rovers
Sheffield Wed. v Crystal Palace
Southampton v Tottenham H.
Wimbledon v Leeds United

First Division
Birmingham City v Oxford United
Bradford City v Crewe Alexandra
Huddersfield T. v Portsmouth
Ipswich Town v Bury
Middlesbrough v Port Vale
Stockport Co. v Wolves
Stoke City v Sunderland
Swindon Town v Norwich City
Tranmere Rovers v Charlton Athletic
W.B.A. v Sheffield United

Second Division
Bristol Rovers v Blackpool
Burnley v Bournemouth
Chesterfield v Wycombe Wand.
Fulham v Northampton T.
Gillingham v Plymouth Argyle
Grimsby Town v Watford
Luton Town v Brentford
Millwall v Wigan Athletic
Preston N.E. v Wrexham
Southend United v Oldham Athletic
Walsall v Bristol City
York City v Carlisle United

Third Division
Cardiff City v Hartlepool United
Chester City v Macclesfield Town
Exeter City v Scunthorpe Utd.
Hull City v Brighton & H.A.
Leyton Orient v Colchester Utd.
Lincoln City v Darlington
Mansfield Town v Barnet
Notts County v Cambridge United
Peterborough Utd. v Torquay United
Rochdale v Rotherham United
Shrewsbury Town v Scarborough

Sunday, October 26
Premiership
Arsenal v Aston Villa
Bolton Wand. v Chelsea

First Division
Q.P.R. v Manchester City

Monday, October 27
Premiership
Leicester City v West Ham United

Friday, October 31
First Division
Portsmouth v Swindon Town

Third Division
Colchester Utd. v Scunthorpe Utd.

Saturday, November 1
Premiership
Aston Villa v Chelsea
Barnsley v Blackburn Rovers
Bolton Wand. v Liverpool
Derby County v Arsenal
Manchester Utd. v Sheffield Wed.
Newcastle United v Leicester City
Tottenham H. v Leeds United
Wimbledon v Coventry City

First Division
Bradford City v W.B.A.
Charlton Athletic v Ipswich Town
Huddersfield T. v Stoke City
Norwich City v Bury
Nott'm. Forest v Crewe Alexandra
Oxford United v Manchester City
Port Vale v Reading
Q.P.R. v Birmingham City
Sheffield United v Tranmere Rovers
Stockport Co. v Sunderland
Wolves v Middlesbrough

Second Division
Bournemouth v Brentford
Bristol City v Oldham Athletic
Burnley v Walsall
Carlisle United v Wrexham
Fulham v Chesterfield
Gillingham v Millwall
Grimsby Town v Southend United
Northampton T. v Bristol Rovers
Preston N.E. v Plymouth Argyle
Watford v Blackpool
Wigan Athletic v York City
Wycombe Wand. v Luton Town

Third Division
Barnet v Notts County
Cambridge United v Torquay United
Chester City v Rochdale
Darlington v Hull City
Exeter City v Peterborough Utd.
Hartlepool United v Brighton & H.A.
Lincoln City v Leyton Orient

Rotherham Utd. v Macclesfield Town
Scarborough v Doncaster Rov.
Shrewsbury Town v Mansfield Town

Sunday, November 2
Premiership
Everton v Southampton

Third Division
Cardiff City v Swansea City

Monday, November 3
Premiership
West Ham United v Crystal Palace

Tuesday, November 4
First Division
Birmingham City v Bradford City
Bury v Nott'm. Forest
Crewe Alexandra v Wolves
Ipswich Town v Stockport Co.
Manchester City v Port Vale
Reading v Sheffield United
Sunderland v Charlton Athletic
Tranmere Rovers v Huddersfield T.
W.B.A. v Norwich City

Second Division
Blackpool v Northampton T.
Brentford v Carlisle United
Bristol Rovers v Bristol City
Chesterfield v Gillingham
Luton Town v Burnley
Oldham Athletic v Wigan Athletic
Plymouth Argyle v Wycombe Wand.
Southend United v Watford
Walsall v Grimsby Town
Wrexham v Bournemouth
York City v Preston N.E.

Third Division
Doncaster Rov. v Cardiff City
Hull City v Exeter City
Leyton Orient v Scarborough
Macclesfield Town v Colchester Utd.
Mansfield Town v Rotherham United
Notts County v Chester City
Peterborough Utd. v Shrewsbury T.
Rochdale v Lincoln City
Scunthorpe Utd. v Cambridge United
Swansea City v Hartlepool United
Torquay United v Darlington

Wednesday, November 5
First Division
Middlesbrough v Portsmouth
Stoke City v Oxford United
Swindon Town v Q.P.R.

Second Division
Millwall v Fulham

Third Division
Brighton & H.A. v Barnet

Friday, November 7
First Division
Manchester City v Huddersfield T.

Saturday, November 8
Premiership
Blackburn Rovers v Everton
Coventry City v Newcastle United
Crystal Palace v Aston Villa
Leeds United v Derby County
Liverpool v Tottenham H.
Sheffield Wed. v Bolton Wand.
Southampton v Barnsley

First Division
Birmingham City v Norwich City
Bury v Portsmouth
Crewe Alexandra v Oxford United
Middlesbrough v Q.P.R.
Reading v Stockport Co.
Stoke City v Wolves
Sunderland v Nott'm. Forest
Swindon Town v Bradford City
Tranmere Rovers v Port Vale
W.B.A. v Charlton Athletic

Second Division
Blackpool v Burnley
Brentford v Bristol City
Bristol Rovers v Fulham
Chesterfield v Grimsby Town
Luton Town v Preston N.E.
Millwall v Carlisle United
Oldham Athletic v Gillingham
Plymouth Argyle v Bournemouth
Southend United v Wigan Athletic
Walsall v Watford
Wrexham v Northampton T.
York City v Wycombe Wand.

Third Division
Barnet v Doncaster Rov.
Brighton & H.A. v Rotherham United
Cardiff City v Torquay United
Hull City v Shrewsbury Town
Leyton Orient v Chester City
Macclesfield Town v Cambridge Utd.
Mansfield Town v Scarborough
Notts County v Exeter City
Peterborough Utd. v Darlington
Rochdale v Colchester Utd.
Scunthorpe Utd. v Hartlepool United
Swansea City v Lincoln City

Sunday, November 9
Premiership
Arsenal v Manchester Utd.
Chelsea v West Ham United

First Division
Ipswich Town v Sheffield United

Monday, November 10
Premiership
Leicester City v Wimbledon

Saturday, November 15
First Division
Bradford City v Tranmere Rovers
Charlton Athletic v Crewe Alexandra
Huddersfield Town v Reading
Norwich City v Middlesbrough
Nott'm. Forest v Birmingham City
Oxford United v Bury
Port Vale v W.B.A.
Portsmouth v Sunderland
Q.P.R. v Stoke City
Sheffield United v Manchester City
Stockport Co. v Swindon Town
Wolves v Ipswich Town

Tuesday, November 18
Second Division
Bournemouth v Southend United
Bristol City v Plymouth Argyle
Burnley v Millwall
Carlisle United v Chesterfield
Fulham v York City
Gillingham v Blackpool
Grimsby Town v Luton Town
Northampton T. v Brentford
Preston N.E. v Bristol Rovers
Watford v Oldham Athletic
Wigan Athletic v Walsall
Wycombe Wand. v Wrexham

Third Division
Barnet v Torquay United
Cambridge United v Brighton & H.A.
Cardiff City v Hull City
Chester City v Peterborough Utd.
Colchester Utd. v Notts County
Darlington v Leyton Orient
Exeter City v Mansfield Town
Hartlepool United v Rochdale
Lincoln City v Doncaster Rov.
Rotherham United v Scunthorpe Utd.
Scarborough v Swansea City
Shrewsbury T. v Macclesfield Town

Friday, November 21
Second Division
Fulham v Gillingham

Saturday, November 22
Premiership
Aston Villa v Everton
Blackburn Rovers v Chelsea
Derby County v Coventry City
Leicester City v Bolton Wand.
Liverpool v Barnsley
Newcastle United v Southampton
Sheffield Wed. v Arsenal
Wimbledon v Manchester Utd.

First Division
Bury v Sunderland
Crewe Alexandra v Stockport Co.
Manchester City v Bradford City
Norwich City v Oxford United
Nott'm. Forest v Charlton Athletic
Port Vale v Sheffield United
Portsmouth v Wolves
Q.P.R. v Huddersfield T.
Reading v Ipswich Town
Swindon Town v Middlesbrough
Tranmere Rovers v Stoke City

Second Division
Bournemouth v Carlisle United
Blackpool v York City
Bristol City v Wycombe Wand.
Grimsby Town v Burnley
Luton Town v Walsall
Millwall v Chesterfield
Northampton T. v Watford
Oldham Athletic v Brentford
Southend United v Bristol Rovers
Wigan Athletic v Preston N.E.
Wrexham v Plymouth Argyle

Third Division
Brighton & H.A. v Cardiff City
Colchester Utd. v Lincoln City
Darlington v Cambridge United
Doncaster Rov. v Rochdale
Exeter City v Shrewsbury Town
Hartlepool United v Barnet
Leyton Orient v Notts County
Macclesfield Town v Hull City
Peterborough Utd. v Mansfield Town
Scarborough v Rotherham United
Swansea City v Chester City
Torquay United v Scunthorpe Utd.

Sunday, November 23
Premiership
Leeds United v West Ham United

First Division
W.B.A. v Birmingham City

Monday, November 24
Premiership
Tottenham H. v Crystal Palace

Wednesday, November 26
Premiership
Chelsea v Everton

Friday, November 28
First Division
Charlton Athletic v Swindon Town

Saturday, November 29
Premiership
Barnsley v Leeds United
Bolton Wand. v Wimbledon
Chelsea v Derby County
Coventry City v Leicester City
Crystal Palace v Newcastle United
Everton v Tottenham H.
Manchester Utd. v Blackburn Rovers
Southampton v Sheffield Wed.
West Ham United v Aston Villa

First Division
Birmingham City v Portsmouth
Bradford City v Norwich City
Huddersfield T. v Bury
Ipswich Town v Nott'm. Forest
Middlesbrough v W.B.A.
Oxford United v Port Vale
Sheffield United v Crewe Alexandra
Stockport Co. v Manchester City
Stoke City v Reading
Sunderland v Tranmere Rovers
Wolves v Q.P.R.

Second Division
Brentford v Wrexham
Bristol Rovers v Millwall
Burnley v Northampton T.
Carlisle United v Bristol City
Chesterfield v Southend United
Gillingham v Grimsby Town
Plymouth Argyle v Oldham Athletic
Preston N.E. v Fulham
Walsall v Blackpool
Watford v Wigan Athletic
Wycombe Wand. v Bournemouth
York City v Luton Town

Third Division
Barnet v Darlington
Cambridge Utd. v Hartlepool United
Cardiff City v Scarborough
Chester City v Exeter City
Hull City v Doncaster Rov.
Lincoln City v Macclesfield Town
Mansfield Town v Leyton Orient
Notts County v Peterborough Utd.
Rochdale v Torquay United
Rotherham United v Colchester Utd.
Scunthorpe Utd. v Brighton & H.A.
Shrewsbury Town v Swansea City

Sunday, November 30
Premiership
Arsenal v Liverpool

Monday, December 1
Premiership
Bolton Wand. v Newcastle United

Tuesday, December 2
Second Division
Bournemouth v York City
Blackpool v Plymouth Argyle
Bristol City v Burnley
Fulham v Brentford
Grimsby Town v Wycombe Wand.
Luton Town v Gillingham
Northampton T. v Chesterfield
Oldham Athletic v Carlisle United
Southend United v Preston N.E.
Wigan Athletic v Bristol Rovers
Wrexham v Watford

Third Division
Colchester Utd. v Cardiff City
Darlington v Shrewsbury Town
Doncaster Rov. v Chester City
Exeter City v Lincoln City
Hartlepool United v Hull City
Leyton Orient v Barnet
Macclesfield Town v Scunthorpe Utd.
Peterborough Utd. v Cambridge Utd.
Scarborough v Rochdale
Swansea City v Rotherham United
Torquay United v Mansfield Town

Wednesday, December 3
Second Division
Millwall v Walsall

Third Division
Brighton & H.A. v Notts County

Saturday, December 6
Premiership
Aston Villa v Coventry City
Blackburn Rovers v Bolton Wand.
Derby County v West Ham United
Leeds United v Everton
Leicester City v Crystal Palace
Liverpool v Manchester Utd.
Newcastle United v Arsenal
Tottenham H. v Chelsea

First Division
Bury v Middlesbrough
Crewe Alexandra v Huddersfield T.
Manchester City v Wolves
Norwich City v Sheffield United
Nott'm. Forest v Bradford City

Port Vale v Birmingham City
Portsmouth v Stoke City
Q.P.R. v Sunderland
Reading v Charlton Athletic
Swindon Town v Oxford United
Tranmere Rovers v Ipswich Town
W.B.A. v Stockport Co.

Sunday, December 7
Premiership
Wimbledon v Southampton

Monday, December 8
Premiership
Sheffield Wed. v Barnsley

Friday, December 12
First Division
Oxford United v Q.P.R.

Second Division
Bristol Rovers v Grimsby Town

Third Division
Cambridge United v Exeter City

Saturday, December 13
Premiership
Arsenal v Blackburn Rovers
Barnsley v Newcastle United
Chelsea v Leeds United
Coventry City v Tottenham H.
Crystal Palace v Liverpool
Everton v Wimbledon
Southampton v Leicester City
West Ham United v Sheffield Wed.

First Division
Birmingham City v Manchester City
Bradford City v Bury
Charlton Athletic v Port Vale
Huddersfield T. v Norwich City
Ipswich Town v Portsmouth
Middlesbrough v Reading
Sheffield United v Swindon Town
Stockport Co. v Tranmere Rovers
Stoke City v Crewe Alexandra
Sunderland v W.B.A.

Second Division
Brentford v Blackpool
Burnley v Wigan Athletic
Carlisle United v Fulham
Chesterfield v Luton Town
Gillingham v Southend United
Plymouth Argyle v Millwall
Preston N.E. v Northampton T.
Walsall v Bournemouth
Watford v Bristol City
Wycombe Wand. v Oldham Athletic

York City v Wrexham

Third Division
Barnet v Macclesfield Town
Cardiff City v Peterborough Utd.
Chester City v Darlington
Hull City v Colchester Utd.
Lincoln City v Hartlepool United
Mansfield Town v Brighton & H.A.
Notts County v Doncaster Rov.
Rochdale v Swansea City
Rotherham United v Torquay United
Scunthorpe Utd. v Scarborough
Shrewsbury Town v Leyton Orient

Sunday, December 14
Premiership
Bolton Wand. v Derby County

First Division
Wolves v Nott'm. Forest

Monday, December 15
Premiership
Manchester Utd. v Aston Villa

Wednesday, December 17
Premiership
Newcastle United v Derby County

Friday, December 19
Second Division
Oldham Athletic v Walsall
Southend United v York City

Third Division
Colchester Utd. v Chester City
Doncaster Rov. v Rotherham United
Scarborough v Barnet

Saturday, December 20
Premiership
Aston Villa v Southampton
Blackburn Rovers v West Ham United
Derby County v Crystal Palace
Leeds United v Bolton Wand.
Leicester City v Everton
Liverpool v Coventry City
Sheffield Wed. v Chelsea
Tottenham H. v Barnsley

First Division
Bury v Sheffield United
Crewe Alexandra v Sunderland
Manchester City v Middlesbrough
Norwich City v Stoke City
Nott'm. Forest v Stockport Co.
Port Vale v Ipswich Town
Portsmouth v Charlton Athletic

Q.P.R. v Bradford City
Reading v Wolves
Swindon Town v Birmingham City
Tranmere Rovers v Oxford United
W.B.A. v Huddersfield T.

Second Division
Bournemouth v Watford
Blackpool v Preston N.E.
Bristol City v Chesterfield
Fulham v Burnley
Grimsby Town v Carlisle United
Luton Town v Bristol Rovers
Millwall v Wycombe Wand.
Northampton T. v Plymouth Argyle
Wigan Athletic v Brentford
Wrexham v Gillingham

Third Division
Brighton & H.A. v Shrewsbury Town
Darlington v Scunthorpe Utd.
Exeter City v Rochdale
Hartlepool United v Mansfield Town
Leyton Orient v Hull City
Macclesfield Town v Cardiff City
Peterborough Utd. v Lincoln City
Swansea City v Cambridge United
Torquay United v Notts County

Sunday, December 21
Premiership
Newcastle United v Manchester Utd.

Monday, December 22
Premiership
Wimbledon v Arsenal

Friday, December 26
Premiership
Arsenal v Leicester City
Aston Villa v Tottenham H.
Bolton Wand. v Barnsley
Chelsea v Wimbledon
Crystal Palace v Southampton
Derby County v Newcastle United
Liverpool v Leeds United
Manchester Utd. v Everton
Sheffield Wed. v Blackburn Rovers
West Ham United v Coventry City

First Division
Charlton Athletic v Norwich City
Crewe Alexandra v Manchester City
Huddersfield T. v Middlesbrough
Ipswich Town v Birmingham City
Nott'm. Forest v Swindon Town
Portsmouth v Q.P.R.
Reading v W.B.A.
Stockport Co. v Port Vale
Stoke City v Sheffield United

Sunderland v Bradford City
Tranmere Rovers v Bury
Wolves v Oxford United

Second Division
Bournemouth v Gillingham
Brentford v Southend United
Bristol City v Millwall
Burnley v Chesterfield
Carlisle United v Blackpool
Luton Town v Northampton T.
Plymouth Argyle v Fulham
Preston N.E. v Oldham Athletic
Walsall v Bristol Rovers
Wrexham v Wigan Athletic
Wycombe Wand. v Watford
York City v Grimsby Town

Third Division
Barnet v Peterborough Utd.
Brighton & H.A. v Colchester Utd.
Cambridge United v Leyton Orient
Cardiff City v Exeter City
Darlington v Macclesfield Town
Doncaster Rov. v Mansfield Town
Hartlepool United v Scarborough
Hull City v Chester City
Lincoln City v Rotherham United
Rochdale v Shrewsbury Town
Scunthorpe Utd. v Notts County
Torquay United v Swansea City

Sunday, December 28
Premiership
Barnsley v Derby County
Blackburn Rovers v Crystal Palace
Coventry City v Manchester Utd.
Everton v Bolton Wand.
Leeds United v Aston Villa
Leicester City v Sheffield Wed.
Newcastle United v Liverpool
Tottenham H. v Arsenal
Wimbledon v West Ham United

First Division
Birmingham City v Tranmere Rovers
Bradford City v Huddersfield T.
Bury v Crewe Alexandra
Manchester City v Nott'm. Forest
Middlesbrough v Stockport Co.
Oxford United v Sunderland
Port Vale v Wolves
Q.P.R. v Reading
Sheffield United v Charlton Athletic
Swindon Town v Ipswich Town
W.B.A. v Stoke City

Second Division
Blackpool v Wrexham
Bristol Rovers v Bournemouth
Chesterfield v York City

Fulham v Bristol City
Gillingham v Brentford
Grimsby Town v Preston N.E.
Millwall v Luton Town
Northampton T. v Walsall
Oldham Athletic v Burnley
Southend United v Wycombe Wand.
Watford v Plymouth Argyle
Wigan Athletic v Carlisle

Third Division
Chester City v Scunthorpe Utd.
Exeter City v Torquay United
Leyton Orient v Doncaster Rov.
Macclesfield Town v Rochdale
Mansfield Town v Lincon City
Notts County v Hartlepool United
Peterborough Utd. v Brighton & H.A.
Rotherham United v Hull City
Scarborough v Darlington
Shrewsbury Town v Cardiff City
Swansea City v Barnet

Monday, December 29
Premiership
Southampton v Chelsea

Third Division
Colchester Utd. v Cambridge United

Tuesday, December 30
First Division
Norwich City v Portsmouth

Saturday, January 3, 1998
Second Division
Blackpool v Bristol City
Bristol Rovers v York City
Chesterfield v Brentford
Fulham v Walsall
Gillingham v Burnley
Grimsby Town v Plymouth Argyle
Millwall v Preston N.E.
Northampton T. v Wycombe Wand.
Oldham Athletic v Wrexham
Southend United v Luton Town
Watford v Carlisle United
Wigan Athletic v Bournemouth

Third Division
Chester City v Cardiff City
Colchester Utd. v Hartlepool United
Exeter City v Barnet
Leyton Orient v Scunthorpe Utd.
Macclesfield Town v Brighton & H.A.
Mansfield Town v Rochdale
Notts County v Hull City
Peterborough Utd. v Doncaster Rov.
Rotherham Utd. v Cambridge United
Scarborough v Torquay United

Shrewsbury Town v Lincoln City
Swansea City v Darlington

Saturday, January 10
Premiership
Arsenal v Leeds United
Aston Villa v Leicester City
Bolton Wand. v Southampton
Chelsea v Coventry City
Crystal Palace v Newcastle
Derby County v Blackburn Rovers
Liverpool v Wimbledon
Manchester Utd. v Tottenham H.
Sheffield Wed. v Newcastle United
West Ham United v Barnsley

First Division
Charlton Athletic v Middlesbrough
Crewe Alexandra v Swindon Town
Huddersfield T. v Oxford United
Ipswich Town v Q.P.R.
Nott'm. Forest v Port Vale
Portsmouth v Manchester City
Reading v Bury
Stockport Co. v Bradford City
Stoke City v Birmingham City
Sunderland v Sheffield United
Tranmere Rovers v W.B.A.
Wolves v Norwich City

Second Division
Bournemouth v Northampton T.
Brentford v Millwall
Bristol City v Grimsby Town
Burnley v Watford
Carlisle United v Southend United
Luton Town v Blackpool
Plymouth Argyle v Bristol Rovers
Preston N.E. v Gillingham
Walsall v Chesterfield
Wrexham v Fulham
Wycombe Wand. v Wigan Athletic
York City v Oldham Athletic

Third Division
Barnet v Rotherham United
Brighton & H.A. v Swansea City
Cambridge United v Scarborough
Cardiff City v Leyton Orient
Darlington v Colchester Utd.
Doncaster Rov. v Shrewsbury Town
Hartlepool United v Exeter City
Hull City v Mansfield Town
Lincoln City v Chester City
Rochdale v Notts County
Scunthorpe Utd. v Peterborough Utd.
Torquay United v Macclesfield Town

Friday, January 16
First Division
Stoke City v Bradford City

Third Division
Colchester Utd. v Torquay United

Saturday, January 17
Premiership
Barnsley v Crystal Palace
Blackburn Rovers v Aston Villa
Coventry City v Arsenal
Everton v Chelsea
Leeds United v Sheffield Wed.
Leicester City v Liverpool
Newcastle United v Bolton Wand.
Southampton v Manchester Utd.
Tottenham H. v West Ham United
Wimbledon v Derby County

First Division
Birmingham City v Huddersfield T.
Bury v Stockport Co.
Manchester City v Sunderland
Middlesbrough v Ipswich Town
Norwich City v Nott'm. Forest
Oxford United v Charlton Athletic
Port Vale v Portsmouth
Q.P.R. v Tranmere Rovers
Sheffield United v Wolves
Swindon Town v Reading
W.B.A. v Crewe Alexandra

Second Division
Blackpool v Bournemouth
Bristol Rovers v Burnley
Chesterfield v Plymouth Argyle
Fulham & Wycombe Wand.
Gillingham v York City
Grimsby Town v Brentford
Millwall v Wrexham
Northampton T. v Carlisle United
Oldham Athletic v Luton Town
Southend United v Walsall
Watford v Preston N.E.
Wigan Athletic v Bristol City

Third Division
Chester City v Barnet
Exeter City v Doncaster Rovers
Leyton Orient v Brighton & H.A.
Macclesfield Town v Hartlepool Utd.
Mansfield Town v Scunthorpe Utd.
Notts County v Cardiff City
Peterborough Utd. v Rochdale
Rotherham United v Darlington
Scarborough v Lincoln City
Shrewsbury T. v Cambridge United
Swansea City v Hull City

Saturday, January 24
Second Division
Bournemouth v Oldham Athletic
Brentford v Watford
Bristol City v Northampton T.

Burnley v Southend United
Carlisle United v Bristol Rovers
Luton Town v Fulham
Plymouth Argyle v Wigan Athletic
Preston N.E. v Chesterfield
Walsall v Gillingham
Wrexham v Grimsby Town
Wycombe Wand. v Blackpool
York City v Millwall

Third Division
Barnet v Colchester Utd.
Brighton & H.A. v Scarborough
Cambridge United v Chester City
Cardiff City v Mansfield Town
Darlington v Exeter City
Doncaster Rov. v Macclesfield Town
Hartlepool Utd. v Rotherham United
Hull City v Peterborough Utd.
Lincoln City v Notts County
Rochdale v Leyton Orient
Scunthorpe Utd. v Swansea City
Torquay United v Shrewsbury Town

Tuesday, January 27
First Division
Birmingham City v Stockport Co.
Bradford City v Reading
Bury v Wolves
Oxford United v Portsmouth
Port Vale v Crewe Alexandra
Sheffield United v Huddersfield T.
W.B.A. v Ipswich Town

Wednesday, January 28
First Division
Manchester City v Charlton Athletic
Middlesbrough v Tranmere Rovers
Norwich City v Sunderland
Q.P.R. v Nott'm. Forest
Swindon Town v Stoke City

Friday, January 30
Third Division
Doncaster Rov. v Scunthorpe Utd.

Saturday, January 31
Premiership
Arsenal v Southampton
Aston Villa v Newcastle United
Bolton Wand. v Coventry City
Chelsea v Barnsley
Crystal Palace v Leeds United
Derby County v Tottenham H.
Liverpool v Blackburn Rovers
Manchester Utd. v Leicester City
Sheffield Wed. v Wimbledon
West Ham United v Everton

First Division
Charlton Athletic v Bury
Crewe Alexandra v Norwich City
Huddersfield T. v Swindon Town
Ipswich Town v Bradford City
Nott'm. Forest v Oxford United
Portsmouth v Sheffield United
Reading v Birmingham City
Stockport Co. v Q.P.R.
Stoke City v Middlesbrough
Sunderland v Port Vale
Tranmere Rovers v Manchester City
Wolves v W.B.A.

Second Division
Blackpool v Wigan Athletic
Brentford v Plymouth Argyle
Bristol City v Wrexham
Burnley v York City
Carlisle United v Wycombe Wand.
Chesterfield v Watford
Gillingham v Bristol Rovers
Grimsby Town v Fulham
Luton Town v Bournemouth
Northampton T. v Oldham Athletic
Southend United v Millwall
Walsall v Preston N.E.

Third Division
Barnet v Cambridge United
Darlington v Brighton & H.A.
Exeter City v Leyton Orient
Lincoln City v Hull City
Mansfield Town v Notts County
Peterborough Utd. v Rotherham Utd.
Rochdale v Cardiff City
Scarborough v Colchester Utd.
Shrewsbury Town v Chester City
Swansea City v Macclesfield Town
Torquay United v Hartlepool United

Friday, February 6
Third Division
Colchester Utd. v Swansea City

Saturday, February 7
Premiership
Arsenal v Chelsea
Barnsley v Everton
Blackburn Rovers v Tottenham H.
Coventry City v Sheffield Wed.
Crystal Palace v Wimbledon
Derby County v Aston Villa
Leicester City v Leeds United
Liverpool v Southampton
Manchester Utd. v Bolton Wand.
Newcastle United v West Ham United

First Division
Birmingham City v Middlesbrough
Bradford City v Charlton Athletic

Bury v Port Vale
Huddersfield T. v Stockport Co.
Norwich City v Manchester City
Portsmouth v Nott'm. Forest
Q.P.R. v Crewe Alexandra
Reading v Tranmere Rovers
Sheffield United v Oxford United
Stoke City v Ipswich Town
Swindon Town v W.B.A.
Wolves v Sunderland

Second Division
Bournemouth v Bristol City
Bristol Rovers v Chesterfield
Fulham v Southend United
Millwall v Grimsby Town
Oldham Athletic v Blackpool
Plymouth Argyle v Carlisle United
Preston N.E. v Burnley
Watford v Gillingham
Wigan Athletic v Northampton T.
Wrexham v Luton Town
Wycombe Wand. v Brentford
York City v Walsall

Third Division
Brighton & H.A. v Torquay United
Cambridge United v Doncaster Rov.
Cardiff City v Lincoln City
Chester City v Mansfield Town
Hartlepool United v Darlington
Hull City v Rochdale
Leyton Orient v Peterborough Utd.
Macclesfield Town v Scarborough
Notts County v Shrewsbury Town
Rotherham United v Exeter City
Scunthorpe Utd. v Barnet

Friday, February 13
Third Division
Colchester Utd. v Mansfield Town

Saturday, February 14
Premiership
Aston Villa v Barnsley
Bolton Wand. v Arsenal
Chelsea v Crystal Palace
Everton v Derby County
Leeds United v Blackburn Rovers
Sheffield Wed. v Liverpool
Southampton v Coventry City
Tottenham H. v Leicester City
West Ham United v Manchester Utd.
Wimbledon v Newcastle United

First Division
Charlton Athletic v Wolves
Crewe Alexandra v Portsmouth
Ipswich Town v Huddersfield T.
Manchester City v Bury
Middlesbrough v Bradford City

Nott'm. Forest v Sheffield United
Oxford United v Reading
Port Vale v Norwich City
Stockport Co. v Stoke City
Sunderland v Birmingham City
Tranmere Rovers v Swindon Town
W.B.A. v Q.P.R.

Second Division
Bournemouth v Chesterfield
Blackpool v Millwall
Brentford v Preston N.E.
Bristol City v Gillingham
Carlisle United v Walsall
Northampton T. v Southend United
Oldham Athletic v Fulham
Plymouth Argyle v York City
Watford v Luton Town
Wigan Athletic v Grimsby Town
Wrexham v Bristol Rovers
Wycombe Wand. v Burnley

Third Division
Barnet v Cardiff City
Brighton & H.A. v Doncaster Rov.
Cambridge United v Lincoln City
Darlington v Notts County
Hartlepool United v Chester City
Macclesfield Town v Leyton Orient
Rotherham Utd. v Shrewsbury Town
Scarborough v Exeter City
Scunthorpe v Rochdale
Swansea City v Peterborough Utd.
Torquay United v Hull City

Tuesday, February 17
First Division
Bury v Stoke City
Charlton Athletic v Q.P.R.
Crewe Alexandra v Birmingham City
Oxford United v W.B.A.
Port Vale v Swindon Town
Portsmouth v Stockport Co.
Sheffield United v Middlesbrough
Sunderland v Reading

Wednesday, February 18
First Division
Manchester City v Ipswich Town
Norwich City v Tranmere Rovers
Nott'm. Forest v Huddersfield T.
Wolves v Bradford City

Saturday, February 21
Premiership
Arsenal v Crystal Palace
Bolton Wand. v West Ham United
Coventry City v Barnsley
Leicester City v Chelsea
Liverpool v Everton

Manchester Utd. v Derby County
Newcastle United v Leeds United
Sheffield Wed. v Tottenham H.
Southampton v Blackburn Rovers
Wimbledon v Aston Villa

First Division
Birmingham City v Sheffield United
Bradford City v Oxford United
Huddersfield T. v Wolves
Ipswich Town v Norwich City
Middlesbrough v Sunderland
Q.P.R. v Port Vale
Reading v Portsmouth
Stockport Co. v Charlton Athletic
Stoke City v Nott'm. Forest
Swindon Town v Manchester City
Tranmere Rovers v Crewe Alexandra
W.B.A. v Bury

Second Division
Bristol Rovers v Oldham Athletic
Burnley v Brentford
Chesterfield v Wrexham
Fulham v Wigan Athletic
Gillingham v Carlisle United
Grimsby Town v Bournemouth
Luton Town v Bristol City
Millwall v Northampton T.
Preston N.E. v Wycombe Wand.
Southend United v Blackpool
Walsall v Plymouth Argyle
York City v Watford

Third Division
Cardiff City v Cambridge United
Chester City v Rotherham United
Doncaster Rov. v Torquay United
Exeter City v Colchester Utd.
Hull City v Scunthorpe Utd.
Leyton Orient v Swansea City
Lincoln City v Barnet
Mansfield Town v Darlington
Notts County v Scarborough
Peterborough Utd. v Macclesfield T.
Rochdale v Brighton & H.A.
Shrewsbury Town v Hartlepool United

Tuesday, February 24
First Division
Birmingham City v Bury
Bradford City v Port Vale
Huddersfield T. v Sunderland
Ipswich Town v Oxford United
Reading v Manchester City
Stockport Co. v Norwich City
Tranmere Rovers v Nott'm. Forest
W.B.A. v Portsmouth

Second Division
Bristol Rovers v Wycombe Wand.

Burnley v Wrexham
Chesterfield v Oldham Athletic
Fulham v Bournemouth
Gillingham v Northampton T.
Grimsby Town v Blackpool
Luton Town v Wigan Athletic
Preston N.E. v Carlisle United
Southend United v Plymouth Argyle
Walsall v Brentford
York City v Bristol City

Third Division
Cardiff City v Rotherham United
Chester City v Torquay United
Doncaster Rov. v Darlington
Exeter City v Brighton & H.A.
Hull City v Barnet
Leyton Orient v Hartlepool United
Lincoln City v Scunthorpe Utd.
Mansfield Town v Macclesfield Town
Notts County v Swansea City
Peterborough Utd. v Scarborough
Rochdale v Cambridge United
Shrewsbury Town v Colchester Utd.

Wednesday, February 25
First Division
Middlesbrough v Crewe Alexandra
Q.P.R. v Sheffield United
Stoke City v Charlton Athletic
Swindon Town v Wolves

Second Division
Millwall v Watford

Friday, February 27
Third Division
Colchester Utd. v Peterborough Utd.

Saturday, February 28
Premiership
Aston Villa v Liverpool
Barnsley v Wimbledon
Blackburn Rovers v Leicester City
Chelsea v Manchester Utd.
Crystal Palace v Coventry City
Derby County v Sheffield Wed.
Everton v Newcastle United
Leeds United v Southampton
Tottenham H. v Bolton Wand.
West Ham United v Arsenal

First Division
Bury v Swindon Town
Charlton Athletic v Huddersfield T.
Crewe Alexandra v Reading
Manchester City v W.B.A.
Norwich City v Q.P.R.
Nott'm. Forest v Middlesbrough
Oxford United v Stockport Co.

Portsmouth v Tranmere Rovers
Sheffield United v Bradford City
Sunderland v Ipswich Town
Wolves v Birmingham City

Second Division
Bournemouth v Preston N.E.
Blackpool v Fulham
Brentford v York City
Bristol City v Southend United
Carlisle United v Burnley
Northampton T. v Grimsby Town
Oldham Athletic v Millwall
Plymouth Argyle v Luton Town
Watford v Bristol Rovers
Wigan Athletic v Chesterfield
Wrexham v Walsall
Wycombe Wand. v Gillingham

Third Division
Barnet v Shrewsbury Town
Brighton & H.A. v Chester City
Cambridge United v Mansfield Town
Darlington v Rochdale
Hartlepool United v Doncaster Rov.
Macclesfield Town v Notts County
Rotherham United v Leyton Orient
Scarborough v Hull City
Scunthorpe Utd. v Cardiff City
Swansea City v Exeter City
Torquay United v Lincoln City

Sunday, March 1
First Division
Port Vale v Stoke City

Tuesday, March 3
First Division
Bradford City v Swindon Town
Charlton Athletic v W.B.A.
Huddersfield T. v Manchester City
Oxford United v Crewe Alexandra
Port Vale v Tranmere Rovers
Portsmouth v Bury
Sheffield United v Ipswich Town
Stockport Co. v Reading

Second Division
Bournemouth v Plymouth Argyle
Bristol City v Brentford
Burnley v Blackpool
Carlisle United v Millwall
Fulham v Bristol Rovers
Gillingham v Oldham Athletic
Grimsby Town v Chesterfield
Northampton T. v Wrexham
Preston N.E. v Luton Town
Watford v Walsall
Wigan Athletic v Southend United
Wycombe Wand. v York City

Third Division
Cambridge Utd. v Macclesfield Town
Chester City v Leyton Orient
Colchester Utd. v Rochdale
Darlington v Peterborough Utd.
Doncaster Rov. v Barnet
Exeter City v Notts County
Hartlepool United v Scunthorpe Utd.
Lincoln City v Swansea City
Rotherham United v Brighton & H.A.
Scarborough v Mansfield Town
Shrewsbury Town v Hull City
Torquay United v Cardiff City

Wednesday, March 4
First Division
Norwich City v Birmingham City
Nott'm. Forest v Sunderland
Q.P.R. v Middlesbrough
Wolves v Stoke City

Friday, March 6
Third Division
Doncaster Rov. v Scarborough

Saturday, March 7
Premiership
Arsenal v Derby County
Blackburn Rovers v Barnsley
Chelsea v Aston Villa
Coventry City v Wimbledon
Crystal Palace v West Ham United
Leeds United v Tottenham H.
Leicester City v Newcastle United
Liverpool v Bolton Wand.
Sheffield Wed. v Manchester Utd.
Southampton v Everton

First Division
Birmingham City v Q.P.R.
Bury v Norwich City
Crewe Alexandra v Nott'm. Forest
Ipswich Town v Charlton Athletic
Manchester City v Oxford United
Middlesbrough v Wolves
Reading v Port Vale
Stoke City v Huddersfield T.
Sunderland v Stockport Co.
Swindon Town v Portsmouth
Tranmere Rovers v Sheffield United
W.B.A. v Bradford City

Second Division
Blackpool v Watford
Brentford v Bournemouth
Bristol Rovers v Northampton T.
Chesterfield v Fulham
Luton Town v Wycombe Wand.
Millwall v Gillingham
Oldham Athletic v Bristol City

Plymouth Argyle v Preston N.E.
Southend United v Grimsby Town
Walsall v Burnley
Wrexham v Carlisle United
York City v Wigan Athletic

Third Division
Brighton & H.A. v Hartlepool United
Hull City v Darlington
Leyton Orient v Lincoln City
Macclesfield Town v Rotherham Utd.
Mansfield Town v Shrewsbury Town
Notts County v Barnet
Peterborough Utd. v Exeter City
Rochdale v Chester City
Scunthorpe Utd. v Colchester Utd.
Swansea City v Cardiff City
Torquay United v Cambridge United

Saturday, March 14
Premiership
Aston Villa v Crystal Palace
Barnsley v Southampton
Bolton Wand. v Sheffield Wed.
Derby County v Leeds United
Everton v Blackburn Rovers
Manchester Utd. v Arsenal
Newcastle United v Coventry City
Tottenham H. v Liverpool
West Ham United v Chelsea
Wimbledon v Leicester City

First Division
Bradford City v Birmingham City
Charlton Athletic v Sunderland
Huddersfield T. v Tranmere Rovers
Norwich City v W.B.A.
Nott'm. Forest v Bury
Oxford United v Stoke City
Port Vale v Manchester City
Portsmouth v Middlesbrough
Q.P.R. v Swindon Town
Sheffield United v Reading
Stockport Co. v Ipswich Town
Wolves v Crewe Alexandra

Second Division
Bournemouth v Wrexham
Bristol City v Bristol Rovers
Burnley v Luton Town
Carlisle United v Brentford
Fulham v Millwall
Gillingham v Chesterfield
Grimsby Town v Walsall
Northampton T. v Blackpool
Preston N.E. v York City
Watford v Southend United
Wigan Athletic v Oldham Athletic
Wycombe Wand. v Plymouth Argyle

Third Division
Barnet v Brighton & H.A.

Cambridge United v Scunthorpe Utd.
Cardiff City v Doncaster Rov.
Chester City v Notts County
Colchester Utd. v Macclesfield Town
Darlington v Torquay United
Exeter City v Hull City
Hartlepool United v Swansea City
Lincoln City v Rochdale
Rotherham United v Mansfield Town
Scarborough v Leyton Orient
Shrewsbury T. v Peterborough Utd.

Saturday, March 21
First Division
Birmingham City v Nott'm. Forest
Bury v Oxford United
Crewe Alexandra v Charlton Athletic
Ipswich Town v Wolves
Manchester City v Sheffield United
Middlesbrough v Norwich City
Reading v Huddersfield T.
Stoke City v Q.P.R.
Sunderland v Portsmouth
Swindon Town v Stockport Co.
Tranmere Rovers v Bradford City
W.B.A. v Port Vale

Second Division
Blackpool v Gillingham
Brentford v Northampton T.
Bristol Rovers v Preston N.E.
Chesterfield v Carlisle United
Luton Town v Grimsby Town
Millwall v Burnley
Oldham Athletic v Watford
Plymouth Argyle v Bristol City
Southend United v Bournemouth
Walsall v Wigan Athletic
Wrexham v Wycombe Wand.
York City v Fulham

Third Division
Brighton & H.A. v Cambridge United
Doncaster Rov. v Lincoln City
Hull City v Cardiff City
Leyton Orient v Darlington
Macclesfield T. v Shrewsbury Town
Mansfield Town v Exeter City
Notts County v Colchester Utd.
Peterborough Utd. v Chester City
Rochdale v Hartlepool United
Scunthorpe Utd. v Rotherham United
Swansea City v Scarborough
Torquay United v Barnet

Friday, March 27
Second Division
Bristol Rovers v Southend United

Saturday, March 28
Premiership
Arsenal v Sheffield Wed.
Barnsley v Liverpool
Bolton Wand. v Leicester City
Chelsea v Blackburn Rovers
Coventry City v Derby County
Crystal Palace v Tottenham H.
Everton v Aston Villa
Manchester Utd. v Wimbledon
Southampton v Newcastle United
West Ham United v Leeds United

First Division
Birmingham City v W.B.A.
Bradford City v Manchester City
Charlton Athletic v Nott'm. Forest
Huddersfield T. v Q.P.R.
Ipswich Town v Reading
Middlesbrough v Swindon Town
Oxford United v Norwich City
Sheffield United v Port Vale
Stockport Co. v Crewe Alexandra
Stoke City v Tranmere Rovers
Sunderland v Bury
Wolves v Portsmouth

Second Division
Brentford v Oldham Athletic
Burnley v Grimsby Town
Carlisle United v Bournemouth
Chesterfield v Millwall
Gillingham v Fulham
Plymouth Argyle v Wrexham
Preston N.E. v Wigan Athletic
Walsall v Luton Town
Watford v Northampton T.
Wycombe Wand. v Bristol City
York City v Blackpool

Third Division
Barnet v Hartlepool United
Cambridge United v Darlington
Cardiff City v Brighton & H.A.
Chester City v Swansea City
Hull City v Macclesfield Town
Lincoln City v Colchester Utd.
Mansfield Town v Peterborough Utd.
Notts County v Leyton Orient
Rochdale v Doncaster Rov.
Rotherham United v Scarborough
Scunthorpe Utd. v Torquay United
Shrewsbury Town v Exeter City

Friday, April 3
Second Division
Southend United v Chesterfield

Third Division
Colchester Utd. v Rotherham United
Scarborough v Cardiff

Saturday, April 4

Premiership
Aston Villa v West Ham United
Blackburn Rovers v Manchester Utd.
Derby County v Chelsea
Leeds United v Barnsley
Leicester City v Coventry City
Liverpool v Arsenal
Newcastle United v Crystal Palace
Sheffield Wed. v Southampton
Tottenham H. v Everton
Wimbledon v Bolton Wand.

First Division
Bury v Huddersfield T.
Crewe Alexandra v Sheffield United
Manchester City v Stockport Co.
Norwich City v Bradford City
Nott'm. Forest v Ipswich Town
Port Vale x Oxford United
Portsmouth v Birmingham City
Q.P.R. v Wolves
Reading v Stoke City
Swindon Town v Charlton Athletic
Tranmere Rovers v Sunderland
W.B.A. v Middlesbrough

Second Division
Bournemouth v Wycombe Wand.
Blackpool v Walsall
Bristol City v Carlisle United
Fulham v Preston N.E.
Grimsby Town v Gillingham
Luton Town v York City
Millwall v Bristol Rovers
Northampton T. v Burnley
Oldham Athletic v Plymouth Argyle
Wigan Athletic v Watford
Wrexham v Brentford

Third Division
Brighton & H.A. v Scunthorpe Utd.
Darlington v Barnet
Doncaster Rov. v Hull City
Exeter City v Chester City
Hartlepool Utd. v Cambridge United
Leyton Orient v Mansfield Town
Macclesfield Town v Lincoln City
Peterborough Utd. v Notts County
Swansea City v Shrewsbury Town
Torquay United v Rochdale

Friday, April 10
Division 2
Wycombe Wand. v Grimsby Town

Saturday, April 11
Premiership
Arsenal v Newcastle United
Barnsley v Sheffield Wed.

Bolton Wand. v Blackburn Rovers
Chelsea v Tottenham H.
Coventry City v Aston Villa
Crystal Palace v Leicester City
Everton v Leeds United
Manchester Utd. v Liverpool
Southampton v Wimbledon
West Ham United v Derby County

First Division
Birmingham City v Port Vale
Bradford City v Nott'm. Forest
Charlton Athletic v Reading
Huddersfield T. v Crewe Alexandra
Ipswich Town v Tranmere Rovers
Middlesbrough v Bury
Oxford United v Swindon Town
Sheffield United v Norwich City
Stockport Co. v W.B.A.
Stoke City v Portsmouth
Sunderland v Q.P.R.
Wolves v Manchester City

Second Division
Brentford v Fulham
Bristol Rovers v Wigan Athletic
Burnley v Bristol City
Carlisle United v Oldham Athletic
Chesterfield v Northampton T.
Gillingham v Luton Town
Plymouth Argyle v Blackpool
Preston N.E. v Southend United
Walsall v Millwall
Watford v Wrexham
York City v Bournemouth

Third Division
Barnet v Leyton Orient
Cambridge Utd. v Peterborough Utd.
Cardiff City v Colchester Utd.
Chester City v Doncaster Rov.
Hull City v Hartlepool United
Lincoln City v Exeter City
Mansfield Town v Torquay United
Notts County v Brighton & H.A.
Rochdale v Scarborough
Rotherham United v Swansea City
Scunthorpe Utd. v Macclesfield Town
Shrewsbury Town v Darlington

Monday, April 13
Premiership
Aston Villa v Manchester Utd.
Blackburn Rovers v Arsenal
Derby County v Bolton Wand.
Leeds United v Chelsea
Liverpool v Crystal Palace
Newcastle United v Barnsley
Sheffield Wed. v West Ham United
Tottenham H. v Coventry City
Wimbledon v Everton

First Division
Bury v Bradford City
Crewe Alexandra v Stoke City
Manchester City v Birmingham City
Norwich City v Huddersfield T.
Nott'm. Forest v Wolves
Port Vale v Charlton Athletic
Portsmouth v Ipswich Town
Reading v Middlesbrough
Swindon Town v Sheffield United
Tranmere Rovers v Stockport Co.
W.B.A. v Sunderland

Second Division
Blackpool v Brentford
Bristol City v Watford
Fulham v Carlisle United
Grimsby Town v Bristol Rovers
Millwall v Plymouth Argyle
Northampton T. v Preston N.E.
Oldham Athletic v Wycombe Wand.
Southend United v Gillingham
Wigan Athletic v Burnley
Wrexham v York City

Third Division
Brighton & H.A. v Mansfield Town
Colchester Utd. v Hull City
Darlington v Chester City
Doncaster Rov. v Notts County
Exeter City v Cambridge United
Hartlepool United v Lincoln City
Leyton Orient v Shrewsbury Town
Macclesfield Town v Barnet
Peterborough Utd. v Cardiff City
Scarborough v Scunthorpe Utd.
Swansea City v Rochdale
Torquay United v Rotherham United

Tuesday, April 14
Premiership
Leicester City v Southampton

First Division
Q.P.R. v Oxford United

Second Division
Bournemouth v Walsall
Luton Town v Chesterfield

Saturday, April 18
Premiership
Arsenal v Wimbledon
Barnsley v Tottenham H.
Bolton Wand. v Leeds United
Chelsea v Sheffield Wed.
Coventry City v Liverpool
Crystal Palace v Derby County
Everton v Leicester City
Manchester Utd. v Newcastle United
Southampton v Aston Villa

West Ham United v Blackburn Rovers

First Division
Birmingham City v Swindon Town
Bradford City v Q.P.R.
Charlton Athletic v Portsmouth
Huddersfield T. v W.B.A.
Ipswich Town v Port Vale
Middlesbrough v Manchester City
Oxford United v Tranmere Rovers
Sheffield United v Bury
Stockport Co. v Nott'm. Forest
Stoke City v Norwich City
Sunderland v Crewe Alexandra
Wolves v Reading

Second Division
Brentford v Wigan Athletic
Bristol Rovers v Luton Town
Burnley v Fulham
Carlisle United v Grimsby Town
Chesterfield v Bristol City
Gillingham v Wrexham
Plymouth Argyle v Northampton T.
Preston N.E. v Blackpool
Walsall v Oldham Athletic
Watford v Bournemouth
Wycombe Wand. v Millwall
York City v Southend United

Third Division
Barnet v Scarborough
Cambridge United v Swansea City
Cardiff City v Macclesfield Town
Chester City v Colchester Utd.
Hull City v Leyton Orient
Lincoln City v Peterborough Utd.
Mansfield Town v Hartlepool United
Notts County v Torquay United
Rochdale v Exeter City
Rotherham United v Doncaster Rov.
Scunthorpe Utd. v Darlington
Shrewsbury Town v Brighton & H.A.

Saturday, April 25
Premiership
Aston Villa v Bolton Wand.
Barnsley v Arsenal
Blackburn Rovers v Wimbledon
Chelsea v Liverpool
Crystal Palace v Manchester Utd.
Derby County v Leicester City
Everton v Sheffield Wed.
Leeds United v Coventry City
Tottenham H. v Newcastle United
West Ham United v Southampton

First Division
Bury v Ipswich Town
Charlton Athletic v Tranmere Rovers
Crewe Alexandra v Bradford City

Manchester City v Q.P.R.
Norwich City v Swindon Town
Nott'm. Forest v Reading
Oxford United v Birmingham City
Port Vale v Middlesbrough
Portsmouth v Huddersfield T.
Sheffield United v W.B.A.
Sunderland v Stoke City
Wolves v Stockport Co.

Second Division
Bournemouth v Burnley
Blackpool v Bristol Rovers
Brentford v Luton Town
Bristol City v Walsall
Carlisle United v York City
Northampton T. v Fulham
Oldham Athletic v Southend United
Plymouth Argyle v Gillingham
Watford v Grimsby Town
Wigan Athletic v Millwall
Wrexham v Preston N.E.
Wycombe Wand. v Chesterfield

Third Division
Barnet v Mansfield Town
Brighton & H.A. v Hull City
Cambridge United v Notts County
Colchester Utd. v Leyton Orient
Darlington v Lincoln City
Hartlepool United v Cardiff City
Macclesfield Town v Chester City
Rotherham United v Rochdale
Scarborough v Shrewsbury Town
Scunthorpe Utd. v Exeter City
Swansea City v Doncaster Rov.
Torquay United v Peterborough Utd.

Saturday, May 2
Premiership
Arsenal v Everton
Bolton Wand. v Crystal Palace
Coventry City v Blackburn Rovers
Leicester City v Barnsley
Liverpool v West Ham United
Manchester Utd. v Leeds United
Newcastle United v Chelsea
Sheffield Wed. v Aston Villa
Southampton v Derby County
Wimbledon v Tottenham H.

Second Division
Bristol Rovers v Brentford

Burnley v Plymouth Argyle
Chesterfield v Blackpool
Fulham v Watford
Gillingham v Wigan Athletic
Grimsby Town v Oldham Athletic
Luton Town v Carlisle United
Millwall v Bournemouth
Preston N.E. v Bristol City
Southend United v Wrexham
Walsall v Wycombe Wand.
York City v Northampton T.

Third Division
Cardiff City v Darlington
Chester City v Scarborough
Doncaster Rov. v Colchester Utd.
Exeter City v Macclesfield Town
Hull City v Cambridge United
Leyton Orient v Torquay United
Lincoln City v Brighton & H.A.
Mansfield Town v Swansea City
Notts County v Rotherham United
Peterborough Utd. v Hartlepool Utd.
Rochdale v Barnet
Shrewsbury Town v Scunthorpe Utd.

Sunday, May 3
First Division
Birmingham City v Charlton Athletic
Bradford City v Portsmouth
Huddersfield T. v Port Vale
Ipswich Town v Crewe Alexandra
Middlesbrough v Oxford United
Q.P.R. v Bury
Reading v Norwich City
Stockport Co. v Sheffield United
Stoke City v Manchester City
Swindon Town v Sunderland
Tranmere Rovers v Wolves
W.B.A. v Nott'm. Forest

Sunday, May 10
Premiership
Aston Villa v Arsenal
Barnsley v Manchester Utd.
Blackburn Rovers v Newcastle United
Chelsea v Bolton Wand.
Crystal Palace v Sheffield Wed.
Derby County v Liverpool
Everton v Coventry City
Leeds United v Wimbledon
Tottenham H. v Southampton
West Ham United v Leicester City

SCOTTISH LEAGUE
FIXTURES 1997-98

(Copyright © The Scottish Football League 1997)

Saturday, August 2nd
Premier Division
Aberdeen v Kilmarnock
Dunfermline Athletic v Motherwell
St. Johnstone v Dundee United

First Division
Airdrieonians v St. Mirren
Ayr United v Greenock Morton
Dundee v Falkirk
Hamilton Academical v Partick Thistle
Stirling Albion v Raith Rovers

Sunday, August 3rd
Premier Division
Hibernian v Celtic

Monday, August 4th
Premier Division
Rangers v Heart of Midlothian

Tuesday, August 5th
Second Division
Clydebank v Brechin City
Stenhousemuir v Queen of the South

Third Division
Berwick Rangers v Alloa Athletic
Cowdenbeath v Dumbarton
East Stirlingshire v Ross County
Montrose v Albion Rovers
Queen's Park v Arbroath

Wednesday, August 6th
Second Division
Inverness Cal. Th. v Livingston
Stranraer v Clyde

Saturday, August 16th
Premier Division
Celtic v Dunfermline Athletic
Heart of Midlothian v Aberdeen
Kilmarnock v Rangers
Motherwell v St. Johnstone

First Division
Falkirk v Ayr United
Greenock Morton v Hamilton Acad.
Partick Thistle v Dundee
Raith Rovers v Airdrieonians
St. Mirren v Stirling Albion

Second Division
Brechin City v Inverness Cal. Th.

Clyde v Forfar Athletic
East Fife v Stenhousemuir
Livingston v Stranraer
Queen of the South v Clydebank

Third Division
Albion Rovers v Berwick Rangers
Alloa Athletic v Cowdenbeath
Arbroath v East Stirlingshire
Dumbarton v Montrose
Ross County v Queen's Park

Sunday, August 17th
Premier Division
Dundee United v Hibernian

Saturday, August 23rd
Premier Division
Aberdeen v Motherwell
Dunfermline A. v Heart of Midlothian
Hibernian v Kilmarnock
Rangers v Dundee United
St. Johnstone v Celtic

First Division
Airdrieonians v Falkirk
Ayr United v Partick Thistle
Dundee v St. Mirren
Hamilton Academical v Raith Rovers
Stirling Albion v Greenock Morton

Second Division
Clydebank v Clyde
Forfar Athletic v Brechin City
Inverness Cal. Th. v East Fife
Stenhousemuir v Livingston
Stranraer v Queen of the South

Third Division
Berwick Rangers v Dumbarton
Cowdenbeath v Ross County
East Stirlingshire v Alloa Athletic
Montrose v Arbroath
Queen's Park v Albion Rovers

Saturday, August 30th
Premier Division
Aberdeen v Dundee United
Dunfermline Athletic v St. Johnstone
Heart of Midlothian v Hibernian

First Division
Airdrieonians v Partick Thistle
Dundee v Raith Rovers

Hamilton Academical v Ayr United
St. Mirren v Greenock Morton
Stirling Albion v Falkirk

Second Division
East Fife v Clyde
Forfar Athletic v Clydebank
Livingston v Queen of the South
Stenhousemuir v Inverness Cal. Th.
Stranraer v Brechin City

Third Division
Berwick Rangers v Arbroath
Dumbarton v Alloa Athletic
East Stirlingshire v Queen's Park
Montrose v Cowdenbeath
Ross County v Albion Rovers

Monday, September 1st
Premier Division
Celtic v Rangers
Kilmarnock v Motherwell

Sunday, September 7th
Second Division
Forfar Athletic v East Fife

Saturday, September 13th
Premier Division
Dundee United v Kilmarnock
Hibernian v Dunfermline Athletic
Motherwell v Celtic
Rangers v Aberdeen
St. Johnstone v Heart of Midlothian

First Division
Ayr United v Dundee
Falkirk v Hamilton Academical
Greenock Morton v Airdrieonians
Partick Thistle v Stirling Albion
Raith Rovers v St. Mirren

Second Division
Brechin City v Livingston
Clyde v Stenhousemuir
Clydebank v East Fife
Inverness Cal. Th. v Stranraer
Queen of the South v Forfar Athletic

Third Division
Albion Rovers v Dumbarton
Alloa Athletic v Montrose
Arbroath v Ross County
Cowdenbeath v East Stirlingshire
Queen's Park v Berwick Rangers

Saturday, September 20th
Premier Division
Celtic v Aberdeen
Dunfermline Athletic v Kilmarnock
Heart of Midlothian v Dundee United

Motherwell v Hibernian
St. Johnstone v Rangers

First Division
Ayr United v Raith Rovers
Dundee v Hamilton Academical
Falkirk v St. Mirren
Partick Thistle v Greenock Morton
Stirling Albion v Airdrieonians

Second Division
Clyde v Brechin City
Clydebank v Stenhousemuir
East Fife v Livingston
Forfar Athletic v Stranraer
Queen of South v Inverness Cal. Th.

Third Division
Albion Rovers v Alloa Athletic
Arbroath v Dumbarton
East Stirlingshire v Montrose
Queen's Park v Cowdenbeath
Ross County v Berwick Rangers

Saturday, September 27th
Premier Division
Aberdeen v Dunfermline Athletic
Dundee United v Celtic
Hibernian v St. Johnstone
Kilmarnock v Heart of Midlothian
Rangers v Motherwell

First Division
Airdrieonians v Ayr United
Greenock Morton v Dundee
Hamilton Academical v Stirling Albion
Raith Rovers v Falkirk
St. Mirren v Partick Thistle

Second Division
Brechin City v Queen of the South
Inverness Cal. Th. v Clyde
Livingston v Clydebank
Stenhousemuir v Forfar Athletic
Stranraer v East Fife

Third Division
Alloa Athletic v Arbroath
Berwick Rangers v East Stirlingshire
Cowdenbeath v Albion Rovers
Dumbarton v Queen's Park
Montrose v Ross County

Saturday, October 4th
Premier Division
Celtic v Kilmarnock
Dunfermline Athletic v Dundee United
Hibernian v Rangers
Motherwell v Heart of Midlothian
St. Johnstone v Aberdeen

First Division
Ayr United v Stirling Albion
Dundee v Airdrieonians
Greenock Morton v Raith Rovers
Hamilton Academical v St. Mirren
Partick Thistle v Falkirk

Second Division
Clyde v Livingston
Clydebank v Stranraer
East Fife v Queen of the South
Forfar Athletic v Inverness Cal. Th.
Stenhousemuir v Brechin City

Third Division
Arbroath v Albion Rovers
Berwick Rangers v Cowdenbeath
East Stirlingshire v Dumbarton
Queen's Park v Montrose
Ross County v Alloa Athletic

Saturday, October 18th
Premier Division
Aberdeen v Hibernian
Dundee United v Motherwell
Heart of Midlothian v Celtic
Kilmarnock v St. Johnstone
Rangers v Dunfermline Athletic

First Division
Airdrieonians v Hamilton Academical
Falkirk v Greenock Morton
Raith Rovers v Partick Thistle
St. Mirren v Ayr United
Stirling Albion v Dundee

Second Division
Brechin City v East Fife
Inverness Cal. Th. v Clydebank
Livingston v Forfar Athletic
Queen of the South v Clyde
Stranraer v Stenhousemuir

Third Division
Albion Rovers v East Stirlingshire
Alloa Athletic v Queen's Park
Cowdenbeath v Arbroath
Dumbarton v Ross County
Montrose v Berwick Rangers

Saturday, October 25th
Premier Division
Celtic v St. Johnstone
Dundee United v Rangers
Heart of Midlothian v Dunfermline A.
Kilmarnock v Hibernian
Motherwell v Aberdeen

First Division
Falkirk v Dundee
Greenock Morton v Ayr United
Partick Thistle v Hamilton Academical

Raith Rovers v Stirling Albion
St. Mirren v Airdrieonians

Second Division
Brechin City v Forfar Athletic
Clyde v Clydebank
East Fife v Inverness Cal. Th.
Livingston v Stenhousemuir
Queen of the South v Stranraer

Third Division
Albion Rovers v Queen's Park
Alloa Athletic v East Stirlingshire
Arbroath v Montrose
Dumbarton v Berwick Rangers
Ross County v Cowdenbeath

Saturday, November 1st
Premier Division
Aberdeen v Heart of Midlothian
Dunfermline Athletic v Celtic
Hibernian v Dundee United
Rangers v Kilmarnock
St. Johnstone v Motherwell

First Division
Airdrieonians v Raith Rovers
Ayr United v Falkirk
Dundee v Partick Thistle
Hamilton Acad. v Greenock Morton
Stirling Albion v St. Mirren

Second Division
Clydebank v Queen of the South
Forfar Athletic v Clyde
Inverness Cal. Th. v Brechin City
Stenhousemuir v East Fife
Stranraer v Livingston

Third Division
Berwick Rangers v Albion Rovers
Cowdenbeath v Alloa Athletic
East Stirlingshire v Arbroath
Montrose v Dumbarton
Queen's Park v Ross County

Saturday, November 8th
Premier Division
Hibernian v Heart of Midlothian
Motherwell v Kilmarnock
Rangers v Celtic
St. Johnstone v Dunfermline Athletic

First Division
Ayr United v Hamilton Academical
Falkirk v Stirling Albion
Greenock Morton v St. Mirren
Partick Thistle v Airdrieonians
Raith Rovers v Dundee

Second Division
Brechin City v Stranraer

Clyde v East Fife
Clydebank v Forfar Athletic
Inverness Cal. Th. v Stenhousemuir
Queen of the South v Livingston

Third Division
Albion Rovers v Ross County
Alloa Athletic v Dumbarton
Arbroath v Berwick Rangers
Cowdenbeath v Montrose
Queen's Park v East Stirlingshire

Sunday, November 9th
Premier Division
Dundee United v Aberdeen

Saturday, November 15th
Premier Division
Aberdeen v Rangers
Celtic v Motherwell
Dunfermline Athletic v Hibernian
Heart of Midlothian v St. Johnstone
Kilmarnock v Dundee United

First Division
Airdrieonians v Greenock Morton
Dundee v Ayr United
Hamilton Academical v Falkirk
St. Mirren v Raith Rovers
Stirling Albion v Partick Thistle

Second Division
East Fife v Clydebank
Forfar Athletic v Queen of the South
Livingston v Brechin City
Stenhousemuir v Clyde
Stranraer v Inverness Cal. Th.

Third Division
Berwick Rangers v Queen's Park
Dumbarton v Albion Rovers
East Stirlingshire v Cowdenbeath
Montrose v Alloa Athletic
Ross County v Arbroath

Saturday, November 22nd
Premier Division
Celtic v Dundee United
Dunfermline Athletic v Aberdeen
Heart of Midlothian v Kilmarnock
Motherwell v Rangers
St. Johnstone v Hibernian

First Division
Ayr United v Airdrieonians
Dundee v Greenock Morton
Falkirk v Raith Rovers
Partick Thistle v St. Mirren
Stirling Albion v Hamilton Academical

Second Division
Clyde v Inverness Cal. Th.

Clydebank v Livingston
East Fife v Stranraer
Forfar Athletic v Stenhousemuir
Queen of the South v Brechin City

Third Division
Albion Rovers v Cowdenbeath
Arbroath v Alloa Athletic
East Stirlingshire v Berwick Rangers
Queen's Park v Dumbarton
Ross County v Montrose

Saturday, November 29th
Premier Division
Aberdeen v Celtic
Dundee United v Heart of Midlothian
Hibernian v Motherwell
Kilmarnock v Dunfermline Athletic
Rangers v St. Johnstone

First Division
Airdrieonians v Stirling Albion
Greenock Morton v Partick Thistle
Hamilton Academical v Dundee
Raith Rovers v Ayr United
St. Mirren v Falkirk

Second Division
Brechin City v Clyde
Inverness Cal. Th. v Queen of South
Livingston v East Fife
Stenhousemuir v Clydebank
Stranraer v Forfar Athletic

Third Division
Alloa Athletic v Albion Rovers
Berwick Rangers v Ross County
Cowdenbeath v Queen's Park
Dumbarton v Arbroath
Montrose v East Stirlingshire

Saturday, December 6th
Premier Division
Aberdeen v St. Johnstone
Dundee United v Dunfermline Athletic
Heart of Midlothian v Motherwell
Kilmarnock v Celtic

First Division
Airdrieonians v Dundee
Falkirk v Partick Thistle
Raith Rovers v Greenock Morton
St. Mirren v Hamilton Academical
Stirling Albion v Ayr United

Sunday, December 7th
Premier Division
Rangers v Hibernian

Saturday, December 13th
Premier Division

Celtic v Heart of Midlothian
Dunfermline Athletic v Rangers
Hibernian v Aberdeen
Motherwell v Dundee United
St. Johnstone v Kilmarnock

First Division
Ayr United v St. Mirren
Dundee v Stirling Albion
Greenock Morton v Falkirk
Hamilton Academical v Airdrieonians
Partick Thistle v Raith Rovers

Second Division
Clyde v Queen of the South
Clydebank v Inverness Cal. Th.
East Fife v Brechin City
Forfar Athletic v Livingston
Stenhousemuir v Stranraer

Third Division
Arbroath v Cowdenbeath
Berwick Rangers v Montrose
East Stirlingshire v Albion Rovers
Queen's Park v Alloa Athletic
Ross County v Dumbarton

Saturday, December 20th
Premier Division
Celtic v Hibernian
Dundee United v St. Johnstone
Heart of Midlothian v Rangers
Kilmarnock v Aberdeen
Motherwell v Dunfermline Athletic

First Division
Falkirk v Airdrieonians
Greenock Morton v Stirling Albion
Partick Thistle v Ayr United
Raith Rovers v Hamilton Academical
St. Mirren v Dundee

Second Division
Brechin City v Stenhousemuir
Inverness Cal. Th. v Forfar Athletic
Livingston v Clyde
Queen of the South v East Fife
Stranraer v Clydebank

Third Division
Albion Rovers v Arbroath
Alloa Athletic v Ross County
Cowdenbeath v Berwick Rangers
Dumbarton v East Stirlingshire
Montrose v Queen's Park

Saturday, December 27th
Premier Division
Aberdeen v Motherwell
Dunfermline A. v Heart of Midlothian
Hibernian v Kilmarnock
Rangers v Dundee United

St. Johnstone v Celtic

First Division
Airdrieonians v St. Mirren
Ayr United v Greenock Morton
Dundee v Falkirk
Hamilton Academical v Partick Thistle
Stirling Albion v Raith Rovers

Second Division
Clydebank v Clyde
Forfar Athletic v Brechin City
Inverness Cal. Th. v East Fife
Stenhousemuir v Livingston
Stranraer v Queen of the South

Third Division
Berwick Rangers v Dumbarton
Cowdenbeath v Ross County
East Stirlingshire v Alloa Athletic
Montrose v Arbroath
Queen's Park v Albion Rovers

Thursday, January 1st
Premier Division
Heart of Midlothian v Hibernian

Friday, January 2nd
Premier Division
Celtic v Rangers

Saturday, January 3rd
Premier Division
Aberdeen v Dundee United
Dunfermline Athletic v St. Johnstone
Kilmarnock v Motherwell

First Division
Airdrieonians v Partick Thistle
Dundee v Raith Rovers
Hamilton Academical v Ayr United
St. Mirren v Greenock Morton
Stirling Albion v Falkirk

Saturday, January 10th
Premier Division
Dundee United v Kilmarnock
Hibernian v Dunfermline Athletic
Motherwell v Celtic
Rangers v Aberdeen
St. Johnstone v Heart of Midlothian

First Division
Ayr United v Dundee
Falkirk v Hamilton Academical
Greenock Morton v Airdrieonians
Partick Thistle v Stirling Albion
Raith Rovers v St. Mirren

Second Division
Brechin City v Clydebank
Clyde v Stranraer

East Fife v Forfar Athletic
Livingston v Inverness Cal. Th.
Queen of the South v Stenhousemuir

Third Division
Albion Rovers v Montrose
Alloa Athletic v Berwick Rangers
Arbroath v Queen's Park
Dumbarton v Cowdenbeath
Ross County v East Stirlingshire

Saturday, January 17th
Premier Division
Aberdeen v Dunfermline Athletic
Dundee United v Celtic
Hibernian v St. Johnstone
Kilmarnock v Heart of Midlothian
Rangers v Motherwell

First Division
Airdrieonians v Ayr United
Greenock Morton v Dundee
Hamilton Academical v Stirling Albion
Raith Rovers v Falkirk
St. Mirren v Partick Thistle

Second Division
Brechin City v Queen of the South
Inverness Cal. Th. v Clyde
Livingston v Clydebank
Stenhousemuir v Forfar Athletic
Stranraer v East Fife

Third Division
Alloa Athletic v Arbroath
Berwick Rangers v East Stirlingshire
Cowdenbeath v Albion Rovers
Dumbarton v Queen's Park
Montrose v Ross County

Saturday, January 31st
Premier Division
Celtic v Aberdeen
Dunfermline Athletic v Kilmarnock
Heart of Midlothian v Dundee United
Motherwell v Hibernian
St. Johnstone v Rangers

First Division
Ayr United v Raith Rovers
Dundee v Hamilton Academical
Falkirk v St. Mirren
Partick Thistle v Greenock Morton
Stirling Albion v Airdrieonians

Second Division
Clyde v Brechin City
Clydebank v Stenhousemuir
East Fife v Livingston
Forfar Athletic v Stranraer
Queen of South v Inverness Cal. Th.

Third Division
Albion Rovers v Alloa Athletic
Arbroath v Dumbarton
East Stirlingshire v Montrose
Queen's Park v Cowdenbeath
Ross County v Berwick Rangers

Saturday, February 7th
Premier Division
Aberdeen v Hibernian
Dundee United v Motherwell
Heart of Midlothian v Celtic
Kilmarnock v St. Johnstone
Rangers v Dunfermline Athletic

First Division
Airdrieonians v Hamilton Academical
Falkirk v Greenock Morton
Raith Rovers v Partick Thistle
St. Mirren v Ayr United
Stirling Albion v Dundee

Second Division
Brechin City v East Fife
Inverness Cal. Th. v Clydebank
Livingston v Forfar Athletic
Queen of the South v Clyde
Stranraer v Stenhousemuir

Third Division
Albion Rovers v East Stirlingshire
Alloa Athletic v Queen's Park
Cowdenbeath v Arbroath
Dumbarton v Ross County
Montrose v Berwick Rangers

Saturday, February 14th
Second Division
Clyde v Livingston
Clydebank v Stranraer
East Fife v Queen of the South
Forfar Athletic v Inverness Cal. Th.
Stenhousemuir v Brechin City

Third Division
Arbroath v Albion Rovers
Berwick Rangers v Cowdenbeath
East Stirlingshire v Dumbarton
Queen's Park v Montrose
Ross County v Alloa Athletic

Saturday, February 21st
Premier Division
Celtic v Kilmarnock
Dunfermline Athletic v Dundee United
Hibernian v Rangers
Motherwell v Heart of Midlothian
St. Johnstone v Aberdeen

First Division
Ayr United v Stirling Albion

Dundee v Airdrieonians
Greenock Morton v Raith Rovers
Hamilton Academical v St. Mirren
Partick Thistle v Falkirk

Second Division
Clydebank v Brechin City
Forfar Athletic v East Fife
Inverness Cal. Th. v Livingston
Stenhousemuir v Queen of the South
Stranraer v Clyde

Third Division
Berwick Rangers v Alloa Athletic
Cowdenbeath v Dumbarton
East Stirlingshire v Ross County
Montrose v Albion Rovers
Queen's Park v Arbroath

Tuesday, February 24th
Premier Division
Dundee United v Hibernian
Kilmarnock v Rangers

Third Division
Arbroath v East Stirlingshire

Wednesday, February 25th
Premier Division
Celtic v Dunfermline Athletic
Heart of Midlothian v Aberdeen
Motherwell v St. Johnstone

First Division
Falkirk v Ayr United
Greenock Morton v Hamilton Acad.
Partick Thistle v Dundee
Raith Rovers v Airdrieonians
St. Mirren v Stirling Albion

Second Division
Brechin City v Inverness Cal. Th.
Clyde v Forfar Athletic
East Fife v Stenhousemuir
Livingston v Stranraer
Queen of the South v Clydebank

Third Division
Albion Rovers v Berwick Rangers
Alloa Athletic v Cowdenbeath
Dumbarton v Montrose
Ross County v Queen's Park

Saturday, February 28th
Premier Division
Aberdeen v Kilmarnock
Dunfermline Athletic v Motherwell
Hibernian v Celtic
Rangers v Heart of Midlothian
St. Johnstone v Dundee United

First Division
Airdrieonians v Falkirk
Ayr United v Partick Thistle
Dundee v St. Mirren
Hamilton Academical v Raith Rovers
Stirling Albion v Greenock Morton

Second Division
East Fife v Clyde
Forfar Athletic v Clydebank
Livingston v Queen of the South
Stenhousemuir v Inverness Cal. Th.
Stranraer v Brechin City

Third Division
Berwick Rangers v Arbroath
Dumbarton v Alloa Athletic
East Stirlingshire v Queen's Park
Montrose v Cowdenbeath
Ross County v Albion Rovers

Saturday, March 7th
Second Division
Brechin City v Livingston
Clyde v Stenhousemuir
Clydebank v East Fife
Inverness Cal. Th. v Stranraer
Queen of the South v Forfar Athletic

Third Division
Albion Rovers v Dumbarton
Alloa Athletic v Montrose
Arbroath v Ross County
Cowdenbeath v East Stirlingshire
Queen's Park v Berwick Rangers

Saturday, March 14th
Premier Division
Celtic v Dundee United
Dunfermline Athletic v Aberdeen
Heart of Midlothian v Kilmarnock
Motherwell v Rangers
St. Johnstone v Hibernian

First Division
Ayr United v Airdrieonians
Dundee v Greenock Morton
Falkirk v Raith Rovers
Partick Thistle v St. Mirren
Stirling Albion v Hamilton Academical

Second Division
Clyde v Inverness Cal. Th.
Clydebank v Livingston
East Fife v Stranraer
Forfar Athletic v Stenhousemuir
Queen of the South v Brechin City

Third Division
Albion Rovers v Cowdenbeath
Arbroath v Alloa Athletic
East Stirlingshire v Berwick Rangers

Queen's Park v Dumbarton
Ross County v Montrose

Saturday, March 21st
Premier Division
Aberdeen v Celtic
Dundee United v Heart of Midlothian
Hibernian v Motherwell
Kilmarnock v Dunfermline Athletic
Rangers v St. Johnstone

First Division
Airdrieonians v Stirling Albion
Greenock Morton v Partick Thistle
Hamilton Academical v Dundee
Raith Rovers v Ayr United
St. Mirren v Falkirk

Second Division
Brechin City v Clyde
Inverness Cal. Th. v Queen of South
Livingston v East Fife
Stenhousemuir v Clydebank
Stranraer v Forfar Athletic

Third Division
Alloa Athletic v Albion Rovers
Berwick Rangers v Ross County
Cowdenbeath v Queen's Park
Dumbarton v Arbroath
Montrose v East Stirlingshire

Saturday, March 28th
Premier Division
Celtic v Heart of Midlothian
Dunfermline Athletic v Rangers
Hibernian v Aberdeen
Motherwell v Dundee United
St. Johnstone v Kilmarnock

First Division
Ayr United v St. Mirren
Dundee v Stirling Albion
Greenock Morton v Falkirk
Hamilton Academical v Airdrieonians
Partick Thistle v Raith Rovers

Second Division
Clyde v Queen of the South
Clydebank v Inverness Cal. Th.
East Fife v Brechin City
Forfar Athletic v Livingston
Stenhousemuir v Stranraer

Third Division
Arbroath v Cowdenbeath
Berwick Rangers v Montrose
East Stirlingshire v Albion Rovers
Queen's Park v Alloa Athletic
Ross County v Dumbarton

Saturday, April 4th
Premier Division
Aberdeen v St. Johnstone
Dundee United v Dunfermline Athletic
Heart of Midlothian v Motherwell
Kilmarnock v Celtic
Rangers v Hibernian

First Division
Airdrieonians v Dundee
Falkirk v Partick Thistle
Raith Rovers v Greenock Morton
St. Mirren v Hamilton Academical
Stirling Albion v Ayr United

Second Division
Brechin City v Stenhousemuir
Inverness Cal. Th. v Forfar Athletic
Livingston v Clyde
Queen of the South v East Fife
Stranraer v Clydebank

Third Division
Albion Rovers v Arbroath
Alloa Athletic v Ross County
Cowdenbeath v Berwick Rangers
Dumbarton v East Stirlingshire
Montrose v Queen's Park

Saturday, April 11th
Premier Division
Dundee United v Aberdeen
Hibernian v Heart of Midlothian
Motherwell v Kilmarnock
St. Johnstone v Dunfermline Athletic

First Division
Ayr United v Hamilton Academical
Falkirk v Stirling Albion
Greenock Morton v St. Mirren
Partick Thistle v Airdrieonians
Raith Rovers v Dundee

Second Division
Brechin City v Stranraer
Clyde v East Fife
Clydebank v Forfar Athletic
Inverness Cal. Th. v Stenhousemuir
Queen of the South v Livingston

Third Division
Albion Rovers v Ross County
Alloa Athletic v Dumbarton
Arbroath v Berwick Rangers
Cowdenbeath v Montrose
Queen's Park v East Stirlingshire

Sunday, April 12th
Premier Division
Rangers v Celtic

Sunday, April 18th

Premier Division
Aberdeen v Rangers
Celtic v Motherwell
Dunfermline Athletic v Hibernian
Heart of Midlothian v St. Johnstone
Kilmarnock v Dundee United

First Division
Airdrieonians v Greenock Morton
Dundee v Ayr United
Hamilton Academical v Falkirk
St. Mirren v Raith Rovers
Stirling Albion v Partick Thistle

Second Division
East Fife v Clydebank
Forfar Athletic v Queen of the South
Livingston v Brechin City
Stenhousemuir v Clyde
Stranraer v Inverness Cal. Th.

Third Division
Berwick Rangers v Queen's Park
Dumbarton v Albion Rovers
East Stirlingshire v Cowdenbeath
Montrose v Alloa Athletic
Ross County v Arbroath

Saturday, April 25th

Premier Division
Celtic v Hibernian
Dundee United v St. Johnstone
Heart of Midlothian v Rangers
Kilmarnock v Aberdeen
Motherwell v Dunfermline Athletic

First Division
Falkirk v Dundee
Greenock Morton v Ayr United
Partick Thistle v Hamilton Academical
Raith Rovers v Stirling Albion
St. Mirren v Airdrieonians

Second Division
Brechin City v Forfar Athletic
Clyde v Clydebank
East Fife v Inverness Cal. Th.
Livingston v Stenhousemuir
Queen of the South v Stranraer

Third Division
Albion Rovers v Queen's Park
Alloa Athletic v East Stirlingshire
Arbroath v Montrose
Dumbarton v Berwick Rangers
Ross County v Cowdenbeath

Saturday, May 2nd

Premier Division
Aberdeen v Heart of Midlothian
Dunfermline Athletic v Celtic
Hibernian v Dundee United
Rangers v Kilmarnock
St. Johnstone v Motherwell

First Division
Airdrieonians v Raith Rovers
Ayr United v Falkirk
Dundee v Partick Thistle
Hamilton Acad. v Greenock Morton
Stirling Albion v St. Mirren

Second Division
Clydebank v Queen of the South
Forfar Athletic v Clyde
Inverness Cal. Th. v Brechin City
Stenhousemuir v East Fife
Stranraer v Livingston

Third Division
Berwick Rangers v Albion Rovers
Cowdenbeath v Alloa Athletic
East Stirlingshire v Arbroath
Montrose v Dumbarton
Queen's Park v Ross County

Saturday, May 9th

Premier Division
Celtic v St. Johnstone
Dundee United v Rangers
Heart of Midlothian v Dunfermline A.
Kilmarnock v Hibernian
Motherwell v Aberdeen

First Division
Falkirk v Airdrieonians
Greenock Morton v Stirling Albion
Partick Thistle v Ayr United
Raith Rovers v Hamilton Academical
St. Mirren v Dundee

Second Division
Brechin City v Clydebank
Clyde v Stranraer
East Fife v Forfar Athletic
Livingston v Inverness Cal. Th.
Queen of the South v Stenhousemuir

Third Division
Albion Rovers v Montrose
Alloa Athletic v Berwick Rangers
Arbroath v Queen's Park
Dumbarton v Cowdenbeath
Ross County v East Stirlingshire

GM VAUXHALL CONFERENCE
FIXTURES 1997-98

(These fixtures are the copyright of the GM Vauxhall Conference and are
reproduced with their permission)

Saturday 16 August

Dover Athletic v Cheltenham
Gateshead v Farnborough Town
Hayes v Halifax Town
Hereford United v Welling United
Kettering Town v Slough Town
Morecambe v Leek Town
Rushden & Diad's v Northwich Vic.
Southport v Hednesford Town
Stalybridge Celtic v Kidderminster H.
Woking v Telford United
Yeovil Town v Stevenage Borough

Monday 18th August

Hednesford Town v Hereford United
Kidderminster Har. v Northwich Vic.
Stevenage Borough v Kettering Town

Tuesday 19th August

Cheltenham Town v Hayes
Leek Town v Southport
Slough Town v Dover Athletic
Telford United v Stalybridge Celtic
Welling United v Woking

Wednesday 20th August

Farnborough T. v Rushden & Diad's
Gateshead v Morecambe

Saturday 23rd August

Cheltenham Town v Woking
Farnborough Town v Hereford United
Hayes v Morecambe
Hednesford Town v Stalybridge Celtic
Kidderminster Harriers v Gateshead
Leek Town v Rushden & Diad's
Northwich Victoria v Kettering Town
Slough Town v Halifax Town
Stevenage Borough v Southport
Telford United v Dover Athletic
Welling United v Yeovil Town

Monday 25th August

Dover Athletic v Stevenage Borough
Gateshead v Northwich Victoria
Hayes v Welling United
Hereford United v Cheltenham Town
Kettering Town v Telford United
Morecambe v Kidderminster Harriers
Rushden & Diad's v Hednesford Town
Southport v Halifax Town
Stalybridge Celtic v Leek Town
Woking v Slough Town
Yeovil Town v Farnborough Town

Saturday 30th August

Dover Athletic v Hednesford Town
Halifax Town v Welling United
Hereford Utd. v Stevenage Borough
Kettering Town v Cheltenham Town
Kidderminster Harriers v Hayes
Morecambe v Telford United
Rushden & Diad's v Gateshead
Southport v Farnborough Town
Stalybridge Celtic v Slough Town
Woking v Northwich Victoria
Yeovil Town v Leek Town

Monday 1st September

Northwich Victoria v Morecambe
Stevenage Borough v Hayes

Tuesday 2nd September

Leek Town v Hereford United
Slough Town v Rushden & Diad's
Telford United v Halifax Town
Welling United v Kettering Town

Wednesday 3rd September

Farnborough Town v Dover Athletic
Gateshead v Southport

Saturday 6th September

Cheltenham T. v Rushden & Diad's
Farnborough Town v Kettering Town
Halifax Town v Yeovil Town
Hayes v Hereford United
Hednesford Town v Woking
Leek Town v Kidderminster Harriers
Northwich Victoria v Dover Athletic
Southport v Slough Town
Stevenage Borough v Morecambe
Telford United v Gateshead
Welling United v Stalybridge Celtic

Tuesday 9th September

Cheltenham Town v Leek Town
Dover Athletic v Yeovil Town
Hereford United v Farnborough Town
Kettering Town v Woking
Slough Town v Welling United

Saturday 13th September

Hereford United v Northwich Victoria
Kidderminster H. v Stevenage Boro.
Morecambe v Hednesford Town
Rushden & Diad's v Farnborough T.
Stalybridge Celtic v Hayes
Woking v Southport

Tuesday 16th September
Halifax Town v Telford United
Hayes v Cheltenham Town
Welling United v Stevenage Borough
Yeovil Town v Kidderminster Harriers

Wednesday 17th September
Farnborough Town v Slough Town

Saturday 20th September
Dover Athletic v Kidderminster Har.
Farnborough Town v Halifax Town
Gateshead v Woking
Hednesford Town v Southport
Kettering Town v Hereford United
Leek Town v Hayes
Morecambe v Welling United
Slough Town v Northwich Victoria
Stalybridge Celtic v Cheltenham Town
Stevenage Borough v Telford United
Yeovil Town v Rushden & Diad's

Monday 22nd September
Hednesford Town v Leek Town

Tuesday 23rd September
Cheltenham Town v Slough Town

Saturday 27th September
Hayes v Hednesford Town
Hereford United v Stalybridge Celtic
Kidderminster Har. v Farnborough T.
Northwich Vic. v Stevenage Borough
Southport v Rushden & Diad's
Woking v Morecambe

Monday 29th September
Kidderminster Har. v Cheltenham T.
Northwich Victoria v Gateshead

Tuesday 30th September
Halifax Town v Leek Town
Woking v Dover Athletic

Saturday 4th October
Cheltenham T. v Northwich Victoria
Farnborough Town v Hayes
Halifax Town v Kettering Town
Hednesford T. v Kidderminster Har.
Leek Town v Slough Town
Morecambe v Dover Athletic
Rushden & Diad's v Woking
Stalybridge Celtic v Yeovil Town
Stevenage Borough v Gateshead
Telford United v Hereford United
Welling United v Southport

Monday 6th October
Hednesford Town v Telford United

Tuesday 7th October
Dover Athletic v Kettering Town
Hayes v Rushden & Diad's

Leek Town v Southport
Slough Town v Welling United
Stalybridge Celtic v Halifax Town
Yeovil Town v Cheltenham Town

Saturday 11th October
Cheltenham Town v Dover Athletic
Farnborough Town v Morecambe
Gateshead v Leek Town
Hayes v Stalybridge Celtic
Northwich Victoria v Hednesford T.
Rushden & Diad's v Hereford United
Southport v Kidderminster Harriers
Stevenage Borough v Woking

Saturday 18th October
Dover Athletic v Stalybridge Celtic
Gateshead v Cheltenham Town
Halifax Town v Stevenage Borough
Hednesford Town v Welling United
Hereford United v Southport
Kettering Town v Hayes
Kidderminster H. v Rushden & Diad's
Slough Town v Morecambe
Telford United v Farnborough Town
Woking v Leek Town
Yeovil Town v Northwich Victoria

Saturday 25th October
Stevenage Borough v Hednesford T.

Tuesday 28th October
Hayes v Woking
Morecambe v Halifax Town
Rushden & Diad's v Kettering Town
Stalybridge Celtic v Gateshead

Saturday 1st November
Cheltenham Town v Halifax Town
Farnborough Town v Welling United
Hayes v Gateshead
Hednesford Town v Yeovil Town
Kidderminster Harriers v Woking
Leek Town v Dover Athletic
Morecambe v Hereford United
Northwich Victoria v Telford United
Rushden & Diad's v Slough Town
Southport v Kettering Town
Stalybridge Celtic v Stevenage Boro.

Saturday 8th November
Dover Athletic v Hayes
Gateshead v Hednesford Town
Halifax Town v Kidderminster Harriers
Hereford United v Yeovil Town
Kettering Town v Morecambe
Leek Town v Stevenage Borough
Northwich Victoria v Farnborough Town
Slough Town v Cheltenham Town
Telford United v Southport
Welling United v Rushden & Diad's
Woking v Stalybridge Celtic

477

Saturday 15th November
Hereford United v Gateshead
Kettering Town v Dover Athletic
Slough Town v Leek Town
Southport v Cheltenham Town
Yeovil Town v Hayes

Saturday 22nd November
Cheltenham Town v Gateshead
Halifax Town v Hereford United
Hednesford Town v Slough Town
Kidderminster Har. v Kettering Town
Morecambe v Rushden & Diad's
Southport v Stalybridge Celtic
Stevenage Borough v Farnborough T.
Welling United v Telford United
Yeovil Town v Woking

Saturday 29th November
Farnborough T. v Kidderminster Har.
Gateshead v Yeovil Town
Hereford United v Dover Athletic
Kettering Town v Stevenage Borough
Leek Town v Cheltenham Town
Northwich Victoria v Welling United
Rushden & Diad's v Hayes
Slough Town v Southport
Stalybridge Celtic v Hednesford Town
Telford United v Morecambe
Woking v Halifax Town

Saturday 6th December
Cheltenham Town v Farnborough T.
Dover Athletic v Woking
Halifax Town v Stalybridge Celtic
Hayes v Telford United
Hednesford Town v Rushden & Diad's
Morecambe v Gateshead
Southport v Leek Town
Stevenage Boro. v Hereford United
Welling United v Slough Town
Yeovil Town v Kettering Town

Tuesday 9th December
Halifax Town v Northwich Victoria

Saturday 13th December
Cheltenham Town v Morecambe
Farnborough Town v Yeovil Town
Gateshead v Stevenage Borough
Hereford United v Hednesford Town
Kettering Town v Welling United
Leek Town v Halifax Town
Northwich Victoria v Southport
Rushden & Diad's v Dover Athletic
Slough Town v Kidderminster Harriers
Stalybridge Celtic v Telford United
Woking v Hayes

Saturday 20th December
Dover Athletic v Northwich Victoria
Farnborough T. v Stalybridge Celtic

Halifax Town v Hednesford Town
Hayes v Rushden & Diad's
Kidderminster Harriers v Leek Town
Morecambe v Kettering Town
Southport v Gateshead
Stevenage Boro. v Cheltenham Town
Telford United v Woking
Welling United v Hereford United
Yeovil Town v Slough Town

Friday 26th December
Cheltenham Town v Yeovil Town
Dover Athletic v Welling United
Gateshead v Halifax Town
Hednesford Town v Kettering Town
Hereford United v Kidderminster Har.
Leek Town v Telford United
Morecambe v Southport
Northwich Vic. v Stalybridge Celtic
Rushden & Diad's v Stevenage Boro.
Slough Town v Hayes
Woking v Farnborough Town

Monday 29th December
Cheltenham Town v Welling United
Dover Athletic v Hereford United
Gateshead v Telford United
Hayes v Northwich Victoria
Hednesford Town v Stevenage Boro.
Kettering Town v Halifax Town
Leek Town v Morecambe
Rushden & Diad's v Kidderminster H.
Slough Town v Farnborough Town
Stalybridge Celtic v Southport
Woking v Yeovil Town

Thursday 1st January
Farnborough Town v Woking
Halifax Town v Gateshead
Hayes v Slough Town
Kettering Town v Hednesford Town
Kidderminster Har. v Hereford United
Southport v Morecambe
Stalybridge Celtic v Northwich Vic.
Stevenage Boro. v Rushden & Diad's
Telford United v Leek Town
Welling United v Dover Athletic
Yeovil Town v Cheltenham Town

Saturday 3rd January
Cheltenham Town v Stalybridge Celtic
Gateshead v Kidderminster Harriers
Halifax Town v Dover Athletic
Hednesford Town v Farnborough T.
Hereford United v Telford United
Leek Town v Kettering Town
Morecambe v Hayes
Northwich Vic. v Rushden & Diad's
Slough Town v Stevenage Borough
Woking v Welling United
Yeovil Town v Southport

478

Saturday 17th January

Cheltenham Town v Hednesford Town
Dover Athletic v Leek Town
Farnborough T. v Northwich Victoria
Hayes v Kidderminster Harriers
Hereford United v Kettering Town
Morecambe v Yeovil Town
Rushden & Diad's v Southport
Stalybridge Celtic v Woking
Stevenage Borough v Halifax Town
Telford United v Sough Town
Welling United v Gateshead

Saturday 24th January

Dover Athletic v Rushden & Diad's
Gateshead v Hereford United
Halifax Town v Slough Town
Hednesford Town v Hayes
Kettering Town v Farnborough Town
Kidderminster Harriers v Morecambe
Leek Town v Stalybridge Celtic
Northwich Victoria v Cheltenham T.
Southport v Welling United
Woking v Stevenage Borough
Yeovil Town v Telford United

Saturday 31st January

Kidderminster H. v Stalybridge Celtic
Northwich Victoria v Leek Town
Yeovil Town v Welling United

Saturday 7th February

Farnborough Town v Leek Town
Hednesford Town v Cheltenham Town
Kettering Town v Gateshead
Morecambe v Woking
Rushden & Diad's v Halifax Town
Slough Town v Hereford United
Southport v Hayes
Stalybridge Celtic v Dover Athletic
Stevenage Borough v Yeovil Town
Telford United v v Kidderminster Har.
Welling United v Northwich Victoria

Tuesday 10th February

Dover Athletic v Farnborough Town

Saturday 14th February

Cheltenham Town v Stevenage Boro.
Dover Athletic v Halifax Town
Gateshead v Rushden & Diad's
Hayes v Yeovil Town
Hereford United v Morecambe
Kidderminster Harriers v Southport
Leek Town v Hednesford Town
Northwich Victoria v Slough Town
Telford United v Welling United
Woking v Kettering Town

Saturday 21st February

Farnborough Town v Cheltenham T.
Halifax Town v Hayes

Hednesford T. v Northwich Victoria
Kettering Town v Rushden & Diad's
Slough Town v Telford United
Southport v Hereford United
Stalybridge Celtic v Morecambe
Stevenage Borough v Leek Town
Welling United v Kidderminster Har.
Woking v Gateshead
Yeovil Town v Dover Athletic

Tuesday 24th February

Hereford United v Hayes
Telford United v Northwich Victoria

Saturday 28th February

Dover Athletic v Telford United
Gateshead v Kettering Town
Halifax Town v Farnborough Town
Hayes v Stevenage Borough
Hereford United v Leek Town
Kidderminster Harriers v Yeovil Town
Morecambe v Slough Town
Rushden & Diad's v Stalybridge C.
Southport v Woking
Welling United v Hednesford Town

Saturday 7th March

Dover Athletic v Gateshead
Kettering Town v Southport
Kidderminster Har. v Hednesford T.
Leek Town v Farnborough Town
Northwich Victoria v Hereford United
Rushden & Diad's v Cheltenham T.
Slough Town v Woking
Stalybridge Celtic v Halifax Town
Stevenage Borough v Welling United
Telford United v Hayes
Yeovil Town v Morecambe

Tuesday 10th March

Kettering Town v Yeovil Town

Saturday 14th March

Cheltenham T. v Kidderminster Har.
Farnborough Town v Telford United
Hayes v Kettering Town
Hednesford Town v Halifax Town
Slough Town v Gateshead
Southport v Dover Athletic
Welling United v Leek Town
Woking v Rushden & Diad's
Yeovil Town v Stalybridge Celtic

Monday 16th March

Stevenage Borough v Slough Town

Tuesday 17th March

Dover Athletic v Kettering Town
Halifax Town v Morecambe
Telford United v Yeovil Town

Saturday 21st March
Farnborough T. v Stevenage Borough
Halifax Town v Rushden & Diad's
Hayes v Southport
Hereford United v Slough Town
Kettering Town v Leek Town
Morecambe v Cheltenham Town
Northwich Victoria v Yeovil Town
Stalybridge Celtic v Welling United
Telford United v Hednesford Town
Woking v Kidderminster Harriers

Monday 23rd March
Kiddermninster Har. v Dover Athletic

Tuesday 24th March
Welling United v Farnborough Town

Wednesday 25th March
Gateshead v Stalybridge Celtic

Saturday 28th March
Cheltenham Town v Kettering Town
Gateshead v Dover Athletic
Hereford United v Woking
Kidderminster Har. v Welling United
Leek Town v Northwich Victoria
Rushden & Diad's v Morecambe
Slough Town v Hednesford Town
Southport v Telford United
Stevenage Boro. v Stalybridge Celtic
Yeovil Town v Halifax Town

Saturday 4th April
Farnborough Town v Southport
Halifax Town v Woking
Hednesford Town v Gateshead
Leek Town v Yeovil Town
Northwich Victoria v Hayes
Slough Town v Kettering Town
Stalybridge Celtic v Hereford United
Stevenage Boro. v Kidderminster Har.
Telford United v Cheltenham Town
Welling United v Morecambe

Tuesday 7th April
Morecambe v Stalybridge Celtic
Southport v Northwich Victoria
Telford United v Rushden & Diad's

Saturday 11th April
Dover Athletic v Slough Town
Gateshead v Welling United
Hayes v Farnborough Town
Hereford United v Halifax Town
Kettering Town v Stalybridge Celtic
Kidderminster Har. v Telford Utd.
Morecambe v Northwich Victoria
Rushden & Diad's v Leek Town
Southport v Stevenage Borough
Woking v Cheltenham Town

Yeovil Town v Hednesford Town

Monday 13th April
Cheltenham Town v Hereford United
Farnborough Town v Gateshead
Halifax Town v Southport
Hednesford Town v Morecambe
Leek Town v Woking
Northwich Vic. v Kidderminster Har.
Slough Town v Yeovil Town
Stalybridge C. v Rushden & Diad's
Stevenage Borough v Dover Athletic
Telford United v Kettering Town
Welling United v Hayes

Saturday 18th April
Cheltenham Town v Telford United
Dover Athletic v Southport
Gateshead v Slough Town
Kettering Town v Northwich Victoria
Kidderminster Harriers v Halifax Town
Morecambe v Stevenage Borough
Rushden & Diad's v Welling United
Stalybridge Celtic v Farnborough T.
Woking v Hednesford Town
Yeovil Town v Hereford United

Monday 20th April
Northwich Victoria v Halifax Town

Tuesday 21st April
Hayes v Dover Athletic
Leek Town v Gateshead
Rushden & Diad's v Yeovil Town
Welling United v Cheltenham Town

Saturday 25th April
Dover Athletic v Morecambe
Farnborough T. v Hednesford Town
Gateshead v Hayes
Halifax Town v Cheltenham Town
Hereford United v Rushden & Diad's
Kettering Town v Kidderminster Har.
Leek Town v Welling United
Northwich Victoria v Woking
Slough Town v Stalybridge Celtic
Southport v Yeovil Town
Telford United v Stevenage Borough

Saturday 2nd May
Cheltenham Town v Southport
Hayes v Leek Town
Hednesford Town v Dover Athletic
Kidderminster Harriers v Slough Town
Morecambe v Farnborough Town
Rushden & Diad's v Telford United
Stalybridge Celtic v Kettering Town
Stevenage Boro. v Northwich Victoria
Welling United v Halifax Town
Woking v Hereford United
Yeovil Town v Gateshead